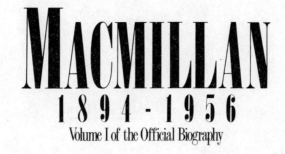

MACMILLAN
1894 - 1956
Volume I of the Official Biography

Also by Alistair Horne

Back Into Power
The Land is Bright
Canada and the Canadians
The Price of Glory: Verdun 1916
The Fall of Paris: The Siege and the Commune 1870–71
To Lose a Battle: France 1940
The Terrible Year: The Paris Commune 1871
Death of a Generation
Small Earthquake in Chile
Napoleon: Master of Europe 1805–1807
The French Army and Politics 1870–1970
A Savage War of Peace: Algeria 1954–1962

MACMILLAN
1894 - 1956
Volume I of the Official Biography
Alistair Horne

MACMILLAN
LONDON

First published 1988 by
MACMILLAN LONDON LIMITED
4 Little Essex Street, London WC2R 3LF
and Basingstoke

Associated companies in Auckland, Delhi, Dublin, Gaborone,
Hamburg, Harare, Hong Kong, Johannesburg, Kuala Lumpur,
Lagos, Manzini, Melbourne, Mexico City, Nairobi, New York,
Singapore and Tokyo

Reprinted 1988

British Library Cataloguing in Publication Data
Horne, Alistair, *1925–*
   Macmillan: 1894–1956
   Vol. 1
   1. Great Britain. Macmillan, Harold,
   1894–1986
   I. Title
   941.085'092'4

   ISBN 0-333-27691-4

Photoset in Great Britain by
Rowland Phototypesetting Limited
Bury St Edmunds, Suffolk

Printed by Butler and Tanner Limited,
Frome, Somerset

To the memory of Andrew Harding

Contents

List of Illustrations

Macmillan

Preface

Boswell claimed (though it could possibly be said he was pleading a special case) that 'nobody can write the life of a man, but those who have eaten and drunk and lived in social intercourse with him'. Or, in the similar advice of that great chronicler of contemporary America, Tom Wolfe, writers 'should spend days if not weeks with their subject'. Although I had been a Macmillan author for almost twenty years, apart from the sporadic encounters of writer and publisher, it was not until the late summer of 1979 that I first got to know Harold Macmillan, then a spry eighty-five. To my considerable surprise, I had been invited to be his official biographer. At first I declined. I had never attempted a biography before – certainly not of a living subject – and, flattering a proposition though it was, I was distinctly uneasy about my qualifications. Finally it was agreed that I should go down to Macmillan's Sussex home, Birch Grove, so that subject and biographer could 'look at each other'. As we walked round and round the garden, lovingly laid out by his redoubtable American mother, Nellie Macmillan, and improved by Dorothy, his wife, I began to realise that he was just about as diffident as I was. I recall making some flip remark about my knowing all too little about British party politics, and not even being sure that I was a very good Tory. He replied, 'Nor was I, dear boy!' The ice was broken; we went into the house, and there began ten of the most rewarding (though demanding) years of my life.

The terms were generous. All his copious papers and his own remarkable store of recollections were put at my disposal. The only major limitation was that nothing should appear in his lifetime – a condition designed to rid us both of inhibitions. The relationship was a curious one. Few biographers of eminent contemporary figures have the enviable good fortune to have access to the memory of their victim during his lifetime. But it also had its disadvantages: in the sheer weight of material amassed, the checking and cross-checking involved, and – not least – the resistance to falling totally under the spell of one of the most fascinating political figures of the twentieth century, not known as the 'old magician' for nothing. We would work often three days at a stretch at Birch Grove (which usually exhausted me more than the octogenarian Macmillan), recording on tape the career of 'this strange, very buttoned-up person', as he liked to describe himself, trying to probe into the many corners left uncovered, or unexplained, by his own voluminous (but impersonal) six-volume memoirs.

As we wandered round the shrubberies and borders of Birch Grove that first day, I remembered his commenting, 'I think gardens should be divided, so you can't see everything at once.' Later I came to recognise the unspoken parallel. Despite the showman exterior, acquired over the years of public life, he was by nature private and deeply reluctant to talk about anything bordering on the personal. Reviewing the first volume of Macmillan's memoirs, *Winds of Change*, his long-time admirer, Randolph Churchill, admitted, 'I have known him upwards of thirty years and I have found it very difficult to get him to talk about himself'; while (reviewing the same volume), a Labour adversary, David Marquand MP, asked rhetorically: 'Why does he shield behind so much armour plating? . . . what is he trying to hide? The obvious answer is, himself. . . .' To me, Harold Macmillan once confessed that the aim of his memoirs had been 'to keep myself out of it'. I told him he had done a good job; thus my hardest task was always to drag him out of his own corner, to winkle the ever-wily politician out of his protective shell. After one par-ticularly arduous session (I think it was over Suez), he jokingly introduced me to neighbours as 'a cross between Boswell and Torquemada!'

Born in 1894, into a strongly Victorian background, Macmillan was brought up to eschew and distrust his own feelings. Yet, with him, emotion never lay very far beneath the surface; on that first day at Birch Grove, I remember his voice breaking and eyes filling with tears as he read to me a desperate memorandum (framed in the 'Muniments Room') that Churchill had written in the darkest days of 1940, exhorting ministers not to lose heart. But, as I came to appreciate, the emotional romantic and the stern pragmatist were but two facets of the same highly complex personality. To the widow of John Wyndham, his *aide-de-camp* and close friend for many years, he was Proteus – the figure of Greek mythology capable of constantly changing his guise in bewildering fashion: 'One moment you had a salmon in your hand, the next it was a horse.' Few men could have been more constituted of paradoxes than Harold Macmillan; it was what gave him his charm (and mischief) as a brilliant conversationalist, and made him an enticing (but elusive) subject for a biographer. Every thought was followed by an afterthought, or two. What looked like white turned out to be black. He was a tease, he loved to *épater les bourgeois* with the remark that he did not really mean – or, perhaps, half-meant. Once when I remonstrated with him over what appeared to be excessive flippancy in the wrong context, he riposted: 'It's very important not to have a rigid distinction between what's flippant and what is serious.' It was, I thought at the time, something of a key to his whole style of government, as well as to his engagingly complex personality.

In conversation, his comment on famous contemporaries was always marvellously vivid, often acid, but almost always coming down on the side of charity. When I asked him why he kept out of his published memoirs (greatly to their loss, and in marked contrast with later political diarists such as Richard Crossman) the more barbed remarks of his unpublished diaries, he replied that such remarks made in the irritation of the moment never represented a considered view. (He added, typically, as an afterthought: 'Also, I wasn't a publisher for nothing; libel's expensive!') But, equally, it seemed to reflect a fundamental kindliness. When he talked, there would be lots of mischief, some penetrating insights, occasional anger, but never enduring malice – which was quite alien to his character. I never heard him express rancour (except, possibly, when discussing the lords of the media); not even towards de Gaulle, the man whom he had saved time and again during the war from the combined wrath of Churchill and Roosevelt, yet who – twenty years later – so bitterly injured him through vetoing Britain's entry into the EEC.

When the news of my commission to write the official biography was first publicised in February 1979, I sidelined with an exclamation remark one report which wrote that it was 'expected to need five years of work'. I reckoned three, at a maximum. In fact it took

exactly ten – more than three years longer than Macmillan was
Prime Minister. If I cannot regret the time spent, I do grieve the
series of personal tragedies, and painful losses, that leadened its
passage. Serena Booker, a brilliant young woman and close family
friend who had worked as a tireless and indispensable researcher (as
well as great morale-booster) for four years, was brutally murdered
while on holiday in Thailand in 1982, in the middle of her work.
Venetia Pollock, another brilliant woman, quite simply the best
editor in the business and also a life-long friend, was stricken with
cancer halfway through the labour of editing a long and complicated
manuscript. The deprivation of her encouragement, and enthusiasm, was all but irreparable. Finally, Andrew Harding, to whom
the dedication of this book had long been promised, who shared
some aspects of the subject's life – Eton, Oxford, wartime Grenadier
Guards – and whose inestimable support over three decades made
this (and many other past books) possible for the author, died
tragically after a courageous struggle against illness, and just before
I was able to tell him that *his* book was finally ready to appear.

This first volume takes Harold Macmillan only through the first
sixty-two years of his life; from birth through his childhood and
family background of the Scottish crofter and his powerful American
mother; Oxford and his five wounds in the trenches of Flanders; his
start as a publisher and entry into politics, the long wilderness years
of the 1920s and 1930s, and the near break-up of his marriage to the
Duke of Devonshire's daughter; the Second World War, and fulfil-
ment at last as Churchill's envoy in North Africa, and his first
encounter with American leaders; followed by the frustrations of six
years in opposition in Clement Attlee's post-war Britain, with
Macmillan playing the role of a leading architect to the Conservative
revival. The Party's return to power in 1951 saw him as a senior
Cabinet minister in all the important posts of first Churchill's, then
Eden's short-lived government. The volume culminates with the
Suez débâcle of 1956 – which was to bring Macmillan, at an age
when most men are thinking of retirement, to No. 10 Downing
Street.

Volume II covers the seven years of his premiership, and the
unexpectedly eventful two and a half decades of his life that remained after his precipitate resignation in 1963.

The web of any biography must be composed of a multiplicity of
strands. For Macmillan, there was an *embarras de richesses*. Apart from

the voluminous tapes I recorded more or less formally in the library at Birch Grove (and over which I can only express gratitude for the subject's extraordinary patience at my prodding and probing), there was a file, marvellously rich – of what I chose to call 'Table Talk': conversation on an infinite range of subjects during meals, walking round the garden, or chatting late into the night over a bottle of whisky, times when the great conversationalist was at his best, when his imagination soared and when a tape recorder would have been intrusive. Trying to emulate Boswell, I jotted down this 'Table Talk' as soon as I could afterwards, while the memory was still fresh. As with the Macmillan diaries, both these sets of source material had of course to be checked, wherever possible, against known facts.

When Harold Macmillan went to the front in 1915, he kept a detailed diary in the form of letters to his mother. Having read many such journals in the course of writing about the two world wars, to me the quality of these unadorned writings is outstanding. After 1918, he stopped keeping a regular diary, concentrating his literary inclinations on publishing and earnest political tracts – except when he made a special trip, as to Stalin's Russia in the 1930s or be-leaguered Finland in 1940. He resumed his diaries, this time in the form of letters to his wife, Dorothy, when sent to the Mediterranean as Churchill's Resident Minister in 1942. Published virtually *in toto* in 1984, they received justifiable acclaim as a remarkable record of men and events – together, perhaps, with some surprise that they could have been penned by the same author of those six rather stodgy and over-length volumes of memoirs. In 1945, Macmillan once again put away his pen until 1950, when the Conservatives at last looked like returning to power. For the next thirteen years he kept a diary faithfully, writing in spidery long-hand (made arduous by a German bullet through his hand in 1915) every night in the small hours after work. The entries totalled some 2000 typewritten pages, which was no mean achievement in itself, and constituted both a boon and a labour to a biographer. Arthur Ponsonby, son and biographer of the great Victorian courtier, Sir Henry, once observed that diaries were 'better than novels, more accurate than histories, and even at times more dramatic than plays'. This could be said of the 1950–63 Macmillan diaries; still unpublished, they are if anything less res-trained, more outspoken, acrid and occasionally savage than the published *War Diaries*, composed as these were under the eye of the wartime censors. His comments on *bêtes noirs* like Diefenbaker of

Canada, or Chancellor Adenauer of West Germany – sometimes even of John F. Kennedy (for whom he had great esteem and personal affection) – are blistering.

Macmillan himself always warned that his diaries should be treated with caution; that, written in the heat of the moment, they were not always factually accurate; nor fair, in that they gave vent to passing piques, which Macmillan would often modify or expunge the following day. But they did represent both the mood and the colour of the times, and what Macmillan himself was thinking at the time, without the influence of self-justifying hindsight. To me, they were also revealing of the man in a way which he perhaps may never have intended. Certainly they provide an invaluable chronicle of his times, and (though heretofore made available exclusively to his biographer) doubtless will be published *in extenso* in the fulness of time.

From 1957 onwards, sparked by the example of Churchill and systematised by his publisher's mind, Macmillan began organising his archives with the clear intent of writing his memoirs one day. When he left office nearly seven years later, it was alleged that (to the considerable embarrassment of the Cabinet Secretary) he had taken with him more copies of classified official documents than any of his predecessors. Whatever the truth (and the Macmillan memoirs were meticulously submitted for public scrutiny), a precedent was set for politicians of both parties. Published by the house of Macmillan, it would hardly have been human if the memoirs did not reflect some self-justification or judicious editing of the underlying material (such as the unpublished diaries); nevertheless, they represent essential background material for any life of Macmillan. To some extent the later volumes have also obviously been overtaken by official material released under the thirty-year rule; I have endeavoured scrupulously to avoid recourse to any British government documents not thus available from the Public Record Office or in the United States under the Freedom of Information Act. Each January there was also the rich crop of new PRO releases to be drawn upon; though I was conscious of the caution by the late Herbert Butterfield: 'The tendency, when new material appears, is to build it into what one already believes about the subject. The true scholar tears down the whole structure of his own belief, and starts again.' More labour for the contemporary biographer.

In addition to Macmillan's own recollections, there was no shortage of writings by others about his times; or of autobiographies by his eminent contemporaries. All of these I used; but of greater value still was the ability to have direct recourse to the memories of many then still alive. I was particularly fortunate in being granted lengthy interviews with four out of five of the Prime Ministers who succeeded Macmillan; Edward Heath alone remained inaccessible. Innumerable people, both in Britain and America alike, gave most freely of their time, recollections and advice. I may have overlooked many to whom I am beholden; if so, I beg their forgiveness, but I must particularly mention the following: Mrs Dean Acheson; Lord Aldington; Robert Amory; Terence Benton; Christopher Booker; Lord Boothby; Robert Bowie; Lord Brimelow; Brigadier Britten; Lord Bullock; Lord Butler; Lord Carrington; William Clark; Sir John Colville; Lord Colyton; Lord Callaghan; Lady Diana Cooper; Brigadier Anthony Cowgill; Quentin Crewe; the Dowager Duchess of Devonshire; the Duke of Devonshire; Ambassador C. Douglas Dillon; Piers Dixon; Avery Dulles; Miss Eleanor Lansing Dulles; Lord Eden; Pamela, Lady Egremont; Penelope Fitzgerald; the Rt Hon. Hugh Fraser MP; Lord and Lady Gage; Lord Gladwyn; W. Averell Harriman; Lord Head; Lord Home of the Hirsel; Lady Lorna Howard; Sir David Hunt; Richard Lamb; Julian Lambart; Lady Marie Lathbury; Lord Longford; Professor Roger Louis; Sir Fitzroy Maclean; William Macomber; Sir Peter Marshall; Ambassador John J. McCloy; Nigel Nicolson; Sir Anthony Nutting; Robert Rhodes James MP; Lord Richardson; Anthony Sampson; Sir David Scott; Lord Sherfield (Roger Makins); Lord Shinwell; Lord C. P. Snow; Lord Soames; Lady Soames; the Rt Hon. Mrs Margaret Thatcher MP; Lord Thomas of Swynnerton; Lady Anne Tree; Lord Trend; Professor D. C. Watt; Sir Dick White; Frank Whitehead; Lord Wilson of Rievaulx; Sir Philip de Zulueta.

No biographer of a living subject could have received greater help, and friendship, from the immediate family, and I am especially grateful for their patience and open-mindedness to Lady Catherine Amery; the Rt Hon. Julian Amery MP; Lady Carol Faber; Julian Faber; Katharine, Lady Macmillan of Ovenden; the late Maurice Macmillan (Viscount Macmillan of Ovenden); Alexander Macmillan (Earl of Stockton).

To Alexander Stockton, my warm appreciation is due as publisher as well as grandson of Harold Macmillan.

Preface

I am particularly indebted to Macmillan Publishers for permission to quote from the Macmillan memoirs, war diaries, etc., and to the Macmillan Trustees for the privileged access, given to me solely, to the Harold Macmillan Archives, including his unpublished diaries of 1950–63.

In the United States, I owe a vast debt of gratitude to the Woodrow Wilson Center of Washington DC, which, by generously granting me a fellowship in 1980–1, enabled me to carry out valuable research on the Eisenhower (and, later, Kennedy) years. In this I was most ably assisted by Neil M. Robinson, appointed as my researcher by the Center. I am additionally beholden to the Dwight D. Eisenhower Library in Abilene, Kansas, and the John Foster Dulles (Mudd) Library of Princeton, New Jersey, whose archives were readily made available to me.

· In the immediate publishing entourage, I feel I owe more special debts of gratitude than on any previous book, and in proportion to the ten years that this work has taken: to my old editor, Alan Maclean, who first initiated the idea that I should be commissioned to write the official life, and who, alas, did not remain to complete the work of editing (my fault, not his, for taking so long); to Ann Wilson, who – an exacting perfectionist – finally took over this arduous labour after Venetia Pollock had, tragically, been forced to abandon it; to Nicky Byam Shaw, my longest surviving friend at court at Macmillan Publishers, for his enthusiasm and good sense at the worst moments; to Philippa Harrison of Macmillan and to Christine Pevitt of Viking Penguin for invaluable support in the latter stages; to Michael Sissons of A. D. Peters, always a constant tower of support and encouragement; to Gill Graham for her able help with the bibliography; and, lastly but emphatically, to Helen Whitten, who over the past five years assumed the work of researcher and most of the seemingly endless task of retyping two long volumes.

Sir Philip Goodhart, Conservative Member of Parliament for Beckenham, to which he was elected shortly after Harold Macmillan came to power in 1957, and which had once been part of Harold Macmillan's own constituency of Bromley, read the manuscript with a penetrating eye for the solecisms that a political innocent might perpetrate; to him I am eminently grateful. He made many admirable suggestions. Any remaining errors of fact or judgement are peculiarly my own.

xviii

Finally, I owe a debt of a different kind to my wife, Sheelin, who knows what it all cost, but whose encouragement never flagged.

Alistair Horne
Turville, August 1988

Part I

A Long Apprenticeship
1894–1939

Chapter One

The Ripening Peach
1894–1914

. . . I owe everything all through my life to my mother's devotion and support. . . .

(HM, Winds of Change*)*

The world was a ripe peach and we were eating it.

(Osbert Sitwell, on England before the 1914–18 War)

King Edward VII Hospital, London 1963

At the private nursing home in Beaumont Street, W1, called King
Edward VII's Hospital for Officers but known more familiarly as
Sister Agnes, the morning of Friday, 18 October 1963, began on a
note of some excitement. Her Majesty the Queen was due at 11 a.m.
to visit her ailing Prime Minister, Mr Harold Macmillan. Nurses
and cleaners bustled and primped, fussed and dusted; private
secretaries and detectives arrayed themselves to keep the press at
bay. The anticipated event would establish precedent, as no reigning
monarch had ever before come to visit a prime minister on his bed
of sickness; but even without precedent, it would have been no
ordinary visit. The circumstances were anything but ordinary,
indeed it might be said that Harold Macmillan was no ordinary
prime minister.

Ten days previously, Macmillan had been expected to announce
his intention of leading the Tories into battle at the forthcoming
General Election. Instead he had been stricken by an unexpected,
and agonising, inflammation of the prostate, which had had to be
removed. In the debilitating aftermath of the operation, Macmillan
had decided that, at sixty-nine, he could not now continue. So the
Party caucuses, cabals and conspiracies had come to Beaumont
Street to discuss his successor. High Tory dignitaries had trooped
in steady procession, one by one, through the tiny hospital bedroom,
each giving his opinion. Always deeply imbued with a sense of
historical precedent and determined to have the transition of power
formally and properly documented, the sick man had drafted a
lengthy letter of resignation for the Queen, which his Private Secretary, Tim Bligh, had handed in at Buckingham Palace at 9.30
a.m.

As 11 a.m. approached, Macmillan, with his acute sense of
protocol, insisted on replacing his pyjama top with a white silk shirt
for the occasion, but as a sartorial compromise he pulled over it one
of his customary well-worn brown pullovers. He was then wheeled
down to the hospital boardroom to await the Queen. 'The poor

4

man had to have a bottle in bed with him,' recorded his personal physician, Sir John Richardson, 'a bell by his side and Sister was outside the door in case he needed help while the Queen was there. He took all this, as everything else, with supreme detachment and dignity. He was very pale and tense and indeed unhappy. . . .'[1]

When the Queen arrived, accompanied by her Private Secretary, Sir Michael Adeane, she was led into the boardroom and remained there alone with the Prime Minister. Macmillan recalled in his diary: 'She seemed moved; so was I. She referred to the very long time I had served her – nearly seven years – and how sorry she had been to get my letter of resignation.'[2] It was a scene that remained etched in Macmillan's memory, and years later he recalled the ensuing dialogue:

> She said, very kindly, 'What are you going to do?' And I said, 'Well I am afraid I can't go on.' And she was very upset. . . . Then said, 'Have you any advice to give me?' And I said 'Ma'am, do you wish me to give any advice?' And she said 'Yes I do'. . . . So then I said 'Well, since you ask for it, Ma'am, I have, with the help of Mr Bligh, prepared it all, and here it is.' And I just handed her over my manuscript . . . then I read it to her, I think.[3]

He went on to explain how he had wanted the memorandum to be in the Queen's archives, 'as a full justification of any action she might take on my advice'.[4] The Queen agreed with his recommendation that Lord Home was the most likely choice to gain general support, and then thanked him. 'We chatted a bit more and then she went away.'[5]

It was, as Macmillan liked to reminisce with detached amusement in later years, 'an extraordinary resignation. . . . the bed covers were down, and concealed underneath the bed was a pail, with a tube full of bile coming out of me. I made my resignation to the Queen of England for an hour, in great discomfort.'[6] The incongruity of the scene was enhanced by the fact that, in their haste, the distraught staff at No. 10 had only been able to provide the most outsize white envelope, many times too big, in which to house the historic document. This the Queen handed to the short and portly Michael Adeane, which, Macmillan's whimsical eye noted as the door to the boardroom opened, 'made him look like the Frog Footman'.[7]

So ended Harold Macmillan's premiership.

The Family Heritage

In the 1960s one fact every schoolchild knew about Macmillan, next to his being author of the remark 'you've-never-had-it-so-good', was that he was the grandson of a Scottish crofter and became the son-in-law of an English duke. (Strictly speaking, it was his great-grandfather who was the crofter, but pride in his origins caused Macmillan habitually to skip a generation.) Daniel, his grandfather, was born the tenth of twelve crofter's children in 1813, amid the clangour of the Napoleonic Wars, little news of which, however, probably reached the bleak northern tip of the island of Arran where the family croft, called The Cock, was situated. Daniel's own grandfather, Malcolm, had been an elder of the Established Church of Scotland and a successful farmer, but under his son Duncan's stewardship, The Cock had not prospered. Life for the twelve children was extremely spartan. Four died early – probably from tuberculosis, of which Daniel himself was incurably stricken before he was twenty. Despite their grim poverty, every spare penny seems to have been spent on education, and Daniel, trudging two and a half miles each day to the tiny local school, somehow achieved a remarkable command of English. In 1824, a year after his father's death and aged only eleven, he left Arran to be bound apprentice to a bookseller in Irvine on the Ayrshire mainland, for the princely wage of 1s 6d a week. Seven years later he moved to Glasgow, and thence – like many ambitious young Scots of the age – to England where, after years of setbacks and repeated ill-health, he and his brother Alexander borrowed £750 with which to set up a bookshop in Cambridge.

In 1843, the brothers established Macmillan and Co., publishers, producing as their first book *The Philosophy of Training* by A. R. Craig. Dealing with the 'improvement of the wealthier classes', it was not exactly a title designed to set the Thames on fire, but very much established the high moral tone the house was to pursue henceforth. A strict Calvinist in his early life, Daniel felt that Mammon was evil and 'requires to be watched and kept under'.

He seems to have driven his small staff like Scrooge: 7 a.m. to 8 p.m. for £60 a year. Despite the ravages of tuberculosis, he was equally exacting of himself, often getting up for work at 3.30 a.m. However, as he grew older Daniel mellowed and finally fell under the influence of Cardinal Newman, whose Anglo-Catholicism came as a blinding ray of light to him. 'You will see that he is no old woman, and that his notions about God are as sublime as anything you have ever read,' he wrote.[8]

In 1857, consumption carried off Daniel Macmillan, aged just forty-four and only seven years after his marriage to Frances Orridge, daughter of a Cambridge chemist. He left behind four children, including Harold's father, Maurice, to be brought up in a large house in the middle-class suburb of Upper Tooting by his brother Alexander and his second wife, a lady of Italian descent, Emma Pignatel. (It perhaps says something about Harold's attitude toward primogeniture, and the female sex as a whole, that he barely mentions the wives of either Daniel or Alexander in his memoirs.) Alexander lived on till 1896 and under him the house of Macmillan flourished and expanded. The career of these remarkable brothers was a typical Victorian success story, with all its stern precepts and morality. Their forceful portraits dominated Harold and his brothers' childhood home; just as, translated in subsequent times, they used to daunt young authors creeping along the corridors of Macmillan's to ask for an advance.

Although Harold never knew Daniel, the crofter-cum-publisher grandfather who died nearly forty years before he was born, to him Daniel seemed 'almost a living person; for we were brought up as children upon the story of his struggles and achievement'.[9] In early childhood Harold read and re-read Thomas Hughes's biographical sketch of his grandfather; one passage in particular appealed to him, a eulogy to self-reliance contained in a letter which Daniel, at twenty, had written to an elder brother censorious of his excessive ambition: 'I do not feel bound to follow in the footsteps of any of my relations. I am here to act for myself. No one of them can stand in my stead in any very important matter. The most important things must be done by myself – alone.'[10] This was to become a creed for Harold: 'I was determined somehow to follow in his footsteps by my own will and effort. Whether this was in the field of art, literature or commerce, I did not know for sure.'[11]

Maurice, Harold's father, was only four when his father died. He was named after one of his godfathers, Frederick Denison Maurice, then an influential writer of the Christian Socialist movement (more jocularly known as 'muscular Christianity'); his other godfather was Charles Kingsley, author of *The Water Babies*, and also published by Macmillan's. With the accent in the family constantly on self-improvement through education, and aided by growing prosperity, Maurice was sent to Uppingham, an old grammar school then being turned into a classic Victorian public school by Edward Thring. From there he went, with a scholarship, to Christ's College, Cambridge, where he got a first in classics. Instead of setting immediately to work in the firm under his uncle Alexander, he spent the next six years as a classics master at St Paul's School in London. A reserved and scholarly man, at the age of thirty he went to Paris where he met, and fell in love with, an American music and art student, Helen Artie Tarleton Belles. Three years younger than Maurice, Nellie – as she was known – was a small, dark-haired woman whose determined features reflected her strong personality. The most incongruous act of Maurice Macmillan's life was almost certainly his marriage to this forceful American woman. Harold, for one, was always baffled as to precisely how they had met and fallen in love. But Maurice and Nellie settled down to conventional married life in London, at 52 Cadogan Place, which remained the family home for fifty years.

Nellie Belles was born in 1856 in the small prairie town of Spencer, Indiana. She was one of three children; her mother had Scottish blood, and her father was a doctor from Kentucky, who supported the North during the Civil War. From conversations in the Belles household, Nellie grew up steeped in the stories of that war. At nineteen a competent singer, she had married a musician called Hill who died six months later; she was never heard to mention his name again. She then persuaded her father to let her go to Paris, where she studied music and sculpture, and gave some concerts at the Madeleine. Her Paris life evidently left a strong mark on Nellie, who would often require her sons to speak French 'downstairs'. She hired French nursery-maids, who, in the best Nancy Mitford tradition, were cordially detested by the English nanny, Mrs Last. (But the French he learned in the nursery, claimed Harold, 'came in very useful when conversing with de Gaulle in later life!')[12]

In Indiana Nellie had been raised in the Methodist Church, and all her life she retained the unassailable Protestant principles of mid-America of that date. When it came to the Church of Rome, these amounted to rooted prejudices; in the words of Harold, 'The most powerful criticism she could make of any argument was that it was "Jesuitical".' Her nonconformist upbringing did not, however, deflect Nellie from being an ardent hostess. Making up for the social shortcomings of an excessively shy husband, she enjoyed entertaining and loved to give dinner parties both in London and later in the Macmillans' home in Sussex. She invited in particular those engaged in literature and politics, and colleagues from such philanthropic bodies as the Women's Liberal Unionist Association and the Ladies' Working Guild filed through the house. But Nellie was, as Harold admitted, somewhat puritanical and one is left with the impression of evenings *chez* Macmillan that were probably yet more formal and stilted than was the norm even of that era.

A Victorian Childhood

Harold Macmillan was born at Cadogan Place on 10 February 1894, in the heyday of the Victorian world. He was the third child and third son; Dan, his brilliant eldest brother, was eight years older than him and Arthur four years older. Though only three at the time, he claimed to recall vividly the Diamond Jubilee procession of 1897, led by the majestic Captain Ames, at 6 foot 8 inches the tallest man in the British Army – though just conceivably his infant memory may have been conditioned by reading Philip Guedalla's colourful account many years later.[13] He remembered too the solemnity, the muffled bands and the black crepe of the old Queen's funeral four years later; he recollected the exhilaration on the news of the relief of Mafeking; he cheered the 'gallant little Japs' in their brilliant performance against the Russian behemoth in the Straits of Tsushima, and – aged twelve at the historic General Election of 1906 – he supported the Liberal, Campbell Bannerman, probably, he thought in retrospect, because the general opinion in the family was for the Conservative, Balfour.

More personally he remembered the clop and jingle of the horse-drawn trams and, from his night nursery in Cadogan Place, the noise of the hammer and anvil from a blacksmith's shop in the mews below. Occasionally, 'to our huge gratification', there would be heard the oompahs of a German band outside, but where other families enjoyed that new contraption, 'with the dog listening to the trumpet-like mechanism through which the sound poured magically from the mysterious box', even the gramophone was disapproved of as 'rather frivolous' in the Macmillan household.[14]

By comparison even with other late-Victorian upbringings, Harold's was an austere one, with little joy or fun to it. He was, he says, 'always anxious lest I might do something wrong or commit some solecism'.[15] His father, Harold recalled as being kind, considerate and generous – not stern, but at the same time taciturn and very controlled: 'Mother would say "Don't do that, that would upset your father" – though you knew it never would.' Maurice had given up smoking at Cambridge, and alcohol at thirty-five, until, at eighty, he was recommended port by his doctors. Possibly there may have been a threat of a drink problem, such as was to plague later generations of Macmillans (though Harold always staunchly claimed that it was inherited purely through the Cavendish line): Maurice himself explained to his sons that it 'might weaken the self-control which he regarded as the essential quality in every man'. It was perhaps an indication of the family atmosphere in which the Macmillan sons were raised.

Maurice regarded the English as being 'rather snobbish, compared with the essential nobility of the Scots', yet transferred his spiritual allegiances to the Church of England. Influenced by Darwin and Thring, he might, thought Harold, even have been called an agnostic, going to church largely from duty. Nevertheless, each day the family went through a Victorian ritual of father reciting aloud the evening prayer, followed by readings from Sir Walter Scott (Harold's favourite was *Guy Mannering*), Tennyson or Shakespeare. A conscientious man of highest Christian principles, Maurice seems to have been something of a workaholic, spending long hours in the office – possibly also to escape from a domineering wife. Shy and retiring, he had few intimate friends – a deficiency Harold himself would share in the course of his own life. But Maurice's small circle did range, eclectically, from the High Tory Lord Robert Cecil to John Morley, the Liberal–Radical, while Arthur Balfour also came to Nellie's salon.

Reading between the lines of Harold's filial loyalty in his memoirs, it sounds as if Maurice was also a faintly dull man, certainly when compared with his father Daniel. Though he had never known his grandfather, Harold admitted that 'he must have been much more amusing than my father!'[16] Maurice was seldom known to express an opinion, except on issues of real importance – when 'his will would prevail'. Otherwise, Harold records revealingly in his memoirs, he 'left the management of his house and everything to do with the garden or our small estate to my mother. In such matters I never heard him express in our presence any opinion, except to approve of what she proposed.'

Harold described his mother as having an:

> unusually strong character. She had high standards and de-manded equally high performances from all about her. She had great ambitions, not for herself but for her children. This was sometimes embarrassing both to my father and us. But I can truthfully say that I owe everything all through my life to my mother's devotion and support. . . .

Others of the family who remembered this American matriarch were less flattering, regarding her as something of a fiend, so tough and powerful as to inhibit all three sons, making them repressed and withdrawn, with the result that, in later life, they all found it difficult to have normal relations with their contemporaries, their own children – and women.

As a child Harold hardly saw his retiring father and took refuge from his forbidding mother and the exacting standards she imposed behind the green baize door, in the bosom of the fiercely patriotic Nanny Last. What affection he found at home seems to have come from Nanny Last; for him she was 'the true centre of life and the only secure world'. With his brothers so much older than him, it must have been a lonely and solitary existence. Occasionally a compliant cook would allow him to sneak out of the back door to the shops. Otherwise his recollections focused on walking with Nanny Last to see the rabbits in the Dell of Hyde Park. Returning, he would always retain a picture of the fish lying on their marble slab outside Mr Vigo's, the fishmonger's shop in Sloane Street, where 'Mr Vigo himself, an immense figure in a blue and white apron, armed with a gigantic skewer for splitting great dripping blocks of ice, used to dominate the scene. . . .'[17] There was the regular visit to the great pantomime in Drury Lane, while a trip to

Kew by horse-bus was a great treat, and an excursion by train even more so. Occasionally the children would be despatched, with Nanny, to the seaside – to 'lodgings with horse-hair sofas and Landseer prints'.[18] The family did not travel abroad; nor was there any personal contact with Nellie's American relatives.

Nellie's thrusting ambition for her three sons impelled them firmly forward. Once, when Harold's own children were very young at Birch Grove – the country home in Sussex bought by Nellie after her marriage – she admonished them: 'Don't kick that door. This house is going to belong to the Prime Minister of England one of these days.'[19] It was her ambition that got Harold to Eton, following Dan, and to Balliol, and into the smart Grenadier Guards; set him on the course to marrying a duke's daughter, and pointed his footsteps towards a political career; and indeed fanned his ambition all through his life. 'You will win through in the end,' his mother would assure Harold at difficult moments, and she would always be there when things went wrong; to purge the friends she considered undesirable, nurse him after he returned badly wounded from the Somme and pick up the pieces when his marriage threatened to founder.

'No-one who has not experienced it,' wrote Harold, 'can realise the determination of an American mother defending her children.' Being so much the youngest, Harold came more under the protective cloak than his two brothers – and there was, inevitably, the reverse side of the relationship. Nellie 'tried to enter into every aspect of her children's life; she wished to know our friends, our amusements, and almost our daily doings.' In her pursuit of the 'highest standards of work and behaviour', Nellie made the future Chancellor of the Exchequer particularly suffer from mental arithmetic: 'She meant to be kind, but was very concerned over my inability to make the appropriate calculations accurately and rapidly.' Harold found her 'maddening on small things, but a rock on bigger things';[20] even six years after her death, when he himself had nearly died in an air crash in Algiers, his first words on coming round were: 'Tell my mother I'm alive and well.'[21] Still later, as Prime Minister, he confided to a friend: 'I admired her, but never really liked her. . . . She dominated me, and she still dominates me.'[22]

With his extremely demanding mother and taciturn, withdrawn father, childhood for Harold must have been far from happy, yet – as in a letter to his long-term confidante Ava Waverley in 1962, he always affected to feel himself 'lucky in my memories', recalling the charm of '. . . Mother's black and white straw hats (like a clergyman) and mutton-chop sleeves and Father's sovereign case, full of gold sovereigns – re-filled daily and carried about at the end of a heavy gold watch-chain. . . .'[23]

Before he was seven, Harold went to Mr Gladstone's day-school, round the corner from Cadogan Place. Gladstone specialised in the classics and was closely connected with Summerfields preparatory school in Oxford, where Dan had already passed through with high distinction to Eton. Once or twice a week an extremely reluctant Harold would also be 'paraded' to Mr Macpherson's Gymnasium and Dancing Academy nearby. He swiftly displayed a marked lack of prowess and enthusiasm for swinging Indian clubs; or, indeed, for any form of athletics. 'How I hated the clubs,' he reminisced to Ava Waverley sixty years later: 'which I always dropped – and the dreadful wooden bars, up which I climbed slower than any other boy. (They were all so agile and so confident – I so unconfident and so shy.) And above all, how I hated the ropes, up which I could not make any progress at all. . . .'[24] Particularly, and most revealingly, it brought back to him 'my perpetual terror of becoming in any way conspicuous . . .'.

This extreme dislike of doing things in public, hardly the ideal talent for a future politician, pursued him right through his youth and into his early days in the army, and to some extent he found himself having to fight against intrinsic shyness throughout his life. A second psychological handicap identified in those early years was a cyclical proneness to despondency, known among Scots as the 'Black Dog'. As a child, he says he found the world generally a hostile and faintly alarming place: 'I was oppressed by some kind of mysterious power which would be sure to get me in the end. One felt that something unpleasant was more likely to happen than anything pleasant.' The Black Dog was to ambush him from dark corners for the rest of his days, and the favourite technique which he eventually developed for coping with the onset of its symptoms was to retreat into himself, accompanied by a Jane Austen novel, sometimes for two or three days at a time.

The third problem he had to overcome was his highly strung nature. It was a constant struggle to discipline, and even repress, his immediate emotions. The image of unflappability for which he

13

became so well known was achieved over many years and was far from being an instinctive characteristic. 'I always felt', he once told the author, 'that one must maintain great control, but it is very exhausting keeping it to yourself. I wasn't really "unflappable", I just had to keep it down.'

Harold may have been made doubly conscious of the need for self-control because his brother Arthur suffered from occasional epileptic fits. Dan, the idolised eldest brother, was packed off to boarding school when Harold was only one; but Arthur, because of the threat of epilepsy, never went away to school. Arthur was not, however, much company for Harold at home; his passionate interest was music, perhaps inherited from Nellie, while Harold admitted to being 'wholly unmusical', and, although they were fond of each other in a brotherly way, they quarrelled incessantly and never became close in later life.

Harold was expected to follow in Dan's footsteps, and in 1903 at the age of nine he was sent to Summerfields, on the outskirts of Oxford, one of England's sterner boarding preparatory schools. In those days, Harold recalled, 'lachrymose farewells' were considered to be bad form, so his 'debut was simple and dignified'. Instead of being driven to the school by his parents like modern children, 'One of my father's clerks took me to Paddington in a four-wheeler with my trunk and my play-box (where, oh where, are all those play-boxes now?), bought me a ticket and handed me over to a junior master who was conducting a number of boys to the same destination. . . .'[25] That first night, after a high-tea of bread and milk, the pale, unhappy little boy wept copiously and to the very last days of his life he recalled being comforted by an older boy, with the words 'don't cry – your situation is bad, but not desperate.'[26] Between Gladstone's and Summerfields, he recalled making one single friend – a boy called Gwynn ('I do not remember his Christian name. We stuck to surnames in those days').

Photographs from Summerfields, and later Eton too, reveal a good-looking boy with a sensitive, full mouth, and a wistful face with a hint of steel in the eyes. He appeared to be clever and bookish, reading widely from G. A. Henty and Conan Doyle to Dickens and Walter Scott. At ten he was already learning the subtle complexities of hendiadys and oxymorons out of a little grammar book of Dan's – which he cherished all his life. But a Summerfields report to his subsequent house master at Eton described him as

'very bright but idle'.[27] A group picture from 1905 shows him as
the central figure in the school play, cast – curiously enough – as
Prime Minister ('though the wig looks more like a Lord Chancellor's', was his comment); otherwise the only other stage role the
future 'actor–manager' could ever remember playing in his youth
was in a crowd scene in *Coriolanus*.

It was from Summerfields that Harold first discovered Oxford.
In those days, he later recalled, the city had only three industries:
marmalade, printing and the University. Once a term, and only
once, parents made 'a somewhat formal visit' to take out their boys.
'There was nowhere to go; there was nothing to go in; there was
nothing to do. So we visited Oxford. . . .' Travelling in a rumbling
horse-tram, 'my mother correctly but not showily dressed, my father
always in a tail-coat and top hat', they alighted at the Randolph
Hotel where they lunched – 'alone and almost in silence', with a
special treat of a glass of ginger-beer. After this cheerful lunch, with
several hours still to be filled in, they explored the colleges of the
University. Too shy to have any contact with the deities that dwelt
inside, Maurice limited his conducted tours to externals. 'Few boys,
between nine and twelve,' declared its future Chancellor, 'can have
known so well at least the exterior of the University.' Seen from a
distance, to young Harold its denizens 'seemed to be so old; so odd;
with such white hair, and such myopic eyes. It was by the spectacle
of these no doubt wise and learned, but queer looking, men that I
was deeply impressed.' With their caps and gowns and semi-clerical
costume, he was also struck by 'what a great part religion must
play in their lives'.[28]

Harold left Summerfields for Eton in 1906, having won the Third
Scholarship; but the achievement was somewhat diminished by the
knowledge that Dan had won the First eight years previously.
Although he revered Dan and they were to remain lifelong friends,
he always suffered from an acute and somewhat resentful sense of
inferiority; it was Dan's school-books and Dan's outgrown clothes
that were handed on to him, and it was Dan who, as a brilliant
classical scholar, always seemed one rung above him. After Eton,
Dan entered Balliol as the Senior Classical Scholar of his year;
Harold gained only an exhibition. Dan graduated with a distinguished First Class degree; Harold says, modestly, he only
scraped a First 'with some difficulty' in preliminary 'Mods' exams;
until, as he put it, he was 'sent down by the Kaiser' in 1914. Though

in early photographs as a young man Dan looked like a Bertie Wooster, he was evidently something of a rake, his escapades with women (in sharp contrast to Harold) causing the family considerable pain. To the outsider, what amounted to Harold's almost hero-worship of Dan all through his life seems not entirely warranted; a brilliant academic mind, a competent publisher and a pillar of the Garrick Club were about the sum of Daniel's achievements.

At Eton, Harold seems to have found few close companions; he was never happy there (though in later life he came to put a brave face on it), and recalled particularly having been plagued with the dread Black Dog. His few lasting friends there, however, included Julian ('Leggy') Lambart (subsequently Vice-Provost of Eton), Harry Willink (later Minister of Health under Churchill, and Master of Magdalene College, Cambridge), and Harry Crookshank, who was to remain one of Harold's very few intimate cronies in his later, political life. Over seventy years later, Leggy Lambart recalled Harold as having shown no particular interest in politics. He thought it was probably from Eton that his passion for the English classics stemmed, but otherwise 'I don't think he had any idea of what he wanted to do.'[29]

Lambart says that he never detected any outstanding sense of humour in Harold, but he was 'devoted' to him, and 'shattered' when he left prematurely. For, after an undistinguished three years, Harold never finished Eton. He seems to have suffered from poor health and in his first half contracted pneumonia, from which he only just survived. Three years later some form of heart trouble was evidently diagnosed, and in 1909 he returned home as a semi-invalid. At various times subsequently the inevitable rumours have arisen that he had had to leave Eton for the 'usual reasons'; though at Eton at that time 'inordinate affection' might hardly have been deemed worthy of expulsion. Lambart remembered his having indeed been very ill, but no hard evidence has ever been produced to back any suggestion of homosexual leanings; certainly nothing beyond what might have been deemed acceptable in an English public schoolboy of the period. And, if there were any such proclivities, given Harold's fastidious nature they would almost certainly have been confined to the emotional and intellectual rather than the physical realm. For a mother like Nellie, Harold's illness and unhappiness would have been enough.

Nellie's reaction, characteristically, seems to have been that Eton had failed her son, rather than the reverse; on the other hand, as the subsequent correspondence with Ronald Knox seems to suggest, there must have been some slight shadow over his departure. In later life, Harold's attitude to Eton was distinctly ambivalent; he wore the Old Etonian tie with addiction (it sometimes seemed to be one of the very few he owned), but he never showed any willingness to revisit the school and it is even uncertain whether he ever went there when his own son, Maurice, was at Eton. It was all very different to the genuineness of his feelings about Balliol College, Oxford. But the really important fact about his leaving Eton was that it necessitated his having a series of tutors, to prepare him for the Oxford scholarship examination. Among them was Ronnie Knox, a friend and Eton contemporary of Dan's, who would become a most profound influence on Harold, but also the source of the first moral crisis in his life – and one of the greatest.

Ronnie Knox

The choice of tutor fell first on Ronnie's older brother Dilwyn, also a brilliant classical scholar, and later a code-breaker of genius. But Dilly was found to be austere and uncongenial, and after a few weeks the relationship foundered. Ronnie, who took his place, was already, at twenty-two, considered one of the most talented young men of his generation, and at Oxford had been at the centre of a group of outstanding undergraduates. A debater of great wit, he had been President of the Union and might well have had a distinguished political career had not the Church posed a prior claim. Indeed, many years after Ronnie's death, Harold Macmillan once speculated – half seriously – on how, if the quirks of history had been only slightly altered, Ronnie might have become Prime Minister and he, Harold, Monsignor Macmillan. Moving himself steadily along the road to full conversion to the Catholic faith, Ronnie was then an ardent Anglo-Catholic, and pressed hard to inject his friends with religious enthusiasm. An immediate sympathy sprang up between tutor and pupil; for Harold, it was the first flowering of an intimate friendship. Speaking of Ronnie Knox, Macmillan in his eighties said:

he was a little bit like Newman . . . he represented the nineteenth century; he was tone deaf, couldn't recognise 'God Save the Queen', but had an extraordinary sense of language. He could write Latin like Ovid. He loved games – chess, acrostics, and would play St Paul's travels like 'Monopoly' – 'Go to Damascus, do not pass Go!' . . . His French style of very incisive thinking was all new to me, and as a boy I found it very attractive. . . . He had no real sense of beauty, or comfort, but a great simplicity. . . . He was sweet and he influenced me because he was a saint . . . the only man I have ever known who really was a saint . . . and if you live with a saint, it's quite an experience, especially a humorous saint . . . and he did have a marvellous sense of humour.[30]

On his side, Ronnie apparently felt that his seventeen-year-old charge was in need of spiritual assistance as well as conventional education, and so he began to explain the hopes and beliefs of the Anglo-Catholics. At Harold's own request, he took him off to an Anglo-Catholic mass. Writing to a friend in October 1910 who had enquired whether he was making Harold a Catholic, Ronnie replied, 'I'm not making him anything yet, but biding my time. I trust I may be sent some opportunity.'[31]

Knox reckoned, however, without the forceful intervention of Nellie Macmillan, with her staunchly Protestant prejudices. A red-blooded American matriarch with innate suspicions about English public-school habits, she was probably apprehensive lest the emotional tenor of the relationship might take an unhealthy direction; she also sensed the possible consequences of Knox's spiritual assistance, and she issued an ultimatum. 'Could you pray for me?' Ronnie wrote to his sister, Winnie, towards the end of October 1910. 'I've got a most heart-rending and nerve-racking dispute going on with Mrs Macmillan, not about money this time, but about things 7000 times more important. Don't tell anyone. . . .'[32] On 4 November he was writing:

She [Mrs Macmillan] (having made certain discoveries) wanted me to promise not to mention anything connected with religion in private conversation to her son. Of course I refused. . . . So I left yesterday; they may want me to come back, but I can't do it under any promises whatsoever. The only thing which complicates the situation is that I'm by now extremely (and not quite unreturnedly) fond of the boy. . . .[33]

Preceding this, Ronnie Knox had penned a letter, several pages long and charged with emotion, to Nellie Macmillan, in which he stated that he could not accept the terms of never speaking to Harold on religious matters: 'because thought is free, and I think talk must be free if proper intimacy is to exist. May I give an example? When I first came here I thought that (for obvious reasons) it would be better if I didn't – whether in public or tête-à-tête – mention anything connected with Eton in Harold's presence.' (Here seems to be a hint at some sort of cloud surrounding Harold's departure from Eton – or at least considerable unhappiness.) Knox continued: 'After about a week, I realised that it didn't matter, and if I hadn't realised that I should hardly know Harold as well as I do. *I couldn't have kept it up*, and I feel that I couldn't keep up a reticence about my view of the Church. . . .'

Invoking his moral conviction that 'all the grace God has given me, is not mine to sell or barter; it must not be squandered at my own pleasure,' he went on, '. . . I needn't – perhaps I can't – explain to you how much mere pleasure it gives me being with Harold but if I bought that pleasure at the price of my own freedom of speech, I should consider it a Judas bargain. . . .' Knox then listed five reasons for not wanting to give up the job, putting 'For Harold's sake first' and finally, and rather pathetically: 'what am I to do when I go away, and how explain my abandonment?' Although he wished to continue to teach Harold, he thought that to live in the same house would not 'be quite tolerable' to him, 'having, if you will excuse my saying so, no-one with whom to discuss my most vital views, at a time when they are particularly effervescent . . .'. He ended by proposing that he live in London and come down to tutor at Birch Grove daily, hoping Mrs Macmillan could 'trust me not to devote hours meant for work to anything in the nature of propagandism'.[34]

This verbose, emotional letter, slightly peevish and morally accusative in tone, yet clearly the product of a twenty-two-year-old in a state of deep distress, hardly recommended itself to Nellie Macmillan, who had the impertinent young tutor shipped off on the first train. Evidence of the speed of his departure comes in a coolly formal valedictory note of 10 November, written on black-rimmed paper from 4 Eaton Place, in which Knox wrote '. . . I need not say how sorry I am that no arrangement could be found,' and ended by asking for his bicycle to be forwarded to Oxford: 'they would pay at that end; my washing too, if it isn't ready before Saturday. I am sorry to trouble you. . . .'[35]

The episode was to have a profound effect on both young men. Knox's biographer, Evelyn Waugh, claims that it 'affected Ronald so painfully that seven years later he set it down as one of his formative experiences'.[36] Knox confessed that it had been the only period 'when I ever experienced before 1915 an attack of what Anglicans call "Roman fever" . . . indeed it was hinted to me at the time [by Mrs Macmillan] . . . that I would have done better to be an out-and-out Roman Catholic. . . .'[37] Reflecting on the episode, Macmillan considered that his mother had 'probably said to Ronnie very firmly – "go the whole way"', thus materially influencing him in his eventual decision to 'pope'.[38]

To understand Nellie Macmillan's stern line with Ronnie Knox, it is worth recalling that her son Arthur, already very much under the influence of Knox, became a high Anglo-Catholic – to Nellie's lasting dismay. Equally, one leading factor must undoubtedly have been her awareness that in the England of 1910 conversion to Roman Catholicism would present an effective obstacle to preferment to senior office under the Crown in either law or politics; and, indeed, for the 'suitable' marriage she desired for all her sons.

Oxford

The lonely adolescent, devastated by the hastened departure of his first close friend, withdrew back into his solitary world, mitigated only by voracious reading – though he never complained of it. Another tutor replaced Knox, but Macmillan never mentioned his name. There can have been little affinity there, but at least he helped prepare him well scholastically for Oxford. The Birch Grove drama of 1910 proved, however, to be by no means the end of the affair. In the autumn of the following year, Harold went up to Balliol to sit the scholarship exam. The first printed paper terrified him:

It seems to have no meaning at all. . . . What is it? Latin? or Greek? It might be Hebrew. . . . You glance around at your competitors. What clever faces! What intellectual brows! What application! They have all begun to write from the very first minute – apparently with easy confidence. Good heavens! Ten minutes have passed – they are running well down the course. You are still at the starting gate. I still have nightmares about examinations. . . .[39]

All through his life he would remember that sensation when he came to give a major speech. Nevertheless, 'a sort of consolation prize', the Williams Classical Exhibition, was awarded him. 'I had not triumphed – but I had not altogether failed.' Dan, however, had won the top classical scholarship to Balliol; 'I jogged along behind; but, still, I jogged.'

The following autumn, 1912, Harold Macmillan went up to Balliol. Ronnie Knox was then Anglican Chaplain at Trinity College; Dan, Harold's rival, had moved on into Macmillan's. Suddenly, for the first time in his life, the sun seemed to burst through the clouds in a blaze of golden glory. His rooms in the front quad were lofty, cold and inconvenient – 'but my own'. To him Oxford represented, at last, escape from 'a home where the discipline was severe and a mother's love almost too restraining', he remarked, with moderation, in his memoirs. 'It was an intoxicating feeling to be on one's own, in a society of countless friends, old and new.' He also soon discovered the delights of alcohol, unknown at home.

Looking back with nostalgia on those early Oxford days, he remembered Talleyrand's remark that anyone who had not known France before the Revolution had never known 'la douceur de vivre'. The Oxford of *Zuleika Dobson* was indeed a sparkling place. 'There is nothing in England,' claimed Max Beerbohm in 1911, 'to be matched with what lurks in the vapours of these meadows, and in the shadows of these spires – that mysterious, ineludible spirit of Oxford. Oxford! The very sight of the word printed, or sound of it spoken, is fraught for me with most actual magic.'[40] At the heart of it lay Balliol, still iridescent in the wake of the great Jowett, whose undergraduates were frequently thought to appear superior, self-satisfied and intellectually arrogant, with what Asquith described as 'a tranquil consciousness of effortless superiority'. It was a rather incestuous little world, where 'the sun rose over Wadham and set over Worcester', where friendships and conversation (especially on religious matters) were conducted in a hot-house atmosphere verging on the precious.

In his first months at Oxford, Macmillan remained painfully shy; a Balliol group photograph of 1913 shows him seated in the back row, outside edge (a position where he was, characteristically, also to be found at meetings of the great in the Second World War). Yet he seems swiftly to have emulated the 'Balliol manner' with enthusiasm, being described by one of his contemporaries as 'tall, willowy, languid'.[41] With a considerable effort of will, hinting at the ruthless determination of later years, he threw himself into almost every possible activity that the University offered; 'I was indeed almost an addict of societies.'[42] His political endeavours verged on the promiscuous; simultaneously he was a member of the Canning (a Tory club), the Russell (Whig or Liberal) and the Fabian Society (socialist). 'In those happy days all was grist to my voracious mill,' he confessed some sixty years later; 'things were much less rigid than now.'[43] But Disraeli had already begun to exert a profound influence on him. At an early date he began to attend the Union, supporting such issues as women's suffrage, but cautiously waiting six months before delivering his own maiden speech. The President of the Union then was Walter Monckton, who was to serve with him in government many years later.

Macmillan was elected Secretary of the Union in November 1913, then elected unopposed (something almost unprecedented) to be Junior Treasurer in March 1914, and – but for the war – would almost certainly have become President. He regarded the Union as a 'good rag', and recalled laughingly in retrospect that the motions were 'mostly old-fashioned, about Charles the First!' Lloyd George coming to speak in 1913 was the most memorable event: 'It was as if a Cleon or a Danton had suddenly invaded our quiet academic groves.' Then with long raven-black hair, Lloyd George gave a wonderful performance – 'the rapid changes from grave to gay – from slow to quick – now menacing, now seductive' – made a profound impression on the young apprentice orator. At the Union he claimed he generally supported the Liberal government, 'especially in its more radical efforts'. One of the first motions he supported, presaging the later radical, was 'That this House approves the main principles of socialism', and in his maiden speech (February 1913) he caused a stir by condemning the public-school system – doubtless influenced by his own less than satisfactory experiences at Eton. *Isis*, the University magazine, rated it 'brilliant'. A polished mandarin style was the vogue of the Union at the time, and Macmillan was in fact mildly criticised for being too slick, for delivering prepared speeches, and for a lack of debating skill. Considering that his display of histrionics on the floor of the Union added to his subsequent reputation as the 'actor–manager', it is perhaps surprising that one of the activities he did *not* undertake at Oxford (or at Eton) was the stage.

In contrast to Eton and his home life, Macmillan made many good and lasting friends at Oxford. There was Walter Monckton, Victor Mallet (later Ambassador to Italy 1947–53), A. P. Herbert, 'Bobbety' Cranborne (the future Lord Salisbury), Vincent Massey (the future Governor-General of Canada), Humphrey Sumner (afterwards Warden of All Souls and his most intimate friend – next to Ronnie Knox), Gilbert Talbot and Guy Lawrence. Ahead of him, Dan's contemporaries, were the 'giants' of pre-1914 mythology, the Asquiths, Grenfells and Shaw-Stewarts. All of them had been educated for what Rupert Brooke described as 'the long littleness of life' expected by the British upper classes in the early twentieth century, and which so few of them were to live to experience. Among the younger Balliol dons Macmillan's favourite was F. F. ('Sligger') Urquhart, who happened to be a Roman Catholic, in fact the first Catholic don at Oxford since the Reformation. This new influence in Harold's life would hardly have been likely to please Nellie, but he was now to some extent at least beyond her reach. Urquhart showed Macmillan 'kindness which I could never repay but I can never forget',[44] and he kept up the friendship until Urquhart's death between the wars.

In the summer of 1913 Macmillan and Walter Monckton were invited by Urquhart on a reading party to his chalet above St Gervais in the French Haute Savoie. It was for Harold a double thrill; he had never been abroad before, except as a boy at Eton on a Hellenic cruise, and then surrounded by schoolmasters and archaeologists; to see Greece was wonderful, but 'there was not much change of atmosphere'. It was a school afloat. Now visiting Urquhart also meant two exciting days and nights in Paris on the way, lodging at the modest and quaintly named Hôtel du Portugal et de l'Univers, then awaking on an overnight train amid the romantic scenery of the Alps. Spent working and reading aloud, plus 'even a little modest climbing' for the essentially unathletic Harold, it was a halcyon summer holiday. In Aubrey Herbert's day, the inspired Sligger's summer reading parties managed to gain four Firsts for the eight Balliol men present, and they undoubtedly gave Macmillan an invaluable academic leg-up.

Of the other congenial dons at Balliol there was A. D. Lindsay, later to become Master, whom Macmillan would support in the famous post-Munich by-election of twenty-five years later against the official Tory candidate, a young barrister called Quintin Hogg – an act that nearly led to expulsion from the Carlton Club. Oxford then was, of course, a world without women; but Macmillan recalls how he 'revelled' in these happy friendships.

The closest of all, however, was – still – with Ronnie Knox.

In 1912 Knox had taken up his new post as Chaplain at Trinity, and had already formed his own 'court' when Macmillan arrived. If anything their relationship now moved on to an even more intense and emotional plane. Towards the end of the war, Knox himself wrote of his Oxford 'circle':

> . . . I have never met conversation so brilliant – with the brilliance of humour, not of wit. The circle is broken now by distance and by death: . . . it was among these that I first began to make proselytes. At the time of which I am speaking, two of them already had adopted what I heard (and shuddered to hear) described as 'Ronnie Knox's religion.' [i.e. at that moment, Anglo-Catholicism]. . . .

He went on to designate them 'B' and 'C' – Guy Lawrence and Macmillan: 'The intimacy I formed with them, combined with their adhesion to my religious views, did much at the time to make me feel comfortable in my then position; and was to do much later, in God's Providence, to make me feel uncomfortable and to quit it.'[45]

At Oxford then, talk – in a rather fervid key – about religion and 'poping' was all the rage. 'One has to remember,' Harold Macmillan once reminisced,

> how different the mood of the day was, how little there was to argue about, because everybody agreed on general principles of morality, unlike now . . . for instance, all well brought up girls

were virgins; so one of the great arguments was on religion. Perhaps they were rather scholastic arguments – possibly in rather a narrow context – and the Protestantism of the public school life I was brought up in all seemed rather arid . . . our arguments were curiously unrelated to life, partly romantic. . . .[46]

Citing a conversation with him at the time, Knox recorded that 'C' (Macmillan) had agreed with 'B' (Lawrence) that the Anglican situation had become impossible; 'he did not, however, urge the same view on me. . . .'[47] From this and the ensuing passage, it sounds as if Macmillan was making the running, but in fact a series of (hitherto unpublished) letters from Knox to Macmillan[48] imply that it was Knox, already well down the road to Rome himself, who was applying constant pressure to his would-be 'proselyte'. They also indicate the very close degree of intimacy and affection between the two friends. On 6 April 1913, Knox was writing:

Harold my dear
    I am so glad you are being happy about the Faith. You see, it often seems too good to be true, so that when I haven't heard from you about it for some time at Oxford, I am always wondering whether you haven't forgotten it all again. I know it's very horrid of me even to feel like that – of course I don't ever really THINK like that – but the people one has prayed about are disappointing. . . . I do think you ought to be thinking about one further step, and that is to say Confession. . . .

In late July, he concluded what he described as 'a very dull letter': 'it wouldn't even matter if you lost it. Except when I mention that I love you very much, Yours most affly, Ronnie.' Two weeks later, on 14 August, he wrote:

Dearest Harold
    I was pained to notice a certain – what shall I call it? – light-heartedness in your reference to our sister church on the continent which has (alas!) fallen into such grievous error. The rapidity with which their services are recited is – I am profoundly convinced – not the least among the many causes which had lost them their hold over the consciences of the masses. . . .

25

A pleading letter from Knox on 17 April the following year suggests, *inter alia*, that – despite the golden age that Oxford genuinely was for Macmillan – there were times even at Balliol when the deadly Black Dog got the better of him:

> Harold dearest
> ... You can't think how much more ambitious I am for you than I ever was for myself, and how much I pray that it will put your nerves right and make you less despondent about Oxford. Jesus wanted you so badly and sought you so carefully, that I am sure he will preserve you for his service ... *please* come to Oxford as soon as you possibly can. You have no need to set an artificial value on yourself by all these dramatic exits and entrances.
> Your always loving Ronnie Knox.

People reading the Ronnie Knox letters in this nasty-minded age would have little difficulty in persuading themselves that, from the exceedingly affectionate – indeed, precious – language employed, Knox and Macmillan were in the middle of a whole-hearted homosexual affair. Penelope Fitzgerald, Knox's niece and perhaps his most sensitive biographer, considered that there was a homosexual element in all the relationships within the 'circle' – 'though not necessarily between Harold and Ronnie'.[49] As she points out, however, this kind of language was not all that unusual between young men of that age at Balliol then. The Grenfells and Patrick Shaw-Stewart habitually addressed each other as 'Dst' – short for Dearest.

There was to be one last, significant exchange in that summer of 1914, after Macmillan, responding to Knox's pleas, had returned to Oxford for the Trinity term. Knox had plans to take a weekend house in Gloucestershire, and to hold reading parties there. Macmillan was invited, but opted out – evidently on the grounds of his mother's disapproval. 'Why should C give any reason for his whereabouts?' Guy Lawrence wrote in pique: 'It's all silly nonsense this truckling to the old-fashioned ignorance of his parents and hanging on to his mother's apron strings. I should like 5 minutes conversation with her on the point.'[50] In the event, none of the Circle was to go, and it proved the beginning of the end of the triangular relationship between Knox and his two 'proselytes'.

Punting, bathing, sitting in the quad, dining and arguing with his friends, debating in the Union and dancing at Commemoration Balls, Macmillan reckoned that golden Trinity term of 1914 to have been the best of all. At the end of it, he passed his 'Mods' triumphantly with a First and could thus look forward to a further two glorious years before taking 'Greats'. There was another beckoning invitation from Sligger Urquhart to return to the Savoyard chalet – for the first week in August. He even had his books – Herodotus and Plato – already packed to go. Like so many who knew that fateful summer, Macmillan remembered a 'cloudless atmosphere with soft, voluptuous breezes and a Mediterranean sky'.[51] 'The world was a ripe peach and we were eating it,' observed Macmillan's contemporary, Osbert Sitwell.[52] On 28 June, Macmillan recalled attending a grand ball in one of London's great houses, and waltzing the night away to Mr Cassani's string band as one detachable stiff collar after another wilted and was replaced in the cloakroom. As he put on his last collar and emerged into the dawn, he heard a paper-boy raucously shouting: 'Murder of Archduke'. To him it had no more significance than it had to any of his fellow guests. But just as Eton had been truncated by the unforeseen, so it meant the end of Balliol and Oxford for Macmillan.

In old age he looked back on this high-point in his life 'with nostalgic regret but with deep gratitude'. Apart from the friendships made, the self-confidence gained, the struggle towards a spiritual resolution, the grounding in rhetoric at the Union, and a First in 'Mods', what had he gained from the education Oxford had to offer in those two short years? Writing in *The Times* two years after his resignation from office, he recalled the words with which his Professor of Moral Philosophy, J. A. Smith, had opened a lecture course in 1914: 'Nothing that you will learn in the course of your studies will be of the slightest possible use to you in after life – save only this – that if you work hard and diligently you should be able to detect *when a man is talking rot*, and that, in my view, is the main, if not the sole, purpose of education.'[53]

Arguably this would prove to be Balliol's greatest gift to Harold Macmillan. Yet, at the same time, if his mother had effectually removed from him his one great friend, so the oncoming avalanche now swept away his golden age of happiness at Oxford.

Chapter Two

Captain Macmillan
1914–1918

. . . of all the war, I think the most interesting (and humbling too) experience is the knowledge one gets of the poorer classes.

(*HM, 27 August 1915*)

The act of death in battle is noble and glorious. But the physical appearance and actual symptoms of death are, in these terrible circumstances, revolting only and horrid.

(*HM, 13 September 1916*)

When the war came, excited crowds in Paris chanted 'à Berlin!' In England young men of Harold Macmillan's age rushed to the colours, so as not to miss a war that was likely to be all over by Christmas. Not quite twenty-one, Macmillan, to his intense frustration, had been operated on for appendicitis just a few days before the outbreak of war. In those days it was a fairly serious operation, requiring lengthy convalescence, and it was not until the autumn that he managed to enter the King's Royal Rifle Corps. Wearing glasses (which later proved awkward under a gas mask) he feared rejection, but 'fortunately the pressure of men going through was very great, and made the medical officers correspondingly lenient.' He was quickly commissioned and found himself a second lieutenant in a training battalion at Southend-on-Sea. The training seemed to bear little relevance to what was going on across the Channel; Macmillan resented the endless parade-ground drill much as he had reacted to swinging Indian clubs in Macpherson's gymnasium as a child, and the evenings were taken up by studying textbooks, relieved only by the discovery of such nuggets as 'Officers of Field Rank on entering Balloons are not expected to wear spurs.' Frustration swiftly returned.

The forceful Nellie came to the rescue, getting him transferred to the far more chic Grenadier Guards, which some of his Oxford friends had already joined and which had already distinguished itself during the famous retreat from Mons in the first days of the war. In his memoirs, he writes with a curiously wry defensiveness of this use of 'pull': 'It was privilege of the worst kind – and so it was. It was truly shocking. But, after all, was it so very reprehensible? The only privilege I, and many others like me, sought was that of getting ourselves killed or wounded as soon as possible.'

There followed more training of the mixture as before, at Chelsea Barracks, with Macmillan actually reporting for duty from the family home at Cadogan Place. Then, in July 1915, he was transferred to a newly formed active battalion, the 4th Grenadiers, at

Marlow. Except for an occasional field exercise life remained 'really like a perpetual garden-party. Glorious weather; lots of friends from London; plenty of visits to London.' Although the war had not ended by Christmas, it still seemed remote and unreal. A photograph of the battalion officers taken just before their departure for Flanders shows Macmillan and a decidedly unmilitary-looking Osbert Sitwell standing next to each other. Macmillan had already begun to sport the military moustache which was henceforth to dominate his features. Osbert (according to his nephew Reresby) was later ordered by his Colonel to improve his aspect by growing one, to which he replied, 'What colour, sir?'[1]

On 15 August 1915, the battalion left for France. Before they sailed, however, there was one last crucial drama to be played out. When Guy Lawrence and Macmillan joined up, Ronnie Knox had remained at Oxford on the grounds that 'the profession of arms was forbidden to the clergy'.[2] Urged on by the war and by the possibility of death, all three had more or less agreed to be converted to Roman Catholicism and it is clear from their letters that now Lawrence and Macmillan were pushing Knox. Lawrence was the first to take the plunge, writing to Knox on 28 May 1915: 'I know I am happy and I only long for you to be happy with me. Come and be happy. "C" will, I think, follow very soon. . . . You've been and still are my best friend, Ron: there is no shadow between you and me.'[3]

On 22 July, Knox wrote to his friend Ted Shuttleworth: 'I didn't pay any attention to the thing . . . until Guy Lawrence and "C" took the line they did. It wasn't simply my two best converts doing it – or rather preparing to do it, for "C" hasn't been received yet; it was more that when they consulted me, I suddenly found that I wanted them to go. . . .'[4] But the very next day Macmillan was himself penning a letter that was to come, evidently, as a total surprise and a bitter disappointment to Knox:

Dearest Ron
    I'm going to be rather odd. I'm *not* going to 'Pope' until after the war (if I'm alive).
    1) My people. Not at all a good reason, which weighs. . . .
[There follow several illegible words, in themselves indicative of how agitated Macmillan's thoughts were at the time of writing this letter.]

2) My whole brain is in a whirl. I don't think God will mind. I mean, I've felt at last after a lot of thought and prayers, that it would be wrong to go now. Because I can't think things calmly now. And I think somehow now that, with my mind as it is, it would be almost a sacrilege. If I get thro', I'll go away from home & you & everything & try & find God's guidance. But I believe now that I may have to *relearn* everything. About now, I think I can't go to Mass at R.C. performances & say my prayers & that be all. . . . I felt a kind of inspiration that was right – lately. . . .[5]

With her powerful Protestant prejudices and unrelenting pressure on Harold ever since the beginning of the Ronnie Knox 'affair', Nellie had won the final round. Harold would never 'pope' now. He would have to 'relearn everything' away from his friends. Two years later, in September 1917, Knox joined Lawrence in the Roman Catholic Church. In *A Spiritual Aeneid* Knox writes of being 'overwhelmed with the feeling of liberty', and finding a 'harbourage'. He ended his *Aeneid* with the interesting prediction that, after the war, 'men will look for guidance to the two institutions which override the boundaries of country – International Socialism and the Catholic Church.'[6] At various times in his life Harold Macmillan, too, would come close to sympathy with both these assumptions.

On his being received into the Church, Knox received a rather sad and self-doubting letter from Macmillan, then recuperating from serious wounds received on the Somme:

My dearest Ronnie

It seems that, for the moment at least, the end of a journey has been reached. Reached, that is, by you and Guy, while I am still lagging, timid, cowardly and faint. I feel sure that you are right. I hope God will bless you & that you will be very happy. I am certain you'll be happier than you have been for years.

From a personal point of view, though, it's rather sad. 3 years ago we were a happy party, & all agreeing & ready to continue together. I feel horribly now like a deserter . . . my dear, it is so sad. . . . Honestly, I don't believe it's all been useless. There is left in me at any rate a memory; an experience never forgotten & still as vivid, or, I hope, a turn of mind, which but for you I should never have had, remains to me – 'for information and necessary action' – if God wills.

Goodbye my dearest Ron. . . .[7]

In August 1918, less than a year after Knox's conversion and before the Armistice, Guy Lawrence was killed. It was a shattering blow to Macmillan and particularly to Ronnie, who wrote to Sligger Urquhart: 'There must be bits of one's heart which can't carry a strong current of emotion and simply fuse (like an electric light).'[8] Guy's death marked the physical end of the inner circle of three, but in fact the 'parting of the ways' (Macmillan's words) had really come with his letter of repudiation of July 1915. Although for the rest of his life Macmillan would always describe Ronnie Knox as 'his dearest friend' and say that 'he was one of those rare friends of youth whom you don't see very often, but you can always take up again where you left off, at once,' the old intimacy was never restored. He wrote to him from the trenches, and Knox came to see Harold in hospital, recovering from wounds towards the end of the war; 'but we never had any close conversations – it was all so exposed in the war.'[9] Knox himself remained bitterly disappointed at Macmillan's 'repudiation'. They would never again talk about religion – 'that was all over, in 1915,' said Macmillan[10] – and it is doubtful to what extent, if at all, Macmillan felt himself able to seek solace from Knox during his own marital crisis in the 1930s, at a time when most men would have particularly welcomed the shoulder of a close friend. Thus, perhaps, all through his life from 1915 onwards, Macmillan was to lack the friend 'that sticketh closer than a brother' to whom one tells all, confides all, from whom consolation is sought.

Yet he never forgot his old friend and tutor, who became a monsignor and the most influential Catholic theologian of his generation. When Macmillan was Prime Minister, in 1957, there was a poignant valedictory scene. Knox was dying of cancer and, on his last visit to London, Macmillan had invited him especially to stay at No. 10, arranging for him to have a last (and hopeless) second opinion. Afterwards he had taken him personally to put him on the train to Paddington, to go to Mells, where he died a few weeks later. Macmillan remarked, 'perhaps without thinking, "I hope you will have a good journey." He replied, "It will be a very long one." To which I said "But Ronnie, you are very well prepared for it." These were the last words we spoke together.'[11] It particularly gratified Knox that the stationmaster raised his hat twice to him as the train pulled out.

Macmillan always remained extremely reticent about his friendship with Knox and about how close he had come to conversion, but although he never 'poped' he remained to the end a dedicated Anglo-Catholic, a church-going believer who took the New Testament with him to the trenches, and – as Prime Minister – showed more interest in Church matters and appointments than perhaps any other incumbent since Gladstone. Religion, tinted with a certain fatalism, was to become 'the strong thing in my life', he once said, explaining his personal creed:

> whatever your views happen to be about practical theology, I don't think a nation can live without religion. . . . if you don't pray every night, and if you don't believe in God, and if you don't think you can serve God eventually, you can't solve all these problems and you can't even survive them. . . . When you give up religion, you give up any kind of idealism. . . .[12]

Flanders

In France, during 1915, Macmillan would need all the strength of his religious convictions. During the Channel crossing he had been amazed by a sumptuous lunch provided for the officers by a wealthy company commander, a genial and portly gourmet called Captain 'Jummie' Morrison; it was presided over by Charles, the *maître d'hôtel* of the Ritz and a posse of waiters all imported for the journey by the generous Jummie. Marching through Le Havre the next day, the battalion drew from French bystanders admiring comments of 'Assurément, ils feront bien peur aux Boches!' – which Second Lieutenant Macmillan relayed with suitable pride in his first letter home to his mother on 17 August. He was to write to Nellie almost daily from the front, and little to anyone else except Knox. '. . . I am very comfortable,' he added, 'and want nothing except 1) *The Ring and the Book* 2) That John's and Pegg will send my trousers. . . .'[13]

Three weeks later he was reporting that his 'library' already consisted of '. . . The Bible – The Imitation of Christ – The

Confessions of St Augustine – the Iliad – Theocritus – Horace.
Odes and Epodes – Poet's Walk – Henry IV – Twelfth Night – The
Winter's Tale – The Poems of Emily Bronte – Maxim Gorky's "Les
Vagabonds" – The Shaving of Shagpat (Meredith) – Lalage's
Lovers (G. Birmingham) – The Ring and the Book – Ruskin's
Sesame and Lilies and Crown of Wild Olive.' It was quite an
unusual collection of reading matter for a twenty-one-year-old
Grenadier ensign on his way to the front; no less unusual perhaps
was the philosophical note on which Macmillan continued:

> . . . I have a friend who was said to have read the Iliad 'to make
> him fierce'. I confess that I prefer to do so to keep myself civilised.
> For the more I live in these warlike surroundings, the more
> thankful I am for all the traditions of the classic culture compared
> to these which journalists would have us call 'the realities of life'
> and are little but the extravagant visions of a fleeting nightmare,
> lacking true value or permanency.[14]

Close to the front he was billeted on a château which he described
with a keen eye for entertaining detail:

> a delightfully musical comedy sort of affair, in the most baronial
> of styles, with spires and stucco, and all the rest. The owner is a
> wine merchant . . . and a most amusing old wife, who is perpetu-
> ally trying to explain that it is only she who is really bourgeois,
> while Leon (the husband) is very *comme il faut*.
> They are really most kind and delightful people. The daughter
> plays the piano very well, and Monsieur Bélanger sings with a
> vast basso voice, rich with the liquor of 60 years. A length of
> black beard – curiously curled – and the most extravagant taste
> in waistcoats – can you picture my home life a little?

He appended the menu for one night's dinner, derived 'partly from
the Govt. "rations", partly from the country, and partly from
Fortnum and Mason . . .'; it comprised eight courses, rounded
off with cigars. 'Such are – at present – the hardships of active
service. . . .'[15]
Apart from eating, he had to train a group of thirty 'bombers'
(though Macmillan wrote constantly complaining that no real
bombs were yet available), and to censor the Guardsmen's letters

home. This latter duty he found laborious, but at the same time appealing in that it afforded him an insight into the lives of his men, the English working class, a breed with whom he had never previously come into contact. It was an insight to which he reacted with a mixture of humour, affection and sensitivity. He wrote to his mother:

> They have big hearts, these soldiers, and it is a very pathetic task to have to read all their letters home. Some of the older men, with wives and families who write every day, have in their style a wonderful simplicity which is almost great literature. . . . And then there comes occasionally a grim sentence or two, which reveals in a flash a sordid family drama. 'Mother, are you going ever to write to me. I have written ten times and had no answer. Are you on the drink again, that Uncle George write me the children are in a shocking state?'[16]

Earlier in the same letter, Macmillan recorded how happy the 'great experience' was making him. It was 'psychologically so interesting as to fill one's thoughts. A company has just passed my house, back from a long route march, singing wonderfully the dear soldier songs, with willy words and willy tunes, but which somehow seem, sung by their great childish voices, from the depth of their very lovable hearts, the most delicate music and the most sublime poetry.'

He had had little chance to meet people outside his own family and friends at school and at Oxford. Most of his friends' fathers were academics, writers or members of the clergy, so about the only contact he had had with the working classes had been restricted to gardeners and domestic servants. Now he rather envied the Guardsmen their easy camaraderie with each other. Apart from sympathy with their plight, he formed at this time a genuine interest in the life of the English working man which was to run through all his political life: it was to become a two-way bond. In the regular 'surgery' he was to hold as a young MP at Stockton, he would find association with his humbler constituents one of the most rewarding aspects of the job, 'not so very different from the relations between a company officer and his men'.

Macmillan's first major confrontation with the enemy took place on 27 September 1915 when the hitherto unblooded 4th Grenadiers were plunged into the epicentre of the battle of Loos. Moving up to the line, Macmillan remembered being addressed by the Corps Commander, who assured them, 'Behind you, gentlemen, in your companies and battalions, will be your Brigadier; behind him your Divisional Commander, and behind you all – I shall be there.' At that point Macmillan heard a fellow officer comment in a loud stage whisper, 'Yes, and a long way behind too!',[17] expressing a scepticism about the qualities of First World War commanders which Macmillan was soon to share in full.

Like so many of the disastrous Allied offensives, Loos began with bright hope. The Highland Division, fighting brilliantly, pushed through Loos and on up to Hill 70 – but only with terrible losses. They then came up against an unexpected second German line. That evening, noted Macmillan:

> A stream of motor-ambulances kept passing us, back from the firing line. Some of the wounded were very cheerful. One fellow I saw sitting up, nursing gleefully a German officer's helmet. 'They're running!' he shouted. The wildest rumours were afloat. . . . But our men were much encouraged, and we stood on that road from 3.30–9.30 and sang almost ceaselessly, 'Rag-time' – and music-hall ditties, sentimental love-songs – anything and everything. It was really rather wonderful.[18]

The next morning they were still waiting; as it transpired later, to allow the cavalry to pass and exploit the supposed breakthrough. But the cavalry's moment never arrived, and later that day things took a sharp turn for the worse, when the 4th Grenadiers found themselves thrown into the heart of the fighting. The Commanding Officer was gassed, his Second-in-Command and Adjutant killed, and in the ensuing confusion the battalion somehow became split in two. Macmillan and his platoon attached themselves to the half whose command had devolved upon the good-living Jummie Morrison. In default of any orders, Jummie attached himself to the neighbouring Guards Brigade. This was broken up by heavy German machine-gun fire, and Jummie's force suddenly found itself isolated, with no one on its right or left. Orders were received to 'crawl back and dig in a little further back on the Hulloch Road', wrote Macmillan in his memoirs: 'but since Jummie could not crawl (he was proud and corpulent), I did not see that I could very well do so either. I therefore walked about, trying to look as self-possessed as possible, under a heavy fire.'

Returning from the front line, Lieutenant Ludlow, the battalion Quartermaster, relayed to Macmillan's old Eton crony, Charlie Britten, this eye-witness account which he passed on to regimental archives:

> The Artillery Commander, when Harold arrived at Loos, was almost demented because there were no Infantry between his guns and the enemy. Regardless of shot and shell, Harold, aged 21, walked up and down the road in full view of the enemy, holding the General by the arm and saying his men would be there in a few minutes and all would be well.[19]

Having already been slightly wounded in the head, Macmillan was shot through his right hand towards the end of the battle and was evacuated to hospital. It was not a serious wound, but it was extremely painful, and he never fully recovered the strength of that hand, which accounts for the spidery handwriting of later age as well as for the limp handshake of which critics occasionally made jest. Writing to his mother from hospital, he affected to have been 'only shaken – "more frightened than hurt". But it has been rather awful – most of our officers are hit. . . . The Guards Division has won undying glory. . . .'[20] Altogether the British lost nearly 60,000 men at Loos – for an advance of a mile or so.

In the aftermath of Loos and right up to the Somme, according to Britten, in the 4th Grenadiers any conspicuous act of courage 'was rated by the Guardsmen as being "nearly as brave as Mr Macmillan"'.[21] What is interesting about this baptism of fire, apart from Macmillan's own reticence in writing about it, as well as a first recorded display of unflappability, is that he received neither official commendation nor decoration for conduct rather more distinguished than that for which many another officer received the Military Cross in the First World War. Britten, who thought the oversight 'deplorable', explained it on the grounds that the Commanding Officer had been gassed, and possibly shell-shocked, and therefore no citation had ever been made.

Leaving hospital shortly before Christmas, Macmillan was sent back to London where he mounted King's Guard for several months.

Dan had meanwhile joined the army, only to be discharged as unfit; while Arthur, because of the threat of epilepsy, had also been rejected for active service. Away from home, Harold found 'the quarters comfortable, and the day spent on guard by no means disagreeable'. Women guests were allowed at luncheon, and the food was excellent. But, like many officers returning from the front, he felt out of place and ill at ease in London, chafing to return to Flanders. In April 1916, he was back there, transferred to the 2nd Grenadiers, and this time in the blood-sodden Ypres salient, distracting himself by reading Richardson's *Pamela*, which, he reported to his mother, was 'vastly entertaining in its mild and uneventful way ... a contrast to everything going on around'.[22]

Some of his letters to his mother almost exult in the joys and dangers of battle while others contain rich imagery and romance with more than a dash of the histrionic that he would come to use with a mastery that steadily increased with age. He seemed particularly aware of the underlying horrors of what war actually meant when it burst upon a peaceful bourgeois world, a theme that was to haunt him and influence his thinking in critical moments ever after. In a letter of 13 May 1916 he describes the machinations of war, ending on a note of patriotic idealism:

Perhaps the most extraordinary thing about a modern battlefield is the desolation and emptiness of it all. . . . One cannot emphasise this point too much. Nothing is to be seen of war or soldiers – only the split and shattered trees and the burst of an occasional shell reveal anything of the truth. One can look for miles and see no human being. But in those miles of country lurk (like moles or rats, it seems) thousands, even hundreds of thousands of men, planning against each other perpetually some new device of death. Never showing themselves, they launch at each other bullet, bomb, aerial torpedo, and shell. And somewhere too (on the German side we know of their existence opposite us) are the little cylinders of gas, waiting only for the moment to spit forth their nauseous and destroying fumes. And yet the landscape shows nothing of all this – nothing but a few shattered trees and 3 or 4 thin lines of earth and sandbags; these and the ruins of towns and villages are the only signs of war anywhere visible. The glamour of red coats – the martial tunes of fife and drum –

aides-de-camp scurrying hither and thither on splendid chargers – lances glittering and swords flashing – how different the old wars must have been. The thrill of battle comes now only once or twice in a twelvemonth. We need not so múch the gallantry of our fathers; we need (and in our army at any rate I think you will find it) that indomitable and patient determination which has saved England over and over again. If any one at home thinks or talks of peace, you can truthfully say that the army is weary enough of war but prepared to fight for another 50 years if necessary, until the final object is attained.

I don't know why I write such solemn stuff. But the daily newspapers are so full of nonsense about our 'exhaustion' and people at home seem to be so bent on petty personal quarrels, that the great issues (one feels) are becoming obscured and forgotten. Many of us could never stand the strain and endure the horrors which we see every day, if we did not feel that this was more than a War – a Crusade. I never see a man killed but think of him as a martyr. All the men (tho' they could not express it in words) have the same conviction – that our cause is right and certain in the end to triumph. And because of this unex-pressed and almost unconscious faith, our allied armies have a superiority in morale which will be (some day) the deciding factor. . . .

He then went on to mention a memorandum circulated by the French on the lessons of Verdun, where – under Pétain – the French army had for months been putting up an inspiring defence in what was the most appalling battle of the war, if not of all history. Macmillan was deeply impressed by Pétain's claim that '. . . "The superiority of mind over matter, of the spiritual over the physical" (queer language to use for an official document from a general!) "is indisputable and decisive".' He ended by quoting the famous Verdun maxim: '". . . Qu'aucun pouce de terrain ne droit être volontairement abandonné . . . *le sacrifice de chacun étant la condition même de la victoire.* [HM's italics]" I have copied these words into my Field Pocket Book. They are very fine. . . .'[23]

Despite the all-dominating actuality of war, Macmillan managed to keep an alert eye on what was happening elsewhere. He expressed sympathy for the embattled government of Asquith, whose ad-vanced Liberal principles of social reform he admired. Of the 'Easter

Week' rebellion which had just broken out, he wrote, on 30 April: 'the scenes in Dublin seem to be very much like those in Paris during the Commune. The real trouble is that the Sinn Fein movement is, as well as disloyal, largely anti-clerical. Therefore one of the strongest powers over them is largely diminished or hampered in its operation.'[24] (Things had not changed much by the 1980s.) For the first time, on 26 May, Winston Churchill, fallen from grace as First Lord of the Admiralty after the Dardanelles, is also mentioned with favour in Macmillan's letters: 'Colonel Winston Churchill's speech the other day has met with a good deal of favourable comment out here. I think he makes some very good points. The very high proportion of non-combatant to combatant forces might be reduced without much difficulty.'[25] All these, and other, letters might be deemed to show an unusual interest in politics for a Guards subaltern.

The deadly summer of 1916 began – with Macmillan asking to be sent '4 pairs of thinnest (white silk) pants', and requesting more books (Aeschylus and Walter Scott), while rejecting with kindly mirth the 'ear-protectors' sent by a well-meaning father: 'you exaggerate in your minds the horrors of war! The noise is not really bad enough to make them necessary.'[26] On 29 June, the eve of the Battle of the Somme, he notes almost in the same breath how he was 'going on with Shakespeare's Comedies' (which he found 'amusing' and 'delightful'), and yet mourning 'with sorrow that another great Oxford friend of mine, Pat Hardinge, has been killed'.[27] One after another his Balliol friends were falling; Gilbert Talbot, son of the Bishop of Winchester and President of the Oxford Union, had been killed at Hooge in July 1915. His death particularly affected Macmillan, as did that of Ivo Charteris, a contemporary in the regiment.

When Kitchener's 'New Armies' went over the top on the Somme on 1 July, Macmillan's battalion was still at Ypres, resting out of the line, but he wrote on 3 July criticising the press for having 'exaggerated our success and our intentions'.[28] On the first he was correct, but not the second; for Joffre and Haig had launched this biggest 'push' yet mounted by the Allies with the clear intent of breaking the Germans' line, and rolling them back out of France. Again, though far removed from the actual scene, he shows a certain awareness of strategic realities: 'the secret was very badly kept, and

I feel sure the Germans knew quite well just when and where we were going to start. I don't believe they knew that the French were going to attack too – hence the French success, which has been so much greater than ours. . . .'[29]

In his letters to Nellie, occasionally the over-mothered little boy would emerge, as when he dwelled at great length on the pain and discomfort of a wasp sting in the trenches, which had swollen up his face. It was in curious contrast to his stoicism in the face of serious wounds; at the same time it revealed a certain tendency to hypochondria, over small ailments, that would be with him all his life. While the Somme raged, Macmillan continued to entertain his mother with cheerful descriptions of the various kind of dug-outs he had inhabited, which differed

as between the Carlton or the Ritz, and some little pot-house in the East End. A dug-out may be a palatial building, or large iron tubing inside, and rows of sandbags on top. Here you can stand up without discomfort. You have a table and chairs, and camp beds. You entertain your friends. You dine at your ease, and sip port and puff at your cigar for all the world as if you were at some rich city banquet. Of such dug-outs is the Kingdom of Heaven. . . .

But a dug-out in the trenches is a very different affair – It's like nothing but a coffin, is damp, musty, unsafe, cramped – 5ft long – 4ft broad – 3ft high. It can only be entered by a gymnastic feat of some skill. To get out of it is well-nigh impossible. . . . It is an evil thing, a poor thing, but (unluckily) mine own and (for the shelter and comfort that with all its failings it contrives to afford me) I love it![30]

Ten days after this letter, Macmillan was wounded for the third time. Out in no-man's land after midnight his patrol was spotted by an enemy bombing post:

They challenged us, but we cd. not see them to shoot, and of course they were entrenched while we were in the open. So I motioned to my men to lie quite still in the long grass. Then they began throwing bombs at us at random. The first, unluckily, hit me in the face and back and stunned me for the moment. . . . A lot of flares were fired, and when each flare went up, we flopped down in the grass and waited till it had died down. . . . it was not till I got back in the trench that I found I was also hit just above the left temple, close to the eye. The pair of spectacles which I was wearing must have been blown off by the force of the explosion, for I never saw them again. Very luckily they were not smashed and driven into my eye.. . . . I thought of you all at home in the second that the bomb exploded in my face. The Doctor told me that I asked for my Mother when I woke up this morning. And now I think of you all, dear ones at home, and feel so grateful that God has protected me once more.[31]

In his memoirs Macmillan writes simply that, the morning after, he was suffering from severe concussion and 'had the worst "hangover" that I can ever remember', so that his corporal was called on to report what had happened after the grenade had exploded: '"Well, sir," he replied, "I saw the German trying to run away. So I 'it 'im, and 'is 'elmet came off. Then I 'it 'im again and the back of 'is 'ead came off."'

For this action Macmillan received a second wound stripe – which he greatly prized – and a commendation from the Brigadier for 'the most useful information' brought in by his patrol, which made him smile, because he did not 'recall that we brought back any special information'. Macmillan refused to be evacuated again to hospital in England, and at the end of July he moved with his battalion to near Beaumont-Hamel. Noting how much more attractive the Somme country was than Flanders, and the gorgeous summer sunshine, his immediate reaction was that it was 'not the weather for killing people'.[32] Having finished the Waverley novels, he spent August reading Boswell's *Life of Johnson*, which he found 'a wonderful book – quite excellent for this life. One can pick it up and dip into it anywhere, for a few minutes.'[33] Poor Nellie Macmillan, obviously worried sick after her son's latest wound, proposed sending him a steel waistcoat, to which he replied politely: 'A *steel* waistcoat is no good at all. It is far too heavy, and is more likely to do harm than good. It will not keep out anything except shrapnel. A bullet wound it makes far worse.'[34] Macmillan, who all his life was possessed by a deep sense of fatalism, said years afterwards that he 'always got the feeling that I shouldn't be killed, I don't know why – absolutely sure of it.' Soldiers had a 'curious feeling' about it. He recalled one young officer friend who, just before going over the top 'came along and cried a little – we were only boys and he behaved very bravely – and he knew he'd be killed, and he was.'[35]

The Somme: A Severe Wound

Macmillan was just about due to go on leave when Haig renewed the useless battering on the Somme, this time with hopes for finally achieving that elusive breakthrough pinned on a bizarre new, and untried, invention called the 'tank'. On 13 September, Macmillan wrote to his mother: 'The flies are again a terrible plague, and the stench from the dead bodies which lie in heaps around is awful. . . .'[36] Several days later she received the letter that all mothers dreaded, signed by the chaplain, Neville Talbot, who, by coincidence, had also been Macmillan's chaplain at Balliol, and brother of his friend Gilbert, killed the previous year. Reporting Harold seriously wounded, Talbot wrote: 'he has two wounds, one in the left buttock and the other in the right leg below the knee. There is nothing broken, and no danger. He has had a trying time but is full of courage.'[37] It was a letter designed to console and allay fears; the main wound was in fact rather more serious than Talbot implied.

The 2nd Grenadiers had been thrown in at dawn on 15 September against a machine-gun stronghold, manned by Bavarians, at Ginchy and close to the famous Delville Wood, right in the centre of the Somme front. It involved a long advance of two miles through terrain flanked by German machine-gunners, whom the novel 'tanks' were supposed to deal with. But, thrown in prematurely by Haig, these either broke down or proved ineffective; Macmillan recalled seeing one of 'these strange objects' bogged down in a huge shell hole. Thus the Germans were able to shoot directly down the ranks of advancing Guardsmen, and they shot well. In Macmillan's account to his mother of what he saw of that day:

> the German artillery barrage was very heavy, but we got through the worst of it after the first half-hour. I was wounded slightly in the right knee. I bound up the wound at the first halt, and was able to go on. . . . About 8.20 we halted again. We found that we were being held up on the left by Germans in about 500 yards

of uncleared trench. We attempted to bomb and rush down the trench. I was taking a party across to the left with a Lewis gun, to try and get in to the trench, when I was wounded by a bullet in the left thigh [apparently at close range]. It was a severe wound, and I was quite helpless. I dropped into a shell-hole, shouted to Sgt. Robinson to take command of my party and go on with the attack. Sgt. Sambil helped me tie up the wound. I had no water, as the bullet had previously gone thro' my water bottle. . . .[38]

He lay in the shell-hole all morning, while the tide of battle flowed back and forth around him – lying 'doggo' and pretending to be dead when any Germans came near, lest they be tempted to 'despatch' him. Though realising that he had been seriously wounded, he was surprised to discover that – unlike the far less dangerous wound through his hand at Loos – 'which was excruciatingly painful, this body blow knocked me out but did not hurt'. Remembering that he had in his pocket a copy of Aeschylus's *Prometheus* (in Greek), which Nellie had sent him, he fell to reading it intermittently: 'It was a play I knew well, and seemed not inappropriate to my position.'

By about 1 p.m., the Germans began shelling their former line, which reassured Macmillan that it was now safely in the hands of friends: 'My hole was twice blown in on the top of me by shells exploding a few yards off. I was beginning now to feel the strain of waiting. I took ½ grain morphia, and succeeded in sleeping till 3.30 p.m. . . .'[39] About half an hour later, he was found by fellow Grenadiers. 'Company Sergeant-Major Norton, a splendid man, I can see him now . . . bottom of shell-hole, sloped rifle: "Thank you, sir, for leave to carry you away," as if he'd been on a parade ground! . . .'[40]

Owing to Macmillan's dazed state of shock, what followed is garbled, but – by any account – it must have represented a remarkable triumph of mind over matter. He seems first to have been taken into the captured enemy trench, where the battalion doctor gave him first aid to his wounds and the Commanding Officer, 'Crawley' de Crespigny, told him, 'Well, I think you'd better be off.' So he and another officer, 'Dog' Ritchie, who had been wounded in the arm only, were taken off on two stretchers under cover of darkness. The Field Ambulance was said to be in Ginchy, but the stretcher bearers did not know the way, and when they eventually reached Ginchy it was being heavily shelled and they could not find the Ambulance. At this point, the two wounded officers conferred and decided not to risk the lives of four able-bodied Guardsmen any further, so they told the bearers to go back to the battalion and they would make what progress they could. In the darkness and confusion of the shelling, Macmillan and Ritchie became separated; then, says Macmillan, for the first time that grim day fear set in. He tried to explain years later:

> bravery is not really vanity, but a kind of concealed pride, because everybody is watching you. Then I was safe, but alone, and absolutely terrified because there was no need to show off any more, no need to pretend . . . there was nobody for whom you were responsible; not even the stretcher bearers. Then I was very frightened. . . . I do remember the sudden feeling – you went through a whole battle for two days . . . suddenly there was nobody there . . . you could cry if you wanted to. . . .[41]

Somehow – he never quite knew how he made it, as his right knee 'was stiff and unusable – and painful' – he managed to drag himself in the dark out of Ginchy and the enemy shelling, and rolled into a ditch. Later (he was unable to remember just how many hours passed) he was picked up by a transport officer of the Sherwood Foresters, who had him put in a horse ambulance cart and taken down further to the proper dressing station. He recalled nothing more until he came to in a French hospital in Abbeville and thence back to 'some distant hospital' in England. From there he wrote encouragingly to his mother on 27 September that the doctor had found no fracture; attributing 'this good fortune entirely to the bullet having passed through the water bottle. If it had not done so, the wound would have been dangerous, and very likely fatal. Such are the mysterious ways of Providence, for which I have to be very thankful.'[42]

The surgeons nevertheless decided that it would be too risky to attempt to remove the bullet fragments from Macmillan's pelvis; they were to be a source of recurrent pain throughout his life, as well as the cause of the shuffling walk that – like the limp handshake – would provide material for satire when he was Prime Minister. Because of the length of time it had taken to get him to proper medical care, combined with the primitiveness and lack of modern drugs in First World War hospitals, the wound closed up before being drained of all infection. Abscesses formed inside, poisoning his whole system.

Had it not been for the redoubtable Nellie's prompt intervention, Macmillan might well have been just one more entry 'died of wounds'. Immediately on his return to England she removed him from the hands of the army butchers and into a private hospital in Belgrave Square, just round the corner from the family house. There was trouble with the War Office, but the 'unlucky general' interviewed by Nellie soon collapsed. Macmillan would always reckon that 'My life was saved by my mother's action.' For the next two years he had to submit to anaesthetic (then of a particularly nauseous variety) each time dressings were changed, as well as a series of disagreeable operations carried out for the removal of fragments of metal and bone. He came to live with pain.

Watching from hospital the long-drawn-out battles of 1917, his youthful enthusiasm gradually turned to disillusion; 'they oppressed me with their futility.' More and more friends died; only a few weeks before the Armistice, the war claimed Guy Lawrence, 'B', the third of the Knox triangle. It was not until about that time that Macmillan himself was finally discharged from hospital – on crutches and still with a tube in the wound, which did not completely heal until the beginning of 1920.

Thus the war ended for Macmillan, undecorated and on crutches, yet alive, but depressed at being removed from the festive rejoicing that followed the Armistice – and much more so at the loss of so many friends. He brooded about the war; when that courageous old Whig grandee, Lord Lansdowne, had published his famous letter in November 1917 pleading for an attempt to seek a negotiated peace, Macmillan like many of his fellow soldiers viewed his intervention with distaste, but later he came to respect this initiative taken by the man who was to become his grandfather-in-law.

Those long months of pain and discomfort in hospital provided a time for reflection and contemplation that were to prove of fundamental importance to Harold Macmillan; something equivalent to what young de Gaulle, also wounded in 1916, was experiencing in a German prisoner-of-war camp. When he was strong enough, he 'struggled through Dante's "Inferno" and "Purgatorio" (Italian on one side of the page, English on the other) . . .'[43] teaching himself Italian on the way. He moved on to Gibbon and Disraeli, thought deeply about the 'two Englands', and about the war leadership, feeling sorry for Asquith ousted by Lloyd George, but glad for the new drive at the top introduced by the fiery Welshman. He also thought intensely about the shape of the post-war world, and particularly the unpromising future of the young working-class soldiers he had come to know and love in the trenches.

The camaraderie of the front line, not least his delight in the discovery of the 'other ranks' and their lives; his admiration for things well done – which he had first noted at the Battle of Loos – imbued him with a lasting respect and affection for the Brigade of Guards. To him it constituted 'the only tolerable form of soldiering, because they always had a view that if anything was done, it must be done as well as possible. . . . I think it created in me a view of perfection, which I didn't have before. . . .' (He added, musingly: 'perhaps it was also a reason I was drawn to the Anglo-Catholics, because all that was beautifully done. . . .')[44] It all made a 'good working rule for civilian life'. At the same time, the slaughters of the Somme and Passchendaele left him with considerable scepticism about the abilities of those in charge which he would bear in mind twenty-five years later: 'The Second War was fought by great generals from their caravans. The First War was conducted by men of lesser quality from their châteaux.' Like many of his generation, he would never either quite overcome his distrust and dislike of Germans, or of anybody who supported them. Later on this was to influence his opposition to Munich, to those found wearing coal-scuttle helmets, be they German, 'White Russian' or Yugoslav Ustashi or Ukrainian, and to Dr Konrad Adenauer. Returning from Adenauer's funeral in April 1967, he remarked: 'The Guard of Honour, all those coal-scuttle helmets . . . they haven't changed!'[45]

If the Great War developed in him personally an innate stoicism, it also endowed him with a sturdy respect for courage in others. With this, too, went a certain contempt for what – resorting to a French 1914–18 usage – he called embusqués, those 'gentlemen of England now abed' who (not necessarily through any seeking of theirs) had missed the war. When it came to 'picking sides' in later life, it was the warriors – the Alexanders, the Lytteltons, Crookshanks, Eisenhowers and Kennedys – to whom he leaned instinctively as his friends, allies and idols, and he would be led into uncharacteristically harsh judgements on those who had not fought, such as Butler, Gaitskell and Foster Dulles, and perhaps, who knows, it may even have played some part in the turning away from Ronnie Knox. This happy breed that had suffered together in battle was indeed, and inevitably, set apart from other men.

It was particularly the memory of all those friends who had died which gave him, he says, almost a sense of guilt about surviving and, in turn, 'an obligation to make some decent use of the life that had been spared to us'. The question was, at what? Returning to finish his degree at Oxford was clearly out. He explained many years later: 'I did not go back to Oxford after the war. It was not just that I was still a cripple. There were plenty of cripples. But I could not face it. To me it was a city of ghosts. Of our eight scholars and exhibitioners who came up in 1912, Humphrey Sumner and I alone were alive. It was too much.'[46] With his beautiful, happy world of pre-1914 Oxford, something had died in him too.

Chapter Three

Marriage and Publishing
1918–1924

*Perhaps there will be storms of wind and rain and high waves
may threaten us sometimes, but we'll always sail on together
bravely, won't we?*

(HM to Dorothy Cavendish, 20 April 1920)

*My brother and I depend very much upon what our grandfather
did. I hope our successors will live by what we are doing now. A
publishing house is a long-term business. It doesn't live from hand
to mouth.*

(HM to George Moore, 1931)

Despite the pain and disability caused by his wounds, let alone the uncertain future of the post-war world, when peace came Macmillan, aged twenty-five, looked forward to it as an attractive, exciting prospect. Like Winston Churchill, he felt this fourth great victory in four successive centuries left Britain in a splendid position – or so it then seemed. On the personal level, he was more fortunate than so many of his fellow veterans in having a job waiting for him in the family firm. For the immediate future, however, he decided to see something of the world; he wanted to be 'away from England, to be away from home, to be on my own'. His first choice was India, where he was invited to go as an ADC to the Governor of Bombay. But the doctors vetoed this. Once again his mother stepped in. She heard that the Duke of Devonshire, then Governor-General of Canada, was looking for a young ADC and, through her long-standing friendship with the Duke's mother, Lady Edward Cavendish, Macmillan was offered the job. This involved staying on an extra year, as a captain, in the Grenadiers.

He reached Ottawa at the end of March 1919. For anyone with an eye for politics, it was an extraordinarily interesting period to be in Canada. After all the blood shed by the Canadians in Flanders, there were strong feelings that Canada had earned her right to a greater say in her own destiny. In 1919, Canada's Grand Old Man, Sir Wilfrid Laurier, the Liberal French Canadian who had done so much to cement the country together, died murmuring 'C'est fini.' Sir Robert Borden, the Conservative Prime Minister who had staunchly aligned Canada with Britain throughout the war and had introduced the unpopular measure of conscription, broke down physically in 1919, after demanding separate representation at the Peace Conference. His successor, Arthur Meighen, struggled nobly against nationwide unrest, both rural and urban.

Above him presided the Governor-General, who, in those days, was far from being a ceremonial cipher; representing both the Crown and the Prime Minister, he was the sole means of communication between the two governments, and thus wielded great power. Victor, the ninth Duke of Devonshire, had been MP for West Derbyshire from 1891 to 1908. He had served under Balfour as Financial Secretary to the Treasury, and had joined Asquith's coalition government as Civil Lord of the Admiralty in 1915. By background he was a born Whig, once remarking to Macmillan during a bad drive on the grouse moor: 'these damned grouse; they won't fly straight – like a lot of Tories!'[1] A man with a walrus moustache and heavy-lidded eyes that gave him a deceptively lugubrious appearance, he was dignified, simple, wise and considerate, characteristics to which Macmillan instinctively responded. The Duke for his part was obviously gratified to have with him an ADC with whom he could intelligently discuss politics – and who was happy to stay up chatting till 3 a.m. Always an owl, Macmillan listened avidly to the political gossip at Government House, and attended parliamentary debates whenever he could.

A strong mutual respect and liking sprang up between the Governor-General and the serious-minded young captain. (If anything, Macmillan may have appeared *too* serious at the time; according to the Duke's grandson, Andrew Devonshire, when visiting Canada as Macmillan's own Minister for Commonwealth Relations in the 1960s, older Canadians remembered him as 'rather pompous, and when they went on skating parties they hoped he wouldn't be there, on duty!')[2] Once again, contemporary photographs show him generally standing awkwardly on the outer fringe of every group, looking in. Nevertheless, it was a cheerful entourage; Macmillan remembered it as being like a 'permanent house-party',[3] and claimed in his memoirs that these ten months in Canada were among the happiest in his life. One other very good reason for this was that suddenly, and for the first and last time in his life, he found himself in love – with the boss's daughter – and within only weeks of his arrival.

Lady Dorothy Cavendish had come to Canada with her father three years earlier and was not quite twenty when she met Harold Macmillan. She had had little formal schooling, and had spent most of her early, probably rather dull life on the vast Devonshire estate of Lismore in Ireland, or travelling between the even more imposing family houses of Chatsworth, Holker Hall and Hardwick in England, keeping out of reach of a reserved and authoritarian mother, Evie Devonshire. Her childhood activities had centred on ponies and hunting, with little time for reading, but she had been raised

53

in an atmosphere steeped in politics. Her elder brother Eddy had been Mayor of Brixton, was a member of the British delegation at the Paris Peace Conference and had just married a Cecil, a powerful clan that had been in the business of politics since Elizabethan days. The two families were in fact doubly interlinked, in that Eddy's brother-in-law, 'Bobbety' Cranborne, the future fifth Marquess of Salisbury, also married a Cavendish. Dorothy's grandfather was the fifth Marquess of Lansdowne, known in the family as 'Daddy Clan', the former Foreign Secretary who had spent fifty years in public service and been author of the controversial 'Lansdowne Letter' of 1917 calling for peace negotiations.

Dorothy had inherited a Cavendish characteristic of being neither clever nor intellectual, but shrewd; in later years Macmillan would freely admit that she was a much better, instinctive judge of character than he ever was, with an unerring knack of spotting what, or who, was a fake. To look at, the young Dorothy was striking rather than beautiful, although a painting of her by Philip de Lazlo, probably somewhat romanticised, shows a sensual mouth and an almost Mediterranean sultriness. In her lack of dress sense she was also every inch a Cavendish. Together with the equally grand Buccleuch clan, the Cavendishes were then nicknamed the 'Grub Club'; both families were so aristocratic, so rich, that there was no need for an outward display of wealth and the women particularly were wonderfully oblivious of what was fashionable.

Sir David Scott, who remembered Dorothy as a child at Chatsworth, retained the image of a very distinct and determined character: 'She was exceptionally friendly . . . thoroughly natural, and sweet, and always gave the impression that she felt fit, on top of the world. . . . She was also very courageous – I remember her telling off her governess.'[4] There was no streak of the Black Dog here – a fact that undoubtedly was to have a healthy, complementary influence on Macmillan as the years went by. Like many others who knew her at various times in her life, David Scott also recalled her engaging humility. She was delightfully free of any kind of snobbery; as a niece remarked: 'she just simply didn't know what the word meant. She would just as soon talk to grave-diggers as politicians, and would be really interested in details like how they dealt with frost in the ground. She *did* fly into terrible rages, she was essentially the peasant, she had a gut reaction to everything.'[5]

This earthiness, noted by many who knew her, again contrasted with, or counterpointed, the cerebral Harold, and her uncontrived 'common touch' was to prove a golden asset. She had a keen sense of humour, especially when it came to spotting human foibles, but probably her most striking characteristic was her natural warmth, combined with an ability to charm. 'Wherever she was, even if there were difficulties,' Macmillan himself recalled towards the end of his life, 'she always had a desire to make everybody happy,'[6] a view that was reinforced by one of her children's contemporaries: 'Whenever she was expected to stay, you knew there was going to be fun – she lit up the room.'[7]

This, then, was the young woman who captured Macmillan's imagination in Ottawa in March 1919. On Easter Sunday he was writing to her, 'Dear Lady Dorothy', describing with dry humour a visit to New York ('an odd mixture of noise and vulgarity') and then (patently set on making a date) turning to golf, at which '. . . I am told that you are the great player of the family, and so I am anxiously awaiting the opportunity to be defeated by you.'[8] By June it was 'Dear Dorothy', telling of a trip to Niagara with the President of Brazil ('I hope to be presented with "The Sacred Order of the Brazilian Nutcracker"!').[9] During a trip to Jasper National Park, amid the wonderful scenery of the Rockies, he knew his 'affections were returned', though it seems that Dorothy took some months longer to make up her mind about marriage. From New York again, at the end of December, he was writing 'My darling Dorothy', and diverting her with anecdotes about English residents there, remarking 'Everybody is always doing something but nothing ever happens!'[10] (Interestingly, although he made much of visiting his mother's home-town in Indiana while in office many years later, there is nothing to indicate that he ever went there while in Canada. By this time, however, both his maternal uncle and aunt had died and there were no close relatives to follow up.)

On 27 December, Macmillan was writing home ecstatically:

My dearest mother,
    It's 'yes'. Boxing Day 1919. No one is to know yet, so *don't tell anyone except Arthur*. I have heaps to write to you about her, but I can't now because I'm too tired. I am the happiest man there has ever been in the world. . . .

Your Harold.[11]

And, a few days later:

> . . . I promised her to write to you about her. And I also promised
> to tell you all her faults! So I'll tell you what she thinks her faults,
> first.

> She is very young and very modest and so a little bit frightened
> of married life. She thinks she will never be able to keep house
> and look after me, and that she will cry when the cook gives notice.
> She is a little frightened that you will think her 'incompetent' or
> 'silly', so you will have to be very very kind to her. . . . but of
> course you will love her enormously, and we will manage some-
> how to run a house. . . . the qualities, I needn't really tell you.
> The kindest heart and the dearest, truthfullest, purest and most
> unspoilt mind. . . . She is superbly beautiful too – at least I think
> so. She is more different to look at than anyone I have ever seen
> . . . she is, oh, I can't say what she is but . . . I love her so much
> I can hardly know what to do or say or think. . . . I feel so happy
> I don't know what to say to you. I am so grateful to you both for
> the way you have looked after and helped me all my life, and
> made this great happiness of mine possible. . . .[12]

On 6 January 1920, Dorothy (though not much of a letter-writer)
was herself writing to her future mother-in-law, echoing her fiancé:

> . . . I am so wonderfully happy – nobody can know how much,
> at being engaged to Harold. I didn't think there could be anyone
> like he is in the world, and I do love him – it's no good trying to
> write how much because it is impossible – I wish that I felt that
> I could make a better wife for him. I'm a perfectly useless person.
> We shall be a pretty comic couple, but I am sure that you will
> help sometimes. . . . I can't in the least write what I want to – I
> just wanted to tell you how wonderfully happy we are and how
> adorable Harold is to me. I dread to think what will happen if
> he goes on spoiling me a quarter as much as he does now![13]

Nellie Macmillan, with all the American mother's fierce ambitions for her son, could hardly have wished for a more aspiring
match, and there were cynics – both then and later – who alleged
that she had engineered his appointment to Ottawa in the first

place in order that the two might meet. But there was equally no doubt, from the tone of his letters both before and after the marriage, that this was a true love match – at least on his side. His previous knowledge of women, as he would often confess, had been almost nil. He had had no sisters; Oxford was very monastic: 'there were women in colleges, but one never saw them';[14] and then came the war, so that his contacts had been limited to the odd dancing partner – and his mother. He admitted to being frightened by women, and rarely made them feel at ease in his company – except, curiously, in his old age. But out of his letters to Dorothy – especially coming from someone whose whole upbringing had trained him to eschew all display of private emotion (although probably he was less inhibited in writing than in speech) – there emerges an almost conventional picture of a highly romantic young man passionately in love. 'My darling,' he wrote on the eve of their wedding:

> I must write the last letter which I shall write before you become my wife. But not, dearest Dorothy, the last love letter you will get from me. For, Dorothy, I shall always be your lover. . . . Perhaps there will be storms of wind and rain and high waves may threaten us sometimes, but we'll always sail on together bravely, won't we? . . . My own darling – I have been sitting thinking of it all. Don't forget it ever, will you? Don't forget the jolly view from the mountain tops, in the dust and heat of the plains. But let us climb all our lives through plains first, and then the lower slopes, and pray to God that we may reach the summit together at the end.
>
> Your devoted Harold[15]

What exactly it was that drew Dorothy to the earnest crofter's great-grandson, the ambitious middle-class publisher's son, with his shy, somewhat stilted manners, his Groucho moustache and the shuffling walk that was a legacy of his war wounds, is less clear. There was the glamour of the wounded hero – but, in 1919, this was sadly not uncommon. When asked the question, one of Macmillan's fellow ADCs, Lord Sefton, remarked 'God knows! Perhaps it was to escape the problems of home, a very tough mother. . . .'[16] As fearsome women, Evie and Nellie seem to have been well matched. A considerable snob, 'Evie Duchess' had

57

apparently set her heart on Dorothy marrying Walter, the future Duke of Buccleuch; but doubtless Harold's romance was assisted by Victor Devonshire's Cavendish lack of snobbery, as well as his own soft spot for his ADC. With one daughter already married to a brewer, Cobbold, the Duke is said to have remarked gruffly: 'Well, books is better than beer.' To members of the Macmillan family, however, there was no doubt that – whether or not she had been driven into an early marriage – Dorothy *was* truly in love with Harold, at least in those first years.

When the wedding took place, on 21 April 1920, the bride's side of St Margaret's, Westminster, was packed with what Macmillan called 'swells' – members of the Devonshire, Cecil and Lansdowne clans, as well as Queen Alexandra and the future King George VI. Not to be upstaged, Nellie packed the right-hand side of the aisle with eminent Macmillan authors, including 'half a dozen OMs'. The most distinguished literary giant present was Thomas Hardy, who was making his final visit to the London he so disliked. Afterwards a glittering reception was held at Lansdowne House, almost the last function to be held there before it passed into the hands of Gordon Selfridge, of department store fame.

Into Publishing

With marriage, Macmillan's Canadian venture of just ten months came to an end. The couple bought a house on the corner of Chester Square, between Victoria and Pimlico, then considered to be modest but respectable, and within walking distance of Macmillan's parents. He recalled that Dickens had once described Cadogan Place, in *Nicholas Nickleby*, as 'the one slight bond that joins two extremes; it is the connecting link between the aristocratic pavements of Belgrave Square and the barbarism of Chelsea.' The same, he felt, could have been said about Chester Square in the 1920s. They lived there for the next sixteen years, bringing up all four children there, while Harold settled down to a life as a junior partner in Macmillan's. Here he was joined by Dan, the revered older brother and classical scholar, who, after being invalided out of the army, had worked with distinction in Paris during the drafting of the Treaty of Versailles. Arthur had taken himself off to practise law.

The House of Macmillan was still very much a family firm, run on the same Victorian principles established by Grandfather Daniel and Great-uncle Alexander eighty years previously. Head of it was Sir Frederick Macmillan, the eldest of Daniel's sons, and the other senior partners were Harold's father Maurice and his first cousin George, son of Alexander. The juniors were George's son Will, and now Daniel and Harold. Under the management of the first generation, the business had expanded successfully and solidly, although annual turnover by the early 1920s was probably no more than £60,000–£80,000 per annum. It had a good, soundly conservative list, based on improving the public mind, coupled with a strong line in theological works. Under the direction of Maurice, Macmillan's moved vigorously into educational publishing and set up branches in Canada and India, Alexander having already launched Macmillan's in New York. The partners took a paternalistic interest in their authors, often above and beyond the call of publishing, which was greatly valued by many of them, such as Lewis Carroll. But their Scottish thrift was not always appreciated. Mrs Humphry Ward, for one, felt underpaid and left.

The Macmillan readers, once headed by Lord Morley, the distinguished radical survivor of Gladstone's Cabinet, set high – sometimes harsh – standards, which were not always proved right. Back in 1868, an unknown twenty-eight-year-old submitted a manuscript entitled *The Poor Man and the Lady* which Morley damned as having 'a certain rawness of absurdity that is very displeasing'. Alexander had added, 'Your pictures of character among Londoners, and especially the upper classes . . . are wholly dark,' but ended on a more kindly and encouraging note: 'If this is your first book, I think you should go on. May I ask if it is, and – you are not a lady, so perhaps you will forgive this question – are you young?' Young Thomas Hardy did 'go on'; was rejected a second time; but on his fourth try was accepted with *The Woodlanders* and was published by Macmillan's for the rest of his life.[17]

Even more searing was the reader's report on W. B. Yeats: 'I shall be sorry to think that works so unreal, unhuman and insincere would be found to have any permanent value. . . . I am relieved to find the critics shrink from saying that Mr Yeats will *ever be a popular author*. I should really at last despair of mankind, if he could be. . . .'[18] Nevertheless, Yeats, too, persisted. On the other hand, *Lorna Doone* was lost 'by an accident', and four overtures by George

Bernard Shaw were rejected. Although Morley commented, 'The writer, if he is still young, is a man to keep one's eye upon,' Shaw failed to pass the ultimate test. Of Shaw's second submission, *The Irrational Knot*, the Macmillan reader wrote, 'There is too much of adultery and the like matters.'[19]

A certain Calvinist morality undoubtedly continued to influence decisions. Hardy's *Tess of the D'Urbervilles* was rejected by *Macmillan's Magazine* because of its 'improper explicitness', and H. G. Wells's *Ann Veronica* was declined by Frederick Macmillan on similar grounds. The relationship with Wells generally was a stormy one; apart from objecting to their prudishness, Wells – in common with the views held by many authors about their publishers before and since – felt that Macmillan's did not sell him hard enough. In 1907, after only 180 copies of *Kipps* had been sold, Wells actually transferred it to Nelson's for a 7d edition – where, within three months, it had sold 43,000, which, as Wells remarked, 'isn't bad for a book left for dead'. Wells wrote to Macmillan's, in terms that were probably not unfair and might have been used by any author to any publisher at any time: 'I like your firm in many ways. I don't think you advertise well. . . . I don't think you have any idea what could be done for me (but that you will of course ascribe to the vanity of Authors). But on the other hand you are solid and sound and sane.'[20] Macmillan's finally lost Wells when (in 1915) they refused to pay what he wanted for *Mr Britling Sees It Through*. On the other hand the partners were capable of spontaneous acts of generosity, such as when Frederick Macmillan tore up a contract for the outright purchase of a book by a schoolmaster called J. R. Green, because it was unexpectedly successful, and substituted it with a royalty agreement that was far more profitable to the author.

In company with other publishers of the time, the senior Macmillans did not believe in publicity, nor in the power of the reviewer to create sales; if a book was good, it would sell itself. Frederick rated highly the importance of the 'traveller', and felt that any sales manager who drove his staff to 'push' a particular book beyond their judgement was mistaken. He himself had been a traveller; in fact, having worked in the firm from the age of fourteen, as the boy who swept the floor in the morning and put up the blinds at night (he was to celebrate his seventieth anniversary in harness shortly before he died in 1936), there was no aspect of publishing he had not experienced. His nephew remembered one among many sound bits of publishing advice he passed on: 'Don't ever have a printing works, because you have always got to find books to keep it busy.' Other houses rejected this principle, and went bankrupt. Frederick's greatest contribution, however – to authors and publishers alike – was his dogged fight, drawn out over two decades, for the Net Book Agreement. During the 1890s book prices had plummeted, slashed by the new reprint libraries; a new novel that had stuck at 10s 6d for fifty years fell to 2s 6d, or even to 6d for a paper edition. Frederick counter-attacked by publishing Macmillan books at 'net prices', and any bookseller who sold them at less had his account closed. Gradually other publishers followed the Macmillan lead, resulting in conclusion of the Net Book Agreement of 1899, which probably saved the book trade from disaster.

The hard-working Maurice had developed little other life outside Macmillan's, except for his club where he repaired to read the evening newspapers; Nellie was allegedly too thrifty to buy them but Maurice never complained, preferring rather to use it as an excuse for escape. At Macmillan's it was he who kept the firm's finances on the ground, whereas George, the theological editor, spent most of his time in the Athenaeum, hobnobbing with bishops. Both he and his son, Will Macmillan, seem to have been something of nonentities, and their branch of the family was in fact bought out by Daniel and Harold in the 1930s. In contrast Uncle Fred hunted passionately, arrived at the office in a Rolls from Devonshire Place and was enormously sociable; Harold remembered him coming to work until he was in his eighties.

These three senior partners met every morning, when Uncle Fred read out the letters addressed to the firm and each of them expressed their view on how to deal with particular affairs. Then, Harold recalled, 'we met at lunch, and naturally my brother and I, and the other, young Will, just sat round and listened. Then they had a glass of madeira and were fed on cake; then we all went off. To miss luncheon was permissible, but rather frowned on.'[21] It was all very Victorian, but Harold Macmillan found it agreeable; on the other hand, with the three old gentlemen so firmly in control, there was little for the next generation to do. He started elbowing a little room at the top for himself by investigating the production end of the business, which he found rather inefficient, and tried to rationalise it by changing paper sizes, so that the same quantity could be used to print more books. Over the next five or six years he gradually took over more of the general books from his uncle, together with some of the top Macmillan authors.

As a breed, authors – and especially venerable ones – are notoriously touchy about being 'handed on' to a younger editor; thus it was a great tribute to Harold that he was able to gain the trust of such notables as Hardy (then regarded as probably the world's greatest living imaginative writer), Kipling, Frazer, Yeats, Hugh Walpole and – among the younger acquisitions – Sean O'Casey and Charles Morgan. He enjoyed his visits to Hardy in Dorset, and remembered him as having 'cheeks like a very battered countryman; pink and wrinkled, rather like a Cox's Pippin'.[22] But he always thought Hardy 'a very bad stylist – self-educated – [he] occasionally would produce classical quotes, as if he had just discovered them; but his great talent was *total sincerity*. That's what made people read him.' Hardy had, he felt, 'a Greek sense of Fate' which Macmillan admitted to sharing. 'But he had a much gloomier view of the world than I do.'[23] Kipling he regarded with even more sympathy when it came to the dread Mrs Kipling, and, as he said many years later, he thought him a better stylist:

> polishing his short stories to perfection . . . but such an unhappy life. . . . he was broken after the war by his only son's death [killed with the Irish Guards]; he didn't recover. . . . then his dreadful wife [he shuddered at the memory] locked him up in the house to write, from dawn till dusk. He used to escape to the Beefsteak, pretending to his wife that he was going to see the banker. At the Beefsteak, he would draw out the most boring member to find something he wanted in a character. The perfect journalist. He is wrongly considered as an Imperialist – his warning of where it would all lead is in *Recessional*. It's such a joy that he is now coming back. . . .[24]

Then there was the harshly rebuffed, very Irish, Yeats, who when he first came to deal with Frederick wore 'sombre clothes, wide black hat, eye glasses on a broad black ribbon and an air of blank, unexpected melancholy'. But on being transferred to Harold, Yeats achieved a remarkable metamorphosis; Irish tweed had replaced the black suit, he wore a coloured shirt, 'his tie flowing through a fine ring'. He used to drop in, unannounced, 'just to chat', and

Macmillan remembered thinking his appearance of the poet and dreamer 'somewhat dramatised'; but 'he was also a practical man, and by no means despised the mundane problems of publishing.'[25]

Of all the authors in the early days, Sean O'Casey was the one with whom Harold considered he was the closest. He and the Irishman who proclaimed himself a Communist and atheist could hardly have been more different; yet, as well as deeming him 'our greatest playwright', he bracketed O'Casey in his memoirs with Ronnie Knox as being 'saintly', which was high praise indeed. Later, O'Casey's widow remained one of his few lifelong women friends. But, although he formed an obvious affection for 'his' authors and their human foibles, he remarked rather revealingly that, with the exception of O'Casey, 'I didn't make friends with them.'[26] Perhaps it was because, as he himself said of Kipling, 'he did not unbutton himself.'

His brother and senior, Dan, was a nervous and shy man who did not find business relations easy, so that Harold was relied on to deploy his latent charm in handling authors. In the course of time he widened his niche in the firm by bringing in his own new authors, such as Lewis Namier, whom he had known at Oxford and whom he admired for being 'the first historian to look at the facts, instead of just reading what other historians had written before him'. Namier in turn brought along 'a clever young man' called John Wheeler-Bennett whom Macmillan liked immensely, and admired for being an amateur who showed academic historians how to write. But it was contemporary economists who interested him most. In 1919, the firm's outstanding book had been *The Economic Consequences of the Peace*, by John Maynard Keynes, one of Dan's closest friends, and a contemporary at Eton. Keynes's theories were greatly to influence Harold the politician, while Harold the publisher was to devote much of his energy to recruiting other modern economists such as G. D. H. Cole, Paul Einzig, Colin Clark and Lionel Robbins.

Meanwhile, Harold's own taste in books was developing: 'I don't like books about action,' he once told C. P. Snow. 'I like books about what's going on in people's minds.'[27] In all matters of choosing authors, Macmillan seemed instinctively to turn for advice to his mother, rather than to his young wife. Nellie had for years operated a literary salon of note – graced, among others, by Henry

James; she used her role as a school visitor (perhaps fairly ruthlessly) to proselytise for Macmillan's educational side; and she had a good nose for a bestseller. In the 1930s, it was she who (with her upbringing in the aftermath of the American Civil War) leaped on *Gone With the Wind* while reading it in proof, virtually grabbing it out of the hands of a rival publisher, Collins, and it was probably her judgement that persuaded Harold to quadruple the (modest) print number initially proposed.

For Macmillan those early years as a publishing apprentice were also a time of married bliss. 'We were young; we were happy; everything smiled on us,' he wrote in his memoirs. Under pressure from Nellie, Dorothy moved out of London during August 1920 to spend much of her time at Birch Grove, where her mother-in-law had arranged a set of rooms for them on the top, 'nursery', floor. Left alone in Chester Square, and with little distraction, Harold wrote to her almost every day, in terms even more warmly demonstrative than during their engagement.

> 12th August 1920
> . . . I am the happiest man in the world, 'cos I've got the world's best wife! . . . by the time you get this, it will be Friday, the world's best and most adorable day and then you will come and meet me, won't you, on the road, and walk across the forest with me. . . .

He continued, revealing a little the pressure and distraction of work already: 'do you mind very much if I don't come till the later train? . . . Only I do hate so much not doing everything you tell me to do!'[28]

After that weekend, he wrote, from Macmillan's: 'My darling one . . . my darling child, goodbye. I love you now about a million times more than last week – always more and more, and you get lovelier all the time. Your own devoted husband, Harold.'[29]

The following March, he was writing in the same vein:

> . . . I love you and want you so much. And I want you to be happier and happier every day and have everything in the world that you want. I will try to give you everything I can; that isn't

much, because I've nothing much to give you, my child, except a most devoted husband's love.[30]

That year, 1921, their first child and only son, Maurice, was born, and two years later came Carol. She would be followed in 1926 by Catherine and finally, in 1930, by the third daughter, Sarah. Dorothy doted on small children and although there was the customary nanny to look after them she probably devoted more attention to them than was usual for mothers of that class and time; it was only as they grew older that she tended to lose interest. Harold himself, like his own father, remained a distant figure to his children; his publishing work and later his political career meant that he saw little of them and, when he did, there was the barrier of his emotional reserve. At first, however, their family life seemed set fair. Harold fretted about Dorothy being bored at Birch Grove with only Nellie for company, but in their initial contentment there is no suggestion that this worried Dorothy. As time went on, as the bride grew into a mature woman, it cannot, however, have always been easy – to put it at its mildest – to live, unfenced-off, in the same house as her strong-willed mother-in-law. To Dorothy, it must have come to seem like exchanging one parental tyrant for another. The seeds of future problems had been sown by the domestic arrangement, which was to continue without much change for sixteen years.

Life at the vast palace at Chatsworth in Derbyshire, where they would generally spend Christmas, equally cannot have been easy for Harold. Although he writes of these Christmases with glowing nostalgia in one of the more colourful descriptive passages of his memoirs, he also notes tellingly: 'The sons-in-law, of course, soon learnt the desirability of sending their families by the early train, and ensuring sufficient important business in London to make it necessary for them to follow later and more comfortably.' There were seven Devonshire sons and daughters, all married and – in the course of time – producing twenty-eight children; one year, regarded by Lady Dorothy 'as the peak of felicity', there were fourteen children under four in the nursery. Together with the attendant nannies, nursery maids, lady's maids and valets, the Devonshire clan added up to some sixty souls; add the other guests and their attendants, plus the servants of the household, and the number gathered under the vast roof must have been about 150 people. Macmillan always relished Lloyd George's famous remark that 'fully equipped Dukes cost as much to keep up as two Dreadnoughts – they were just as great a terror and they lasted longer.' The children delighted in this exciting world, where they were pampered by the servants. As each family arrived, in a never varying ritual, they would be formally received at the top of the great stairs by Granny Evie, the austere mother from whom Dorothy had sought to escape in marrying Harold. Incapable of feeling the cold and oblivious to her surroundings, Evie presided over houses where water left in wash basins froze overnight and the nurseries were uncarpeted. This physical frost apparently also extended to her relationships with children; Dorothy inherited her own great fund of natural warmth from her father, who was devoted to his offspring.

Macmillan remembered the snowy Christmases, accompanied by skating and tobogganing, with keenest pleasure – 'the beauty of the great trees in the garden and park, and the house shining with a strangely golden glow in the rays of the low winter sun'. He also relished the space the huge house provided to escape (especially from the argumentative Cecils), and to read. Although Andrew, the present Duke of Devonshire, considered that Macmillan had a great feeling for Chatsworth and a genuine love for it, these memories must have been partly glossed with the rosy tint of time. His early affection for the old Duke had grown into a genuine love on both sides, with Harold becoming the favourite among all the sons-in-law. He would still stay up with him till three or four in the morning, discussing politics and humouring the Duke's strong Whig sensibilities. However, in his later years, the Duke suffered a stroke which changed his whole personality. Although he and Macmillan remained deeply attached to each other, from being one of the most jovial of men, he became gruff, unapproachable, even morose. The old Duke's tragic affliction, which rendered him at times almost demented, cast a sombre shadow over life at Chatsworth.

Whereas the post-Second World War generation of Cavendishes recalled with joy how Macmillan induced 'great life' into an otherwise rather dull and serious scene by his acting and spirited playing of 'The Game' (his favourite performance was to don a loud check jacket and impersonate a bookie), in the 1920s and 1930s he seems often to have appeared out of place. He was bored by the great Devonshire passion, horse-racing, and in turn he bored them by pontificating. The Cecil clan patronised him and made little bones about regarding the publisher as being 'in trade', and socially rather bourgeois; at the same time, politically, they became suspicious of his radical views and what they regarded as his opportunism. His powerful Cecil brother-in-law by marriage, 'Bobbety' Cranborne, the future fifth Marquess whom Macmillan would cheerfully allow to resign from his first Cabinet, apparently neither liked nor trusted Harold.

A more raffish brother-in-law, James Stuart – outstandingly good-looking, successful with women and capable of being crushingly rude (Macmillan regarded him, in his capacity as Chief Whip to Churchill from 1942 to 1945, as 'the only man I think I have ever known who rather frightened Churchill')[31] teased Harold unmercifully, although, later, in politics he was to become one of his closest friends. At Chatsworth, Stuart would mock him about the Christmas presents he gave, because they were always so carefully chosen as to be 'just right' – perhaps a shade too much so. Harold did, however, learn to become an excellent shot on the Devonshires' moors, a pleasure that was important to him until, at the age of eighty-four, his eyesight had deteriorated to the point where he could no longer see the birds. But his dress on the grouse moor sometimes drew amused comment; Lord Home recollected him as being the only person he ever knew who wore spats. Harold seems to have cultivated egregiously unmodish clothes, perhaps in emulation of the young Disraeli, or maybe to redress his lack of confidence in the Chatsworth world. Staying there in the late 1930s, Lord Longford remembered Macmillan being still 'a rather sad figure – rather isolated in these circles'; while his own son, Maurice, went so far as to suggest that those Chatsworth days must have been 'absolute hell' for his father.[32]

Into Politics

Meanwhile the influence of his political father-in-law, his insight into Canadian politics, his thinking and reading during the months in hospital, had all combined – fanned by the pressing ambition of Nellie, and despite his having a perfectly good job as a publisher: in 1923, at the general election of December that year, Harold decided to try to stand for Parliament. From the days of hope and euphoria of 1919, the political scene in Britain had changed with brutal swiftness. Throughout 1920 the post-war boom was at its height, but by that winter slump and unemployment were already reaching out their ugly fingers. On 25 August 1921, by which time the number of unemployed had risen to the alarming figure of two million, Macmillan was writing to Dorothy:

> I go to a meeting of the Employers' Federation at 11 a.m. tomorrow and we have to decide whether to hold out or not. I hope we shall not give way, as the last bonus of 5/- was given 'to meet the rise of 15 points in the cost of living' and as the cost of living has now fallen by 50 points, it doesn't seem unreasonable to ask for a 5/- reduction in wages.[33]

The 'honours' scandals at home, Ireland, the cost of the Treaty of Versailles, and the threat of a new war with Turkey abroad added to the government's unpopularity. At the famous Carlton Club meeting of 19 October 1922, the Conservative leaders sounded the death-knell to the great wartime coalition, and an election was called the following month. Lloyd George found himself a prime minister without a party, and although he contemptuously dismissed the platform of 'Tranquillity' proclaimed by his Conservative opponent, Bonar Law, as 'not a policy, but a yawn!', he misinterpreted the mood of the country. Bonar Law won, and at fifty-nine the Welsh wizard lost power, never to regain it.

Macmillan watched the election of 1922, in which some of his friends had already been involved, with growing excitement. Within seven months, however, cancer had forced Bonar Law to resign, and a new election was called. Macmillan was somewhat torn by whether to range himself with the Tories or alongside his long-time idol, Lloyd George. Was he Conservative or Liberal – or even Radical? But it looked as if the Liberal sun had set. It was thus as a Tory candidate that Macmillan offered himself for the general election of December 1923. Diffidently he went to Conservative Central Office and asked for the chance to gain experience by contesting a tough seat. He was told: 'We've got the very thing for you . . . Stockton-on-Tees . . . you can't possibly win it.' The Conservatives in Stockton must have reckoned themselves fortunate to find such a suitable candidate asking for their nomination. At that time a Conservative candidate who stood for a constituency without a strong local party association was generally expected to finance the campaign out of his own pocket and the cost – about £200–£300 – was enough to ensure that there were comparatively few people who wanted to fight hopeless seats such as Stockton. That Macmillan could readily afford this sum is indicative of how prosperous the publishing house had become.

Discovering the north-eastern shipbuilding area of Stockton, depressed as it was and by nature a Liberal–Radical seat, was exhilarating to the young candidate still in his twenties. For all his theoretical contact with politics, it was his first 'rough and tumble of the market place'. In Stockton he inherited an 'uneducated, illiterate Cockney agent', but Macmillan was soon recognising his loyalty, and it was a measure of the flair he was to show years later in office for selecting the right man for the job that he resisted pressures to sack him. Together they went on to fight five elections, and Macmillan claimed that he 'never had a better friend'.

Dorothy, though still nursing Carol, plunged herself with typical gusto into the election campaign within days of its starting. Under the dowdy pudding-basin hat of the times, the Duke's daughter appeared on election posters throughout Stockton, plain and earnest, calling upon constituents: 'May I appeal to YOU to VOTE for my Husband. I know that he will serve YOU faithfully and carry out all he has promised to do.' Macmillan was amused to note that all his electoral meetings seemed to be arranged in a Stockton infants' school, 'whether by malignance or stupidity'; and he always remembered the spectacle of his stout north-country supporters 'trying to squeeze into those puny forms'. One of his most devoted Party-workers told him the blunt home truth: 'You are no speaker, but you're a good lad,' yet he was not discountenanced.

When election night arrived, Macmillan came within 73 votes of winning the seat, against both a Liberal and a Labour candidate. Dorothy, he claimed mischievously many years later, 'achieved great fame and notoriety by going to sleep during the count, which was thought to show a great type of Cavendish phlegm and self-control!'[34] The close result was considered a success, and Captain Macmillan remained on the books at Stockton. He did not have to wait long. The Parliament of 1923–4 was one of the shortest, and most dramatic, in British history. Ramsay MacDonald, heading a new political constellation, a Labour government, but in a weak minority position, lasted less than a year. In October 1924 the third general election in two years took place. This time Baldwin came in on a Conservative landslide of 419 seats to 151 Labour and only 40 Liberals – the Liberal collapse heralding the two-party system which was to remain largely unchanged throughout Macmillan's career. At Stockton, thirty-year-old Harold Macmillan won by over 3000 votes, and for him a new life began.

Chapter Four

The Great Divide
1924–1931

*The memory of massive unemployment began to haunt me then and
for many years to come.*

(*HM, recalling Stockton in the 1920s*)

*I have often since found that when a line of action is said to be
supported 'by all responsible men' it is nearly always dangerous
or foolish. . . .*

(*HM, on restoring the Gold Standard, 1925*)

Stricken with massive unemployment, Stockton in the 1920s was one of the most depressed – and depressing – areas of Britain. In the early days of the industrial revolution Stockton had been a boom town, port for the flourishing Durham coal mines and home of the world's first railway. Later in the nineteenth century, the shipbuilding industry had given Stockton's prosperity an additional boost, while the demands of the First World War had filled the shipyards. Then came the post-war slump. The yards closed and rotted away, and the river warehouses fell into decay. When Macmillan first stood for the constituency in 1923, national unemployment figures were already 2.1 million; by 1931 they had reached the 2.7 million mark, and there was no welfare state, no adequate dole or social security system to fall back on. In Stockton itself during this period, Macmillan assessed the unemployment rate to average between 25 and 30 per cent, although at one point nearly half the male population was out of work.

Macmillan's knowledge of industry was confined to printing and publishing. He had never set foot inside the vast ironworks, shipyards or heavy engineering plants that formed the heart of Tees-side. He soon found, however, that one of the most rewarding aspects of the job lay in dealings with his constituents; the plight of the many disabled, and unemployed, ex-servicemen particularly touched his heart, and he admired the wry optimism with which the grimmest street in the worst slum always seemed to be called 'Paradise Row'. But much as Macmillan might have liked to claim the 'common touch' and to have established close personal links, shyness and diffidence inhibited him. The awkwardness that he often felt, and showed, when he came into contact with people was especially marked in his early political career. He took refuge behind a mask of distant formality; he appeared the aesthete; he had no natural gift as a public speaker and showed little sign of the exceptional skill that he would later develop. What came out at Stockton was the voice of the Oxford Union: it did not fit, and

Macmillan knew it. One constituent, Miss Amy Cooke, remembered in her eighties, half a century later, how speaking 'really took it out of him; he was very shy, but then when you got to know him there was enormous charm and warmth – he couldn't .be anything but sincere.'[1] Qualms about public speaking would remain with him all through his political life and even as Prime Minister the preparation of a major speech would make him physically sick.

Macmillan at this time was far from unflappable and later admitted that he had never liked the rougher side of politics, adding revealingly that when he had to face 'heckling and din', he would say to himself: '"My mother would know how to do this, or she would approve of my doing it", and that would make it much easier.'[2] Far more than his mother, however, Macmillan's greatest asset at Stockton was his wife. Over fifty years later local people who remembered Dorothy Macmillan as the young MP's wife all spoke warmly of her social gifts. 'He was very halting as a speaker, almost had a stammer – it was she who brought him out.' 'Oh, she was wonderful – knew everybody's face – she really made it for him.' 'She was very much loved. There was really no one like her. I would say she was the greater part of his success here.'[3] Macmillan himself, revisiting Stockton in 1979, graciously paid tribute to 'my dear wife, who was so much more responsible than I for winning the hearts, if not the votes, of Stockton'.[4]

Dorothy was undoubtedly helped by the political background in which she had been raised, but it was her genuine interest in people's lives that endeared her to her husband's constituents. 'She treated the people at Stockton rather as she did the tenants at Chatsworth,' said Macmillan, 'talking to them completely naturally – because she was a child of nature – and people are very quick to see what is genuine or fake.'[5] In her knack for remembering people's faces and their problems (something Macmillan was never so good at), she had something of the extraordinary facility of the Queen Mother. Many people indeed considered that Macmillan might well not have held troubled Stockton but for Dorothy. She never let the constituency, or him, down; she was always there when needed, whatever the other complications of her life.

For all his diffident manner and uninspiring public speeches, there was no question about the emotions which Stockton's plight induced in Macmillan. They were to be a prime conditioning factor in his domestic political thinking throughout the rest of his career. In one of the more moving passages of his memoirs, he describes how, by 1931:

Many men, and indeed whole families, had been without work and wages for long periods, with corresponding difficulties and hardships. Their clothes were worn out; their furniture in disrepair; their savings gone; their homes dilapidated. Weekly sums of money, drawn from whatever source, which might have been adequate for a man out of work for a few weeks, were cruelly insufficient for men involved in what had become almost permanent unemployment. This, of course, especially affected the older men, who found it more difficult to move to more hopeful areas or to adapt themselves to new skills.

I shall never forget those despairing faces, as the men tramped up and down the High Street in Stockton or gathered round the Five Lamps in Thornaby [one of the more affluent middle-class districts]. Nor can any tribute be too great to the loyal, unflinching courage of the wives and mothers, who somehow continued, often on a bare pittance, to provide for husband and children and keep a decent home in being.

One of the few bright spots was the establishment of a new chemical industry – soon to be known as ICI – across the River Tees at Billingham. But what, in practical terms, could a young, newly elected backbencher do about Stockton's plight? He organised the purchase of a derelict shipyard and turned it into a training centre and club for the unemployed, financing it partly, it seems, out of his own pocket. He tried to get the old people out of the slums, to have charabanc party trips – 'some of them had never moved out since their grandfathers had left the farms on the Yorkshire Dales and come in as puddlers or steelmen'.[6] But these actions were but nibbles on the fringe. What was needed was an imaginative, and radical, policy to deal with the problem of unemployment and poverty on a national scale. It was the quest for such a policy that canalised Macmillan's energies and kept him in the House of Commons, or locked away in his study, for long hours during his first apprenticeship years as an MP; while abroad, it seemed at the time, 'we felt reasonably secure.'

In the Commons

On 30 April 1925, Macmillan made his maiden speech in the House, during the debate on the government's Budget, lending what *The Times* described as 'undubious and provocative acceptance' to Chancellor of the Exchequer Winston Churchill's more 'social' proposals, such as those on old-age pension and tax remissions, and roundly assailing the socialist ex-Chancellor, Philip Snowden, for his niggardly criticisms. (Macmillan would later remark pungently how little sympathy he had 'with those who, writing from pleasant suburban retreats or comfortable editorial chairs, dilate upon the disciplinary values of pre-war conditioning. It was my fate to live with the problems of heavy unemployment for fifteen years.') Making this first speech was, Macmillan recalled, as alarming as any experience 'except for "going over the top" in war'. He discovered the seating of the House to be 'so arranged that when you stand up to speak, the bench in front of you seems to catch you just below the knee and gives you the impression that you are about to fall headlong over'. On re-reading his maiden speech four decades later, Macmillan found it 'more controversial than convention normally expects or allows'; to the lay reader it also seems ponderous for a young MP. But it was well applauded and brought Macmillan a certain notoriety.

He now began to write articles on rating reform, housing and slum clearance; one such, dated September 1925, contained his slogan for 1951: 'Housing is not a question of Conservatism or Socialism. It is a question of humanity.' In Westminster he never missed an opportunity to bring pressure on the government to deal with the unemployment and poverty problem. 'It was not popular. Some of the north-country members supported me of course, but most Tories did not sit for depressed areas – not many won seats in them – although some of them supported me.'[7]

At the start of his parliamentary career, he had a high regard, even affection, for the Conservative Prime Minister, Stanley Baldwin – then at the peak of his very considerable powers. He felt that Baldwin's great electoral triumph of 1924 was due to his reputation for decency and fair-mindedness, which had won the support of working men and women throughout the country. He looked on Baldwin as something of a Disraeli, bent on bridging the 'Two Nations' and committed to do something about unemployment and industrial reform; his heart was in the right place. Yet, early on, Macmillan began to be troubled by Baldwin's ambiguousness on tariff reform. To safeguard depressed British industry, Macmillan believed that some degree of protectionism was essential. Baldwin had declared before the 1924 election that he could not tackle unemployment until he was relieved of the pledge against protection by the former Conservative Prime Minister Bonar Law, but a year later Macmillan was disillusioned to find that he was proceeding 'to bind on himself the same or very similar shackles as his predecessor'.

In 1926 the coal dispute broke out, leading to the nine-day General Strike in May. Working conditions in the mining industry, a legacy of the Victorian era, had deteriorated further with the general depression and an attempt by mine owners to cut wages and extend working hours to meet the financial crisis was bitterly resisted. A government enquiry under Sir Herbert Samuel was set up, which reported in March, but the dispute remained unresolved and the TUC finally called for a nationwide strike in support of the miners' case. The dispute – Macmillan concluded in retrospect – could, and should, have been avoided 'if the owners had unequivocally accepted and if the Government had undertaken to give immediate effect to the recommendations of the Samuel Commission as to the reorganisation of the industry. . . . But Conservative opinion was not yet prepared for so drastic an interference of the State with industry.' Here, clearly, Macmillan was already somewhat out of sympathy with Conservative opinion.

In one of his earliest letters to Winston Churchill, he wrote from Stockton on 10 April of the 'appalling conditions in this area', adding how 'the patience and endurance of the workers as a whole is really remarkable. Certainly adversity brings out greater virtues than prosperity in all classes, but particularly so among the working people.'[8] During the General Strike the North-east had remained reasonably calm but he was left with a sense of 'sorrow and shame that there should be strife on such a scale between two sections of our own people. War is bad enough; anything like civil war is a thousand times worse.' If unemployment on Tees-side affected him deeply, the shock of the General Strike was also to leave its mark when he came to deal with the trades unions himself, several decades later.

He would always consider that Baldwin alone, remaining calm and moderate throughout the crisis, had saved the country from disaster; yet, noting how strangely moods of energy and lethargy alternated in the Prime Minister, he reckoned that the General Strike had left him exhausted. Slowly disenchantment with the Baldwin government set in. In 1927 Macmillan supported its Trades Disputes Act, which was designed to prevent another general strike. But he did so with misgiving that its powers might be too repressive, and thought that it should be 'accompanied by a progressive programme of social reform and industrial reorganisation carried out in a constructive spirit'. During the second reading of the Bill, in May 1927, he warned the House that if it was 'to be the prelude to a general swing to the right, if it means the beginning of reactionary policy, then I am bound to admit it means the beginning of the end of this party of which I have the honour to be a member, and it means also the end of all the members of the moderate party opposite. It means that the parties . . . are captured by the extremists.'[9] Tough talk for a new young backbencher. The following year Macmillan, with seven others, voted against his party over a bill designed to revise the Poor Laws, on grounds of its lack of humanity: 'It was the first time I had done so. It was to prove during the next ten years by no means the last.' On this occasion, however, Macmillan succeeded in winning the small concession sought by him and his fellow rebels.

Like so many other Members, Macmillan had initially found the House of Commons and its atmosphere remarkably like going back to school. The ministers and leaders of the Opposition sitting on the front benches reminded him of 'the top boys of the sixth form'. From among these gods, the new boy sought a super-hero, and found one outside his own party in the shape of Lloyd George. He remembered the powerful impact the Welshman had made on him the first time he had seen him in action at the Oxford Union; he liked his radicalism, and especially his concern about unemployment. He was also enthralled by his artistry in the House:

I can see him now: the wonderful head, the great mane of white hair (turned from raven black to pure white during the few years of the war); the expressive features, changing rapidly from fierce anger to that enchanting smile, not confined to the mouth, but spreading to his cheeks and eyes; above all, the beautiful hands, an actor's or an artist's hands, by the smallest movement of which he could make you see the picture he was trying to paint.

On one occasion in the early years, when Macmillan anticipated the worst after launching a rash dart at him, Lloyd George totally disarmed him by saying: 'I saw very well what you were doing the other day. You were trying to disguise your revolt against your Tory front bench by a side-attack on me. It is an old trick and I have done it many times. But you are a born rebel.'

A friendship sprang up between them, and the former Prime Minister gave the new boy hints about speaking in the House; hints that were badly needed, for Macmillan's performance at Westminster was as lacklustre as it was in the homelier surroundings of Stockton. In 1927, James Johnston, a *Yorkshire Post* journalist, wrote prophetically of him: 'He is one of the few promising men whom this Parliament has produced. He has the affinity with the spirit of the age and understanding of Parliamentary ways which guarantee success in the political life of the future. Some day he will be one of the guiding forces of the Conservative Party. . . .' But he also remarked: 'He is an enthusiast who does not enthuse. There is no declamation in his speeches, no skilful manipulation of voice, no display of studied gesture.'[10]

Lloyd George showed him how to vary the pace and the pitch, and he also taught him 'to use his arms; not wrists, not hands, not ineffective posturing, but the whole of the arms and shoulders, even the back in a total integration of body into words'.[11] As Macmillan himself recalled, after one speech Lloyd George offered him the shrewd critical advice:

> You made an essay, which was a very good essay, in an economic journal. You made about 25 points, all leading on to one another – that's not the way to speak. You want to make one point, if you are a back-bencher; two if you are a Minister; possibly three if you are Prime Minister, but better still two. . . . The art of speaking is to leave on the audience a clear picture of what it is you want. Not to write an essay about it.[12]

While struggling to master the art of oratory, Macmillan was also busy compiling a booklet called *Industry and the State* which, published in the spring of 1927, came to be regarded 'as a manifesto of the progressive wing of our party'. Among other radical ideas, it proposed that collective bargaining should be given statutory authority; and the extension of joint industrial councils with increased powers, and of trade boards. Macmillan's fellow authors were three other young MPs, Bob Boothby, Oliver Stanley and John Loder; together they formed the nucleus of a Tory progressive group later to be nicknamed the YMCA. This marked the beginning of an important and long-lasting political alliance with Boothby. To his surprise, Macmillan received a congratulatory note from Neville Chamberlain, then Minister of Health, saying that although he could not agree with everything put forward he thought the booklet would be 'stimulating' to members of the Party. (Nevertheless, he never addressed Macmillan again during the rest of that Parliament.)

Sitting ten feet away across the gangway, a new Labour MP was shortly to have similar thoughts: 'When he began to talk about public utilities,' remarked Emanuel Shinwell, 'I began to show interest; I thought, that's curious for a Tory. Some of his ideas were rather half-baked . . . but interesting. He was not a true Socialist, it was sort of Fabian stuff . . . but he was *compassionate* – one of his great attributes.'[13] Macmillan's own side of the House soon began to hold similar views to Shinwell's; he was 'suspected of being pink by that extraordinary right-wing of the party', remarked his future colleague, Rab Butler.[14]

Through Bob Boothby, Macmillan began to enjoy Churchill's company. Boothby claimed Macmillan was his 'closest political friend' in the 1920s: 'He was certainly the bravest of us, the only one who resigned the Party Whip,' he told the author.[15] At the age of twenty-six, Boothby had become Churchill's Parliamentary Private Secretary in 1926 and for the next thirteen years he remained extremely close to him, often speaking to the great man with a bluntness few (and certainly not the young Macmillan) would hazard. In October 1926, Boothby had written to Churchill a typically outspoken letter, explaining why the coal miners believed the government had let them down, and damning it as 'a government of reaction'.[16]

For any young MP, Churchill's company in those days must have been extraordinarily stimulating. He was, recalled Macmillan, 'unique, wayward, exciting, a man with a peculiar glamour of his own, that brought a sense of colour into our rather drab political life'. He had, so it seemed, lived several men's lives already: journalist, Liberal, First Lord of the Admiralty, soldier, historian, now Tory Chancellor of the Exchequer – and what more might there be to come? His circle of friends, wrote Macmillan, would sit round, sometimes late into the night, smoking, drinking and arguing, and of course listening. . . . It was the first time that I had come across this kind of method of conducting political talk. . . . To sit and talk to Churchill was like young men at Oxford arguing with dons or even professors – and plenty of drink and cigars provided. To be sent for to Neville Chamberlain's room was more like an interview with the headmaster.

All these activities in the House kept Macmillan extremely busy, but he had developed a consummate skill in dichotomising his two professional lives. Dennis White, who worked in Macmillan's from 1926 onwards, remembered how Harold Macmillan would come in every morning from nine-thirty till one, and do a full day's work as a publisher, before going off to the House.[17] This concentration left all too little time for Dorothy and the children.

In 1926, the year their third child, Catherine, was born, the Macmillan home at Birch Grove was rebuilt by Nellie into an imposing mansion, a great neo-Georgian barrack of a house, one of only two or three such major works of residential construction undertaken during the depression; its cornerstone was laid by five-year-old Maurice. Much of the house seemed to be kitchens and servants' quarters, and in these vast back areas the old-fashioned bells, still extant at the end of Harold's life, told their story of a matriarch-dominated household: 'Mrs Macmillan' (Nellie); 'Mr Arthur' (brother); 'Mr Harold'; 'Lady Dorothy's sitting room'; 'Master Maurice, day nursery'. Through his distinguished marriage, Harold had established himself as Nellie's clear favourite, on whom all her ambitions now centred. She was down on Dan's wife, Betty, who was considered 'Welsh and unsuitable', while the gentle, religious and intelligent Arthur, already in disfavour for his Anglo-Catholicism, in her eyes had also married beneath him; his wife Peggy was the peace-maker of the family. Ruthlessly, the two older brothers were ruled out of their birthright to Birch Grove, Nellie persuading the compliant Maurice to leave it entirely to Harold and Dorothy – with the proviso, disastrous as it turned out, that she be allowed to stay in the house until her death. Throughout his life, Harold apparently suffered a repressed sense of shame at the way his brothers had been treated, and constantly tried to make amends.

As designed by Nellie, the house was impossible to divide – with the consequence that mother-in-law was perpetually on top of the young couple. For a born gardener like Dorothy, brought up in the great terraces of Capability Brown's Chatsworth, conflict in the garden at Birch Grove must have proved at least as grievous. Her mother-in-law planted bedding-out begonias, in a very municipal way, which contrived to flower only when Dorothy was in residence, while Dorothy planted bulbs that flowered chiefly when Nellie was there. It seems to have been a strange horticultural feud. All Harold and Dorothy's children united in disliking their American grandmother; Carol, the eldest daughter, remembered as a child finding her mother sticking pins into an effigy of Nellie.[18]

It cannot have been a particularly happy environment for the children, perhaps least of all for Maurice, who also suffered from Dorothy's quite explicit preference for girls. He revered his father, but – because they saw so little of each other – both found it difficult to put out an affectionate hand to the other. 'He could be embarrassing when he tried to show affection,' Maurice once remarked; 'he couldn't cope with personal problems, his own, or mine. There was always a distance between us.'[19] Harold also erred, thought C. P. Snow, by being 'constantly under the impression that Maurice could do anything, perhaps asked too much of him'.[20] For much of Maurice's life, the pressures, the expectations were to prove too great. He, in his turn, would serve in the wartime army, go into politics and make a dynastic marriage by marrying the Hon. Katharine Ormsby-Gore, daughter of Lord Harlech and related back to Dorothy's family through a Salisbury grandfather. Carol would marry a wartime Welsh Guardsman and member of a famous Lloyds broker family, Julian Faber; and Catherine, by marrying Julian Amery, MP and son of Churchill's close associate Leo, would create yet another political dynastic link within the Macmillan clan. Sarah, the youngest, would remain rather the outsider, and was to die at a tragically early age.

The conversion of Birch Grove may have marked a turning point in Harold and Dorothy's marriage, without Harold in his political and publishing preoccupations being aware of how Nellie's potent influence and constant presence could undermine his marital relationship. He never ceased to recognise that out of Nellie's iron will and driving ambition was forged his political future, and, whatever the later personal cost, he made his mark during these first years in Parliament in the mid-1920s.

Macmillan himself regarded the publication of *Industry and the State* as the most productive period of his thinking, but perhaps a more significant contribution at this time was on derating, to alleviate the weight of taxation on industry by reducing the rates levied by local authorities. He noted wryly that it was 'not a popular line either in the party or generally throughout the country', especially in the more prosperous areas; it was however vigorously supported by Boothby, Stanley and Loder. Macmillan's view was that British industry could never be reanimated (nor unemployment reversed) while laden with unfair burdens. Hence it should be relieved of paying rates to local authorities. He laid particular emphasis on the so-called 'devastated areas' such as Tees-side, where the burden was most disparate and the rates 'bore no relation to profit, but were a very heavy charge upon costs'. Eventually he broached his scheme to Winston Churchill, who was taken by it and gradually adopted it as his own idea.

In the spring of 1927, Churchill proposed that factories and farms should be relieved of £30 million in rates, half the cost of which should come from economies in government spending. That December he took Macmillan completely into his confidence, and Macmillan responded with nine pages of notes – which formed the basis for a powerful Churchillian memorandum to the Cabinet. On 1 January 1928, Macmillan followed it up with a twenty-page letter to Churchill from Chatsworth. 'Christmas, with its accompaniment of large numbers of children to be amused and vast quantities of pheasants to be shot, is not conducive to serious thought,' he began diffidently; then went on to remark appreciatively how 'you have always been most kind to those of us who are ordinarily classed merely as troublesome young men. . . .' The language was ponderously learned and contrived; he wondered whether 'the rescue of the industrialist Andromeda from the clutches of the socialist dragon will have an excellent effect on the character of the dragon'.[21] It was not quite Churchill's style, but the solid arguments put forward, and the way in which points were advanced to meet a likely counterattack by the Minister of Health, Neville Chamberlain, clearly impressed him and four days later he wrote the young backbencher a flatteringly grateful letter:

It is always pleasant to find someone whose mind grasps the essentials and proportions of a large plan. I made you party to it because I was sure you would enrich its preliminary discussion, and also because – though you may have forgotten it – a chance remark of yours about the rating system, made more than two years ago, first implanted in my mind the seed of what may become a considerable event. . . .[22]

On 15 January Churchill told him that he considered his statement so lucid and well balanced that he had sent it to the Prime Minister. Baldwin was 'extremely complimentary'; Chamberlain, apprehensive about the electorate, was rather less so. He belittled the scheme as 'characteristic of Winston in its ingenuity, audacity and vagueness',[23] and later in the year he wrote acidly of its actual progenitor: 'On the backbenches Harold Macmillan speaks often and well. [Few, except so arid an orator as Neville Chamberlain, can have shared this last sentiment at the time.] He is patronised by the Chancellor, I think, through the influence of R. Boothby who is the Chancellor's PPS and a friend of Macmillan. But both of them are rather mistrusted by the rank and file. . . .'[24]

On 14 March, Macmillan wrote another, five-page, memorandum in support of Churchill after he and Boothby had spent a morning at the Treasury. It ended: 'if this plan goes awry, we shall see the eventual and perhaps early dissolution of the Party. If it goes right, it will put new life into the Party. It will provide constructive policy other than Protection. . . . It will consolidate the moderate vote. . . .'[25]

In the following February, the massive Derating Bill passed on its third reading, although the inevitable compromises had whittled it down. It was a major achievement, and a personal triumph for Macmillan, who reflected that its main principles have 'stood the test of time and experience'. A month later, Macmillan had a new memorandum in the post to Churchill, this time proposing Budget cuts together with a whole new set of vigorous policies designed to appeal to the voters at the forthcoming election. He urged that modernisation and research were the key to industrial revival, rather than tariffs and protection, and proposed the slogan 'Modernisation at Home, Markets Abroad'. Churchill responded by discussing with Macmillan some of the economic policies that would be unveiled in his forthcoming Budget. Macmillan wrote back with enthusiasm, talking excitedly about 'The Vision Splendid' and 'The Grand Policy' – a phrase that would ring an echo, though in different contexts, four decades later.

The whole derating saga reveals how progressive was Macmillan's thinking at the time. It was also, historically, a factor in exacerbating the already tetchy relations between Chamberlain and Churchill – and thus between the Minister of Health and the Chancellor's young allies. But its importance lay above all in the personal link which it established between Macmillan and Churchill, a link that would never be broken and would eventually bring Macmillan to supreme office, as Churchill's natural heir. Macmillan recalls in his memoirs how excited he was to be taken into Churchill's confidence at that time, and admitted that 'it was the making of my political life, in a sense.'[26]

The Year of the Great Crash

Nineteen-twenty-nine was a year of disaster throughout the world; it was also one of the most wretched in Harold Macmillan's life. On 8 February, he wrote prophetically to Dorothy: 'perhaps you were right about politics but we shall probably not have to travel backwards and forwards to Stockton much longer.' On 30 May, Baldwin went to the country on the feeble slogan of 'Safety First'. His government's record of achievement was not a bad one but the country did not think it good enough: once again Ramsay MacDonald became head of a Labour government dependent on Liberal support. At Stockton, wrote Macmillan in 1975 with the dispassion of time, 'My unhappy constituents did not want "safety" – which meant hanging about the streets or haunting the factories in despair. Safety meant the dole. They wanted work. So they very properly voted me out, and I had to confess, in my heart, that I could not blame them.'[27]

But that was not how he felt at the time. Hugh Dalton, successfully elected for Labour in another Durham seat, recalled seeing Macmillan, as the train to London moved out, standing at a window 'with tears streaming down his cheeks' bravely calling for three cheers for Baldwin.[28] For once emotion had broken through habitual stern reserve.

His self-control was, however, far more severely tested that year when he realised that his wife had fallen irrevocably in love with Robert Boothby, and he with her. Six years younger than Harold, one of his closest friends and vital political allies, Boothby possessed a strikingly attractive personality: he was moreover considered *the* coming man. Brilliant, a remarkable speaker, eccentric, ahead of his time, many saw him as a potential prime minister. The antithesis of his friend, Harold Macmillan, he affected total self-assurance; quoting a journalist who had praised him as being 'always ahead of his time, and always right', Boothby declared, 'From this conclusion I cannot dissent.'[29] Extremely good-looking, he dressed with careless raffishness, in complete contrast to Macmillan with his unstylish clothes, gold-rimmed glasses, unappealing bushy moustache and toothily diffident half-smile. (Indeed in some of the photographs of those days Harold looks more like one of Lenin's early collaborators than a duke's son-in-law). Boothby on the other hand dashed about in an open, two-seater Bentley and was socially at ease wherever he went, be it to Hatfield, Chartwell or Chatsworth. He would lean back in his chair, casually relaxed, and talk about his passion for jazz, for the music of Gershwin, and his addiction for Hemingway.

Boothby would proclaim 'my religion is humour' and demonstrate this with uninhibited zeal which often went too far. Interviewing Hitler in the 1930s, he was asked – with reference to the Polish corridor – how he would have felt had Germany won the war and driven a corridor between England and Scotland. 'You forget, Herr Hitler,' Boothby replied, 'that I come from Scotland. We should have been delighted.'[30] Hitler had not smiled, and indeed his sallies were by no means enjoyed by all, but Dorothy Macmillan clearly found them to her liking and he no doubt found a natural foil in her.

Attractive to both sexes, Boothby on his own admission enjoyed being 'chased all over the place' by homosexuals in Nazi Germany. Endowed with the worldly allure of a rising star, he had a strong streak of the bounder in him as well as an element of irresponsibility. He admired – and obviously envied – Lloyd George's remarkable private life and his ability to get away with 'two wives, two homes and two families'.[31] Boothby's engaging capriciousness, however, had a self-destructive factor built into it. 'I don't think you will ever get high office . . . because I don't think you really want it,' he was told, perceptively, by a great political hostess of the time, Mrs

Ronnie Greville.[32] Others too recognised flaws: Shinwell felt he preferred love to life, Anthony Head considered he had absolutely no principles, and eventually even his champion Churchill became worried by the defects in his character.

At a house party at Bowood, the Marquess of Lansdowne's Wiltshire seat, to which both Dorothy and Boothby had been invited, an incident took place which, Boothby was to claim, cemented his attraction in her eyes during the early phases of the romance. In the course of a silly game, Lady Henry Bentinck, who was described as a 'sheep disguised as a shepherdess', lost her glasses and the party broke up with a certain amount of hilarity at Lady Henry's expense. A few days later Dorothy received a packet containing a pair of broken glasses, accompanied by an invitation to lunch. Boothby had stepped on the glasses, and then concealed the deed.

It is not hard to imagine the appeal for Dorothy of Boothby, in comparison with Macmillan. One was a dashingly handsome bounder, the other worthy and almost dowdily prosaic. Boothby appeared destined for stardom – not so Macmillan; and the Cavendishes were traditionally drawn to success, in whatever field. Cavendish women also had a reputation for being highly sexed, and it seems that Macmillan – like Churchill – attached little importance to the physical aspects of love. There may well have been something cloying in Harold's love; from the letters of those early days there emerges occasionally a sense of devotion bordering on the dutiful, suggesting that he may have at times treated Dorothy as a surrogate mother-figure. And there was of course the added marital hazard of cohabiting with a formidably strong-willed mother-in-law: one of Dorothy's own daughters-in-law thought that 'It must have been like a strait-jacket.' Bob Boothby took her away from all that, amused her and probably made her feel truly herself for the first time.[33] Boothby's explanation was that '... Harold couldn't express emotions, that was the fault of it all.... he didn't give her what she needed, he was so involved in politics, all the time.... she was bored stiff in the 1920s by political meetings....'[34]

The attraction that Dorothy Macmillan held for Boothby, apart from her obvious charm, is perhaps partly that she gave him self-confidence; ostensibly full of bounce, Boothby was insecure in his social origins. Moreover, she could give the politician on the make the *entrée* to other doors vital to his ambitions, just as she had for her husband. But whatever the underlying reasons, the attraction was genuine and intense. If Boothby's earthy, reckless sense of humour struck a chord in Dorothy, it was because she too had a touch of the daredevil; she once took part in a mock 'burglary', equipped with masks and toy pistols, of the house of a pompous royal equerry.[35]

The relationship, in one form or another, was to continue until Dorothy's death in 1966, and its impact on Boothby's life was total. 'Even now, when the telephone rings,' he admitted in old age, 'I still expect to hear her voice saying "It's me" – that was how she always spoke on the telephone. . . .'[36] In his memoirs he declared that the years 1925–35 were ones of 'sheer enjoyment' for him; yet he also developed a habit of referring, privately, to what had happened in 1929 as 'the Great Crash'. It was 'a real tragedy, but we couldn't avoid it. . . . it was on the scale of Wagner, George Sand, if you like Parnell. . . .' In old age, telling all, he claimed on the one hand that 'it wasn't an affair in the modern sense. It was a romantic friendship in the true Victorian tradition';[37] while on the other hand his *ex post facto* view of the dominating love of his life also contained a curious blend of romanticism and self-pity that sometimes verged on the unchivalrous, and of exhibitionist vulgarity. To him Dorothy was 'a very powerful woman':

> she drove me, and also Harold in a different way. . . . I think she was always interested in power. . . . She never suffered a pang of remorse, or she never showed it, anyway – absolutely none about me or Harold. . . . She was certainly not the sweet, simple, good, quiet lady – how little people knew! . . . Several times I got engaged, once in Venice, but Dorothy came all the way from Chatsworth to pursue me there. . . . she was absolutely unafraid of anything. . . . She broke off my engagement, and stopped me twice more from getting married. . . . she was relentless, there was a streak of cruelty in her, I have to admit, and very selfish. But we were absolutely fixed upon each other. . . .[38]

In fact, Boothby, in 1935, married Diana Cavendish, a cousin of Dorothy Macmillan. But the marriage lasted only two years and he did not marry again until 1967, a year after Dorothy's death.

If the years that followed 1929 were 'sheer enjoyment' for Bob

Boothby, they must have been unadulterated hell for Macmillan. The electorate had deprived him of his seat in the Commons; Boothby had taken away his wife. His early letters to Dorothy leave one in no doubt of the depth of his affection for her – and he remained very much in love with her. An intensely proud and private man, he was now grievously wounded both in pride and in privacy. For it was simply not in Dorothy's nature to weave a tissue of lies, let alone to hide anything. Through letters left around, telephone calls made *fortissimo* with doors ajar, the Macmillan children learned about the affair in their teens. 'What he minded most,' in his son Maurice's opinion, 'was being dishonoured.'[39] Though people talked less (when he heard of the affair, King George V was said to have ordered 'Keep it quiet'),[40] and gossip columnists were both less efficient and less unprincipled in the 1930s, everybody in the small world of society soon came to know about the Dorothy–Boothby relationship. Respect for Harold Macmillan and awareness of his misery probably helped staunch this knowledge from seeping out to a wider public. But knowing that 'everybody' knew, while trying to keep up pretences, could only have exacerbated the pain for Macmillan. Characteristically he was inhibited from pouring out his soul to anyone, probably including his oldest and dearest friend Ronnie Knox. The sole exception seems to have been his mother. The wound festered inside him.

At an early stage in the affair he seriously considered starting divorce proceedings; on the other hand, he seems to have lived in dread of Dorothy's leaving him for Boothby, and there was a moment when that seemed a distinct possibility. In the strictest conjugal sense, the marriage was finished, with Dorothy Macmillan recorded as declaring on more than one occasion, 'I am faithful to Bob'. When Sarah was born in 1930, it was generally accepted that Boothby, not Macmillan, was the father. Eventually Macmillan dropped ideas of divorce, and endeavoured to achieve a *modus vivendi*. Here it is impossible not to see the influence of Nellie Macmillan, aware as she would have been of the consequences that divorce, in the 1930s, might have had on her son's political future. During one of the rare – and demonstrably painful – occasions that he ever discussed his marriage, he said:

> . . . I never loved anyone but her – never had a woman friend, or even knew anyone. On her side, there were transient things –

unimportant. What counts are the fundamentals. . . . I had everything from her, owed everything to her. . . . She filled my life; I thought in everything I did of her . . . she was devoted to me. . . . We were very close; I told her I'd never. let her go – it would have been disastrous . . . a hopeless fellow. And what's physical love? She wanted everything. She had it. In middle age, things pass; I said jokingly, 'Now you've had everything, husband, children, home, a lover, what more?' In the way women do, she said it was my fault . . . but what's physical love compared to things you share, interests, children? . . . But it took a lot out of me, physically. . . .[41]

Somehow, Dorothy Macmillan managed a double life, being in daily contact with Boothby, travelling at home and abroad with him whenever possible, yet at the same time running a household for her husband and – most important – never once letting him down when needed at Stockton or at the hustings. In return, Macmillan always treated Boothby in public with the utmost civility. Indeed, it was he who as Prime Minister bestowed a peerage on Boothby; though when Boothby wrote asking for it (with similar insensitivity, he had also evidently expected a Cabinet post), Macmillan's faithful Private Secretary, John Wyndham, pocketed the letter for several days out of concern for the hurt it might inflict. Macmillan's reaction was, 'of course he must have it.'[42] Nevertheless, the 'arrangement' of the 1930s concealed a world of heartbreak for Harold Macmillan. 'He had a sad lonely life really,' remarked his sister-in-law 'Moucher', Dowager Duchess of Devonshire. He was an old-fashioned man, she felt, who would have liked to have come home to his wife at five o'clock each evening, but she wasn't there. 'If your wife is a great anxiety to you, it is pretty grim.'[43] In his diary for 29 November 1930, Harold Nicolson recalled a dismal house party at Cliveden which included Boothby and the Macmillans: 'Great sofas in vast cathedrals. Little groups of people wishing they were alone. . . . After dinner, in order to enliven the party, Lady Astor dons a Victorian hat and false teeth. It does not enliven the party.'[44]

As the years passed, life went on at Birch Grove, but with a certain separateness and lack of warmth, Harold reading at one end of the house, Dorothy and the children playing games at the other end. Gradually, as both grew older, and the physical side of the passion between Dorothy and Boothby ran its course, a new relaxed attachment, affection – and, indeed, devotion – grew up between the Macmillans, cemented during the premiership years. In Harold Macmillan's own words, 'In doing what was difficult, I had my reward in the end.'[45] Or, as Dorothy's niece, Andrew Devonshire, remarked, 'I think their life was one of the greatest arguments against divorce.'[46]

Many of those, like Pamela Egremont, who knew Macmillan well over long periods of his career believe that he might never have emerged as Prime Minister but for 'the grit in the oyster' provided by the Boothby tragedy, which gave him that extra thrust to get to the top. His long-time colleague, and rival, Rab Butler, considered that Macmillan '*did* suffer greatly, it *did* depress him, but he would never admit it; the extraordinary thing about Harold was that he had such moral strength. . . . Boothby did have a depressing effect, but not on his moral character, which was so strong . . . but perhaps it did enhance his character.'[47]

Macmillan himself admitted that 'all this personal trouble then did strengthen my character'.[48] The dignity and selflessness with which Macmillan comported himself throughout must – in the long run – have aided his public advancement, at the expense of Boothby, once considered the more brilliant but whose judgement was being increasingly exposed to doubt. Yet in some ways the anguish of the 1930s probably gave Macmillan a cynicism about life which had not existed before, and which was to manifest itself much later. It also created certain blind spots that would – for instance – bear grave consequences during the Profumo case which, three decades later, would mark the beginning of the end of his public life.

While Macmillan was trying to save his marriage, he also needed to revive his parliamentary career. In the immediate aftermath of the 1929 general election it was by no means clear that Stockton could easily be won back. It seemed sensible to look for a new seat. Within weeks he received an overture from the Hitchin Conservative Association to stand for their constituency. The sitting member, Major Guy Kindersley, wanted to retire and it was agreed in December 1929 that a by-election should take place in the following spring.

Notionally, Hitchin was a safe seat in the comfortable and relatively affluent Home Counties which would involve Macmillan in far less travelling and absence from London. In view of the recurring pain of his war wounds and more particularly on account of the gnawing anxiety about his marriage, this must have been a serious personal consideration in weighing up the offer. In theory, he had been promised the support of Lord Beaverbrook – then threatening to split the Tory Party on the issue of Empire Free Trade. But Beaverbrook's support was ever an unpredictable asset, and there was a danger that he might suddenly put up an 'Empire Free Trader' for the seat; there were also disturbing noises from the National Farmers' Union (whose President was a constituent), added to which there was a Liberal threat to back the socialists over the tariff issue. So the seat was much less safe than it looked even before Kindersley began to wobble over his decision to resign.

But there was more to it than that, and it hinged significantly on Macmillan's whole political credo. On 27 May 1930, *The Times* published a letter by Macmillan commending Sir Oswald Mosley for sticking to his election pledges to reduce unemployment, and for resigning as a junior minister in Ramsay MacDonald's government. Macmillan had then gone on to criticise the Conservative government. Two days later he received a telegram from Beaverbrook, with the assurance 'IF I CAN SUPPORT YOU IN ANY DIRECTION AT THIS MOMENT PLEASE LET ME KNOW'; but this coincided with an acidly prefectorial note from Kindersley, still firmly in the saddle: 'Don't do it again or I may find myself compelled however reluctantly to fight Hitchin again, which would be a bore. . . .'[49]

When the Hitchin Conservatives had first made their approach to Macmillan, they were well aware that he stood on the radical wing of the Party, but his views were still perceived to be compatible with mainstream Conservative policy. The sharp tone of Macmillan's letter now suggested that their potential candidate was drifting out of the mainstream altogether, and the Hitchin Conservatives began to have second thoughts. In September, after he had been attacked in the right-wing *Patriot* for being a free-trader and for threatening to vote against Baldwin, Macmillan wrote a twelve-page letter of self-justification to the Association Chairman, Lieutenant-Colonel Sir Charles Heaton-Ellis, couched in coolly ponderous terms. Refusing to yield an inch on the 'radicalism' that was so upsetting the right-wingers of Hitchin, Macmillan declared: '. . . I shall be deterred neither by the frontal onslaught of acknowledged

enemies nor by the less reputable attacks of nominal allies. . . .'[50]
By February 1931 Kindersley had changed his mind and informed
Macmillan that he was now definitely not going to stand down.
The flirtation with Hitchin ended frigidly, with Kindersley writing
no longer 'My dear Harold', but simply 'Dear Macmillan'.

Meanwhile Ramsay MacDonald's economic problems made it
probable that Stockton could be regained at the next general election. Stockton had, however, adopted a new Conservative candidate, Leonard Ropner. Fortunately, the popularity which Harold
and Dorothy had gained during his past five years there now came
to his assistance. Some of the letters received after his 1929 defeat,
notably from working-class constituents, attest to the affection in
which he was held. One spoke of the pleasure of 'working with one
of the greatest ladies in the country and one of the finest gentlemen';
many expressed appreciation for his having found them a job.
'Don't be too downhearted,' wrote another (on 12 June 1929): 'I
am certain there is a great future for you, men of your Character,
sincerity of Duty, Honour and Straightforwardness can ill be spared.
It is men of your type that are required to carry out those great
ideals of Lord Beaconsfield, therefore as an humble deciple [sic]
myself, I say Go Forward, more determined than ever, and I hope
I shall live to see the day that you get the Reword [sic] that you
deserve, and your great ambition Realised. . . . "God bless you
Both."'[51]

In March 1931, Macmillan received an appeal signed by many
of his former supporters in Stockton urging him to return. Clearly
under some pressure, Leonard Ropner did the gentlemanly thing
and – pleading 'family bereavement and ill health' – withdrew
his candidature. Macmillan accepted Stockton's 'all-is-forgiven'
invitation conditionally:

> . . . I cannot now bind myself to stand for Stockton for more than
> one election. . . . My reasons for this are personal. I do not yet
> know whether I shall be able, in several years time, to stand the
> strain that will be involved, and I might find it necessary, for
> business and other reasons, to seek a constituency nearer
> London. . . . I am not quite so vigorous as I was. Neither my
> wife nor I, with the various claims upon our time, could do quite
> as much travelling up and down between London and Stockton
> as we used to do.

He ended: 'You know how fond of Stockton my wife and I are, and how proud of our connection with it. . . . I expect that many people will think me rather foolish to give up one of the safest seats in England; but I really do love the North, and we shall be very happy to be amongst you again.'[52] In fact, of course, the option of Hitchin was no longer open to him anyway.

Thus ended Macmillan's Hitchin flirtation. On the one hand a constituency nearer London might possibly have helped his marriage; on the other hand, the probability was even greater that his political career would have advanced no further. He would never have been happy in a rich, middle-class constituency in the 1930s. At 'dear old Stockton', as he called it in later life, he was both known and established, and – however precarious his tenure . there – it provided him with the ideal platform from which to shout out for industrial reform. The lure of another safe seat (Finchley) in the South returned, briefly, at the 1935 election, but he decided he could not desert Stockton, and he was to remain there until the 1945 débâcle.

Macmillan's defence of Mosley in what Rab Butler described as a 'long magisterial letter' to *The Times* had wider repercussions. Macmillan had suggested ironically that Mosley had 'broken the rules of the political game' by saying what he meant and meaning what he said, and then went on to declare that if the rules were not changed 'many of us will feel that it is hardly worth while bothering to play at all.' Apart from outraging Hitchin, this provoked an acid reply, signed by Butler and three other Tory MPs: 'When a player starts complaining that "it's hardly worth bothering to play" the game at all, it is usually the player and not the game who is at fault. It is then usually advisable for the player to seek a new field for his recreation, and a pastime more suited to his talents.'[53] The letter marked the first salvo fired between Butler and Macmillan, who were to be both rivals and colleagues for the rest of their political lives. Baldwin also attacked Macmillan obliquely in a speech about people who 'hunted with packs other than their own',[54] and Macmillan now came close to accepting Butler's caustic advice.

After his resignation from office in disgust at the government's reneging on its electoral promises, Mosley had been expelled from the Labour Party altogether, and early in 1931 he had founded his New Party, with proposals for a planned economy that particularly appealed to Macmillan and his parliamentary friends. His New Party would soon move towards Fascism, and Mosley would become the fallen angel of the 1930s, but in 1931, aged only thirty-five, he was still widely regarded as the golden boy of British politics. He and Macmillan became very close. This provoked a stinging letter from a new correspondent, Margot Oxford (widow of ex-Prime Minister Asquith), all about team-work, straightness and fair play:

> You cd. all do a fresh deal now with Baldwin if you wd get together and if you sway towards Mosley, Winston or any other false God you do no good at all in politics and the X bench [cross-bench] mind is sterile. Tom [Mosley] has played the fool to a degree I never thought possible as he is very clever – but not quite as remarkable as he thinks he is. Come and see me. . . .[55]

Five days later brought another lecture from Lady Oxford, warning of the evils of 'groups *outside* the existing parties':

> if they *were* to succeed we would be like France; clerical, anti-clerical, agricultural and anti ditto, centre, left-centre, right, half right, etc. all *very* boring; I shd avoid Winston, he has *no* political insight or glimmer of gratitude or loyalty. Try and get together all the young ones. Men who coin phrases to cover their changing convictions are no good – I have seen too many of them in politics.[56]

Over the next two months Macmillan's political antennae began to quiver, and he was having second thoughts about Mosley. Meeting him on the train to Oxford, Harold Nicolson, who had been one of the first to join Mosley's New Party, noted in his diary for 30 May 1931 how Macmillan took 'the usual young Tory view that his heart is entirely with the New Party but that he feels he can help us better by remaining in the Conservative ranks. . . . He anticipates the present Government being in power for another two years, followed by a Tory administration lasting some three years. He feels that five years from now, the New Party will have its great opportunity.'[57]

Fascism, however, would soon derail Mosley, and within a matter of months the much-vaunted New Party proved itself a broken reed, with policies irrelevant to the problems for which it had been founded. Such is the peril for those who found new political parties in Britain. Macmillan said of Mosley in retrospect: 'A certain arrogance and impatience brought an end to his parliamentary career. When he later took refuge in an extra-parliamentary movement, and tried to bring Fascism into England, he was doomed. . . .' And 'Great talents and great strengths of character were thrown away in vain. Had he waited, he might have been supreme. He struck too soon, and fell for ever. In politics, as in many other things, the essence of the game is "timing".'[58]

One net gain of the flirtation with Mosley was to bring Macmillan a new collaborator in the shape of Allan Young, a young ex-Marxist from the Clyde who had been Secretary of the New Party and had contributed many of the best ideas in its manifesto. Together with another ex-Marxist, John Strachey (later to become a minister in the 1945 Attlee government), Young left the New Party in disgust at its slide towards Fascism, and teamed up with Macmillan as his economic adviser. A more important consequence of the Mosley interlude, however, was that it afforded Macmillan an invaluable lesson in patience, as well as in the folly of seeking remedies outside the existing party framework. Not for the last time, impatience and audacity carried him to the brink of the abyss, while a certain prudence caused him to draw back before it was too late.

Chapter Five

The Wilderness Years
1931–1939

It is very difficult for those whose memories do not go back to the twenties and thirties to have any conception of the virulence with which the role of the State in a modern economy was contested.

(*HM*, Winds of Change)

Let us either settle with Germany now, or coerce her now. But don't let us purchase an uncertain peace at a terrible price to be paid later.

(*HM, the* Star, *20 March 1936*)

In 1931 Macmillan suffered a collapse. A recurrence of troubles from his wartime wounds – coupled with a deliberately vague diagnosis of 'neurasthenia' – provided a smoke-screen for what in fact seemed to have been a full-scale nervous breakdown. The exact details were kept extremely quiet within the family, through the efforts of Nellie. One of the few to have an inkling of just how desperate Macmillan was over Boothby was Lord David Cecil, the younger brother of Bobbety Cranborne, who recalled him once banging his head against the wall of a railway compartment in sheer despair. Inhibited as he always was about baring his soul to others, the extent of Macmillan's anguish was also revealed when he confided to a woman friend, 'I just can't go on'; this was reinforced years later when the old family nanny hinted darkly to one of the Macmillan children of a suicide attempt.[1]

To recover, he was sent by Nellie for several months to a sanatorium at Neu Wittelsbach, near Munich. On 16 September, he was able to reassure her that the doctor had found 'no organic disease, only nervous prostration'. Five days later there followed a letter saying that Dr Lampe 'thinks I have only just avoided a complete breakdown. . . . I think if I can have this cure and get properly rested I can face my other troubles. Perhaps it won't be so long as seems now probable. One never knows. . . .' The next week he was complaining of 'rather a battered feeling . . . the same kind of experience after Loos or after the Somme. But I was younger then, and had (I suppose) more resilience. . . .' Revealing his anxiety, and that he was not in touch with his wife's movements, he asked his mother whether Dorothy had been to Birch Grove. His thoughts then turned abruptly to the British political scene. There was growing talk of an imminent general election to replace Ramsay MacDonald's flagging National Government; 'if there is an election,' continued Macmillan in his letter to Nellie, 'I think I shall make an effort to come home. I want to get into the H of C, because

I think it wd make my life much easier. The doctor seems rather uncertain as to whether I ought to risk the effort. . . .'[2]

Nevertheless, with the kind of phenomenal display of will-power that had characterised his survival on the Somme fifteen years earlier, and despite the misgivings of his German doctors, he was back at Stockton the following month, fighting for re-election. The effort was worth it; loyally supported by Dorothy, his majority over Labour rose from a hoped-for 3000 or 4000 to just over 11,000. In one of the greatest landslides in British history, the Conservatives came back with 473 seats, supported by a further 81 miscellaneous allies. But for all Macmillan's satisfaction, personal and professional, at getting back into politics, it is clear from a letter of 5 November 1931 to his constituency Chairman, Ernest Appleton, that his recovery was far from complete. Macmillan thanked him for his help in the election,

> not only with political work, but (which I most especially appreciated) you have taken so much trouble in so many ways to spare me and make this easier and more comfortable for me. . . . as I expected I am suffering from a bit of reaction and my leg is getting rather bad again. But I do hope to get better gradually. I should not attempt to do anything in Stockton or in parliament until I am fit. . . .[3]

Yet convalescence soon took the form of plunging himself with almost frenetic energy into political activities. It was not until 1933 that he allowed himself anything resembling a proper holiday. He then travelled on a boat to Dalmatia and Greece, taking with him twelve-year-old Maurice. Having been such a distant parent, this voyage of mutual discovery between father and son proved to be a pleasure to both. Many years later, Maurice recalled realising 'for the first time how vulnerable he was, as opposed to being remote, and also the immensely important role played by my grandmother'.[4] In a letter to Nellie, Harold himself wrote with touchingly warm affection and praise for Maurice as a travelling companion, and remarked how greatly he himself was benefiting from the cruise: 'it makes me feel young to be back in the classical atmosphere. . . . my "middle age" troubles seem far behind, and I seem to be back in those happy years of pre-war Oxford.'[5] Yet, on his return, inevitably the domestic strains continued.

Birthday-greetings telegrams to his parents during the years 1933–4 bear the revealing signature 'Harold. Maurice. Carol.' Dorothy's name was conspicuously absent.

A First Visit to Russia

In September 1932 Macmillan made a five-week trip to Russia with his new friend and collaborator, Allan Young. While it formed part of the programme of physical recovery after his breakdown, he also went out of curiosity to visit a country where 'planning' was a holy word. Visitors to the infant Soviet Union in those days, such as Bernard Shaw and Nancy Astor, travelled 'more with the purpose of talking than of listening', observed Macmillan; it was all taken too earnestly, or not earnestly enough. Macmillan himself, once again keeping a journal in the form of letters to his mother, combined the serious with the sardonic. He and Young travelled mostly second class, and sometimes 'hard', in hopes of having a 'better chance of seeing ordinary people'. Travelling out on a small steamer, the SS *Cooperazia*, his first impressions would not be unfamiliar to tourists to the Soviet Union half a century later; the taps produced no hot water, and the itinerary was subject to frequent change. He noted, with respect, how much of the hardest work on board ship was done by female sailors, and was amused by its holy-of-holies, called the Lenin Room, which struck him as a parody of the chapel of a French château; he found the revolutionary rituals held there 'all very queer, but they seem to take it very seriously.' At Hamburg he was distressed to see vast quantities of German steel being taken on board, because 'Germany is giving Russia the longer credits which we refuse,' credits that were in fact being financed out of *British* loans, instead of orders coming to poor Stockton.

In Leningrad he was taken to see the Anti-Religious Museum situated in the old Cathedral of St Isaac (still a top tourist attraction). He found it 'one of the queerest exhibitions I have ever seen', and asked Nellie to try to 'imagine H. G. Wells using *The Golden Bough* to produce a popular skit on religion suited to the intelligence of the junior classes of an English elementary school. . . .' At Tsarskoe Selo (now Pushkin) Palace, he was delighted to come across a picture of his father-in-law, in his ducal Coronation robes, bearing the inscription, 'Typical Boyar of the old regime in

Capitalist countries, living on the exploitation of the working classes'. In Moscow the Intourist guide pressed a reluctant Macmillan (to whom prison reform was never to be a matter of high interest) to visit what was obviously a show prison, for worst offenders. The inmates, he was told, could come and go as much as they liked, and were allowed a week's holiday a year; apparently only two had ever failed to return. Macmillan noted sardonically that perhaps it did not speak very favourably for conditions outside the prison compared with those inside it. Later he came closer to the truths of Gulag on meeting a young engineer returning from Siberia, who had seen forced labour camps for kulaks from Astrakhan whose treatment was so bad that their only hope rested on a Japanese invasion of Russia.

From Moscow, Macmillan and Young floated down the Volga, via Nizhni-Novgorod, to the great new industrial city of Stalingrad. On the boat he found a 'crusading' enthusiasm for the new system, which was to be repeated in their subsequent visits to factories at Kharkov in the relatively prosperous Ukraine, where the atmosphere reminded him of an American city during a boom. Back in Moscow, Macmillan busied himself in discussions with trade commissars as well as doing some private business for Macmillan's with the state publishing house. He affected pleasure at learning that the system had 'no literary agents to bother about', and admiration that Stalin's last book had had an advance print order for 3½ million copies. The Russian sense of humour commended itself greatly to Macmillan. Among the contemporary jokes he brought back to England was one about a self-important man who pushed himself to the head of a long queue outside a shop, shouting 'Out of the way, I have a permit not to stand in the queue,' to which the crowd replied, 'You silly fool. This is the queue of people who have a permit not to stand in the queue!' It was an anecdote he would enjoy making use of when at the Ministry of Supply during the war.

Macmillan returned from the trip with a strong affection for what he had seen of the ordinary Russian, plus an enduring interest in the idiosyncrasies of the Soviet system. He admired the nation's stoicism in the face of grinding privation, but reckoned that its main fault lay in the fact that, although having barely emerged from feudalism, it was now trying to pass to state capitalism without going through the development which the industrial revolution had brought about in most Western countries. He had also seen enough of the inefficiencies of Stalinism to help him recognise some of the problems created by central economic planning. Leaving Russia for the West was, he often used to remark, like passing into Alice's looking-glass world where everything was the opposite to what one expects. Who were the lunatics? Those inside, or those outside?

Macmillan the Pamphleteer

By the end of 1931, the world recession seemed to have reached its ugly trough. In Britain unemployment had soared to the 2.7 million mark; exports had sunk to £461 million, compared with £839 million two years previously. America's own grave sickness at home, accompanied by the suspension of foreign lending abroad, had had a disastrous effect on world recovery. Macmillan, a staunch supporter of the gold standard, was deeply critical of the new President, Franklin D. Roosevelt, elected for the first term in November 1932, in his refusal to help restore the international monetary system through fixed currencies that would be attached to the price of gold. Macmillan felt that there was an impelling need for international, rather than national, action in establishing exchange rates.

The terrible winter of 1932/3 saw the unemployment rate reach 27 per cent on Tees-side. The shipyards at Stockton were collapsing through empty order books – and 'lack of effective organisation to win and hold what markets might become available'. A sad letter of May 1932, written reluctantly by his old Stockton friend and supporter Billy Ellis, tells of the impossibility of maintaining four children on £2 a week: 'we all need footwear, underwear and top clothes, as we have not been able to renew the same as they have worn out. . . . You will appreciate I think why I was not at the Thornaby dinner. I could not afford 2/6. . . . I am forced to tell you the true position and seek your aid, as I would not let anyone else know. . . .'[6] Macmillan sent Ellis a cheque for £5, and received a touchingly grateful acknowledgement. In December of the same year the Mayor of Stockton was reporting to him that the Medical Officer of Health had examined one set of schoolchildren in Stockton and found 80 per cent of them suffering from under-nourishment.

A month later he was informed of one family who had 20 shillings a week to provide food for eight adults.

For Macmillan, now, more than ever before, unemployment was the overriding preoccupation. From the backbenches he watched in mounting frustration the government's piecemeal efforts to cope with its causes; he and his allies began to conclude gloomily that 'the disease was more deep-rooted' than they had previously imagined, and that 'the structure of capitalist society in its old form had broken down, not only in Britain.' Some radical new thinking was required.

Over the next six years Macmillan began to express his ideas in a series of tracts, pamphlets and books, culminating in 1938 with *The Middle Way*, which epitomised his whole philosophy. Much of the leg-work, and brain-power, was provided by Allan Young. But the endeavours of both were heavily tinted with the principles of the Macmillan house economist, John Maynard Keynes, on deficit budgeting, spending one's way out of recession (i.e. inflation), and the pursuit of a middle course between egalitarian socialism and a collapsing *laissez-faire* capitalism. Keynes's belief in the need for centralised planning of the economy Macmillan adopted with increasing zeal. His first effort was a sixteen-page pamphlet called *The State and Industry* (not to be confused with his earlier pamphlet, *Industry and the State*) which he circulated privately in March 1932. Two months later he produced a longer, more ambitious document, *The Next Step*. This recommended, *inter alia*, reflation to 1928 price levels through a policy of cheap money for industrial borrowers, and the creation of a broadly based Investment and Development Board designed to direct investment into the most beneficial channels. These first pamphlets evoked an enthusiastic response from Keynes, coupled with the criticism 'you are not nearly bold enough. . . .'[7]

Over the course of that year Macmillan continued to air his views in the leading national and provincial journals. 'Slowly but surely,' he claimed, 'planning (once a dirty word) was becoming respectable.' In a debate of March 1933, he urged as a remedy to deflation the immediate lifting of restrictions upon public expenditure, and stressed that housing must come first. In view of the realm where Macmillan was first to make his name in Churchill's post-war ministry, this was an interesting priority to be selected. In December

1933 he published the first book under his sole authorship, called *Reconstruction: A Plea for a National Policy*, which pursued in greater detail the case for planning made in his earlier tracts. He admitted that some of his proposals bore points of similarity with the Soviet system and with Mussolini's corporate state, but he stressed that the idea of planning was neither Fascist nor Communist, and ended by warning that, if capitalism did not reform itself, these two 'movements of revolution which rest upon passion' would overthrow reason. Sent a copy, Baldwin (with little evident enthusiasm) promised to 'read it carefully'. The socialist *New Statesman* praised *Reconstruction* as a 'bold and thoughtful scheme of national economic planning'; but *The Economist* thought it 'an oddly half-baked book'.

Inside the House Macmillan continued to be critical of the government's half-hearted efforts to combat unemployment: 'Mr Disraeli once said that he saw before him a bench of extinct volcanoes. I would not be so rude but there are a few disused slag heaps which might well be tidied up.'[8] Of the project to send four commissioners to 'investigate conditions in the depressed areas', he remarked acidly: 'I am glad that there has been on this occasion a visit from Whitehall to the Passchendaele of Durham and South Wales.'[9]

In March 1935 fourteen MPs joined him in publication of a booklet called *Planning for Employment*, and a movement was formed called the Next Five Years. Its leader was a born rebel, Lord Allen of Hurtwood, a man of great moral courage who had begun life as a conscientious objector and extreme left-wing socialist and who, in the great split in the Labour Party of 1931, had thrown in his lot with Ramsay MacDonald. Macmillan regarded him as 'one of the most remarkable men whom I have known and one of the most attractive'. Under his leadership, it was hoped to lay down a blueprint for a New Deal for Britain, which was set out in a booklet called *The Next Five Years*. Macmillan played a leading role in developing its economic themes, extending those that he had put forward previously. Looking back on it forty years later, Macmillan remarked:

At the time it seemed to lean rather more to the Left than to the Right, especially with regard to the proposals for an increase in public or semi-public control of utilities such as transport, gas and electricity. Today, however, it would seem to be rather Right-

Wing; so far have we travelled in these years. But what were more novel were the policies for industrial organisation including the participation of labour. . . .

The *New Statesman* welcomed the book for its 'socialist' line, but – significantly – its editor G. D. H. Cole, though impressed, found it 'too democratic for the Conservatives and too unsocialistic for Labour'.

With the approach of the 1935 general election, however, the work of the Next Five Years group became 'somewhat confused' because of Lloyd George's effort to recapture the centre of the political stage with his New Deal, a programme that bore embarrassing resemblance to that set out in *The Next Five Years* booklet. The troubles also seem to have stemmed from Macmillan's susceptibility to the Welsh wizard's spell, coupled with a return of thoughts about forming a new Centre Party. In his memoirs, Macmillan brushes aside talk about the Centre Party, but that there was something of this sort in the air is suggested in an interview he gave to the *Star* on 25 June 1936, as part of a series the paper was running on the prospects of a British popular front (currently much in vogue in France). Of the Conservative establishment, he wrote damningly (together with perhaps a jab at his beer-business brother-in-law) that 'A party dominated by second-class brewers and company promoters – a Casino Capitalism – is not likely to represent anybody but itself.' The remark characterised the contempt he was beginning to feel for the Tory Party; but he was equally critical of Labour: 'after ten years of no imagination, no drive, all we are left with is men like Attlee and Lansbury who are quite incompetent to govern an Empire.' Macmillan came out in favour of a new constellation, headed by Labour's Herbert Morrison (who was, at least until the 1945 Labour government, to be a hero of his), a Labour Party stripped of its left, 'a fusion of all that is best in the Left and Right and . . . a Left Centre rather than a Right Centre'.[10] This sounds like a social-democrat party much ahead of its time. The *Star* interview was followed by two rather dampening letters, from Lloyd George and from another Welshman, Aneurin Bevan.

At the November 1935 general election (Macmillan's fifth in twelve years), Lord Allen, the one-time left-winger, had been Macmillan's most effective supporting speaker at Stockton, and had paid him a generous compliment: 'He could have earned the ordinary plaudits of his party. He could have gained a career, honour and comfort; instead he has insisted in making an independent contribution. . . . He has shown courage, persistency, and, above all, gentleness in the way of expressing his opinions which is beginning to win the hearts of the people all over the country.' Macmillan, who had fought the campaign largely on the Next Five Years theme, won by a majority of 4000 over his (female) Labour opponent; the Liberal lost his deposit. Baldwin, heading a National Government, came to power with a majority of 249, although Labour gained 154 seats compared with 52 in 1931. By the following year, in a debate on the depressed areas of 7 May, Macmillan was expressing impatience at the 'little headway' achieved by the Next Five Years group; it made him feel 'rather sad and old'. When the group set up a journal, the *New Outlook*, he immediately wanted to use it for politically effective propaganda, rather than for airing academic views, as envisaged by Lord Allen. Macmillan swiftly brought it under his control, so much so that, by June 1936, Allen was complaining wearily: 'I am compelled now to see that much of the trouble during the last 2½ months has been due to one man, Mr Macmillan, functioning on every committee and attempting the guidance of practically all our activities.'[11]

Macmillan in his memoirs admitted, 'I have no doubt that he was right and that I was impatient,' but in the meantime a new factor had arisen to divide the two men – Hitler. Like many other men of good will, Allen, a gentle soul, had gone to see the Führer and had come away with hopes that he could be tamed by appeasement. By 1938, Macmillan and Allen had drifted apart. The *New Outlook* had collapsed after about a year's existence and the Next Five Years group wound itself up in November 1937. To some the episode seemed to suggest for the first time a new toughness in Macmillan, not previously detected in his political technique.

The Middle Way

Restless as ever, and still aided by Allan Young, Macmillan now set to work on a full-scale book which was to incorporate all his thinking on economics over the past decade. It was published in June 1938 under the not very inspiring title *The Middle Way*. Many years after his retirement, when asked if he had re-read it recently, he replied, 'No – it's unreadable, I should think!'[12] This was not just excessive modesty; containing a wealth of detail on such riveting matters as milk distribution, it was remarkably stodgy and made no concessions to readability – despite the author's experience as a publisher! Yet it was an important, and – for its time – in many ways a revolutionary document. His main contention was that society should be reorganised 'in such a way as to bring the economic system under conscious direction and control, and that the increased production should be directed towards raising the standard of living and security of all the people'.[13] It was this notion of 'levelling-up' rather than down which chiefly distinguished his arguments from those of contemporary socialism, and, indeed, was a tenet to which he would passionately adhere throughout his premiership. He strongly rejected the socialist view that held it necessary to reduce the incomes of one class in order to increase the incomes of another.

As might have been expected, the nub of his argument harked back to his persistent quest for the still deficient 'comprehensive scheme of national planning'. Quoting a statistic that nearly 30 per cent of the British population lived below the hunger level, Macmillan urged the introduction of a minimum wage, as 'a measure of social justice, lifting up to a tolerable human standard the unfortunate families now living in conditions that are a disgrace to the community'. It would also provide a 'stabilising factor' in the economy. Macmillan recommended trades union participation in setting progressive rises to this minimum wage, which to begin with he based on figures that would seem unbelievable half a century later, even allowing for inflation: 53 shillings per week for a man with a wife and three children. He followed up with short-term proposals for dealing with the 1.5 million unemployed. Earlier that same year, he had observed in the House with the biting irony for which he was becoming recognised: 'Unemployment is not in itself a harmful thing. When it is unemployment of the upper classes it is called leisure. The real problem is that of not having enough money.'[14] As well as adhering faithfully to the doctrines of Keynes (as, indeed, did most of *The Middle Way*), these proposals also mirrored Roosevelt's public works schemes: 'A great deal of useful work might be accomplished in the improvement of amenities, the tidying, cleaning, and beautifying of localities, or in the carrying out of a number of socially useful tasks that would otherwise have been neglected.'[15]

Some of the more revolutionary notions of *The Middle Way* included the nationalisation of the coal mines (where the miners were still enduring 'conditions of poverty that are shameful') and an extension of public control over the energy-producing utilities in general. A National Nutrition Board, which should 'regard itself as an expression of the organised consumers' needs', would handle the distribution of dairy products, bread, flour, sugar and potatoes, and would run National Bakeries, producing a standard loaf.

There was the far-reaching proposal to replace the Stock Exchange by a new National Investment Board, to 'eliminate the speculative evils . . .' but 'preserve a reasonable liquidity of investment. It should be possible to do so without allowing an important financial institution to become a casino.'[16] This, coming from the man who as Prime Minister would introduce the lottery of Premium Bonds is worth noting. Macmillan, however, did not endorse Labour's intent to nationalise the banks, nor Labour's plans for assuming 'a measure of public control' over land, transport and finance. This offended his entrepreneurial philosophies, inherited from his hard-headed crofter ancestry. On the other hand, he was eager for trades union participation in his proposed planning bodies. Thus, under his planned economy, there would be room for both state and private enterprise.

The same kind of flexible approach was applied to the problem of balancing Britain's foreign trade, which he believed could no longer be solved 'by the simple device of clapping on a tariff'. He also considered it 'economic lunacy to go on producing particular goods at high-production costs at home when the balance of advantage has clearly shifted to another country which is anxious to sell them to us at the cheaper price. . . .'[17] (Many years later, when considering the problems of British Leyland threatened by Japanese competition, this was a basic wisdom to which Macmillan would frequently return.) Often quoting Keynes, he urged that there had to be a close nexus between foreign trade policy and that of the domestic economy: 'if we plan the one, we plan the other.'[18]

In pressing his pursuit of a middle way between what he described in his memoirs as the opposing evils of 'the intolerable restriction of a totalitarian State and the unfettered abuse of freedom under the old liberalism', Macmillan concluded with an eloquent plea that all classes must share in his new 'dynamic of social change', and the new prosperity which he hoped it would create:

if the poor are to do the driving, and the rich stubbornly to resist, if, at this critical moment, we hesitate to be guided by the British tradition of peaceful change, then we shall move stage by stage towards the embitterment of class antagonism and the decay and destruction of our democratic institutions. . . . Without tolerance there is no freedom. In the absence of freedom, every form of cultural progress is stultified, distorted, and destroyed. . . .[19]

Among his contemporaries, *The Middle Way* certainly caused more of a stir than anything Macmillan had produced previously. The Tory back (and front) benches growled distrustfully, though to young Tories then at Oxford, like Hugh Fraser and Edward Heath, *The Middle Way* provided a message full of hope. In the *New Statesman* Macmillan once again received an accolade from G. D. H. Cole, while still further to the left, Ellen Wilkinson, Labour Member for stricken Jarrow, then known as Red Ellen for her fiery extremism, sent her congratulations. Even the loyal Macmillan nanny was heard to exclaim, 'Mr Harold is a dangerous Pink.'[20] Macmillan himself came to regard *The Middle Way* as his political testament. Certainly, it foreshadowed many of the courses of action that he would pursue both as Chancellor and as Prime Minister, behind which there would remain the influence of those good Keynesian principles of eschewing deflation at any cost. But if Macmillan's Conservative colleagues in the 1930s had actually read the whole of his book they would undoubtedly have shared nanny's views. It is difficult to imagine that the author of *The Middle Way* could have stood as an orthodox Conservative candidate if a general election had been held in 1939 or 1940. His Party career may well have been saved by the onset of the war. Meanwhile, before there was any prospect of *The Middle Way* proposals being tested in practice, rearmament in face of the threat of Hitler, however half-hearted, was bringing its own unattended end to Britain's depression.

Macmillan and Churchill: The Threat Outside

During the early 1930s Macmillan and Churchill had drifted apart, first of all over India. Churchill, the dedicated paladin of Empire, the romantic imperialist, was bitterly opposed to any policy that might lead to Indian self-government. He went as far in his views as to remark that Gandhi should be 'bound hand and foot at the gates of Delhi and trampled on by an enormous elephant ridden by the Viceroy'.[21] In January 1931 he resigned from Baldwin's Shadow Cabinet in protest at its promise of support for the portended India Bill. Macmillan considered that, on this issue, Churchill diverged from the mainstream of Conservative opinion, and, although Churchill was able to gain the backing of nearly 100 Tory MPs, Macmillan was not one of them. In his memoirs, Macmillan quotes one sentence from a speech in December 1934 by Baldwin advocating India's evolution towards self-government, the words of which were to leave a deep – indeed historic – impression upon him: 'There is a wind of nationalism and freedom blowing round the world and blowing as strongly in Asia as anywhere in the world.'

Churchill would not hold office until called back at the beginning of the Second World War, and – at a time when his genius was most needed by the country – the effectiveness of his pleas for rearmament and resistance to Hitler was impaired because of doubts about the soundness of his judgement in the light of his India policy. As far as it concerned their relations, Macmillan remarked, 'I didn't want to quarrel with him so I rather dropped out of his circle.'[22]

A second factor that helped to keep Macmillan out of the Churchill circle was the presence of Bob Boothby, now at the peak of his intimacy with Churchill. Also, much as Macmillan was drawn by Churchill's personality, it seems to have been a one-way attraction in those early days. Possibly, like many of his other parliamentary contemporaries, Churchill found Macmillan too earnest; he was not 'fun', something that was so important to Churchill, especially in those unrelievedly sombre years out of office. Macmillan, too, differed with Churchill over the abdication crisis of 1936. The latter was romantically loyal towards Edward VIII, whereas Macmillan believed, as he revealed in a letter to Baldwin, that 'you are dealing with eternal verities here from which no deviation is possible without disaster. . . . The slightest weakness now would be a shattering blow to the whole basis of Christian morality, already grievously injured during recent years.'[23]

But as the 1930s progressed Churchill and Macmillan were gradually drawn together again in common cause against rising dictators abroad: together they felt in honour bound to attack a complacent and appeasing Tory government. However, it was initially Anthony Eden, rather than Churchill, who provided Macmillan with a rallying point on foreign affairs, and made him forsake his interest in the domestic scene.

Appointed Under-Secretary of State at the Foreign Office in 1931, under Sir John Simon, and later Sir Samuel Hoare, Anthony Eden made the most spectacular rise in politics of any young man entering Parliament just after the First World War. Universally popular and dedicated to his work on collective security at the League of Nations, Eden drew the strong support of Macmillan and his Next Five Years group. In 1935, the year of Mussolini's invasion of Abyssinia, Macmillan delivered a speech in the North, calling for the need to face 'the new barbarism' which he saw entering the world, and for the British to 'be prepared to fight for a collective system if we want peace'. December of that year saw the conclusion of the shabby and shady Hoare–Laval Pact, wherein the British Foreign Secretary was bamboozled into a deal which removed the teeth from any League sanctions against Mussolini, allowed Italy a free hand in Abyssinia, and virtually signed the death warrant of the League. *The Times* of 18 December published a letter from Macmillan which ended on an acidly prophetic note: '. . . I have never attended the funeral of a murdered man; but I take it that at such a ceremony some distinction is made between the mourners and the assassins.'

Macmillan found himself – once again – at odds with a government which, by its irresolution, had sacrificed the principle of collective security, while, at the same time, by its superficially hostile noises towards Italy, it had only succeeded in pushing that country into the arms of Hitler. He deeply sympathised with Eden who, in the absence of his boss (in the middle of the crisis Hoare had inconveniently chosen to break his nose skating) had to defend a policy for which he held scant respect against hot questioning in the House. Macmillan was delighted when, a few days later, the broken-nosed and humiliated Hoare was forced to resign, and was succeeded by thirty-nine-year-old Eden.

At about this time Macmillan seems to have moved back into Churchill's orbit. He recalled:

. . . I met him somewhere and he said 'You haven't been to see me lately'. So I came back and sat hours drinking with him. There was a row of people, Brendan [Bracken] and Co. . . . Then after that, he would come over for lunch and I would go over there [to Birch Grove and Chartwell] and tell him when something was going to happen, or he would hold forth about it. . . . 1936, when the Germans reoccupied the Rhineland, that was the great moment. It was then that Churchill said to me, 'Well it's now inevitable, and we shan't win.'[24]

Opposing the Dictators

Hitler's marching back into the Rhineland, demilitarised under the post-1918 peace treaties, marked a turning point in Macmillan's outlook on foreign affairs and also a first mild rift with the policies of his friend Eden, who considered that public opinion in neither Belgium nor France would support action against the Germans returning to 'their own back garden'. Churchill, with reason, regarded March 1936, rather than Munich in 1938, as the moment when the cause of stopping Hitler was lost. Macmillan wrote a forceful and far-sighted article in the *Star* of 20 March 1936: 'We have an uneasy conscience about Germany. We are not happy about the Treaty of Versailles. . . . We remember what we refused to Liberal Germany and have been forced to allow to Totalitarian Germany. We remember the humiliations of Stresemann and Brüning; and we wonder how far we have been responsible for the triumph of Hitler.' For these concessions, wrongly timed, Macmillan unequivocally blamed Baldwin and MacDonald – 'Just as they shirked the social and economic problems. . . .', they had, he continued on a prophetic note, 'elevated inactivity into a principle and feebleness into a virtue. . . . There will be no war now. But unless a settlement is made now . . . there will be war in 1940 or 1941. . . . Let us either settle with Germany now, or coerce her now. But don't let us purchase an uncertain peace at a terrible price to be paid later.'

Among the letters that this article provoked was one from a distant acquaintance, a Mr T. Pellatt writing from the Bath Club:

My dear Harold

I KNOW you will forgive me calling you by your Christian name. . . . I MUST be able to say to myself 'I called by his Christian name this man, WHO IS NOW PRIME MINISTER. . . . Yes – YOU WILL

SOMEDAY be Prime Minister. . . . You are a very VERY brilliant man. I NEVER flatter.[25]

The last sentence of the *Star* article contained the nub of Macmillan's reproaches against Britain's handling of the dictators in the second half of the 1930s. Over Abyssinian sanctions, there had been two clear options: to resist Mussolini resolutely, and bring him down; or to be conciliatory, at the expense of Abyssinia, with the aim of keeping Italy out of the Nazi camp. But in attempting to pursue a pusillanimous course between the two, Britain had lost on both.

When the final instalment in the Hoare–Laval traduction of Abyssinia occurred, Lloyd George, in what Churchill once described as one of the greatest parliamentary performances of all time, lashed Baldwin and Chamberlain for permitting the torch of their election pledges in support of collective security to become 'dimmed': 'Tonight it is quenched – with a hiss; a hiss that will be re-echoed throughout the whole world. . . . Tonight we have had the cowardly surrender, and *there* [pointing to the Treasury bench] are the cowards. . . .'[26] After the Foreign Affairs debate on 23 June 1936, Macmillan and one other Tory MP, Vyvyan Adams, not merely abstained but voted against the government, and the following week Macmillan resigned the Whip. This was – and is – a backbencher's ultimate protest against his party's policies. Henceforth he was as committed as Churchill to pursuing the twin chimera of opposing the dictators and of rearmament. Although Macmillan supported the rearmament programme primarily on grounds of national interest, there was also – as he admitted years later – a more parochial dimension to his thinking: 'it might give us some work in the north-east!'[27] In a Britain befuddled by appeasement, the road was a lonely one. Of all the Baldwin–Chamberlain rearmament team the only one who impressed Macmillan was the Minister for Air, Philip Cunliffe-Lister. Against all odds he did much to lay the foundations for Britain's wartime air expansion, including production of the Spitfire – and was then forced to resign in despair at Chamberlain's policies in the summer of 1938.

On top of all the political demands on Macmillan's life, in the late 1930s a series of family bereavements imposed their own additional burdens. In March 1936, his father died, a few weeks short of eighty-three, and having continued to work at Macmillan's until he had become all but blind. Only a few weeks earlier, George, son of Alexander and also one of the three partners of the second generation, had died. Finally, that June, Frederick Macmillan died, aged eighty-four. The removal of all three senior partners within four months suddenly devolved great responsibility and extra work upon Harold and Daniel. Over the next three years – and indeed through the war – Daniel, whom Harold gratefully regarded as 'a protecting and loving friend' as well as older brother, was happy to bear the brunt so that Harold could devote most of his energy to politics. Nevertheless, Harold somehow managed to find enough time to continue to be a serious, thrustful and hard-bargaining publisher. Rache Lovat Dickson, who joined the company as assistant editor about that time, recalled how at first he found Harold Macmillan rather remote and absent-minded, but: '. . . I was to learn that he was much more of a publisher than I had suspected, and that beneath that bland appearance of a typical young Conservative politician of the '30s, he hid an extremely keen and incisive brain. . . .' What equally impressed Lovat Dickson was Macmillan's decision to publish a book by Arthur Bryant, in favour of Munich, which struck him as being 'against all this strange man was doing; burning up his energy, hardly stopping to eat or rest, while he travelled the country and spoke out against the Munich settlement. . . .' Macmillan explained: '"We are publishers, not policemen. Everybody should be free to say what they like." '[28]

In 1937 there was a much greater blow when Harold's beloved mother Nellie died, aged eighty-one. She had never quite recovered from her husband's death eighteen months earlier: 'Even her indomitable courage was quenched. She had almost lost the will to live,' wrote Macmillan. In her last years, Nellie, 'ambitious for my success', had become sadly confused by Harold's apparent isolation in the political wilderness. But – as always – she had backed him to the hilt, and her death was a grievous loss to him; 'it deprived me of a rock-like, unshakeable support'. Given the dominant role that his mother had played throughout his life, this was almost an understatement. Her death left him peculiarly alone, and vulnerable, in his personal life. He and Dorothy now moved permanently to Birch Grove, which they henceforth had completely to themselves and their children, and which to some extent must have made their life together easier. By the end of the 1930s, the worst of the pain over his wife's liaison had probably been drawn away. Despite Boothby's constant entreaties, Dorothy had agreed never to leave Harold. Boothby, in despair, had married in 1935 Diana Cavendish, a cousin of Dorothy's; it was a brief marriage and he returned to his *grande passion*. Harold, acceptant but often miserably unhappy, found a welcome distraction in 'burning up his energy' in a life dedicated to politics, and with what was left absorbed by publishing.

From Abyssinia and the Rhineland, the way led inexorably to the *Anschluss* of Austria in March 1938, and on to Munich that September, a *via dolorosa* well travelled by subsequent historians. Baldwin, whom Macmillan rated the most powerful Prime Minister since Walpole and who succeeded in reuniting the nation, but failed to give it strength, had retired; Chamberlain came. Charitable often to the point of blandness in his memoirs, about the best thing Macmillan could find to say about the new Prime Minister was: 'If he had none of Baldwin's lethargy, he had little of Baldwin's imagination. Baldwin had always been uncertain of himself; Chamberlain was only too sure that he was right on every question. . . . Had Chamberlain retired or died in 1937, he would have gone down to history as a great social reformer and a great administrator.' He added some years later, 'I didn't like Chamberlain – he was a nice man, but I thought he was very, very middle class and very, very narrow in view.'[29]

However, Macmillan now rejoined the Party faithful in the belief that Chamberlain would provide a more robust policy than his predecessor. But if Macmillan in general supported Chamberlain's endeavours on the domestic front, he soon found himself opposed totally to his foreign policy. On 20 February 1938, he and the anti-appeasers were profoundly shocked by the sudden and unexpected resignation of Eden; Churchill, wrote Macmillan, 'was almost in despair over the catastrophe'. Simultaneously came the resignation of Eden's Under-Secretary, Lord Cranborne – Macmillan's kinsman by marriage. Encouraged by Churchill, Macmillan and some twenty Tory MPs abstained in the ensuing debate; apart from Churchill and his lieutenants, Brendan Bracken and Boothby, the abstainers included such names as Harold Nicolson, General Louis Spears, Anthony Crossley and Ronnie Cartland. This group, Macmillan said, were regarded as 'habitual suspects' by the Whips, but this time they were supported by 'respectable figures' like Sir Joseph

Nall (a rather right-wing industrialist), Leonard Ropner, Robin Turton, Dick Briscoe, Paul Emrys-Evans and Hamilton Kerr. (The last-named, later MP for Cambridge, became one of the leading Tory protagonists of Macmillan-for-Premier in the early post-war era, and later his PPS.) Altogether the twenty dissidents represented the hard core forming the anti-appeasement lobby. Eden was succeeded by Lord Halifax, whom Macmillan respected for his strong religious convictions, but thought too gentlemanly to face Hitler, lacking 'the strength to succeed where Eden failed'; as a result the foreign policy was Chamberlain's.

With Eden's resignation, events began to accelerate. On 11 March 1938, Hitler moved into Austria. Looking ahead with 'sombre expectancy' to the next blow, Macmillan wrote in the *Northern Echo* on 18 March, warning of Hitler's designs on Czechoslovakia and calling for the inclusion of Churchill in a new national government as a demonstration to the world that Britain meant business. He admitted that he was of two minds whether Britain should make an invasion of Czechoslovakia a *casus belli*, but urged, 'if we mean to do so we had better say so now, that is if we mean to join with Russia and France; and not when it has happened.' This was very much in line with his theme, all along, that whatever Britain did decide it was essential she should make her intentions totally clear in advance. With his sense of history this was where, he felt, Sir Edward Grey had failed so badly in 1914.

The first of Chamberlain's three flights to Germany had impressed Macmillan; it was after all courageous of a statesman, rising seventy, to undertake what was in those days no easy journey. However, after Chamberlain's second meeting with Hitler, at Bad Godesberg, Macmillan was one of seven Tory MPs (including Boothby and General Spears) to sign a petition to Halifax urging that no further pressure be put on the Czechs to accept Hitler's terms. Yet on the eve of Chamberlain's third departure for Munich in September, Macmillan had the honesty to remember standing up in the House and sharing the general emotion, and the country's natural sense of relief. But 'then I saw one man silent and seated – his head sunk on his shoulders, his whole demeanour depicting something between anger and despair. It was Churchill.' Immediately after Munich, nevertheless, he remembered thinking: 'My son would stay at school and go to Oxford in the autumn. . . .'

When the degrading terms of Munich became known, there was

much talk that younger members of the Cabinet – Walter Elliot, Oliver Stanley, Malcolm MacDonald – would resign; in which case, Macmillan considered, the government would surely have been brought down. In fact, only one man, Duff Cooper, First Lord of the Admiralty, resigned – with words that marked his finest hour: '. . . I have ruined, perhaps, my political career. But that is a little matter; I have retained something which is to me of great value – I can still walk about the world with my head erect.'[30] According to his wife, Diana Cooper, when she telephoned the news to Churchill, 'His voice was broken with emotion. I could hear him cry.'[31] Macmillan, congratulating Duff Cooper, called his resignation speech 'the finest thing I've heard since I've been in the House; the deep sincerity gripped even those members who disagreed with your argument. I can assure you that it has heartened a great many of us more than you know.'[32]

Duff Cooper now joined the Tory dissenters. After Munich their numbers reached some thirty, divided between Churchill's group – nicknamed the Old Guard – and Eden's, who were known as the Glamour Boys. Macmillan says he attached himself to the latter, 'but also kept in close contact with Churchill and acted in a sense as a link between the two bodies'. Working behind the scenes, out of the limelight, Macmillan seems to have played a key role in attempting to create a cross-party front against Chamberlain and appeasement; his 'left-wing' domestic policies gave him, alone among the Tory dissidents, the credentials to hold out a hand to the Labour leaders. Accordingly, at nearly midnight on 3 October, the day after Duff Cooper's resignation, Macmillan, with Churchill's blessing, sought out Dr Hugh Dalton, an Old Etonian Labour MP. He told Dalton that 'loyal' Tories were pressing for a general election, in which they hoped that Chamberlain, as the Saviour of Peace, would sweep the country. Any Tories who opposed the government in the forthcoming debate on Munich would be 'marked down for destruction' and would find 'official' Tory candidates run against them at the election. Despite this threat, Macmillan was anxious to co-ordinate a hostile amendment with Labour, and – beyond that – to try to arrive at a united anti-appeasement policy. He suggested that Attlee and Dalton should meet Churchill the next day, and late that same night he took Dalton round to Brendan Bracken's house in North Street, where the doctor 'found Churchill, Eden, J. P. L. Thomas, Bracken and some others'.[33]

Three days later, following the post-Munich debate in which the dissident Tories abstained, the far-left Labour MP Stafford Cripps visited Dalton 'and urged that we should make common cause with the anti-Chamberlain Tories'. Cripps and the wily doctor, however, also saw more parochial advantages to be gained from the Munich crisis. Although the Labour Party was unable to gain power by itself, 'to split the Tory Party would be real big politics'.[34] The Tory dissidents may well have sensed this, and have taken fright. Dalton recorded that he saw Macmillan again,

> and told him that Attlee, Morrison and I would probably be willing to meet three or four of them. He was pleased at this, but said there was some difficulty within their group. Eden and some others were very moderate and wanted 'national unity' with everybody, while Churchill and Duff Cooper were out for Chamberlain's blood and inclined to join with anyone else to get it. . . . Now that the threat of an early General Election had receded, the moderate Tories, I thought, would probably draw back into their shells. . . .[35]

The following week Dalton had a third meeting with Macmillan, and noted that the Tory dissidents still seemed divided on tactics: 'Macmillan himself would like to see a "1931 in reverse" . . . an influential breakaway from the Conservative Party and a union of Labour with Tory dissentients to form a new "National Government".' Macmillan yet again was toying with the notion of a new 'Middle Way' coalition party, this time to meet an external threat. To Dalton he proposed four lines of joint attack on Chamberlain's policy towards Hitler. But, says Dalton, 'even this modest programme evaporated. Macmillan sounded Duff Cooper, who would not come without Eden, and Eden would not come at all. Churchill was quite willing to come, but in view of the refusal of the others, we on our side thought it best to call a halt. . . .'[36] So once again Macmillan was frustrated, and (though he said nothing of it in his memoirs) registered private doubts about Eden's reliability as an ally.

In the critical post-Munich debate, Chamberlain was more robust than expected and received wide support on both sides of the House. There would be no general election over Munich. Chamberlain's position in the country, Macmillan noted, 'was overwhelmingly strong'; at the same time he recalled Munich dividing it, even within families, with unparalleled bitterness. On Guy Fawkes Day, 1938, at Birch Grove the Macmillans dressed their guy in a frock coat, black Homburg hat and rolled umbrella. Some relatives staying were much offended. The scene was heightened by the presence of some forty Czech refugees, a number of them Jews, to whom the Macmillans and neighbours had provided shelter. Given the emotions generated by Munich, it is a testimony to Macmillan's magnanimity that his memoirs contain so conspicuously little rancour towards Chamberlain. He made due allowance for the debilitating influence of Britain's haunting memories of the horrors of 1914–18. Yet, he wrote that he felt at the time, 'we ought to have fought at Munich'; and in later life nothing was to alter that conviction.

As the slide to war accelerated, Macmillan remained one of the foremost dissenters to keep up pressure on the government. At a by-election at Oxford, he outraged many colleagues by supporting an Independent candidate, Dr A. D. Lindsay, the Master of Balliol, on an anti-appeasement ticket against the official candidate, a brilliant young lawyer called Quintin Hogg. By the quirks of fate, one of Macmillan's more enthusiastic undergraduate backers was a Balliol organ scholar, Edward Heath; while, in 1963, Macmillan's two favourites for his own succession were to be first Hogg, and second another appeaser – Alec Douglas-Home. Hogg got in at Oxford, though with a nearly halved majority, while Macmillan was threatened with withdrawal of the Whip, the prospect of an official Tory candidate being put up against him at Stockton at the next election, and – fate worse than death – ejection from the Carlton Club. None transpired.

Next he produced a pamphlet, entitled *The Price of Peace*, in which he urged again that Britain should make her position to Hitler totally unambiguous (though he reckoned Poland would now probably 'adjust herself' to German designs), and rearm with renewed vigour. He had already called for National Service (though it was his government that would eventually abolish it in 1960) and he spoke up for an 'alliance of peace-loving powers' headed by Britain, France and the USSR, combined with an effort to gain US support. In February 1939, he followed up this tract with another, *Economic Aspects of Defence*, in which he was helped by a Macmillan author, economist Dr Paul Einzig, and the Hungarian-born Thomas Balogh, who was to become chief economic adviser in the 1960s to Macmillan's rival, Harold Wilson. Facing the probability of war squarely, he pressed for a translation to rearmament of the industrial efficiency principles he had propounded the previous year in *The Middle Way*; strategic materials, such as pig-iron, should be stockpiled and a Ministry of Supply should urgently be created. Little could he have foreseen that this last would furnish him with his first government post. In June, four months later, Chamberlain belatedly acquiesced and the Ministry Macmillan had clamoured for was duly set up.

By the end of March 1939, Chamberlain had thrown British policy into reverse by issuing his guarantee to Poland; 'demented pledges, that cannot be redeemed. . . .' was how Lloyd George rated them, in default of any Soviet commitment. Macmillan agreed; and so did Hitler. On the 29th, Macmillan joined with Churchill, Eden and Duff Cooper in a motion calling for the formation of a national government. The following week, he was lunching at Chartwell when Mussolini invaded Albania, on Good Friday. He recalled vividly his first glimpse of Churchill springing into action:

> Maps were brought out; secretaries were marshalled; telephones began to ring. 'Where was the British fleet?' That was the most urgent question. That considerable staff which, even as a private individual, Churchill always maintained to support his tremendous literary and political effort was at once brought into play. It turned out that the British fleet was scattered throughout the Mediterranean. . . .

Deeply impressed, Macmillan continued: 'I shall always have a picture of that spring day and the sense of power and energy, the great flow of action, which came from Churchill, although he then held no public office. He alone seemed to be in command, when everyone else was dazed and hesitating.' Four days later, Harold Nicolson found Macmillan 'enraged' that Chamberlain should be remaining in power, and at the same time fulminating against Eden and his followers for being 'too soft and gentlemanlike' in their attitude to Chamberlain.[37]

In May, Chamberlain half-heartedly began talks with the Russians in an eleventh-hour attempt to bring them into the kind of firm alliance that Macmillan – and Churchill – had been urging. Then, on 22 August, came the bombshell of the Molotov–Ribbentrop Pact. Using words that he would repeat in a different context a generation later, Lord Cranborne wrote to Macmillan on 30 August declaring that the Pact 'would go down to history as one of the classical examples of being too clever by half'. Indeed, noted Macmillan, 'clever' though it seemed, 'in the end, Germany paid a frightful forfeit.' It did, however, make war in 1939 just a matter of timetables. On 1 September, Hitler's Panzers crossed the Polish frontier. Two days later the sirens sounded in London.

Part II

The Second World War
1939–1945

Chapter Six

'Winston Is Back!'
1939–1942

I began now to think of war not as young men think of it, with the natural buoyancy of youth, but with the realism of middle age. . . .

(*HM*, The Blast of War)

That Macmillan would in time reach the top I had privately considered possible during the war when he was my parliamentary secretary at the Ministry of Supply.

(*Herbert Morrison*, An Autobiography)

In late August 1939, Macmillan was on a short sailing holiday in the Channel with a parliamentary colleague, Wyndham Portal. Putting ashore at Poole Harbour on the 23rd, they read in the papers news of the Nazi–Soviet Non-Aggression Pact. Macmillan at once realised that this meant 'either another easy victory for Hitler or war under the worst possible conditions, with Russia neutral, Czechoslovakia already overwhelmed, and France and Britain powerless to bring any effective aid to Poland, whose independence they had guaranteed'.[1] The latter prospect was what he had most dreaded ever since Munich, and before. He immediately set off for London, to witness days of confusion in the Commons. At dawn on Friday, 1 September, Hitler's Panzers invaded Poland. After a two-day wait which agonised and infuriated Churchill and his supporters, Neville Chamberlain finally declared war. His dispirited broadcast was heard by Macmillan at a gathering in Ronald Tree's house in Queen Anne's Gate; he and the other members of the Eden Group present then walked over to Parliament as the air-raid sirens announced the first false alarm of the war. Leaving the brief session in the Commons that Sunday morning, Macmillan recalled a sense not of fear but of awe, intermingled with guilt: 'We few survivors of the First War seemed to have failed in our duty and to have betrayed our fallen friends. How strange it all was – the repetition of 1914 but without the glamour!' His first thought was for eighteen-year-old Maurice, up at Balliol, as he himself had been twenty-five years earlier: he would go to the war, but would he come back?

On the Sunday afternoon following Chamberlain's declaration of war, Churchill was invited to take over the Admiralty, which sent a historic signal out to the Fleet, 'WINSTON IS BACK'; but as the glum months of the 'Phoney War' dragged on, it was evident that – under Neville Chamberlain – there were going to be no jobs for the Churchill supporters and opponents of Munich. Macmillan felt both ill-used and useless. He tried to get back into his old regiment, the Grenadiers, 'but they didn't want me . . . sick and old'.[2] With some bitterness, he thought that perhaps the best he could do would be to offer his services to drive an ambulance for the Cuckfield Rural District Council.

For Macmillan personally, the immediate future seemed to hold depressingly little. Having put so much of himself, his energy and intellect into politics – to the extent of bringing about at least in part the breakdown of his marriage – what did he have to show for it? He was now forty-five, had served fifteen years on the back-benches and, unlike his fellow dissidents, Eden and Duff Cooper, had never once held office. He would describe himself in his memoirs as having, through his economic tracts in the 1930s, become 'in a minor way, something of a national figure';[3] but so far as the wider public was concerned, the accent should indeed have been on the word 'minor'. His name appears surprisingly seldom in any of the accounts of these times by contemporaries. Harold Wilson thought that Macmillan's attachment to the Whig tradition might well have led him to cross the floor of the House – as Churchill had done twice – 'had he not looked across that great divide at the Parliamentary Labour Party of those days, and decided there was nowhere to cross to . . .'.[4] It was also harder for him to forget that, much as in ideological and human terms he might sympathise with the Teesside unemployed, he was himself, both by inheritance and marriage, a man of wealth and privilege. He was speaking with more than a touch of truth when, in 1938, he teased Frank Pakenham, later Lord Longford, who was trying to woo him for Labour: 'When I consider the prospect of associating with your wild young men of the Left, I have to remember that I am a very rich man!'[5] Macmillan would never be able to accept egalitarian socialism.

Thus by the outbreak of war Macmillan did not seem a likely candidate for office, and had few followers. He himself admitted many years later that at the time it did indeed rankle that 'men who – without conceit – were clearly inferior to me in ability or brains, were continually promoted. It was a little painful, but I accepted it . . .'; on the other hand, with the philosophic detachment of old age, he recognised the benevolent hand of fate: 'of course, if I had accepted a post under Chamberlain, I would almost certainly have disappeared without trace.'[6]

In his first wartime contributions from the backbenches, Macmillan returned to his early love – a planned economy. He was shocked by the inept complacency of the Chamberlain government, and the painfully slow pace of mobilisation – especially in the realm of munitions supply, and despite the mystifying fact that there continued to be a large reserve of unemployed labour. During the first important debate on economic warfare held on 18 October 1939, he rose to criticise the 'almost complete statistical blackout' which, on top of the physical blackout every night, had closed in on the House. He savaged John Simon, the Chancellor of the Exchequer, for having made 'a very characteristic speech. . . . I do not think I have ever listened in so long a time to so little being said,' and then went on:

> It has been long recognised that if it came to war, war would be totalitarian, and we now learn in actual practice the full significance of that phrase. It means that the total energy of the nation has to be organised and directed to secure the maximum results and, therefore, that every error of policy or administration, even on the remote fringes of economic activity, will be paid for by a prolongation of the struggle and the consequent sacrifices of additional lives. . . .

He stressed the urgent need for a strategically planned economy. The newly formed Ministry of Supply (which he had called for repeatedly in pre-war years) was doing its best, but it had started too late. And he ended an intervention that could have been little palatable to Chamberlain with the warning: 'We "muddled through" the last war, and in doing so, we needlessly sacrificed hundreds of thousands of young lives – among them those gallant, heroic leaders of men whose loss has been sadly missed from our councils these last 20 years. . . . We cannot – we dare not – "muddle through" again.'[7]

Speaking to his constituents at about this time, he warned them of the dangers ahead, forecasting that Germany would inevitably attack Holland and Belgium. On 17 January 1940, he was exhorting the House not to swallow government propaganda and delude itself that Germany was in a desperate economic plight: 'They have made very long, careful and exact preparations during the years in which we have been living in a fool's paradise, making barely any preparations for war. . . .'[8] On 1 February he was pleading for a War Cabinet that would operate as 'a corporate body' under a strong personality, and making reference to Churchill and the battle he had waged 'alone for ten years'.[9] On 8 February, he was hammering home to the House once again that 'The purpose of economic planning is just the same whether in peace or in war. It is ultimately to utilise to the full the human and material resources of the nation. In peace it is butter, and in war it is guns and butter.'[10] Meanwhile, he was also contributing an article for *Picture Post* in which he outlined a possible organisation for a United Europe that might emerge as a result of the war.

In the context of the Phoney War, none of this was notably heady stuff, and Macmillan confessed later that – had it not been for the war and the sense of obligation it imposed – he might have left Parliament at this time to concentrate on publishing with his brother Dan. As it was, he continued to play an active role in the firm. On Friday, 1 September, he addressed the staff with a morale-boosting speech, and scribbled out a suitably resolute press release: 'Macmillan and Company Ltd. . . . wish to state emphatically that they propose to carry on their business at St Martin's Street, London W.C.2, until they are either taxed, insured, A.R.Pd or bombed out of existence.'[11] In anticipation of severe aerial bombing, part of the deep basement which housed the stock was reinforced with girders and made habitable for the staff, and a supposedly unique fire-watching system was inaugurated with spotters installed on the roof. Many of the younger employees left to join the armed forces but despite all the difficulties, exacerbated by a growing shortage of paper, publishing went on: appropriately, a new one-volume edition of *War and Peace* was brought out; as in 1914–18, works on travel and scholarship appeared without interruption, including Rebecca West's classic on Yugoslavia, *Black Lamb and Grey Falcon*, and the *Journals of Dorothy Wordsworth*. Other eminent authors published during the war included Osbert and Edith Sitwell, Eric Linklater, Maurice Bowra, Charles Morgan, Storm Jameson and Pearl Buck. As the war progressed, such deeply moving personal battle accounts as Richard Hillary's *The Last Enemy* also came to Macmillan's.

The war, too, had had its immediate effect on Macmillan's home life. Under the refugee scheme, some forty young children from a school in London's Balham were evacuated to Birch Grove for the duration of the war. After Munich, Macmillan had already made plans for giving up the whole house and had packed all furniture into the drawing room. He and Dorothy now moved into a neighbouring small house on the estate, Pooks Cottage, where they remained until 1952. In London they moved out of the house in Chester Square and into a *pied-à-terre* at 90 Piccadilly, where Harold spent much of the week alone. At Birch Grove the gardens laid out by Nellie Macmillan and later lovingly nurtured by Dorothy grew derelict; but Dorothy, with her affection for young children, played a constant role in the welfare of the evacuees at Birch Grove and established herself as a beloved figure in many youthful memories.

As the autumn turned to winter, the war dragged on, treacherous in its stagnation. Poland had been crushed with terrifying speed and brutality by the German Panzers, while Britain and France sat inert behind the Maginot Line, unable, or unwilling, to lend teeth to their guarantees to the Polish ally – much as Macmillan had foreseen. Discontent and frustration with Chamberlain mounted. On 29 September, after Hitler had ripped out the heart of Poland, Soviet troops stole in by the back door and occupied eastern Poland up to the notional Curzon Line. Not long thereafter Stalin moved in on the three Baltic states: Estonia, Latvia and Lithuania. In a style to which the West was then unaccustomed, patriots and anti-Communists disappeared in countless thousands; in the Katyn Forests a large proportion of the survivors of the Polish officer corps were brutally murdered. To British, and French, public opinion this was nothing more than a recurrence of the instinctive acquisitiveness whereby Russia would bite chunks out of her neighbours whenever historically the opportunity presented itself; worse, in the prevailing context, these were acts of the jackal against nations paralysed, or mauled, by the common enemy.

Finland

On 30 November, Soviet Russia struck with all its might against tiny Finland. With resort to the kind of double-speak that would become more familiar in the post-1945 world, the USSR invoked a mutual-assistance pact which it claimed to have concluded with a new 'Finnish Democratic Republic', a fictitious body led by a Communist agitator called Otto Kuusinen. To the amazement of the West, for weeks on end tiny Finland – only four million strong – fought back with unheard-of gallantry, inflicting heavy casualties and defeat after defeat upon the ponderous Soviet mammoth which was pinned down on the Mannerheim Line. In this 'Winter War', where the lowest temperatures for 100 years were registered, the Red Army's ineptitude caused many false conclusions about its overall combat value to be drawn by analysts abroad – especially in Berlin. Filmgoers in Britain and France were treated weekly by Movietone News and Pathe News to fresh sagas of Finnish heroism, and, in these countries where attempts to conclude an alliance with the Soviets had foundered during the inter-war period upon deep-seated mistrust of the Bolshevists, hatred for the Soviets began almost to eclipse that felt for Hitler's Germany.

Declaration of war over Poland seemed to have been succeeded by a new moral passion to make this now a crusade to rid the world of *all* totalitarian evils. And, since Stalin had signed the Non-Aggression Pact with Hitler, had joined in the partition of Poland and was now attacking neutral Finland, what was there to choose between the two dictators? To Franco-British strategists, too, was there not here also perhaps a chance of opening a 'second front', to strike back at Hitler by grabbing the Scandinavian iron-ore re-sources essential to the German war effort? Gamelin, the French generalissimo, was being urged by the ultra-right-wing General Weygand (his eventual successor) to break the back of the Soviet Union in Finland.

With hindsight it is easy to see that any course of action that might have brought about war between the Soviet Union and the West would have been a calamity; but this is to ignore the mood of the time – and Harold Macmillan was as much in tune as anyone with public sentiments over Finland. Early in January he joined with alacrity – encouraged by Churchill – a government working committee, set up by that well-known man of action, Leo Amery, to help organise aid to Finland and to recruit an international volunteer force. On 5 February, with the Mannerheim Line still holding firm, the Supreme War Council in Paris provisionally agreed to send two British divisions and some 50,000 French troops to help Finland. These could not reach Finland until April, and their arrival and supply would be dependent upon the acquisition of the Norwegian iron-ore port of Narvik. Thus was a dual-purpose blow to be struck against the Nazi–Soviet war machine; and thus was neutral Norway to become – through strands of extraordinary complexity – enmeshed eventually in the loom of war.

131

Five days after the Paris decision, Macmillan and Lord Davies, former Radical MP and PPS to Lloyd George, were despatched by the Amery Committee as a fact-finding delegation to Finland, accompanied by Colonel Serlachius, the Military Attaché from the Finnish Embassy. Promises of aid to Finland also seem to have been accompanied by a curious amount of free-booting. On the day before his departure, Macmillan received a note from Bob Boothby, offering 75,000 Mauser (German) rifles 'from a Belgian company with which I am connected'. There followed a further inventory of munitions from foreign sources, many from Italy, and Boothby would follow this up with a telegram to Macmillan while in Finland: 'MATERIALS SPECIFIED NOW AVAILABLE AND NECESSARY OFFICIAL REPRESENTATION SHOULD BE MADE BY FINNISH GOVERNMENT WITHOUT DELAY.' History does not reveal what there might have been in the deal for Boothby.[12]

This was Macmillan's first official job abroad and, respect for the Finnish courage tempered by his own frustration at not yet having received any other war appointment, he set off with something of the high excitement with which he had gone to France in 1915. At this very moment, however, the Soviets were bringing up some thirty divisions and better-trained troops heavily equipped with artillery and tanks, to launch a final offensive in the Karelian Isthmus north-west of Leningrad. Passing through Stockholm on the way, Macmillan recorded in his diary a note of comic relief:

> Lord Davies has left his teeth in the train. Great confusion, followed by much diplomatic activity. . . . Lord Davies has lost his passport. . . . Lord Davies's passport has turned up, but not his teeth. . . . As the Malmö train connects with the Berlin train, it is thought that the teeth have been stolen by a Gestapo agent. . . .[13]

With Lord Davies reunited with his bridgework, and Macmillan equipped with a conspicuously tall white fur hat (which he would proudly flaunt on his visit to Khrushchev, as Prime Minister in 1959), the delegates finally reached Helsinki, where they promptly called to see the Prime Minister, Risto Ryti. He gave them bad news about the new Russian offensive, where 1000 planes at a time had been thrown in. Macmillan learned that the Finns now had only about 100 planes in all, and were so short of shells that the artillery was not allowed to fire until the Russian infantry were actually attacking; whereas on one sector of two miles the enemy gunners had been expending 300,000 shells in a day. Later Colonel Serlachius showed Macmillan Soviet tanks which the heroic Finns had knocked out by prising open the turret hatches, and throwing 'Molotov cocktails' inside. By such means they claimed to have destroyed 400 tanks. But it was clear to Macmillan that this kind of heroism would not suffice for long. There were also reports that the Russians had breached the Mannerheim Line at several points. On the 15th, Macmillan boldly telegraphed Chamberlain:

EXPERT MILITARY OPINION HERE ADMITS SITUATION VERY GRAVE (STOP) UNLESS FURTHER MATERIAL AID CAN ARRIVE RAPIDLY POSITION WILL BECOME CRITICAL (STOP) URGENT NEED ARTILLERY ALL CALIBRES . . . BOMBERS AND FIGHTERS (STOP) IF THESE MADE AVAILABLE AT ONCE BELIEVE POSITION CAN BE HELD TILL THAW GIVES SHORT RESPITE (STOP) AFTER THAT OUR VOLUNTEERS OR TROOPS COULD OPERATE HERE. . . .

For double assurance, he also signalled Churchill – begging him to ask to see the cable to the Prime Minister – so as to be certain that 'urgent action' was taken. Despite all the hints of serious deterioration at the war front, Macmillan gave heed to hopeful notions of the Finnish General Staff that, with the availability of three foreign divisions, a spring offensive might be possible which would cut the thin Soviet line linking Murmansk to Leningrad.

Lord Davies having fallen ill, Macmillan was taken alone to visit a sector of the central front, near Kajaani, commanded by a General Toompo. Equipped with a white camouflage sheet to conceal his conspicuous dark fur coat, Macmillan was forced by air-raid warnings to leap off the train at regular intervals into waist-deep snowdrifts. Reaching the front he heard repeated accounts of the slaughter of ill-trained Russian troops, and was shown one large group of corpses apparently liquidated by their own commissars – doubtless *pour encourager les autres*: 'We were particularly impressed by the nature of the wounds which had caused their death. In nearly every case, the Russians had been hit in the head or in the neck.' The bravery and extraordinarily high morale of the Finnish soldiers he saw (who reminded him of the Guards) struck a strong warrior chord in Macmillan. But, on return to base, he was warned by Colonel Serlachius that the situation down in the critical Isthmus was now too desperate for him to get there, or to see Field-Marshal Mannerheim, Finland's legendary Commander-in-Chief. After a fatiguing series of journeys under constant air attack, Macmillan reached Vaasa on the Gulf of Bothnia on 22 February. He and Lord Davies then flew out to Stockholm, and thence eventually to London.

His Finland trip made a deep impression on Macmillan, and – always one to be attracted by courage – he retained for the rest of his life 'a vivid memory of those gallant and fearless people'. In 1979, he fulfilled a dream by returning to Finland for the first time since the Winter War, where he was welcomed by some of his old hosts. Meanwhile, a further episode with a link to the distant future occurred on Macmillan's way home. This was a meeting with a young volunteer, one of the first 200 already bound for Finland, called Harold Evans.* Macmillan's accounts of Finnish heroism greatly inspired Evans, although the war was to end too early for him to play a part. Trapped in Finland after the German invasion of Norway, Evans spent the next eighteen months using his experience as a journalist on the *Sheffield Telegraph* to run a newspaper for the British Legation. The next time Macmillan met Harold Evans was in 1957 when he was appointed the new press secretary at No. 10 Downing Street.

Pessimistic though he was about the outcome in Finland, Macmillan returned to Westminster full of fight. On 2 March, Premier Daladier of France announced that he was ready to send volunteers to Finland, even though there was still no commitment from either Norway or Sweden to permit their transit. Reluctantly, Chamberlain agreed to launch the Narvik operation. But on the 13th, the Mannerheim Line having finally cracked and the key bastion of Viipuri captured, brave Finland was forced to sue for peace. Macmillan, however, remained 'obsessed by the Finnish tragedy'. On 19 and 20 March, the Commons debated British support for Finland, and Macmillan entered the lists with a powerful attack on Chamberlain, backed by a well-prepared use of facts and figures

* Later Sir Harold Evans, not to be confused with the former editor of *The Times* of the same name.

that he had gained on his Finnish trip. He began gently enough, recognising that the Government would have had to overcome perhaps impossible obstacles in order to rescue Finland, but:

> Perhaps the most damaging criticism of His Majesty's Government is that, having begun to regard the Finnish war as part of the strategic front, they did not move with sufficient rapidity or with sufficient determination into this position; that they hovered between two policies, and that at the end of this affair we have, by universal consent, obtained a maximum of disadvantage with a minimum of advantage. . . .[14]

This point, highly germane to the backbenches' mounting dissatisfaction with Chamberlain's conduct of the war in general, Macmillan pressed home with considerable effect. Then he accused the Prime Minister of having blatantly misled the House. On the 13th, Chamberlain had assured MPs that, of the Finnish government's repeated appeals for munitions, 'every one of these requests has been answered'; yet now, noted Macmillan, he had climbed down to saying feebly 'Every request was considered so far as it was possible.' This was not at all the same thing; and item by item Macmillan proved how the Finns had been let down, quoting a British telegram which had been sent as late as 12 February: 'None of the weapons or munitions which your country requests can be spared from our resources.' This led to an angry exchange between Chamberlain and Macmillan, from which the Prime Minister came out worst.

Macmillan noted with relief that, throughout the debate, both Churchill and Eden were conspicuously absent from the government bench; 'this made my task easier.' He wound up with a forceful passage:

> As to the general lessons of this episode, I do not know enough of the strategy of war to know whether on the whole we have gained or lost. . . . But it does, I think, throw a piercing light on the present machinery and method of government. The delay, the vacillation, changes of front, standing on one foot one day and on the other the next before a decision is given – these are patently clear to anyone. The moral of the history of these three

months to be drawn for the future is, to use the phrase of Burke, 'a proof of the irresistible operation of feeble council'. . . .[15]

These were words that undoubtedly remained in the minds of Members during the ensuing debates which saw the end of Chamberlain. As Macmillan admitted in his memoirs, it was one of those rare experiences 'of starting with a hostile audience and winning it over to my side', and his speech unmistakably shook the government. It was also – though this could hardly be predicted at the time – to be the last intervention Macmillan would make from the backbenches until his resignation almost twenty-five years later.

In the course of his speech, Macmillan once again harked back to the wild optimism he had found in Finland, remarking that, had the promised volunteers arrived in time, 'another week might have made the whole difference.' In the light of what we now know of the subsequent history of the Second World War, the thought of what *might* have happened had British troops reached Finland in time, with a totally unprepared Britain possibly plunged into war with the USSR as well as with Germany, makes the blood run cold. It was a disaster from which Britain, and France, were saved by only a matter of days, if not hours, through Finland's capitulation. Macmillan's role in the story was perhaps one instance where the swordsman had escaped the confines of reasoned intellect. Embroilment in Finland was, as Macmillan admitted later in life, an error of judgement – though not of honour, or of heart – and it was an error in which he was in a large and distinguished company at the time.

On 29 March, Macmillan sent a poignant thank-you letter to his Finnish host, Colonel Serlachius, in which, after describing his return to England and the subsequent events, he said:

you know that I feel that a great part of the fault is our hesitation and weakness. There seems to be some fatal inability in modern democratic governments to make up their mind until it is too late, and I am afraid that this is another case of which there have been many examples before. I do not know how I can write to you or what to say. Sometimes I feel that none of you will wish to think of, or to hear from your English friends again. . . . there is nothing now that I can say which can be of any help, except to send you my profound homage. I have never been anywhere

where I was so much impressed by both military skill and civilian courage. . . .[16]

So ended the sad tale of the Winter War. The train of powder it had ignited, however, continued to burn with fateful consequences, bringing a sudden and violent end to the Phoney War. After months of deliberation, at a meeting of the Allied Supreme War Council on 28 March, Churchill finally persuaded Chamberlain to mine the Leads, the Norwegian coastal waters, down which crept the German iron-ore boats. But by this time the ample warning of British intentions had been in Hitler's hands for several weeks and – with characteristically brutal speed – he acted to forestall them. On 5 April, the day after Chamberlain had made his famous and foolish speech about Hitler having 'missed the bus', some 10,000 German troops were 'embussed' for Norway aboard merchant ships and colliers in one of the most daring strokes of the war. In taking this gamble, Hitler may well have received encouragement from the Commons debate on Finland in mid-March, containing as it did Macmillan's detailed revelations of the true state of British unpreparedness – although Macmillan had previously recommended to Chamberlain that this debate be held in private session. On 9 April, Denmark fell with hardly a shot fired; by the first week in May the British expeditionary force had been forced out of all Norway, bar a precarious toe-hold in Narvik. Finland had brought down Daladier in France and had badly shaken Chamberlain; the Norwegian débâcle despatched him.

The Fall of Chamberlain: A Job for Macmillan

Writing to his travelling companion, Lord Davies, on 8 April, Macmillan observed: 'I do not go to the films; but my daughters tell me that when the Prime Minister appears now on the news reel scarcely anyone applauds. I am sorry to say that this is also true of my daughters!'[17] The wave of anger that swept the country at Britain's inability to save Norway also threatened to engulf Churchill, as the Minister directly responsible for the Royal Navy's reverses. This was a source of deep worry to Macmillan and his fellow dissidents, who were now more bent than ever on seeing Chamberlain replaced by the First Lord, and it was not in

Churchill's nature to pass the buck. On 7 May began the historic two-day debate that was to destroy Neville Chamberlain. The mortal shot was fired by the redoubtable backbencher Leo Amery; his speech, recalled Macmillan, 'was the most formidable philippic which I have ever heard delivered by a former Minister against a lifelong friend and colleague'. It culminated with the memorable quotation from Oliver Cromwell to the Long Parliament: ' "You have sat too long here for any good you have been doing. Depart, I say, and let us have done with you! In the name of God, go!" ' Macmillan would remark that it was one of the mysteries of politics why Leo Amery did not reach a higher position: 'he had a far better grasp of world affairs than all the Hoares and the Simons put together. He also had what many lacked – courage, physical and moral. . . .' In fact, in those frenetic May days, Amery after his famous speech was briefly considered as the possible successor to Chamberlain.

Little good was done to Churchill, however, by the appearance, in his full uniform as an Admiral of the Fleet, of the First World War hero, Sir Roger Keyes, who rent the Admiralty for the Norway fiasco, as a representative of the 'fighting and "sea-going" navy'. Churchill, thought Macmillan, was saved on the second day of the debate by savagely witty advice from Lloyd George that reduced the House to laughter: 'The Rt Hon. Gentleman must not allow himself to be converted into an air-raid shelter to keep the splinters from hitting his colleagues.' That evening Macmillan, seeing Churchill in the smoking-room, wished him good luck with his winding-up speech for the government, but added that he hoped it would not be too convincing: ' "Why not?" he asked. "Because," I replied, "we must have a new Prime Minister, and it must be you." He answered gruffly that he had signed on for the voyage and would stick to the ship. . . .'

Meanwhile, Macmillan, who had maintained from the Munich era his old connection with Hugh Dalton, reported back to the 'Watching Committee', which had been set up by Lord Salisbury and was composed of most of the pro-Churchill Tories, on what the Labour Opposition was going to do. On the morning of 8 May he heard that they were going to demand a vote. Preserved in the Birch Grove archives is the Chief Whip's note of a three-line whip that historic night: 'A division of the utmost importance may take place, and your attendance by 10.30 is most particularly requested. David Margesson.' The division, recalls Macmillan, 'was the most tense that I have ever known'. The count was Ayes 281, Noes 200 – a majority of only 81 instead of the customary 240 or more. Macmillan had been one of the thirty-three members of the backbench '1922 Committee' to vote against the government. There were shouts of 'Resign!' from the Labour benches, and Colonel 'Josh' Wedgwood started singing 'Rule Britannia'. A largely tone-deaf Macmillan tried to join in, unharmoniously. In the various cabals and meetings that took place during the following hectic day, Macmillan spoke out strongly against Halifax, whom the Party stalwarts were canvassing to succeed Chamberlain, and in favour of Churchill. To the very last Chamberlain tried to cling on: 'like trying to get a limpet off a corpse' Bracken remarked to Macmillan in a furious mixing of metaphors. However, at dawn the next day, Friday, 10 May, came the long-dreaded news that Hitler had attacked the Low Countries in an all-out *Blitzkrieg*. The Phoney War, with which Chamberlain would forever be identified, was over and there could be no further delay in creating a new British government. At 6 p.m. that evening Churchill saw the King and accepted the commission which he was to hold for five years.

It was during those balmy May days, when the Panzers were slicing with terrifying speed through the French defences at Sedan, that Churchill called for Macmillan. Of his new coalition Cabinet, Churchill remarked, 'I have formed the most broad-based government that Britain has ever known'; it extended from Lord Lloyd of Dolobran (a diehard Tory of the extreme right) to Ellen Wilkinson (more popularly known as Red Ellen). Notwithstanding the stigma of Munich, Macmillan's old rival and future lieutenant, Rab Butler – eight years his junior – was called on to stay at the important post of Under-Secretary of State for Foreign Affairs; 'I wish you to go on with your delicate manner of answering parliamentary questions without giving anything away,' Churchill instructed him with perceptive irony.[18] Most of the rebel Tories of the 1930s were rewarded for their loyalty to him during the Wilderness Years: Duff Cooper became Minister of Information (succeeded by Brendan Bracken in July 1941); Lord Cranborne Paymaster-General; and Boothby Parliamentary Secretary at the Ministry of Food. The Labour leader, Herbert Morrison, was appointed Minister of Supply, and Churchill asked Macmillan to go there as his Parliamentary Secretary. 'Would that be agreeable to me?' Macmillan recalled him saying. 'I said, yes it would, and so it was settled.' After sixteen frustrating years, he had finally made it. The post was not exactly grand or glamorous; however, it was one for which Macmillan in his repeated pre-war calls for such a ministry, as well as his theoretical expertise in planning, was admirably equipped.

Macmillan took up his new post at one of the blackest moments in British history. By the fifth day of Hitler's onslaught in the west, the battle had been virtually lost by France. On 20 May, the first Panzers reached the Channel, cutting off the British expeditionary force and the cream of the French Army. A month later France signed an armistice, and Britain was alone. Miraculously, the bulk of the British forces escaped from the trap at Dunkirk, but they had left behind them virtually all their heavy equipment, the equivalent to the arms of eight to ten divisions. This included 45,000 vehicles, nearly 700 tanks and some 2500 assorted artillery. Threatened by imminent invasion, Britain was denuded of weapons. It fell to the Ministry of Supply to replenish this armoury, while still engaged in the seemingly impossible task of trying to equip an army expanded (on paper) from six divisions to fifty-five on the outbreak of war. The Ministry of Supply also had to provide the machine-tools to turn out the weapons, and control the factories in which they were made as well as finding the raw materials required. It was a daunting task, and Macmillan found his new boss, Herbert Morrison, 'a little dazed' by it all. Before the war, Macmillan had admired this little Cockney for his political courage; he had been Macmillan's choice for leader of a popular front in 1936. But Macmillan thought him now out of his depth: 'I doubted if he really understood the problems which confronted us.' In his own memoirs, Morrison wrote, 'Supply was hardly a post to run after,'[19] and he was not unhappy when Churchill transferred him to the Home Office after five months.

Thus from the first a great deal of responsibility devolved upon Macmillan, and at last he was able to put into practice some of his theories of *The Middle Way* on economic organisation and planning. The scope of his work was immense: 'the collection of railings (repeated almost every week); the Flax Control Board; the uses of glycerine; the provision of sawmills; the utilization of waste leather; the sales of newspapers in the street; the future of the organ-building trade; the likely yield of the wool-clip; the collection of kitchen waste (a special favourite); the provision of steel helmets for Home Guard,

Harold Macmillan, aged four.

Harold Macmillan's parents: Maurice Crawford Macmillan, in 1882, aged twenty-nine, and Helen Belles, in Indiana in the 1880s, before her marriage to Maurice.

The three Macmillan brothers at
Cadogan Square. Left to right:
Arthur, Daniel and Harold.

At the Eton Wall Game.

Monsignor Ronald Knox, tutor to Harold Macmillan between Eton and Oxford.

At the Oxford Union, 1912. (Harold Macmillan seated second from left.)

Balliol, 1913. (Harold Macmillan seated third from right, back row.)

4th Battalion Grenadier Guards, England, August 1915. (Harold Macmillan is third from right, standing; on his right, Osbert Sitwell.)

Second Lieutenant Macmillan, Grenadier Guards, France, 1915.

Dorothy Macmillan, by Philip de Laszlo, 1920.

Relaxing at Government House, Canada, 1919. (Harold Macmillan and Dorothy Cavendish at right of picture.)

Harold Macmillan marries Lady Dorothy Cavendish, 1920.

The Duchess of Devonshire, 'Evie', with Rachel and Dorothy, May 1922.

Harold and Dorothy Macmillan with Maurice, Carol and Catherine, 1930.

Catherine, Carol, Sarah and Maurice at Birch Grove on the outbreak of war.

Boothby with Churchill, then Chancellor of the Exchequer, 1928.

Electioneering at Stockton.

Early influences: John Maynard Keynes and Sean O'Casey (two eminent Macmillan authors); Lloyd George and Oswald Mosley.

Finland, 1940, with Lord Davies.

At the Ministry of Supply. Lord Beaverbrook returns from Moscow in 1941, with Harold Macmillan on his right.

John Wyndham, later Lord Egremont,
Private Secretary to Harold Macmillan
when he was British 'Minister Resident' in
the Mediterranean.

With Churchill, Casablanca, 1943.

Two future Prime Ministers.

nurses and midwives. . . .' One of his earliest functions was to
receive from 'a truly Elizabethan character', the Earl of Suffolk, a
quantity of heavy water which he was engaged in smuggling out of
France, and which – although Macmillan was of course totally
unaware of this at the time – was subsequently to be used in the
fabrication of the atom bomb. But his main contribution was one
of organisation: setting up area boards to decentralise production
(a hotly disputed issue); arranging for closer liaison between government, industry and labour; and chairing the Industrial Capacity
Committee, to which all these activities were answerable. One of
his lieutenants in charge of the key function of machine-tool control
was an able industrialist called Percy Mills, who so impressed
Macmillan that he was to bring him into his government – as a
non-political outsider – twenty years later. When supplies from
America began to flow in, this also came within Macmillan's
competence.

In the House he was frequently called upon to answer questions
on behalf of his chief. Here he was not at his best; though he says
he 'began to learn the technique', he dreaded question time and his
circumstantial manner tended to irritate questioners. Morrison,
however, recognised his energy and capability in a back-handed
compliment in his memoirs (written when Macmillan was Prime
Minister and he and Morrison had been political enemies for many
years): 'That Macmillan would in time reach the top I had privately
considered possible during the war when he was my parliamentary
secretary at the Ministry of Supply. He then showed how ambitious
he was. Indeed, in his loyalty to me his advice for my advancement
tended to occupy his mind to such an extent that I had to remind
him that we had a war job to do and that personal careers were not
important.'[20]

In October 1940, Morrison was replaced by Sir Andrew Duncan,
a typical Lowland Scot whom Macmillan found 'cautious, diligent,
orderly, unimaginative, but efficient . . . an agreeable and easy chief
to serve'. The Blitz, however, now descended, and Harold Nicolson
recalled meeting Macmillan on 15 October,

sadly contemplating the ruins of Leicester Square. He tells me
that he had been in the Carlton Club last night when the bomb
fell. He had been having a glass of sherry before dinner with
David Margesson. They heard the bomb screaming down and

ducked instinctively. There was a loud crash, the main light went out and the whole place was filled with the smell of cordite and the dust of rubble. The side-lights on the tables remained alight, glimmering murkily in the thick fog which settled down on everything, plastering their hair and eye-brows with thick dust. They saw through the fog the figure of Quintin Hogg escorting old Hailsham from the ruins like Aeneas and Anchises. . . .[21]

For Macmillan, whose eyesight was never his strongest point, the blackout was a nightmare: in November he was knocked over by a taxi in the dark. It seems to have been another lucky escape: 'I was much bruised, but no bones were broken, and after a few days I could go back to work. But it gave me a shock.' Morrison urged him to sleep in the large air-raid shelter under the Ministry but Macmillan, after trying it one night, disliked it greatly and did not use it again. So, while Dorothy stayed at Pooks Cottage in Sussex, Harold continued to live in his rooms at 90 Piccadilly, groping his way through the darkness and bombs each night, getting down to the country only for an occasional weekend. Then, on returning to 90 Piccadilly one evening, he found a note from his servant, saying 'Your rooms have been blown in. I have put some things in Mr. —'s room.' His next move was to a flat belonging to one of his authors, Hugh Walpole, where he stayed until 1943. Meanwhile, the House of Macmillan in St Martin's Street also had a close shave when a bomb demolished Hamptons, fifty yards away.

Yet spirits remained high, boosted by occasional exhortations from Churchill like this memorandum which Macmillan kept framed at Birch Grove long years after the war:

STRICTLY CONFIDENTIAL
In these dark days the Prime Minister would be grateful if all his colleagues in the Government, as well as high officials, would maintain a high morale in their circles; not minimising the gravity of events, but showing confidence in our ability and inflexible resolve to continue the war till we have broken the will of the enemy to bring all Europe under his domination. . . .

The war headlines said little to maintain this confidence, given the state of acute debility that persisted in Britain's armed forces, and her isolation as the solitary nation still confronting Hitler. Then, on 22 June 1941, Hitler invaded Russia. Almost immediately Macmillan's Ministry found itself charged with sending steadily mounting quantities of arms and munitions to the new ally. To meet these heavy demands Lord Beaverbrook was appointed to the Ministry of Supply with almost dictatorial powers, and with Macmillan, who became spokesman in the House of Commons, as his second-in-command.

In all things, Max Beaverbrook was a controversial figure, but there was no disputing his dynamic appeal. As Minister of Aircraft Production, he had thrown his prodigious energy, and his powerful propaganda machine, into some campaigns of dubious value – such as pressurising British housewives to surrender their irreplaceable aluminium saucepans for melting down into Spitfires. Nevertheless, he had injected an unmistakable new vigour into the British aircraft industry. Macmillan had first known him in the late 1920s. Like many, he was both repelled and fascinated by 'this strange attractive gnome with an odour of genius about him', as Diana Cooper once described him.[22] Macmillan well knew 'the Beaver's' reputation for driving underlings into the ground and for gaining possession of their souls, and at first he seems to have been somewhat daunted. Many years later, Michael Foot claimed, unflatteringly, to recollect seeing Macmillan, on what he thought was probably his first visit to Beaverbrook's country house at Cherkley, 'waiting in a lounge outside the library, and I remember him giving me a great eulogy of what he thought of Beaverbrook, full of flattery, and it was obviously planted to be passed on by me – so of course I did – and Beaverbrook laughed. I remember then thinking how unctuous and grandiloquent Macmillan was at the time.'[23]

Macmillan's own account, however, suggests that he soon took the measure of his new boss:

> . . . I made up my mind that the only way to treat Max was to be very aloof from him. I never went into his room and talked. About 8 o'clock – I always stayed in the Ministry till about nine – he'd say 'You haven't been to my room, come and see me there.' I'd say: 'You didn't send for me.' 'Well, come to dinner. . . .' 'I was going out with some friends.' Then he'd say, 'Will you come to stay at Cherkley with me?' I was very pompous and said, 'Of course – what are we going to discuss?' 'No, we're just going to

have a party.' I'd reply, 'Usually when I'm asked to a country house party, my wife has been asked with me.' 'Oh no, it isn't that kind of party.' 'Well, I think perhaps I won't come. . . .' 'Oh well, I'll get Dorothy to come.' 'Of course that would be delightful. . . .'

He tried to trap me. . . . He couldn't resist seducing men in the way he seduced women. And once a man was seduced by him, he was finished. I've seen two or three people ruined by it.[24]

Once Macmillan had established their relationship on a sound footing and settled down to working under the new regime, he found the task 'thrilling' and 'fun' (the latter word was to become a cipher for his highest approbation). Life with Beaverbrook was certainly gruelling; appearing to need no sleep himself, he had a habit of ringing subordinates at three or four in the morning from wherever in the world he happened to find himself. He saw his chief role as co-ordinating arms and supplies between the US, Britain and the Soviet Union. This involved much flying to and fro – high altitude providing, incidentally, about the most satisfying relief from the chronic asthma which plagued the press magnate. During his Minister's prolonged absences, Macmillan found himself virtually in charge of the Ministry of Supply. Here one of his more testing responsibilities was to keep the peace between Beaverbrook and the powerful trades union leader, Ernest Bevin, appointed by Churchill as Minister of Labour and generally enjoying his full support. The clash was as much one of personalities as principles; Beaverbrook, says Macmillan, 'could not refrain from teasing his solid opponent who seemed often slow in his reaction and ponderous in his movements. Bevin was the bull with many taurine qualities; Beaverbrook was the matador.' Beaverbrook often resorted to highly unofficial, even piratical methods to acquire the labour for his factories, which enraged Bevin. While doing his best to keep the peace, Macmillan appears to have defended his chief robustly; he wrote to Bevin in November 1941: '. . . Lord Beaverbrook says that the difficulties about the Production Executive are your own fault.'[25]

Eventually the infighting led to Macmillan doing himself out of a job. On 28 October 1941, after some damaging criticism of the government in the Commons, he drafted a minute to Beaverbrook characteristic of Macmillan the planner: 'A Production Ministry (to include Labour) is absolutely necessary. . . . All our troubles flow from trying to substitute inter-departmental committees for a head. When we have a head, all the other parts of the body will work harmoniously together. That's the whole story – except to add that there is only one man in the country who will be accepted for a moment as head – yourself.'

After much argument, on 2 February 1942, Beaverbrook told Macmillan that he had decided to accept a new post of the sort proposed in Macmillan's memorandum. But there would have to be changes in the Department's representation in the House of Commons. Three days later Macmillan bade goodbye to the Ministry of Supply.

Looking back on Beaverbrook in wartime, Macmillan saw him as 'a very tortured figure . . . almost Jekyll and Hyde'.[26] Vindictive, cruel and often small-minded as Macmillan recognised him to be, 'he radiated strength, authority, determination and energy'. In his wartime relationship with Churchill, Beaverbrook, he thought, had played a strangely beneficial role, the importance of which Macmillan never fully appreciated until he was Prime Minister himself:

> On the whole nobody ever comes to see you if you are Prime Minister. . . . The nice people don't come because they don't want to be thought courtiers, and the tiresome people – you don't want to see them. But Max recharged the old boy's batteries. I bet you the night that the two battleships were sunk [*The Repulse* and *The Prince of Wales*, on 10 December 1941], Winston sat alone and nobody blew in to have a jolly whisky and soda. But Max might have done – and would have stayed till four in the morning, and drunk with him and told him stories, to take his mind off it. . . .[27]

Often while Macmillan was with Beaverbrook at the Ministry of Supply he recalled his saying that he was going to see Churchill that night – and it was always in the bad times. As regards their own relationship, Macmillan asserted that 'until the end of his life I received nothing but kindness.' Preserving his soul intact against this extraordinary force in the earliest days, but also fighting battles on his behalf, evidently paid dividends many years later. Even when Macmillan, as Prime Minister, was pressing hard for Britain to join the EEC, 'which was exactly the opposite of Max's policies, he never allowed a personal attack on me [in the Beaverbrook press].'[28]

To the Colonial Office

More immediately, there was another important bonus for Macmillan to derive from his collaboration with Beaverbrook. It probably brought him closer than ever before to Churchill – and more favourably under his scrutiny. Beaverbrook, unhappy at losing Macmillan on taking over the new Ministry, apparently put in a good word for his former lieutenant to Churchill. On 5 February 1942, Macmillan became Under-Secretary at the Colonial Office. With him he was permitted to take his Private Secretary, John Wyndham, who was henceforth to fill an important role in his life until Wyndham's early death in 1972. It was a modest promotion, though Macmillan remarked jocularly at the time that it 'felt like leaving a madhouse in order to enter a mausoleum'. Meanwhile, Rab Butler had once more moved ahead of him up the political ladder to become Minister of Education, a post which he held with utmost competence and reforming zeal until the dissolution of Churchill's wartime coalition in 1945.

The Secretary of State for the Colonies was another peer, Lord Moyne, so Macmillan once again had substantial responsibilities as ministerial spokesman in the Commons. After less than three weeks, Moyne was replaced by Lord Cranborne, already doubly related to Macmillan by marriage, and now Maurice Macmillan was about to marry a Cranborne niece. Macmillan found him, an old friend from both Eton and Oxford days, easy to get on with and – at this time – sharing a similar point of view. At first, Macmillan admitted that his knowledge of colonial affairs was limited, having concentrated in the past largely on domestic economic matters or foreign policy; and once again, he took over his new post against a sombre background of military disasters.

Within the first two weeks, Singapore had surrendered, accompanied by the loss of Hong Kong, Malaya, Borneo and much of Burma. With them went 60 per cent of the world's tin, and 90 per cent of its rubber production. Ceylon and possibly India looked like being next on the Japanese programme. In North Africa, the bastion of Tobruk fell to Rommel in June, together with 33,000 men, and the Churchill government tottered; so did public morale. But there still remained fifty-five colonial territories, with some sixty million inhabitants, scattered across the globe. Macmillan's job was to act more or less *in loco parentis* to these, keeping them happy and loyal, but chiefly ensuring the supply of their vital raw materials for the war effort; which brought him back into contact with his old colleagues at the Ministry of Supply. Initially the Ministry of Works tried to fob off Macmillan and his staff with gloomy offices in a decaying Whitehall building. But, displaying a remarkable talent on the first of many such occasions, John Wyndham discovered that the Scottish Office had departed to Edinburgh for the duration, and he 'commandeered' their pleasant quarters in Lord Melbourne's old house.

Macmillan's tasks were many and diffuse. They included composing a suitable response to the touching proposal made by a chieftain to have himself and his three sons dropped by parachute on Berlin with a view to killing Hitler with bows and arrows; 'an ambitious but, alas, impractical plan'. More serious was Macmillan's endeavour to ensure the supply of cocoa from the Gold Coast (later Ghana) by establishing a streamlined West African Produce Control Board to stabilise and fix prices for both producer and customer, which was basically Lord Woolton's Ministry of Food. With cocoa prices at an all-time high, revenue was immense. But instead of distributing all the profits to the producer and customer, Macmillan's Board diverted a considerable proportion into a special fund, earmarked to aid West African development in the post-war world. When Ghana achieved its independence in 1957, Macmillan claimed that the fund stood at about £400 million; Nkrumah, he said 'blew the lot!'[29]

Unfamiliar as this new scene was to him, Macmillan's mind was soon racing ahead to think about the future status of Britain's colonial empire, beyond the war. In a speech in the House, on 24 June 1942, he posed the rhetorical question of why the colonies were poor:

Because of capitalist exploitation, or because of insufficient capital? Because they are too much governed, or too little governed? Because there are too many white planters and settlers, or too few? . . . No. They are poor because they are just beginning. They are four or five centuries behind. Our job is to move them, to hustle them, across this great interval of time as rapidly as we can.

Already one could detect just a preliminary zephyr of the winds of change. He continued, noting how 'the Empires of the past have

died because they could not change with the times. . . . By contrast
our Empire has had the great quality of adaptation. By that it lives.'
The future governing principle of the colonial empire should be
'partnership between the various elements'. All should be treated
as a whole; 'we want no depressed areas', and there would have to
be long-term investment on capital development.[30]

Meanwhile, within the confines of the Colonial Office, Macmillan
was hatching even more revolutionary-sounding schemes. In 1923,
his own father-in-law, when Colonial Secretary, had laid down the
principle of native 'paramountcy' for Kenya, which meant eventual
African predominance. The British settlers had protested robustly,
and policy through the 1920s and 1930s had vacillated back and
forth. By 1939 the 3000 white settlers of 1911 had multiplied to
nearly 30,000; some of them were extremely wealthy and had
occupied much of the best land. The African population, with its
rapidly expanding birthrate and reduced infant mortality, was
beginning to feel land hunger. These pressures were particularly
acute in Kikuyu tribal areas. In July 1942, Sir Arthur Dawes,
Assistant Under-Secretary at the Colonial Office, produced a paper
for his chief, Sir George Gater. Having discarded the idea of self-
government for the settlers along the lines of Southern Rhodesia, this
cautiously recommended a form of federation embracing Kenya,
Tanganyika and Uganda, providing a framework for a solution
most likely to satisfy the demands of the whites, Africans and the
100,000 or more Asians who lived in the three colonies. Beyond
remarking, however, that if African aspirations were not met Britain
– like George III and Lord North – faced losing the whole continent,
Dawes's paper made scantest reference to the most pressing need
of the Africans in Kenya – land.

Macmillan responded to the Dawes paper with a critical memorandum the following month, in which he warned that a clash was
bound to come: 'The Whites cannot afford economically to abandon
their supremacy. The Government will be torn between the rights
of the settlers and their obligations to the natives. Even if the federal
solution proposed by Sir Arthur Dawes were to be put into effect
now, the land-hunger and the pressure of the natives will not be
relieved.'[31] He went on to suggest a quite different and much more
radical policy that all or some of the land in the Highlands now

belonging in fee simple or long leasehold to the settlers be nationalised and two kinds of farms, State farms and Collective farms, be
created. These would be based on the Russian system, of which
Macmillan had received a glimpse (perhaps tinted with rather too
rosy a hue) in 1932. The Collective farms would be a group of small
farms, by implication in African hands, organised to form an
efficient unit.

Macmillan foresaw that the scheme would initially provoke 'excited protests' from the white settlers (which was probably a major
understatement), but eventually they would be persuaded of the
advantages it held for them. They would be able to recover the
capital sunk into their farms; which, given the uncertainties of war,
might have considerable attraction. They would have *security of
employment*, and pensions, as managers in the government service.
Or, if they didn't fancy the scheme, 'they can return to England.'
As for the Africans, they would 'obviously stand to gain in every
way'; their wages and conditions of employment would be protected
by the government, and they would be enabled to leave the native
reserves and settle on the prime-quality land hitherto earmarked
for the Europeans in the 'White Highlands'. Macmillan admitted
that, apart from resistance from the white Kenyans, the Kenya
government would have to become very efficient – 'for it will be
running the largest single agricultural business in the Empire'. And
it would be very expensive; but, concluded Macmillan ominously,
'it will be less expensive than a civil war'.[32] That 'civil war' came
with Mau Mau ten years later.

The Macmillan proposals met with a cool reception in the
Colonial Office, criticism tending to be based on the adverse
reactions they would arouse in Rhodesia and South Africa at a time
when their support was vital to the war effort. After Macmillan left
the Colonial Office, a few months later, the whole issue seems to
have been pigeonholed, perhaps in the classic civil service expec-
tation that, if nothing was done, the inconvenient problem of Kenya
would just go away. However, as far as Macmillan's own future
policy towards Africa was concerned, these 1942 proposals are very
relevant. They show him thinking ahead about the long-term future
of the African population, and about the necessity for fundamental
change in colonial Africa. At the same time Macmillan was expressing impatience at American interference in British colonial affairs,

following the US entry into the war. Of Roosevelt he noted acidly in his memoirs: 'Apparently unconscious of conditions either in Harlem or in the Deep South, he expressed concern about the low standard of living in many of the West Indian islands.'

That Macmillan was also thinking ahead on other fronts is indicated by an entry in Harold Nicolson's diary, dated 23 October 1942:

> Harold says that the British people are now supremely prosperous and happy. Were it not for the bombing, they would be perfectly content. [This is perhaps somewhat of an exaggeration.] But that they dread for the future. If the present system can give them security and employment, they will support it: but if we fail to do so, we shall be swept away, politely but firmly. He regards extreme Socialism as inevitable, with the Conservatives standing, not so much for property, as for private lives. He is confident and interesting.[33]

In the course of his life Harold Macmillan came to develop a marked and almost oriental fatalism about life, which sometimes seemed at odds with his devoutly orthodox Christian beliefs. In his later years he would often remark that he had always followed the principle of 'take it as it comes, it never turns out as you expect.'[34] Now, in the autumn of 1942, fate took an unexpected hand in his career. The immediate catalyst assumed the form of Sir Stafford Cripps. Macmillan was by no means alone in considering Cripps, a teetotaller and vegetarian so far to the left that he had been expelled from the pre-war Parliamentary Labour Party, to be a strange man, with a remarkable propensity for annoying Winston Churchill. During the desperate winter of 1941–2, Cripps nevertheless had suddenly achieved fame and popularity as British Ambassador in beleaguered Moscow. On his return it was clear that he would have to be given a ministerial post, but he infuriated Churchill by also demanding a place in the Cabinet. Eventually he was pacified by being made Lord Privy Seal and Leader of the House of Commons, as well as receiving a seat in the War Cabinet; but within nine months the Commons had been thoroughly alienated by his personality and Churchill irked by his badgering about how to run the war. In September 1942, Cripps offered his resignation and two months later he was slotted into Beaverbrook's old post as Minister of

Aircraft Production, where he remained more or less peacefully for the rest of the war.

The translation of Cripps, however, set in train a government reshuffle in which Lord Cranborne was removed from the Colonial Office to take over Cripps's role as Lord Privy Seal. His post was then taken by Oliver Stanley. One of the ablest of Macmillan's contemporaries, Stanley was already being talked of as a potential successor to Churchill. He was a close friend of Macmillan, who greatly admired him. But Stanley as Colonial Secretary could speak for himself in the House of Commons, which meant a *de facto* demotion for Macmillan, who, for eighteen months under Lords Beaverbrook, Moyne and Cranborne, had been the Minister responsible to the Commons. He thought seriously of resigning and there was even talk about his being given a peerage. He decided to tackle Churchill about his future. But by this time the Anglo-American expeditionary force had just landed in North Africa, and Churchill had other problems on his mind than the woes of a junior minister. Instead Macmillan in November unburdened his heart to Churchill's intimate, Brendan Bracken. After being shown Macmillan's draft letter of resignation, Bracken strongly advised him to do nothing, be patient and wait. Fortunately, Macmillan accepted this advice.

A month later Churchill sent for Macmillan. He began by quizzing him about how far he had followed political developments in French North Africa since the Allied landings there on 8 November. Macmillan's response was evidently satisfactory. Churchill then went on to explain how, because of the complexity of the various rival French representatives, he intended appointing a British Minister Resident to represent the government at Allied Force Headquarters in Algiers. The Minister would be of Cabinet rank, though not a member of the War Cabinet – unlike his opposite number (and Macmillan's friend and contemporary) in Cairo, Oliver Lyttelton – and he would report directly to the Prime Minister. He could also retain his seat in the House of Commons: 'It would be an adventure of a high order. This post was at my disposition. It was for me to decide.'

In fact Macmillan was second choice, the post having already been offered to his friend, Captain Harry Crookshank, who had also been seriously wounded with the Grenadiers in the First World War. Still plagued by these wounds, Crookshank had turned down the job, pleading that he could not face the sand and the flies. Macmillan had no such inhibition. Although Churchill suggested that he take a few hours to think it over, Macmillan accepted 'immediately and gratefully'.

Chapter Seven

The Hinge of Fate
December 1942–June 1943

He [Macmillan] will be, I am sure, a help. He is animated by the friendliest feelings towards the United States, and his mother hails from Kentucky [sic]. . . .

('*Former Naval Person*' *to President Roosevelt,*
27 December 1942)

Among the many sobriquets or code-names for de Gaulle in common use at Allied Force Headquarters during the war, perhaps the most popular was 'Ramrod'. This nickname recalled the famous definition of a man who was alleged to have all the rigidity of a poker without its occasional warmth.

(*HM*, Pointing the Way)

For all his enthusiastic alacrity in accepting Churchill's offer of December 1942, Macmillan remarked to a friend that, in North Africa, he was probably being sent to 'a political Siberia'.[1] His doubts were compounded when, two days after his appointment, on Christmas Eve, the news came through of the assassination in Algiers of the French leader Admiral Darlan. For a moment he wondered whether there was still going to be a job. Nevertheless, he set to with energy to gather together a staff and prepare his journey. The staff consisted of two secretaries – Miss Campbell, who had been Macmillan's secretary in the Colonial Office, and a Miss Williams – and his old colleague and Private Secretary John Wyndham. Roger Makins, chosen from the Foreign Office to be his diplomatic adviser, was not yet ready to leave, so a temporary replacement, Pierson ('Bob') Dixon, was to join him in Algiers. Good choices, like many of Macmillan's wartime aides, both men were later to rise to the top of their profession: Makins (later Lord Sherfield) as British Ambassador to Washington during Suez, and Dixon (later Sir Pierson Dixon) as Macmillan's Ambassador to Paris during the crucial EEC negotiations in the 1960s.

In many ways, however, the most important member of the little troupe was John Wyndham. Aged twenty-two to Macmillan's forty-eight, Wyndham was heir to Petworth House in Sussex, and had become known to Macmillan through family social connections. Harold Evans, press secretary to Macmillan when Prime Minister, describes the John Wyndham he knew in the 1960s in an admirable portrait that would almost certainly have been as valid for 1942:

> Physically he might have been invented by P. G. Wodehouse – tall, willowy, stooping and peering through spectacles with exceptionally thick lenses. . . . He more than pulled his weight in a role difficult to define – a combination of ADC, observer and commentator, contact man, cheerful but determined 'fixer', good companion and court jester. . . .[2]

When completing the Positive Vetting Questionnaire instituted by the Macmillan government, Wyndham would answer the question 'Are you in debt?' with a response indeed worthy of Bertie Wooster: 'Yes . . . about £1 million.'

But despite appearances and his anomalous role in the Macmillan household, he was considerably more than just a 'court jester'. The flippant façade masked great ability and sensitivity, a combination which Macmillan always admired. He had a deep knowledge of English literature, which allowed him to keep up with Macmillan's allusions with ease and often cap his quotations. Though he disguised it well, Wyndham also suffered acutely from melancholia, which enabled him to recognise the moments when Macmillan was seized by the Black Dog, and to cajole him out of it in a way not given to any member of his own family. In fact, he came to be almost a surrogate son to Macmillan. The relationship was somewhat akin to Churchill's affection for, and dependence upon, the egregious Brendan Bracken. And – psychologically – it was just as hard on Macmillan's only son Maurice as it was on young Randolph Churchill. Eccentric, slightly raffish, totally uninhibited in the presence of the high and mighty, and given to the use of appalling language of Restoration earthiness, John Wyndham helped open Macmillan's eyes to, and keep him in touch with, a more worldly world to which part of him longed to belong; in doing so, he undoubtedly helped Macmillan escape from that carapace of donnish pomposity. The one person who could tell his chief 'you're being stupid',[3] he remained totally dedicated to Macmillan for the rest of his life; in Algiers, he was to prove an invaluable aide to the new Minister Resident.

For his new appointment, Churchill wished Macmillan to wear uniform, but Macmillan suggested that a Captain of the Reserve, even of the Grenadier Guards, 'would not cut a very impressive figure' among all the generals and high brass assembled in North Africa. 'I see your point,' remarked Churchill, climbing down: 'You mean that between the baton and the bowler there is no middle course.' So Macmillan continued to sport the incongruously baggy trousers and rimless glasses that gave him an air of an early Bolshevik leader. On 31 December, the little party set off, Miss Campbell wearing a round straw hat, which she apparently considered appropriate to the African continent, her pockets stuffed with chewing gum and raisins; their limited luggage included two typewriters 'stolen from the Colonial Office'. The small, twin-engined Lockheed Hudson taking them described a wide circuit out into the Atlantic, to avoid Luftwaffe Messerschmitts, landed at Gibraltar, and finally reached Algiers on 2 January.

Initially they were lodged in the Hotel Aletti, but within a few days John Wyndham – displaying the talents he had used to 'commandeer' the Scottish Office for Macmillan when at the Colonial Office – had mysteriously laid his hands on a 'rich and sumptuous villa' that was to be the envy of his colleagues. 'I have never lived in such strange luxury,' Harold wrote to Dorothy on 26 January: 'Everything is of marble or gold. All the pictures are Botticellis or Murillos. . . . All the furniture is antique, or semi-antique. . . . You look out upon the blue waters of the Bay on the one side, and backwards to the hills on the other.'[4] She would, he thought, be entranced by the sun and the flowers. It was all in extravagant contrast to the austerity and deprivations of wartime England. He hoped she would think of coming out soon to visit him.

The Americans

At 4 p.m. on the day of his arrival, Macmillan was summoned to see General Dwight D. Eisenhower, the Allied Commander-in-Chief, at the elegant Hotel St Georges, high up above Algiers, which had now become Allied Force Headquarters. Macmillan was warned that the interview might be 'rather sticky', and this proved no exaggeration. The pressures that the newly appointed general-issimo was himself experiencing were revealed in a letter from Eisenhower to General Ismay, dated 16 December 1942: 'Upon reaching here I sensed that every individual was suspicious of everybody else – every man was sure all others were crooks and liars. . . .' To counter this unwholesome atmosphere, Eisenhower explained that he had set out to establish for himself 'a reputation for the most straightforward, brutal talk that could be imagined . . . just a man too simple-minded to indulge in circumlocution. . . .'[5] It was an image that he would maintain successfully when he became President of the United States ten years later, and perhaps thus helped explain how, having passed through a formidable system of sentinels and passes, Macmillan was greeted coolly by Eisenhower, who asked him blankly 'what have you come for?' Macmillan recorded in his memoirs:

> I tried to explain that I thought my appointment had been arranged between the President and the Prime Minister. 'But I have been told nothing of it. You are a Minister, but what sort of Minister are you?' 'Well, General,' I said, 'I am not a diplomatic Minister; I am something worse.' 'There is nothing worse,' he replied.

To this, Macmillan ventured: 'Perhaps you will think a politician even more troublesome.' The General evidently did not disagree, and although Macmillan went on to explain that his role would be to relay the Prime Minister's feelings 'on anything that comes up', the conversation, he said 'began to languish'.

Either Macmillan's recollection is at fault here, or there had been a hiccup in communication between Washington and Algiers, or else the Americans were not being entirely ingenuous. When Macmillan reported to Churchill (on 9 January 1943) that Eisenhower had been 'very much nettled' by Britain's alleged failure to notify him of Macmillan's appointment, Anthony Eden scribbled plaintively in the margin of the letter, 'But we did notify.'[6] In *The Second World War*, Churchill published a telegram to Roosevelt dated 27 December 1942, in which he declared:

> the War Cabinet attach much importance to Macmillan's appointment and arrival [at Algiers]. We feel quite unrepresented there, yet our fortunes are deeply involved, and we are trying to make a solid contribution to your enterprise. Murphy's [Eisenhower's State Department adviser] appointment has already been announced, and I hope you will agree to my publishing Macmillan's.[7]

From the *War Diaries* of Oliver Harvey, not published until 1978, one learns that there had already been some controversy over Macmillan's appointment between Churchill and the Americans, with Eisenhower expressing reluctance to have Macmillan in North Africa looking after British interests, rather than having him attached to his own staff, like Robert Murphy. Harvey, who was then

Private Secretary to Eden, notes already on 20 December that this would have been 'an impossible position for a British Minister and would stultify him from the start. Roosevelt seems determined to keep us out of effective say in N. Africa. It is disquieting for the future of Anglo-American cooperation. I gather that even PM is becoming slightly peeved at the Presidential methods. . . .'[8] Churchill, however, had had to climb down after some argument, and finally agreed to send Macmillan officially only 'to assist' Murphy. None of this was vouchsafed to Macmillan, and it was all to make his road a stonier one in the early days.

This conflict in the record reveals the existence of potential schisms in this first joint Anglo-American operation, within a few weeks of the landings in North Africa. Thus Macmillan was at once thrown in at the deep end in his prime task of mediating and liaising between Churchill and Eisenhower (and behind him Washington and ultimately the all-powerful paraplegic in the White House).

After the coolness of his initial reception by Eisenhower, Macmillan says that he tried to thaw the ice by bringing up his American antecedents: '"My mother was born in Indiana," I said, "at a little town called Spencer. So I am a Hoosier."' Coming from the small town of Abilene in the nearby state of Kansas, Eisenhower received this disclosure with 'obvious pleasure, and after that we got on better'. In fact, Eisenhower then treated Macmillan to an hour's run-down on his political problems in Algiers. Chief of these were his dealings with the French, and the mauling he had received at the hands of the Anglo-American press for maintaining relations with the late Admiral Darlan, branded as a Vichy reactionary. He greatly resented this, and failed to understand 'why these long-haired, starry-eyed guys keep gunning for me. I'm no reactionary. Christ on the Mountain! I'm as idealistic as Hell,' Macmillan quoted him as saying.

Macmillan came to enjoy Eisenhower's forthright soldier's vocabulary. He felt that Ike's antipathy to having a British minister round his neck, 'who might make trouble for him in all sorts of ways', could be overcome. Indeed he was to be proved right; immediately after their first meeting, on 2 January 1943, Eisenhower wrote to the Combined Chiefs of Staff: 'Mister Harold Macmillan has just reported . . . and explained his mission in this theater. I am convinced that he will be most helpful and, since he is obviously concerned only with assisting me to the utmost, it appears that no further definition of his status, as requested in my 3670, is necessary.'[9]

From the C-in-C's office, Macmillan was led in to see his opposite number, Robert Murphy. A tall lanky Irish–American of about fifty, Murphy was – unlike Macmillan the politician – a career diplomat from the State Department. In the summer of 1940 he had been the Chargé d'Affaires of the American mission in unoccupied France, and in 1941 he had been the senior American diplomat in French North Africa, when he had skilfully handled the negotiations with the French authorities to minimise the opposition to the Allied landings in North Africa. As Eisenhower's political adviser, he had a direct line to Roosevelt, much as Macmillan did to Churchill, but he seems often to have been kept isolated from State Department lucubrations and suffered from the additional disadvantage of being (as Macmillan put it in a despatch to the Foreign Office) 'a prisoner of his past' with the French, in that he had served before the Allied landings in both Vichy and Algiers.

To begin with, Macmillan encountered with Murphy the same kind of 'awkwardness' that Eisenhower had shown; at this stage in the war, few Americans had had any personal dealings with the British, and mistrust was endemic. Macmillan determined to gain Murphy's confidence and to work as closely as possible with him – to the extent of ensuring that, when he obtained an office, it was next door to his American colleague.

In his memoirs Murphy would pay Macmillan the tribute that, although he had not brought to Algiers 'any exceptional knowledge of French or African affairs. What he did bring was exceptional common sense and knowledge of British politics. . . .' No American, he thought, would have suspected Macmillan's Midwest ancestry, but he respected the fact that 'in dignity, voice, manners, dress, and personality – [he] was and still is almost the American popular image of an English gentleman. . . .' He added, with more than a slight note of envy, that 'Macmillan's Government kept him better informed than my government did me.' In retrospect, Murphy recalled that more than once he had learned first from Macmillan of vital decisions taken in Washington, but praised the tact with which Macmillan always behaved towards him: 'his political weight in London was vastly greater than mine in Washington, but I cannot recall a single instance when he invoked this to swing the balance of opinion at Allied Force Headquarters.'[10]

Macmillan reciprocated Murphy's feelings, though he was occasionally less generous to him in private than in his published memoirs. In a despatch to the Foreign Office of 9 January, he remarked that Murphy was 'certainly over-worked and not very orderly in his methods. He is a diplomat and not an executive. . . .'[11] Whereas in his memoirs, Macmillan praised Murphy for his readiness 'to see both sides of a question', in his unpublished diaries he would, with some impatience, expose the reverse side of this attribute as 'an incurable habit of seeing every kind of person and agreeing with them all in turn'.[12] Nevertheless, over the long term, Macmillan agreed in general with Murphy's summing up of their relationship: 'We got along famously together.'

Speaking of his wartime relationship with the Americans in general Macmillan was very fond of remarking, with just a touch of cynicism, how it was preferable for the British always to play a secondary role, to be a deputy or a number two, while letting the US counterpart be number one; 'this way you could often get them to do what *you* wanted, while they persuaded themselves it was really all their idea!'[13] Richard Crossman, as Director of Psychological Warfare in Algiers, recalled Macmillan instructing him along precisely those lines, and then continuing on a theme that was equally to become a favourite hobby-horse of Macmillan's:

'We, my dear Crossman, are Greeks in this American empire. You will find the Americans much as the Greeks found the Romans – great big, vulgar, bustling people, more vigorous than we are and also more idle, with more unspoiled virtues but also more corrupt. We must run A.F.H.Q. as the Greek slaves ran the operations of the Emperor Claudius.'[14]

Again, some might find a trace of cynicism. But there was nothing cynical, contrived or disingenuous in Macmillan's new-found affinity for the Americans. Just as the requirements of the job did indeed bring out in him a remarkable capacity for the 'delicate diplomacy' noted by Bob Murphy, so contact with Americans seemed to bring out in Macmillan other characteristics that had lain dormant. Perhaps it was the genes of his mother finding an outlet; but in any event the vitality, spontaneous warmth, breezy informality and generosity endemic to the Americans among whom he now lived sparked off something in him. A new Macmillan, relaxed and at ease, more self-confident and less pompous, began to emerge; and this in turn undoubtedly contributed to the success of his relations with his US colleagues.

. . . And the French

Testing as they sometimes were, Macmillan's dealings in the Mediterranean with Britain's new ally were almost always enjoyable. The same could not be said of his dealings with her old ally, the French. The second of Macmillan's main tasks, coping with the French authorities in Algiers, and their labyrinthine intrigues, was to tax all his ingenuity. The trouble all stemmed from the political instability of France that had followed her crushing defeat in 1940, and the fact that the British and Americans had backed rival French horses, as well as having very different views on the political future of French North Africa.

When the Germans had overrun northern France in 1940, Marshal Pétain, as head of the defeated French, had made an armistice with Hitler and set up his headquarters for the unoccupied zone at Vichy. The Germans agreed at this armistice not to occupy the French African colonies so long as they remained loyal to Pétain, and they allowed a French army of 120,000 men to remain in North Africa. Pétain's Delegate-General in charge of Algeria, Morocco and Tunisia was Maxime Weygand and Pétain had instructed him to repel all invaders, be they Axis or Allied. After the fall of France, Britain had given her unwavering support to Charles de Gaulle and his Free Frenchmen, who were installed in London, whereas the Americans had recognised a multiplicity of French authorities: Marshal Pétain in Vichy, de Gaulle in London and those parts of the French African empire that had gone over to the Free French, and Admiral Robert in Martinique. This policy reflected Roosevelt's distrust of de Gaulle, his intent to assure the French people a free political choice after liberation, his desire not to provoke Pétain but coax him away from collaboration with the Germans, and his hope of keeping the Germans out of French North Africa.

As a result of their split policy, the Americans had also hoped, when they landed in Algeria under General Eisenhower in

Operation Torch on 8 November 1942, that the Vichy French troops would rally to the Allied cause. With this in mind, they had smuggled a senior French soldier, General Giraud, known as 'King-Pin', into Algeria before the landings. A tall and dapper, unmistakably French four-star general who had commanded the crack Seventh Army with distinction during the Battle for France in 1940, Giraud had recently escaped from the supposedly escape-proof German prisoner-of-war fortress of Königstein: the circumstances of this, and his subsequent 500-mile trek across Nazi-occupied Europe, conspicuous figure that he was, remain mysterious. Very privately, Macmillan would often express suspicions, because of the trouble that Giraud was to cause the Allies in North Africa: 'The Germans must have given him a railway ticket!'[15] Whatever his military qualifications, and bravery, King-Pin's political acumen was virtually nil, and what there was seemed orientated towards the narrow right wing. Diana Cooper described him unkindly, but accurately, as 'a more wooden Kitchener of Khartoum',[16] while Eisenhower had been infuriated by him when, at their first meeting, he 'even made a point of his *rank*. Can you beat it? Yet he's supposed to be the high-minded man that is to rally all North Africa behind him to save France.'[17] To his American mentor, Lieutenant-General Mark Clark, Giraud is also supposed to have confessed, 'I am not a politician. I am a soldier. All I want is the post of commander-in-chief.'[18]

And indeed this is what the Americans, carrying a reluctant Churchill with them, tacitly promised Giraud if he united the French troops behind him. Because poor Free French security had contributed to the failure of the attempt to seize Dakar in 1940, the Americans were adamant that de Gaulle should not be informed of Operation Torch until the landings had actually taken place; they considered him to be excessively political and therefore wished him to be kept out of the North African cauldron at all costs. Although he still championed de Gaulle, Churchill, reluctantly, acquiesced with Roosevelt, thereby inflicting a wound to de Gaulle's pride that would ever remain unhealed. In the event, Giraud turned out to be a busted flush. The army of North Africa did not follow his lead, and some of the Allied landings were fiercely opposed, costing the lives of over 500 Allied servicemen. This slowed up the drive eastwards, which in turn permitted the establishment of a Wehrmacht force in Tunisia before the Allies could get there.

The Americans were already feeling disillusioned over Giraud's performance, when they were faced with a new factor on the Algiers scene. Admiral Darlan, viewed by Churchill as a 'dangerous, bitter, ambitious man'[19] and a dedicated Anglophobe who – after Pétain – was the most senior figure in the Vichy government, had come to Algiers to visit his son, seriously ill with polio, on 5 November. The Allied landings three days later caught him there. Ever prone to play the Vichy card, and perhaps additionally influenced by sympathy because of his own suffering from polio, Roosevelt urged that the Allies dump Giraud (despite American undertakings to him) and back Darlan. But London, where Darlan was regarded as a dedicated foe, representing a regime which the British public despised, was outraged. Churchill's characteristic view of the whole issue was robustly stated in a message of support sent to Eisenhower on 14 November: 'Anything for the battle, but the politics will have to be sorted out later on.'[20]

Nevertheless, Churchill was subjected to bitter attack in England, and on 10 December called a Secret Session in the Commons to meet his critics. Here he made one of his greatest speeches, describing the French dilemma to the House of Commons on 10 December in magisterial terms which Macmillan would remember in all his dealings with de Gaulle over the next twenty years:

The Almighty in His infinite wisdom did not see fit to create Frenchmen in the image of Englishmen. In a State like France, which has experienced so many convulsions – Monarchy, Convention, Directory, Consulate, Empire, Monarchy, Empire and finally Republic – there has grown up a principle founded on the *droit administratif* which undoubtedly governs the action of many French officers and officials in times of revolution and change. It is a highly legalistic habit of mind. . . . Much therefore turns in the minds of French officers upon whether there is a direct, unbroken chain of lawful command, and this is held by many Frenchmen to be more important than moral, national, or international considerations. From this point of view many Frenchmen who admire General de Gaulle and envy him his role nevertheless regard him as a man who has rebelled against the authority of the French State, which in their prostration they conceive to be vested in the person of the antique defeatist who to them is the illustrious and venerable Marshal Pétain, the hero of Verdun, and the sole hope of France. . . .[21]

Churchill himself remarked of this speech that he could not remember any other 'where I felt opinion change so palpably and decisively'.

The outcry over Darlan was finally, and conveniently, stifled, when, two weeks later, he was assassinated by a twenty-year-old French youth, Bonnier de la Chappelle, with obscure motives. The Americans, with some embarrassment, were now forced to fall back on their first bedmate, Giraud, who received the imposing title of High Commissioner for French North and West Africa, and additionally that of Commander-in-Chief. From London de Gaulle promptly suggested coming to Algiers for discussions, but Giraud replied evasively, declaring that the time was not yet opportune. Another wound was inflicted on the *amour propre* of the proud Brigadier-General. And meanwhile, despite Montgomery's victory at El Alamein, the Germans were still in French North Africa, in strength.

Macmillan's first official duty, acting jointly with Robert Murphy in this intricate Franco-Anglo-American web, was to ask Giraud – in the name of Eisenhower – to remove from North Africa the French Royalist Pretender, the harmless Comte de Paris. Macmillan at once saw the historical irony of the situation: 'How strange it seemed, indeed how impudent, that Murphy and I should go to a French general to secure the expulsion from a French territory of the descendant of the longest line of kings in Europe.'

Casablanca

On 12 January, less than two weeks after his arrival, Macmillan received a telegram informing him that under the code-names of Admiral Q and Air Commodore F respectively, and supported by a vast court of generals and other notables, Roosevelt and Churchill were shortly to meet at a 'summit' conference in Casablanca. Macmillan and Murphy were summoned to attend: 'Certainly all this looked like being more fun than sitting at home in the impressive but dreary surroundings of Whitehall. I had been right to be patient; but this reward was something beyond my wildest dreams.'

Privately, Macmillan christened the two potentates 'the Emperor of the East and the Emperor of the West'; because it was indeed, he wrote in his diary, 'like a meeting of the later period of the Roman Empire'. He noted with regret, however, that the 'Red Emperor', Stalin, could not also have been in attendance. The 700-mile flight from Algiers in Eisenhower's personal Flying Fortress was an eventful one, with three out of its four engines breaking down in succession. In their encampment at Anfa, just outside Casablanca, Macmillan found the two emperors massively protected by guards with 'tommy guns and sawn-off shotguns and all sorts of weapons of that kind', he wrote to Dorothy.[22] On the evening of his arrival, Macmillan was called in to visit the Emperor of the West at his villa. There he found Roosevelt 'in a great bed on the ground floor. He was indeed a remarkable figure: the splendid head and torso full of vigour and vitality; below, concealed by the coverings, the terrible shrunken legs and feet. . . .' At the head of the bed sat Churchill, while Eisenhower stood rigidly to attention, which later provoked Macmillan (doubtless with that favourite image of Greeks and Romans somewhere at the back of his mind) to whisper to Murphy, 'Isn't he just like a Roman centurion!'[23]

Of his first encounter with Roosevelt, Macmillan recorded in his memoirs, 'The President was particularly charming to me. There was a great deal of joking.' This published statement seems, however, to have sweetened considerably the real impact Roosevelt made on him. 'He was a man to whom I took an immediate suspicion,' he remarked on more than one occasion subsequently: 'he threw up his hands when I walked in, and he said "Harold, I *am* glad to see you." Well, that was absolutely insincere. I had met him only once before, in America. . . . And to me that was displeasing. . . . He tried to charm everybody. . . . He lived on charm. . . . Even thought he could charm Stalin.'[24] Later Macmillan came to resent bitterly the ease with which his idol, Churchill, seemed to be taken in by this facility of Roosevelt's: 'Churchill had a certain naivety in his character. . . . He hated disbelieving in people. I don't think he realised how devious FDR could be. . . . To me he seemed false. . . .'[25]

If this excessive display of familiarity at their first meeting at Casablanca was to set Macmillan on his guard, it had a rather different effect on the Roman centurion. Obviously puzzled at the effusiveness – even by American standards of warmth – of his leader's greeting, Eisenhower remarked to Macmillan:

'You never told me you were a friend of the President's.' And I said, 'Well, I'm not really but we have some mutual friends and connections.' And he said 'I didn't know you were on Christian name terms with him.' And I said, 'I'm not. He is with me, but I'm not with him.' He said, 'Well, you're funny people, English people. If you'd been an American you would have told me this before.'[26]

In retrospect, Macmillan always reckoned that Eisenhower's appreciation of his never trying to exploit acquaintance with Roosevelt considerably enhanced his standing in the General's eyes. Before Casablanca, Macmillan felt that he had still been slightly kept at arm's length by Eisenhower, reluctant to have him on his staff in the first place, and treated rather as a subordinate official. From Casablanca began a real friendship and growing mutual affection between the two.

The overall purpose of the 'emperors'' meeting at Casablanca was to hammer out a future Allied war strategy, in its widest aspects. Admiral King, the American naval chief, wanted all resources switched to the Pacific, once North Africa had been cleared. The US Army Chief-of-Staff, General Marshall, urged the priority of an early build-up in Britain for an invasion of France; this in turn reflected Soviet pressures for a Second Front. The British supported a pursuance of operations in the Mediterranean, to knock Italy out of the war and liberate Greece. Here was a basic divergence of interests; to the Americans, the Mediterranean was but 'a temporary battleground and little more',[27] whereas to the British it was a vital route to the Middle East and India. The differences caused by these decisions of high policy agreed at Casablanca were later to involve Macmillan closely. During the conference, however, what preoccupied both himself and Murphy most was the problem of the French.

While ever loyal to his former chief, Murphy in his memoirs notes critically of Roosevelt at Casablanca that 'His mood was that of a schoolboy on vacation, which accounted for his almost frivolous approach to some of the difficult problems with which he dealt. . . .'[28] This frame of mind may in part have been accounted for by Roosevelt's delight in escaping from the hothouse atmosphere of wartime Washington, but in no way did it help in dealing with de Gaulle – whom at times he refused to take seriously. As Murphy also reveals, Roosevelt suffered additionally from the continuing disability of being unable quite to decide whether the Allies had 'occupied' or 'liberated' French Africa. In a letter to Murphy's office of 2 January 1943, he had declared: 'I feel very strongly that, in view of the fact that in North Africa we have a military occupation, our CG [Commanding General] has complete control of all affairs, both civil and military. Our French friends should not be permitted to forget this for a moment. . . . the French people will be able to settle their own affairs when the war ends. . . .'[29] This remained very much his attitude at Casablanca. Yet he was not even totally consistent here, chiding Murphy for having given a written pledge to Giraud before Torch that the USA would guarantee to return to France every part of her empire. Murphy recorded without enthusiasm that 'Roosevelt's intense personal interest in French affairs was not always helpful. . . . the President discussed replacement of French officials and changes in French laws in Africa as if these were matters for Americans to decide. . . .'[30] Basically Roosevelt remained steadfastly opposed to the creation of anything resembling a French 'provisional government'.

Enter de Gaulle

At Casablanca Roosevelt made it quite plain that he still regarded de Gaulle as just another French general – and a tiresome one at that. British relations with de Gaulle were, however, of quite a different order. While admitting what a 'difficult person' he was, Macmillan had stressed to Murphy how much de Gaulle's determination to carry on the fight against Nazi Germany had meant to Britain, at a time when the odds had seemed so hopeless:

> Macmillan declared that British self-interest and prestige and honour all demanded that the British government should support de Gaulle's political aspirations. The French leader was determined to push his own London Committee into the African administration, and Macmillan said that the British government felt bound to support that objective insofar as it could be satisfied without endangering military operations. . . .[31]

Churchill's own attitude to de Gaulle was always one of ambivalence and dilemma. The dilemma – and it assumed particularly large proportions in North Africa – was that, however much he supported de Gaulle's cause, when it came to a choice between that and his 'special relationship' with Roosevelt, the latter would take precedence. His personal feeling towards de Gaulle was one of true love–hate, varying from immense admiration to total exasperation. At the time of Casablanca it was exasperation that ruled. Within the British Cabinet the heaviest support for de Gaulle came from Anthony Eden, always a dedicated Francophile. But from now on in North Africa de Gaulle's most staunch defender was to be Harold Macmillan.

While at the Colonial Office in London, Macmillan had had two meetings with de Gaulle and had been impressed by him on each occasion. When once tackling the Prime Minister about being less intolerant of de Gaulle's 'prickliness', Macmillan recalled saying to him,

> 'Supposing Hitler and Sea Lion had succeeded and the King had fallen, but supposing we had got to America and made a government in exile there, what would you have thought it your duty to do to the Americans? To insult them at every point, and stand up for the past. . . . We would have felt it necessary to stand up and be *ultra* rigorous about the rights of the British Empire. . . .' He said, 'Yes, I see that. . . .'[32]

Macmillan had come to Algiers with an ignorance which had led to early blunders; first, he had raised no objections to Marcel Peyrouton, with an unsavoury past as Vichy's Minister of the Interior, staying on as Governor-General of Algeria; and secondly he had probably underestimated the problems of squaring the French circle. Yet he had gone to Casablanca with a scheme for a union between de Gaulle and Giraud which looked forward to the post-war world. Pierson Dixon, the Foreign Office official attached to Macmillan who could therefore be assumed to speak with Macmillan's voice when reporting back to London, wrote in January that whatever regime was set up in Algiers would inevitably be a pattern for the post-war government in France. Thus 'the Administration must be staffed by men of liberal ideas and must proceed in its acts upon liberal lines.'[33] As Macmillan then regarded Gaullism as being 'broadly a movement of the Left', it would provide an essential leavening to the ultra-conservatism of Giraud and his followers; for 'Neither America nor Great Britain wish to become the instrument for forcing a kind of junta of semi-fascist Generals into power.'[34] This was, essentially, to be the backbone of British policy over the next five months.

Macmillan and Murphy together put forward the scheme for a union based on joint political leadership between Giraud and de Gaulle. But Giraud at once objected that a four-star general could not serve side by side with a mere brigadier, and the whole project was thrown into jeopardy by the emperors deciding arbitrarily to summon de Gaulle to Casablanca from London. Macmillan had warned Churchill that de Gaulle might well resent being invited to French territory by two foreigners, and recommended that the invitation come instead through the offices of General Giraud. Nevertheless, to Churchill's rage, de Gaulle 'was very haughty and refused several times',[35] whereas Giraud had accepted an invitation to Casablanca at once. Churchill retorted on 18 January with a furious blast, to be suitably edited by Eden for onward transmission to de Gaulle:

> The fact that you have refused to come to the meeting proposed will in my opinion be almost universally censured by public opinion. . . . The position of His Majesty's Government towards your Movement while you remain at its head will also require to be reviewed. If with your eyes open you reject this unique opportunity we shall endeavour to get on as well as we can without you. The door is still open.[36]

In his covering message to Eden, he added 'Here I have been all these days fighting de Gaulle's battle. . . .' (In fact most of the 'fighting' seems to have been waged by Macmillan, trying to mollify his chief on de Gaulle's behalf.) Churchill concluded:

> If in his fantasy of egotism he [de Gaulle] rejects the chance now offered, I shall feel that his removal from the headship of the Free French Movement is essential to the further support of the movement by HMG. I have doubted very much whether we should go so far to give him a further chance, but this must really be the last. . . . I think for his own sake you ought to knock him about pretty hard.[37]

The 'knocking about' had some of the desired effect. On 22 January de Gaulle arrived in Casablanca, but was at his arrogant worst. At one point, rage provoked Churchill to shake his finger in de Gaulle's face and to lapse into his famous *franglais*: '*Mon Général, il ne faut pas obstacler la guerre!*' After a while, Roosevelt became even more impatient than Churchill with the endless intransigence of de Gaulle on what he considered to be points of principle. Draft after draft was framed by Murphy and Macmillan in an attempt to find a formula for French political union. It was typical of Giraud, who, observed Macmillan pungently, 'had no political sense or interest in larger issues, that he accepted each of them in turn without a murmur. It was equally typical of de Gaulle, whose purposes were highly political and whose suspicions had been thoroughly aroused, that he turned them down one after another.'[38] From seeing de Gaulle in action, Macmillan swiftly concluded that he would triumph eventually over General Giraud, who was so untutored in the craft of politics. Accordingly, for the remainder of the conference Macmillan fought tooth and nail to persuade both of the emperors to give de Gaulle another chance.

All through the night of 23 January, the last night of the historic conference, Macmillan and Murphy wrangled with de Gaulle in the President's villa, trying to extract a final communiqué announcing his willingness to set up a joint 'Comité de Guerre' with Giraud, a point which he had already conceded in principle. But, at the eleventh hour, de Gaulle jibbed again, stating in his memoirs that the draft communiqué 'had the triple disadvantage of being dictated by the Allies, of implying that I renounced whatever was not merely the administration, and last of pretending that we had reached an agreement, when in fact we had not'.[39] He declared to Macmillan that he would only give an oral 'agreement to agree'. On the edge of despair, Macmillan felt that only some public act could prevent de Gaulle backsliding again after the Conference adjourned. The British and American press had by this time assembled, to learn – to their amazement – for the first time of this meeting of the two emperors. Photographers were busy and, at Macmillan's instance, he and Murphy pushed the two French generals out into the limelight; there de Gaulle and Giraud, 'in a picture which went round the world, were seen to be shaking hands with the best approach to a smile that they could manage'. Roosevelt found the scene hilarious, and dubbed it henceforth 'the shotgun wedding', in which de Gaulle was the unwilling 'bride'.

Thus ended Casablanca. The British strategy, to gain first priority for the Mediterranean war, had been accepted; but perhaps of greatest historic consequence were the two words let slip by the Emperor of the West – 'Unconditional Surrender'.

Oliver Harvey confided in his diary, 'PM has come back even more anti-de Gaulle than when he left. . . . He now talks of breaking him. . . .'[40] The wayward General, however, received unexpected support from a high place to which Churchill was ever heedful; King George VI wrote in his diary, also on 9 February, '. . . I warned Winston not to be too hasty with de Gaulle. . . . I told Winston I could well understand de Gaulle's attitude. . . .'[41] Back in Algiers, Macmillan was also more sanguine about the future. Four days after Casablanca, he was reporting to Major Desmond Morton, Churchill's personal assistant: 'I think frankly the Americans would have liked to see the fall of de Gaulle. Although, in certain moods, the PM talked big about breaking him, I knew well that in his heart he was very anxious not to be forced to do so. . . . So he was really relieved when he came, and I think pleased at the modest degree of cooperation between the two French generals which was reached. . . .'[42]

In personal terms, Casablanca had fascinated Macmillan: 'Never had I mingled with this high political and military society or been made privy to such vast and enthralling issues. And all this in the first three weeks of my new appointment!' He might well have claimed, too, that at this first experience in high-level diplomacy he had acquitted himself with great distinction. On 4 February there arrived an accolade from Eden in London, praising his efforts for having 'contributed as much as anything to the progress made. Please accept my thanks and congratulations.'[43]

Macmillan now had to devote all his talents to winning over a reluctant Murphy (who had come away from Casablanca regarding de Gaulle as a 'Frankenstein Monster of which we ought to welcome the opportunity to rid ourselves . . .'),[44] as well as to thrusting the reluctant 'bride' and 'groom' into closer conjugal relations with each other. Hardly had he returned to Algiers than he found himself at the centre of a small storm which might have had grave repercussions on Anglo-American amity had it not been handled with utmost diplomatic skill. Macmillan in his memoirs calls it 'the Anfa mystery', after the Casablanca suburb where the conference had taken place.

Shortly after the emperors had departed, Macmillan had picked up an exchange between Bob Murphy and Harry Hopkins, Roosevelt's envoy-extraordinary, to the effect that there had been private negotiations between Roosevelt and General Giraud. The genesis of this, it transpired, had been a shadowy ultra-right-wing businessman with substantial vegetable-oil interests in North Africa, Jacques Lemaigre-Dubreuil. Before Casablanca, Lemaigre-Dubreuil had gone to Washington to lobby energetically on Giraud's behalf, and he had apparently succeeded in gaining a certain influence with Secretary of State Cordell Hull. Returning to Casablanca, Lemaigre-Dubreuil drafted a memorandum which he persuaded Giraud to take to Roosevelt on the last day of the conference, and endeavour to get his signature for it. In it the USA, *and Britain*, committed themselves to recognising that the French Commander-in-Chief in Algiers would be invested with 'the right and duty of preserving all French interests in the military, economic, financial and moral plane'.[45] By implication this plenipotentiary would be Giraud; no mention was made of de Gaulle.

This memorandum appears not to have been seen by Murphy, and certainly not by Macmillan or any of the British delegation. But, acting on suspicion, three days later Macmillan managed to smoke out from Murphy two documents based on the Lemaigre-Dubreuil memorandum which had been approved by Roosevelt. One contained the loaded words: 'it was agreed between the President of the United States, the Prime Minister of Great Britain and General Giraud that it was their common interest for all the French fighting against Germany to be reunited under one authority, and that every facility would be given to General Giraud in order to bring about this reunion.'[46]

Macmillan refused to believe Churchill could have agreed to such 'misleading and indefensible' phrases, which would have placed Giraud firmly in the saddle. He insisted that they should be referred back to London – where they were repudiated with 'emotion and even anger'. After an interval of some four months the documents were rephrased in innocuous terms, giving de Gaulle equal standing with Giraud. To cause the Americans the least possible embarrassment, it was suggested that Roosevelt had been guilty solely of carelessness, not taking in the full significance of what he was signing. But Macmillan in his memoirs many years later condemned it as a 'reprehensible action on Roosevelt's part, and the use of

Churchill's name was unpardonable.' In private he went even further, evincing it as an example of Roosevelt's 'deviousness' and of trying to put one over on Churchill. Macmillan's alertness here undoubtedly averted far-reaching consequences for the Allies, while his diplomatic skill prevented charges of ill-faith escalating into a rift between them. When de Gaulle, however, eventually got wind of the Anfa documents, it only hardened his mistrust of US intentions.

Macmillan continued to press de Gaulle's cause as well as the need for a unified French authority. On 20 February, William Strang of the Foreign Office was reporting to Eden what clearly represented the forward thinking of Macmillan: 'The French Empire should be an ally in every sense of the word; French armies should participate in the reconquest of France; and France should be present at the victory. For the future, we should hope that France would be a strong and independent power, acting with Russia and ourselves for the containment of Germany.'[47] He was able to add, 'General Eisenhower agrees generally with our views, and it now appears that Mr Macmillan is bringing Mr Murphy round.' Eden appended an 'I agree' to the memorandum.

At this point, however, an accident occurred which nearly brought the Resident Minister's career to an untimely end. On 21 February, at Churchill's instance, Macmillan flew off to Egypt on another intricate mission involving the French, accompanied by John Wyndham and a French admiral with his staff. A powerful French battlefleet had been 'neutralised' at Alexandria since the fall of France. Its commander, Admiral Godfroy, had consistently refused to accept orders from anyone but Pétain; now, with the German occupation of unoccupied France, which had followed the Allied landings in North Africa, Macmillan's task was to persuade Godfroy to hand over his ships to the Allies in North Africa. However, the plane, a small unconverted Hudson bomber, failed to take off from Algiers airport, crashed and caught fire at the end of the runway. Macmillan, trapped in the co-pilot's seat, had considerable difficulty in extricating himself through the overhead escape hatch.

Characteristically both he and John Wyndham subsequently made light of the episode, Macmillan writing in his diary about the difficulty of 'middle-aged and rather portly publishers, encumbered by the weight of their own dignity and a large green Ulster overcoat, trying to spring through a smallish hole about the height of their head. . . .'[48] John Wyndham was to recall his chief's moustache 'burning with a bright blue flame',[49] while Macmillan fabricated a good story out of how the French Admiral had walked up and down on the tarmac, wailing: '"Ma casquette; ma casquette! J'ai perdu ma casquette." To this lament, I replied, or so it was alleged, "I don't care a damn about your casquette. J'ai perdu my bloody face."'

In fact Macmillan's burns were extremely serious, his eyesight possibly saved only by his glasses, and he seems to have behaved with conspicuous courage. John J. McCloy, Roosevelt's Assistant Secretary of War, had been sent out to bolster Murphy and had landed at Algiers at the instant Macmillan's plane crashed. Seeing the burning plane, he had run over to see if he could help: 'They said "there's a fellow going back into the plane" – It was Macmillan going back . . . to get out a Frenchman. It was the most gallant thing I've ever seen, and I'd been in the first war and seen plenty of gallantry then. . . .' A few days later he visited Macmillan in hospital, on official business, and found his face completely covered in a plaster cast, like some member of the Ku Klux Klan:

> All he had was a space for his mouth and eyes – talking through this hole about the Darlan Jewish decrees. I was at a complete loss, because I couldn't see his expression, I couldn't see whether he was laughing or serious. . . . the next time I saw Macmillan was at the Cairo Conference – of course, I didn't recognise him, until some ADC pushed a note to me: 'Why are you cutting me?!' I was always lost in admiration for Macmillan from that moment onward; his name to me connoted courage.[50]

Concussed, Macmillan seems to have imagined he was in the Somme clearing hospital of 1916, and his first thought was to ask that a message be sent to his mother, now seven years dead – rather than to his wife. His face and lips permanently bore the mark of the burns. He was in bed a week, then – against the advice of his doctors – insisted on flying on again to Cairo to complete his mission, still covered in bandages. Finally, by August 1943 the French warships successfully reached French North Africa, after sailing round the Cape.

By a curious coincidence, Macmillan was in hospital simultaneously with Churchill, knocked down by pneumonia as a result of the strain of his North African trip. While Macmillan distracted himself with Gibbon, Churchill recalled reading *Moll Flanders* in bed; such was their difference in literary taste! From his hospital bed, Macmillan wrote a relaxed and chatty letter to Eden, expressing detached amusement at French intrigues and full of enthusiasm about his work:

> I feel so happy to be out of it [backbiting in the Commons] and so sorry for you. The purely Balkan politics we have here are more to my liking. If you don't like a chap, you don't deprive him of the whip. . . . You just say he is a Monarchist, or has plotted to kill Murphy, and you shoot him off to prison or a Saharan concentration camp. Then a week or two later, you let him out and make him Minister for something or other. It's really very exhilarating. . . .
>
> P.S. The French have two great words here, which they use perpetually. Everything is 'indispensable', and that means they make no effort to do it. Or else it is 'inadmissible'. That means they do it all the time.

He also thanked Eden for having sent him 'a most excellent assistant in Roger Makins. I find it hard to live up to his very high standard of work; and I am afraid I shock him sometimes. But he has a very good sense of humour, and is in every way most reliable. . . .'[51]

News from Home

Following his accident, Macmillan telegrammed Dorothy in Sussex in much the same vein as he wrote to his mother a generation and a war earlier:

> Please send immediately in bag black walking shoes from flat, also brown ditto from home, also brigade tie [his only concession to the uniform he had declined to wear], also handkerchiefs, also two ordinary day shirts and collars, also two or three suits underwear, also dressing gown, bedroom slippers from home and one pair pyjamas. Also bath sponge. We have all had a wonderful

escape and I am only one even slightly injured. Alas my poor coupons.*[52]

On 23 February, Dorothy wrote back in a similarly matter-of-fact manner:

My dear Harold,
I was very disturbed this morning to hear of your accident . . . we all wonder where you were going in your aeroplane! They really are horrible things.
Love, Dorothy[53]

During these early days apart while Macmillan was establishing himself in Algiers, their correspondence had continued on a more or less weekly basis; his in the form of a diary, rather as he had written to Nellie Macmillan in the First World War, and possibly with a view to future publication. Eventually published when he was ninety,[54] in retrospect, the diaries provide a vivid and immediate picture of the war, while they also reveal much more of the man than emerges from his own volume of memoirs of the period. They show a man of courage, energy and shrewd pragmatism, almost always good-tempered and optimistic, and with a new self-confidence as he took his biggest single leap towards No. 10. He wrote with the humour and unaffected relish for description of the true diarist (flying over the endless Sahara he summed it up as 'so much bunker and not enough fairway'). While writing its eight hundred pages, a marked stylistic improvement from his writings of the 1930s, he somehow also found time (as in the trenches of the First World War) to read the works of some forty of his own favourite authors, and in addition to explore a Greek or Roman ruin whenever time permitted.

Dorothy's letters, on the other hand, were fewer and full of domestic news – long, chatty and friendly, but somewhat detached and impersonal. On 5 February, before his accident, she had written: 'It's fantastic at home. The yellow crocuses are out, the Japonica in flower, the daffodils right up, catkins in flower. . . . I hope the socks are allright. Is there anything else you want?' On 9

* During the Second World War clothing was strictly rationed, and purchasable only in exchange for coupons.

February, her letter of greetings on his forty-ninth birthday referred to Casablanca: '. . . I should think your last visit from the PM must have been great fun. I am told that he is delighted with you and thinks you are doing amazingly well. . . . all of which is very satisfactory.' Five days later she was chatting:

> I am trying to teach myself to type so I hope you won't mind me practising on you. . . . it has to me several drawbacks; I find it very much more difficult to spell, and therefore find myself saying things quite different to what I mean to. Also typing things give [sic] away one's bad English much more than writing. . . . Blake is anxious lest the pheasants start laying too soon. He says the partridges are pairing now. He is also nervous lest we have not left sufficient cocks. Blake is always full of fears of some sort, so I expect all is well really. He suspects Aron, one of the remaining Czech refugees of poaching. . . . Both your old bosses seem to be giving tongue a good deal. Beaverbrook sounds as if he is getting a bit restless, critiseing (I never could spell that) Aircraft Production a good deal . . . Herbert Morrison makes weekly vast orations. I suppose he is out to be PM one day. . . .[55]

On 24 February, Macmillan was writing back from hospital, expressing concern about how Dorothy was going to manage without a cook in wartime Sussex – 'You will have to get Nanny back again' – and fretting that Carol, the oldest daughter, might marry out of boredom 'some terrible poop in order not to be an ATS [Auxiliary Territorial Service; Women's Army]. . . . it really is very hard on girls of her age. . . . Perhaps she had better come out on our staff here – then she could marry John, which would be very agreeable, for he already treats me like a father. . . .' He complained about the hospital routine: '. . . I am getting a little too old. . . . I do *not* like to go to sleep at 9 pm and be woken at 6 am. Nor do I like prunes and rice.'[56]

Having finally got to Cairo, he enjoyed describing to Dorothy the incongruous scenes on the roads there:

> first you pass a flock of sheep, with lots of black and white lambs. Next comes a General, in a Humber; next a herd of goats, usually black – sometimes black and white – with lots of kids. Next

perhaps an Egyptian or European magnate in a Rolls Royce, then lots of camels, with men precariously perched on their backs; then a water-buffalo and calf being led out to pasture; then a cow or two and some calves. Altogether an extraordinary mixture of more or less biblical scenes and modern life.[57]

His letters to Dorothy over the following months show a typical father's concern about his children. There is more worry in March about Carol not receiving a large enough allowance to enable her to live in London: '. . . I feel so distressed about her and feel I have muddled her career. But really this horrible war has upset everything so badly. . . .' In April he was worrying about Catherine: 'She should persevere with her art, but of course (*like me*) she is naturally lazy. It takes time to learn how to work and it was always a great effort for me when I was young. Gradually one gets the habit of it. But I still do like loafing.' And later, in July: 'She is really a very strange child – very like Maurice. I am afraid this excessive introspection and interest in herself is inherited from her Father and his family. . . . I don't know why I write like this, but I feel most of my letters (like Catherine's) are terribly egotistical. So I feel I must tell you how much I think about you all. . . .'[58]

The same files at Birch Grove also contain many loving letters from twelve-year-old Sarah about horses and school. Either Sarah and Macmillan wrote more to each other, or else more of her letters were kept; whichever way, it seems indicative of special affection, even though – on Harold's part – also inhibited. His letters are those of a man not knowing quite what to say to a twelve-year-old girl, with love constantly struggling to break through. On 28 January, he wrote, for example, from Algiers: 'this is a funny place. It is very hot in the day and very cold in the night. The sun is quite lovely, and so are the flowers.'[59]

The letters between Harold and Dorothy at this time, now in their twenty-third year of marriage, suggest a couple who have come to terms with their marital problems. He missed her, and clearly longed for her to join him. Occasionally, when his spirits were low and in company with very intimate friends, he would let his hair down and reveal the still unhealed misery about his wife's continuing relationship with Bob Boothby. But, by 1943, on the whole the anguish seems to have abated; there being no greater opiate than the unrelenting pressure of work, and the fascinating times he was living through in North Africa.

For female company Macmillan seems to have depended largely on his loyal and efficient secretary, Miss Campbell of the comic hats, who stayed with him right through to the end of the war. Following his plane crash, he was dictating to her from his bed: 'She seemed not to be too terrified by my appearance, which is now frightful, as my lips are just about to come off, revealing (I hope) a sort of Cupid's bow behind, that will be very attractive. . . .'[60] And on 29 July he was reporting:

> Miss C and Miss Williams remain excellent workers. The Sergeant-Archivist is in love with Miss W and since this passion seized him has neglected his work. Fortunately this is done by a large, plain, red-faced and red-armed girl who has arrived recently and is very good. I suppose she will soon be a spoilt beauty in Algiers, where there is a definite shortage and therefore a correspondingly enhanced value put upon feminine society. . . . But I must turn to graver themes more worthy of a Resident Minister.[61]

Of the many glamorous French ladies and American women war correspondents, some who doubtless tried to captivate the now influential grass-widower, he wrote with characteristic amused detachment: 'My neighbour at lunch is a lady of great sprightliness and charm, Comtesse de Rose – a brunette, who fascinates us all here and is (in a society very lacking in women) the universal standby at all our parties. She is coy, *espiegle*, captivating – and not too clean. But there it is; *on fait de son mieux*.'[62]

Macmillan Saves de Gaulle

On 12 June 1943, Dorothy wrote a letter in which her earthy common sense managed to encapsulate the principal headaches that Macmillan had had to face over the four and a half months since Casablanca: 'One wonders if it will ever be possible for these two generals to agree about anything. . . . It would surely be possible to get many of the things de Gaulle wants if he was a little more tactful. In point of fact, I suppose he wants everything, but should he have it?. . . .'[63] During this time Macmillan had had to fight, not on two but on three fronts: to press Giraud to make his administration more liberal and purge it of Vichyite influences; to make de Gaulle less intransigent; and finally to protect him from the wrath of Churchill and Roosevelt. The endless bickering between the French leaders was also having its demoralising impact on their juniors. In the spring of 1943, a young French officer, Jules Roy, recalled how 'When I rushed to Algiers to discover how long it would be before we would have our weapons, I returned crushed. Generals and politicians were fighting among themselves and attempted their own little revolutions within government and military headquarters. . . .'[64]

Macmillan was helped by the favourable turn the war was taking in North Africa; in February Montgomery's victorious Eighth Army had reached Tunisia and by April it had linked up with Eisenhower's Anglo-American forces pushing eastwards. It was clear to any Frenchman that the days of Vichy and its servants were numbered. Nevertheless, although the shotgun wedding between the two generals had formally taken place at Casablanca, there was no sign yet of the honeymoon. By May, an exasperated Roosevelt was suggesting to Churchill that de Gaulle be sent off as Governor to Madagascar. Had it been seriously meant, Churchill might well have been happy enough to acquiesce. Repeatedly, it was left to Macmillan to pick up the pieces. On one occasion, he took the responsibility on himself, in the absence of Eisenhower, to recommend to Churchill that de Gaulle not be permitted to make a premature trip to Algiers – for his own good. On another, later, occasion it was Macmillan who persuaded Eisenhower to disregard an order from Roosevelt to have de Gaulle sent back to London. Macmillan himself at times became infuriated by de Gaulle's hauteur. The two code-names alternately used for him seemed curiously apt – 'Wormwood' and 'Ramrod'. Of the latter, Macmillan remarked years later, with some acidity, that it recalled 'a man who was alleged to have all the rigidity of a poker without its occasional warmth'.[65] Even de Gaulle remembered Macmillan 'violently irritated, crying "If General de Gaulle refuses the hand which is stretched out to him you must know that America and Great Britain will abandon him altogether and that he will not be anything any more."'

Privately, in his despatches to Churchill, Macmillan tended to express a little more confidence that external influences would make de Gaulle more disposed to be reasonable in the long run. During one of the worst crises with de Gaulle in early May, Macmillan portrayed him reassuringly as simply one of those 'difficult' race horses 'which either refuse to come to the starting gate at all, or insist in careering down the course before the signal is given, or suddenly elect to run on a racecourse different from the one appointed by the Stewards of the Jockey Club.' He knew Churchill well enough to appreciate how much the imagery of the turf would appeal to him.

In contrast, Macmillan regarded Giraud as an 'old-fashioned, but charming colonel, who would grace the Turf Club'. He came to like him, despite his hopelessness as a political animal; 'he is really so nice and also so stately and stupid.'[66] For Giraud's own obstinacy towards union with the Gaullists, and tardiness to purge the reactionaries from his own ranks, Macmillan – in the intimacy of his diaries – largely blamed the shortcomings of Bob Murphy. On 23 April, he was writing: 'My American colleague is very difficult to handle. He seems to be without any fixed purpose and is affected by every change of mood of local opinion or Washington rumour.'[67] And three days later: 'My colleague Murphy is back at his old tricks and trying to impede the union [of de Gaulle and Giraud] without quite consciously admitting (even to himself) that he is doing so. . . . The position of these negotiations is becoming very acute because Giraud is turning stubborn. I am convinced that this is because he believes that he can rely on American support.'[68] To counterbalance this State Department line, Macmillan came to rely – and with evident success – on his burgeoning personal friendship with Eisenhower, who, when required, could bring the considerable weight of the Allied military machine in Algiers to bear on Giraud.

Amid all this turmoil, Macmillan unexpectedly acquired an invaluable ally in Jean Monnet, a cosmopolitan French business-man who had been sent to Washington to work on the Allied Purchasing Council. There he earned considerable respect in high places, and at the end of February 1943 he was sent by Roosevelt to Algiers with the ostensible task of supervising arms shipments to the French forces, as promised at Casablanca. In this he obviously wielded great power, but he also achieved the unique distinction of gaining the confidence of both de Gaulle and Giraud. Macmillan (in his memoirs) would say that 'France owes much to Jean Monnet.

His work at Algiers was absolutely vital to any solution. He was the lubricant, or even catalyst, between the two bitterly opposing factions. . . .'

Almost immediately, Macmillan and Monnet established an identity of aims. Both looked far beyond the immediate problem of de Gaulle versus Giraud to the need for a strong France in post-war Europe, and both agreed that this was one of the most important issues facing Britain's wartime foreign policy. They also agreed on the priority of creating a provisional French government, as a political rather than a military entity, able to speak on equal terms with the US and British governments. Although he did not like de Gaulle, and viewed his long-term ambitions with mistrust, Monnet soon came to share Macmillan's view that he was the only figure around which such an administration could be shaped. But Monnet felt strongly that Cabinet responsibility, not personal autocracy, was essential: once metropolitan France was liberated, it was imperative that there be free elections. Macmillan and Monnet prepared the framework of union between Giraud and de Gaulle on this basis.

By the end of April, something like an agreement had been reached. On 4 May, however, from London de Gaulle launched a blistering attack on Giraud's regime, of which Monnet said in a letter to Harry Hopkins that it reminded him 'of the speeches that Hitler made before the Czecho-Slovakian affair'.[69] For a time it looked as if the whole British policy was on the brink of collapse, with Giraud threatening to break off negotiations. Once again it fell to Macmillan to smooth down ruffled feathers.

At this time his somewhat battered morale was considerably restored by words of praise from Admiral Cunningham, the greatly respected British naval commander in the Mediterranean. 'Minister,' he said, '. . . You have made a striking success here, far greater than I thought possible. You have raised British prestige enormously. Do not worry about your trouble. I should certainly find it necessary to say that if you are not supported at home, I could not continue to command the Mediterranean fleet.'[70] Too modest to repeat this in his memoirs, Macmillan added in his diary: 'This was half-serious and half-joking, but rather nice all the same.'

Persuading Giraud that it was absurd to break off negotiations just because 'one politician made an offensive remark about another', he drafted for him an adroitly worded despatch to send to de Gaulle. In it were stated two key principles for the future French Committee for National Liberation, which Macmillan had drawn up with Monnet: Cabinet *not* personal government; and observance of the terms of the French constitution that provided for the re-establishment of a legal government in post-war France. This in effect meant extracting from de Gaulle a public undertaking that he would not seek to impose a personal dictatorship after the liberation. If de Gaulle accepted these two principles, then he could come to Algiers; if not, he must stay in London.

On 13 May all Axis troops in Tunisia surrendered to General Alexander, and de Gaulle realised he now had no option but to give in and accept the Macmillan–Monnet terms. The surrender meant that Africa was at last clear of the Axis; after El Alamein, here was the second great victory for the Western Allies in the Second World War. At no subsequent time would British arms play so preponderant a role in the victory, nor did British prestige ever stand higher. It was a source of particular pride to Macmillan, and he records with a glow how a week later – through the courtesy of Eisenhower – he and Bob Murphy were among the few civilians to stand on the saluting base at the great victory parade held in Tunis.

Tactfully, Eisenhower had a resplendently uniformed Giraud placed at his side, and the parade was headed by French Spahis, magnificent with their white horses and red cloaks. They were followed by a large American contingent which – in the eyes of Montgomery's Eighth Army that had been slogging across Africa for the past three years – looked almost indecently well heeled. But, according to Macmillan, the real surprise of the day came from the British, who had made a major effort of stage-management. Pipers collected from the whole of the British First and Eighth Armies, all the Highland regiments, the Scots Guards, the Irish Guards, led the troops in desert-stained battle-kit, slow-marching past the saluting base. There was 'hardly a dry eye of the older ones amongst us. . . . at that moment they were masters of the world.'[71] To Macmillan, Eisenhower was ecstatic in his admiration of the British contingent. Returning to Algiers in the Commander-in-Chief's plane, as they flew over the first convoy to attempt the Mediterranean passage since 1941, Macmillan remarked to Eisenhower: '"There, General, are the fruits of your victory." He turned to me and said, smiling through his tears, for he was deeply moved, "Ours, you mean, ours – that we have all won together."' It was a peak in Anglo-American concord, perhaps not to be attained again until the honeymoon between Kennedy and Macmillan himself two decades later.

There was a light note struck at the ending of all the magnificence, when into Eisenhower's departing aeroplane an emissary from the new Bey of Tunis tossed to Macmillan and Murphy two gaudy decorations, the Tunisian 'Medal to be Proud Of', First Class. Noting that the colours coincided with the MCC's, Macmillan sent his back to Birch Grove, where Lady Dorothy promptly relegated it to the children's dressing-up cupboard. There then ensued a long correspondence with pompous Foreign Officials, who pointed out that it should be returned since ministers were not permitted to accept decorations from other powers. (Macmillan seems to have had a predilection both for foreign orders and for teasing officialdom about it, with a gaudy miscellany of decorations and sheikhs' daggers 'disappearing' into the unfathomable dressing-up cupboard during the course of his career.)

After the 'grand day' in Tunis, Macmillan, to ensure that there would be no reneging by de Gaulle this time, decided to fly to London on 21 May. For the flight Eisenhower loaned Macmillan a B–17 Flying Fortress, with the cordial farewell: 'Come back as soon as you can. I don't want to be without you.' Macmillan had not misjudged the need for urgency. Unless his mission to London was successful, he reflected, the '. . . Gaullists and Giraudists, now that there are no Germans to fight, will soon start a civil war amongst themselves . . .'.

While in London Macmillan saw a telegram from Churchill in Washington, where he reported 'a very stern mood' about de Gaulle. For the umpteenth time, Roosevelt was pressing Churchill to break with de Gaulle forthwith. On the 23rd, a lengthy despatch was sent from Eden to Churchill, bearing the unmistakable imprint of Macmillan, and urging the Prime Minister to reconsider, on the grounds that the union was nearer than it had been at any time; that there was no likelihood of any of the present members of the French National Committee continuing to function if General de Gaulle were removed; and that there was a danger that, if de Gaulle were driven out of public life at this moment, they would not only make him a national martyr but would find themselves accused, by both Gaullists and Giraudists, of interfering improperly in French internal affairs – with a view to treating France as an Anglo-American protectorate.

Not for the first, or the last, time Macmillan had saved de Gaulle. He had also stuck his neck out with Churchill, by suggesting that agreement over French union was closer than it really was. Everything depended on his now being able to deliver the goods. On 29 May, Ramrod and his entourage left London; de Gaulle himself gave this shameless account of the leave-taking: 'Mr Eden good-humouredly said: "Do you know that you have caused us more difficulties than all our other European allies put together?" "I don't doubt it," I replied, smiling also, "France is a great power."'[72]

In Algiers the reception accorded de Gaulle, orchestrated by Macmillan and very different from that at Casablanca four months earlier, certainly helped support this claim. He arrived in a French plane; General Giraud was at the airport, with a French guard of honour, and a band played the 'Marseillaise'; American and British officials stood *behind* the French, and finally de Gaulle was driven off in a French car. In a letter to Dorothy of 31 May, Macmillan wrote:

> General de Gaulle's mood seemed to vary from comparative calm to extreme excitability. He was clearly very hostile both to the Americans and, to a somewhat less extent, to the British. In the course of conversation he observed that the Anglo-Saxon domination of Europe was a mounting threat, and that if it continued, France after the war would have to lean towards Germany and Russia. Monnet still finds it difficult to make up his mind as to whether the General is a dangerous demagogue or mad or both.[73]

When one considers de Gaulle's policies of two decades later, the penultimate sentence seems to convey more the thoughts of a prophet than of a madman.

On 1 June Murphy and Macmillan called on de Gaulle, who gave his views on the character a French administration should assume. On this occasion, recorded Macmillan, 'de Gaulle was at his best, and my colleague was much impressed. He set out his deep feelings in a powerful and even noble way. Naturally there were some harsh phrases. But it was clear to us both that here was a more powerful character than any other Frenchman in or outside France.' In vivid terms he described the moral revolution going on in France, as a consequence of the terrible humiliation of 1940. Murphy was clearly moved; then, as the meeting broke up, de Gaulle took his arm and said: 'Why do you not understand me? Why do you always interfere with me? It is a mistake France will not understand, why your politicians are against me. I represent future France, and it will be better for us all if you support me.'[74]

The following afternoon Macmillan met de Gaulle alone to discuss last-minute hitches in the path to union (Giraud having just threatened to resign, alleging fears of a Gaullist coup), and de Gaulle assured Macmillan that he would create no further difficulties. Delighted, Macmillan asked if he might speak 'quite frankly' to him, and 'whether he would mind my speaking in English as it would be easier'. (Many years later, in their complex negotiations over the Common Market, the question of Macmillan's command of French when speaking to de Gaulle without interpreters was to raise some speculation.) His oratory rising to the exalted sphere to which de Gaulle's speeches so often aspired, Macmillan then told him of his First World War experiences, as an appeal to the emotions which he would not be above resorting to at various crises in his later political career. He related how '. . . I had been wounded on French soil on three occasions; I had lost many of my best and dearest friends. . . . We formed an affection for France which had never been broken. . . .' His appeal cannot have been lost on de Gaulle, who had also been wounded (and taken prisoner) in 1916. Macmillan went on to suggest that the Frenchman's views on social matters were probably very similar to his own. After the war, he foresaw that: 'Great wealth would pass away. Property would be regarded as a trust, for the general benefit. We hoped to see the transformation from one society to another without revolution or disturbance, and it depended in my country as in his, on whether men of progressive opinions could work together and inspire the necessary changes.'

He begged for patience and for him not to miss this opportunity to join honourably with Giraud in the proposed union. He then dangled the broadest of hints in front of de Gaulle: 'I felt sure that as the weeks and months went by he could, without straining the law, or acting in any way unconstitutionally, obtain for himself and those who were with him the reality of power.' Macmillan recorded that the General listened politely and attentively, remarking that he had always felt that Macmillan understood him.

De Gaulle Wins

The impact of Macmillan's words must have been considerable – equally his ultimate intervention with Giraud. Despite more last-minute hitches, on 3 June, the long-awaited French Committee of National Liberation (FCNL) was finally formed. Its function was 'to exercise French sovereignty' and 'to direct the French war effort in all its forms and all places', and de Gaulle and Giraud were to serve as its Joint Presidents. In Algiers to discuss plans for the coming invasion of Sicily, Churchill and Eden were on hand to witness the final consummation of the shotgun wedding arranged at Casablanca. After six months of intrigues, manoeuvrings and exhausting negotiations, French unity had finally been established. On 5 June, de Gaulle wrote Macmillan a letter expressing what was perhaps the nearest Ramrod could come to gratitude: '. . . I would like to tell you how much I appreciated the action which you have exercised here in the name of the government of which you are a part, and to what point your sympathy is precious to me, which permits me also to call it our friendship. . . .'[75]

But this was by no means the end of 'the French problem'. In the first place, the FCNL had to gain respectability through official Anglo-American recognition, the mere fact of which was obviously galling to French pride. The opening plays of the FCNL were not auspicious. On 7 June General Giraud signed a series of decrees which – to Robert Murphy – was tantamount to having 'practically signed away all his powers to de Gaulle'. When Murphy pointed this out to him, 'as sympathetically as I could', the politically inept soldier exclaimed: 'But I was never told that!'[76] A few days later, Giraud threatened resignation, but, in the usual Algiers paradox, it was de Gaulle who actually resigned. Using all his diplomacy, and urging patience, Macmillan eventually coaxed him back, while at the same time having to mollify a still-sceptical Churchill, powerfully influenced by a relentlessly hostile Roosevelt. On 11 June, Macmillan received a signal from Churchill questioning the wisdom of early recognition, and referring him to Matthew vii, verse 16: 'Ye shall know them by their fruits. Do men gather grapes of thorns, or figs of thistles?' Macmillan, the scholar, could not resist retorting: 'See Revelations, chapter ii, verses 2–4 inclusive . . . "I know thy works, and thy labour, and thy patience and how thou canst not bear them which are evil. . . . Nevertheless I have somewhat against thee, because thou has left thy first love. . . ." '[77] On receiving this audacious riposte, and checking the biblical reference, Churchill flew into a rage, but then evidently saw the humour of the allusion.

Strongly backed by Macmillan, Churchill countered Roosevelt's opposition with resort to mild sophistry:

> What does recognition mean? One can recognise a man as Emperor or as a grocer. Recognition is meaningless without a defining formula. . . . Macmillan tells us repeatedly that the Committee is acquiring a collective authority and that de Gaulle is by no means its master . . . he strongly recommends a measure of recognition.[78]

Two days later Churchill was still vexedly complaining of de Gaulle to Macmillan: 'Why can he not be a patriot, and sink his personal vanity and ambition? Then he might find friends who would recognise the good that is in him.'[79]

In mid-June King George VI visited Algiers and presented Macmillan with a first-class diplomatic conundrum. The Prime Minister had advised, in rather governessy terms, that he should not invite the French to lunch with the King unless they were 'behaving well'. Were they? asked George VI. 'No, Sir,' replied Macmillan. 'Some have resigned; others are threatening resignation. I can't say that they are behaving well.' Nevertheless, he urged the King to hold the lunch on the grounds that 'it may do good, and it can do no harm.' The King laughed, and – according to Macmillan – the lunch party was a 'great success'.

Afterwards Macmillan told de Gaulle that he planned to spend the afternoon motoring to Tipasa to bathe, on which de Gaulle asked if he could accompany him. So, for three and a half hours, the two drove, strolled through the magical Roman ruins, and talked together 'on every conceivable subject – politics, religion, philosophy, the Classics, history (ancient and modern) and so on. All was more or less related to the things which fill his mind.' Then Macmillan went and bathed naked in the sea, while 'de Gaulle sat in a dignified manner on a rock, with his military cap, his uniform and belt. . . .' Many years later he could still remember 'with pleasure' that afternoon 'with this strange – attractive and yet impossible – character'.

On 2 July, Giraud, invited by Roosevelt, left for the US – rashly as it turned out. Roosevelt reckoned that a glittery reception in the White House would give Giraud irresistible panache in Algiers, but in fact, in Giraud's absence, it left the field there wide open to de Gaulle. By the end of July, de Gaulle agreed to a new compromise – wisely, in that it was greatly to his advantage. While he and Giraud were to continue signing all orders jointly, he would become, in effect, sole Prime Minister, which Macmillan foresaw would mean Giraud concentrating more and more on purely military matters, leaving political questions in de Gaulle's hands: 'At last he [de Gaulle] is beginning to learn a little patience.'[80]

Meanwhile, Roosevelt's interferences on behalf of Giraud had only backfired badly against him among the rest of the FCNL, which regarded them as flagrant violations of French sovereignty. One by one Roosevelt's excuses for withholding recognition were whittled away, and finally – on 26 August – it was accorded. The terms varied, however, between the Allies, with the American formula phrased in the most lukewarm language. 'This statement,' it concluded, 'does not constitute recognition of a government of France or of the French Empire by the Government of the United States.' The British position was exemplified by Churchill's assurance to Roosevelt in July: 'My chief desire in this business has been to keep in step with you.'[81]

In contrast, the Soviet Union, swift to spot a long-term advantage, committed itself in far more generous terms than either of the other two allies, recognising the FCNL as 'representing the state interests of the French Republic', and as 'the sole representative of all French patriots in the struggle against Hitlerism'.[82] This would provoke from de Gaulle several utterances in September and October to the effect that France 'must be with Russia in the future'.[83] Thus was the mould already setting on certain aspects of Gaullist foreign policy of two decades later; de Gaulle would neither forget, nor forgive, what he construed to be the insulting pusillanimity of *les Anglo-Saxons* over recognition of the FCNL, and there would always be a temptation to play the Russian card.

In Algiers, however, Macmillan was overjoyed with the crowning of his efforts, realising that 'de Gaulle now found himself Prime Minister of what was in effect the Provisional Government of France'. His headaches were still not over, though, with the two French generals continuing to show a regrettable propensity to bury the hatchet in each other. Nevertheless, his achievements had by any yardstick been outstanding, and of historic importance. He had saved de Gaulle, and had placed him in a position of power – though with appropriate democratic safeguards. He had seen the necessity, in 1943, to think of the shape of post-war France, and by enabling the provisional government of the FCNL to come into being he probably saved France from a Communist-led civil war following the liberation. He had been well supported from London and given general guidance by the staunchly Francophile Eden at the Foreign Office, where Macmillan's efforts had not gone unnoticed: 'He has been indefatigable in his efforts to bring the different warring elements together and it is probably only thanks to his patience, perseverance and powers of reason that the Committee . . . ever came into being.'[84] He had also made a large contribution to the cause of Anglo-American friendship, which had helped his own friendship with Eisenhower. Indeed, to use the words of one of his critics: 'It would be difficult to exaggerate the extent of Macmillan's sway over Eisenhower and Murphy.'[85]

Macmillan himself chiefly found pleasure in the verdict of one British newspaper, which suggested that he had been assisted by 'an imperturbability which it is almost impossible to rattle'. This had certainly helped to calm temperatures in the hothouse atmosphere of Algiers and was, he thought in retrospect, possibly the foundation of the legend of 'unflappability' that was to serve him well many years later. His success in handling de Gaulle – and Eisenhower and Churchill – had, all in all, made it the most satisfying year in his political career to date, and possibly the happiest.

Chapter Eight

Viceroy of the Mediterranean
July 1943–November 1944

I think I might even win the next election at Stockton as the man who drove Fascism out of North Africa and dethroned King Victor Emmanuel in Italy!

(HM, War Diaries, *3 November 1943*)

. . . not even the Prime Minister in Britain enjoyed quite such unquestioned prestige as Harold Macmillan had earned for himself both in his own British staff and in Ike's entourage. . . .

(Richard Crossman, Sunday Telegraph, *9 February 1964*)

Macmillan's newly recognised quality of unflappability was to prove invaluable as the war in the Mediterranean spread ever wider. After the clearing of Axis troops from North Africa in May 1943, the Allied military strategy – as agreed at Casablanca that January – was to invade Sicily, swiftly followed by a landing on the mainland of Italy. With the war over in North Africa, Macmillan's function of Resident Minister there looked at first as if it might be at an end; but he was not withdrawn, and in June 1943 he received a formal directive from Churchill to play the same advisory role to Eisenhower (and Alexander) in Italian affairs as he had done with the French. Meanwhile, still based in Algiers, he continued to be involved in French affairs until the beginning of 1944, when Duff Cooper took up his appointment as first British Ambassador to the provisional French government. The ill-defined nature of Macmillan's office, which was to come under challenge from various directions over the next eighteen months was a reflection of the increasing discord at the highest level between the Allied leaders over the administration of the territory about to be conquered, or liberated, from the enemy. It was thus without any specific authority, or instructions, that Macmillan now became involved in Italian political affairs.

The assault on Sicily, Operation Husky, began on 10 July, under the immediate command of Alexander. It is not now regarded as one of his or Eisenhower's finest campaigns. Gaps in the overall planning led to a conflict over tactical objectives between the two strong-willed army commanders, Montgomery and Patton, in which in turn lay the seeds of resentments that would mar Anglo-American military relations for the rest of the war. The attack began badly, in adverse weather, with half the British gliders from this first airborne operation falling into the sea – a failure which would have its repercussions on the much more audacious scheme shortly to be conceived for the mainland proper. Nevertheless, in thirty-eight days an attacking force of thirteen divisions succeeded in wresting

Sicily with its extraordinarily difficult terrain from more than thirteen enemy defending divisions, at a cost of 31,000 Allied casualties to estimated enemy losses of 170,000. Husky also achieved one clear-cut political result: on 25 July Mussolini was toppled, and the Italians began to sue secretly for peace terms.

The complex task of negotiating armistice terms acceptable to the Italians fell largely to Macmillan and Robert Murphy. On first hearing that Mussolini had been overthrown and King Victor Emmanuel had, nominally, resumed control of his realm with the aged figure of Marshal Badoglio taking over the government, Eisenhower's reaction had been immediately to broadcast a message of encouragement to the King. Macmillan and Murphy were forced to point out to the simple soldier that Allied Force Headquarters lacked the authority to take such a political initiative; Washington and London would have to be consulted first. Eisenhower, recalled Murphy, 'replied rather wearily that in the old days, before rapid communications, generals were free to do whatever they thought best; nowadays an opportunity could be lost while officers argued back and forth.'[1]

Amid these deliberations, Roosevelt's Secretary of War, Henry Stimson, arrived in Algiers via London. He had not been impressed by British arguments that, since the invasion of Sicily had (as the British predicted) precipitated the fall of Mussolini, all efforts should be concentrated on pursuing the war to Italy proper. (Nor was he evidently very impressed by the military success of Husky to date.) On the contrary, Stimson reflected an intensification of the suspicions that had surfaced at Casablanca regarding British motives in the Mediterranean. Eisenhower was told that on no account was he to get too heavily embroiled in an Italian campaign that was no more than a sideshow; the Second Front in northern France was still to be given overriding priority. Stimson's line was strongly reinforced by a cable on 12 August to Eisenhower from the US Chief of Staff, General Marshall, currently attending the Quebec Conference with Roosevelt and Churchill. Consequently, says Murphy – and Macmillan agreed – 'Eisenhower never did have the formidable expeditionary force which was generally supposed available for use in Italy. That is why the capture of Rome, hopefully expected in the autumn of 1943, was delayed until June 1944.'[2]

This backdrop to Anglo-American divergences was to influence the course of the Italian peace initiatives which began in early

August, first in Lisbon then in Madrid. Two Italian generals, Castellano and (later) Zanussi, met secretly with General Walter Bedell Smith, Eisenhower's Chief of Staff, and Brigadier Kenneth Strong, British Chief of Intelligence at AFHQ. The meeting was confined to a strictly military level, lest Churchill and Roosevelt be accused of 'making a deal with Fascists', and the two Allied generals were not empowered to negotiate on a broader basis than 'unconditional surrender'. At the same time, bureaucrats in London and Washington were still bickering over a lengthy document of surrender terms comprising some forty clauses. These clauses were to become known as the 'long terms'.

Meanwhile, back in Algiers only five days after the news of Mussolini's fall, Macmillan, according to Richard Crossman, had 'quietly proposed that since neither the British nor the Americans could get any policy directive from home we should draft our own Anglo-American directive to ourselves, and send it via the combined Chiefs of Staff to the White House and No. 10'. Crossman, who, though subsequently a prominent political adversary of Macmillan, continued to regard his performance in the Mediterranean with little short of adulation, goes on to claim: 'Within a day we had done the job, and from that moment on we realised that Eisenhower's Anglo-American command under Macmillan's leadership could always in an emergency reckon on bickering between London and Washington which could only be ended by our proposing the solution.'[3]

Although Macmillan in his memoirs never actually claimed to have initiated the proposal, he was indisputably the author of the 'directive', which formed the basis of the 'short terms' eventually to be accepted by the Italians. These comprised ten simple, and purely military, conditions, in which the words 'unconditional surrender' were 'studiously avoided'; Eisenhower was instructed to produce, if requested, the 'long terms', covering all political, economic and financial matters. But these were still being argued over. So Eisenhower asked Macmillan to fly to London and clear the air.

In his *War Diaries*, Oliver Harvey, then Eden's Assistant Under-Secretary at the Foreign Office, entered the following item for 9 August:

A.E. [Eden] wants to reply [to the Italian peace emissaries] that Badoglio must first offer unconditional surrender and after that we will communicate our terms. Macmillan over here. Also Swinton.* A.E. as usual most reluctant to see either. . . . he won't share anything and he hates even discussing it with his colleagues, all of whom bore him![4]

The passage is perhaps as indicative of Eden's character as of the stresses between him and Macmillan, already apparent in 1943. Nevertheless, Macmillan returned from London having gained approval for his short terms, so that Eisenhower – by the time of the first meeting between the Italian and Allied generals in mid-August – had full authority to negotiate.

At this meeting, however, General Castellano caused consternation by making proposals that went well beyond what was anticipated by Eisenhower. 'They were not so much concerned', says Macmillan, 'with the terms of an armistice as with the conditions for a new alliance. Castellano made it clear that they were envisaging a complete reversal of Italian policy: they wished to abandon their German allies and join the British and Americans. This would be a new "combinazione" and, he trusted, a very happy one.'

Having had three years in which to gauge the Italians' military potential as 'allies', the Anglo-Americans were less enthusiastic, if not positively sceptical. Immediately, all they wanted from the Italians was help to ensure an unopposed landing. The Italian negotiators were told that Italy would have to 'work her passage', a slogan that would, eventually, evolve into the formula of 'co-belligerence'. Another delay ensued while this and the Macmillan short terms were referred back to Rome. A deadline for acceptance was set for midnight on 30 August.

Meanwhile, the Allied long terms had finally reached AFHQ, forty-two clauses long, drafted largely, it seems, by the nimble pen of Gladwyn Jebb, who many years later admitted that these had been a mistake and that the short terms had been much better.[5] To the recipients at the time, the document was, in the words of Macmillan, 'a planner's dream and a general's nightmare'. All those concerned at AFHQ felt the terms to be excessively, and unrealistically, harsh – placing as they did complete control of every aspect of Italian affairs into Allied hands. When General Zanussi was shown them privately, he remarked that, whereas the Italians

* Lord Swinton, Cabinet Minister Resident in West Africa.

might easily accept the short terms, he deplored the decision to force so humiliating a surrender on Italy; and more time would be required to study these long terms.

Meanwhile the Germans were steadily building up their forces south of Rome. Strongly backed by both the US and British military, Macmillan cabled London urging that the armistice be accelerated by settling for the short terms and dropping the long. In Churchill's absence at Quebec, his deputy, Clement Attlee, sent 'a very confused reply' suggesting a compromise whereby the long terms should be presented to the Italians only after they had signed the short. The straightforward Eisenhower grumbled that it was a 'crooked deal';[6] Macmillan, always the politician holding that the ends justified the means, particularly in war, decided 'come what may, to use my own discretion. Anyway, Sicily was quite a long way from Whitehall.' In the event, the opprobrious long terms were quietly shuffled away – though not before they had added to the lethal delays that afflicted the impending landings, or induced stresses between the Allies and their new 'co-belligerent' partner. Macmillan's dismissive comment in his memoirs was that the long terms 'need never have been written, and all the bother about getting them signed was only a waste of time'.

By the time the talks with the Italians reconvened at the end of August, General Zanussi had introduced a new proposition: the Allies should land an airborne division near Rome, which would immediately be supported by six well-equipped Italian divisions. Together these could easily deal with the one and a half German divisions in the area, and they could also seal off the three German divisions around Naples. Thus the Allies could capture Rome, and also rally to the Allies a substantial part of the Italian armed forces. Murphy found Zanussi an eloquent advocate, and both he and Macmillan were at once enthusiastic about the scheme. When put to the military, Eisenhower's staff planners (especially the British) supported it – provided the Italians were serious. But General Matthew Ridgway, commander of the division that would be involved, the US 82nd Airborne, and his deputy, General Maxwell Taylor, had doubts. Pressed by Murphy and Macmillan, however, Ridgway finally agreed, provided that 'the two double-damned political advisers went to the Rome landings. . . . "It's a deal," we told Ridgway.' Later, when the operation was definitely approved by Eisenhower, Macmillan and Murphy informed him that, by agreement with Ridgway, they themselves would be going; to which the General responded drily, 'There's nothing in the regulations which says diplomats are not expendable.'[7]

Meanwhile at the grove in Cassibile (which, as Macmillan the classicist noted, was exactly the place where the Athenians had surrendered to the Syracusans in 413 BC) a new hitch arose as soon as the Italian envoys arrived to sign the armistice at Alexander's headquarters. The Allied negotiators were incensed to be told that – despite the offer of the airborne drop – the Italian generals had no authority from the King to sign anything in advance of the Allied landings. It was clear to Macmillan that the Italians were procrastinating, in the hope of a better deal.

Supported by Murphy and Bedell Smith, he now used his influence with Alexander, sending him a message suggesting that the time had come for a display of firmness. The Commander of Allied Forces, recalls Macmillan,

> played up frightfully well. He appeared in a car with a jeep in front and a platoon of Guardsmen, wearing a brass hat, beautifully polished boots and gold spurs, and well-cut trousers. . . . He advanced, wouldn't shake hands with them, and said, 'Gentlemen, what's all this about? Are you here as plenipotentiaries? If so, you will sign. If you're spies, I'll put you under arrest. Will you please think about it during the next hour.'[8]

Claiming to have seen that morning an intercept cable from Badoglio that contained instructions to sign, Alexander with every semblance of cold fury threatened to bomb Rome if the armistice were not signed within twenty-four hours. Then he marched out. His performance delighted Macmillan, although it narrowly missed turning into *opera bouffe*, for the pomped-up General had to scramble over a stone wall before getting into his car, and after delivering his tirade he had to crawl along behind the wall in his tight boots, in order to reach Macmillan's tent and report progress.

The armistice was not finally signed until the afternoon of 3 September. At dawn, Montgomery's troops had already begun to cross into the toe of Italy, over the Straits of Messina. The main Allied landings, at Salerno, south of Naples, which were supposed to coincide with the public announcement of the armistice, did not however take place until 9 September, in the teeth of fierce German resistance. That same day the Germans seized control of Rome, and King Victor Emmanuel fled to Brindisi. The airborne landing, which was to be accompanied by Murphy and Macmillan, never took place.

At great personal risk, Maxwell Taylor had been smuggled into Rome to make contact with General Ambrosio, the Italian Chief of Staff, and General Carboni, commander of the key armoured corps. Both had, by 7 September, clearly lost their nerve, for fear of what the Germans might do to them, with Carboni telling Taylor (with less than total truth, as it later transpired)[9] that the airfields were in German hands and his tanks nearly out of fuel and ammunition. Taylor returned to the 82nd Airborne's Licata base in Sicily, where some sixty Dakotas were already loaded, to give a thumbs-down verdict. Back in Algiers, and still awaiting orders to embark, Macmillan gloomily learned that the 'adventure' was definitely off. He wrote tersely: 'I much regret this. . . .'[10] By 10 September, the Germans – with nineteen divisions now operative in Italy – had mopped up the elite Italian units round Rome, and Rommel had occupied the Alpine passes – expressing surprised delight that the Allies had been so slow to take advantage of the Italian collapse. Thus the unfortunate Italians got the worst of both worlds, having switched sides and now being exposed to the Germans without any Allied troops to protect them.

Macmillan in his memoirs wrote that, apart from his own acute personal disappointment, 'the failure to risk the airborne division proved a fatal impediment to our hopes for the early capture of Rome and added enormously to the difficulties of the long struggle from one end to the other of the Italian peninsula.' After the war, Murphy held to the view that the US airborne commanders had misjudged the situation, and that the Rome landings should have taken place. Alexander himself had reckoned that – with Italian help – he could have taken Rome by mid-October.

But was the operation ever technically possible? Many years later, General Gavin, the distinguished subsequent commander of the 82nd Division who led it through Arnhem, told the author that he had regarded the operation as 'totally hopeless. . . . there would have been no means of supplying the force once it had landed; the Italians were quite unreliable, and there was a complete lack of anti-tank weapons for dealing with heavy German tanks.'[11] On top of that, he might have added the demoralising effect of the unhappy experiences in those first airborne landings in Sicily just two months previously.

At various times Macmillan has been blamed for the delays in the Italian armistice, the fateful forty-five days during which the Germans consolidated their hold. But the causes of procrastination lay in London, Washington and Rome. Had it not been for Macmillan's invention of the short terms, the delays might have been even worse. Macmillan himself points to the shortage of landing craft – due to the limitation imposed by US strategic misgivings – which, in the event, enabled Alexander to land no more than three divisions on the bloody beaches at Salerno. There was also the fact, which the Italian negotiators were unable to comprehend, that fighters based in Sicily could not operate north of Naples.

Nevertheless, the whole business of the Italian armistice undoubtedly increased friction between Macmillan and Eden back in London. On 1 September, Harvey in his diaries reflected the Foreign Office's irritation:

> Macmillan and Eisenhower are being incredibly wooden and obstructive over the armistice arrangements. . . . Eisenhower is in a fright over his operations and seems now to think the Italians must be won over to us. We are heading for a new Darlanism and what a row it will cause. We blame Macmillan for being stupid over this. He at least should have more sense. The only way to get anything out of the Italians is to go on hammering them.[12]

Meanwhile, Macmillan was echoing a similar degree of impatience with 'my colleagues in London', doubtless with Eden specifically in mind. 'I wish some of them would come and try landing on a defended and mined beach out of a barge, in which one has been three or four days at sea (and sick half that time) in the middle of the night!'[13]

To assuage their personal frustration over the aborting of the Rome landing, on 12 September Murphy and Macmillan launched their own private invasion of the Italian mainland. From Tunis they flew in a Flying Fortress to Taranto, together with General Maxwell Taylor (who spoke some Italian) and a British General, Sir Frank

Mason-MacFarlane, the Governor of Gibraltar, who had been designated to lead a military mission to the Italians, with Murphy and Macmillan as political advisers. Circling round the great Italian naval base, they noted with concern a number of Italian warships beneath; had they heard about the armistice, or would they open fire? After some nervous manoeuvring, the B–17 landed safely and the next day the party moved on to 'capture' Brindisi, and locate the government of King Victor Emmanuel and Marshal Badoglio, which had taken refuge there.

Macmillan's new task became that of trying to create a new, more liberal and broad-based Italian regime, which meant first settling the future of the King and his dynasty. His and Murphy's dealings with the Italians were not helped by General Mason-MacFarlane, who was unable to conceal what was then the standard British Army attitude to all Italians – one of blunt contempt. He termed Badoglio a 'has-been' and the seventy-three-year-old King 'gaga'. By November, Macmillan would write acidly in his diary: '*I do not see why great dynastic changes – for good or ill – should be made by a couple of generals . . . of low rank and limited political experience. . . . The problem may be solved by the Italians themselves, without intervention from us*' (Macmillan's italics).[14]

In September 1943, however, both Macmillan and Murphy were sympathetic towards the little King, feeling that he had done more than was generally credited in forcing out Mussolini. Macmillan, an instinctive monarchist, was strongly inclined towards the Savoy dynasty as being 'the only thing that could be said to be Italian. . . . what else was there?'[15] To him it was a unifying force, and the one counterweight against the serious threat of a Communist take-over in Italy. Churchill, too, was prepared to go to almost any length to save the King. Churchill's support prolonged the King's reign for several months, but, in the long run, American pressure proved too strong. Roosevelt was up for re-election in 1944 and the vote of the anti-monarchist New York Italians was of some importance to him. On 11 April 1944, at his villa in Ravello, a tearful King Victor Emmanuel, in the presence of Macmillan and Murphy, abdicated in favour of his son Umberto, who – temporarily – became regent. Shortly thereafter the liberal Bonomi government was instated, which would contain those great post-war European politicians, de Gasperi and Giuseppe Saragat.

In January 1945 Macmillan was to revise at least momentarily his personal opinion of Victor Emmanuel when he discovered that the King's cousin, Prince Doria ('a remarkable man – a real mediaeval saint, of spotless reputation'),[16] had written to the King, begging him not to go to war with England in 1940. The King had not replied, giving the letter instead to Mussolini, who threw Doria into prison. Macmillan thought the story 'dreadful': 'After all, he need only have burned the letter. I am now so glad that I bullied him at Ravello. [It] removes any qualm I had about the King. . . . He says he is cold at Ravello. . . . Let him perish of cold. Even a Stuart King scarcely did such a dirty trick. . . .'[17]

As the campaign dragged on, Macmillan, the classical scholar in love with Italy, seems to have been more genuinely concerned with the plight of the Italian civilians than were many of his contemporaries. On a visit to Naples in January 1944, he noted how it was still in a terrible condition. War destruction had rendered thousands homeless,

> There is only a minimum subsistence ration of food (125 grammes a day of bread). . . . The Germans destroyed or carried off 92 per cent of the whole stock of sheep and cattle and 86 per cent of the poultry. There is a flourishing 'black' market. . . . There is a very bad clothing situation – no boots or shoes or underwear. There is very little soap. With all this, typhus is naturally beginning. . . .[18]

Matters got progressively worse as each new segment of Italy was liberated, and by July Macmillan recorded press reports that one out of every two babies in Rome was dying, while tuberculosis was carrying off some 200,000 Italians a year throughout the country.

By now Macmillan had finally moved from Algiers to the Allied headquarters at Caserta, lodged in the vast eighteenth-century palace that reminded him of Chatsworth ('only five or six times as big')[19] and on whose ponds American generals were given to landing in seaplanes. There he remained for the rest of the war. In late 1943 he had been appointed the UK High Commissioner to the Advisory Council for Italy, and in his eyes one of the principal villains on the Italian scene was the American-inspired Allied Military Government of Occupied Territories (AMGOT), which was top-heavy and inefficient. The Americans favoured direct military control of all liberated territories, while Macmillan – with equal consistency – as early as August 1943, before any landing on the Italian mainland had taken place, was recommending that civil administration take over just as soon as was practicable. He was incensed by the repeated intrusion of domestic American politics on to the Italian scene, a policy 'that wasn't to help feed the Italians or to get them out of their difficulties, it was to give good jobs to people strong in the New York Italian community – make them all colonels. They didn't care tuppence about what the Italians really needed. . . . a vast Tammany Hall, I had to get rid of them. . . .'[20]

And he did, eventually. From the beginning he resisted, successfully, the imposition of Mayor Fiorello La Guardia of New York on AFHQ; while a bitter and off-the-record letter to his friend Alexander, of 21 October 1944, reveals his views of the American ally:

> In spite of all the talk . . . which the President has adopted relating to Italy, no (repeat no) additional supplies of wheat or other foodstuffs have been offered to us from the Combined Chiefs of Staff. . . . I made a suggestion to General Wilson [the new Supreme Commander of the Mediterranean] that we should threaten to reduce the food ration still further and to announce the reduction before . . . the Presidential election. That might bring them to their senses. . . . what I now fear is that once polling day is over, neither the President nor the Combined Chiefs of Staff nor any other American authority will bother two hoots about the Italians, having secured the votes of their American relations. . . . just as the authorities will not send us food, neither will they send us sufficient transport.[21]

Enter the Soviets

In all his Italian dealings, as in those with the French, Macmillan warily noticed the increasing importance of the Soviet presence. This first took the shape of one Alexander Bogomolov, an ex-professor of Marxism turned diplomat, formerly Russian Ambassador to Vichy, then posted to Algiers as Ambassador to the FCNL in October 1943. A 'large-limbed man with loose clothes, white hands and a fat white face' and a delicate stomach, Bogomolov was a good choice. He swiftly ingratiated himself in Algiers, where he made himself so approachable as to gain the congenial nickname of Bogo. He disarmed John Wyndham by laughing uproariously (and perhaps excessively) at *Three Men in a Boat*. With the French, and subsequently the Italians, Bogo played skilfully on Anglo-American differences. According to Murphy, he lavished on de Gaulle 'the formalities customarily accorded to a Chief of State. These courtesies cost nothing and paid off handsomely.'[22]

Before the end of 1943, Bogo was reinforced by a far more sinister and effective figure – Andrei Vyshinsky, the dreaded prosecutor during the purges of the 1930s, and an intimate of Stalin, who sent him to be the Soviet representative on the newly formed and all-powerful Advisory Council for Italy. To Macmillan, Vyshinsky at first sight looked beguilingly benevolent, 'exactly like Mr Pickwick',[23] and he exuded even more dangerous charm than Bogo. It was Macmillan's first contact with Russians since his visit to the USSR, and he could not quite visualise in Vyshinsky 'the cruel persecutor of the Russian terror . . . the gloating, merciless, bloody figure of which we read six or seven years ago'.

In December 1943, he recorded that Vyshinsky wanted to know how many Fascists had been tried and shot since the capture of Sicily. 'The best that Harold [Caccia, Macmillan's Foreign Office adviser in Italy] could do was to murmur something about nearly 1,500 in prison – but Vyshinsky obviously thought this a very poor result of three months' work.'[24] By March 1944, Macmillan summed up the two Russians in his diary:

> Bogomolov is naturally shifty; Vyshinsky naturally frank. Vyshinsky would laugh with you, and then pull out a revolver and shoot you quietly through the back of the head. Bogomolov would entertain you to a series of rather dreary repasts where you would be slowly poisoned in indifferent French wine.[25]

Like most Anglo-Americans at that time, including Churchill and Roosevelt, Macmillan clearly remained half-shocked and half-amused by Russian expressions of bloodthirstiness, and their calls for wholesale purges of Italians. He seemed hardly able to take them at their face value – an inability that was to have relevance at the close of the war. Neither Macmillan nor Murphy, however, were under any illusions about the aims of Soviet *realpolitik* as the war progressed up Italy towards the industrial north. Murphy, writing clear-sightedly, though *ex post facto* long after the damage had been done, said that 'the political operations of the Soviet Government in Italy were more important in the long run than either the German or the Allied military operations. . . .'[26]

On landing in Naples in January 1944, most of Vyshinsky's vast team 'disappeared' – patently, Macmillan noted, to establish intimate contact with the Italian Communist Party. Later that year, Bogo – almost *en passant* – suggested that the world-famous Italian Communist leader, Palmiro Togliatti, might return home, after seventeen years' exile in the USSR. Suddenly, Togliatti was there, and almost overnight the Italian Communist Party, though outlawed for two decades under Mussolini, emerged as one of the most potent influences in Italy – and, indeed, Europe.

Togliatti was a great deal more than just a national party leader; he was one of the aces in the pack of international Communism over two generations, until he died in 1964. In Italy, the roots of his power were generously fertilised by the general benevolence shown towards the Communists by Rooseveltian America, as well as by strong Allied support for the Communist partisans and by the adroit way in which Togliatti's Soviet masters, Bogo and Vyshinsky, contrived to exploit Anglo-American political and strategic differences. Over the delicate issue of the future of the monarchy, the Italian Communist Party played its hand with consummate skill, by showing willing to join a government before the issue was resolved; which, says Macmillan, succeeded in making the position of the liberal and moderate parties 'very uncomfortable'. From his Italian post – but in one of his other roles – Vyshinsky, according to Murphy, 'simultaneously organised several satellite governments in eastern Europe so effectively that they remained intact through years of post-war strains. . . . Vyshinsky and his fellow operators achieved maximum results at minimum cost. The Communist base in Italy, unlike those in eastern Europe, never required any Red Army garrison to hold it. . . .'[27] Meanwhile, the arrival of Josip Broz Tito in Italy on 4 June 1944 heralded the advent of a new Communist headache for Macmillan.

The Cairo Conference

These inroads created by Soviet policy in the Mediterranean stemmed from decisions of high policy and strategy that lay outside the competence of Macmillan, or Murphy. Macmillan was particularly taken by two remarks made by Churchill in November 1943. He had flown to Gibraltar to meet the Prime Minister on HMS *Renown* and then went on to attend the Cairo Conference between Churchill and Roosevelt, with the Anglo-American Chiefs of Staff (plus – on occasions – China's *generalissimo*, Chiang Kai-Shek). In an after-dinner conversation, Churchill remarked to Macmillan that Cromwell was a great man, but 'he made one fatal error. Born and bred in fear of Spain – Spain was claiming and holding the hegemony of the world – he failed to see in the decline of Spain the rise of France: Richelieu, Mazarin: hence Louis XIV, hence the Marlborough wars, hence the long struggle for Europe. Will that be said of me?'[28] With this appeal to his sense of history, Macmillan knew exactly what Churchill meant. Hitler was already beaten; but what sort of threat would the victorious Russians – with whom 'our American friends' were at that moment rather obsessed – present in the post-war world? The problem at the end of 1943 was how far the Soviet imperialism would stretch, and how to keep it as far away as possible to the east.

The second remark by Churchill concerned the Chief of Staffs system, which he said 'leads to weak and faltering decisions – or rather indecisions. Why, you may take the most gallant sailor, the most intrepid airman or the most audacious soldier, put them at a table together – what do you get? *The sum of their fears.*'[29] If his remark about Cromwell revealed Churchill's fear about Russian intentions, this second remark expressed his misgivings that, given the 'extreme rigidity of the combined Chiefs of Staff system, and of our American Allies generally', little could be done about it. With both, Macmillan was totally in accord, and – as a consequence – he got himself involved in strategic planning that was, strictly speaking, well outside his brief.

The Cairo Conference was a preliminary to the 'Big Three' meeting with Stalin at Teheran, and at Cairo Churchill tried for the last time, and failed, to persuade Roosevelt to expand the fighting in the Mediterranean. They thus arrived at Teheran (which was not attended by Macmillan) in a state of disagreement, to the delight of Stalin, who found himself with what amounted to a casting vote on Anglo-American strategy. He gave all-out support to Roosevelt over priority for a 'second front' in France (Operation Overlord), and was also quick to support Roosevelt's suggestion for a second landing in the south of France (Operation Anvil), with divisions diverted from Italy. At the same time, he made plain his disapproval of the Allies pushing into the north of Italy. For, as the Chief of Imperial General Staff, General Alan Brooke, noted in his diary: 'such an advance led too directly towards Yugoslavia and Austria, on which, no doubt, he had by now cast covetous eyes.'[30] It was also at Teheran that were laid the foundations of the Yalta agreements, the cause of so much trouble for Macmillan in later years.

At Cairo, Macmillan had been asked by Churchill for his opinion on whether General Maitland Wilson or Alexander should succeed Eisenhower as SACMED (Supreme Allied Commander, Mediterranean), as Eisenhower was earmarked to head the forthcoming invasion of France. Macmillan opted categorically for his friend Alexander, giving in writing some cogent reasons – among them that 'he has now learnt the quite difficult art of managing Americans' (this, no doubt, instructed by Macmillan himself!). In doing so, Macmillan aroused Brooke's displeasure. 'I shall have heavy work ahead,' he complained in his diary. 'The trouble has been caused by Macmillan, who has had a long talk with the PM suggesting Alex was the man for the job, and that he, Macmillan, could take the political load off him. He . . . evidently does not understand what the functions of a Supreme Commander should be. . . .'[31] Brooke distrusted Macmillan's motives, on the grounds that he 'knew he could handle Alex, and that he would be a piece of putty in his hand; but on the other hand Jumbo Wilson was made of much rougher material which would not be so pliable.'[32]

In the event, Brooke's candidate won. Alexander was, however, finally promoted to be SACMED a year later. In the meantime he remained as Commander-in-Chief, Italy, where his relationship with Macmillan grew ever closer. Indeed, so close was their friendship by mid-1944 that it was hard to decide who was influencing whom. Churchill's CIGS had a point when he stated forthrightly that 'some of us had doubts as to whether Macmillan or Alexander was Supreme Commander of the Mediterranean.'[33]

During the Cairo Conference, a new crisis had blown up with the French. This time it was over Syria and the Lebanon, French mandates since 1918, which had been in a state of turmoil –

tragically familiar to more contemporary observers – since their liberation from Vichy by British forces supported by the Free French. Via a famed but autocratic Francophile, General Sir Louis Spears, who had been appointed as Minister to the Levant by Churchill, strong British pressure was applied on the French to hold free elections. When elections were held, the British and the French both accused each other of trying to rig them; but in the event the anti-French Nationalists won a resounding victory. The French responded, on 11 November, by arresting the Lebanese President, Prime Minister and three other ministers.

In Algiers, de Gaulle and the FCNL were outraged by Spears's high-handedness and what they construed as interference in a purely French sphere, aimed at pushing France out of the Levant. Churchill was enraged, once again, by the stubbornness of de Gaulle, and Macmillan was called in, once again, to mediate. In his diary of 15 November, Macmillan noted that the Prime Minister had 'asked a great deal about the French situation. He is still violently anti-de Gaulle but as always if you maintain a point with energy, he is prepared to listen.' On the following day, he returned to the old theme:

> [Churchill] is naturally very incensed at Giraud's disappearance from the political field, since he regards the 'co-presidency' as the basis on which British and American recognition were granted. But he knew in his heart that it was only a temporary expedient. . . . What he fears is a sort of de Gaulle dictatorship, hostile to Britain and mischievous if not dangerous. . . .[34]

Macmillan felt, with some irritation, that Spears – an old friend and fellow MP from pre-war days – had overreacted and antagonised the French unnecessarily. At Cairo he observed Roosevelt once again browbeating Churchill on a familiar theme: 'that France could not recover; that Indo-China should not be returned to her control; that Dakar, in West Africa, should pass under American protection . . .'. These were but new variations on the anti-colonial threnodies at Casablanca the previous year.

Lubricated by Macmillan, a compromise was eventually worked out over the Lebanon, though he found it one of the most exhausting crises he had had to deal with to date. Then, hardly was the dust settled in the Levant, than de Gaulle unleashed a new drama with the arrest and threatened prosecution – on grounds of collaboration – of three senior French officials. Peyrouton and Boisson, the ex-Vichy Governors-General of Algeria and French West Africa respectively, had both been given assurances of protection by Churchill and Roosevelt personally, for their help in facilitating the Allied landings of 1942; the third, Flandin, had been an old political friend of Churchill's from the days of the Rhineland crisis of 1936. When Churchill heard the news, he was recovering from pneumonia at Carthage, and reacted 'in a most excited mood, roaring like an excited bull down the telephone . . .'.[35] The following day, 22 December, Macmillan feared he might have an apoplectic fit. Roosevelt carried Churchill's anger one step further, by despatching 'the most extraordinary telegram' to Eisenhower, ordering him to direct the FCNL 'immediately to set free and discontinue the trial' of the three officials.[36]

This peremptory telegram 'fairly put the cat among the pigeons'. It was difficult to see how Eisenhower, who was away in Italy, could refuse to carry out his President's command, the enforcement of which might well require Allied military action against the FCNL; this would in turn destroy all that Macmillan had so laboriously built up with de Gaulle. Macmillan, who in any case sympathised with the French to the extent that Boisson anyway 'was a brutal and cruel man', having harshly maltreated torpedoed British seamen interned under his governance, persuaded Eisenhower's deputy, General Bedell Smith, to defer action for two or three days.

Meanwhile, Macmillan risked another sally at the still ailing Churchill, who now 'seemed rather alarmed at the avalanche which he had started' with Roosevelt. Whereas the President was manifestly still determined to find any excuse to be rid of de Gaulle, Churchill's sentiments, Macmillan went on to note, were more complex: 'He feels about de Gaulle like a man who has quarrelled with his son. He will cut him off with a shilling. But (in his heart) he would kill the fatted calf if only the prodigal would confess his faults.' Churchill telephoned Bedell Smith while Macmillan was actually in the room, to growl: 'Keep Harold up to the mark. He is much too pro-French. He will not carry out my policy or my wishes. I rely on *you*!'[37] Macmillan attributed this surliness to the pneumonia and domestic tenseness over his troublesome son, Randolph, but could not help feeling hurt and alarmed. He had also received no response from Eden, to whom he had sent a telegram asking for support.

He tried appealing to Churchill's sense of history, using – as he had done in the past – an analogy between the British revolution of 1688 and de Gaulle's accession to power. But:

> The liberation of France would be by British and American armies. They looked forward to it with desperate longing. But the fact that they could do so little to achieve it added to the burden of bitterness and shame. The one thing they could do at once was to set about a series of State trials. . . . The emotions were partly revenge, partly ambition, and partly the taking of political positions for the future.

By Christmas Day, Macmillan visiting Churchill found that he had made one of his amazing recoveries and had just consumed a sumptuous Christmas dinner, washed down liberally with champagne. He toasted Macmillan 'in most eulogistic terms', and that evening – dressed in a flamboyant Chinese dressing gown that made him look like 'a figure in a Russian ballet' – bade farewell in positively warm-hearted and forgiving terms. '"Perhaps you are right,"' he admitted. '"But I do not agree with you. Perhaps I will see de Gaulle. Anyway you have done very well." Then he took my hand in his in a most fatherly way and said "Come and see me again before I leave Africa, and we'll talk it over."' Macmillan was 'deeply touched, and my love and affection for him came flowing back.'

The next day he found that the situation had been miraculously reversed. Under pressure from Churchill, Roosevelt had sent a telegram completely backing down; there would now be no intervention by Eisenhower. Even de Gaulle compromised by postponing the trials of the three Vichyites until after the war.

Ten days later Macmillan handed over formally to Duff Cooper in Algiers, thereby more or less relinquishing his association with French affairs and de Gaulle – for the time being. It was just about time; he had confided in the privacy of his diaries during the last tussle with Churchill: 'It is really getting beyond a joke and much as I love Winston, I cannot stand much more. . . .'[38]

Feeling the Strain

There were several times during this Mediterranean period when the stress and pressure of work proved too much for Macmillan. In October 1943, after a flying visit to London which had infuriated Eden, he was taken ill with a fever that his army doctor, Colonel John Richardson (later Lord Richardson, who was to remain Macmillan's physician and devoted friend until retirement), diagnosed as a 'bad state of exhaustion approaching prostration'. The conflict with Anthony Eden that was beginning to build up at this time may well have contributed to Macmillan's physical collapse. Oliver Harvey recorded in his diary for 8 October how, on the eve of Eden leaving London for Algiers:

> Macmillan has suddenly appeared to AE's fury. . . . He is being packed off again. Macmillan is anxious to maintain a sort of *droit de regard* over all our French and Italian relations from his post at Eisen-HQ. AE does not wish to encourage this and part of the idea of the appointment of Duff and Charles* to the French and Italians is to cut him out of the picture. I can't think why he dislikes Macmillan (though he certainly is a bore) and is even jealous of him.[39]

The presence in Algiers of Eden and his staff, 'all making separate and impossible plans', did nothing to mitigate Macmillan's illness and accompanying depression. In a glum bout of the Black Dog, he wrote to Dorothy: '. . . I wish I were at home and could see you and the children. One gets intolerably lonely and depressed here if one stops work for a minute. So tomorrow I shall abandon my rest cure, which if it may benefit my body only makes my mind disturbed and melancholy. Heaps and heaps of love to you all. . . . Your devoted Harold.'[40]

His letters to Dorothy around this time reveal his homesickness and how much he was missing his wife and family. Laconically, he admitted in his memoirs that he could not shake off his depression. 'The only thing that comforted me was the news of the birth of my first grandson.' Perhaps wishing to atone for his deficiencies as a

* Sir Noel Charles, made High Commissioner in Italy, with the rank of Ambassador the following year.

father, he showed much interest in the birth of this baby, Alexander, the eldest son of Maurice and Katie (Ormsby-Gore). On 17 August, he had written to Dorothy: '. . . I have a feeling (and a great hope) that it will be a boy. Do you remember all the excitement about Maurice? I remember . . . generally living in a world of panic and excitement. No other baby had ever been born before. I expect Maurice will feel like that, so you will have to support him. . . .'[41]

On 11 October, after receiving the telegram informing him of Alexander's birth the previous day, he told her, 'I cannot tell you how much I was pleased. . . .' And three days later he was writing: 'I cannot get over my pleasure about the baby. Do write me details – weight, eyes, hair etc. I do hope he won't have the Ormsby-Gore mouth and teeth. . . . Honestly, I am so happy about it. I feel a new interest in everything and that so many things become worth while – planting trees for instance and publishing books!'[42] Detectably, his morale improved, to the extent of being even able to discern in de Gaulle 'a sense of humour (rather puckish)'.

Dorothy kept up her chatty, affectionate letters in response. On 23 November, after Macmillan had been designated UK High Commissioner to the Advisory Council for Italy as well as Political Adviser to the Supreme Allied Commander in the Mediterranean area, she wrote teasingly to him:

> At last we know what you are. From the wireless tonight you seem to have got two names as well as keeping your old one. It all sounds very imposing!. . . How lovely the country sounds after the rain. I have always wanted to see that sudden blossoming of all the flowers. I wonder you have not all gone crackers with the difficulties and complications of setting up the Italian government, but as you rightly say all situations have been complicated since you arrived in Algiers! I love the way you have to switch from French politics to Italian governments and then suddenly to locusts. . . . it is staggering what you do get through. . . .[43]

It was not, however, all toil and stress for Macmillan. A visit to Alex's headquarters always provided the kind of relaxation that most appealed to him. As guardsmen who had known each other since the First World War, Macmillan and Alexander already had much in common. But after arriving in Algiers Macmillan had found himself enchanted by 'the character of this very remarkable man. He has quite extraordinary charm. He has made simplicity the rule of his life. The whole atmosphere of the camp is dominated by his personality – modest, calm, confident. . . .' This simplicity and modesty was repeatedly remarked on by Macmillan in his diaries; but (as he would often comment in later life) he saw Alex's true genius in his being 'an artist. . . . all the really great men, whether Winston, Alex or Charlie Chaplin, have always been artists.'[44] Macmillan once likened Montgomery to Wellington, but he regarded Alexander as 'the greatest general since Marlborough, in commanding coalitions'.[45]

Alexander's biographer, Nigel Nicolson, commented judiciously on how Macmillan 'conceived for Alexander an esteem and affection which made him the hero of his wartime volume of memoirs. He saw in him all the qualities which he most admired, and many of which he shared, chivalry, ease, firmness, and unshakable faith in victory, a patrician use of great power, a capacity to set worry aside. . . .'[46] Macmillan described how he found the atmosphere of Alex's quarters in Tunis 'rather like a large country house. You come to meals and otherwise attend to your own business. There is plenty of quiet amusement available – sightseeing, bathing or just agreeable conversation with the other guests. . . .' Outside of 'business' sessions, the conversation thoroughly matched Macmillan's own style – 'a little history, a little politics, a little banter, a little philosophy – all very lightly touched . . .'. There was talk about the campaign of Belisarius, about Cardinal Wolsey's bad breath, about how Frederick I of Prussia recruited his Guards, about the merits of classical versus Gothic architecture, about how best to drive pheasants, and about the antecedents of the Duke of Buccleuch's huntsman.

Alex, on his side, made a practice – from Tunis onwards until the end of the campaign – of inviting Macmillan to attend his daily War Room conference whenever he was near Command Headquarters. For him, a visit from Macmillan constituted 'happy days'; he was 'a delightful companion who was both wise in advice and always amusing; a man of great intellect, morally and physically brave, but far too reserved to show these admirable qualities outwardly . . .'.[47] The last judgement showed a rare perceptiveness of the real Macmillan.

Apart from these visits to Alex, Macmillan always derived benefit from the occasional free, and carefree, hours when he could travel with John Wyndham to the ruins of Tipasa and Djemila in Algeria, or through Algerian Kabylia, or to Carthage and the classical sites of Italy, or to observe a majestic eruption of Vesuvius. Always he continued his voracious reading: Trollope, Dickens, Jane Austen, Rebecca West, Trevelyan's *Social History*, Disraeli, Boswell ('just the thing for air travel').[48]

He also managed to find time to contemplate the shape of post-war England, and his own future. Rereading *Sybil* and *Coningsby* yet again, he found encouragement in reflecting that 'the young men in the Tory Party now read his [Disraeli's] novels and study his life with the same enthusiasm as we did thirty years ago. . . . There is some pretty good material about if one can only give it a chance.'[49]

Observing the nude soldiery bathing off the North African coast, he was given to speculate:

The more I see of this army the more I wonder what they will make of England after the war. Will they be soothed in the syrup of Beveridge? Will they be victims of that Pied Piper Morrison? Will Dick Acland and Priestley cash in on their vague aspirations and sentiments?* Or will they be able (as we failed to do 25 years ago) to construct a virile creed, firmly based on the glories of the past but looking avidly to the new duties and ambitions of the future Empire? It is all very strange and makes me feel very old.[50]

He was not yet fifty.

In January 1944 he was ruminating with some uncertainty about his own political destiny:

I cannot make up my mind whether I shall ever be able to face a Stockton election again. It's a sort of nightmare. Probably in the end I shall decide to go through with it. . . . Of course if I stay in politics and remain a Minister, I must have a seat where I can get elected. I wonder what the chances would be at Stockton; I imagine they only think I am neglecting my war duty by paying no attention to them. And, of course, very few of the new electorate will have heard of us. I suppose there will inevitably be a swing

* The MP Richard Acland, with J. B. Priestley, had founded in 1942 the Common Wealth Party, which advocated public ownership on moral grounds.

to the Left. Curiously enough, I think what the people still want is a 'Middle Way'. . . .[51]

The following month, on his fiftieth birthday, he gloomily recorded: 'It is terrible to reflect on all the follies and mistakes of so many years – so much attempted, so little achieved.'[52] It was at about this time, also, that Dr John Richardson recalled asking Macmillan whether he thought he would ever become Prime Minister. He replied, in a remarkably accurate prediction, 'Every politician can wonder and hope, but all I can say is that if I do become PM it will be in about twelve years.'[53] He was a year out.

Links with Home

In January 1944 Eisenhower was summoned back to England to command the Overlord forces for the June invasion, and later in the year Bob Murphy would follow him. Macmillan was sad to bid farewell to his American friends, particularly Ike. Although his enthusiasm for Murphy had slightly waned over the handling of the 'Italian problem', Murphy would write to him in the warmest terms in September: '*Partir, c'est mourir un peu*. In this moribund state then I want you to know how hard it is for me to realise the flight of twenty months of delightful association with you. . . . I believe you know how much I admire you as a person and your ability as a representative of your country. A more abundant supply of that rare article – Harold Macmillan – would make this world a far more attractive habitation.'[54]

But, as Eisenhower left, Macmillan's old colleague Duff Cooper arrived in Algiers as Ambassador to the French, and he and Diana Cooper quickly injected a new, lively note. Initially the Duff Coopers (never backward in accepting hospitality) were irked that Macmillan did not instantly place his villa at their disposal, in that he had no wife and four or five empty rooms (though he appears to have fed them every day). But Diana, with her remarkable powers of perception, soon recognised Macmillan as a fine man of 'life and vision'.[55] Writing to a friend in England, she predicted, 'One day he'll be Prime Minister. I've put my money (nay, my shirt) on him. He's my horse.'[56] Years later, when he was Prime Minister, she always referred to him as 'my horse' and gave him in memento an ivory steed that assumed pride of place in the library at Birch Grove.

Among his staff, too, Macmillan drew almost universal affection and respect. As that future socialist Cabinet Minister, Richard Crossman, wrote many years afterwards: 'What I remember chiefly about Macmillan was his buoyancy. And no wonder; not even the Prime Minister in Britain enjoyed such unquestioned prestige as Macmillan had earned for himself both in his own British staff and in Ike's entourage. . . .'[57] When Crossman was gravely ill, back in England in late 1943, his wife wrote to Macmillan:

> Yesterday he asked me if I would write you a line for him. Several times he has said that his visit to Algiers was probably one of the happiest times of his life. . . . The other day when he was at a very low ebb, he made me smile by saying 'Nowadays, I sometimes think what I would like my last words to be and, I'm awfully sorry, but they're not addressed to you, they are to Harold Macmillan. Tell him that I wanted to go on working with him.' . . .[58]

In February 1944 Macmillan himself was again stricken down with illness, this time with acute and painful eczema on his hands. Though partly attributable to the burns suffered in his plane crash the previous year, it also seems to have had as much of a neurasthenic cause as his earlier illness, and he was forced to take a month's leave in England. From the emotional tone of his letters to Dorothy, he clearly yearned for her company, despite all that had gone wrong with the marriage. Frequently he tried to delight the gardener in her with descriptions of the carpets of wild gladioli and irises produced by the Algerian spring. Replying to a description she had sent of a visit to Chatsworth on a spring day, he wrote:

> Alas, I fear I cannot write now what I would like to – but I read and re-read your letter and could see Dorothy Cavendish – first a little girl I never knew with pigtails – then Canada – and then the young woman and always that love of trees and woods and streams which I (poor fool) dared to imprison in the stucco and railings of Chester Square. Dear, dear Dorothy – please forgive me. . . .[59]

There was seldom a shortage of dramas on the home front to distract him. In March 1944, he was being consulted by the distraught wife of his agent in Stockton and telling Dorothy:

Apparently that silly fat husband of hers has fallen in love with a French nurse. He is thoroughly entangled and I have got to disentangle him. It's a great bore – because he was a *very* bad agent and I should prefer to see him settle down in Algiers than return to Stockton, if I only thought of my interest. But I suppose I must try and do something. . . .[60]

Cupid was also capable of striking closer to home. A letter of 15 January shows Macmillan worrying about his eldest daughter: 'How strange Carol is! I know she will either have a tremendously successful and useful life or a disaster of equal proportions. I worry rather over her, because she is so like us both – sensitive, passionate, irresponsible in certain moods. She has your greatest quality – honesty of mind.'[61] Three months later Carol married a dashing Welsh Guards officer, Julian Faber.

Carol's marriage provoked further pangs of sentiment in Macmillan, stuck away as he was in the Mediterranean. There were times when he wished his job could be wound up, so that he could come home. Writing to Dorothy on 19 April, he found it hard to realise where the years had gone: '. . . I do wish we had some more children – very small. Dear Carol . . .'.[62] He hoped that Dorothy might be able to come out and join him '*very* soon'. On their twenty-fourth wedding anniversary two days later, the wild anemones and cyclamen he had seen flowering while on a visit to Alex at Caserta made him recall nostalgically Chatsworth and Birch Grove.

The following day he was exulting that she was on her way to join him in Algiers for what would be a four-month visit. 'Hurrah, hurrah! It is splendid and we are all much excited. It will be such fun. . . .'[63] There followed joyous days of picnics and bathing expeditions to Macmillan's favourite haunt, the enchanted sea-lapped Roman ruins at Tipasa, west of Algiers ('the old city in its garden of myrtle and figs and greenery as romantic as ever. . . .'),[64] or to the wild mountains of Kabylia. Often they were accompanied by John Wyndham; while Dorothy bathed, Harold would spend the day lazing in the sun and reading *Coningsby*, as his old friend, Ike, led the great invasion into Normandy. With her earthy forthrightness, Dorothy immediately endeared herself to all who met her, trumping even Diana Cooper by swimming uninhibitedly 'in the buff', like the British soldiery, off Algiers. In July she accompanied him as he left Algiers permanently for Caserta, after nineteen months in North Africa: 'without much regret, but grateful for an experience which has been the most interesting, even exciting, of my life . . .'.[65] Typically, about all that Macmillan records of Dorothy's visit in his memoirs was that 'She was to stay for four months . . .', but in effect these were clearly some of the happiest months of the war for him.

At Odds with Eden

In the long year between the Italian armistice and Macmillan's transfer to Caserta from Algiers, there were times when his diaries show him feeling out of the centre of the war, frustrated and wanting to be sent home. Nevertheless, through energy and ability, coupled with ambition, he was all the time increasing his actual base of power, insubstantive as it appeared – much to the growing displeasure of Eden at the Foreign Office. From their tentative collaboration on the Conservative backbenches, Macmillan was aware of Eden's highly strung temperament and jealous nature. A clash seemed inevitable. From the beginning Eden had been unhappy about Churchill's appointment of Macmillan to Algiers, reporting as he did direct to Churchill and short-circuiting the Foreign Office, and it was probably in part to pacify Eden that Churchill had kept Macmillan's function ill-defined and anomalous.

The arrangement had worked reasonably smoothly until the Italian armistice, but by 2 January 1944 Bob Dixon, now Eden's Principal Private Secretary, was recording in his private diaries a 'latent crisis' in the Foreign Office over the function of the two Ministers of State in the Mediterranean: 'AE's feelings about HM are really the difficulty. . . .'[66] In March Noel Charles was brought back from Brazil by Eden to take over as future Ambassador to Italy, but when Dixon spoke to Macmillan (who was then on a visit to London) about it:

it was disconcerting to find that he had no intention of allowing NC to replace him as High Commissioner in Italy yet. He seems to think of Noel merely replacing Harold Caccia and acting as the Resident Minister's Deputy. This will never be accepted in the FO. There is no real job left for HM in the Mediterranean, and I think he knows this and would like a Department at home but sees no prospect of getting one. He is even casting sheep's eyes on the FO, AE having somewhat imprudently told him of his own difficulties in carrying that office together with the Leadership of the House. . . .[67]

Macmillan's own account of this was that:

the FO, of course, want their own man (Charles is a professional diplomat). I do not mind, as I think anyway my job is an impossible one and the more ambassadors, etc., I have to manage the merrier. I already have Duff Cooper, [Ralph] Stevenson (Yugoslavia), Leeper (Greece), Steel (F.O. chap for Roumania, Bulgaria, etc.). Now I shall have Charles (for Italy). Nevertheless, I expect there will still be something to do, because all the generals hate the Foreign Office men and distrust them profoundly. So I have no doubt there will be quite an amusing task in reconciling them and getting some reasonable decisions made. . . .[68]

In May, Macmillan despatched a memorandum on a general policy for Italy,[69] which was critical of the Foreign Office's 'dangerously blind view'[70] and clearly impressed Churchill. Macmillan complained of the lack of any positive policy to preserve the fabric of Italian social, economic and religious life, and thus avert the dangers of Communism on the one hand and Fascism on the other; the economic crisis in Italy was 'not being tackled with any real grip'; and, in addition, he was receiving 'no guidance or directive of any kind' on British policy for the Balkans. Macmillan's aim was for an early conclusion of a peace treaty with Italy which Eden, whose reputation had been so closely linked with combating Mussolini's imperialist ambitions, thought should be concluded only when the war with Germany was finally over. To someone as authoritarian in his control of British foreign policy as Eden was, Churchill's interference was bad enough, but such an intervention by a junior with an anomalous post must have been intolerable. On 9 May Macmillan was told firmly by the Foreign Office, 'The time is not yet ripe for any such fundamental change in our relations with

Italy.'[71] Three days later Macmillan waspishly told Anthony Rumbold:* 'The fact is that the Secretary of State [Eden] is very prejudiced against the Italians. He does not realise that they are largely responsible for the success of his political career. What are we going to do about it?'[72]

On 17 June, less than two weeks after D-Day, Alexander showed Macmillan a personal telegram to Churchill, 'couched in strong and even eloquent language'. Alexander pointed out that Kesselring's armies in Italy were beaten, and that there was nothing to prevent him marching on Vienna. Instead of Anvil (the projected landing on the French Riviera), he proposed 'an operation eastwards to cross the Rivers Po and Piave, seize Trieste and the Istrian Peninsula, and march through the Ljubljana Gap threatening Vienna'. In this Alex was strongly supported – and, indeed, influenced – by his political adviser. Code-named with geographical appropriateness Armpit by Alexander and Macmillan, it was the genesis of the much disputed 'Ljubljana Gap' strategy.

Alexander, says Macmillan, asked him to fly to London to support his telegram to Churchill. Accordingly, he set off, accompanied by the Chief of Staff to SACMED, General Gammell, 'on an undertaking far outside the most liberal interpretation of my functions', but with little apparent hesitation. Arriving in London on 22 June, Macmillan at once aroused Churchill's ardent enthusiasm for Armpit, it being, of course, very much in step with his (as well as Macmillan's) forward political thinking – to forestall the Russians advancing too far into Central Europe. But, however politically desirable, 'a powerful statement of the case' by the Prime Minister met with Brooke's equally powerful opposition on the grounds that it was militarily impracticable and 'not based on any real study of the problem'.[73] The seal was set on it on the 28th, when the American Chiefs of Staff replied with 'not only a brusque but even an offensive refusal to accept the British plan . . .'. Roosevelt was insistent that Anvil, the ancillary thrust through the south of France, to which he felt he had committed himself to Stalin at Teheran, was to go ahead. Churchill was incensed; Macmillan flew back to Italy, deeply disappointed.

To the end of his life, Macmillan argued that the failure to pursue

---

* Sir Anthony Rumbold, later Ambassador to Austria; at this time a Second Secretary on Macmillan's staff.

the Ljubljana Gap strategy was a tragic mistake, writing in his memoirs that it 'might have altered the whole political destinies of the Balkans and Eastern Europe. . . . But apart from Roosevelt's desire, at that time, to please Stalin at almost any cost, nothing could overcome the almost pathological suspicions of British policy, especially in the Balkans. . . .' The war, thought Macmillan, could have ended 250 miles east of where the Iron Curtain eventually dropped, with Vienna and Prague firmly in Western hands.

Since 1944, the argument has raged over the feasibility of Armpit. More recently, historians in sympathy with Brooke have condemned it on tactical grounds. Whatever the military verdict, however, there is no doubt that Armpit vigorously enhanced Macmillan's political reputation with Churchill – as well as his friendship with Alex. At the same time, it brought him into further conflict with Eden. Macmillan recorded that the Foreign Secretary was 'put out' by his unheralded visit to London to plead the case of Armpit versus Anvil; it was in sharp contrast to his friendly reception by Churchill, who told him that the Foreign Office was rather annoyed at him coming without permission, but went on to say that 'I am very pleased you have come. You are not a servant of the Foreign Office. You are my servant and colleague and you must do whatever you like.'[74]

Eden's side of the picture comes over clearly in the diaries of Sir Robert Bruce Lockhart, head of the Political Warfare Executive and closely in touch with Eden's circle at the Foreign Office. Bruce Lockhart recalled how Macmillan, on 22 June, had expressed himself 'a great admirer of the PM', who:

for all his tiredness and old age was still far the cleverest man we had. Macmillan was not so flattering about Anthony who, he said, seemed so far away when he [Macmillan] saw him . . . that obviously he was taking nothing in. Said Anthony had too much for any one man to do, should give up the Foreign Office where he was handicapped by Winston's constant interference. . . . Cranborne could do the job well. . . . 'there ought to be a change. I think I could get on with the "old boy" [Winston] better than most people.'[75]

'Macmillan obviously has ambitions to be Foreign Secretary,' concluded Bruce Lockhart, returning to the theme three days later:

Anthony [Eden] is also much worried by the activities of Harold Macmillan who not only is having some success with the PM on questions of Mediterranean strategy, but is also interfering with Italian and Balkan affairs and is upsetting our representatives, Noel Charles and Lord Moyne, in those areas. Trouble was that now we had ambassador in Algiers to French, ambassador in Italy to Italians, Resident Minister in Cairo for Middle East and Balkans, etc., there was no proper post for Macmillan in Mediterranean unless, as he seemed to wish, he usurped functions for the Foreign Secretary. Anthony said: 'We already have two Foreign Secretaries (i.e. himself and WSC); I am not going to have a third!'[76]

In July Macmillan received a stinging but also somewhat contradictory rebuke from Eden for his handling of talks with Tito, to which he snapped back: 'I find it difficult to reconcile the severe, not to say wounding censure in the first sentence of your telegram with the tenor of the remaining portion. It seems to me that like Balaam you started out to curse but remained to bless. . . .'[77] The following month Churchill himself, with Bob Dixon – representing Eden – arrived in Italy to decide, among other things, on the political chain of command. Macmillan's stock with Churchill had undoubtedly risen since the spring; nevertheless he had to battle for his existence every inch of the way. Churchill could blow hot and cold. On 11 August, Dixon noted, 'The PM very critical of the FO. . . .', accusing it of being 'inconclusive': '"If you ask the FO to write you a paper, you add up the paragraphs with odd numbers, and you get one opinion, add up the paragraphs with even numbers and you get another: and no conclusion. . . ."'[78]

Three days later, Churchill, replying to a Macmillan note advocating the Italian peace treaty, pitched in on Eden's side:

I cannot see what advantages we gain or disadvantages we seek to avoid by making this untimely peace with Italy when the Armistice terms provide for everything. Surely the peace terms should wait until the general Peace Conference. Besides this, the present Government have absolutely no representative authority. They hold office only as a result of their own intrigues. The industrial [and strongly Communist] north has no representation and may easily repudiate what is signed behind their backs. . . .[79]

The following day, on top of this somewhat reproving note, Macmillan got wind of a plot to have him ousted – probably tipped off by Randolph Churchill, who had also turned up in Rome and was to become a life-long ally. Macmillan wrote in his diary that he had confronted Bob Dixon with the charge that he had been sent out to Italy to abolish the post of Resident Minister, Mediterranean, 'to which he has rather shamefacedly admitted. If only Anthony had told me straight out that he wanted to get rid of me I would willingly have resigned. Indeed I have told both him and the PM that I am ready to wind up the show at any moment. But I resent being got out by the back door. . . . I shall now fight for my position to the bitter end.'[80]

On the next day, 16 August, after a dinner with Churchill, he recorded that 'We had one tiff, but I answered him back. I am sure this is the right way to treat him. He then becomes very amenable and pleasant. If you let him go on, he tramples on you.'[81]

Churchill told Dixon that he was toying with the idea of appointing Macmillan to succeed General Mason-MacFarlane as head of the Allied Control Commission, the executive body now in charge of Italy, then added, rather lamely, 'He must have a job for HM. There was nothing available at home. . . .'[82]

Macmillan had meanwhile submitted a far-reaching memorandum, another of his famous 'think-pieces', on the reorganisation of the Mediterranean Command. Generals – and diplomats – should be subordinate to the politicians (e.g. himself); further, the Command should be divided into a Central Mediterranean and an Eastern Mediterranean theatre. The advantages would be 'that we should obtain a free hand in Greece and elsewhere in this area to use British power as we thought fit . . .',[83] i.e. without American interference. It was all radically at odds with Eden's thinking.

The arguments continued for a week, and for a while Macmillan's chances looked dim. In fatigue coupled with a touch of the Black Dog, he seems to have come close to throwing in his hand. But by 21 August the tide had turned in Macmillan's favour. 'Further telegrams prepared on Greece,' he wrote jubilantly in his diaries: 'I fear Anthony may not like the decision. . . . I cannot help being amused by Bob Dixon's predicament. He came out with orders to abolish me. In the first days he has given me Greece. Tomorrow he has got at least to get me out of Italy! Roger [Makins, Macmillan's chief Foreign Office adviser] is triumphant. . . .'[84]

Macmillan's own triumph at the discomfiture of Eden's envoys was complete the next day, when Churchill refused to go along with Dixon's efforts to elevate Noel Charles at the expense of Macmillan. 'When Charles cried out piteously, "But what am I to do?" he replied, "What do Ambassadors ever do?" . . . He wants *me* to be head of the Control Commission and run the new policy. He will *not* have a [preliminary peace] treaty, but he wants a steady process of relaxation of control. This, he says, is the task of the politician not the diplomat. . . .'[85] By Dixon's account, Macmillan had thrown down his gauntlet, and suggested that he be withdrawn. Churchill had promptly picked it up and said to Macmillan '"Certainly you mustn't be withdrawn. I will make you head of the whole show. . . ."'[86]

Macmillan, exhausted, had won almost all the points. Although he was forced to yield to Eden's viewpoint that a peace treaty with Italy should be concluded only when the war with Germany was finally over, he had got through the general policies he believed in. But the battle lines with Eden for future years had been drawn up.

On 14 September Churchill wrote to Roosevelt,[87] telling him that he proposed to appoint Macmillan to the office of Chief Commissioner of the Allied Control Commission, formerly held by General MacFarlane, 'in order to have more political knowledge and experience in this post, so full of economic and political issues and so important for the welfare of the Italian people'. Macmillan would remain as British Minister Resident at Allied Headquarters and British Political Adviser to the Supreme Allied Commander.

Thus Macmillan had got rid of his *bête noire*, the Italophobe Mason-MacFarlane, and the Americans tacitly handed the reins of administering Italy to Macmillan. On 10 November, he became Acting President of the Allied Commission, the Supreme Allied Commander being the (nominal) President. At last Macmillan's status was regularised, and he found himself in an executive role. In practical terms, conditions of life for the Italians greatly improved: 'Power became increasingly available; transport was gradually provided. The Italian Government began to function with reasonable independence. . . .' In political terms, Macmillan's accretion of personal power was immense, and it was no exaggeration to term him, as did John Wyndham, 'Viceroy of the Mediterranean by stealth'.[88]

Chapter Nine

Greece and Victory
October 1944–May 1945

I have decided that in sieges it is permissible to drink the former ambassador's champagne.

(HM, during siege of Athens Embassy, December 1944)

The Americans wanted to 'liquidate' as soon as possible the whole situation arising from the war in Europe.

(HM, War Diaries, 2 January 1945)

Macmillan's involvement in Greece began with a 'vague understanding' early in 1944 that the country, when liberated, would
come under his responsibility. This had been confirmed by
Churchill during his visit to Italy in August, after which
Macmillan had found himself established as *de facto* 'Viceroy of the
Mediterranean'. But instead of his involvement comprising, as in
Italy, the relatively simple task of organising the economy, assuring
food supplies and laying the foundations for self-government, Macmillan found himself being sucked into the vortex of a full-scale
civil war. The Greek political scene was far more confused and
fragmented than the French and Italian put together, and considerably more lethal. During the years of pre-war instability, power
had wobbled back and forth between Venizelist Republicans, the
monarchy and a military dictatorship, with the Communists a
constantly menacing force in the background.

Since it was Churchill who had courageously, but hopelessly,
gone to the aid of Greece against the Axis in March 1941, the task
of liberating her was also allotted to Britain in the autumn of
1944. Meanwhile, however, as the German grip slackened, vigorous
resistance groups had established themselves within the sanctuary
of rugged mountain areas. As in other occupied countries, the first
group to arise, as well as the best organised and most ruthless, was
Communist-controlled – the National Liberation Front (EAM),
with its guerrilla/military formations of ELAS, both in turn subordinate to the Greek Communist Party (KKE). Later, other groups
sprang up, notably EDES, of republican but anti-Communist persuasion. All were kept going by British arms and supplies. But by the
summer of 1943, as well as killing Germans, ELAS – strengthened by
arms received from the capitulating Italian forces – began to attack
and try to eliminate its non-Communist rivals. Local order was
further weakened by the fact that both the King, George II, and
the lawful government were in exile. On top of the miseries of

German occupation and starvation, by the winter of 1944 the wretched Greeks faced mounting civil war.

Predictably the future of the King of Greece had provoked serious dissension between that dedicated monarchist, Winston Churchill, and an ailing Roosevelt. Finally it had been agreed that the King should not return to Greece until after the German withdrawal, and that a plebiscite should be held thereafter. The Americans offered to help with relief and rehabilitation, but made it clear in advance that they would accept no other responsibility. Thus, from the start, Macmillan and the British would be on their own. On 8 October, Churchill and Eden, on their way to Moscow, joined a major conference at Caserta, attended by representatives of the various Greek factions. Here Macmillan was the principal architect of an important accord whereby the warring guerrilla leaders undertook to place their forces under the orders of General Scobie, the British commander-designate of Allied Forces in Greece. It was also decided that he should go forthwith to Athens and endeavour to set up a Regency Commission, as a kind of caretaker body. News from Greece made maximum haste essential; ELAS were now reported massacring civilians in the Peloponnese; the Germans were withdrawing rapidly (they left Athens on 13/14 October), and the Communists looked as if they might seize power any minute. (Fortunately, noted Macmillan in his memoirs, 'they waited another six weeks'.)

On Friday the 13th, inauspiciously, Macmillan set off aboard the cruiser HMS *Orion*, the Admiral's flagship, accompanied by General Scobie. The *Orion* was well in the van of a fleet of over a hundred ships, preceded only by busy little mine-sweepers; behind came a Greek battleship bearing the Greek government of George Papandreou with the British Ambassador, Rex Leeper. It was an eventful voyage. The fleet had barely entered Greek waters when German mines began to explode all round, and a British sweeper was blown up, followed by two more. Then 'a small water-ship . . . struck a mine very near us – just off our starboard bow – and went down like a stone. Twelve men were saved, the other ten or fifteen were drowned.'[1] A number of mines cut from their moorings by the sweepers drifted dangerously down the line, to be fired at by a variety of weapons. It reminded Macmillan (who could seldom resist resorting to field sports for a good analogy) of 'trying to shoot rabbits in thick bracken. The mine is hard to see and hard to hit.'

227

He found it altogether 'a thrilling experience – it really gave one an idea of the problems confronting a navy today. . . . Fortunately we were not troubled with enemy aircraft. Only one approached us (a Ju. 88) and was promptly shot down by Spitfires. . . .' Here was the kind of physical action that Macmillan, the swordsman, had been longing for ever since September 1939, and from now on his diaries take on a new tone of excitement.

The fleet reached Piraeus on the 17th, but the Greek government refused to land – because it was a Tuesday. Baffled at first, Macmillan subsequently discovered that this was the day of the week when Constantinople had been captured by the Turks in 1453 and there was a widely respected Greek tradition that nothing should ever be initiated on a Tuesday. Twelve years later, when Macmillan as Foreign Secretary was faced with the problem of Cyprus, he would remember this incident as an example of the undying feelings of the Greeks about the Turks. When Macmillan did land the following morning, all his classical background responded to the sense of occasion. It was an emotional day. Together he and General Scobie drove from Piraeus into Athens 'through crowded streets, filled with cheering crowds, like an election day at home. Whenever a British uniform appeared, great enthusiasm and applause. . . . I did my part and encouraged General Scobie to do the same, bowing, waving, blowing kisses etc. from the open car.'[2]

Alas, the euphoria was not long-lived, as it soon appeared that the Papandreou government had little influence outside Athens. During those initial honeymoon days, however, Macmillan managed to push through some important measures providing food and stabilising the drachma. So appalling was inflation that the price of a newspaper rose from 2 billion drachma to 4, then to 10 billion, and when the currency was finally stabilised (by Sir David Waley, brought in from the Treasury by Macmillan) the rate was 50,000,000,000 old drachmas to one new. Churchill flew in on his way back from Moscow, to report a bizarre agreement whereby the USSR, in return for being granted '90% predominance in Rumania' had agreed to permit the British to exercise 90 per cent influence in Greece, against a Russian 10 per cent. How it was intended that these mystical percentages could be measured out as if by some alchemist was never clear, though Macmillan at the time was curious about what would come out of the Soviet 10 per cent. The answer was not long delayed.

Meanwhile, exigencies in Italy required him to flit repeatedly back and forth to Caserta, where, already at the beginning of November, he found the Americans 'up in arms' at British actions in Greece. The British press was no less critical. On 28 November the Communists repudiated the undertakings to Papandreou, with the EAM police refusing to hand in their arms; in Athens there were fierce demonstrations against both Papandreou and Leeper. On 2 December a general strike was unleashed by the Communists; there were riots in Athens, martial law was declared and the police opened fire on the rioters. In London much of the British press spoke loosely about the 'Fascist' Greek police, while Churchill was enraged by an article in *The Times* which opened with the words: 'The seeds of civil war were well and truly sown by the police of Athens today.'[3] But this was, in effect, the day that civil war did break out in Greece.

On 5 December, General Scobie records visiting Papandreou and finding 'him and his Cabinet in a state of despondency verging on panic'.[4] Harshly, Leeper told Papandreou, 'Mr Churchill once described you as a second Venizelos. Many people today are calling you a second Kerensky.'[5] Scobie himself was a deeply worried man, having just received an order from SACMED for the return of the key 2nd Para Brigade (presumably for operations in northern Italy where the Yugoslav partisans were creating a new problem). He considered this unit essential for keeping order in Greece, and took the initiative of wiring directly to Churchill to have the order reversed.

Clearly someone in the higher councils of war had made a grave error in assessing the military strength of ELAS; Leeper for one never thought the numbers of British troops adequate in case of major trouble. Macmillan, meanwhile, was in London during these early days, preoccupied with Italian problems. On 8 December, he went to the House of Commons to hear Churchill give 'a superb parliamentary performance' against some bitter attacks. One particular phrase stuck in his mind: 'Democracy is no harlot to be picked up in the street by a man with a tommy gun.'[6]

If British parliamentarians and press were hostile, possibly even more disturbing to Macmillan, as to Churchill, was the virulence of the American reaction. In Athens, during the early days when the British were most hard pressed, the Americans had gone out of their way to display neutrality, travelling about the city with stars-and-stripes on the bonnets of their cars. In the States, there was ill-informed comment that the British were primarily interested in restoring the Greek monarchy. Roosevelt's new Secretary of State, Edward Stettinius, sharply criticised British policy and the involvement of her troops in Athens. British wartime propaganda was to blame, Macmillan thought, for building up the resistance fighters, in Greece as elsewhere, as Byronic idealists when in fact 'with all their patriotism, they had become the instrument of Communist ambitions'. He noted sadly at the time how Britain had 'drifted apart from our American ally'.[7] Already strained over the de Gaulle versus Giraud controversy, over Mediterranean high strategy and over the administration of Italy, it was Greece – as Macmillan saw it – that marked the breakdown of the wartime honeymoon.

Churchill was evidently much dejected, and fatigued, by this discord, and the night after the Commons debate Macmillan found him 'in rather a petulant mood'. He accused Macmillan of deserting his post, to which Macmillan replied firmly that he had been summoned back from Athens, and – on Churchill's own orders – was bound for Washington for top-level talks on Italy. The Prime Minister, according to Macmillan, then 'rambled on in rather a sad and depressed way',[8] countermanded his orders and asked him to hurry back to Athens, which, Churchill wrote in a note the following day, 'seems to me to be a field of action incomparably superior to what was mapped out for you in Washington'. This was exactly Macmillan's view, and with alacrity he and John Wyndham sped back to Greece on 11 December.

Under Siege

Joined by Alexander, they arrived in Athens to discover that the rebels were now holding four-fifths of the city, and all the hills round it, with the British forces and the Embassy besieged in a small central area. After an hour's delay, because the road was under shell-fire, 'we left for General Scobie's HQ. Alex was in one tank, I in another. (The room provided for a middle-aged politician is not great.) It was quite an interesting progress and I could see through the periscope what was going on. . . .'[9] The news Scobie gave could hardly have been worse; the British had been badly caught by surprise; the insurgents controlled the power station, the main airport and access to the ports. The British had no secure base from which to operate and only an estimated three days of ammunition and six days of food left. Alexander promised to send supplies and two fighting divisions from Italy, but warned that December was not the best month for landing them on the open beaches of Phaleron Bay.

Alex's pronouncement, 'You are in a grave situation',[10] seemed somewhat superfluous, and on reaching the British Embassy Macmillan speculated about whether he was committed to suffer the fate of Gordon of Khartoum. One thing was certain: it was imperative to find a political solution with the utmost despatch. He was fortunate to find an able collaborator in Rex (later Sir Reginald) Leeper. Meeting Leeper for the first time in Rome that summer, Macmillan had not been unduly impressed: 'I like him well enough, but he is terribly vague, incompetent, and donnish. He is clever, but in a negative and irritating sort of way.'[11] Later Macmillan came to realise that the 'vagueness' concealed a brilliant classical mind and a remarkable grasp of the swiftly changing kaleidoscope of Greek politics. 'He understood the Greeks, and they understood him. . . . he was not easily taken in. If he believed in mankind, he had a healthy distrust for most men, and all politicians.'

Leeper (who had initially held reservations about finding himself under Macmillan) was equally taken by his boss, and at one point threatened to resign if another Cabinet minister were sent to replace him in Athens. 'He was always looking ahead,' Leeper wrote subsequently in his memoirs, 'foreseeing the next difficulty and taking steps to forestall it. . . . His advice on immediate issues was as wise as his vision in anticipating future developments was constructive. . . .'[12] By the following June, the ubiquitous Bruce Lockhart was recording in his diaries that Leeper now regarded Macmillan as 'his latest hero', and would have liked to see him take over the Foreign Office – 'if anything happened to Anthony'.[13]

Together, under the worst of auspices inside the besieged British Embassy, Macmillan and Leeper got down to distilling a political potion, which, certainly at the time, looked as though it would indeed need to have magical qualities. Alexander claims that it was Macmillan who advanced the claims of Archbishop Damaskinos, Archbishop of Athens;[14] but Macmillan more modestly accorded the initiative to Leeper who, he said, 'had no difficulty in persuading us that the King should be asked to agree to the Archbishop being appointed Regent'. Either way, it was a solution that strongly appealed to all three.

Dedicated monarchist that he was, Macmillan did not have quite the same enthusiasm for preserving the monarchy in Greece that he had shown over Italy. He was not over-impressed by King George II, a homosexual, who had sat it out in exile in London and Cairo, where Macmillan felt he 'hadn't done much good'. He also realised that, in the hearts of many Greeks, George II was associated – rightly or wrongly – with the forces of reaction. Personally, Macmillan preferred the brother, later King Paul. At the same time, Macmillan had constant misgivings about the Allied policy of giving all-out support for left-wing resistance, or partisan movements, simply because they killed Germans. He would often cite Wellington's simple wisdom in declining to inflame Spanish–American revolutionaries against Napoleon: 'I always had a horror of revolutionizing any country for a political object. I always said, if they rise of themselves, well and good, but do not stir them up; it is a fearful responsibility.'[15]

As Macmillan explained his position many years later, in 1944 Greece there was no such thing as an indigenous royal dynasty. It was German or Danish: 'not at all like the monarchy that starts with Edward the Confessor. It hadn't a great connection with the country. But it represented something.' It was quite clear that it was difficult to run a constitutional monarchy in Greece, but the situation at that time struck him as 'absurd'. It was:

> as if the whole of England was split between Conservatives and Liberals, and we were allowing ourselves to be taken over by a Communist revolution. On the whole the Venizelists were, rather like in England, the City, rich merchants, and the monarchists were peasants, the people. . . . the obvious way to bring them together was to have a Regency, because by that means you preserved the principle of the monarchy; you allowed it to be established whenever it was suitable, for example, by plebiscite once the rebellion had been crushed, but you got both sides to strike at the Bolsheviks.[16]

It was now a matter of winning over the King, the various squabbling Greek political leaders, Winston Churchill and the

Americans to support the key personality at the heart of the Leeper/ Macmillan proposition. Initially all opposed it with varying degrees of vehemence.

Macmillan had been instantly struck by Archbishop Damaskinos when he first set eyes on him, at an armistice ceremony: 'This splendid figure – well over six foot – in black robes, with a black hood draped over his Orthodox hat, and a long black ebony cane with a silver top, intoned a blessing in a fine musical baritone, with appropriate hierarchical gestures, dignified, traditional, and immensely impressive.'[17] Alexander equally admired the Archbishop (who, apparently, had been a champion wrestler in his youth) as 'a strong character, fearless and incorruptible', who had stalwartly refused to knuckle under to the Germans. 'He was to prove a great friend of Britain,' noted Alex, who however 'surmised at the time that the Prime Minister was unlikely to approve of him, since he would consider that his sympathies inclined too much to the Left.'[18]

This was hardly an understatement. At one point Churchill convinced himself that Damaskinos was both a Quisling and a Communist; he spoke of him to Macmillan as a 'pestilent priest, a survival from the Middle Ages', and expressed grave fears that the Archbishop would make himself into a dictator supported by the left wing. He took a similar line in his correspondence to Roosevelt. Nevertheless, Macmillan continued undaunted with his struggle to pressurise the Greeks into accepting the 'pestilent priest'. On 13 December, General Scobie records the King still rejecting Damaskinos, but 'Macmillan sent a cracking reply asking for an answer today.'[19]

Meanwhile, a serious and indeed menacing battle was going on around the now besieged Embassy. On 13 December, Macmillan recorded in his diary how 'a very heavy attack was made on us last night. The rebels rushed the HQ of one of our armoured brigades and got in. The fighting is still going on there now. It is about 300 yards from the Embassy.'[20]

Inside the Embassy were some fifty people, including servants and guards, sleeping in the passages because the front rooms had had to be evacuated, and all cosseted by Mrs Leeper – 'a really splendid woman', commented Macmillan, 'who presided with grace and dignity over the many weeks of the siege', feeding the inmates on reduced army rations of bully-beef and biscuits. Because of rebel action, there was no heat, light or mains water, though 'we have fortunately filled all the baths; we have a lily pond in the garden; and today we have found a disused well, which will probably give us at least water fit for cooking and some washing'.[21]

The shortage of water, however, was mitigated when – early on in the siege – Macmillan stumbled on the intact wine cellar that had belonged to Sir Michael Palairet, British Ambassador when the Germans had seized Athens. He ordered that the locked door be broken down, which appears to have provoked one of the few disputes between Macmillan and his host, Leeper, with the latter insisting that the contents were the private property of his predecessor. As a burst of automatic fire hit the outside of the Embassy, Macmillan reputedly sat down and wrote on a slip of paper: 'I have decided that in sieges it is permissible to drink the former ambassador's champagne. Harold Macmillan, Minister of State.'[22] For the rest of the siege morale was maintained at the expense of the absent Sir Michael.

Into what John Wyndham described as this 'odd house party' had arrived as Press Attaché Osbert Lancaster, cartoonist, classicist and erudite wit, whom Macmillan regarded as 'a great addition . . . a tower of strength, common sense and fun'. Certainly the combination of Lancaster, Wyndham and Macmillan must have done wonders to induce an atmosphere of gaiety into an otherwise grim situation. Down in the half-basement, more or less out of bullet range, they set up what Macmillan nicknamed 'Pratt's Club', comfortably supplied with champagne and booze from the looted ambassadorial cellar; 'there is a little party there every evening before dinner, with some of the girls, which helps to cheer things up.'[23]

The Embassy, painted pink and therefore a conspicuous target, was under constant fire at close range. Exercise was limited to a small part of the garden, and even that risked a sniper's bullet. The lanky John Wyndham tried skipping until a bullet struck at his feet. In full sight of all safely inside the Embassy, he threw himself for cover into the herbaceous border, 'only to hear the Ambassadress cry from behind the French window: "Oh, John, not the dahlias!"'[24] With bullets playing round him, the unfortunate Wyndham was then enjoined by Osbert Lancaster to keep the sniper 'in play', while an armoured car was called up to pick him off. During another attack, Wyndham admitted that while reading for distraction a copy of Gibbon 'bound in blue cloth . . . I found that I had sweated so much that the blue had come off on the palms of my hands'. Later that same night, he ended a draft despatch to Eden, which reported that 'the enemy were at the gates' (as indeed they were), on a typically Wyndhamesque note of the kind that always endeared him to his boss: 'therefore, Sir, I may cease to have the honour to be Your obedient servant. . . .'[25]

Macmillan seems to have taken the daily risks with a mixture of unflappability and almost enjoyment. He and the Ambassador insisted, as a matter of principle, on using the official study, remarking in his memoirs only that 'the bullets came through the window, but there was a corner in which one could sit without undue risk'. In fact the walls around the Ambassador's desk were pitted with bullet holes, and to reach it he and Leeper had to enter the room by a side door, then creep around the floor to reach their chairs out of sight of the snipers. During one conversation a bullet actually hit the wall two inches from Macmillan's head; the two men stopped talking; the Minister Resident silently edged his chair out of the line of fire, then resumed the conversation. When not engaged in conference in the Embassy study, Leeper noted that Macmillan insisted on working 'in some discomfort in half a room in the Chancery', to show the Embassy staff as well as the Greeks that 'he had not come to supplant me'[26] – a display of tact that much gratified Leeper (and doubtless helped placate Eden).

Out on the streets it was even more dangerous. The talented Harold Caccia, who had succeeded Roger Makins as Macmillan's right-hand man from the Foreign Office (and was again to succeed Makins as Ambassador to Washington in 1956), narrowly missed death when his jeep was destroyed by a rebel shell. Outside Athens, too, the news continued bad, with ever increasing stories of appalling left-wing atrocities making a political solution all the more urgent. On 16 December, Macmillan recorded visiting General Scobie's headquarters – 'Got through without a bullet. . . . The military situation should begin to improve, as Hawkesworth and the 4th Division are arriving.' From there he went to see Damaskinos: 'My opinion of his Beatitude is confirmed each time I see him. About the rebels, he wishes to be quite firm; but he wants no counter-revolution. I said that was a proper distinction between the condonation of sin and its forgiveness. This pleased him.'[27]

*

In selecting and then winning over the Archbishop for the immensely delicate and taxing role Macmillan wished to impose on him, that youthful influence of Ronnie Knox, together with his abiding faith and interest in church matters, must have served him in good stead. The King, however, remained obdurate, while – in interesting contrast to his son four decades later – Prime Minister Papandreou would countenance no compromise, or conciliation, with the Communists. From London, Churchill continued to growl, unhelpfully. He still regarded Damaskinos as a Quisling and Macmillan and Leeper as 'two fuzzy-wuzzies',[28] evidently feeling that Macmillan was exceeding his brief. An angry telegram reached Macmillan on the evening of the 19th: 'He is annoyed with me for having pressed the regency with arguments about the political position at home and Anglo-American relations instead of confining myself to purely Greek considerations.'[29] He decided that night to run the gauntlet out of the Embassy the next day, and make a flying trip to Caserta. There were urgent matters involving other parts of his far-flung and expanding 'vice-royalty', and he badly needed support over Greece from his friend Alex. Accordingly Alexander sent Churchill a strongly worded telegram, culminating with the warning: 'I earnestly hope that you will be able to find a political solution to the Greek problem, as I am convinced that further military action after we have cleared the Athens–Piraeus area is beyond our present strength.'[30]

Macmillan followed this up with a personal letter to Eden, carried by a returning officer, and containing an acid criticism of the considerations of higher strategy which had led to the Greek débâcle in the first place: 'Since the dispositions made were suitable to a jamboree and not to a battle, we only just avoided a large-scale massacre of soldiers and diplomats. . . .' He went on to stress once more his and Alex's conviction that 'there is no (repeat no) military solution,' while condemning the Greek King for citing 'constitutional niceties' as a reason for his obduracy. 'All I can say is, "Constitution my foot". He did not care two hoots about the Constitution when he made Metaxas dictator. As for the politicians . . . they beat anything I have yet seen in the Mediterranean. . . .' He then put to Eden the natural volatility of political opinion: 'For instance, can you tell me whether the Conservatives or Labour will get in at the next election? I am certain that there is a large amount of sympathy with EAM in Greece, that a moderate, reasonable, progressive policy could detach the vague, radical element from the hard, Communist core.'

He seems to have flown back to besieged Athens that same day far more despondent than his memoirs reveal. In his diary entry for the 21st, Scobie recorded that Headquarters was 'full of cheer', because things seemed to be going well at last. The army was indeed doing a remarkable job, in relief and reconstruction as well as in just keeping the peace. ('Our enemies described us as an army of occupation in Greece,' wrote Leeper. 'An army with occupation would be nearer the mark.')[31] On Macmillan's arrival, however, Scobie 'found everyone in a terribly depressed state'.[32] Macmillan reported that Alex feared an enemy offensive on the west coast of Italy, and that therefore troops might actually have to be transferred *back* from Greece, rather than vice versa. (In northern Europe, Field Marshal von Rundstedt had just launched his surprise, sledge-hammer offensive through the Ardennes, which had thoroughly caught the Allies off balance and created something close to panic among the higher echelons everywhere.) According to Scobie, Alex's message via Macmillan was that he, Scobie, might therefore have to make peace; and he claims that he made a forthright response to Macmillan (perhaps rather uncharacteristic of a fairly junior general), to the effect that if peace was made now 'the cause would be lost and Greece would inevitably yield to Communism. For the sake of Britain, the Empire and the world in general, we must bring this issue to a victorious conclusion. I had no intention of making peace at present.'[33]

By Christmas Eve, Macmillan was noting that 'the sniper who shoots down our *street* is being active, but he seems to be letting us alone in the garden.'[34] In fact, however, the tide had turned; moreover, Macmillan and Alex in their combined intercessions with Churchill and Eden had made a far more powerful impact than they realised at the time.

Christmas came. And what a Christmas it was in the beleaguered British Embassy! Mrs Leeper somehow made Christmas trees out of nothing; Osbert Lancaster snipped out illuminated silhouettes of the Virgin and the Holy Child in the manger, and the Kings and Shepherds; there was carol-singing and midnight mass in the Ambassador's drawing room. While guns fired in the background, the officiating vicar had to arrive by armoured car, to deliver what Lancaster described as 'a seasonable and apposite' sermon, by referring to the Herald Angels as 'God's airborne division'. In the middle of the service, John Wyndham was called to the signal office, where a cryptic telegram had just arrived from Churchill, announcing that he was despatching 'an important envoy' by air to Athens the very next day.

The envoy turned out to be no less than Churchill himself, accompanied by Eden. Macmillan, Alex and Leeper drove out to the airport, each in a separate armoured car. There, in bitterly cold weather, with a biting wind blowing down from the mountains, Macmillan met the surprise visitor who – contrary to his expectations – 'was in a most mellow, not to say chastened, mood'.[35] In a gentle vein, Churchill chided him for his disregard of danger, and begged him to take more care. Macmillan riposted: 'Why bother? The food here is already killing me!'[36] Given the quite extraordinary risks the Prime Minister himself was taking, his concern for Macmillan was almost ironic.

After about two hours' discussion inside the freezing plane, Churchill agreed to Macmillan's plan. Rather than being lodged in the bullet-riddled Embassy, for Churchill's own safety it was decided he should stay aboard the cruiser *Ajax*, one of the victors of the Battle of the River Plate, now anchored off Piraeus. When Archbishop Damaskinos came aboard for his first meeting with Churchill, Alexander, who was in the room at the time, noted that 'Winston, slumped on the sofa, looked bored and obviously dubious about the prospects of the meeting. Then a magnificent figure of a man appeared in the doorway – strong, virile, well over six feet, with his black beard and his great head-dress which made him look like a giant.' Churchill, who – so Alexander sensed – had fixed in his mind that he was going to meet 'a politically slick cleric and a man of little real importance', rose to his feet in astonishment. From then on, the two immediately hit it off: 'Winston', commented Alexander, 'had found his man – thanks to Harold Macmillan.'[37]

The occasion had, however, nearly been wrecked at the outset when the Archbishop, in all his Metropolitan finery, arrived on the ship in the midst of a rowdy fancy-dress Christmas party. The sailors, in Churchill's own account, 'thought he was part of their show of which they had not been told, and danced around him enthusiastically. The Archbishop thought this motley gang was a premeditated insult, and might well have departed to the shore, but for the timely arrival of the captain, who after some embarrassment, explained matters satisfactorily.'[38]

The following evening, Churchill, girt about with a large pistol, accompanied Damaskinos, Eden, Alexander and Macmillan to a crucial conference in the Greek Foreign Office. In a bleak room, unheated and dimly lit by only a few hurricane lamps, all the Greek principals – including the three Communist leaders – were present. There was still the sound of firing outside. After an all-night session, an accord emerged; as Macmillan had originally proposed, the Archbishop was appointed Regent and General Plastiras, an anti-Communist republican, became Prime Minister. The Communists were effectively kept at bay, and a truce followed early in January. Churchill wrote to his wife, Clemmie: '. . . I have made friends with the Archbishop, and think it has been very clever to work him in as we have done, leaving the constitutional questions for further treatment later.'[39] It was oblique but high praise for Macmillan's role. Back in London, Churchill extracted from the reluctant King of the Hellenes an official proclamation appointing Damaskinos Regent.

Meanwhile, a ton of dynamite was discovered in the sewers beneath Scobie's headquarters in the Hotel Grande Bretagne. (Scobie remarked that if it had gone off the principal victims would have been the hostile British correspondents lodged there.) At home, it was a moment of considerable anxiety with the Germans' Ardennes offensive still causing alarm and V–2s falling with increasing regularity on London. The mandarins of the Foreign Office were appalled 'by the light-hearted nature of PM's escapade', recorded Bruce Lockhart: 'Prime Minister of Britain going away in very bad weather to settle a squabble in a very small country. No security arrangements would have been made, etc.'[40]

Nevertheless, it was undoubtedly Churchill's personal intervention that tipped the balance with the Greek politicians, and ultimately saved Greece from Communist subjugation. As he wrote himself: 'When three million men were fighting on either side on the Western Front and vast American forces were deployed against Japan in the Pacific the spasms of Greece may seem petty, but nevertheless they stood at the nerve-centre of power, law and freedom in the Western world.'[41] Here was certainly one occasion when Churchill got his priorities right. Possibly more than any other act, it confirmed the grandeur in Macmillan's eyes of 'this indomitable old man' who six weeks later was to return 'to receive the greatest ovation that any foreigner has ever received in the ancient city of Athens'.

Truce in Athens

When John Wyndham saw Macmillan back in Rome on 1 January 1945, he found him 'terribly tired', but justly jubilant at what had been achieved.[42] By early January a truce had been established, with British forces controlling Athens and all Attica. As more and more appalling stories of Communist atrocities and brutal abductions of civilians came to light, so gradually the attitude of the press at home shifted. For Macmillan, the line taken by the press over Greece left him with a mistrust for *The Times* ('pitifully ignorant and dangerously pedantic') that he could never quite shake off. He had also noted, bitterly, the impotence imposed on British action by American hostility, a lesson he would have to relearn a dozen years later at Suez. Although he had personally revelled in the dangers of the siege – 'It was all great fun,' he would exuberantly claim in his eighties, confessing unashamedly: 'I enjoy wars; any adventure's better than sitting in an office!'[43] – he was also able to philosophise on the basic tragedy of the Greek civil war, whereby disunity of the bourgeois parties had opened the door to Marxism and revolution. 'The issue of the second half of the twentieth century,' he wrote prophetically in his diary on 11 January, 'will not be monarchism v. republicanism, but a liberal and democratic way of life versus the "proletariat dictatorship of the Left" and the police state.'[44]

As one of the combatants, and a considerable expert on Greece, C. M. Woodhouse, remarked, Macmillan himself had displayed 'almost unerring judgement' in dealing with the 1944 crisis.[45] Approbation for Macmillan's role was not, however, universal within the British corridors of power at the time. General Alan Brooke, the CIGS, commented in his diaries that Alexander, 'in his absorption in the Greek episode, was being too much influenced by his very able partner, the Resident Minister of State. . . .'[46] Macmillan's contribution had been incalculable, and if Greece had enhanced his admiration for Churchill, the reverse was indisputably true; for here, in the Prime Minister's entourage, was one of those rare people who had showed that he possessed both the strength of character and now the self-confidence to stand up to this terrifying colossus – and get it right.

By a miracle, the precarious truce held up. During it Macmillan managed to snatch a few moments to visit the sites of Ancient Greece in which he had been steeped since childhood. There was a visit to the Acropolis in brilliant sunshine, then pottering about old streets that disclosed fragments of temples and market-places. A flight down the Gulf of Corinth delighted him with 'a splendid view of Mount Parnassus – snow-covered – and of the great mountains of Peloponnese on the southern shore'. In the evenings he would read Bertrand Russell's *Power – A New Social Analysis*: 'witty, pungent, philosophical, whimsical and bitter. I enjoyed it.'[47]

On another trip to the Royal Palace at Tatoi, accompanied by Osbert Lancaster and the Leepers, Macmillan noted compassionately the misery of the Greek peasants, scrabbling for firewood, miserably dressed. The palace itself, occupied by ELAS during the civil war, presented 'a horrible scene of dirt and destruction: every chair ripped of its covering (no doubt for clothing), furniture smashed, the filth of a monkey house in every room, and some unburied and putrefying corpses. Such was the result of an occupation by the noble army of ELAS, so beloved and admired by *The Times*,' he added bitterly. In sharp contrast, the Greek spring was bursting out with new hope. 'Crocuses, anemones – white, blue and crimson – wild aubretia, cyclamen, and thyme,' Macmillan described to his garden-loving wife: 'You, dearest Dorothy, would have been in ecstasies of pleasure.'[48]

On 14 February, urged by Macmillan, Churchill on his way back from the Yalta Conference flew in triumph to an Athens at peace, and ecstatic. Some 50,000 Greeks thronged Constitution Square to greet him. It was a perfect day of Athenian early spring and, compared with that bleak Christmas Day of armoured cars and gunfire of just six weeks previously, the atmosphere reminded Macmillan of 'a football match, or a race meeting in peace-time'. In the crowd he detected 'a sense of relief, as well as of triumph; a feeling of gratitude and pride, of a people who had been through a hard and gruelling test . . .'.[49] As the sun dropped below the Acropolis, Churchill made an unprepared but memorable speech, culminating with the words: 'Let party hatreds die. Let there be unity. Let there be resolute comradeship. Greece for ever! Greece for all!'[50] Later that afternoon, Macmillan took his friend Alex to Marathon, where he enjoyed pointing out to him that the Persians had come within twenty-six miles of Athens, compared with the seventy miles from Cairo where Alexander had found Rommel when he took over command.

There were still years of hard struggle before the Communist guerrillas were defeated in Greece, in which the recalcitrant Americans would have to bear the financial burden, but Macmillan often speculated subsequently on what had persuaded the Soviet hand to hold off when all Greece could so easily have been seized, militarily, during that grim winter of 1944. He reckoned Stalin must have been deterred by the resolution shown by the Churchill government, and decided 'to call off this attempt and wait for a better occasion'. For Macmillan himself, there was one last, gratifying incident remaining. When Archbishop Damaskinos gave up the regency in September 1946, two years before his death, he wrote glowingly to him: 'With feelings of love and gratitude I send my warmest greetings to my dear Mr. Macmillan, whose admirer and devoted friend I shall always remain, and I pray that the Grace of God may always rest upon him and that he may be blessed with happiness in his great country.'

After a semblance of peace had been restored to Greece in February, Macmillan once more had to concentrate his energies on Italy, where problems, old and new, had been mounting up. Although his forces had been diluted and diverted to other fronts, Alexander had thrust across the Arno and broken through the Gothic Line, fanning out into the Lombard Plain. By the end of April he was reaching out for the great northern cities of Turin, Milan and Trieste, and – with more of Italy cleared of the enemy – he was pushing on the doors of Austrian Carinthia. With every fresh square mile of territory occupied, Macmillan's headaches – and Alex's – multiplied. Yet it was clear that the end of the war could not be far off. Not for the first time Macmillan, amid all his immediate preoccupations, found himself thinking about the shape of post-war British politics, and his own place there. As soon as the war ended, there was bound to be a general election; would he stand for Stockton again? And, if so, would he be re-elected?

Back in September 1944, he had received an enticing proposition from his friend, and successor in Algiers, Duff Cooper. Knowing that he was about to be appointed Ambassador in liberated Paris, and would therefore have to give up politics, Duff Cooper had 'offered' Macmillan his parliamentary seat of the St George's division of Westminster. Embracing Mayfair and Belgravia – the wealthiest residential areas in London – St George's was probably *the* safest Conservative seat in the whole country.

At first Macmillan was clearly taken by the proposition, writing to Duff Cooper on 4 October that he would be very glad to have his name put forward but, with his habitual political prudence, he begged Cooper to keep the matter secret: 'I have not yet written to the Chairman of my Association at Stockton and do not propose to do so until I have definitely arranged some other less exacting seat. It would be very embarrassing to me if my name were mentioned in connection with St George's and then it did not come off.'[51]

When Macmillan claimed in his memoirs that it did not take him long to make up his mind, he was not being entirely candid. He was evidently still mulling over the proposition in March 1945, when Lord Beaverbrook intervened with a letter 'imploring me not to give up Stockton for St George's' and making a high-handed offer that, if Macmillan lost Stockton, whoever won St George's would be shuffled off into the Lords to make room for him. In his diary Macmillan noted, 'I am really rather annoyed about all this fuss,' but he reluctantly felt he had to acquiesce: 'I have no agent, no association, and no funds! . . . It seems my fate to try to get away from Stockton but never to achieve it!'[52]

So much for 'dear old Stockton'. Nevertheless, his decision to eschew St George's was not formally announced until 26 April, the same day he offered himself for re-election at Stockton. The clinching arguments, he said, were the same 'which had actuated me fifteen years before at Hitchin. . . .'

Important as this was to him, during these last months of the war in Europe, Macmillan could have had only the most fleeting moments for such personal considerations. The pressures were greater than they had ever been. As Acting President of the Allied Council for Italy, he was responsible for all the mountainous problems of food, the reconstruction of industry and the rehabilitation of hundreds of thousands of liberated Italian prisoners-of-war; each of these problems escalated as the Allies thrust deeper into the industrial north. Up in the north the Communist-controlled Italian partisans were also becoming increasingly active, well organised and armed. The recent bitter experiences in Greece were not forgotten, and Macmillan thought it essential to absorb these partisans into either the British or Italian armies, in order to get hold of their weapons. Unless they were 'disarmed', a revolutionary situation, as in Greece, seemed likely to occur.

On 8 February Macmillan wrote a despatch along these lines to Sir James Grigg, Secretary of State for War. To retain control over the Communist groups right from the start, Macmillan, with the full support of Alex, arranged for the infiltration of British officers and 'reliable Italians' into the partisan bands. At the same time he was warning Eden, 'We do not want to see Italy break up and/or "go Communist".'[53] Gaining Foreign Office support to this end, he pursued vigorous action to strengthen the political hand of the infant Bonomi government against Communist activities.

While he was fighting these battles, Macmillan noted with some disillusion how he could count less and less on American co-operation. Already in January 1945 he was recording that 'the Americans want to "liquidate" as soon as possible the whole situation arising from the war in Europe.' The blow that struck all the Allies alike on 12 April – the death of Roosevelt – also had its profound effect on a whole range of American policies, while in his first few weeks in office the new President, Harry Truman, who was a stranger to the realities of power, tried to find his feet.

Tito – A New Threat

America's apparent apathy played its role in a new problem that was to become the most critical of any that confronted Macmillan and Alexander as the war drew to a close: the threat to Trieste and north-eastern Italy by Marshal Tito's Yugoslav forces. Eden had done his best to limit Macmillan's involvement in Yugoslav affairs, and to prevent any contact with Tito himself. Thus it had not been until August 1944 that Macmillan had his first meeting with this new rising star on the Mediterranean scene, when Brigadier Fitzroy Maclean (who had commanded the British Military Mission to Tito's partisans since the previous year) had brought him to lunch at Macmillan's villa in Caserta.

Macmillan was clearly struck by Tito's forceful personality, but determined to take a no-nonsense line with him. He firmly refused to have Tito's personal bodyguard standing in the dining room during lunch; instead they stood in the passage, but 'we shall gradually reduce them to standing outside the house'. Tito, he wrote, was 'quiet, well behaved, interesting and seemed reasonable. I think he is very much on his best behaviour. It is difficult to form an estimate of his quality. He obviously has character and power of command. He is shorter, stockier, and even fatter than I expected, but he has a certain dignity which is impressive. . . .'[54] Macmillan had already spotted the contradictions into which Churchill's declared policy of supporting anyone who would fight the Germans was bound to deliver him: 'it is difficult to be a Communist in Yugoslavia and a Royalist in Greece. . . .'[55] On the other hand, if he were cold-shouldered by the Americans and the British, Tito would inevitably be pushed further into the arms of the Russian bear.

In September 1944 the Soviet forces had entered Yugoslavia, linking up with the partisans. A new strident tone entered Tito's voice; he 'has been behaving rather rudely to us', Macmillan noted mildly in his diary for 24 November. Elated by the liberation of their country, largely by their own heroic efforts – inspired by Communist ideology and heavily armed by Soviet weaponry, the Yugoslav partisans had suddenly transformed themselves from an essentially guerrilla organisation into one of the most powerful, and determined, armies on the European battlefield. Tito had made quite plain his territorial claims on the Italian provinces of Istria and Venezia Giulia, with their substantial Slovene and Croat populations. It was equally plain that he would occupy these areas before Alexander could arrive with any sensible forces. Because Trieste in Venezia Giulia was, among other things, essential as a supply port, Alexander on his own initiative flew to see Tito in Belgrade. The result was highly unsatisfactory. Macmillan noted vexedly in his diary for 20 February 1945: 'Of course, this matter (which may easily become urgent) ought to have been dealt with at the [Yalta] Conference. But they [the Foreign Office and State Department] either overlooked it or shirked it.' He found it difficult to see how Tito's forces were going to be ejected.

On Alexander's return, a tense meeting took place between himself and Macmillan, out of which emerged two proposals: to divide Venezia Giulia into two zones, leaving the eastern zone to Tito; and to establish a military government over the whole region, in which the Yugoslavs would be allowed to participate. This would, Macmillan thought, avoid any danger of *de facto* political recognition. Both proposals were vigorously opposed by Eden and the State Department, Eden making it plain that Macmillan was once again exceeding his brief. But as Macmillan complained in his memoirs, 'nobody was prepared to answer Alexander's vital question. If the Yugoslavs opposed his occupation of the whole of Venezia Giulia, was he to use force?'

By 26 April, Macmillan was still complaining that they had no instructions. He succeeded, however, in carrying a proposal that Alexander should 'content himself with trying to get Trieste and the Robertson (or Wilson) line. This can be defended against Tito and/or Stalin as a *military* necessity to secure Allied communications into Austria.'[56] The line to which Macmillan referred was to be roughly the line along which the issue was finally resolved nearly ten years later in October 1954. But in the late spring of 1945, as the German collapse released Yugoslav units which then met the thin British advance guard face to face, so the menace grew to the gravest proportions. The Americans began to switch their policy to what Macmillan considered to be 'a very pedantic attitude. They thought we must occupy and govern *all* Venezia Giulia. This is quite unrealistic.' Moreover, the US War Department wanted 'to use *no* American troops and the President is beginning to take fright. Unless we are very careful, it will be another Greece – with us carrying the baby, as usual. . . .'[57]

As the men on the spot, both Alexander and Macmillan felt themselves far better qualified to judge the realities of the situation than either Eden in London or the Pentagon in Washington, from whom they had been receiving minimal guidance. Alexander (always a cautious general; certainly no George Patton) had been badly shaken by the success of the last-gasp Rundstedt offensive in Belgium and by the realisation of how dangerously depleted his own forces in northern Italy had become by the demands of Greece. Weak as he was, and with his lines of communication seriously extended by the weeks of swift advance, Alexander made it plain to Macmillan that he felt he was in no condition to face a new military threat from Tito, particularly as support from the Americans was questionable.

Macmillan was equally sensitive to the psychological problems involved. 'I am very tired – and very worried about this Tito affair,' he wrote on 9 May, the day after the German surrender:

> ... I feel that we must be very careful. Neither British nor American troops will care for a new campaign in order to save Trieste for the 'Eyeties'. On the other hand to give in completely may be a sort of Slav Munich. Nor do I know what advice to send London. It is difficult to guess what will be Winston's mood. I do not want to excite or depress him. So far, we have only reported events and devoted the rest of our efforts to advising Alex so as to keep him on the right line and avoid any traps. . . .[58]

In trying to head off a confrontation with Tito over disputed Venezia Giulia, Macmillan admitted in his memoirs that Alexander and he 'were acting beyond, or even contrary to, our instructions, but by now we had some experience of this . . .'. Here, then, was set the scene for a major human tragedy, which was to return to haunt Macmillan in his last years.

Meanwhile, in February, following the Yalta Conference, Macmillan had met General Anders, commander of the Polish II Corps that had heroically fought its way up the length of Italy with the Allies. The Yalta agreements to repartition Poland had reduced Anders to near despair, and there followed a 'painful' monologue in which Anders declared that 'Poland was finished, betrayed by her allies. It was now merely a question of time before all Europe would succumb to Bolshevism.'[59] It was, Macmillan recalled, a 'terrible evening'.

After nearly six hard years of war, the leaders on the British side were beginning to show marked signs of battle fatigue as the end drew near. Macmillan was no exception; between January and April 1945, seven trips (in an uncomfortable B–25 twin-engine bomber) are recorded to Greece, and six separate visits to the Italian front. On his last trip to Greece, in mid-April, he admitted to falling asleep several times while in conference with Leeper and the new Greek Prime Minister, Admiral Voulgaris. Occasionally, in quest of solace or stimulant, he would drink too much. Henry Hopkinson, then a career diplomat serving under Macmillan on the Commission for Italy and later to become a close political colleague of both

Macmillan and Eden,* recalled him returning from one of his excursions to Greece at about this time: 'he was rather tight and at the end of a long table I can still see him criticising loudly Anthony's policies – and gesticulating – in the middle of which he suddenly fell over backwards. . . .'[60] The episode stuck in Hopkinson's mind (he remained throughout a staunch supporter of Eden) 'as an act of disloyalty towards Eden even then'; but it was probably at least as revealing of Macmillan's own exhaustion as of the state of discord that had come to exist between the two politicians.

Back in Italy, on one of his tours to the front, Macmillan had a last fleeting moment of personal glory in the expiring war. On 23 April, he and his escort encountered an American infantry battalion 'advancing in rather a gingerly fashion' on the city of Modena, apparently still occupied by the enemy. Ever the swordsman, Macmillan decided to beat the Americans into Modena. There was, he recorded, a little desultory sniping still going on, but 'our arrival at the Municipio (or Town Hall) caused some excitement. There was a lot of shouting and embracing. The leader of the partisans kissed me on both cheeks on being told that I was the famous Haroldo Macmillano – said by the BBC to be the ruler and father of the Italian people. . . .'[61]

Suddenly in the midst of all this rejoicing, a two-hour duel flared up between the partisans and Germans and Fascists who had taken up positions in nearby windows. The partisans, firing off a motley of arms in all directions, caused the Minister Resident 'more alarm than our opponents', but eventually it was all over and Macmillan and his entourage left, claiming 'we had "liberated" Modena'.

Afterwards Macmillan slipped away for a few days' repose to Assisi, visiting St Francis's monastery and the churches and what he decided was the most beautiful place almost in the whole of Italy. It was at Assisi that he heard both of the grisly hanging of Mussolini and his mistress, and of the German surrender in Italy to Alexander, on 29 April. Churchill paid a warm tribute to Alexander, and it was a particular source of joy to Macmillan that, after so much hard slogging, his friend and chief should have received the honours of the first major German surrender before the conquest of Berlin. As it was a purely military matter, Macmillan felt it proper to continue to lie low at Assisi, where he noted simply in his

* He became Lord Colyton in 1956.

diary that 'with all his power of evil, his strength, his boasting', Hitler had lasted twelve years, whereas, in contrast, 'St Francis did not seem to have much power, but here in this lovely [place] one realises the immense strength and permanence of goodness – a rather comforting thought.'[62]

When the long-awaited actual day of peace came on 8 May, Macmillan recalled years later the curious sense of emptiness, of flatness. He longed to get back to England, and felt that, after two and a half years in the Mediterranean, his job was completed. Yet, in the chaotic aftermath of war, though there remained little more than two weeks for him in his post as Churchill's Minister Resident, there was no opportunity for the indulgence of anything resembling emptiness. The collapse of Germany, if anything, exacerbated most of the problems Macmillan already had on his plate. Having marched all the way from El Alamein, Alexander had now acquired boundaries for his command – and thus for Macmillan's 'vice-royalty' – which were vastly over-extended. He had to face on the one hand the ever mounting pressure by the Yugoslavs and their Soviet backers, and on the other hand the appalling problems of supporting and relocating the tragic flotsam and jetsam of war that the tide had washed into Alexander's inflated command.

It was out of these unexpectedly harrowing last days that grave charges emerged to assail Macmillan over thirty years later: the forced repatriation to the Soviet Union and Tito's Yugoslavia of White Russians and anti-Communist Yugoslavs.

Chapter Ten

A Tragic Epilogue
May–June 1945

I thought we had arranged to send all the Russians back to Russia.

(Churchill to the Foreign Office, 28 October 1944)

It's rather as if you had been fighting alone for four years with the Campbells as your ally – then they ask you to hand over the MacFarlanes and the MacTaggarts to them.

(HM, on the Yugoslav repatriations)

By May 1945, in the Austrian province of Carinthia there were nearly 400,000 German troops who had surrendered to Lieutenant-General Charles Keightley's (British) V Corps; among them were approximately 40,000 Russians who, to some extent or other, had been associated with the Nazi armed forces. According to the Yalta Repatriation Agreement signed on 11 February 1945, all Soviet citizens liberated by the British, and all British subjects liberated by forces operating under Soviet command, were to be handed over. This Agreement was interpreted as meaning that all Soviet citizens captured while serving or having served with the Germans were to be repatriated, forcibly if necessary. The Soviet government were reciprocally committed to the safe and swift repatriation of all British and American POWs liberated from Nazi camps in Eastern Europe. The United Kingdom government did not regard as Soviet citizens those White Russian émigrés who had escaped Bolshevism in the wake of the 1917 Revolution.

Among the surrendered Russians, who included an estimated 11,000 women and children 'camp followers', were upwards of 4000 of these old émigrés, some serving with Cossack and Caucasian units who had operated under German command in Yugoslavia and Italy, others who had served in a separate formation known as the Russian Defence Corps (*Schutzkorps*), or 'Rogozhin Corps' after the name of its commander. The Rogozhin Corps claimed to be the last surviving unit of the old Russian Imperial Army, and had found refuge since the Russian Civil War in Yugoslavia, where – during the Second World War – it had taken part in operations against Tito's partisans. Among those serving with General Domanov's Cossacks within the 15th SS Cossack Cavalry Corps, commanded by a German general, von Pannwitz, were – notably – two ex-White Russian generals, Krasnov and Shkuro. None of these White Russians was liable to repatriation under the Yalta Repatriation Agreement. Yet by the end of May 1945, amid scenes of frightful brutality in which women and children 'dependants' were involved, they along with most of the 40,000 had been handed over to troops commanded by the Soviet Marshal Tolbukhin. Some of those repatriated committed suicide; some were summarily executed; most were despatched to labour camps, where many did not survive the abominable conditions. Krasnov, Shkuro and some of the other old émigrés were eventually executed after a period of imprisonment.

The details of this harrowing story were revealed first by Lord Bethell,[1] and then expanded upon in a series of books by Nikolai Tolstoy, culminating in *The Minister and the Massacres*, which was published in 1986.[2] This focused the burden of blame sharply on Macmillan, who was alleged by Tolstoy to have 'conspired' to send the old émigrés to their doom, and thereby deliberately to have contravened agreed British policy. Tolstoy further alleged that in doing so he deceived the Allied Commander-in-Chief, his old friend Alexander, with equal deliberation. No coherent motive was given except a concluding innuendo that Macmillan was in some way in thrall to the Soviet KGB.[3] These charges constituted the most serious ever made against Macmillan in his lifetime, to the extent that, at one time, even his own son-in-law, Julian Amery (who had served with the anti-Communist Albanians during the war), was led to regard the repatriations as 'one of the few blots on Harold that I can think of'.[4] Thus the charges demand detailed examination, part of which is to be found in the form of extended notes at the back of this book.

The nub of all the allegations against Macmillan centres on a meeting between him and General Keightley at Klagenfurt on 13 May 1945, but they also have to be seen in the light of the circumstances in Europe as the fighting ceased in 1945, and of the British government policy behind the Yalta terms and its interpretation.

The Yalta Agreement had been made at a time when relations with the Soviets – crucially important to the Churchill government – were already deteriorating, but the real horror of Soviet brutality in Eastern Europe, on both a national and an individual level, was not yet fully appreciated. As Churchill confessed later: 'I felt bound to proclaim my confidence in Soviet good faith in the hope of procuring it. . . . Our hopeful assumptions were soon to be falsified. Still, they were the only ones possible at the time.'[5]

The British government policy to repatriate all Soviet citizens, including civilians, had been discussed at three Cabinet meetings over the months before the Yalta Conference. As early as 24 August 1944, Sir James Grigg, Churchill's Secretary of State for War, had written a note to Eden which showed Cabinet members fully aware of the likely consequences of their policy: 'the dilemma is so difficult that I should like a Cabinet ruling as to its solution. If we hand the Russian prisoners back to their death it will be the military authorities who do so on my instructions and I am entitled to have behind me, in this unpleasant business, the considered view of the Government'.[6] On 4 September 1944, the Cabinet met to give Grigg the backing he needed, agreeing to send back all Soviet POWs then in British hands, irrespective of their wishes. A minute from Churchill to Eden of 18 January 1945 further indicated the bent of British policy at this time: 'Why are we making a fuss about the Russian deportations in Roumania. . . ? It is understood that the Russians were to work their will in this sphere. Anyhow we cannot prevent them.'[7]

On 29 January, Churchill and Eden had set off for Yalta, Churchill with a temperature of 102 degrees. Two days later the Cabinet met to approve the draft agreement to be considered at Yalta. In Churchill's absence, it was chaired by the Deputy Prime Minister, Clement Attlee, and attended by two other leading Labour members of the wartime coalition government, Bevin and Morrison (both future Foreign Secretaries), as well as sixteen other ministers and Sir Orme Sargent, the Deputy Under-Secretary of State for Foreign Affairs. There was discussion of a Soviet proposal that any reciprocal agreement to cover the repatriation of prisoners-of-war 'should be extended to all liberated Soviet and British subjects'.[8] The 'general view' of the Cabinet, comments Martin Gilbert, was to accept this Soviet proposal, which meant that 'any Soviet citizen who was liberated in western Europe should be "repatriated" to Russia, not merely those who had fought in the German ranks, or aided in some way the German policy of persecution. . . .'[9]

On 15 February, three days after the Yalta Agreement had been made, Churchill and Eden passed through Athens, where they gave Macmillan a first-hand account of what had transpired. The importance of Soviet relations for both military and political reasons was forcefully impressed on him. Both Churchill and Eden were seriously concerned by reports of Soviet harsh treatment of British POWs; and one of the most cogent issues on the agenda was the repatriation of these prisoners. By the time of Yalta they were still believed to number an estimated 50,000. This proved subsequently to be exaggerated; nevertheless, given the conditions in Soviet-occupied Eastern Europe, the importance of precipitate action assumed a special dimension.

Following the Yalta Conference, the Combined Chiefs of Staff issued a directive to Eisenhower and Alexander to give immediate effect to the agreement. AFHQ transmitted instructions accordingly to the British forces under their command (including Eighth Army HQ, which was the immediately senior formation to Keightley's V Corps) in letters of 6 and 15 March.[10] The letter of 6 March stated, *inter alia*, that 'all persons of undoubted Soviet citizenship will be repatriated irrespective of their own wishes'; but 'any person who is NOT a Soviet Citizen under British law will NOT be sent back to the Soviet Union unless he expresses a desire to be so.' It then spelt out its definition of what constituted a Soviet Citizen, under British law, 'in order to assist in determining the nationality of prisoners of war':

all persons coming from places within the boundaries of the Soviet Union as constituted before the outbreak of the present war. All persons coming from territories west of such boundaries have Polish or Baltic state nationality unless there is evidence to show in particular cases that they have acquired Soviet Citizenship by their own voluntary act. A man who has served in the Soviet Army is not a Soviet citizen if he comes from territories west of 1939 boundaries of the Soviet Union unless he has acquired Soviet Citizenship. . . .

The object of this definition was clearly to enable Balts and Poles to escape the Soviet net. British officers and men of the Eighth Army had fought all the way up Italy alongside the heroic Poles of General Anders' army and would have felt particularly ill-disposed to any further betrayal of the Poles. In retrospect, the AFHQ Advocate-General's office, although briefed presumably by the Foreign Office, erred in not specifically excepting also any Russian citizens who had left the Soviet Union *before 1939*. Possibly, AFHQ in March 1945 was not expecting to find any such old Russian émigrés in its bag in Carinthia. But whatever the excuse, the omission was a grave one.

The AFHQ follow-up letter of 15 March, dealing chiefly with administrative procedures, if anything tightened the noose around the émigrés' necks by inserting the further word 'civilian': 'The provisions of this directive apply to all Soviet citizens, *civilian* or military, who come under British control, from whatever source, irrespective of whether they have served in enemy forces or not. . . .' Superseding previous directives, it was these two letters that provided the authority to be used by V Corps for implementing the repatriation policy for the Russians. Copies were also sent to the 'British Resident Minister'. They would have been the last rulings that Macmillan and V Corps received before the meeting of 13 May.

The Yugoslav Threat

In purely military terms, the position of all Alexander's forces in the north, but particularly that of Keightley's V Corps, appeared very precarious in the spring of 1945. Intelligence reports showed that, as the war ended, Soviet troops had begun building defensive installations in Austria, including anti-aircraft guns at a time when the Luftwaffe was no longer operative, while messages of unprecedented virulence were passing back and forth between Churchill and Stalin.

The flurry of signals from AFHQ to Whitehall and Washington, and between Truman and Churchill, reveals how seriously the potential dangers of the Trieste and general Yugoslav situation were viewed, and the strength of the concern about the problems that could ensue if operations had to be mounted. With hindsight, the scale of the problems was over-estimated, but there is no doubt that *at the time* all involved treated the situation as very sensitive. This was true even more of AFHQ than at Whitehall, although Churchill had been forcibly impressed at Yalta by Stalin's boast that the Yugoslavs now fielded twelve divisions, compared to liberated France's eight. Alexander's alarm is clear from his signal to the Combined Chiefs of Staff on 11 May, in which he stated: 'even if the Russians did not give [Tito] material support, but . . . nevertheless he decided to resist us by force, I should require a total of 11 divisions. . . .' This estimate assumed that 'my forces would display the same fighting spirit and high endeavour in battle as hereto. In

view of the announcement of VE Day, and the long publicity given
to Tito's operations in aid of the Allied cause, I am doubtful whether
in fact this would be the case. . . .'[11] Throughout the Allied forces,
intense admiration had indeed come to be felt for the exploits of
arms of Tito's partisans. Alexander went on to note that his total
strength was eighteen divisions, of which only four were British,
and, of the remainder, most could not be counted on to engage in
any action against the Yugoslavs.

On 12 May, Alexander asked Macmillan – who was due to depart
finally for England in two weeks – to go to Treviso to confer with
the Eighth Army commander, General Sir Richard McCreery, and
to discover at first hand what was really happening. It was also
Macmillan's brief from Alexander to explain to McCreery the
reasons why any armed confrontation with the Yugoslavs had
to be avoided. The previous morning a harassed McCreery had
requested from Alexander full authority to use force; to which
Alexander, at top speed, had replied that same evening that he was,
'at this very moment', in direct contact with London, Washington
and Belgrade, where matters were being discussed 'on the highest
level', that the Eighth Army commander did not understand how
serious the implications were, and that Macmillan would explain
when he arrived.[12]

Macmillan found McCreery 'worried, and a little sore over his
lack of information'. The conversation seems to have concentrated
on the Yugoslav threat, with no discussion of the fate of the surrendered White Russians and Cossacks. Macmillan showed the General
the most recent interchange of top-level telegrams, which he considered 'helpful from the psychological point of view, since it put
the General and his staff in the picture'. After visiting General John
Harding, commanding XIII Corps, and an old friend from the
North African campaign, he returned to Venice with McCreery's
Chief of Staff, Brigadier Floyd. Macmillan was sufficiently relaxed
after his day's work to do some swift sightseeing, and to experience

a great thrill to go down the Grand Canal – past the Ca' d'Oro
and the great Renaissance palaces – and stop opposite the Salute
and the Custom House – all intact and all with the same calm,
satisfied beauty, at once confident and nostalgic. We dined at the
Grand Hotel. The food (British rations) was excellently cooked.
The wine was very good. The waiters attended us as deftly and

reverently as no doubt they had the German officers until a few weeks ago.[13]

After dinner they flew back to spend the night at Treviso, at Eighth Army HQ.

Macmillan's Meeting with Keightley

The following morning, 13 May, Macmillan (accompanied by his deputy Philip Broad, Brigadier Floyd, Group Captain Constantine Benson, chief of the Allied Military Government Section at Eighth Army, and 'one or two other Eighth Army officers'),[14] flew to Klagenfurt to visit General Keightley at HQ V Corps, the force in the most vulnerable position. It seems that the initiative for this further trip came from Macmillan, acting on Alexander's brief; though Macmillan's own recollection years later was that he had responded to an urgent *ad hoc* request for a visit from General Keightley.[15] Macmillan spent some two hours with Keightley. This was a top-level policy meeting which was attended by the relevant staff officers from Eighth Army and V Corps. No records were preserved.

With Keightley now dead, the most important survivor of his entourage was the senior staff officer, or BGS, of V Corps, Brigadier Toby Low – who later became Lord Aldington. Low, not yet thirty-one and one of the youngest brigadiers in the British Army, had already won the DSO and MBE, the French Croix de Guerre and the American Legion of Merit, in fighting the Germans. A qualified barrister, nurturing political ambitions, he would be elected Tory MP for Blackpool North in the 1945 general election that was already on the near horizon in May 1945. Looking back to that time, Lord Aldington stated that he was not at the crucial meeting of 13 May between Keightley and Macmillan, but that he had been involved in drafting the signal to General McCreery that followed it.[16] Macmillan himself recalled that most of the meeting was occupied in discussing the Yugoslav problem. It was, he noted in his diaries, 'a source of trouble and anxiety', and 'We have to look on, more or less helplessly, since our present plan is *not* to use force and *not* to promote an incident. . . .'[17] This was the burden of the message he brought from Alexander; at the same time, the need was underlined to clear the area at the earliest opportunity as a contingency for possible operations against Tito. But in the last few minutes, Keightley, said Macmillan, without prior warning, consulted him on how to deal with the 40,000 Russians, for whose repatriation Marshal Tolbukhin was forcefully pressing.[18]

In both his memoirs and his diary entry for 13 May, Macmillan stated that among the surrendered Germans were 'about 40,000 Cossacks and White Russians, with their wives and children'. 'These were', he wrote in his memoirs, 'naturally claimed by the Russian commander, and we had no alternative but to surrender them. Nor indeed had we any means of dealing with them had we refused to do so.' His more detailed diary entry reads:

> To hand them over to the Russians is condemning them to slavery, torture, and probably death. To refuse, is deeply to offend the Russians, and incidentally break the Yalta agreement. We have decided to hand them over (General K. is in touch and on good terms with the Russian General on his right), but I suggested that the Russians should at the same time give us any British prisoners or wounded who may be in his area. The formal procedure is that they should go back through Odessa (which I understand means great hardship). I hope we can persuade the local Russians to hand them over direct (we think he has 1,500–2,000) and save them all this suffering, in exchange for the scrupulous adherence to the agreement in handing back Russian subjects.

(The numbers of British prisoners may have been exaggerated in Macmillan's mind at the time, but he would naturally have felt more concern at their fate than at that of any pro-German 'White Russians'.)

Immediately after Macmillan's departure from Klagenfurt, Keightley was warned that their sector was about to be flooded with yet another 300,000 Germans and 200,000 Croats, moving north-westwards from Yugoslavia, and posing one further nightmare for V Corps. This subsequently proved to be a wild exaggeration. Later that same day, Macmillan went on to record a 'robust' message from the US:

> The Americans have suddenly hardened; the President [Truman] will not be 'pushed about' any more. He proposes a stiff note to

Tito, amounting almost, if not quite, to an ultimatum. This, of course, entirely alters the position from last Thursday (when General McNarney told us categorically that his orders were that American troops were not to be used in the Jugoslavian affair). I at once telegraphed to Churchill saying that the position seemed to me radically changed (I wonder for how long!). . . .[19]

He ended a long day with a 'pleasant dinner' with his friend Alex, listening to a tired Churchill on the radio.

Back in London, Churchill's Private Secretary, Jock Colville, was writing similarly in his diary entry of 14 May: 'The Americans seem willing to stand four square with us and Truman shows great virility; but Alexander has alarmed them – and incensed the P.M. – by casting doubts on the attitude of the Anglo-American troops, should there come an armed clash with the Yugoslavs. . . .'[20]

That same day Keightley signalled McCreery at Eighth Army.

On advice Macmillan have today suggested to Soviet General on Tolbukhin's HQ that Cossacks should be returned to SOVIETS at once. Explained that I had no power to do this without your authority but would be glad to know Tolbukhin's views and that if they coincided with mine I would ask you officially. Cannot see any point in keeping this large number of Soviet nationals who are clearly great source contention between Soviets and ourselves.[21]

A similar message, with the request 'Please inform MACMILLAN', was despatched by V Corps to AFHQ.[22] At AFHQ, General Robertson, Alexander's Chief Administrative Officer, promptly telegraphed back to V Corps the confirmation that 'all Russians should be handed over to Soviet forces at agreed point of contact established by you under local arrangement with Marshal Tolbukhin's HQ. . . . steps should be taken to ensure that Allied PW held in Russian area are transferred to us in exchange at same time. . . .'[23] It would have been General Robertson's responsibility that the Field Marshal saw this telegram, or was at least cognisant of its import.

Over the next two weeks, British V Corps went ahead with arrangements to repatriate the 40,000 or so Russians in their hands, which included the old émigrés and families and camp followers. According to the records, Macmillan had no further involvement, following his return to Caserta, but it is on Keightley's words 'advice Macmillan' and on Macmillan's own apparently ill-defined blanket phrase 'Cossacks and White Russians'[24] that blame for sending back the 'non-Soviet citizens' has been laid at his door.

Questioned three and a half decades later about it,[25] Macmillan – despite his normally phenomenal memory – was hazy in his recollections of the Keightley conversation. He stressed that he had been sent to Klagenfurt as Alexander's agent, but with full *advisory* powers only; he could initiate no orders to the military.[26] The 'White Russian' problem had not, Macmillan recalled, been on the agenda and, when popped in by Keightley during the last ten minutes or so of their two-hour meeting, no specific names of White Russians were ever mentioned.[27] Concerning the fateful words contained in his memoirs, and the underlying diaries, 'and White Russians', Macmillan declared forthrightly, on more than one occasion, 'I may well have said "we'd better send them all back". . . . Quite possibly we did send back the White Russians, by mistake. . . .' Both he and Keightley, as well as the other senior officers in the chain of command between Alex at AFHQ and Carinthia, should, he admitted, have been aware of the Yalta ruling that excluded the 'old' White Russians (though the unclear form in which this was passed down is shown in the key AFHQ letter of 6 March). In the general confusion of the moment, it is also arguable that the AFHQ rulings governing Soviet citizenship may well have been insufficiently clear in their implications even to Brigadier Low's attuned legal mind, but that he complied with them as he understood them. Macmillan, confiding in extreme old age what he would wish to be handed down in his official biography, was prepared to 'take the blame' for sending back the White Russians 'by mistake', 'but I can only be charged with giving bad advice, or the wrong advice – advice going beyond Yalta. I would not go into the witness box and say that I did not give such advice. . . . I cannot be charged with giving orders. I am unable to say *who* might have given the executive order.'

Macmillan also emphatically dismissed any suggestion that he might have sought *ad hoc* advice from Eden, the Foreign Office or the Cabinet in London. Eden was in the US and physically out of touch; any communication to him 'would have gone through AFHQ, and there would have been a record'. There was none.

Though he never made any attempt to pass the blame down the

line, he felt that possibly his 'advice' to Keightley might have been 'misinterpreted', or that 'somebody' in V Corps had exceeded his brief. His diary entry for 13 May shows him to have been fully aware of how dire the consequences would be for the repatriated; nevertheless he remained unrepentant over their fates – even of the 'old émigrés' who may have been wrongfully handed back, of whom he once remarked: 'All they could think of was Russia and the Russians; it was rather as if we had been pushed out of England to Canada, then if the Nazis had attacked, we got up and turned on the Canadians, thinking that the Nazis were going to get us back home. . . .'

In this context, the bitterness that prevailed in 1945 among the British combatants towards the Germans or *anybody* wearing a coal-scuttle helmet cannot be understated. The shooting war had only just ended, Belsen and the full horror of the concentration camps only just revealed, and soldiers who had been shot at by men in German uniform were unlikely to enquire too closely whether these were Germans or press-ganged Russians, let alone 'old' or 'new' Russians. Nor would most soldiers have, as of May 1945, concerned themselves too deeply in the fate of such unfortunates (although attitudes changed later among the men who actually had to herd them into the transports themselves). British Army sentiment was probably exemplified by a subsequent comment of Brigadier Toby Low: 'we were not awfully sorry for them, because they had been fighting for the Germans.'[28] It was a sentiment that Macmillan – with his own grim experiences of the First World War – wholeheartedly shared.[29]

Many of the 'Victims of Yalta' had quite appalling reputations. The track record of Cossack, Ukrainian or White Russian units fighting alongside the Germans is one of beastliness often paralleling or even exceeding that of the worst SS units. In northern Italy and Carinthia, where they were finally rounded up, the Cossacks – employed by the Germans to hunt down partisans in the last stages of the war – left an outrageous trail of murder and rape. Macmillan's own oft-repeated stigmatisation – 'they were terrible people – like Genghis Khan' – was almost certainly shared by many of the British officers with local knowledge. Patrick Martin-Smith, a British liaison officer in north-east Italy who had observed at first hand the behaviour of Domanov's Cossacks in 1944, remarked: 'It is not surprising therefore if Mr Macmillan could see very little reason why the Cossacks should not be handed over in May 1945. Certainly none of us did when the matter arose at the time. . . .'[30]

Five days after his return from Klagenfurt, Macmillan sent one of his regular letters to Sir James Grigg, the Secretary of State for War (who had been so unhappy about the repatriations back in August of the previous year), reporting on his meeting with Keightley:

> . . . I must say the troops are behaving with amazing self-control and good humour in a very difficult situation; but I think something must be done soon to bring it to an end – I mean at any rate within the next three or four weeks. Otherwise the temper of the troops will be too hardly tried. The utter confusion in these areas is really astonishing. . . . In Austria one British [i.e. V] Corps seemed to be charged with:
> (a) Disarming, shepherding and feeding about 400,000 Germans.
> (b) Dealing with the White Russians and Cossacks, together with their wives and families, serving in these German forces.
> (c) Dealing with Ustashis, Chetniks and other Yugoslav refugees, deciding which, if any, are to be handed back to the Tito troops etc.
> (d) Standing their ground against a very large force of Yugoslav troops and partisans who have invaded Carinthia.
> (e) Coming to some arrangement with large Russian armies on their Eastern flank. . . .
> General Keightley did not seem unduly depressed at the size of his problem. . . . But at the same time it is very disagreeable and one does not quite see how it can be straightened out without some lapse of time. As I write I have just heard that Tito has made a prevaricating and unsatisfactory reply to the Anglo-American démarche. I do not know what the outcome will be. It is now out of our hands here. . . .

He ended: '. . . I have been down at A.F.H.Q. more than at Rome lately because of this Yugoslav crisis – the Field Marshal likes me to be about so that we can talk things over. . . .'[31]

This letter suggests several things: that Macmillan's visit to Keightley had not resolved the matter, and that there had been no further intervention by the Minister Resident; and that, far from working behind his back, Macmillan was in closer contact with Alexander than ever.

The Role of V Corps

Meanwhile, on 14 May, the day that Keightley sent his signal on 'advice Macmillan' to McCreery, the Eighth Army diary entry states that 'the refugee and PW situation V Corps area becoming unmanageable and prejudicing operational efficiency of Corps. Essential to clear it immediately in view of the political situation.'[32] It was an understatement. Civilisation had all but broken down. Armies of 'displaced persons' were drifting from one end of Europe to the other amid Brechtian scenes reminiscent of the Thirty Years' War; all had to be fed, and administratively 'tidied up' by the victorious Allied armies. But these armies, and especially the British, were themselves physically and mentally exhausted. Decisions of great magnitude were being taken daily, not in the boardroom atmosphere of a peace-time headquarters, but by harassed and overworked young company commanders, often in their mid-twenties, out in the field.

This was reflected by Alexander signalling for help, in almost desperate tones, to Eisenhower, on 17 May. Stating that the prisoners in his area now totalled about 220,000, with Croat and Slovene refugees still pouring in, he stressed:

> With possibility of hostilities in Austria against Yugoslavs, it is essential to free my L. of C. [Line of Command] immediately from this embarrassment. . . . My situation . . . in Austria is one with which it is impossible for me to deal. . . . My earnest appeal to you is to come to my assistance as regards surrendered German armed forces including Cossacks. . . . The only alternative is that as matter of operational and administrative necessity I shall be compelled to disband them, which would produce confusion in contiguous German territory under your command. . . .[33]

The same day Alexander sent an 'Emergency' signal to the Combined Chiefs of Staff in Washington, in which he pressed urgently for direction regarding the final disposal of three particular groups: 50,000 prisoners, including 11,000 women, children and old men, who had 'been part of German armed forces and fighting against the Allies' (i.e. the Cossacks); Chetniks, presently estimated to total 35,000; and German Croat troops numbering 25,000. To return these people to their country of origin might, Alexander stated, 'be fatal to their health'.[34]

On 18 May, the minutes of the Chiefs of Staff record that in response to Alexander's urgent pleas for help, Admiral Sir Andrew Cunningham 'suggested that Field Marshal Alexander should be instructed to hand over to the Russians all Cossack prisoners of war, and pointed out that under the Yalta agreement, they would in any event have to be repatriated to Russia'.[35]

The formal reply to Alexander, approving retrospectively the transfer of Cossacks overland to the Russians, did not arrive until 20 June,[36] by which time the damage had been done; but it is clear from internal notes in Whitehall in May to the Chiefs of Staff Secretariat that the Cossacks had to be treated as Soviet nationals and returned. Telephone calls between Whitehall and AFHQ would have reflected this.

On 21 May at a meeting at V Corps headquarters chaired by Brigadier Low, where the situation remained tense, it was confirmed which Russian formations should be handed back and which should not. Among those *not* to be handed back were Rogozhin's White Russian *Schutzkorps*, while among those to be returned was General von Pannwitz's 15th SS Cossack Cavalry Corps, mainly comprised of Soviet citizens under the AFHQ definition given on 6 March, but also including some Russian émigrés as well as German and other nationals. It was decided – again at V Corps level, contrary to AFHQ policy, and without any further 'advice Macmillan' – *not* to effect positive screening for non-Soviet citizens among the formations that were to be repatriated, on the grounds that this would inflame the remainder and thus make repatriation very difficult except by the use of considerable force. As confirmed by Brigadier C. E. Tryon-Wilson, the Senior Administrative Officer at V Corps, verbal instructions to divisional and brigade commanders were in accordance with the decision not to screen formations to be sent back.[37]

An important memorandum, entitled 'Definition of RUSSIAN NATIONALS', was signed by Brigadier Low and sent to V Corps units on 21 May.[38] It incorporated, correctly, the established ruling on Soviet citizenship, but – apparently for the first time – introduced the rider of 'living within the 1938 boundary of the USSR'. It referred to doubts which had been raised within V Corps about the treatment as Soviet nationals of 'certain formations and groups', and then went on to state categorically that the Rogozhin *Schutzkorps* 'will NOT be treated as SOVIET NATIONALS until further notice'.

Yet, among those that were to be treated as 'Soviet Nationals' were listed by name the reserve units of Lieutenant-General Shkuro; on the other hand, the order went on to specify that 'Any individual although of RUSSIAN blood who, prior to joining the GERMAN forces, had not been in USSR since 1930, will NOT until further orders be treated as a SOVIET NATIONAL. . . .' Why the arbitrary date of 1930 had been picked out of the blue is not known, and the order appears contradictory, in that while the first part had embraced Shkuro and the other 'old émigrés', the second part clearly exempted them. At the same time, Krasnov and Shkuro had, very honourably, not come forward to be treated differently from their unit or their fellow Cossacks.[39]

The V Corps order of 21 May stressed that 'Individual cases will NOT be considered unless particularly pressed', and – further – that 'In all cases of doubt, the individual will be treated as a SOVIET NATIONAL'. Low, in retrospect, regarded the order as 'absolutely clear. . . . you would treat all these Russians as Soviet Nationals, unless they complained. . . .' As a lawyer, he agreed that it was a case of Roman as opposed to British law, with the onus on the prisoners to prove they were not Soviet citizens.[40] The overriding requirement on 21 May had been: send back the Cossacks; and with them went Krasnov and Shkuro.

No signals or messages during the period up to the actual repatriation of the Cossacks referred to the émigrés as such. The protests that went up the line to higher authorities from many of those involved, including the divisional commanders Arbuthnott and Murray, were about sending back the Cossacks in general, some of whose leaders had been named as specifically wanted by the Soviet authorities; the émigré problem was never in itself raised.

On 22 May, at a conference of V Corps commanders, authority – brutal in its implications – was given to 'shoot at Cossacks to enforce evacuation' if necessary.[41] The same day, General Morgan at AFHQ signalled General McCreery that authority to hand Russians over was granted, provided that force was *not* used.[42] On 23 May V Corps requested agreement to use force, and stated incidentally that 'force was not mentioned by Macmillan'.[43] No written reply to this request has been found. On 24 May, Eighth Army HQ issued instructions: 'all Russians who are Soviet citizens to be handed back without use of force, otherwise to be evacuated.'[44]

The same day, Keightley gave an order which seemed at odds with V Corps' 'Definition' of three days previously: 'It is of the utmost importance that all the officers and particularly the senior commanders are rounded up and that none are allowed to escape. . . .'[45]

In sum, the V Corps principle – ruthless in its interpretation under the pressure of events – was, when in doubt, repatriate. On 25 May, V Corps confirmed to Eighth Army and higher headquarters that 42,000 Cossacks handed over to Russia were 'Soviet citizens within the definition of AFHQ (6th March) letter'.[46]

Macmillan's Visit to Chequers

Meanwhile, on 18 May, Macmillan in his office in Caserta had received an unexpected telegram from Churchill, summoning him back to England for consultations. Before leaving, he had had yet another conversation with Alexander about the Yugoslav threat, during 'rather a confusing day' of telegrams from Eden in Washington, reporting vacillating American moods: 'Apparently Alex's military appreciation . . . has rather worried them. . . .'[47] Alexander had pointed out that, 'coming immediately after V.E. Day and following months and years of praise of Tito by press and B.B.C., it was not just too easy to ask them suddenly to embark on operations on a considerable scale against Yugoslavia. . . .' Macmillan commented, reassuringly, that the reliability of the Allied troops could be expected to improve as they 'get to know and dislike the Jugoslavs. They will see the so-called Jugoslav administration, thieving, raping, and killing; and they will not like it.' He remained sharply sceptical about American intentions:

If the Americans are undecided and get cold feet they will naturally try to cover themselves. And it is easier to put the blame on Alex or me than to shoulder it themselves. Meanwhile, the President says he cannot make war against the Jugoslavs unless they 'attack' our troops. But as they are in possession and keep moving in more forces, of course they will not 'attack' us. The point is unless we can push them out by force, there is no way of ejecting them.[48]

On the 19th Macmillan flew in a B–25 bomber to England, staying three days at Chequers with Churchill, to whom he relayed the foregoing exchanges with Alexander. That first night, he recorded in his diary 'a lot of talk – chiefly on the political situation at home . . . then a lot of talk (till 2 p.m.) about Tito'.[49] Jock Colville noted that Macmillan, who had been:

> summoned from Italy because of the Venezia Giulia crisis, arrived at tea-time with Robert Cecil, who is acting as his ADC. The P.M. was still loitering with his geese and goldfish pond (recently plundered of their, to him, precious occupants by a thief or an otter – it was long before anyone dared break the news) at Chartwell and so I took Macmillan and Robert up to Beacon Hill. I don't like the would-be ingratiating way in which Macmillan bares his teeth. . . .[50]

In this setting, the following day there were more discussions about Tito and the Yugoslav threat, intermixed with a great deal more about Macmillan's own political future. Meanwhile, however, domestic politics intruded, overshadowing all else. Churchill had written to Attlee, the Leader of the Labour Party, suggesting that the war coalition should continue till after the defeat of Japan, but this was sharply rejected on the evening of the 21st. Macmillan noted that 'Winston was hurt at the unnecessarily waspish and even offensive tone of Attlee's reply. It arrived during dinner. . . . Most of the evening was spent in drafts and re-drafts for the PM's reply to Attlee, at which we all tried our hand.'[51]

During these discussions, Churchill offered Macmillan first the Air Ministry – if the Conservatives were returned to power – and then the Ministry of Labour. Macmillan declined the latter, on the grounds that he felt he had been 'too much out of politics for this job'.[52] Finally it was settled that he should become Minister for Air forthwith. He returned to Italy on the 22nd, spending the evening again with his friend Alex, to whom he reported on the Chequers talks, as well as confiding in him Churchill's instructions to relinquish his post as Resident Minister and return home permanently to take up his new job on the 26th.

On the 23rd, Churchill's coalition government resigned, and a 'caretaker' interim regime took over, which must, in itself, have provided a potent enough distraction from the concurrent issue of the Russian – and Yugoslav – repatriations. Macmillan noted how Churchill had been 'much encouraged by Truman's forthright attitude' (the President had sent a strong message to Stalin asking the Russians to restrain Tito), but nevertheless he felt that the Chequers meeting 'did not greatly advance the situation with which I was chiefly concerned' – namely, the Yugoslav threat in Carinthia and northern Italy. He observed of Churchill, palpably worn out by his five years as war leader, that he had lost some of his old capacity to focus on problems: 'It takes rather a long time now to talk with PM. He thinks and talks of so many things at once. . . .'[53]

There is no reference in either the diaries or memoirs to the White Russians, or specifically to his visit to Keightley in Klagenfurt; nor, when questioned about it nearly forty years later (he was then approaching ninety), did he have any recollection of the subject having been broached at all at Chequers. Yet it seems, on the face of it, unlikely that Macmillan would not have made some reference to the human suffering involved in the thousands of Russians and Yugoslavs 'milling around', or to the fate that the repatriates could expect – or, in the case of the Yugoslavs, were already experiencing.[54]

In any event, orders were now put in train reversing, or at least slowing down, the repatriation decisions. By the time they were enacted, however, tragically most of the damage had been done by the local military authorities.

The Yugoslav Repatriations

Even before the Russian repatriations had begun, anti-Communist Yugoslavs (described by British officialdom alternately as 'dissidents' or 'anti-partisans') were being handed over to Tito's forces, with consequences similarly grim to those suffered by the Russians. Macmillan, as Alexander's political adviser, was charged nearly forty years later by Nikolai Tolstoy with being chiefly responsible 'for arranging the surrender of more than 70,000 [Yugoslav] men, women and children to certain death, torture and imprisonment'.[55] As before, the deception was allegedly set up during Macmillan's Klagenfurt meeting on 13 May with General Keightley of British V Corps.

The background circumstances, as well as the charges, parallel the saga of the White Russians – except that the fate of the Yugoslav 'anti-partisans' was not laid down by Yalta. There was the general picture of chaos in the area, and alarm, from Alexander downwards, that the situation was drifting dangerously close to war, under the most disadvantageous terms, with the Titoist Yugoslavs. There was the consternation at the lack of firm support from the US under its new President, and the same continuing bitterness of the British Army towards anyone caught in German uniform. Equally, as with the Cossacks, there was little enthusiasm in the British Army for the anti-Communist Yugoslavs, some of whose factions – notably the Quisling Croat Ustashi – had appalling reputations for brutality. There was the same unawareness, or willing disbelief, of the full brutality of Tito's OZNA secret police towards 'dissidents'. Finally, there was the wartime commitment of Churchill to Tito.

The situation was made the more complex by the savage civil war, or rather wars, that had been fought in the artificially created nation of Yugoslavia for the previous four years. The fate of the defeated Chetniks, the royalist nationalist Serbs led by General Mihailović, should command more sympathy than the 'White Russians'; they at least had fought against the Germans, with characteristic Balkan fervour, in the early days of the post-1941 resistance. Then they had been dropped by Churchill, on the simple principle that the partisans killed more Germans. After all the wartime bloodshed and suffering, the partisans were filled with bitter vengefulness as they advanced towards the north-west, pushing before them a panic-stricken mêlée of Chetniks, Ustashi, Slovene Domobran militiamen and anti-Communist civilians, all heading for sanctuary in Italy or Carinthia. The number repatriated by force or guile, and subsequently killed or imprisoned by Tito's men, varies wildly from Tolstoy's 70,000 downwards, but, whatever the figure, the repatriations reflect badly on the British.

Conflicting Orders

The signals emanating from AFHQ during this crucial period are strangely contradictory. They reflect the confusion of the moment, as well as of Yugoslav factionalism, where there was a tendency to tar all 'anti-partisans' with the brush of the disgraced Ustashi; but they provide no serious evidence to suggest that Alexander and Macmillan were travelling along different tracks. For example, a signal from AFHQ on 9 April to the Allied headquarters of the Balkan Air Force advised that surrendered Yugoslav Quisling forces 'should be handed over forthwith to Tito's Yugoslav forces', i.e. push them back as soon as possible.[56] But a minute from AFHQ's largely American-staffed G–3 Branch to the Chief of Staff decreed, in direct contradiction of this, that such forces surrendering to the Fifteenth Army Group should be 'evacuated in the normal way for PW. The question of their further disposal should then be taken up through Governmental channels . . .',[57] i.e. they should *not* be pushed back.

On 28 April, Macmillan received a telegram from the British Ambassador recently arrived in Belgrade, Sir Ralph Stevenson, warning that the 15th Army Group 'would shortly be meeting with considerable anti-partisan Yugoslav forces whose total strength is believed to be over 200,000 men. . . . These anti-partisan Yugoslavs, without exception, completely compromised by open collaboration with the Germans. . . .' Nevertheless, Stevenson urged that they should not be handed over to the Titoist forces but be 'disarmed and placed in refugee camps'.[58] This latter was the agreed Anglo-American policy promulgated to AFHQ on 2 May, and the following day the Eighth Army issued instructions that Chetniks and other anti-partisans were to be regarded as surrendered personnel and their disposal was to be decided at governmental level. On 13 May, Macmillan had his fateful meeting with General Keightley at V Corps, of which he wrote in his diaries concerning the Yugoslav problem:

> thousands of so-called Ustashi or Chetniks, mostly with wives and children, are fleeing in panic into this area in front of the advancing Yugoslavs. These expressions, U. and C., cover anything from guerrilla forces raised by the Germans from Slovenes and Croats and Serbs to fight Tito, and armed and

maintained by the Germans – to people who, either because they are Roman Catholics or Conservative in politics, or for whatever cause are out of sympathy with revolutionary Communism. . . . (This is a very simple formula, which in a modified form is being tried, I observe, in English politics.)

After this last sardonic aside, he simply states: 'We had a conference with the General and his officers covering much the same ground as those with Generals McCreery and Harding yesterday. He gave us his story and we gave him ours. I feel sure it was useful and helpful all round.'[59]

It was then that the need to 'clear the sector' urgently was agreed upon in Keightley's HQ.[60] The urgency was emphasised by reports reaching Keightley, after Macmillan's departure, of the impending arrival in V Corps of 200,000 Croat 'anti-partisans'. These warnings later proved to be grossly exaggerated, in that most of the Croats had already been turned back at the Austrian frontier. Nevertheless, this faulty intelligence formed an important factor in V Corps' future dispositions.

The next day, 14 May, General Robertson, Alexander's Chief Administrative Officer at AFHQ, issued operational instructions to the Fifteenth Army Group and Eighth Army: 'all surrendered Yugoslav nationals remaining in German forces to be handed over to Yugoslav forces.'[61] There is no evidence that Macmillan intervened here.

Twenty-four hours later, Robertson received a protest from Alexander C. Kirk, Murphy's successor from the State Department, firmly opposing any forced repatriation of anti-Communist Yugoslavs: 'such contemplated violation agreed Anglo-American policy cannot be justified on grounds of administrative expediency.'[62] But that same day, AFHQ signalled to MACMIS in Belgrade (Brigadier Fitzroy Maclean's mission to Tito), with copies to the Fifteenth Army Group and Eighth Army, that approximately 200,000 Yugoslav nationals in the German armed forces had surrendered in Austria: 'We should like to turn these over immediately to Marshal Tito's forces and would be grateful if Marshal Tito would arrange to instruct his Commander to accept them and to arrange with GOC V Corps the rate at which they can be received and handed over.'[63] On 17 May, a reply from Tito's Cabinet accepted the return of the 200,000. In fact, these Yugoslavs were evidently turned back before they crossed the frontier and did not surrender to V Corps.[64] However, Stevenson's telegram may explain the alarm into which Macmillan, Alexander and V Corps were precipitated. They also indicate that the principle of repatriation on a massive scale had been approved by Alexander himself, who could not conceivably have been unaware of the telegram to MACMIS of the 15th – the *key* telegram.[65]

Nevertheless, as of 18 May, Macmillan in his letter to Sir James Grigg at the War Office was treating the repatriation of the Yugoslavs from Austria as a question that was still open; when he mentions Ustashi, Chetniks and so on, he uses the phrase 'deciding which, if any, are to be handed back . . .'.

By 23 May, Alexander was signalling a clear directive to his subordinate formations, 'No Yugoslavs who have come into the hands of Allied troops will be returned direct to Yugoslavia or handed over to Yugoslav TPS against their will.'[66] The timing is significant, coming immediately after Macmillan's return from the Chequers meeting and coincidental with Churchill's own apparent change of heart. It also followed some sharp divergences with the US. Much later, in August, when Alexander was called on by an angry Washington to justify the repatriations, his deputy told Kirk that '. . . Macmillan had concurred in proposed action. But in any event Supreme Allied Commander took the decision because of conditions existing of which he was better aware than [State] Department.'[67]

The last, somewhat acid comment shows just how out of phase British and US policy had been during the last critical days of the war, when Truman was taking over from Roosevelt with so little preparation. Kirk told Alexander sharply that the US had nothing to add to their original protests about the repatriations 'except to point out to him again that Resident Macmillan acted contrary to policy agreed upon after consultation by Department and Foreign Office'.[68]

It seems, however, that the Foreign Office policy had not been so clearcut. In an 'informal ephemeral minute for the benefit of my successor' of September 1945, John Addis of the Foreign Office's Southern Department noted that, in response to Alexander's urgent plea for a directive on 17 May, 'we at first gave the advice that while the Chetniks should be retained as disarmed hostile troops, the Croatian Ustasa should be pushed back into Yugoslavia. . . .' After the US objected, the Foreign Office retracted, accepting that 'all Yugoslav

Quisling formations should be treated alike and retained.' Instructions, however, were apparently not sent out to AFHQ until 20 June, and meanwhile 'we learned incidentally . . . that while the question of principle was still under discussion . . . V Corps had agreed to hand over Croats to Yugoslavia and 900 Croats were transferred on the 24th May. We never saw any of the telegrams from the military authorities in Italy reporting this transfer. . . .'[69]

Repatriations of Yugoslavs by V Corps had, however, begun well before the 24th. On 17 May, V Corps had issued orders that *all* Yugoslav nationals were to be handed over to Tito's forces; they were to be 'disarmed immediately but will NOT be told of their destination'.[70] Two days later it was agreed with the Yugoslav Army, at V Corps level, that 'V Corps will return all Yugoslav nationals in Corps area (including Chetniks and White Guards etc.).'[71] On 23 May, Eighth Army headquarters, evidently uneasy, asked AFHQ for agreement that V Corps should continue the existing arrangements for handing over 'anti-partisans', of whom 'considerable numbers have already been handed back'. The signal noted that the Yugoslav Army was now asking for the return of 'all' Yugoslav nationals, including Chetniks, and it ended with what appears to be V Corps' self-initiated extension of the Yalta Agreement governing Soviet repatriations: 'Consider policy should be for all nationals, i.e. persons born within the pre-1939 frontier of an allied country, to be handed over to all concerned except only such as are required for offences against British.'[72]

The tone of all these headquarters communications tends to support the view that the Yugoslav repatriations stemmed less from wider political commitments than from local military decisions – particularly those by HQ V Corps. In defence of its actions, the former Brigadier Low subsequently explained that the line of communication between Carinthia and Italy would have been blocked if all the 'anti-partisans' had been sent to Distone as required by AFHQ.[73] Thus, against both AFHQ intentions and Eighth Army operational instructions that only those Yugoslavs who wished to return were to be repatriated, but in an attempt to obey their injunctions to avoid the use of force, V Corps (as of 17 May) had indulged in this deplorable act of deception, by pretending that the Yugoslavs were being despatched to Italy. Once again, V Corps had exceeded its brief. It was never suggested subsequently by Lord Aldington, however, that the use of deception, or of force, had in any way been part of the 'advice Macmillan' of 13 May.[74]

Lord Aldington claimed that all his actions were reported back to Eighth Army and ultimately AFHQ every evening, and denied that he had been party to any sort of 'bargain' with the Yugoslavs. There was, however, little doubt that V Corps had more practical reasons for getting rid of the Yugoslav refugees than the White Russians. Tito, apparently under Soviet pressure, *did* withdraw over Carinthia and Trieste. How much this climbdown was influenced by British propitiation of Tito through handing over the wretched 'anti-partisans', while at the same time demonstrating that Alexander's forces were preparing to fight, if need be, by 'clearing the area', remains an open question.[75]

Shortly before Macmillan died, in December 1986, Lord Aldington said to Julian Amery, and he repeated the statement several times subsequently, that the decision at Klagenfurt of 13 May had been purely 'military' and V Corps would have carried it out regardless of Macmillan's 'political advice'. Macmillan could 'have objected on political grounds, certainly';[76] but the inference is that it might not have made much difference. Lord Aldington's admission was fundamental to the case against Macmillan, and, if it could have been made several years earlier, the old statesman would doubtless have been saved much distress in his last years.

Blunder or Conspiracy?

That there was a grievous blunder committed, starting at Yalta and to which Macmillan was party at Klagenfurt on 13 May, and which resulted in the deaths of Russians who should not have been handed over to the Soviets (as well as those who, under the strictest interpretation of Yalta, could not have escaped the net – and several thousand Yugoslavs), seems irrefutable. But the most invidious charge made against Macmillan is that, instead of only being involved in a terrible blunder, he deliberately conspired to deceive his close personal friend, Alexander. This now seems to have been effectively scotched, not least by the latest evidence which reveals convincingly just how many other people at various army HQ levels were party to the Macmillan 'conspiracy'.[77] As for motivation for such a conspiracy, nothing intelligible has ever been advanced – unless one were to give credence to the innuendo of Macmillan being in the thrall of the KGB. The whole record of the sturdy line he took in support of Armpit, the 'Llubljana Gap' scheme to get into Central Europe ahead of Stalin; of his struggle to keep the Communists at bay in Greece, and the Italian partisans in Northern Italy, speaks for itself. Had he still been involved in some underhand conspiracy, he could hardly have allowed the entry about the 'White Russians' and his painful moral dilemma to stand in his diary entry for 13 May, or then to publish it after the Tolstoy attack had been made. Any such conspiracy would inevitably have been revealed to Alex by the time of Kirk's reproving letter of 14 August, if not much earlier. Yet there is no evidence that Macmillan's role in May 1945 ever diminished his friendship with Alex subsequently – nor his standing in Churchill's eyes.[78]

Finally, there is no satisfactory evidence to suggest that Alexander would have behaved differently to Macmillan on 13 May at Klagenfurt. The humanitarian Alexander was appalled by the frightful scenes of Communist brutality that followed the actual handovers, and eventually intervened to put a halt to them; yet it is one thing to have had a premonition of the fate that might have been in store for the repatriates (as had Macmillan – witness his diary entry of 13 May), and another to have received first-hand accounts from the outraged commanders involved of the extent of the barbaric dreadfulness on the part of the Soviets and Titoists that accompanied the actual handovers. After questioning Macmillan himself on no less than eight separate occasions, I was left with the strong personal feeling that he – equally a deeply humane man with a rooted abhorrence of Communist excesses – was far more tormented by the episode of the repatriation, and the Tolstoy allegations, than he ever let on. Nevertheless, whatever remorse he may have felt privately, in public Macmillan remained unrepentant about what had happened, and ready to shoulder whatever blame attached to him. Commenting nearly forty years later on the Yugoslav repatriations, he used a Highland parallel: 'It's rather as if you had been fighting alone for four years with the Campbells as your ally – then they ask you to hand over the MacFarlanes and the MacTaggarts to them.'[79]

At Klagenfurt, it was Macmillan the pragmatist that took precedence over the sentimentalist. The impression is that he acted, as did Alexander initially, in conformity with the general mood of the time, supported by the US and with no guidance from a tired and distracted Churchill. On 13 May 1945, he had been faced with a crisis that demanded an instant, practical solution, and he responded with counsel of ruthless pragmatism, which may well have been compounded by the element of pessimism within his character, as well as by sheer physical fatigue. He had given his 'advice', painfully aware of what it might mean for the repatriates, responding reflexively to a problem put to him without warning, perhaps in a manner reminiscent of Henry II and Thomas à Becket. V Corps, alarmed by its immediate predicament, subsequently went ahead with the repatriations, exceeding its brief or directly contravening the confused orders from AFHQ. It could be argued, however, that the actions of V Corps had averted a collision with Tito's forces, thereby saving British lives and possibly Carinthia too.

In the hindsight of forty years later, unconditioned by the chaotic context of Europe at the end of the war, the morality of the repatriations is easy to question. Where Macmillan's critics go radically wrong, however, is in veering towards the 'conspiracy' rather than the 'muddle' theory of history, thereby perpetuating against him a disgraceful slur, on the least substantial evidence that devolves almost exclusively from what he did, or did not, say at that one meeting at Klagenfurt on 13 May 1945; of which there is no transcript or minute. If there was a 'muddle', with tragic consequences, what is now certain is that there was no plot or conspiracy by Macmillan with General Keightley, Brigadier Low or any other person. And, ultimately, it is surely towards the corrupt and inhuman system that indiscriminately executed, tortured or despatched to Gulag the repatriated Russians and Yugoslavs that the weight of anger should be directed, and not against the muddling British – and certainly not against Macmillan specifically. Though it in no way helps exonerate Harold Macmillan, it should perhaps be noted *en passant* that, in the days of peace and prosperity of the 1970s and 1980s, successive British Conservative and Labour governments have followed the practice of handing back to the Chinese Communists the hundreds of thousands of Chinese men, women and children who have tried to find a haven in Hong Kong – a practice which has aroused not the slightest protest.

Dealing with the Yugoslav challenge was Macmillan's last mission in his two and a half years as Churchill's Resident Minister. After he left Italy permanently on 26 May, a combination of increased

American firmness and pressure from the Kremlin led to a containment of Titoist revolutionary zeal. The demarcations proposed under the 'Morgan' or 'Robertson' line, whereby Tito kept Fiume and Pola, and Trieste remained in Allied hands, were accepted and stood (despite continued minor squabbles) until the final treaty of October 1954 when Trieste reverted permanently to Italy. It was a compromise partition that had come essentially from the politician's brain of Macmillan, and for which he had had his knuckles rapped by Eden. But he found irony in the fact that what he felt could have been achieved by Alexander on his 21 February visit to Belgrade, 'had it not been so summarily rejected by distant governments in London and Washington unacquainted with the difficulties and dangers on the spot', was finally to be ratified only a decade later.

On 24 May there were many warm but regretful leave-takings in Caserta. Alex 'came early and stayed to the end'. The next day Macmillan flew to Rome for a farewell audience with Pope Pius XII, who presented him with a fine silver medallion. Macmillan found him a 'poor, solitary figure', much concerned and saddened at the darkness of the future.[80] He then went to call on Bonomi, the Italian Prime Minister, who was full of doubts about whether he was going to survive the present governmental crisis. Shades of Italian political history to come! On the 26th, accompanied by the faithful John Wyndham, he flew off home in the Field Marshal's private Dakota, seen off by Alex himself, plus a galaxy of British and American officers. 'After so long and enthralling an assignment,' he recalled, 'the final scenes were rather saddening.' At any rate it had been a unique experience: 'It is the end of a chapter – "Mediterranean merry-go-round or from DARLAN to TITO"' was the final entry in his wartime diaries.[81]

It was certainly a chapter that formed the most decisive part of his career to date, as well as defining – or at least helping him to find – his true character. He had left London in 1942 an unknown politician. By any standard, his wartime achievements in the Mediterranean had been remarkable, and they established him as a public figure of considerable weight, both in Britain and with his wartime American colleagues. It was into Churchill's orbit, shrouded as it was with the mists of post-war uncertainty, and menace, that Macmillan now flew back to England at the end of May 1945 as one of the grandees of the inner Tory councils.

Part III

From Electoral Defeat to No. 10
1945–1957

Chapter Eleven

A New Britain
1945–1950

. . . it was not Churchill who lost us the election – if anything we would have got through clinging on to his coat tails – it was the shadow of Neville Chamberlain. . . .

(HM, BBC interview, 9 September 1969)

The Somme drained off what should have been the leadership, and now our country is in irreparable decline – under your gang.

(HM to Richard Crossman,
quoted in Sunday Telegraph, 9 February 1964)

Despite the saddening severance of his wartime Mediterranean ties, after two and a half years' absence Macmillan was eager to pick up with home life again. There were three recently born grand-children, Maurice's sons Alexander and Joshua, and Carol's daughter Anne, whom he had not yet seen. There were the tasks of restoring the run-down Birch Grove estate and of revitalising the family publishing firm. And there was the question of reweaving the fragile strands of his marriage. After years of enforced absence during the war, hundreds of thousands of servicemen shared the same anxieties, but for Macmillan, given all that had passed before, these carried dimensions of extra sensitivity.

In the months following his return, however, Macmillan hardly had time to contemplate, let alone enjoy, family life. Even before he had had a chance to recuperate from the telling exertions of the war years, the forthcoming general election on 5 July was absorbing all his thoughts and energy. The office to which he had returned, Secretary of State for Air in the caretaker government, did not involve him directly in planning electoral strategy; but he was, for the first time, a participating member of the Cabinet. Back in April he had written rather aloofly from Italy to Sir Edward Grigg:*

. . . I suppose all my colleagues in England are discussing internal politics. Here they seem rather remote and, to tell the truth, rather boring. It sounds a pompous observation, but I am so impressed with the immense problems confronting Great Britain in the field of economic and foreign policy that I find myself rather remote from the kind of things that seem to interest the Conservative Central Office and party machine. . . .[1]

* Minister Resident in Cairo following the assassination of Lord Moyne; he later became Lord Altrincham.

This was something of a pose. In Italy he had indeed been thinking about wider aspects of domestic policy – such as how a future Conservative administration would propose to remove all controls during a time when world shortages were going to be very harsh, and on how to graft a more 'socialist' planned-economy approach on to the Tory tradition. But, nevertheless, the infighting of internal politics, and electioneering, was grist to his mill, and he returned to England full of enthusiasm for the party-political fight.

This fizz soon began to drain out of him, however. He found 'a certain flatness and frustration' being in the caretaker government: 'The Prime Minister was away at Potsdam, dealing with enormous questions of which we heard only distant and occasional echoes, Cabinets were few and uninspiring. . . .' He felt depressingly out of touch, and indeed out of key, with the 'new' Britain from which he had been away for so long. It was a drab, exhausted country, embittered by enduring privations, rationing of food, clothing, petrol – of almost everything; nearly all the old assumptions were now under question. Among the working class the egalitarian experiences of war had brought forth a new articulate self-confidence that cried out for radical solutions. Opinion polls indicated that the political change people most commonly wanted was a withering away of class distinctions. Thoughts about a Utopian, socialist new world that *had* to follow on as a well-earned reward for the suffering and futility of 1939–45 had been fanned by such popular organs as *Picture Post* and the *Daily Mirror*. The Beveridge Report on social security, which was to lay the foundation for the welfare state, had become essential – indeed, popular – reading. Because of its heroic performance in the war, the Soviet Union had come to be regarded by the left with starry eyes, blind to the well-publicised defects of the pre-war era and unheeding of more recent Stalinist excesses.

Thus there was altogether a new revolutionary mood in the air, quite different to what Macmillan recalled in his dealings with his friends, and allies, in the pre-war Labour Party. By comparison, Macmillan, the rebellious Tory of the 1930s, appeared – in the words of Robert Blake – to have been 'not a very exciting sort of rebel'.[2] On top of this, there was the problem of fighting an election against such socialist issues as nationalisation of coal, which Macmillan had himself once espoused so ardently, back in the 1930s. It was the beginning, as he himself admitted, of an unhappy interlude.

*

So much time had elapsed since Macmillan had last had to deal with party-political issues that he felt 'a little at sea'. Even at 'dear old Stockton' he was not really at home any more. Things had moved too fast. His Labour opponent, George Chetwynd, a personable young man who had served in the Army Education Corps and worked hard in the constituency while Macmillan was an 'absentee landlord', was fairly typical of the new socialists. Macmillan's old pre-war ally, Hugh Dalton, wrote of Chetwynd: 'Excellent and pleasing young candidate, but don't think he can beat Macmillan. His organisation is very poor and they have an old Agent who seems half asleep, but I should expect Macmillan's to be very good.'[3] Such pessimism about the election results was widely shared in the Labour Party at the time, while the remarks about the quality of Macmillan's agent are interesting given his own doubts expressed during the latter stages of the war.

In his campaign, Macmillan went into bat ponderously on 'The Middle Way': 'In the realm of national economic planning we shall hold a wise balance between the field suited for private enterprise and that allocated for ownership or control. . . . the Government will follow the national characteristic – a middle course avoiding equally the extreme of *laissez-faire* and that of collectivist control for its own sake.'[4]

The electorate were not stirred. Emanuel Shinwell, one of the socialist big guns sent down to help Chetwynd, mocked Macmillan with telling effectiveness and with a felicitous mixing of metaphors by terming him a 'mugwump' ('a person who sat on the fence with mug on one side and his wump on the other'), and observing that 'If you stand in the middle of the road, it is well known that you stand to get run over. . . .'[5] Many years later Shinwell liked to reckon (with little historical support, however) that this sortie possibly cost Macmillan the election.[6]

Shinwell himself was opposed at the nearby north-eastern seat of Seaham by twenty-four-year-old Maurice Macmillan, making his political début in a hopeless contest. Before the election he received the following advice from his father, then still in Italy, which is revealing both in its perceptiveness and in the somewhat patronising style to which he was often wont to resort henceforth in his dealings with the socialists at large:

you will find Shinwell a very tiresome man in outward manner – sneering, offensive and truculent. Underneath he is rather a good chap, suffering from an intense inferiority complex, due partly to his birth, which is Polish. You'll have to work out a careful plan. I think if he is treated with extreme courtesy, at the same time making the points against him strongly and clearly, he can be irritated into making possibly rather a fool of himself. . . .'[7]

At Stockton Macmillan seemed an alien, uncomfortable with the Tees-side proletariat, whom he treated rather as he might tenants of Birch Grove or Chatsworth, or the Guardsmen of the First World War, or the soldiers of 1943–5 (with whom he had had only somewhat oblique dealings in the Mediterranean). The style was all wrong. Once again, as before the war, it was Dorothy, loyally at his side as at every election, who showed herself much more at ease – and much more popular.

From the beginning, the apathy of the electorate forewarned Macmillan that the election was lost before it started. When the results came out on 26 July – they were announced three weeks later to enable the overseas service vote to be counted – there were 'no crowds, no enthusiasm; it was a dull formality'. Chetwynd had won by an easy majority of 8664. (Shinwell beat Maurice by 32,000 votes.) Macmillan noted wryly that there was a certain symmetry: in twenty-two years he had fought six elections at Stockton, and won three and lost three.

The overall result of the general election paralleled Macmillan's defeat at Stockton in an unprecedented swing to the left. Ever loyal to Churchill, Macmillan maintained that it was not he but 'the shadow of Neville Chamberlain'[8] that had lost the election. Insofar as the British electorate wanted a change from the old, traditionalist, blimpish Conservatism as represented by Chamberlain, this was true. But it was also true that Churchill, out of key like Macmillan, and still exhausted from the demands of the war, fought a lacklustre campaign, and largely on the wrong issues. The Tories regarded the triumphant war-leader as their strongest card; that was an inevitable, but questionable, judgement. Churchill's instinct was to fight the election on the heroic issues of the war, and the wider challenges of the peace; but the electorate, weary of global responsibilities, preferred, less adventurously, to seek a new deal at home. As Churchill confided in gloom to his physician, Lord Moran, 'I have no message for them now. . . . I feel very lonely without a war.'[9]

There were many like Vita Sackville-West, to whom Churchill's speeches in 1945 came over as 'confused, woolly, unconstructive and so wordy that it is impossible to pick out any concrete impression from them'.[10] At Walthamstow in the East End, at what should have been the Party's climactic address, Churchill was actually booed into silence by a crowd of 25,000 amid shouts of 'What about jobs?' and 'What about houses?' Elsewhere, more reverent crowds turned out to cheer him – but voted against his Party.

In Opposition

In an unexpected landslide for Clement Attlee and the Labour Party, the 398 Conservative MPs had been reduced to 213. For the first time in history Labour commanded a clear majority in the Commons; it could do anything it wanted. On the last page of the Chequers' visiting book, Churchill wrote glumly, 'Finis'. Harold Nicolson, defeated like Macmillan, voiced the sentiments of many a fallen MP: 'I feel sad and hurt, as if I had some wound or lesion inside. But I cannot make out what is the centre of this sadness. Naturally I mind leaving the House and being outside public life. . . . But there is something else. . . . I hate uneducated people having power; but I like to think that the poor will be rendered happy. This is a familiar conflict.'[11]

In the bitterness of defeat, Macmillan himself may well secretly have echoed some of this, as well as wishing that he had not rejected Duff Cooper's offer of the safe seat at St George's. It was the end of Stockton – until he took his earldom there nearly forty years later. The defeat came at a crucial moment in Macmillan's career. His claim to a place in the inner circle of the Tory Party was still tenuous and if he was now forced to wait for two or three years before a by-election in a winnable Conservative seat, the whole impetus of his political career would be lost. By an astonishing stroke of luck for Macmillan, however, a suitable seat for him to contest became vacant almost immediately.

During the three-week gap between the election and the announcement of the results, Sir Edward Campbell, the long-serving Conservative Member for the constituency of Bromley, died. Bromley, a middle-class suburb of south London, lay on a direct line between Churchill's home at Chartwell and Westminster, and Churchill's views on the selection of a candidate clearly carried great weight with the Bromley Conservative Association. One of the contenders was Churchill's son Randolph. As a staunch fan of Macmillan, he instantly stood down, declaring that 'no one has a greater claim'.[12] On 16 November, Macmillan was back in Parliament with a respectable and – for the first time – safe majority of 5557.

In the new Commons, Macmillan found himself ranged against one of the most able governments in modern times. It was also one of the most powerful; as one of its new young MPs, Woodrow Wyatt, wrote many years later, it was 'the only Labour Government ever to be confident in its complete control of its followers and policies'.[13] Its leaders had greatly benefited from five years' practical experience of governing under the wartime coalition. There were times during Churchill's many absences when, as his deputy, 'Little Clem' (Ernest Bevin's nickname for Attlee) had virtually been Prime Minister on the home front, and with the passage of time his stock has risen steadily, to the point where he is now regarded as one of the great British Prime Ministers of this century. His successor, Harold Wilson, attributed Attlee's strength in Cabinet to 'his business-like control of its proceedings and his utterly clear capacity for summing up its decisions'.[14] From Macmillan's memoirs he emerges as 'much underrated' and 'one of the best chairmen I have ever sat under'. Attlee was expert at delegating, and it was through numerous ministerial Cabinet committees over which he ruled that there came to pass the staggering amount of legislation that reached the statute books between 1945 and 1951. He was also helped immeasurably by having a totally loyal and dependable lieutenant in the square shape of Ernest Bevin, who – as well as being Foreign Secretary – maintained the closest touch with the trades unions, over which he wielded unprecedented influence.

Macmillan also admired Attlee's capacity to be 'a good butcher' in dealing with his colleagues – a quality which he himself was to emulate two decades later. In the House the new leader was preeminently calm and unexcitable under fire, and Macmillan observed with respect how his dry, unemotional method often gained substantial tactical victories over the great orator, Churchill. In sum, 'if Attlee lacked charm, he did not lack courage. If he drifted into difficulties, he generally found a way out of them. . . .'

As Leader of the House, there was Macmillan's former boss at the wartime Ministry of Supply, Herbert Morrison. He represented 'the Centre, even the Right, of the Labour Government', and on matters such as nationalisation of public utilities, railways and coal 'our views were not very far apart'. (As socialist measures bit deeper and tempers frayed, Macmillan's views on the Labour leaders generally and Morrison in particular would acquire much more virulence.) Attlee's first Chancellor of the Exchequer, Hugh Dalton, Macmillan 'always liked, although to many people he was unattractive and even repellent'. He was 'a twister', Macmillan acknowledged, 'but he was a patriot, he supported us before the war.'[15]

But to Macmillan, 'in many ways the most brilliant and the most memorable', the 'most exciting' and perhaps the most attractive of all the 1945 Labour team, as well as proving to be an unexpectedly good Minister of Health, was Aneurin Bevan. This 'eccentric and uncontrollable star' of the left was simultaneously a 'poet' and a 'Jacobin', thereby gaining from Macmillan what was just about his highest acclaim for a public figure – that of being 'an artist'. He could understand how the nightmare experiences of unemployment in the mining valleys of South Wales conditioned Bevan, and were responsible for his more emotional outbreaks against the Tories. When Bevan died, in 1960, Macmillan paid a moving tribute to him in the Commons:

> he was a genuine man. There was nothing fake or false about him. If he felt a thing deeply, he said so and in no uncertain terms. . . . he expressed in himself and in his career, in his life, some of the deepest feelings of humble people throughout the land. . . . beneath the charm and ebullience of his Celtic temperament, he was a deeply serious man.[16]

According, however, to Bevan's biographer, Michael Foot, Bevan did not reciprocate Macmillan's encomia. Of *The Middle Way* he once remarked 'He still doesn't know where he is. He and all his middle-of-the-roaders are the parasites of politics.'[17] It is easy now to forget just how radical, indeed revolutionary, were the policies – and language – of the 1945 socialists; Bevan outraged the Tories when in May 1948 he declared that he held them to be 'lower than vermin'. Yet many in the Party were well to the left of Bevan – or had at least started there. Among them was young Major Denis

Healey, a Communist Party member until the Non-Aggression Pact
of 1939, and who during the 1945 election praised the 'socialist
revolution . . . firmly established in many countries in eastern and
southern Europe . . .'.[18] Then there was John Strachey, the Minister
of Food and another ex-Communist, and – behind the scenes –
such figures as the left-wing intellectual chairman of the National
Executive, Harold Laski, much hated by the Opposition, who –
they thought – regarded the war as having been but a kind of second
act to the Russian Revolution.

Remarkably, 'Chairman' Attlee largely succeeded in keeping under
his stern control all the various radicals, Jacobins and revolutionaries that comprised the Labour forces in 1945, and exploited his
imposing majority to push through a truly astounding body of
legislation. In the 1945 Labour government's first nine months, no
less than 75 Bills were introduced, while during the whole of its five
years 347 Acts were implemented. They began with nationalisation
of the Bank of England. Then followed nationalisation of coal, steel,
railways, gas and electricity; the commitment to full employment
and economic planning was buttressed by the retention of wartime
controls, rationing and food subsidies – so as to maintain the
principle of 'fair shares for all'. But, above all, there was the creation
of the National Health Service and the consolidation of the welfare
state, as prescribed by the wartime Beveridge Report. *Pari passu* the
Empire was transformed by bestowal of independence upon India,
Burma and Ceylon – a process over which Attlee himself assumed
personal charge; millions of men were demobilised from the armed
forces with remarkable efficiency, and NATO was founded – not
least through the forceful inventiveness of Ernest Bevin. It was
decided that Britain should go-it-alone to become a nuclear power,
and, against all odds, towards the end of its term Labour managed
to achieve a vigorous recovery in British exports.

What nobody, however – neither Macmillan in the 1930s, nor
the Labour Utopians in 1945 – appreciated was just how much
the welfare state and nationalisation were going to cost. Britain,
moreover, was virtually bankrupt. Statisticians estimated that the
war had cost Britain some £7300 million, or the equivalent then of
a quarter of the national wealth. Much of this was accounted for in
the destruction of such capital assets as shipping and housing, but
£4200 million had disappeared in the sale of foreign holdings to

finance war munitions. The income on these foreign holdings had been vital in helping to pay for British imports before the war, and now, simply to maintain the pre-war level, Britain's run-down industry would have to increase exports substantially over the pre-war level – regardless of the vast consumer demands of the denuded home market. On top of this, to pay for the war Britain had increased her external debts from £476 million in 1939 to £3355 million in June 1945. For the past four years, only American Lend–Lease had, in effect, kept Britain going. Then, suddenly, seven days after the end of the Japanese War, President Truman discontinued Lend–Lease. This move should not have come as a total surprise to those who followed American congressional affairs, but the timing created a severe shock. It was – says Macmillan – a 'devastating blow, struck without warning and without any attempt at negotiating'. In the House, the American action provoked 'strong feelings on all sides'. Britain faced bankruptcy.

Macmillan's old hero and author from the inter-war years, Maynard Keynes, who had already played an important role in the Bretton Woods conference the previous year when the International Monetary Fund and the World Bank were launched, was des-patched to Washington to negotiate a vast new dollar loan of $3750 million. Although fatally ill with heart disease, Keynes was brilliant in his eloquence, and was accorded the veneration of a demi-god by Rooseveltian Treasury officials, such as he was little accustomed to at home. The Keynes Mission succeeded – but at an excessively heavy price. Departing from the generally pro-American tone of his memoirs, Macmillan records that 'many Ministers were disturbed – and even disgusted – by the harshness of the terms and the arrogant tone of the American Administration. The Opposition leaders were equally divided. . . .'

Even the new American loan was insufficient to meet all Britain's needs under Labour. Chancellor Dalton's determination to main-tain a policy of 'cheap money' with bank rate at 2 per cent (a figure that, in later years, looks like something out of the *Arabian Nights*) soon led to what he aptly called the problem of 'the vanishing dollar'. By the end of July 1947 only $1000 million of the $3750 million US loan remained; by September the sum had drained away to $400 million. Labour's predicament had been greatly exacerbated by the bitter winter of 1946–7, one of the grimmest in living memory. Museums had never been so well attended, as people huddled into them for warmth. The lights went out in the shops and strikes multiplied. Coal supplies dwindled, railways broke down, electricity was cut off, and unemployment soared to over two and a quarter million – all with catastrophic effects on the crucial export trade. There were angry outcries of 'Starve with Strachey and shiver with Shinwell', the Ministers of Food and Fuel respectively.

Savage austerity measures were introduced by Sir Stafford Cripps, then Minister of Economic Affairs, to cut foreign expenditure. The government introduced the Transitional Powers Bill, giving itself powers unprecedented in peacetime, including the direction of labour. Somewhat excessively, Churchill condemned it as 'a blank cheque for totalitarian government', although it did mark for Macmillan the moment when the prestige of the Labour government had fallen to its lowest point. What Dalton called the *annus horrendus* ended with his bringing down the temple on his own head. 'DALTON LEAKS' triumphed the Tory press at Dalton's venial error in letting slip details of his November Budget on his way to the House of Commons. He resigned, to be replaced by the puritanical Cripps.

A pacifist on the extreme left before the war, Cripps now – suitably – became the archpriest and symbol of socialist austerity. Macmillan recalled that the vegetarian, teetotal and monastic-looking Cripps was 'said to live on water-cress grown off the blotting paper of his desk!'[19] With his brilliant legal mind, lofty ideals, strict asceticism and frequent 'appeals to a higher power', Cripps had a curiously daunting effect on Macmillan, who rarely criticised him with impunity: 'when I said we lived in a world of fish and Cripps I was very much attacked.'[20] By early 1949, under Cripps's 'Austerity Programme', the British meat ration was reduced to 8d a week, lower than at any moment during the war, while even bread was rationed for the first time. Morale sank dismally in a lacklustre world where conversation dwelt chiefly on survival and on whether coal stocks would hold out, and editors tried bravely to distract readers with trivia, the glitter of Hollywood and scandal – habits that were to die hard – rather than talk about the socialists' Brave New World.

Macmillan soon established himself as one of the Opposition's principal spokesmen on industrial and economic matters, while his wartime experience also meant that he was sometimes called on to speak about foreign affairs. Under the Churchillian system of

Opposition, there was no formal Shadow Cabinet; all the Privy Councillors sat on the Opposition front bench but – in contrast to subsequent practice – no one was allocated a specific function. Macmillan regarded this as the best technique of opposition: 'It would be bad enough being Postmaster General anyway,' he once remarked, 'but supposing you're stuck with it as "Shadow" for four years, what would you do?'[21]

He inevitably found himself having to back what was the approved Tory line, and the line, especially in the early days, came from the top. He was, in any case, unshakable in his loyalty towards his old wartime chief, although, privately, he often regarded Churchill as sadly miscast as a Leader of the Opposition in peacetime. Disraeli's maxim that 'there are few positions less inspiriting than those of a discomfited party' was certainly true of Churchill and the Opposition leaders in the months following the 1945 Tory defeat. The blandness of Macmillan's memoirs masks the true bitterness he and other Tory leaders felt at the time, as when Labour members stunned them by singing the revolutionary 'Red Flag' in the House, or when Bevan made his 'vermin' attack. Yet on some issues – such as nationalisation of coal – his own past views from the *Middle Way* years committed him to temper his criticism as Opposition spokesman.

One of the chief speakers during the debates on the Coal Industry Nationalisation Bill in 1946, Macmillan records half-heartedly how: 'since I felt the issues were really settled beyond recall, it was best to attempt some philosophic approach to the general problems.' When it came to the later readings on the Coal Bill he tried to introduce an alternative plan that would do more to 'humanise' the face of nationalisation. As envisaged by the Labour ministers, the new scheme – Macmillan complained – did not allow for any co-partnership (as was to become a principle in post-war Germany) or participation in the affairs of the industry by the mine workers. 'This is not socialism,' he declared, 'it is state capitalism' – thereby earning the approval many years later of Ian Gilmour, one of the leading 'wets' under Thatcherism, who remarked that he 'had history on his side'.[22] In retrospect, Macmillan himself liked to think that it was not until his appointment of Lord Robens in 1961 that progress was made with the human side of the mining problem.

Macmillan attacked the socialists for their food and housing programmes, and – as a pre-war planner himself – was on sound ground when he constantly lambasted them for lack of a coherent plan: 'they preached planning and practised confusion.'[23] He made a special – and popular – Aunt Sally out of socialist intellectuals like Laski, as 'those clever men who in every age were always wrong' and who were dragging their party 'down the slippery slope to Communism'.[24] Typical of Macmillan of the time was the pun he coined – 'let sleeping dogmas lie'. Writing in the *Daily Telegraph* of 3 October 1946, he castigated the ruling hierarchy for their claim to 'the pompous infallibility which is one of the most tiresome of Socialist characteristics . . .', and called for an 'alliance, or fusion' of Conservatives and Liberals to combat the new menace.

It was the evident profligacy of the socialists, determined to pursue their Utopia in the welfare state, to drive the nationalisation programme ruthlessly from target to target, as well as pursuing such costly follies as the Groundnut Scheme in East Africa, all regardless of the financial facts of life, that most drew Macmillan's fire in opposition. He became swiftly disenchanted with the costliness, and inefficiency, of the kind of centralised planning, as put into practice by Labour, which he had himself called for so vigorously in the 1930s. He was also shaken by Keynes's dire warnings on the country's financial prospects, which predicted terrible times ahead for any government. He constantly hammered away on the dangers of a return to unemployment, which, as with the financial crisis, he insisted only dramatically increased productivity could cure.

It was three years since Macmillan had spoken in Parliament, and he found himself badly out of phase with the style, as well as the new mood, of the House. He readily conceded that, at least initially, he fell into the error of attempting too many jokes, and that his speeches were 'over-prepared and indulged in too many paradoxes and epigrams' (a charge he would later prefer against Harold Wilson). He dubbed Morrison 'the Artful Dodger', Bevan 'the fat boy in Pickwick', depicted Attlee as 'born to doodle while Europe burns', and compared socialists attacking monopolies to 'Satan rebuking sin'. He adopted many Churchillian mannerisms, not always successfully. To his old friends now seated on the government side of the House, the new Macmillan was positively irritating. 'The studied Edwardian elegance of his despatch-box manner,' said Richard Crossman, 'the mannered witticisms and the whole style of professional party polemics which he so consciously adopted – everything about him disconcerted.'[25] Crossman, remembering the wartime chief he had admired in Algiers, was further disconcerted when one evening Macmillan complained for an hour of the decadence of Britain.

Michael Foot recalled that he 'could hardly bear to listen to Macmillan speak [he was] so affected, pompous and portentous, and so artificial'.[26] Macmillan's biographer and left-wing adversary, Emrys Hughes, accused him of having cultivated 'an oratorical style of the Gladstonian period. He would put his hands on the lapels of his coat and turn to the back benches behind him for approval and support. He would raise and lower his voice and speak as if he were on the stage. . . . His polished phrases reeked of midnight oil. . . . Did he know when he was acting and when he was not himself?' Where was the teaching of Lloyd George?

On the other hand, Hughes admitted that Macmillan was 'the Tory Front Bench speaker who could most easily raise the temperature of the House' and if the socialists thought him 'flippant, superficial, supercilious and arrogant', the battered Tories loved it and regarded him as 'clever, hard hitting, forceful, convincing, eloquent, one who knew all the tricks of the Parliamentary game . . .'.[27] Watching him in action in 1946, the perspicacious Bruce Lockhart considered that Macmillan 'may yet succeed Winston. He has grown in stature during the war more than anyone. . . . He was always clever, but was shy and diffident, had a clammy handshake and was more like a wet fish than a man. Now he is full of confidence and is not only not afraid to speak but jumps in and speaks brilliantly. He has a better mind than Anthony. . . .'[28]

Personal Pessimism

There did indeed seem to be a change from the Macmillan of the 1930s. There was less theoretical idealism and more pragmatism – and more of the cynicism that infuriated the socialists. There was also perhaps more of the duke's son-in-law, and less of the crofter's grandson; the figure fitted more easily into middle-class Bromley than grimy, proletarian Stockton. The frustration of his present position, however, caused him at times to sink into pessimism;

his memoirs of the period repeatedly use the words 'unhappily', 'melancholy', 'futility' and 'disillusionment'. After what he described as the 'heroic age' of the British Empire at war, the extraordinarily swift ebb of Britain's relative strength and standing in the world subsequently was particularly painful to the patriot in him; while his own sudden reduction from being 'Viceroy of the Mediterranean' to just another fallen politician induced frequent bouts of the Black Dog which never lay far beneath the surface of his psyche. From being the fulfilled man of action in wartime, there returned something of the gloomy, frustrated and pessimistic figure of the 1930s.

It was this Macmillan that enounced Cassandra-like utterances about the inevitability of Europe being overrun by the Communist hordes, that bemoaned to Richard Crossman about how the nation was in 'irreparable decline' because its leadership had been killed off on the Somme, and that groused to Harold Nicolson about the great difficulties of persuading the British working class of the necessity of work. 'They have no conception', Nicolson recorded him as saying in November 1945, 'of the meaning of natural wealth, and have been taught that it is merely the profits of the rich. They think that they can now be idle, and that in some manner the Government will provide. He says, and I agree with him, that France will become a prosperous power long before we do.'[29] It was a very different tone to the Macmillan of Stockton in the depression years.

Once again, during this period, there were moments when Macmillan seriously contemplated quitting politics to become a full-time publisher. As it was, in deepest frustration at Westminster, he often deflected his energies to St Martin's Street. (C. P. Snow recalled a 'shamelessly poaching letter' of about 1947, aimed at prising him away from Faber's;[30] more letters followed, until, when Snow wrote his best-seller, *The Masters*, Macmillan succeeded, and kept him ever after.)

After the initial rapture of homecoming, his former discomforts at the family hearth also reasserted themselves. When he wrote in his memoirs, 'I felt myself almost a stranger at home,' although he was referring specifically to his political life, the utterance might as well have applied to other worlds. The birth of successive grandchildren did not seem to arouse in him the same excitement as had the birth of the first, Alexander, and for all the affection that he might have longed to pour out on first and second generation alike, there was still that quality of remoteness in their relations that seemed beyond his power to eschew. There were further complications. As the children grew up, Dorothy's lingering attachment to Boothby became an increasing factor in all their lives – with all the attendant strain that came from such awareness. It was at this time, too, that it became clear that Maurice was suffering from alcoholism, an affliction that all four children were to suffer at one time or other, to lesser or greater degree. But with Maurice it would always be a source of particular distress to his father, and a disappointment which, proud and ambitious for his only son, he did little to hide.

Thus, the late 1940s was not a happy time for Macmillan. Yet, at the same time, he was gradually finding a cause, and canalisation, for the vast reserves of energy and the idealism that were still there, intact, after the war. It was provided abroad by the vision of European unity and, at home, by the reconstruction of the battered Conservative Party.

The Tory Road to Recovery

Once the first harsh shock of being out in the wilderness had passed, the Tories had set to to muster their forces, to re-examine their philosophy, their policies and their image. The war had despatched many of the old-style Tory leaders, the cohorts of Chamberlain and Baldwin, and some promising new talents had emerged. Oliver Stanley, Macmillan's old Secretary of State at the Colonial Office, was, according to Michael Foot, the Opposition gun most feared by the government.[31] Macmillan himself was always convinced that had Stanley not died tragically early in 1950 he would have become Prime Minister after Eden. Then there were two able colleagues of Macmillan's from his First World War days – Harry Crookshank and Oliver Lyttelton; David Maxwell-Fyfe, who was to act as the master-mind behind the 'democratising' of the selection of Conservative candidates; and Lord Salisbury – Bobbety – the right-wing conscience of the Party.

Of all the new talents in the Party, however, none was more important than the brilliant, enigmatic figure of R. A. ('Rab') Butler, with his crippled right hand and the eyes of a Chinese mandarin. Educated at Marlborough, Rab had gone on to get a double first in French and History at Cambridge. Eight years younger than Macmillan, he was to form with him a love–hate relationship that became an accepted fact of life in Tory inner circles as the years went by. While Macmillan recognised and admired the intellect of his colleague and rival, Rab's cerebral and subtle intellectualism was not quite congenial to him, and he tended to condescend to him as an *embusqué*, someone (through no fault of his own) who had taken part in neither world war and – worse – had been an appeaser. Macmillan could never quite forgive Butler for his association with Chamberlain's appeasement policy when he became Under-Secretary to Halifax at the Foreign Office after Eden's resignation in 1938. At his unkindest, Macmillan rated him as 'the most cringing of Munichites'.[32] Butler had, however, gone on from the Foreign Office to the Board of Education (where Churchill thought he could 'do no harm'), to make his name with the 1944 Education Act, which is still regarded as one of the most far-reaching reform measures of our time, and had proved himself to be a formidable power on the domestic scene.

At times, in retrospect, Macmillan would describe Butler as 'a born don'; at other times, as 'a Monsignor in the Vatican': 'I always thought of him', he would say with a not-unaffectionate chuckle, 'wearing a soutane. He would have been marvellous in medieval politics, creeping about the Vatican; a tremendous intriguer, he always had some marvellous plan . . . and he loved the press. . . .' He sweetened the pill: 'But charming, and awfully nice. . . .'[33]

Despite the differences – or perhaps because of them – Macmillan and Butler provided admirable foils for each other, in a quite remarkable partnership lasting almost twenty years. Butler recognised Macmillan as having been

reared in a very tough school in politics. Permanently influenced by the unemployment and suffering in his constituency in the North-East. . . . the fact that he had spent much of his early life as a rebel while I was a member of the despised and declining 'establishment' underlines a difference of temperament between us. It may also lie at the root of our future relationship. But in political philosophy we were not far apart. . . .[34]

He admired some of the economic doctrines of *The Middle Way* and, most importantly during the critical opposition period, both men saw eye to eye over the new, middle-of-the-road, modern-minded Tory Party that *had* to emerge from the ashes of the old.

With their minds on higher things, both Churchill and his *prince-héritier*, Eden, were happy to leave reconstruction of the Tory Party to others. In the summer of 1946 Churchill, by what Macmillan dubbed 'a stroke of genius', invited Lord Woolton to be Party Chairman. Woolton, who had been the immensely successful, and popular, Minister of Food during the war, was a name known to every household. Macmillan rated him 'the best salesman in the world'.[35] Under Woolton's able and congenial chairmanship, Butler was put in charge of the moribund but key Research Department. Into it he recruited a 'brains trust' of brilliant young men, among them Iain Macleod, Enoch Powell and Reginald Maudling. John Wyndham, who went to work there after 1945, found Old Queen Street a stimulating place, with these future political stars in a state of constant ferment and argument. Rab's influence over both the thought and its expression produced from his 'Brains Trust' was decisive.

Following the Party conference at Blackpool in October 1946, a committee was set up under Butler to produce a document restating Conservative policy. From the Opposition front benches, Macmillan was one of those most closely involved. Already by the summer of 1946, he had put in some serious political thought on reshaping the Party. In one of the more profound philosophic passages of his memoirs, he argues how Peel had been 'the first of modern Conservatives', insofar as he understood that after a major débâcle a party could only be rebuilt by means of 'a new image'. Peel had achieved this in part by changing the name of the party from Tory to Conservative, and Macmillan began to float ideas about a 'New Democratic Party'; Woolton was more in favour of calling it the 'Union Party'.

On 3 October 1946, to coincide with the opening of the Party conference, Macmillan published an important article in the *Daily Telegraph*, under the heading 'Anti-Socialist Parties Task: The Case for Alliance or Fusion'. Stressing the damage that socialism had already done in Britain, he urged that Liberals and Conservatives get together, either by integration or by alliance, 'to promote a policy, not of passive anti-Socialism, but of an active and dynamic character. It must be positive as well as negative. . . .' The theme of alliance with the Liberals was one to which Macmillan would return frequently over the next few years; after a by-election at Leicester in the autumn of 1950, at which the Liberals had not put up a candidate, he wrote in his diaries that, to obtain an alliance with the Liberals, it would be worthwhile 'to offer proportional representation in the big cities in exchange. . . . It could do no harm and might do good. How else are the great Socialist "blocs" to be eaten into. . . ?'[36]

Both his ideas of changing the Party name and seeking a common cause with the Liberals, however, came to nothing. After the 1946 Party conference, Brendan Bracken reported triumphantly to Beaverbrook:

> The neo-Socialists, like Harold Macmillan, who are in favour of nationalising railways, electricity, gas and many other things, expected to get great support from the delegates. . . . It turned out that the neo-Socialists were lucky to escape with their scalps. The delegates would have nothing to do with the proposal to change the party's name. They demanded a real Conservative policy instead of a synthetic Socialist one so dear to the heart of the Macmillans and the Butlers, and it gave Churchill one of the greatest receptions of his life.[37]

In fact, however, the setback to 'the Macmillans and the Butlers' was purely temporary. Out of the committee headed by Butler there emerged, by May 1947, an important policy document called the *Industrial Charter*. Macmillan had had a significant hand in drafting it; as Crossbencher in the *Sunday Express* remarked, without enthusiasm, it read like 'a second edition' of *The Middle Way*, and, although Butler was the overlord, the *Charter* was a triumph for much of Macmillan's pre-war thinking.[38] In Macmillan's own words, it

> proved our determination to maintain full employment, to sustain and improve the social services, and to continue the strategic control of the economy in the hands of the Government, while preserving wherever possible the tactical function of private enterprise. Our purpose was 'to reconcile the need for central direction with the encouragement of individual effort'. We also accepted

as irreversible the nationalisation of coal, the railways, and the Bank of England, and the impossibility of unscrambling these scrambled eggs. . . .

The same themes were developed further in *The Right Road for Britain*, published in 1949, and other similar policy documents evolved under Rab's guidance, with the accent becoming slightly more conservative as the realities of power approached. To a gathering of young Oxbridge Tories at the Coningsby Club, Macmillan once declared that the essence of all politics was 'the struggle to occupy No-Man's-Land – to seize the middle ground'.[39] This was something he believed throughout his life, and it was what the Butler–Macmillan reforms of the Party were all about. Occasionally he was tactically apprehensive when he saw the Labour Party trying to steal their clothes, in its fits of what right-wing critics came to dub 'Butskellism'. Writing to his old friend, Alex (then Governor-General of Canada), in February 1948, he noted how 'the Labour movement as a whole is turning towards the centre. The Communist, semi-Communist and fellow travellers are less popular.' Although he welcomed this 'in the national interest', he added that it 'may be politically unfavourable' to the Tories.[40]

Macmillan became, as his biographer Anthony Sampson has observed, 'the main salesman' of the new image, and a very enthusiastic and persuasive salesman he was too. Young candidates and older backbenchers alike flocked to ask him to speak at their meetings. 'His speeches were marvellous,' recalled Nigel Nicolson, 'covering the whole sweep of politics, and he used to ask for our opinions – it soon developed into a kind of seminar – he made us feel that we counted for something.'[41] The young particularly were warmed by his interest in them and by his capacity for offering friendship. With a new-found eloquence and display of self-assurance he was able to tell the '1900 Club' in a speech on 27 June 1949 that the 1945 defeat had transformed the Party, and that 'it was surprising how good' the reformed Party machine had become.[42]

Occasionally Macmillan's reforming zeal would result in his knuckles being rapped by Churchill. In February 1948, for instance, he sent off a long memorandum, blaming the Party for 'failing to take the initiative', and suggesting the establishment of a 'Managing Committee – comparable to the War Cabinet' to take over planning functions from the 'more ponderous shadow cabinet'. Churchill replied tartly: 'I do not agree with what you propose and I do not think our colleagues would do so either. . . . I propose to continue the present system as long as I am in charge. I do not think things are going so badly. . . .'[43]

The matter was dropped. Nevertheless, Macmillan seldom showed fear of tackling Churchill. When Churchill was preparing a major speech on the financial crisis in October 1949, Macmillan wrote to him:

The keynote of your speech should be – there is a way out. That is what the people want to hear. They are *bored* – bored stiff with the inter-party slanging match. They don't want to think of you as a party leader. You have never been a good party man; they want to think of you as a national leader. They want to hear that there is a way out. . . .[44]

Whatever failings Macmillan saw in Churchill as the Opposition party leader, he retained all his wartime admiration of him for his role in international affairs after 1945. While helping to create the new Conservative image at home, Macmillan had been following closely events abroad, where Churchill and Foreign Secretary Ernest Bevin were playing key parts, and it was here that he found the second major outlet for his frustrated energies and hopes.

Chapter Twelve

The Cold World Outside
1945–1950

*Incomparably one of the vital issues of the day is the survival or
decay of Europe. . . .*

(HM, speaking at Bromley, June 1947)

*With Communists we cannot say it with flowers. . . . The cold
war must be fought with as much energy and singlemindedness as
the shooting war. . . .*

(HM, House of Commons, 23 March 1949)

However mountainous the problems with which the Attlee government had to wrestle at home between 1945 and 1950, Macmillan was the first to admit that those overseas were even more baffling. Attlee's initiation in the world arena came when he went to take over from Churchill and Eden at Potsdam in July 1945, accompanied by sixty-four-year-old Ernest Bevin. It was the change in participants that brought home abruptly to the world at large how Britain had now been relegated to second place in the Anglo-American alliance.

A few days after the Potsdam Conference ended, the first atomic bomb fell on Hiroshima and Japan surrendered the following week. The Second World War had ended, but without any caesura Britain found herself in the grip of the cold war with Soviet Communism. One after another, satellite 'People's Republics' were set up in liberated Eastern Europe, and on 5 March 1946 Churchill made his historic speech at Fulton, Missouri, warning that an Iron Curtain had rung down in Europe. Six months later he was making a clarion call for European unity at Zurich. That December the Communist Vietminh took up arms in Indo-China.

In March 1947, the US – at last recognising the Communist threat – committed herself to provide aid to Greece, under the 'Truman Doctrine'. Three months later, Secretary of State General Marshall was making his first proposals for the inspired European Recovery Programme that was later to bear his name, and the following April the Organisation for European Economic Co-operation (OEEC) was established. Meanwhile, the Communist seizure of power in Czechoslovakia in February 1948 for the first time aroused the West – especially the US – fully to the realities of the cold war, and by the following year the North Atlantic Treaty Organisation (NATO) had been created to defend Western Europe.

In May 1948, the month that the Council of Europe was established, the three Western occupation zones in Germany were incorporated into the Federal Republic, and the subsequent proclamation of the German Democratic Republic in the Soviet zone set the seal on what had already long been a fact of life: the division of Germany. June saw the beginning of the Berlin blockade, which was to run for eleven months until Western determination to maintain the lifeline to Berlin by airlift caused the Russians to back down, bringing with it one of the West's first tangible successes of the cold war. Within a further six months, in October 1949, the Chinese People's Republic took over in Peking, and about the same time the USSR exploded her first atomic bomb. On 25 June 1950, North Korea – backed by the USSR – invaded the South.

Moreover, these five years saw the creation of Israel and the independence of India and Pakistan. The first Attlee government thus marked an epochal period of history in which the world was largely reshaped. And for at least two years from the end of the war in Europe, Britain, though weakened in material terms, carried the lonely torch as well as much of the burden of the cold war.

The problems that beset Ernest Bevin as Foreign Secretary were thus enormous. Chosen by Attlee over Hugh Dalton because he wanted 'a tank rather than a sniper', Bevin was left to run foreign policy almost entirely without interference from his chief (in sharp contrast to the regimes of Churchill, Eden and Macmillan himself). He is now increasingly regarded as one of Britain's outstanding Foreign Secretaries; he was certainly the first to have to face up to living in the Big Power world where Britain's natural role exceeded the nation's means.

Soon after Potsdam it became abundantly clear to Bevin, as it did to Churchill – and Macmillan too – that British policy would be opposed by Stalin. Although resolutely anti-Communist, Bevin never sought confrontation with the USSR, but awareness of the threat world-wide made him determined to resist Stalin all along the line. For the best part of two years, it was a lonely resistance; whether through blindness in Washington, or instinctive distrust of a socialist Britain, Bevin could scarcely count on support from Truman any more than he could from Stalin. Despite her wartime pioneering, Britain was not going to be helped to build an atomic bomb, while American big-business interests, too, wasted no time in seeking to capture British markets in Latin America, and her holdings in the Middle East oilfields. The Palestine issue in particular did much to alienate US public opinion, and it was not until the coming of George Marshall as US Secretary of State, in 1947, and the common threat of Berlin and Prague, that something approaching the wartime 'special relationship' was re-cemented. Bevin's great contribution to international affairs was in helping to end America's post-1945 neo-isolationism. He was, moreover, principal architect – on the European side – of both the European Recovery Plan and NATO.

During the Bevin era, Macmillan constantly fretted at Britain's debility in the world arena and – given his wartime experiences – especially at the falling away of the 'special relationship'. Yet, though he held the socialists responsible, he seldom blamed Bevin personally, and then only during Bevin's last year when his powers were noticeably declining. He came to have considerable respect for Bevin's record in dealing with the Russians and much of the criticism he would make of the Labour government for its feebleness in tackling the Communist threat was the conventional rhetoric of political opposition.

Because of his close involvement in international affairs during the war, Macmillan frequently spoke from the Opposition front bench on the momentous world issues now facing the Attlee government. Called to lead his first Commons debate on 20 February 1946, he suggested that Soviet policy was chiefly concerned, defensively, with the creation of 'a new *cordon sanitaire* . . . of States made satellite and dependent . . .'.[1] He supported this with a historical review of the many invasions of Russia, from both east and west, and suggested that her need for security could only be reconciled 'by direct and personal negotiation'. These were themes developed, with some consistency, from his trip to the USSR in the early 1930s, from his wartime experiences and right through to his own premiership.

Two weeks after Macmillan's speech, however, came Churchill's Fulton speech, with its much tougher talk about the Iron Curtain and outspoken comparisons between Communism and Fascism. Coming so soon after the joint Allied victory over Germany, it embarrassed Washington and the Attlee government alike, as well as some leading Conservatives – including Anthony Eden. Macmillan himself still felt some doubts about whether Churchill had not over-simplified the moods and motives of those in control in Russia. 'Was Stalin really so powerful?' Deeply impressed by what the Russians had suffered from Hitler during the war, he could not quite make up his mind how real was the Soviet fear of Germany, or how much it contained an element of opportunism. After Fulton, however, influenced as always by his leader, he swiftly picked up the Churchillian refrain, adding his own conviction as Stalin's aggressiveness proved Churchill right. Six months later, Macmillan was chastising government circles for the 'semi-religious Socialist fervour' with which they claimed 'only a Government of the Left in Britain will be able to reach amicable friendship and comradeship with the Union of Soviet Republics. Only a Socialist Government can obtain concord with a Communist Government in Russia.'[2]

By the time of the Berlin blockade, in 1948/9, evoking his pre-war stance against Chamberlain, he was attacking the airlift as 'an act of political appeasement' and stating that it would have been better 'to face the issue squarely'. This should have been by economic boycott of the Soviet zone and the threat of military force (although these were measures from which, when Prime Minister, he was himself to shrink during the Berlin crisis of 1961). He continued his speech in the Commons by warning: 'Do not give away guns in order to get butter. . . . Step by step the cold war must be won. If the way be long and weary, let us have courage and faith. For this is no ordinary journey that we must travel together. It is, perhaps, the last Crusade.'[3]

It was, indeed, in almost religious terms that Macmillan, like Churchill, came to see the struggle against Stalinist Communism. In an interview with *The Recorder* of 26 February 1949, he spoke of the need to 'go back to the broad principles on which Western Christendom is based. . . . Today the position of the Christian World is not unlike that of the 5th Century AD at the time when the invasions of the Goths ultimately led to the break-up of the Roman Empire. What saved civilisation was the conversion of the conquerors to Christianity. . . .'[4]

This crusading stance against Communism was very far from the US views in the first post-war years. Again, because of wartime commitments, one of Macmillan's deepest concerns in this period was the fate of Greece, which was threatened anew by Communist domination. By 1947, it was clear that Britain, faced by bankruptcy, could no longer afford to sustain the Greek government without American assistance, which had not been forthcoming. Then, in March 1947, President Truman called upon Congress to take over Britain's burden by giving military and financial aid to both Greece and Turkey, including a gift of $400 million. In a foreign affairs debate in the House on 16 May 1947, Macmillan rejoiced 'that the United States have taken a decision, a non-party decision, binding equally upon Republicans as upon Democrats, to abandon isolationism . . .'. Had there ever been, he continued, 'a more dramatic reversal of policy than that of the United States towards Greece in two short years? . . . Has there ever been a more sensational justification of what we did . . . in the winter of 1944? . . .'[5]

Gratifying as it was to see British policy – his policy – vindicated, Macmillan observed that 'America had now been forced to stake out strategic positions in Europe as her defence against the potential thrust of an expansionist Russia. . . .'

Macmillan recalled all too vividly how, with Roosevelt, there had been 'hardly any moment in the war, however grave, at which the President did not find an opportunity to drag in his anti-colonial bias, based on very little real knowledge but much vague prejudice', and he continued to chafe at the assaults which the US maintained on Britain's imperial position – or what remained of it – after the war. The most serious issue that divided Britain and the US in these years was Palestine, where – to American Jewry as well as to wider sections of US public opinion – Bevin and his policy was seen (rightly or wrongly) to be pro-Arab, if not actively anti-Jewish.

In 1939, when war with Hitler had appeared imminent and the Foreign Office had deemed it vital to placate the strategically placed Arabs, Britain had produced the much criticised White Paper setting strict limits on Jewish immigration to Palestine, where Britain still exercised uneasily the Mandate granted after 1918. During the Second World War, this had compounded the tragedy of the holocaust, and in 1945 there were many thousands among the survivors desperate to flee Europe for the Promised Land. Efforts by a joint Anglo-American committee to arrange the immediate entry to Palestine of 100,000 Jews were rejected. Under the aegis of the Jewish extremist Stern Gang and Menacheim Begin's Irgun, terrorism reared its ugly head for the first time in the post-war world. On 22 July 1946 the government offices in Jerusalem's King David Hotel were blown up by Begin's men, with a loss of nearly a hundred people, many of them young female employees. As terrorism and punitive counter-measures escalated, so did bitterness in both Britain and the US.

Macmillan, following Churchill, had strongly opposed the original White Paper, and now both found themselves in a minority in the Conservative Party in supporting the Zionist cause. Macmillan recalled Churchill making a speech in the Commons on 1 August 1946 that 'was one of the most powerful and courageous that I have ever heard him deliver'. It ended with a pronouncement that 'shocked the great majority of Members on all sides'. 'Our friends in America', Churchill declared, must be told firmly that 'either they should come in and help us in this Zionist problem, about which they feel so strongly, and as I think rightly, on even terms, share and share alike, or that we should resign our Mandate . . .'.[6]

Macmillan thought that Churchill, even though out of power, might have succeeded in swinging American opinion, but the essential co-operation was not forthcoming. In September the following year, amid mounting disorder, the Labour government announced its intention to end the Mandate.

A Passage to India

Of far greater consequence than Palestine to Britain at the time was, however, the future of that 'jewel in the crown' of Empire, India. Macmillan had never seen eye to eye over India with the imperialist Churchill, dating back to the debates on Indian home rule of the 1930s. Nevertheless, in 1946, he was appalled when, after Cripps and the antique Lord Pethick-Lawrence had returned from one of several missions to the sub-continent, Attlee announced that its future was a matter to be decided, not by the British government, but by the Indians themselves. Macmillan thought this an outrageous 'abdication of duty as well as of power'.

By the end of 1946, deadlock over India seemed complete and Macmillan decided to pay a visit there, to 'see what was going on', although the purpose of the trip was as much to fly the flag as publisher at the various Macmillan establishments in India. It was the kind of trip where he might well have taken along his son Maurice; nevertheless he was in fact accompanied by his old wartime aide, John Wyndham – plus St Augustine's *Confessions*, Plato's *Republic*, Mrs Humphry Ward's *Robert Elsmere*, Byron's *Don Juan*, Ainsworth's *Tower of London*, Aldous Huxley, A. E. Mason and Agatha Christie.

On their way in January 1947, they made a brief detour via Iran.

309

The Russians had just, under Anglo-American pressure, withdrawn from their wartime occupation of the north but the whole country filled Macmillan with foreboding. Visiting the Abadan oilfields in the south, which were soon to cause a major crisis for Britain, Macmillan thought it one of the grimmest places he had ever seen: 'like a bit of Hell pushed up. . . . no vegetation of any kind, no greenery, no water, nothing – but these eternal hills . . . one horrid desert knoll after another . . .'.[7]

In Teheran he had a gloomy conversation with the young Shah's Minister of Labour. After the long dictatorship of Reza Pahlevi, Macmillan found the moderate politicians of Iran 'fatally weakened'; 'In spite of the country being absolutely full of money, no internal loan can be raised. . . . No one has sufficient confidence in the regime to lend for a long term loan. Insecurity has made very high interest rates a normal thing.' Iran's greatest problem, Macmillan thought, was the rampant cost of living, which an incompetent and corrupt administrative machine made virtually impossible to contain.

Arriving in India from austerity Britain in that terrible winter of 1947, Macmillan found life in the last days of the Raj quite extraordinary. He stayed first in Government House, Bombay, where 'Servants abound. It is really quite embarrassing. Each one has a separate task and does nothing but this – a perfect trade union. One does the flowers, another calls you and draws the bath; another brings drinks; another messages. . . .' With this plethora of servants, dressed in the splendid red surcoats, red turbans and white trousers, inherited from the emperors, 'You are never alone. . . . at home there are too few servants; here there are really too many.'

Moving on to Delhi, Macmillan found the atmosphere unreal, and very sad. 'All power is oozing away and only the shell is left. And that is made the more oppressive because the outward symbols of imperial power remain. In the vast palace of New Delhi . . . Guards are mounted; the royal (or viceroyal) state is maintained, the toast of the King–Emperor is drunk each night at dinner.' Although British and Indians alike were talking openly of '"when India is free", nobody really believes that anything but chaos will follow'. Macmillan felt that the British were running away; 'We are deserting, and if we are to go, we can never return. . . .'

He was haunted by the lonely, 'almost pathetic figure' of the

Viceroy, that distinguished soldier, Field-Marshal Lord Wavell: 'Charming, sincere, cultivated – but no politician, and hopelessly bemused by the Congress Party here and the Socialists at home. He confessed to me that the Cabinet mission (he cordially hates Cripps) had twisted him and confused him. . . .' With few advisers and confidants, and no clear knowledge of either what he ought to do or what the government in London intended, Wavell seemed a man resigned, sitting 'alone in his great room, with the paintings and prints of all the viceroys, knowing that he will be the last . . .'. (In fact, of course, Wavell was succeeded by Mountbatten, for whose abilities Macmillan had a far higher regard.)

One of the first Indians Macmillan met was a man with whom he would, later, as Prime Minister have a long and warm relationship – Pandit Nehru: 'high-class Brahmin of Kashmir, intellectualist, philosopher, writer; nationalist, socialist, revolutionary; exquisite and even flowery in taste. . . . Many years of prison life – or rather preventive detention – have left a mark upon him. He is, I should judge, torn between bitter hatred of the British and a desire to be fair and objective. . . .' Nehru struck Macmillan as 'very nervous, jumpy and strained', and he rather doubted his political stamina: 'He is not a man for storms; only a stormy petrel.' As Macmillan admitted, his later relationship with Nehru as a Commonwealth Prime Minister was to prove him wrong.

Macmillan was also taken aback by the inflexibility of the Moslem leaders. Liaquat Ali Khan 'spoke with more bitterness than I expected, for he has the reputation of being a moderate man . . .'. The formidable Jinnah, already ageing, he found 'a man of striking appearance – thin, almost emaciated, with long bony fingers and a strangely shrunken, skull-like head. His voice is low and very beautiful, under wonderful control. The orator, indeed the actor, are clearly a great part of the man.'

Jinnah warned him that a united India, then still the notional hope of the British government, was 'an impossibility'; for India was 'a continent – or sub-continent – not a nation'. Fatalistically, he predicted civil war, 'and chaos and destruction and rivers of blood'. Save partition, he could offer little hope by way of a solution. Jinnah died the following year; Liaquat Ali Khan, Pakistan's first Prime Minister, was assassinated in 1951. In retrospect, Macmillan felt that, had Jinnah survived, Pakistan might have had a more stable future.

Although it was, primarily, as a publisher that Macmillan had gone to India, that part of his trip occupies only a few lines in his letters and diary. The chief purpose of the first Macmillan staff meeting he attended, was 'of course, to ask for more wages', but in Calcutta he came up forcibly against the nightmare prophesied by Jinnah. During the recent disturbances, the location of the Macmillan building there had 'been a disadvantage. Most of the staff are Hindus and this is rather a Muslim quarter. The killings were on a scale quite beyond what we were led to believe at home. . . .'

Macmillan left India shocked and depressed by what he had seen. He admitted to having no profound knowledge of Indian affairs, nor do his diaries reveal any great empathy; 1947 India was, he decided, 'the most snobbish and aristocratic country I have ever seen. Everybody looks down on everybody else. Everybody kicks the man immediately below him. . . .' In contrast to Churchill (or his Macmillan author, Rudyard Kipling), Macmillan was moved much more by present realities than by the awe and symbolism of Britain's imperial past, and his experience of the country in 1947 was undoubtedly to influence him when it came to the 'winds of change' era.

Passing through Cairo on his return to England, Macmillan heard the news that Wavell had been sacked and replaced by Mountbatten, and that Attlee had announced to the Commons the 'definite intention' of transferring power into Indian hands 'by a date not later than June 1948'. When the debate on the government's plans took place the following month, March 1947, Churchill gave what Macmillan described as a 'sombre peroration', deeply regretting the ending of Britain's imperial past. Macmillan's feelings were torn between his belief in home rule for India and his loyalty to Churchill, and between sympathy for Attlee's position and disapproval at the hasty manner in which the Labour government was handing over power. He found himself in a difficult position. When called upon to speak for the Opposition during the second reading of the India Independence Bill in July 1947 (Churchill was away ill), Macmillan limited his remarks to praising Britain's past contribution to India.

The following month, the new independent dominions of India and Pakistan came into being. After that the dominoes fell rapidly:

Burma in January, and Ceylon in February 1948; and the first steps were taken towards decolonialisation in the Caribbean, Malaya and West Africa. Thus, Macmillan later wrote, the direction of the 'wind of change' was 'already set by the time the Conservative Party came into power in 1951'.

In November 1949, Macmillan declaimed to the House: 'We are in the Commonwealth; in the same family. We know and trust each other. . . . The stronger and better the British Empire, the greater will be our contribution to the recovery and security of Europe.'[8] This was not just lip-service to the more fervid imperialists within the Tory Party; nevertheless, Empire and Commonwealth were never to have for Macmillan quite the same degree of priority as for other Tory leaders, such as Lord Salisbury.

Towards a United Europe

In referring to the Empire in terms of the 'recovery and security of Europe', Macmillan was very much in accord with Churchill, whose call for a united Europe was part of the grander, global theme of building up resistance to the menace of Communism. In his visionary way, Churchill had already been talking about a Council of Europe even before El Alamein in 1942. At Zurich on 19 September 1946, six months after his Fulton speech, he made the second of his great post-war speeches, about the need to unite Europe, and early in 1947 he founded the non-party United Europe Movement. Macmillan was a natural choice for the committee, on which one of the leading activists was Churchill's son-in-law, Duncan Sandys; other Conservative members included David Maxwell-Fyfe (who had prosecuted the chief German war criminals at Nuremberg), David Eccles, Peter Thorneycroft and Bob Boothby. Incomprehensibly to Macmillan, Anthony Eden 'stood aloof'. On the Labour side, their opposite numbers comprised Herbert Morrison, Hugh Dalton, William Whiteley – the Chief Whip – and Maurice Edelman, who was one of the few totally convinced Europeans on that team. Labour's attitude to Europe received its guidance from Attlee, who, in the view of his successor Harold Wilson, distrusted continentals on the basis of his army experiences between 1914 and 1918.[9]

In May 1948, a vast Congress of Europe was held in The Hague, consisting of eight hundred delegates, among them several former

Prime Ministers, no less than twenty-nine former Foreign Ministers, and some Ministers in office. It was, said Macmillan, 'a grand affair'; however, already his keen political ear was detecting how 'a considerable portion of the Conservative Party were doubtful and even anxious about this new movement', on the grounds that it might prejudice Britain's position in the Empire and Commonwealth. Among the Labour delegates, he claimed to note with equal concern a tendency 'to promote the concept that the liberties and prosperity of Europe were only safe in Socialist hands'. At a meeting in London Macmillan warned strongly of the illusion of a socialist united front to resist Communism. 'We shall never unite Europe by dividing ourselves.' Prophetic words!

From the Hague Congress followed the foundation of the Council of Europe, meeting in Strasbourg for the first time in August 1949. It was, Macmillan recalled, 'certainly a thrilling moment'. The three years that he would subsequently sit at Strasbourg provided him with a deeply satisfying oasis in an otherwise forlorn political desert. Europe, at least initially, gave him a new purpose, a new focus for idealism. Dealing with foreigners and wider foreign issues invoked the excitement, as well as the attendant skills, of his wartime years in the Mediterranean. He spoke good French (thanks to Nellie Macmillan) and – although his prickly friend from Algiers days, de Gaulle, had temporarily quit the political scene in a huff – Jean Monnet, whom Macmillan vastly revered and who had helped him save de Gaulle in 1943, had now re-emerged as the catalyst for Europe. Macmillan was also impressed by the new French leaders like Bidault and Schuman: 'keen, amusing, deeply religious, and patriotic men. They are very different from the old French politicians. . . .'[10] Getting to know 'almost every distinguished personality in Europe' was to be a great help for the future.

Macmillan's enthusiasm for Europe at the time seemed boundless, almost excessive. One political commentator recalled how 'Macmillan put an arm on my shoulder and spoke with a fervour which I thought embarrassing about his belief in the European idea'.[11] On 17 August 1949, he went so far as to table an amendment in the Assembly proposing that 'The Committee of Ministers shall be an executive authority with supranational powers. The Committee shall have its own permanent secretariat of European officials. . . .' Presaging the Brussels apparatus of the EEC of two decades later, it was a proposal that the Liberal *News Chronicle* rated a 'political bombshell'.[12]

Churchill was the obvious star of the proceedings at Strasbourg in August 1949. He received frequent and moving orations, though he was, so Macmillan claimed, somewhat put out to discover that the public holiday on the day he received the Freedom of Strasbourg was given not in his honour, but because it happened to be the Feast of the Annunciation. Otherwise Macmillan remembered Churchill revelling in his position, declaring, 'This is the best fun I've had for years and years. . . .' The 'fun', however, was somewhat marred at an early stage by internecine bickering among the British delegates; evidently Herbert Morrison was the main problem. 'Having absolutely no knowledge or experience of foreigners,' Macmillan wrote acidly to Dorothy on 10 August, 'Herbert clearly thought that he would reproduce Westminster at Strasbourg. He would "lead" the House; we should be a docile and patronised Opposition. The "foreigners" would stand in awe of British prestige. . . . He was going to alter the rules; he was going to elect the officers. . . .'[13]

It was hardly a promising beginning; nor, alas, was it uncharacteristic of British attitudes toward Europe in general. Morrison irritated the French by some undignified horse-dealing over the office of vice-president; he embarrassed the British and (according to Macmillan) 'amazed' the Europeans by making a public scene over the payment of £2 a day to one of the Conservative delegates. In contrast to the immense success of Churchill, Macmillan noted with growing impatience 'the morose jealousy of Morrison or the frightful "*faux bonhomme*" business of Dalton. . . . in general all countries are annoyed by the British rudeness and boorishness, as exhibited by the Socialists. They seem to behave as the traditional 19th century Englishman in Paris. The difference is, however, that they are more rich – now we are bankrupt. . . .'[14] Even Hugh Dalton made an unflattering comparison between Morrison and Macmillan: the latter speaking in French and to the point, the other in English, long-windedly and unintelligibly, with no interpreter present.[15]

Progressively Churchill came to dominate this first session, while the British socialists, by resorting to obstructive proceduralism when they found themselves outvoted, 'put the Assembly against them. By the end, they voted alone, abandoned in disgust by the

Continental Socialists. . . .' Again, this alienation was a harbinger of what was to become a sadly familiar pattern.

Although at the end of August, Churchill suffered a minor stroke, it did not impede him from making perhaps his greatest contribution to the Strasbourg session. Speaking about the problem of Germany, he paused, looked round the chamber and in a dramatic outburst,

> demanded almost fiercely, 'Where are the Germans?' He pressed for an immediate invitation to the West German Government to join our ranks. . . . 'We cannot part at the end of this month on the basis that we do nothing more to bring Germany into our circle until a year has passed. That year is too precious to lose. If lost, it might be lost for ever. It might not be *a* year. It might be *the* year.

Given how much of his life had been dedicated to mortal combat against them, Churchill's determination to bring the Germans back into the fold so soon after the war was an imposing monument to his magnanimity, and it had Macmillan's full admiration. By his own admission, Bevin could never entirely stifle his dislike for the Germans; Macmillan with his many war-wounds also always had his difficulties, but – like Churchill – he saw the grander design. 'You cannot', Macmillan once observed, 'have two enemies, and Churchill's move followed logically on the Fulton speech.'[16]

Macmillan had had considerable reservations about the wisdom of the Nuremberg trials, while his Italian experiences made him unhappy about prolonging denazification in Germany. Already back in February 1946 he had made a moving appeal in the House for an early 'accommodation' with Germany before it was too late and she once again became a menace to peace. He warned: 'Germany, now cast down, despised, shunned like an unclean thing, will once more be courted by each of the two groups [the West and the Soviet bloc], and from a starving outcast she will become the pampered courtesan of Europe, selling her favours to the highest bidder.'[17]

In March 1949, addressing the Commons about European fears – and particularly French fears – over the future of Germany, he declared: 'The only guarantee is if the soul of the German people is won for the West. If Germany enters a West European system, as a free and equal member, then indeed German heavy industry can be subjected to control; but not an *invidious* control directed against Germany alone. . . .'[18]

Consequently Macmillan was well suited to be charged by Churchill with pressing the issue of German entry at Strasbourg, which he wholeheartedly supported. On 30 March 1950, a formal invitation was issued to Dr Adenauer's Federal Germany, and it was accepted: 'a decisive step had been taken towards reconciliation and unity.' By the winter of 1950, too, the generous American-financed European recovery programme was bringing a revival of prosperity to much of Western Europe, including Germany and Great Britain.

By that time, the first general election in Britain since 1945 had been held. After the terrible winter of 1947 and the savage austerity measures introduced by Cripps to meet the economic crisis, things had seemed to go better for Labour. In March 1949, the government was able to remove the unpopular measure of clothes rationing. The balance of trade was looking up. At that time, Macmillan, who often betrayed a curious blend of antipathy and admiration towards Cripps, admitted that 'our Conservative outlook seemed rather grim. We could protest against Cripps and his philosophy, but it certainly seemed to be winning through.' Remarkably enough, not a single seat had been won back by the Conservatives in parliamentary by-elections up to 1950 and Macmillan felt that the 'Government was still riding high upon the worldwide reputation of Cripps as a kind of cross between a priest and an economist'.

Then in April 1949 Cripps introduced his last Budget before the coming general election. In his first Budget he had hit the rich with a 'once for all' capital levy, which had at least pleased the Labour left, but this second Budget, by its neutrality, satisfied no one; there were no cuts in government expenditure, and no incentives to stimulate Britain's stagnant industries. To George Wigg on the Labour backbenches it was a 'Tory Budget'; to the Tories it represented a definitive admission of the failure of socialism. It was to prove, Macmillan said, 'a milestone to Conservative victory and a tombstone in the Socialist graveyard'. Almost immediately Britain was plunged into a new dollar crisis, and in September – after long denials that any devaluation was intended – Cripps devalued the pound from $4.03 to $2.80.

In the February 1950 general election, the socialists, in their policy document *Labour Believes in Britain*, fought the campaign on the now jaded issue of still further nationalisation. The most successful Tory propaganda card of the campaign, next to the still vigorous figure of Churchill himself, was Woolton's selection of 'the Radio Doctor', Dr Charles Hill, who, with his atonal daily advice on constipation and other medical matters, had made himself a household name across the country. Macmillan fought his campaign unashamedly on the 'middle ground', if not *The Middle Way*, and romped home at Bromley with a majority of 10,688. He noted how both parties had tended to move towards the 'middle ground', with all but a few of the extreme left of the Labour Party losing their seats and all but three of the 100 Communist candidates forfeiting their deposits. Yet it was a disappointing result for the Conservatives, with Labour actually increasing its overall poll, although the swing to the Conservatives of 3 per cent was enough to reduce the Labour lead from 166 to 17 over the Tories.

In the spring of 1950, France's Robert Schuman announced, as something of a bombshell, his plan to pool Franco-German coal and steel production; in fact it precisely embodied the points made by Macmillan in his Commons speech of March 1949. The Schuman Plan, the rock on which the European Economic Community was to be built, was more than just a coal and steel pool; behind it lay the loftiest hopes for ending, once and for all, the centuries of murderous Franco-German rivalry.

Its architect was one of the European trio of Christian Democrats who represented the peak of idealism about Europe, leading it on the path towards reconstruction and reconciliation. The others were Adenauer and de Gasperi; all three, one from the Rhineland, one from the Tyrol and the third from Alsace, came from regions which had been subject to the most bitter nationalist rivalries throughout history, and all were deeply imbued with the European spirit. Macmillan described Schuman as 'this strange, melancholy, quixotic figure, half politician, half priest'.[19] With gentle mockery he enjoyed recalling French cartoons at the time which depicted that eminently respectable Catholic statesman embracing a tart, above the caption 'Monsieur Schuman et sa poule'.[20] In fact, he had the highest regard both for Schuman and his 'pool', especially since Schuman's chief adviser was Macmillan's old friend from Algiers days, Jean Monnet.

On 15 August 1950 Macmillan praised the Plan before the Strasbourg Assembly as being 'not just a piece of convenient machinery. It is a revolutionary, and almost mystical conception. . . .' Within a few days of the announcement of the Schuman Plan, Macmillan had, however, noted with alarm the tepid reaction in British government circles. At a speech in London on 17 May he endeavoured to counteract this by praising Schuman's proposals as 'an act of high courage and of imaginative statesmanship. . . . I hope that British statesmanship will at least be equal to this new responsibility.'

On 13 June, however, the worst fears of Macmillan and the 'Europeans' were confirmed: Attlee made a formal statement that Britain was not willing to join the six European nations in their preliminary discussions of the Plan. In retrospect, this was a crucial milestone in British post-war history; 'the greatest mistake of the post-war period', said Dean Acheson.[21] With Bevin by now ill, and Attlee and Chancellor Cripps both out of the country, it appears that the issue was never dealt with by the Cabinet in full session; and that the vital decision was taken by Herbert Morrison – tracked down in the Ivy restaurant, after an evening at the theatre. 'It is no good,' he said. 'We can't do it, the Durham miners won't wear it.'[22]

Speaking to his own constituency about the British rejection, Macmillan employed phrases that, sadly, he would have to repeat for another occasion twelve and a half years later:

> This has been a black week for Britain; for the Empire; for Europe; and for the peace of the world. . . . without British participation, Franco-German unity may be a source not of security but danger. . . . In the not too distant future, we may have to pay a terrible price for the isolationist policy which British Socialism has long practised. . . .

Macmillan's mounting exasperation with Labour policy towards Europe is betrayed in his diaries for 1950. A speech made on 13 November about the European Movement by the now ailing Bevin (for whom his respect had largely evaporated), he rated 'the worst oration I have ever heard. . . . It does seem to me extraordinary that our Government should be both negative and rude. In normal life, if one is unable to agree, one tries to be specially courteous in the manner of the refusal. Even publishers do not insult the authors whose MSS they decline. . . .'[23]

He was shocked at the rough way Bevin had treated Guy Mollet, the distinguished and anglophile French socialist leader, who, recorded Macmillan, 'still does not want to push his quarrel with the British Socialists *à l'outrance*. But he realises the great gulf that has sprung up, and that faced with the choice between the international tradition of Socialism and the "Socialist planned economy", the British Labour Party have definitely decided in favour of the latter. . . .'[24]

In October Macmillan was already acidly blaming the deterioration of Franco-German relations over the newly projected 'European Army' upon 'the failure of British diplomacy under the vain and aging Bevin to play any effective role. . . . All this comes from Attlee's inertia and Bevin's jealousy . . .'[25] – jealousy aroused presumably by Churchill's continuing triumph at Strasbourg.

It was not only the Labour government that gave Macmillan cause for concern; there was also a strong undercurrent of opposition within the Tory Party towards the Schuman Plan or anything that involved surrender of British sovereignty to supranational authorities. In June Macmillan had addressed an urgent minute to Churchill, pointing out that the Schuman Plan 'may well be a major turning-point in European history. It is certainly a turning-point in the fortunes of the Tory Party. This issue affords us the last, and perhaps only, chance of regaining the initiative. . . .' He chided Churchill, 'You started United Europe. . . .' Therefore Churchill alone 'must give the lead for which *Britain, the Empire, Europe* and *the world* have been waiting. Everyone looks to you. . . . You cannot let down all Europe.'

These strong words suggest that Macmillan was already sensing a change of heart in his hero and leader. On 20 June Boothby wrote on similar lines to Churchill, ending by pointing out that Churchill had 'got the Labour Party on the run' and could win the next election, if only he now provided 'the leadership for which the whole western world is praying'.[26] At about the same time, a newly elected Tory Member – Edward Heath – was making a maiden speech in the Commons which strongly urged co-operation with Europe.

Under all these pressures, on 27 June 1950, Churchill rose in the House to accept, without hesitation, the principle of abrogation of national sovereignty – provided the conditions and safeguards were satisfactory. Soaring to those well-known heights of oratory, he recalled the risks and sacrifices Britain had made during the war, then pronounced solemnly, 'The Conservative and Liberal Parties declare that national sovereignty is not inviolable, and that it may be resolutely diminished for the sake of all the men in all the lands finding their way home together.'[27]

Thus encouraged, Macmillan at Strasbourg on 15 August made his eulogy about the Schuman Plan being an 'almost mystical conception'. Later in this same session, Schuman paid Macmillan the high compliment that he had 'done more for France than any man, even including Churchill'.[28]

Yet it was clear that Macmillan too was already being pulled in different directions, over three different issues: first, how far could Britain go down the road of a 'federal' as opposed to a looser 'confederal' Europe; secondly, where would the supranationalism of the more dedicated French 'federalists' lead Britain; and, thirdly, could there be a clash of priorities between Commonwealth and Europe? An article he wrote in the *Manchester Dispatch* of 11 October 1949 betrayed the inner conflict: 'The Empire must always have first preference for us: Europe must come second in a specially-favoured position. Politically, strategically and economically, Britain is part of Europe, though she is also head of the Empire. We cannot isolate ourselves from Europe.'[29]

On the dangers of excessive supranationalism, he cautioned the European Assembly the day after his encomium on the Schuman Plan: 'Our people are not going to hand to any supranational authority the right to close down our pits or steelworks.'[30] When he introduced a resolution to bring the Schuman Pool within the framework of the Council of Europe, Monnet expressed concern to Schuman that this would turn the High Authority into nothing more than a committee of representatives from the coal and steel industries.

Although there is no doubting Macmillan's total commitment to Europe at this juncture, at the same time he was asking himself – how much would the British electorate accept? The general election six months earlier had brought in a severely weakened Attlee government; there was the prospect of an imminent Conservative victory. The determination – as the socialist years of 'mismanage-ment' clocked up – to get back into power, and stay there, was an overriding consideration and inevitably tempered Macmillan's stance towards Europe at this point.

In the autumn of 1950 a new factor arose to challenge the 'European-ism' of British politicians of all hues – the European Defence Community. On 25 June 1950, North Korea – with massive Soviet backing – had invaded South Korea. Once again the West looked dangerously vulnerable, and especially in Germany where the frontier between East and West assumed the potential menace of Korea's 38th Parallel, and where a dangerous military vacuum beckoned. In face of this new aggressive mood of the Communists, the NATO council launched the proposal of rearming West Ger-many at its meeting in New York in September. The big issue was how to reconcile this with European (and notably French) fears of a remilitarised Germany, and on 24 October France came up with the Pleven Plan, to evolve into the ill-fated European Defence Community (EDC), which envisaged integration of German forces on the 'combat team' or brigade level.

Nobody in England much liked the idea; Macmillan considered the scheme 'more calculated to alleviate the fears of the French than to strike terror into the Russians', while Churchill deprecated 'this vast Foreign Legion' as a 'sludgy amalgam'. Before it was finally demolished by the French themselves, the EDC plunged Europe into three years of time-wasting argument during which recriminations grew and enthusiasm for the 'European Idea' waned – especially north of the Channel.

These prolonged debates over Europe had a significant influence on Macmillan's thinking when it came to European issues in the late 1950s and early 1960s. Much has been made of a despairing remark made by him and picked up by Hugh Dalton following one of the Strasbourg meetings in 1950:

> . . . I think Europe is finished; it is sinking. It is like Greece after the second Peloponnesian War. Athens and Sparta are quarrelling and Philip of Macedon is watching and waiting to strike. I have been reading Thucydides lately and it is just like our times. If I were a younger man, I should emigrate from Europe to the United States. . . .[31]

This gloom, though typical of Macmillan in his bouts of pessimism at the time, cannot be taken as a true reflection of his thinking. There were already the tugs in other directions; above all there was the potent influence of Churchill. Over Europe, Macmillan and the other European enthusiasts were to some extent like a string of light bulbs attached to a powerful dynamo – Churchill; as long as the dynamo rotated, they emitted a bright light, but when the dynamo faltered, or stopped, or even reversed its direction, their light dimmed accordingly. As Macmillan noted, Churchill's Zurich cry, 'Let Europe unite', was an emotional appeal, not a considered programme. In one of his rare criticisms of Churchill, at the time of the early debates over creation of a European army, Macmillan recorded that although Churchill 'contemplated a system in Europe in which Britain should play a leading role, not merely cheer from the sidelines . . . [he] had no clear or well-defined plan. He was then in Opposition, deprived of the vast machinery at the disposal of Ministers. He was an old man trying to give a new lead to the world which he had helped to save. . . . It was for others to find detailed solutions. . . .'

Macmillan thought it was a weakness of Churchill's approach that he had made 'no attempt to devise a constitution for Europe, whether political, military or economic'. Equally the criticism that Macmillan himself, in tune with his leader and the vast majority of his fellow Tories, had begun to blow hot and cold over Europe, had a certain validity – at least by the beginning of the 1950s.

Chapter Thirteen

Under Churchill:
Houses and Defence
1951–1955

I've never enjoyed three years more. . . . It was great fun.

(HM on period as Housing Minister)

*I am not persuaded that our membership of NATO is enough. . . .
If the EEC proposals should come into being they will separate
us from our most important Continental neighbours.*

(HM, March 1952)

After Attlee had scraped in again at the 1950 general election, Macmillan noted gloomily in a memorandum on electoral strategy that 'unless there is a dramatic change in either the economic or the political situation, another election will not produce a substantially different result.'[1] That 'dramatic change', however, was provided by the Korean War and its economic consequences. Meanwhile, the socialists managed to limp along in office for the next nineteen months, during which Macmillan watched with mounting aggravation the flailings of the government in its death throes.

In his memoirs he summed up 'the great Labour Parliament' as 'one of mixed triumphs and tribulations. Many of the questions raised in these five years are still with us. How to get expansion without inflation; how to carry the burdens as well as enjoy the advantages of a reserve currency.' To his diaries at the time, however, he exposed a far more pungent exasperation with the socialist 'experiment'. Commenting on how ill Bevin looked in November 1950, Macmillan fumed: 'What is strange is that he (and his friends) still seem quite unable to grasp the complete and utter failure of the policy for which he has been responsible during 5 years. The Socialists as a whole are beginning to have a sort of fumbling idea that all is not well. This does not prevent them from booming away the old familiar clap-trap. . . .'[2] His personal bitterness was shown during the preparations for his daughter Catherine's marriage to Julian Amery in 1950, when, his son-in-law recalled, Macmillan struck off the invitation list all the socialist leaders, including Attlee, who had been old political friends of Julian's father, Leo Amery. 'He hated them all at that time.'[3]

It was Attlee's harsh misfortune that ill-health removed in a matter of months between October 1950 and March 1951 two of his ablest lieutenants, Cripps and Bevin, followed in April by the resignation of Aneurin Bevan. Returning home from a short visit to Scandinavia in March 1951, Macmillan found the Commons 'completely out of control, like an unruly class under a weak French master. Everyone freely insults each other and combines in insulting the Speaker. I have never seen anything like it before. . . .'[4]

Cripps was succeeded at the Treasury by Gaitskell, and the sight of Hugh Gaitskell delivering his first Budget did nothing to appease Macmillan: 'a pupil of Mr Dalton. He has imitated his rather pedantic style, tedious expositions of the obvious, weak gestures, and irritating smile.'[5] His full spleen, however, was reserved for Herbert Morrison, Bevin's successor as Foreign Secretary. Despite their recent differences, to Macmillan Bevin had still been 'the strongest figure in the Labour Government'. In April 1951, the month of Bevin's death – only weeks after his resignation – Macmillan wrote that he had been in many respects 'a very bad Foreign Secretary', whose Palestine policy was 'absurd', making Britain 'equally odious to Jew and Arab'; and his attitude to united Europe was 'petty'. Nevertheless, 'he has done one immense service to Britain and the world. He has imposed upon an unwilling and hesitant party a policy of resistance to Soviet Russia and to Communism. A Tory Foreign Secretary (in the immediate post-war years) could not have done this.'[6]

Morrison's accession to the Foreign Office was rapidly followed, on 2 May 1951, by the sudden move on the part of the Iranian government, led by the eccentric Dr Mossadeq, to 'nationalise' the British-owned Anglo-Iranian Oil Company. The Americans, noted Macmillan, 'were certainly unhelpful. Perhaps the oil interests were jealous; perhaps the politicians were not sorry to see Socialist Britain hoist with her own petard. . . .' Having accepted the principle of nationalisation at home, the Attlee government was indeed vulnerable, and Morrison – to the rage of Macmillan – made the poorest of showings. He expostulated in his diaries, following a Commons debate on 21 June: 'In all the years I have been in the House, I have heard nothing like it from a Foreign Secretary at such a moment. . . . This dirty little Cockney guttersnipe has at last revealed himself for what he is, "a third-rate Tammany boss". . . . Even the imperturbable Rab was white and quivery with rage. . . .'[7]

Eventually, in the summer of 1953, Mossadeq was arrested by the Iranian Army; the Shah, brought out of exile and helped by the new British administration, regained the power that he was to wield for another two and a half decades, and an agreement was patched

together with the British oil interests. Not, however, before the
sound-waves set up by Mossadeq's action had caused echoes that
were to have devastating consequences for British interests elsewhere in the Middle East. Five months after Mossadeq's grab for
Anglo-Iranian, Egypt was denouncing the Anglo-Egyptian Treaty
of 1936, on which rested Britain's continued presence on the Suez
Canal.

It was, however, the Korean War as much as any concatenation of
internal events that precipitated the fall of the Attlee government
in 1951. Evoking his involvement in high strategy during the war
years, the Macmillan diaries contain some ambivalent, and occasionally perhaps surprisingly 'dovish' undertones towards Korea;
while, in retrospect, they also display considerable strategic
prescience about the perils of the West getting 'bogged down' in
Far Eastern conflicts.

Following General MacArthur's inspired amphibious landing at
Inchon, things had started to go badly wrong for the UN troops
and on 27 November 1950 Macmillan recorded news that between
'100,000 and 200,000 Chinese' had unexpectedly intervened in
North Korea: 'Meanwhile, with typically British escapism, the
House of Commons is thoroughly enjoying itself discussing whether
the Festival of Britain amusement park should or should not be
open on Sunday afternoons.'[8]

Three days later he noted that 'the real argument against the Far
Eastern war is a military one. Our weakness (that is, of the Free
World as a whole) is so marked, that it is surely very risky to get
involved more and more deeply in this part of the world front. . . .'[9]
Though he felt confident that US nuclear superiority would deter
the Russians from taking advantage of this Western military weakness to attack in Europe, he feared that possibly Korea could be a
feint to pin the Americans down there, while the Russians might
'start a drive in the Middle East, where the prize is really great –
the greatest source of oil supply in the Old World'. Already, in his
thinking, Macmillan was placing the highest priority on the West's
strategic position in the Middle East.

After a talk the following week with Sir David Kelly, the British
Ambassador in Moscow, he was reflecting on the 'dilemma' of the
wider, and perennial, strategic issues which the Shadow Cabinet
had just been discussing:

If we wait for the showdown with Russia, we may well be weaker (relatively) in 3 years than we are now. For the degree (if any) that we have caught up on conventional weapons may be more than balanced by Russia's increased power on unconventional weapons. Should we then hurry on the conference and the show-down now? Peace by ultimatum! Either you agree to our terms, covering the whole field, including Central and Eastern Europe – or we will destroy you![10]

(At this point Macmillan was forced to interrupt his rhetorical question to note, with some irritation, that he had been side-tracked and 'made to agree to become chairman of the party housing committee. . . . It really is a great bore, as I am already overworked and since I know absolutely *nothing* of the matter it will mean a lot of work. . . .')

On 11 December, he was back pondering 'the real problem': whether it was best to buy time to precipitate a showdown. The greatest danger, he felt, lay in Europe 'being gradually driven in on herself, as first the Far East and then Middle East are overrun or so dominated by fear of the Communist powers that all our influence disappears. . . .'[11] Two days later he was reacting more hawkishly, echoing Churchill's fears: 'Whatever might be the technical advan-tages of not "getting bogged down" in Korea, I am sure that a moral defeat would mean the end of the white man's position in the East and that the moral collapse might easily spread to the West. If Indo China goes, Siam follows. Then Malaya falls. . . .'[12] This was a precursor of the much later, and oft-despised, domino theory, and Macmillan's doubts about the Korean involvement were sub-sequently to have an important influence on the views he put many years later to President Kennedy when the US was about to be embroiled in Laos.

The Korean War provoked constant worries about the state of the Anglo-American relationship, and anger at the government's attitude: 'Tomorrow has no meaning for Attlee. He never thinks beyond "today". Thus the close relations between the US and the UK have not been continued. . . . Even the Churchill–Roosevelt treaty about the use of the atom bomb (under which neither power might use it without the agreement of the other) has been allowed to lapse.'[13]

There was the disturbing revelation on 14 December that General

MacArthur received his instructions not from any UN or Anglo-American staff organisation, but from the American Chiefs of Staff. British views about advancing beyond the 'waist' – roughly the line of the North–South Korean border – had not been heeded. 'We are treated worse than General de Gaulle or exiled governments during the war.'[14]

A visit from Prime Minister Menzies of Australia a month later found Macmillan still worrying on the same theme. From Menzies's account of his recent visit to Tokyo and his interview with MacArthur, Macmillan concluded with some alarm that 'The General seems to live in a more and more fantastic atmosphere of royal pomp, surrounded by obsequious "Yes-men". His political and military plans are not revealed to anyone – least of all to Washington.'[15] For all MacArthur's shortcomings, Macmillan was now persuaded that the British government should come out with a moral condemnation of China, if for no other reason than to 'do something to bridge over the dangerous rift that is obviously threatening between London and Washington'.[16]

He was infuriated by British pusillanimity, and sounded off again at *The Times*, which was 'playing as unpatriotic a role (from the highest motives) as it did in Mr Chamberlain's days'. But it was for the declining Attlee government that he reserved his spleen until the Chinese menace was gradually contained in Korea. 'MacArthur is domineering, but at least knows what he wants,' wrote Macmillan with grudging admiration on 7 April 1951. 'The British Government, weak and divided, exercise little or no influence on events.'[17]

Macmillan, however, later admitted that shortly after the shock of the North Korean assault revealed the global weakness of the West, Attlee had in fact reacted with singular courage, introducing legislation to increase defence spending to £3600 million in over three years, thereby creating six to ten new army divisions. The measures were warmly supported by the Tories. Then, in January 1951, with even greater courage, Attlee raised the ante to £4700 million. The question immediately arose: how was Britain, in her continuing financial straits, to raise the money? At his first Budget in the spring of 1951, Gaitskell proposed a modest increase on tax rates, then attacked the new Sacred Cow of socialism, the National Health Service, by introducing charges on false teeth and spectacles. On 23 April, Aneurin Bevan resigned, somewhat disingenuously widening the dispute to claim he was resigning over rearmament.

This had not been the issue, and Macmillan thought Bevan had 'double-crossed' his colleagues. The Labour Party was split wide open; and defeat lay inexorably ahead at the next general election. At the same time, Attlee's rearmament drive was to present the incoming Tories with the legacy of a built-in inflation factor that would never quite go away.

Labour's reverses finally forced them to call an election in October. That month Macmillan castigated Morrison in his diary as 'the meanest man I know . . . utterly incapable of magnanimity', in an unnatural outburst of savagery that was provoked by the level at which Labour was fighting the election. As characterised by the tasteless *Daily Mirror* headline, 'WHOSE FINGER ON THE TRIGGER' (which provoked even Churchill to sue for libel), Labour's campaign centred on a warmongering scare, launched back in May when Hugh Dalton had declared: 'If we get Churchill and the Tory Party back at the next election we shall be at war with Russia within twelve months.' Given that it was Labour who had launched the new arms programme, the campaign was as hypocritical as it was irresponsible.

On the other side, the Tories based their campaign, once again, on the Butler–Macmillan *Right Road* platform, with Churchill delivering one of his finest broadcasts since the war. They cashed in heavily on the electorate's fatigue with the years of Crippsian austerity, following on all the drawn-out deprivations of the long war. Foremost among the Conservative promises of a better life was the pledge to build 300,000 houses a year, which had come to be adopted in an almost haphazard fashion at the pre-election Blackpool Party Conference of October 1950. Macmillan was not even sure he had been present when the pledge was adopted. He thought it all began as a kind of auction: 'they got excited, and said two hundred . . . fortunately Fred [Lord Woolton] stopped the bidding at three hundred, otherwise I don't know what would have happened!'[18] Two months later, he had very unwillingly found himself chairman of the housing committee, quite unaware that it would mean a vital step up on his way to the top.

When the election votes were counted the results were, once again, disappointing to Tory hopes. The country was still split down the centre, with the socialists again actually increasing their overall vote. Because of the distribution of seats, however, the Tories managed just to scrape in with a majority of twenty-six over Labour and seventeen over all parties combined. Although he was gratified that his own majority rose by some 13 per cent, Macmillan considered that the Party's total majority, resulting from a national swing of only 1.1 per cent, was 'enough but only just enough'. The slimness of the margin was to bedevil Conservative policy-making, curbing its audacity for many years to come. The experience of the cataclysm of 1945, followed by those six frustrating wilderness years, was repeatedly to set a limit on the political risks Tory leaders would be prepared to take henceforth. Macmillan himself would never let the Party forget how traditional values had been swept away at home, but – more especially – how Britain's voice had been weakened abroad during the Attlee government.

If the election results were a disappointment to Macmillan, no less disappointing was the division of spoils among the victors. Churchill decided to keep for himself the post of Minister of Defence; Macmillan thought, rightly, that this would prove too much for him to cope with at the age of seventy-seven. Equally unwise, in his opinion, was making Eden both Foreign Secretary and Leader of the House of Commons, where, with so small a majority, the pressures would impose a heavy strain on a man already recognised not to be in the most vigorous health. With Butler appointed Chancellor of the Exchequer, and his friend Oliver Lyttelton given the Colonial Office, the road upwards looked effectively blocked, once again, to an ambitious politician.

The New Government

It was not until 28 October, three days after the election, that Macmillan received a call summoning him to Chartwell. There he found Churchill, so he records in his memoirs, 'in a most pleasant, and rather tearful mood. He asked me to "build the houses for the people". What an assignment!' Macmillan was taken aback. 'I knew nothing whatever about the housing problem except that we had pledged ourselves to an enormously high figure, generally regarded by the experts as unattainable. . . .' The interview terminated with Churchill declaring in all solemnity: 'It is a gamble – [it will] make or mar your political career. But every humble home will bless your name if you succeed.'

Macmillan asked Dorothy, who had driven over to Chartwell, for her advice, 'which from a long experience I knew to be generally sound. She was in no doubt at all that I ought to accept. I had always agreed to do anything that I had been asked by Churchill, and it had up to now succeeded.' So Macmillan went back and accepted the post.

His account minimises the initial frustration and distress he felt on being offered a post which colleagues like Maxwell-Fyfe regarded as 'a backwater'. Christopher Soames, then a young ADC to his father-in-law, remembers 'Harold coming down fuming after his appointment; "If he wants to kill me politically, then let him do it, but not this way. . . !" He felt there was no way he could possibly build 300,000 houses.'[19] Though loath to admit it, he also felt let down by his old wartime boss. In his diaries Macmillan reveals that, before discussing the proposal with Dorothy, he had already sought the advice of Bridges and Brooks, respectively head of the civil service and Secretary to the Cabinet, who were both also at Chartwell. His mind seems finally to have been made up by the arrival of his old friend, Harry Crookshank, who 'thinks I had better take it on'. But, on accepting, 'I begin to realise what a terrible burden I have undertaken. Churchill is grateful and will back me; but I really haven't a clue how to set about the job. . . .'[20]

The new Churchill administration immediately found that the crisis inherited from its predecessors was even worse than anticipated. By the end of the year, the balance of payments deficit approached £600 million, and the Treasury mandarins warned Churchill that the country was 'heading for early bankruptcy' unless stringent measures were taken. Churchill, the 'warmonger', was forced to cut back the Attlee rearmament programme, principal cause of the financial crisis. Butler, the new Chancellor, ordered an immediate slash of £360 million in imports; raised bank rate to 2½ per cent, then again to a staggering (by current precedents) 4 per cent in March the following year. The foreign travel allowance was cut to £25 per year. It looked as if (despite election promises) austerity was there to stay; and so too were wage inflation and military expenditure, twin bugaboos that throughout the Churchill administration were to conspire to reduce Britain's industrial competitiveness at a time when the war-ruined economies of her European neighbours were just beginning to catch up (although, between

1952 and the 1955 election, unemployment never rose above 2 per cent, nor inflation above 3 per cent).

Macmillan – ever loyal to his wartime chief – would always vigorously defend Churchill's personal performance, at least in the early days of his new administration. Serving with him was, Macmillan once said, 'like constantly having tea with Dr Johnson'.[21] He described with admiration Churchill's many-faceted accomplishments, as seen on a visit to Chartwell in 1951: 'he was continually distracted by one of his new hobbies – an indoor aquarium with tanks of tropical fish, minute but very lovely. He was quite fascinated by their delicate beauty. On this occasion he gave me an inscribed copy of Volume IV of his war history, *The Hinge of Fate*.'[22]

He noted (and it was to influence his own style of Cabinet management) Churchill's addiction to the written word. Unlike Lloyd George, who 'regarded conversation as a method of doing business', Churchill looked on it 'as an amusement, as a source of ideas. But he never did any business by conversation, never. Everything was in writing.' On the other hand, Macmillan also recalled how Churchill 'unlike perhaps more shy, or more pompous ministers', encouraged conversation, as a kind of 'free-for-all': 'We might all have been undergraduates sitting in Balliol. . . . But out of three hours' conversation, he'd probably remember something. He was a most dangerous man to talk to because he'd say "Two years ago, you said something to me". And I had entirely forgotten about it. . . .'[23]

Macmillan studied Churchill in Cabinet with amused respect, recalling one particular meeting, in October 1952, after the morning press had been full of sensation about a footman running amok in the Earl of Derby's house and shooting dead two butlers. Churchill particularly wanted to avoid discussion that day on the continuing presence of British forces in Egypt, so – to pre-empt Eden – he launched forth in mock horror with an attack on the Home Secretary Maxwell-Fyfe, accusing him of permitting 'anarchy' to break loose in Britain. With the somewhat pompous Maxwell-Fyfe rising to the tease, Churchill managed to keep up the filibuster long enough for the Cabinet to be adjourned before the unwanted item had come up. 'There were those who held that this was a sign he was gaga,' commented Macmillan; 'But he certainly wasn't – it was just very skilful manoeuvring.'[24]

Sadly for Macmillan, his deep affection for Churchill continued to be largely unreturned; although there was no doubt about Churchill's recognition of Macmillan's professional ability. Churchill's youngest daughter, Mary Soames, felt that there was an obsequious element in Macmillan's deference to her father that did not appeal to him; he still often found Macmillan pompous, even boring. Clementine Churchill, always strongly protective of Churchill in his friendships, never liked or entirely trusted Macmillan, a view which was confirmed by Churchill's former Private Secretary, Sir John Colville.[25] This coolness towards Macmillan was to increase as 'Clemmie' came to regard him as leader of the cabal that was pressing the old warrior to retire.

Building the Houses

Having once recovered from his initial discomposure at the appointment as Housing Minister, Macmillan threw himself into the task of meeting the Tory pledge to build 300,000 houses a year with impressive energy. He was much helped from the very beginning by Churchill according him total licence to 'do it in any way you like',[26] as well as offering his fullest support. Always genuinely concerned with improving the quality of life of the 'ordinary man', Churchill told Jock Colville shortly after the 1951 election that his policy was going to be 'houses, red meat, and not getting scuppered'.[27] This priority meant that Churchill would almost invariably back Macmillan's pleas for more finance against Butler, striving to balance the books at the Treasury. Was his housing programme, Macmillan enquired, to be sacrificed so as to 'bring comfort to the acute speculators of Brussels and Zurich?'[28] His demands, inflationary in themselves, provoked a first clash of wills between Butler and Macmillan. Macmillan won, defeating Butler's desire to cut subsidies for housing.

The housing problem confronting Britain in 1951 was partly the legacy of the nineteenth century, greatly exacerbated by the Second World War when one house in every three had been either destroyed or damaged, and none had been built. Under the socialist government, hampered by shortages of materials and skilled labour, as well as by austerity cuts and all manner of restrictive regulations, house building had reached a maximum of somewhere over the

200,000 mark. Macmillan's basic philosophy, as stated in the Commons in December 1951, was one which would remain at the heart of Conservative principles throughout the Macmillan premiership – and, indeed, was continued through to the Thatcher era: 'We wish to see the widest distribution of property. We think that, of all forms of property suitable for such distribution, house property is one of the best.'[29]

Macmillan's campaign involved the unfettering of private industry from incentive-killing controls, and his first move was to set up something like a wartime headquarters, called a Minister's Council, to co-ordinate strategy. He operated with a combination of cajolery, threat and sheer political cunning, and – as in wartime – showed great skill and sensitivity in choosing his team of key subordinates. Those he inherited in the Ministry of Housing did not all fill him with an excess of confidence. 'It is rather a bore', he wrote testily in his diary, 'that the Permanent Secretary, Sir Thomas Sheepshanks, is so useless. . . . He reminds me of Will Macmillan [his cousin] (who, according to Uncle Fred, ought to have been a civil servant).'[30] With Sir Thomas's flaccid hand on the tiller no houses would be built at all, Macmillan felt. Fortunately, within the Ministry there was a brilliant and hyper-energetic woman, Evelyn Sharp (later Dame Evelyn), who was soon to become the first female Permanent Secretary of an important ministry, and whom he regarded as 'without exception the ablest woman I have ever known'.

From outside, Macmillan imported a self-made Birmingham businessman, Sir Percy Mills, whom he had worked with and regarded highly when Mills had been Controller-General of Machine Tools at the wartime Ministry of Supply. Mills was to act as an industrial confidant to Macmillan for many years; with natural good manners, he could get on with almost anybody, although senior civil servants were often upset by the intrusions of one who had no other title than that of 'unpaid adviser'. As his Junior Minister Macmillan brought in a cocky and talkative MP whom he came to admire more than almost any of those whom he promoted after 1957 – Ernest Marples. Also an entirely self-made man, Marples was the son of a labourer, whose own father had been head-gardener at Chatsworth; educating himself, he had sold newspapers, become a bookie's 'dodger', then started his own engineering company. When war came, he joined up in the ranks and became 'a pauper again' – a factor which most contributed to Macmillan's respect for him: 'He was a Sergeant-Major, never got a commission, came back, started up Marples–Ridgeway. Up to a point, he was a genius. He had no vision – unlike all those people at Oxford who *talk* – but he brought in American principles of business and construction. . . . He introduced the first solar house.'[31]

Aged forty-five and brimming over with ambition, Marples had burst into Parliament at the 1945 election, often amazing his public school colleagues with his combination of blue suit and orange-brown shoes. As put by Anthony Sampson: 'Between Macmillan, with his languid style, and Marples, with his boasting efficiency, there existed an alliance of mutual advantage, between the amateur and the professional.'[32] Recognising his debt, Macmillan said simply, 'in fact, Marples made me PM: I was never heard of before housing. . . .'[33] One of Marples's many practical contributions was to introduce what Macmillan nicknamed 'the boneless wonder', a form of concrete construction requiring virtually no timber – timber that had to be imported with Butler's scarce dollars.

Macmillan was also much helped by a pre-war ally from anti-appeasement days, Lord Swinton, who now held the key post of Churchill's Minister of Materials and was able to funnel to Macmillan vital stocks of steel, which was still strictly rationed. 'I always gave him what he wanted,' said Swinton, 'though there were plenty of rival claimants baying like hounds at feeding time.'[34]

Meanwhile Percy Mills's job was to set up ten Regional Housing Production Boards – an experiment in practical decentralisation which had occupied Macmillan's thoughts even before the *Middle Way* era. The aim was to speed up construction by reducing shortages of both materials and land. To help achieve this latter priority Macmillan pushed through a Bill to repeal socialist legislation that had imposed, in 1947, a development charge on building land.

Macmillan's legislation created one unforeseen, tragic consequence. Early one morning in 1952 he found himself summoned peremptorily to the Churchillian bed chamber, to find the Prime Minister angrily puffing a cigar in bed, with his pet budgerigar perched on his head, and brandishing the *Daily Mirror* at him: 'Have you not heard of Pilgrim's suicide? You are responsible for Pilgrim's death. How are you going to make an atonement?' For a moment, Macmillan thought the Prime Minister had gone mad, but he discovered that Mr Pilgrim was an Essex smallholder who had bought half an acre of land in 1950 at a price artificially inflated by the Labour government development charges of £400. When he came to sell it, under the new Macmillan rulings, all he could get for the land was £65, and, having borrowed money for the original purchase, the financial loss so preyed on his mind that he committed suicide. Always one to rush to the support of the victimised 'little man', Churchill had been incensed by the potential unfairness of the legislation as it stood. The Macmillan Bill was duly amended. When it was finally enacted, in November 1954, Evelyn Sharp wrote a generous letter to Macmillan, taking responsibility for and expressing distress at the 'atrocious first drafting', and saying that 'your handling of the Bill has been the most brilliant thing I have ever seen. . . . I do not know anyone else who could have done it. . . .'

Macmillan's programme was also assailed by natural forces beyond his control. In August 1952, a violent storm dumped nine inches of rain on Exmoor, leading to a devastating flood that swept away much of the pretty Devonshire coast town of Lynmouth, drowning many people and causing widespread evacuation. The damage to housing was enormous. Macmillan was promptly on the scene, wearing a rustic cloth cap and declaring that the havoc reminded him of 'Wipers' (Ypres, largely destroyed in 1915). Some of his more staid colleagues grumbled that this was showmanship, of the brand increasingly associated with the new, self-assured Harold Macmillan; nonetheless, the success of the Minister's presence was unmistakable. The following year an even graver and more widespread disaster struck, in the shape of floods down the east coast from the Orkneys to Kent, on a scale hardly ever experienced in the British Isles. Some 25,000 houses were flooded and the total damage set at about £50 million.

Macmillan's legislation undoubtedly did much to break the log-jam on private construction. At the same time, setting a precedent Margaret Thatcher was to follow many years later, he also author-ised local authorities to sell off council houses – of which some 3000 were in fact sold before the 1955 election. (Not always seeing eye to eye with her predecessor on economic matters, Thatcher was full of respect for Macmillan's handling of housing: 'He didn't say "no, this can't be done or this will be blocked by the civil service", he *did* overcome, he dominated his civil servants – they didn't dominate him. . . .'[35]) Gradually the election pledge figure came within reach. By the end of 1952, aided by a year of generally good weather, totals already reached 240,000 houses built, as against 195,000 for 1951. At the Conservative Party Conference of 1952, Macmillan was given a standing ovation. The next year the figures were 318,000, and on 1 December 1953, Macmillan was able to announce to a jubilant Tory Party that the famous target had been reached, and indeed exceeded. (The next thing, he remarked in irony, was that he would be accused of over-production.)

Few doubted Macmillan's personal success in energising and directing the building crusade. 'He exuded enthusiasm – his zeal was infectious,' wrote his Parliamentary Private Secretary, Reginald Bevins (who became Postmaster-General in the Home government). 'He was really superb at handling people, tactful, courteous, never giving much away.'[36] Even adversaries like Hugh Dalton and Michael Foot had to recognise the marked superiority of the Tory housing record under Macmillan; although some houses which they built, Dalton wrote, 'had lower standards than most of ours. But . . . it was the totals of new houses which counted with public opinion and public comfort, and led towards the "affluent society".'[37]

Both then and much later, however, Macmillan's building crusade has drawn criticism – much of it on technical grounds. The high-rise horrors that have defaced many British cities, even disasters like the collapse of the Ronan Point tower block in London in 1968, and the legacy of shoddy workmanship, have been blamed on the Macmillan era. Kingsley Martin, editor of the *New Statesman*, grudgingly thought that Macmillan had been 'handed success on a plate', at the expense of sacrificing other priorities.[38] Various other critics thought that road construction, school building and industrial expansion had suffered as a consequence of the 300,000 programme.

Accelerating the rate of new house building represented only part of Macmillan's brief; the second was to clear slums and to improve the vast backlog of existing housing that had lapsed into disrepair. Here Macmillan was probably less successful. There was serious criticism that the priority on new building had led to neglect of repairs urgently needed in rent-restricted houses. One of

Macmillan's last initiatives at the Ministry was, in 1954, to draft the Repairs and Rent Act, which would enable landlords to raise rents to more realistic levels. His civil servants, however, held him responsible for giving owners far too little to spend on repairs and urged a substantially higher increase in rent than Macmillan had felt was politically acceptable. At the other end of the spectrum, Macmillan's critic Emrys Hughes regarded his Rent Act as 'the greatest act of appeasement to the property owning classes that could have been devised. . . . It reduced their [the poorer tenants'] standard of living because it sent up their rents. It led to demands for increased wages which helped to bring about inflation and financial crises later on.'[39] The problem was left to Macmillan's successors to try to solve; they never have, and British rent, leasing and real estate laws have remained a dreadful jungle.

Whatever the criticisms, however, Macmillan's success at Housing did his Party immeasurable political service in advance of the next election. It left on the electorate an indelible impression that the Tories were a party that got things done. Certainly, as the veteran Labour leader, 'Mannie' Shinwell, saw it, Housing made Macmillan at last a national figure, poised on 'a stepping stone to eventual leadership'[40] – although a *Daily Mirror* popularity opinion poll held in the summer of 1954 gave Eden 52 per cent as Churchill's successor, and Macmillan less than 2 per cent.

Macmillan had never quite succeeded, much as he had tried, in getting on close terms with the working class; one of his gentler Labour critics, Maurice Edelman, noted that 'His sympathy was undoubted; his manner was all wrong. His forays were like those of a public school missionary to the East End. . . .'[41] Yet, in May 1953, it was Harold Macmillan who was chosen to give the first-ever party political broadcast on television – which was generally rated a success. Thereby began a long love–hate relationship with the new medium. More than ever before he was becoming a familiar – and popular – figure in the House Smoking Room, held to be an important weathercock of party political success. Certainly, Macmillan himself was always quite unequivocal about what Housing had meant to him in personal terms: 'I've never enjoyed three years more . . . three of the happiest years of my life . . . it was great fun. . . .'[42]

Family Problems

Macmillan's febrile political activity left less opportunity than ever for family life. With Dorothy much of the time at Birch Grove, Harold operated from a flat in the West End in a state of semi-bachelor neglect. Visiting him there one day, Maurice's wife Katie found the lamp-shades undusted; writing on them with her finger 'DUST ME' she found the words still there two weeks later. In his memoirs, however, Macmillan writes of the 'happy years' of the early 1950s: 'My children were married, grandchildren were beginning to appear, and our life at home and among our friends was gay and stimulating.' Characteristically, these lines embrace the whole of his domestic life for the period; there is no suggestion of any troublesome clouds. Yet these were also the years when Maurice, working at Macmillan's and frustrated (temporarily) in his own political ambitions, was afflicted with his worst bouts of alcoholism. Harold – so controlled a personality himself – was intolerant of what he regarded as lack of self-discipline on the part of his son. He was sometimes provoked into almost physical rage, but otherwise retreated into cold disaffection. In November 1954, his diaries contain the brief entry: 'Went to see Maurice, who is in a nursing home, doing a cure. The poor boy is not strong and I am getting more and more anxious about him and his future – also about what is to be done about Macmillan and Co.'[43] In fact, it was another five years before Maurice, with immense will-power and after great suffering, finally conquered the problem, although his health never recovered.

Meanwhile, though the principals were now well into middle age and Macmillan himself had – to some extent – come to live with it, the Boothby–Dorothy love affair still rumbled on, taking its toll among the younger generation. It was evidently at an undergraduate ball in Oxford that Sarah was casually told that Boothby was her true father. According to a don who consoled her afterwards, Sarah was shattered. On 30 July 1953, Macmillan recorded laconically in his diaries: 'Sarah's wedding. A most happy and successful day.'[44] But this revealed nothing of the heavy clouds which preceded the event.

Earlier Sarah had discovered she was pregnant; it appears that Dorothy had pressed Sarah to have an abortion on the grounds that otherwise 'it will ruin your father's career'. Those who knew her well reckoned that it was the abortion (which left her sterile), more than the revelation about Boothby, which led Sarah on the fatal road of drink. To Boothby, Sarah's abortion was the 'one thing I could never quite forgive Dorothy, the one wicked thing she did. . . . I think it was all part of her guilt conscience, but it killed Sarah. . . .'[45] If Boothby's assertion was true, the tragic episode reveals how ruthlessly, in the duality of her attachments, Dorothy was dedicated to furthering her husband's ambitions in his public life.

The distance between Macmillan himself and his daughter is perhaps implicit in Sarah sending a letter rather than speaking to her father about a date for her marriage. 'Darling Daddy,' her letter of 28 April 1953 began, 'I am so sorry to worry you when you are busy, but as there never seems very much time to talk to you I thought I would write.' She hoped that the marriage could take place 'fairly soon'. Her mother was urging her to wait another six months, but Sarah could 'not see that six months would help very much'. Writing back, her father proposed that the wedding be fixed for a date between July and the end of September: 'You have had a long wait and a very difficult time, which I think you got through with great courage and good sense, but we must get it right at this stage.'[46]

Only days before Sarah's wedding at the end of July Macmillan was carried off for an operation to remove a gallstone. For some months previously he had been tormented with acute pain: 'Indeed, I scarcely knew how to get through my last speech.' Under the skill of his doctor from North African days, John Richardson, the operation was wholly successful. Yet a couple of months later he was confiding to his journals that 'I have been rather troubled to find that I am still rather easily tired and even "shaky" when it comes to any but written work. . . .'[47] The following May, now sixty, he was still forced to admit that he felt 'very tired. The truth is, that my work is getting rather too much for me, with all the speaking engagements which I have unwisely accepted. Then I take so much trouble about my speeches – 4 or 5 hours' work on each.'[48] At least he suffered no longer from the nervous ailments that had plagued him both before and during the war, and his fatigue symptoms remained a well-kept secret. To his colleagues he seemed to have regained much of his old verve.

At the same time Britain herself was entering a new mood of self-

confidence. In February 1952, King George VI had died unexpectedly. Macmillan was saddened by the death of the man whose quiet
courage he had greatly admired during the war years, and he noted
how, in his career as an MP, he had already sworn allegiance to
three monarchs. Yet the coming of the new young Queen, whose
coronation provided a first glittering pageant in the dreary post-
war world and coincided with Edmund Hillary's ascent of Everest,
seemed to offer promise of a 'new Elizabethan age'. Like many of
his countrymen, Macmillan welcomed the wave of revived patriotic
pride it heralded.

Minister of Defence

In a reshuffle of the Churchill Cabinet announced on 18 October
1954, Macmillan was moved from Housing to be Minister of
Defence, to replace his old wartime friend, Alexander, who had
proved less than a success in a political role. It was an important
promotion, though – in the five brief months it lasted – it proved
to be the least happy post Macmillan ever held. At first it was
suggested he should replace Harry Crookshank as Lord Privy Seal
and Leader of the House, which, out of loyalty to an even older
friend than Alex, he refused. When Eden first mooted the idea of
Defence, Macmillan was hardly enthusiastic: '. . . I explained that
I thought this was a bad idea. There was nothing to do. . . .'[49] But
what else was on offer? The Foreign Office was the only post that
he really coveted, yet so long as Churchill remained Prime Minister
and Eden Foreign Secretary there was clearly no opening there.

It was a considerable understatement when Macmillan, in his
memoirs, says that his period at Defence 'was somewhat frustrating'.
Rather more characteristic of what he really felt was a private
explosion picked up by the ubiquitous Lord Moran after three
months in office: 'Winston ought to resign. He didn't interfere in
my housing, just left it all to me. But since I became Minister of
Defence I have found that he can no longer handle these complicated
matters properly.'[50] It was true; Churchill's style of government
tended towards allowing his ministers freedom of action without
interference, but Eden at the Foreign Office and Macmillan at
Defence were the unhappy exceptions. As it had been throughout
the war, often to the exasperation of his service advisers, strategy

and the minutiae of defence matters continued to be Churchill's particular reserve. Thus the flow of memoranda to Macmillan was incessant – and exasperating.

'I was a failure,' Macmillan confessed many years later, 'and I rather slacked; but how could you be any good under Winston, who knew more about defence than anyone else. . . . I wasn't even allowed to introduce a White Paper!'[51] This sense of impotence was confirmed by his Parliamentary Secretary at the Ministry, Lord Carrington, who regarded it as 'a hopeless role', for the additional reason that 'we had no power to take any decision at all, over the Service Ministers'.[52]

Nevertheless, it was an office that did give Macmillan the opportunity for serious reflection on British defence requirements. One of his first visitors was Field-Marshal Montgomery, now in his late sixties. Monty at once put the need for integrated services under a single Minister with real power. Macmillan was interested. A few months later Montgomery followed up with a 'Private and Top Secret' memorandum, which started on the pessimistic premiss that NATO as a whole was 'in no position, today, March 1955, to fight a war and succeed'.[53] Among a number of forward-looking points he made was that, with the progress in development of vertical take-off aircraft (then very much in its infancy), navies should go for smaller and cheaper carriers. Armies of the future would require 'air transport on a vast scale'; but this would have to be provided by air forces. None of this projected modernisation could be achieved under the present system, whereby both at home and within the NATO alliance, each service tried to be self-contained. What was needed was 'joint defence, both internationally and from the inter-Service point of view'.

On his first incursion into NATO enclaves, Macmillan found himself immediately at one with the abrasive little Field-Marshal on the NATO ministers of defence: 'they have what they call a private meeting with about a thousand people in the room, and everybody talks one after another, and they have a restricted meeting with only three hundred, and finally they do a little business after dinner . . .' said Macmillan. Because Stephanopoulos, the president of NATO for 1954, 'seemed deaf, blind and terribly nervous, this tended to lengthen the proceedings . . .'.[54] The standard of work achieved did not impress him. On the other hand, he greeted with enthusiasm West Germany's accession to NATO through the medium of the Western European Union (WEU). After much coming and going, France's Mendès-France had finally vetoed the European Defence Community, towards which Macmillan had been as lukewarm as Churchill. Getting the French to accept West German rearmament within the WEU framework, as the alternative to the EDC, and in exchange for a British undertaking to maintain four divisions on the continent until the year 2000, had been a great diplomatic coup for Eden personally, but in the background the hand of Macmillan was also evident.

It was during his stewardship of Defence that Britain committed herself to developing her own hydrogen bomb. At a NATO meeting in December 1954, Macmillan challenged the view that 'these new weapons, revolutionary as they are, have lessened the chances of peace. On the contrary, I believe they have enormously increased them by adding so greatly to the power of the deterrent. . . .' Henceforward, Macmillan's philosophy on defence became dominated by the principle of the 'independent deterrent'. In the Ministry of Defence, Macmillan's eyes focused on what seemed to be the disparately large conventional forces maintained by Britain's hard-pressed economy. As of 1954, 800,000 men were serving in the three services; 300,000 of them were National Servicemen, and there was an additional reserve of 600,000. While the two years' National Service stood, Macmillan noted that 'this method of maintaining distant garrisons was becoming more and more expensive'. In a memorandum to Churchill of 2 February 1955, Macmillan warned that if National Service was cut, however, 'There would be no safety margin for anything like another Korea.'[55] As events were to prove, whether Macmillan or Churchill were ultimately to blame, it was the shortcomings of the conventional forces that would hamstring British action at Suez the following year more effectively than any other single factor.

In Churchill's last two years of office, an almost obsessive fear of a nuclear holocaust came to dominate his mind. It also brought him into conflict with the Americans. At the time of the Korean War, he had warned the House of Commons that within three or four years the Soviets would possess a stockpile of atomic weapons 'sufficient to cause a catastrophe at any time they wanted'. His fears were intensified by what he construed to be US sabre-rattling; in early 1953 Secretary of State John Foster Dulles had introduced the philosophy of 'massive retaliation', and about the same time had given birth to the new and flesh-creeping word of 'brinkmanship', or the art of moving up to the brink of the nuclear abyss. Churchill was fearful that the Americans might use their temporary nuclear superiority, acquired through recent development of the H-bomb, to seek a 'showdown' with the Russians – or with the Chinese supporting Ho Chi Minh's war against the French in Indo-China. The British people, he reckoned, were little aware of what was happening in the jungles of South-east Asia, 'but they did know that there was a powerful American base in East Anglia.' Use of nuclear weapons in Indo-China might escalate to 'an assault by hydrogen bombs on these islands . . . and of all the nations involved, the United States would suffer least.' Equally, according to Macmillan, Churchill had been 'deeply wounded' by the election 'warmonger' cries and felt that he had to 'make a final contribution to peace and by personal discussion with Stalin's successors – that was the main reason why he stayed so long in office. . . .'[56]

Churchill had few illusions about the prospects of a thaw with the Russians, remarking sombrely in Macmillan's hearing that 'the terrible fact is that the Soviet Government fears our friendship more than it fears our enmity'. Nevertheless, two months after Stalin's death, Churchill on 11 May 1953 roused himself to deliver a powerful speech in which he called for Three-Power talks with Stalin's successors, on the basis of the old wartime model, and in an endeavour to remove Russian anxieties. The following month, Churchill suffered a major stroke; visiting him in September, Macmillan found him still talking about making a personal visit to see Stalin's successor Malenkov in the USSR. The initiative had, in the meantime, become more pressing as the Soviets had already exploded their first H-bomb the previous month. At the Bermuda Conference that December, Churchill – still showing some traces of his stroke – persisted on the same theme with the Americans. Eisenhower and Dulles were, to put it mildly, apathetic – so, too, was Eden. Eisenhower had an aversion to these sort of conferences, and – in the wake of the bloodily suppressed East German uprising of June 1953 – Dulles particularly thought that little could be achieved by Summit talks with the Russians at this point. Thus, for Churchill, Bermuda was a disaster – and so too was the Berlin Conference of Foreign Ministers, which opened the following month (January 1954) in an endeavour to resolve the division of Germany.

There was another element; at the end of the Truman era, Eden had returned from a visit to Washington in January 1952 and had shocked the Cabinet by his impressions. He had been, recorded Macmillan in his diaries, 'forcibly struck – indeed horrified at the way we are treated by the Americans today. They are polite; listen to what we have to say, but make (on most issues) their own decisions. Till we can recover our financial and economic independence, this is bound to continue. His other impression was the extent to which the "politics" of the Presidential year dominated the whole scene and all American thought. Everything they did, or refused to do, in the sphere of external policy, was caused by this naive pre-occupation. . . .'[57] It was a lesson that both Eden and Macmillan would have forgotten by the time of the next US presidential election, in the autumn of 1956.

With the advent in 1953 of the beloved Ike of wartime memory, Churchill persuaded himself that the old 'special relationship' between himself and Roosevelt could be reincarnated. This was not at all how Eisenhower, and even less so John Foster Dulles, saw it. At face value, Eisenhower displayed all the wartime camaraderie and respect for Churchill. But, privately, both he and Dulles doubted whether the old warrior was up to his present responsibilities; nor did they trust Churchill's capacity to get the West involved in any repeat of Yalta with the USSR, just as, in reverse three decades later, Western Europe was alarmed at the prospect of a summit between Gorbachov and an elderly President Reagan.

These hints seem to have been only partially picked up by Churchill as he soldiered on in his grand belief that, singly, he could make that 'final contribution to peace' by a personal initiative with the Russians. In June 1954 he told Eden that he was thinking of retiring by the end of the following month, but an invitation from Eisenhower made him take heart. Following that Washington visit, Churchill and Eden returned on the *Queen Elizabeth*. The Geneva Conference, which was to set the seal on France's defeat and withdrawal from Vietnam, was then still under way. In the course of the long sea-voyage, and very much against Eden's advice, Churchill despatched what Macmillan in his memoirs describes as 'rather a fulsome message to Molotov, suggesting a personal meeting between himself and Malenkov'. Although Churchill made it clear that the Americans were not committed, Eisenhower was 'amazed', Dulles appalled – and so was Eden.

Not consulted in advance, the Cabinet in London rose up in arms. 'Now the fat's in the fire,' Macmillan wrote in his diary for 9 July. Salisbury, leader of the right wing, was threatening to resign, with Macmillan begging him 'to hold his hand'. To Eden he wrote: 'The effect on the Government might be fatal, and on the Party also. It would be a grievous wound to you and your chance of starting off with a fair wind. We must stop it, somehow. . . .'[58] Macmillan's immediate reaction, however, was that Eden himself 'ought to have resigned on the boat'. The day after what Macmillan recorded as being 'the most dramatic Cabinet which I have attended', he confided to his diary one of his bitterest criticisms of Churchill: he 'is now quite incapable – mentally, as well as physically – of remaining Prime Minister . . . his judgment is distorted. He thinks about one thing all the time – the Russian visit and his chance of saving the world – till it has become an obsession.'[59]

In the course of time, however, and the temporising of successive Soviet notes, Churchill's enthusiasm for his one-man mission to Moscow waned; then, suddenly – on 8 February 1955 – Malenkov was sacked and replaced by the duo of Bulganin and Khrushchev.

The Tories Abandon Europe

Commenting on the strength and greatness of Churchill's remarkable mind, Macmillan remarked how it 'tended to concentrate upon a single major problem'. But, especially in old age, this could also prove to be a major defect, so that his 'obsession' with the Moscow initiative exacerbated his blindness to more immediate issues – notably Britain's role in Europe. Conversations with Churchill after his return to power had swiftly led Macmillan to conclude that 'he had now abandoned or postponed any effort to realise his European conception'. Churchill's attitude towards the Schuman Plan, as of the end of 1951, was that Britain 'should be with it though they could not be of it'.[60] What Macmillan saw as Churchill's strange unwillingness to defend the ideas and ideals which he did so much to promote in opposition still provides one of the most inexplicable and least satisfactory aspects of his peacetime administration. His impatience with the French was particularly marked; at the Bermuda Conference of 1953, Eisenhower's press assistant, James

Hagerty, was shocked at the 'complete and utter disdain' with which Churchill had treated the French delegation. He had ignored Bidault, offering Eisenhower a drink but not the Premier of France. Hagerty later reflected that the difficulties with France in the ensuing decade might well have stemmed from this kind of treatment. Churchill's tergiversation over Europe was a source of bitterest disappointment to the 'Europeans' in his Cabinet – of whom Macmillan had always been counted as one of the leaders.

Boothby, a dedicated 'European' and lifelong admirer of Churchill, voiced the common frustration when he wrote that the whole idea of an integrated European army 'was in fact blown up by Churchill's government of 1951'.[61] He was also not off target when he accused Eden of being 'primarily responsible' and of having done 'a hatchet job'. Records and correspondence of the time leave little doubt of Eden's coolness towards the European Common Market that was in the making, or of how this led to a marked alienation from colleagues in the government like Maxwell-Fyfe, Duncan Sandys, David Eccles and notably Harold Macmillan. As Churchill was obsessed with his mission to Moscow, so Eden's energies as Foreign Secretary were focused upon grand projects of peacemaking in Indo-China and upon menaces in the Middle East. He stated his attitude to European *integration* categorically in January 1952: 'This is something which we know, in our bones, we cannot do. . . . For Britain's story and her interest lie beyond the continent of Europe. Our thoughts move across the seas. . . .'[62] To Macmillan, in retrospect, Eden was motivated by patriotism – 'I think he was unaware of the changes in the world which had taken place as a result of the Second World War' – and by the British tradition, 'a dislike of foreigners and a determination to avoid permanent entanglements. These were very much Foreign Office principles.'[63]

Unmistakably, the great dead hand of the Foreign Office, coldly sceptical about prospects of European unity, rested heavily upon Eden's shoulder. At its head during the crucial years of 1953–6 was a cynical, diminutive Irishman, Sir Ivone Kirkpatrick, who tended to read the future excessively in terms of the past. A young diplomat in Hitler's pre-war Berlin, he held the German character to be largely irredeemable; in 1953 almost his final act as the last British High Commissioner in West Germany had been to arrest six neo-Nazis on what seemed to be the slenderest evidence that they were planning a *putsch*. With little reluctance, the Foreign Office marched in step with Kirkpatrick, refusing to accept that the French and Germans could ever successfully bury the hatchet and join in an integrated Europe, and believing that their rivalry would inevitably cause such European institutions as the Coal and Steel Pool to collapse. France's rejection of the European Defence Community in 1952 (in which Churchill's own aloofness, unexpected by the Europeans, had played an unmistakable role) lent powerful weight to this argument. Therefore Britain had to remain wary, if not distant. This was the sermon preached, with considerable influence, through the 1950s and even into the 1960s.

Macmillan was among the leaders of the 'Europeans' whom Boothby accused of doing nothing to challenge the Churchill–Eden line in the 1951 government. At the Ministry of Housing, Macmillan was, however, far removed from the European cockpit at a crucial time; as he told Eden plaintively in a letter about the European Movement in November 1951, 'I am now entirely enveloped in clouds of bricks and mortar.'[64] In January 1952 he wrote to Eden expressing his fears that the Germans would come to dominate the Schuman Plan, or possibly throw in their lot with the Russians, if Britain did not take a lead; his warning was dismissed with this acid marginal note by a junior Foreign Office aide: 'The S of S knows of this letter and the enclosures but does not want to read them at the moment.'[65]

Macmillan found little encouragement within the Cabinet; nevertheless, in March he was writing to Churchill in unusually acrid terms, after the Foreign Office had circulated what he dubbed 'a quite dreadful paper' which Eden had endorsed: '. . . I feel bound, before returning to my "rabbit hutches" from a short expedition into world politics, to send you, with apologies but affection, the attached note.' In it, he expressed his 'disappointment at the course of the discussions at last Thursday's Cabinet on the future of the Council of Europe and European unity generally'. Referring to the 'growing sense of confusion and dismay' among Conservatives who had supported the European Movement, he protested that the continued opposition of the Foreign Office 'appears just as strong under your administration as under the previous one'. This was 'quite inconsistent' with the pronouncements made by Churchill, and by Eden, while in opposition. He did not think that British membership of NATO was enough; it was only by extending

Britain's leadership of the Commonwealth to Europe that she could bring to bear 'the influence in world affairs which should be ours. It is no longer a case of choosing between the policies of Marlborough and Bolingbroke, but of combining them.'[66]

This was a clear statement of Macmillan's feelings at that time, and – over a period of days – he came closer to resigning from the government than on any other occasion in his career. In his memoirs he states that he held back partly because he found little support within the Cabinet, except from Home Secretary Maxwell-Fyfe, but above all because of his 'affection for and loyalty to Churchill'. Later in life he reckoned (revealing also his abiding fear of a party political defeat) that his resignation 'would have been a terrible mistake. We only had a sixteen majority and no enthusiasm in the country whatever for Europe.'[67] But he always felt that the coolness shown to Europe by the Churchill administration was a major mistake; had Britain been involved in the drafting of the Common Market institutions from their very inception, then they might have assumed a less rigidly bureaucratic and supranational form.

Nevertheless, the privacy of Macmillan's diaries shows that he was increasingly suffering from bouts of pessimism towards Europe and the Europeans – which may well have conditioned his restraint about resigning. On 18 February 1952, for example, he was writing: 'The facts of European life remain. The French are frightened of the Germans; the Germans are frightened of themselves. (For they know that Hyde is there, always ready to replace Jekyll.) . . . Churchill seems to make no effort for the European conception. His eyes are on Russia.'[68] Jock Colville's diary entry for 31 May indicates how Macmillan's thoughts were running just two months after he had been voted down in the Cabinet: 'Harold Macmillan said to me at the Turf yesterday that he thought development of the Empire into an economic unit as powerful as the USA and the USSR was the only possibility. . . .'[69]

Churchill Retires

By the spring of 1953, the British press had begun to criticise Churchill's lack of grasp. Such doubts about the fitness of his old hero to remain at the helm had already begun to affect Macmillan. They were closely coupled with fears of the effect that long-protracted delay in the succession was having on the *prince héritier*, Eden. In December 1951, Macmillan, complaining in his diaries about the difficulty of collaborating with 'a queer man' like Eden, had remarked: 'If he had the first place, he might easily rise above all these faults. It may really be that he has been Prince of Wales too long.'[70] In June the following year, he was expressing worries about the lack of any 'real directing hand or inspiration' in the Cabinet: '. . . I fear the old man will decide on a "Samson" attitude. If he goes he will pull the whole temple down with him. . . . Yet, if he stays – without a policy – he will drift to an inglorious decline. I try to tell him this . . . but it is not easy to move him. . . .'[71]

During 1953, he and Eden discussed several times, and evidently in the most amiable terms, the need for Churchill to retire. Politically, the time seemed ripe since 'a Socialist victory at the next General Election no longer seemed inevitable. . . .'[72] Eden told Macmillan that the Queen had disclosed to him that the King, just before his death, had intended talking to Churchill about his 'plans'.

Then, three months later, Eden was carried off to hospital for an operation on his afflicted spleen; Churchill's resignation had to be at least temporarily shelved. With Eden out of action, the burden on Churchill increased and in June he suffered his major stroke. It was a well-kept secret, but when revealed to his intimates it came as 'a terrible shock to us all. . . . Many of us were in tears.'[73] Suffering himself from the gallstone which had to be removed a few days later, Macmillan went down to see Churchill at Chartwell on 2 July. 'At dinner, he talked so much at the beginning that he slobbered over his soup. He poured out some champagne with a steady hand, and cried out "You see, I don't spill precious liquor!" . . .'[74] Though distressing, Macmillan found the atmosphere curiously 'not oppressive', and within weeks the tough old man had made a remarkable recovery.

Talk about the succession was postponed yet again, though it continued to preoccupy Macmillan's thoughts. When the Eccleses and Wooltons came to lunch at Birch Grove in December, the general view was 'that we shall drift on to disaster . . . unless Churchill goes . . .'.[75] In March the following year, Churchill confided to Rab Butler over dinner, pathetically: 'I feel like an aeroplane at the end of its flight, in the dusk, with petrol running out, in search of a safe landing. . . .'[76]

July 1954 brought the row over the telegram to Malenkov, and in its wake Macmillan wrote with unaccustomed fierceness in his diaries:

We must have a completely new Cabinet and Government, representative of the party. The present Cabinet does *not* represent the party. It is a Churchill creation, and based on the practice of war, not of peace. . . . All of us, who really have loved as well as admired him, are being slowly driven into something like hatred. Yet we know that illness has enormously altered and worsened his character. He was always an egoist, but a magnanimous one. Now he has become almost a monomaniac. . . . It breaks my heart to see the lion-hearted Churchill begin to sink into a sort of Pétain. . . . Lady C longs for him to resign. Lord Beaverbrook (out of mischief) urges him to stay.[77]

Macmillan now took the lead in persuading Churchill to go. In the course of several meetings during 1954, Churchill confided to Macmillan his reservations about Eden's calibre ('he thought Eden sometimes shrank from anything except the FO . . .').[78] This, coupled with dedication to his Soviet initiative, was what caused him to procrastinate. In August, over a lunch at Chartwell that lasted till 4 p.m., Macmillan attacked the Prime Minister for not being fair to Eden, and badgered him to declare his intentions. 'Churchill naturally did not much like this,' Macmillan recorded in his memoirs, 'but as always treated what I said calmly and courteously.' Macmillan made it clear that of course he, as 'the younger son', had nothing to gain from the inheritance, and therefore it was easier for him to 'speak to his father about the wisdom of handing over'. The result of the confrontation, however, was only a forthright letter to Eden, which began by remarking pointedly that 'We have both had a hard fifteen months. . . . I was much grieved and troubled by your illness and the uncertainty as to whether and when you could return . . .', and continued: 'I have no intention of abandoning my post at the present crisis in the world. . . .' The only thing he could promise was a 'thorough reconstruction of the Government'.[79]

Macmillan pressed him to announce his resignation before the Party conference in October, which would leave nearly two full years before a general election would have to be held, and he followed up with a letter on 2 October urging that 'the most important thing now is Anthony's position'. He hoped Churchill would come to a clear decision about the date of the handover, and inform Eden: 'Otherwise I fear we may lose him now, as well as the Election, when it comes.' Matters, however, were allowed to drift on into the autumn. Delegated by his Cabinet colleagues, Macmillan had another go at Churchill in November, when he recommended that the Prime Minister (who was about to celebrate his eightieth birthday) should announce his retirement early in the new year, with a view to an April election; this, Macmillan thought, given the threat of economic problems ahead, would present the most propitious timing. Churchill seemed receptive, then once again reneged. In his diary for 22 December, Macmillan recorded a painful session between Churchill, Eden, Salisbury, Woolton, Butler, Crookshank, James Stuart and himself: 'Nominally it was to discuss an election. Actually, it was to discuss how long Churchill should stay. He now suggests July 1955! Eden is in despair. The Government business creaks along. Stuart thinks he will never make any decision again about anything, and will stay till he dies or the Parliament ends in 1956!'

When Churchill's physician, the indiscreet Lord Moran, came to lunch at Birch Grove early in January 1955, he cast new doubt on whether the *prince héritier* could stand the strain. 'If the artificial bile channel (or whatever it is) "silts up again" (so Moran said) it will be very serious.'[80] By Moran's own account of this lunch, 'Harold defended Anthony' and then surprised him with his impassioned declaration 'Winston ought to resign. . . .' Later he noted, with respect, that of all Churchill's friends who felt he should go, 'only Harold Macmillan had the guts to say so' to his face, and it was only when Macmillan had 'made his position untenable that Winston recognised that he must go'.[81]

On 26 February, at Chartwell, Churchill confided to Macmillan that he had now fixed a date for his retirement: 5 April. But as late as mid-March he was still showing signs of wanting to backtrack, using the excuse of needing to attend a prospective Western summit conference. Eden was 'distraught', and 'blurted out "I have been Foreign Secretary for 10 years. Am I not to be trusted. . . ?"' This was, wrote Macmillan, 'the most dramatic, but harrowing discussion at which I have ever been present'.[82] Finally, on 17 March, following a lunch with Churchill and Field-Marshal Montgomery, Macmillan recorded an end to 'the crisis of indecision.

He will retire before Easter. Monty was in good form and did his best to cheer things up.'[83] The date of 5 April was now definite.

Sadly, the old Titan laid down his office almost 'not with a bang, but a whimper', for his resignation occurred in the middle of a press strike. Macmillan admitted in his diaries, 'Now that he has really decided to go, we are all miserable.'[84] At his farewell Cabinet meeting, Macmillan recalled that 'Anthony made rather a flat speech, then we all shuffled out. It was hard to say anything. . . . Norman Brook said to Winston, to cheer him up, "By the way did you know that General X died this morning, except for yourself the last of the survivors of Omdurman?" Winston's response was "How very *civil* of him!" . . . that was a combination of all the wit and egotism, his half-laughing at himself, his remarkable choice of words!'[85]

For all the struggle it had taken to get Churchill to accept the inevitable and resign, and for all the defects of his last years, Macmillan for one recognised that 'no Minister out of office has ever had such an effect on foreign policy'. Equally, in his last administration he brought the country to a high degree of economic recovery from the level inherited in 1951; he had ended rationing, and achieved full employment 'without undue inflation'. Whereas the Holy Grail of a summit with Stalin's successors lay manifestly beyond Churchill's waning powers, 'he nevertheless', wrote Macmillan (doubtless thinking of his own démarche four years later), 'set the Western statesmen on a path which they have subsequently pursued.'

For Macmillan personally, given his profound devotion to Churchill, and admiration for all that he had stood for during the war, it had required considerable courage to act as spokesman for the 'cabal' asking Churchill to make way for Eden. He had risked his friendship with his old chief – though, in fact, his outspokenness had probably enhanced it, even if he had not in any way raised his stock with Clementine Churchill. At the same time, following the farewell dinner at No. 10 on 4 April, Lord Woolton entered in his diary with whimsical detachment: 'Very amusingly Harold Macmillan again stopped and posed in the middle of the roadway before joining me in my car and then waved to the crowds as we passed them. I agree that a public man has to be something of an actor; I wonder whether it is really necessary to be a showman as well!'[86]

Chapter Fourteen

Under Eden: From Foreign Office to Treasury
May 1955–July 1956

Since my introduction to diplomacy during the Mediterranean campaign, I had regarded the Foreign Office as the summit of my ambitions. If only I could achieve this post and hold it for three or four years I could then happily retire.

(HM, Tides of Fortune*)*

He looks so old and he shambles badly, but it is promotion and makes him nearer premiership.

(Diana Cooper, on HM becoming Chancellor)

'The Great Commoner' had been most circumspect in giving no advice to the Queen on his succession, but there was never any doubt that it would be Eden, and from April until 26 May the Conservatives flung themselves into preparing for the next general election. Whatever doubts Macmillan and his colleagues may have had about Eden, they were evidently not shared by the electorate at the polls in May 1955. The Korean War had ended, and so had the French involvement in Indo-China. The Abadan oil crisis had been settled favourably, with Mossadeq comfortably replaced by the omnipotent and pro-Western Shah. An agreement had been signed with the Egyptians to pull the last British troops out of Suez, after much unpleasantness in Cairo. Butler had reduced taxes, Macmillan had achieved his housing target, and there was relative peace with the unions.

In this first election campaign where the small screen played an extensive role, Macmillan wrote with undue modesty of being 'cast in a minor role in another television performance. It was a curious and not altogether satisfactory experiment. Ten newspaper editors asked questions and five Ministers sat in a row like school-boys to answer them. . . .' In fact, a Gallup poll gave Macmillan 41 marks out of 100 as a performer; Attlee got only 28.

When the votes were counted on 26 May, the Conservatives were shown to have gained more votes overall than Labour, for the first time since 1935. From seventeen, the Tories increased their majority to a comfortable fifty-nine. Macmillan bestowed due praise on Eden for having 'given us a splendid lead – he never put a foot wrong during the whole campaign.' Macmillan's own majority at Bromley was increased by over 1000. Of even greater personal satisfaction was the success of his son Maurice, standing for the first time at Halifax, after four previous failures. Harold went up to speak for him, and Maurice got in with a 1500 majority, representing a 2000 vote swing from Labour. 'It is really splendid – so good that he has *won* a seat, and all on his own. . . . Dorothy is in the seventh heaven and really happy.'[1]

So began the brief and tragic Eden era, which in effect had already opened with Churchill's resignation on 5 April. In the new Cabinet then formed by Eden, Macmillan had received the job he coveted more than any other – Foreign Secretary. Butler stayed on as Chancellor of the Exchequer, his fifth year in the post. But Macmillan was very much Eden's second choice. As he remarked pointedly in his memoirs, Eden would have preferred Lord Salisbury, but was dissuaded by the inconvenience of having a Foreign Secretary in the House of Lords. (This was not an inconvenience that subsequently deterred either Macmillan or Mrs Thatcher.) Thus Eden's choice fell, 'reluctantly', on Macmillan: 'I felt that his active and fertile mind would team well with the high quality of Foreign Office leadership under Sir Ivone Kirkpatrick.'[2]

Macmillan accepted the post with full enthusiasm, reflecting on how proud his mother would have been. He said many years later that he had reckoned that 'if Anthony's government lasts five years, I'll be 65 or so and I will have had five years at the Foreign Office. Then I shall retire. That will be enough. . . . That was my natural hope and ambition. . . .'[3]

With his wartime experience, as well as his acquaintance with European politics and politicians through Strasbourg in the 1940s, Macmillan felt particularly well fitted to be at the Foreign Office. There he found many old wartime subordinates, like Roger Makins (currently Ambassador in Washington), Harold Caccia and Pierson Dixon, all of whom had risen to the higher echelons. Over it all reigned Sir Ivone Kirkpatrick. His cynicism appealed to Macmillan, and they got on well together; 'very unconventional, quite a character. Very strong will. . . . he was always right, awfully bright. But he couldn't keep to a point – this enormous department rather worried him. . . . great memoranda and jaw, jaw, jaw. . . .'[4]

Macmillan's earliest briefings left him 'rather horrified. . . . There is trouble in every part of the world and (what is worse) fundamental disagreements as to *method* (not as to objective) between UK and USA.' He at once found himself flung into an unexpected flurry of travel. Instead of sitting at their desk in London, as in the old days, modern Foreign Secretaries, he found, had become little more than 'peripatetic salesmen'. But his first two tasks, at any rate, were not disagreeable.

May 1955 took him to Paris for the 'solemn and moving scene' of NATO receiving – at last – a rearmed West Germany into its bosom, for which Macmillan and Churchill had fought so hard in the late 1940s. Here Macmillan had his first official encounter with his American opposite number, John Foster Dulles. Discussing British proposals for a heads-of-state meeting to discuss German reunification with the Russians, Dulles asked Macmillan whether the Vice-President, Richard Nixon, might come instead of the President. 'Thinking this was a joke, I told him of the famous music-hall joke. "Poor Mrs Jones, what a terrible thing has happened to her!" "What has happened to her?" . . . "Why, she had two fine sons. One of them went down in the *Titanic*, the other became Vice-President of the United States. Neither of them was ever heard of again. . . ."' The stern and unbending Dulles did not immediately respond to Macmillan's peculiar sense of humour. Later, however, 'he laughed outright (rare for him) and said "I guess poor Nixon wouldn't like that." So it was dropped. The President will come. So we have brought off the first *grand coup*. . . .'[5]

After Paris Macmillan went on to Vienna for the signing of the Austrian Treaty. It was, he rightly reckoned, one of the most extraordinary episodes in post-war diplomacy. For nearly eight years the Russians had sat on the terms of the agreement, which was to return Austria her independence and bring about the withdrawal of the 60,000 Soviet occupation troops. Then, suddenly, after the death of Stalin, the Russians announced they were ready to sign. All the details had been worked out well in advance of Macmillan coming to the Foreign Office and he admitted, 'I got all the credit, but it wasn't anything to do with me at all!'[6] On 15 May, Macmillan, Dulles, Pinay and Molotov signed the Treaty in the sumptuous Belvedere Palace. It was sunny springtime, and a festive occasion with many receptions and vast cheering crowds. Even the steely Molotov seemed to warm to the atmosphere. Seeing him for the first time, Macmillan noted that he was 'smaller than I had supposed and older (we are all older!). He is grey, not black any more; a very pale pasty face; a large forehead. . . . He wore a very respectable black suit – and looked rather like a head gardener in his Sunday clothes. . . .'[7] (Twenty-five years later Pinay and Macmillan returned to Vienna to celebrate the anniversary as the sole representatives of the original signatories, both now in their late eighties. They tried to tease Molotov's granite-faced successor, Gromyko, with Pinay asking, 'Your colleague, who signed the Treaty with us – I forget his name – *ah, oui, ce gentil Monsieur Molotov* – whatever happened to him?', knowing perfectly well of Molotov's disgrace. Quick as a flash, Gromyko replied: '*Il est libre, mais très malade!*')

In July came the Geneva conference on German reunification, with the heads of state meeting in advance of the foreign ministers, as Macmillan had originally proposed. Here Macmillan first set eyes on the new Soviet duumvirate; Bulganin, he thought, 'looks like a Radical–Socialist Mayor of a French industrial town. He might be *un bon papa.* . . .'[8] Khrushchev, on the other hand, 'is the mystery. How can this fat, vulgar man, with his pig eyes and ceaseless flow of talk, really be the head – the aspirant Tsar – of all these millions of people and this vast country?'[9] Macmillan continued to find Molotov, surprisingly, displaying an 'unexpected attractiveness and even softness'. He noted Soviet reservations about their Chinese ally, and was left with a strong feeling that they really wanted *détente* with the West, not war. As Geneva ended, Macmillan shocked Foreign Office purists with his jaunty music-hall quip: 'There ain't gonna be no war!' With nothing concrete decided, there was not exactly going to be peace, either.

When the foreign ministers resumed their sessions at Geneva in the autumn, Macmillan found Molotov his old aggressive, unconciliatory self. In a 'cassant tone', 'he refused free elections for Germany altogether. He practically claimed that Germany could only be united as a Communist and satellite state.'[10] In the light of what was to happen in Hungary the following year, Macmillan came to attribute the Soviet hardening of line to growing unrest in the East European satellite. Nevertheless, he, characteristically, derived some almost frivolous pleasure from a frustrating experience. He wrote to Dorothy on 5 November, describing a farewell dinner given by the French:

The food and wines were magnificent. The guests were rather gloomy. Pinay (who is very bourgeois) could not conceal his animosity towards his chief guest (Molotov). Dulles sulked. The British affected great gaiety. After dinner, all sorts of little whispering groups were formed – like diplomats in a film. It was great fun. . . .[11]

It was also 'fun' to ridicule Molotov's absurd claim that the East German government had been elected by 'free elections'. Macmillan could not resist pointing out that they were elected by over 99 per cent of the votes: 'any man or any party that can get 99% of the votes in a free election are not politicians – they're walking miracles.' This caused some amusement among the French and American delegations. When Prime Minister himself, however, Macmillan was to invoke the 'Geneva spirit' of bonhomie achieved at that initial conference in his own attempts to reach accommodation with Khrushchev.

Just before the Geneva 'Summit', a conference was held at Messina comprised of foreign ministers and technical experts from the European countries forming the economic unit of the 'Six'. Invited to participate in what proved to be the foundation of the EEC, Eden snubbed the offer. Macmillan's own excuse was that he was too heavily involved in the Cyprus crisis. The truth was that Eden, strongly supported by Butler, now dominated a Cabinet lukewarm about collaboration with the Six and where the rival pull of Commonwealth ties assumed precedence. Within the Foreign Office, no less a personage than Gladwyn Jebb, who was later to become the greatest enthusiast of European unity, was convinced that the Six would fail in their ambitions. Following agreement at Messina, however, the Spaak Committee was formed to pursue the technical work of drafting an agreement, which eventually led to the signature of the historic Treaty of Rome in 1957.

The British remained sceptical; Macmillan wrote in his diary for 14 December 1955, while on a visit to Paris:

The French will never go into the 'common market' – the German industrialists and economists equally dislike it, although Adenauer is attracted to the idea of closer European unity on political grounds. This, of course, is very important, and I made it clear that we would welcome and assist the plan, although we could not join. . . .[12]

The entry reveals once again the Foreign Office influence.

Macmillan did, however, win a round with Eden in persuading the Cabinet to send to the Spaak Committee meeting in Brussels a 'representative', rather than an 'observer'. But the representative, Russell Bretherton, was only an official from the Board of Trade, and, although a 'pro-European' himself, his instructions were clearly to place a damper on any move towards the creation of supranational institutions. As the Messina powers were now already committed towards this goal, the British attempt to torpedo it as well as the style of the rebuff generated the worst possible feelings. Macmillan told the Six coldly, 'There are, as you are no doubt aware, special difficulties for this country in any proposal for a "European Common Market".' The British government would be 'happy to examine, without prior commitment and on their merits, the many problems likely to emerge from these studies'.[13] It did not wish to duplicate the functions of the OEEC (Organisation of European Economic Co-operation), which were to pursue the same broad ends of trade expansion and industrial collaboration as set out under the original Marshall Plan, and which had no supranational powers. This could hardly have sounded more lukewarm, and aroused further resentment against Britain. In the meantime Macmillan, removed from the Foreign Office to the Treasury, had begun to contemplate free trade alternatives to the Common Market.

Macmillan has been rightly criticised for coming under the Foreign Office spell and 'blowing cold' at this critical moment in the development of the EEC. Foreign Office policy is revealed in a memorandum from Sir Ivone Kirkpatrick, dated 25 November 1955, which declared that 'Messina is a doubtful, if not actual wrong approach, and OEEC is a better one. . . .'[14] At about this same time even Gladwyn Jebb appended to a brief on the Common Market the lethal words: 'embrace destructively'. Macmillan's own lame reasoning in 1955 was that it was 'too late' to reverse the Attlee government's original decision not to enter Schuman's Coal and Steel Community, and that neither the British electorate nor the Commonwealth were ready to accept the EEC with its supranational elements.

He had, in justification, come to the Foreign Office only two months before Messina, and was therefore largely executing Eden's established policy of the cold shoulder. Yet, it cannot be denied that a firmer, more dedicated stand by Macmillan might have reversed it. In the passage of time he was contrite about this failure, writing in his memoirs that the Eden Cabinet should have been 'more alert' to the dangers of remaining aloof from Messina, and that it had erred in not recognising the real depth of Franco-German reconciliation.[15]

Among other criticisms of Macmillan's role as Foreign Secretary was his handling of the Cyprus crisis, which landed in his lap in 1955. That year serious terrorism broke out against the British troops there, directed by EOKA and supported by mainland Greeks in support of 'Enosis', or union of the island with Greece. The Colonial Secretary, Alan Lennox-Boyd, in May declared Cyprus to be essential to Britain's world-wide strategy. By June 1956, the month before Nasser moved on the Suez Canal, Eden was putting it even more graphically: 'No Cyprus, no certain facilities to protect our supply of oil. No oil, unemployment and hunger in Britain.'[16]

Macmillan's first thought was that, knowing the Greeks of old, 'It should be possible to organise a pro-British party among the Greeks. After all, Xerxes had no difficulty. . . .'[17] After this hope proved unrealistic, the Foreign Office involved itself in what was then a Colonial Office problem when Macmillan suggested that, since Turkish interests – including a substantial Turkish minority – were involved, Turkey should be brought in with the idea of establishing some sort of 'tridominium'. Consequently, a tripartite conference was arranged in London in August 1955, presided over by Macmillan. He seems to have had a somewhat Salomonian solution in mind: 'We expected the Turks to accept. If the Greeks also agreed, we would put forward definite proposals for constitutional progress in the island. If the Greeks refused, at least Britain's position at the United Nations would be strengthened. . . .' The conference was condemned as 'a trap' by the Greek Cypriot leader, Archbishop Makarios, and it broke up in deadlock; there were savage riots against the Greeks in Izmir and Istanbul, and terrorism increased in Cyprus.

In September, Macmillan requested the British UN delegation to appeal to Dulles to cease interfering: 'You should impress upon him how deeply hurt we shall all be here if we cannot rely on American help in matters of this kind. We on many occasions have subordinated our particular view to the common interest of the team.'[18] At the same time, Macmillan was expressing displeasure with the 'almost Byzantine incompetence of the Colonial Office. . . . The Governor . . . seems ineffective, even for a Wykehamist, and without any faith in the sacredness of his mission.'[19] The offending Governor was replaced by Field Marshal Sir John Harding, representing a harsher line of anti-terrorism. An exasperated Macmillan was reminded of 'one of those irritating puzzles that we had as children, when it was almost impossible to get all the balls into their respective holes at the same time. One could perhaps get in the Turks and then the Greeks; but immediately Archbishop Makarios would suddenly pop out.'

Macmillan was castigated for his proposal to 'stir up the Turks' in order to counterbalance Greek agitation. But, given Turkey's proximity to Cyprus and her fears of finding a·Communist regime taking over in the island, as well as her genuine concern for the Turkish minority, she would almost inevitably have been drawn into the issue eventually. Meanwhile, by March 1956 any hope of a quick settlement was relinquished, with the exile of Archbishop Makarios to the Seychelles. A solution over Cyprus – what Macmillan was to rate as 'one of the most baffling problems which I can ever remember' – was now deferred until his premiership.

Hardly had the Cyprus conference drawn to its disappointing conclusion than another problem hit Macmillan from a different direction. Ever since the two British Foreign Office defectors, Burgess and Maclean, had disappeared back in May 1951, the British press had rumbled on, their suspicions unallayed. Now revelations published by a Soviet defector – Vladimir Petrov – brought the whole story to the boil again. In November 1955, Macmillan was called upon in the Commons to defend the Foreign Office, which had come under severe attack. During the debate a new factor was thrown at the government in the shape of the 'Third Man'.

Primed by a journalist, Colonel Marcus Lipton on the Labour benches questioned Macmillan point-blank: was 'Kim' Philby the 'Third Man' who had tipped off Burgess and Maclean? Macmillan, knowing that MI5 had Philby in its sights but had not yet accumulated enough evidence to convict, was thoroughly embarrassed, and – under parliamentary rules where a question demands an answer

– had little option but to respond: 'I have no reason to conclude that Mr Philby has at any time betrayed the interest of this country, or to identify him with the so-called "third man", if indeed, there was one.'[20] Macmillan's bland response was to come back to plague him in years to come. Philby was delighted; years later he admitted that Lipton's crudely phrased question had been 'a gift' to him – for 'by naming me he virtually forced Harold Macmillan to clear me. . . .'[21]

On 8 October, Macmillan wrote in his diary that he had 'warned' Eden that 'we should have to *do* something about the Burgess and Maclean affair. I do not, of course, want an enquiry into the past. But I think something is needed to satisfy the House of Commons and the public about the future. . . .'[22] On the 19th, he wrote a note to the Cabinet, proposing that a general enquiry into security problems be set up, preferably under the chairmanship of Lord Radcliffe. Eden was not favourably inclined, and the proposal was shelved.

Reprehensible as was Eden's torpor, Macmillan could not escape his share of the responsibility, both in 1955 and later. Espionage and security were always to be something of a blind spot in Macmillan; he took the general, perhaps over-gentlemanly view that, to obtain the ideal level of security, one would have to adopt the measures of a police state, 'which are distasteful to our national sentiment . . .'. As he put it in a television interview with Ian Trethowan:

> the espionage or defection of anybody in a policy department is not very important. What does he give them? A few memoranda, which from my recollection of Government memoranda never come down on one side of the question or the other. He takes a few things. The really dangerous espionage is technical. Some machine, some improvement, which probably has a life of what, a year at most? I think it's all rather exaggerated. . . .[23]

This did show, however, an insensitivity to the fundamental demoralisation that unresolved fear of traitors in their midst could cause in government departments, let alone among the public at large; and not to mention the considerable damage it did to Anglo-American relations.

The Middle East

It was during Macmillan's Foreign Office tenure that the storm clouds gathered in the Middle East. Back in 1952 Britain had again committed herself to honour the 1936 Treaty with Egypt, which involved the removal of the last British troops based on the Suez Canal by 1956. Consistently taking the tougher line on any withdrawal without adequate safeguards, Macmillan had had frequent clashes of opinion with Eden. How Macmillan's mind was already working is shown from his diary entry of 18 August 1953, concerning the right of Britain to return to the Suez base: 'Of course, there will be quibbling. . . . But, in the event of war, there will be no quibbling, and the Americans would support us. . . .'[24]

Over the next few years this was to become a recurrent theme; yet when Eisenhower presented a revolver to General Neguib, the new leader of Egypt who had ousted the obese and corrupt King Farouk in 1952, it seemed a symbolic portent that the US would not necessarily support British policy towards its former fiefdom. Eden was outraged by this American 'gaffe'. In November 1954 the much more dynamic, strident and – to the British – more menacing figure of Gamal Abdel Nasser in turn ousted the easy-going Neguib. He immediately began preaching the cause of pan-Arabism, with its corollary of ridding the Middle East of foreign influences. Within the year, Nasser had taken the first step along this risky road by making overtures to the USSR for the purchase of Soviet and Czechoslovak arms. As Britain had just signed the final evacuation accord, Macmillan was thoroughly alarmed by this 'new and sinister element'.

Macmillan's fears of a threat to the Middle East centred on losing the oil that was vital to Britain's survival. One of his earliest involvements while Foreign Secretary was as party to an exotic and mysterious scheme, entitled Project Alpha, sired jointly by Eden when still at the Foreign Office, and Dulles. Alpha ingeniously proposed to end the Arab–Israeli deadlock by providing a land corridor between Jordan and Egypt, across the Israeli-held Negev. To sweeten the pot, Britain and America were also to provide substantial funds to enable Israel to compensate the Arab refugees displaced in the 1948 war. No reference to Alpha was made in either the Eden memoirs or his official biography, though he put much energy into it. Macmillan in his memoirs, too, is dismissive, describing it as 'fantastic' and 'Dulles's pet idea'. 'Like the White Knight, he claimed it proudly as his own invention. . . .'

Macmillan, however, seems to have been open-minded towards it: 'It might be a prologue or an epilogue – Alpha or Omega. . . .' he wrote in a minute in May 1955,[25] and for a while Alpha appears to have been discussed seriously by both the Israelis and the Egyptians.[26] Gradually the scheme fell apart through its own impracticality, but as much through changes of mind on the part of Dulles and Eden. A typical Foreign Office brief of the time recommended that, 'at each state' HMG should 'try to see that we are in a position where the blame for failure can be laid wholly or at least partly on Israel'.[27] That so little was made of Alpha in Macmillan's memoirs may be explained partly by the fact that it failed, by a certain embarrassment in both the US and Britain at this wheeling and dealing so reminiscent of pre-1918 diplomacy, and not least by Macmillan's own resentment at Eden's constant interference and insistence on handling the Alpha negotiations himself. Suez was in any case to administer the *coup de grâce* to it.

Macmillan's unpublished diaries for 1955 reveal his leaning marginally towards Israel (in contrast to the traditional attitude of the Foreign Office), coupled with early 'hawkishness' towards Nasser – and the ambivalence of Dulles. Writing about the Egyptian arms deal on 23 September, Macmillan recorded: '. . . I am proposing to Dulles a *very* stiff and almost threatening protest to Nasser. We really cannot allow this man, who has neither the authority of a throne nor of a Parliament, to destroy our base and threaten our rear. . . .'[28] Two days later he was commenting with concern on Eisenhower's illness (he had just suffered a coronary thrombosis); it would mean, Macmillan predicted, 'that the Republicans will be fighting for their lives, instead of having the "walkover" which they have been expecting. This in turn will reflect itself in their foreign policy.' November 1956 would prove him correct though not entirely for the right reasons. 'They will be much more sensitive to pressure groups, like the Jews. . . .'[29]

At this time of Eisenhower's debility, Macmillan saw the Russians moving 'into a field from which hitherto they had kept studiously aloof', and feared that they would not be cajoled out of this new move by Eden or anyone else. A visit on 29 September from the Egyptian Foreign Minister, Mohamed Fawzi, did little to dispel

Macmillan's misgivings: 'a pretty smooth customer, sly and insinuating. . . .'[30]

On 2 October, Macmillan during an appearance at the United Nations dined with Dulles at his Washington home, together with Vice-President Nixon, Allen Dulles of the CIA and General Douglas MacArthur, in retirement since his sacking by Truman for having overstepped the mark in Korea. Secretary of State Dulles

> took the gravest and most pessimistic view. The evidence was piling up – the Egyptian deal was not an isolated event. The Russians were corrupting also Syria, Saudi Arabia and trying Libya. They would soon start on Iraq. . . . Dulles asked if we had enough troops to re-occupy Egypt and I said 'not in Suez. They are moving out fast. But it could be done from Cyprus, no doubt.'[31]

It was an intriguing preview of what was actually to take place the following year. In October 1955, however, Macmillan concluded that this 'did not seem practical'; 'So it comes to a mild squeeze on Egypt, and benefits to the loyal Arabs – Jordan, Iraq, etc. Let unpleasant things begin to happen to Nasser, and pleasant things to the others. . . .' The 'mild squeeze on Egypt' related chiefly to the major project, now in the offing, to build with foreign money the Aswan Dam, with its promise of vastly increasing irrigated farmland in the narrow and over-populated Nile Valley, together with an immense hydro-electric scheme. Presciently, Macmillan saw the vital importance of securing this contract for an Anglo–German–French consortium, backed by America: 'it will regain Western prestige in Egypt. It matters much more to them than arms. But it will be very bad if we miss the chance and let the Russians slip in again. . . .'[32]

The 'pleasant things' to which Macmillan referred had to do with the newly formed Baghdad Pact. Under strong American pressure, this had come into being earlier in 1955, as a 'northern tier' defence grouping, both to forestall Soviet moves on the Middle East and to act as a counterweight to Egypt and Syria. The first members with Iraq were Turkey and Iran; Britain had joined the Pact in April, followed by Pakistan, and it was a British priority to get the key state of Jordan to join too. Britain committed herself to help the signatories with arms supplies, notably with Centurion tanks to the friendly government of King Feisal and his veteran premier, Nuri es-Said, in Iraq. Meanwhile, the Pact's US progenitor had promised all support – provided there could be a settlement of the Arab–Israeli dispute. This was about as realistic as pigs on the wing and Dulles' ambivalence was – as Macmillan had predicted – exacerbated by the prospect of the concessions that would have to be made to woo the Jewish vote in America for the 1956 presidential election.

Meanwhile, the Soviets used the singularly unmenacing Baghdad Pact as a pretext to press the arms deal still harder with the Egyptians. Israel became increasingly nervous. In May 1955, Moshe Sharett, the Israeli Prime Minister, had asked the US for a positive guarantee. The legal-minded Dulles, however, had taken the line that it was impossible to guarantee frontiers which had not been agreed between the various parties. Macmillan came under growing pressure from elements in the Tory Party, mostly on the right, to come to Israel's help by concluding a definite treaty with her; a proposition to which he personally was by no means averse. Talk grew of the possibility of a major pre-emptive attack by Israel, while a clear clue to how the US might regard such an attack was given to Macmillan by Dulles in an informal chat during the second Geneva Conference, on 27 October 1955. Dulles told him that he had categorically warned Premier Sharett recently that 'the United States would not stand for a preventive war launched by Israel.' Macmillan's diary entry for that day noted: 'It is clear that the Americans are becoming as worried as we are about the situation in the Middle East. The difficulty is to get them to act with any speed. Yet, without them, with our slender resources, there is little that we can do.'[33]

In the US Dulles had warned Vice-President Nixon on 17 October that the Middle East had become so 'filled with danger that we could lose the whole Arab world if we play this on a partisan basis'.[34] Nevertheless, when Macmillan pressed him to tackle the Soviets over the arms deal with Nasser, he had declined on the grounds that he did not wish to exceed his sick President's brief, based on not upsetting the peaceful *status quo* between the major powers.

Amid the intensifying gloom that surrounded the Middle East, Macmillan could record one small success. In the autumn of 1955, Saudi Arabia made a move to take over Buraimi Oasis, which Britain reckoned lay in the territory of her clients, the Trucial States of the Gulf. Because the Saudi representative had resorted to bribery, Macmillan repudiated an arbitration agreement and a small force was sent to occupy the disputed oasis; to which, wrote Macmillan in his memoirs, the Saudis 'had no real claim but which was vital to our oil interests'.

The legal position, Macmillan admitted in his diary for 18 October, was 'rather tricky (the Attorney-General was rather wet about this) but the political situation is urgent. We must act, firmly and quickly, if we are to retain our prestige and hopes of more oil in this area.'[35] Significantly, he wrote in his memoirs, 'In all the circumstances I thought it wiser not to consult the United States or even the old Commonwealth territories about our decision. . . .' Neither Dulles nor the Commonwealth appeared to show any undue distress at not having been consulted over the British occupation of the tiny oasis at Buraimi, though Dulles did evidently murmur to Macmillan at Geneva a few days later that the State Department had been 'upset because they had had no prior warning'. Macmillan parried this by explaining that his decision had been taken out of 'anxiety to avoid involving him in any accusation of complicity, and with this explanation he appeared satisfied'. With Suez looming up, a minor but important precedent of non-consultation was perhaps established here.

On 21 December 1955 Macmillan was transferred from the Foreign Office to succeed Butler as Chancellor of the Exchequer. When Eden told Macmillan of his intentions, it came – to put it mildly – as a 'shattering blow'. He had thought himself ideally suited as Foreign Secretary, and was thoroughly enjoying the job. It had not been easy. Just as he had suffered from Churchill's repeated interference when Minister of Defence, so Macmillan had found Eden determined to go on running his own policy at the Foreign Office.

Macmillan admitted that he was infuriated by Eden's interference, remarking of his replacement by the relatively unknown Selwyn Lloyd:

There is no point in having a weak minister – you must have somebody who can say exactly what he means; not just simply a state secretary. It was quite clear that Eden wanted to get rid of me; he kept on sending me little notes, sometimes twenty a day, ringing up all the time. He really should have been both PM and Foreign Secretary. . . .[36]

As Sir Nicholas Henderson aptly notes in his excellent memoir, *The Private Office*, by tradition all foreign secretaries, 'unless merely their Master's voice, are as little inclined to welcome interference from No. 10 as Prime Ministers are disinclined to resist the lure of playing *la grande politique* in the international arena'.[37]

There were those who regarded Macmillan as a disaster at the Foreign Office. Lord Kilmuir, the former Sir David Maxwell-Fyfe who was to become Macmillan's Lord Chancellor, thought that his appointment by Eden was 'a major error of judgement',[38] given that Eden wished to maintain control of foreign policy. Critics concluded that Macmillan's nine-month stint was a failure, but also found it difficult to disentangle how much policy was his, and how much Eden's; others rated him one of Britain's worst foreign secretaries. Written four days before Macmillan left the Foreign Office, a *Times* leader declared that the public had 'no very clear-cut idea' either of his foreign policy or of the man himself.[39] But such opinions possibly suffered from being written too close to the event.

One important colleague who did not share this low opinion was Macmillan's American opposite number, John Foster Dulles. From the moment of that first tricky meeting in Paris in May 1955, their personal relations had steadily improved. Although Macmillan always harboured reservations about Dulles, he managed to keep them to himself. Back in 1953, in one of his most critical strictures against the Americans, he had written that Dulles appeared 'to be the most dunder-headed man alive', who moved 'from blunder to blunder'.[40] Shortly after taking over as Foreign Secretary, Macmillan had a long telephone conversation with President Eisenhower, during which his old friend had observed: 'Foster's a bit sticky at first, but he has a heart of gold when you know him. You have got to get to know Foster.'[41] Eden never 'got to know' Dulles, and was daggers-drawn with him from the time of the Indo-China crisis of 1954, when Dulles convinced himself that Eden had welched on a joint commitment that would have helped bail out the hard-pressed French at Dien Bien Phu. Shortly after Eisenhower's exhortation, however, Macmillan admitted that he had begun to understand Dulles's 'strange and complex character', as well as his lawyer's dedication to legality. 'With all his faults – his agonisingly slow speech [which infuriated the restless Eden], his unwillingness to look you straight in the face, his deviousness of method – there was something engaging about him if you could penetrate the surface. His rare smile had great charm. . . .'

During the late months of 1955, Macmillan had extensive dealings with Dulles over the Middle East, and on 27 October he recorded in his diary a long philosophic talk with Dulles about the future, the likelihood of Eisenhower winning again and the two of them continuing to collaborate. 'We might together change the history of the world,' expatiated Dulles:

> We must disprove the slanders against the old Western civilisations; show that 'Colonialism' was a fake charge; prove the immense benefit that the British Empire had been and was; and lead the young nations to our side. Much study should be given to this, and to the philosophic attack on the heresies and falsity of the Communist doctrines. . . .

'All this was very surprising and rather impressive,' concluded Macmillan.[42]

By the time he left the Foreign Office in December, Macmillan felt sincere regret at losing contact with Dulles; 'for I had not found it too difficult to bring him round to our point of view . . .'.[43] He was skilful in playing up to Dulles's considerable ego, making a delicate show of deference to his long experience of foreign affairs: 'I am just a child in these matters. I have been building houses. You must teach me. . . .' had been his opening line.[44] Writing to Macmillan from Washington on 22 December, Roger Makins reported that 'Foster had drawn me aside in the State Department and said how deeply distressed he was at the change, how well you had been working together, and what a pity it all was. . . .' It would thus be no exaggeration to acclaim Macmillan as having been, of Dulles's three British opposite numbers, the one with whom he had got on best.

Macmillan's successful relationship with Dulles should certainly be taken into account when evaluating Macmillan's career at the Foreign Office. The indications suggest that – had Macmillan remained one more year – the catastrophic Anglo-American schism over Suez would never have happened. Certainly this is what

Macmillan himself always thought, privately, in retrospect. All through his life he remained bitterly resentful of Eden's decision to move him, and regarded it as disastrous in national terms. He consistently held Eden to have been motivated simply and unworthily by jealousy. This view was vigorously disputed by Philip de Zulueta, who served both Eden and Macmillan: 'I tried repeatedly to get him [Macmillan] to see that it was purely because Rab wanted to go. . . .'[45] Rab's wish to move was undeniable; he had held the office of Chancellor over four difficult and arduous years; his post-election autumn Budget, which had increased the cost of 'pots and pans', had been a political and public relations fiasco; and his beloved wife, Sydney, had died of cancer the previous December, leaving Rab's morale and energy both severely undermined. Nevertheless, what was of predominant importance was how Macmillan himself regarded Eden's decision, in view of how this was to affect his role in the cataclysmic Suez crisis that was so soon to assail Britain.

Eden and Macmillan

The curious and capricious personality of Anthony Eden stemmed no doubt in part from his extraordinary family background. Eden's father was a highly eccentric figure, locally nicknamed 'the Bloody Baronet': excessively irascible, and hypersensitive to noise, his idea of hell was a dog barking or children whistling in the street. His children grew up terrified of him. Timothy Eden, Anthony's oldest surviving brother, noted how, in later age, his father would 'not tolerate contradiction' and could only see the righteousness of his side of any issue. Moreover, 'his fierce resentment of the slightest criticism made him too susceptible to flattery, and he was therefore constantly deceived. . . .'[46]

Despite his great charm, integrity and genius for diplomacy, Anthony Eden seems to have inherited a fair measure of parental foibles, which illness evidently exacerbated. Rab Butler, in one of his pungent asides, said that 'Anthony's father was a mad baronet and his mother a very beautiful woman. That's Anthony – half mad baronet, half beautiful woman.'[47] Butler also noted Eden's acute sensitivity to all forms of criticism, while many of his contemporaries shared Butler's opinion of the feminine ingredients of his character.

Macmillan – already dedicated to the pursuit of unflappability – was one contemporary who could never quite come to terms with the highly strung atmosphere with which Eden surrounded himself habitually: 'He'd have a mass of people round when he was trying to write a speech. How he ever wrote it I can't imagine. Everybody talking; a tremendous flap went on. . . . He was always very excitable, very feminine-type, very easily upset, easily annoyed. . . .'[48]

Eden was certainly long on sensitivity, though short on a certain quality of sensibility about the feelings of others and about how they would react under given circumstances. Compared with Churchill, Attlee or Macmillan, he found the art of delegation difficult. These defects also affected his capacity to make and retain friends. Already by the end of 1955, Eden had alienated many powerful allies who might otherwise have helped him ride out the crisis of the following year. His coolness towards Europe had upset men like Maxwell-Fyfe, Eccles, Sandys – and of course Macmillan himself; Butler nourished the grudge that Eden had been responsible for defeating his plan, as Chancellor, to make the pound convertible in February 1952; while Macmillan would never quite forgive Eden for sacking him from the Foreign Office, just when things were beginning to get interesting at the end of 1955. Abroad, Dulles was totally estranged. Thus Eden could really count on no friends in high places in the Cabinet of 1955–6, or outside it.

Perhaps his best friend was his fiercely loyal second wife Clarissa, much younger than himself and a Churchill. She was unforgiving towards those who criticised him or who – like the powerful Lady Pamela Berry, wife of the owner of the *Daily Telegraph*, or the mischievous Randolph Churchill – questioned whether Eden physically was up to being Prime Minister. There were also loyal and close collaborators who, like Philip de Zulueta, felt that Clarissa's influence on Eden was 'disastrous'; she had a habit of 'always stirring up Anthony when he didn't need it, and did not calm him'.[49] She tended to make him more, not less neurotic. In his oblique manner, Rab also commented on the raggedness of Eden's nerves; waiting for the succession, he thought, 'did not suit Anthony any more than it had suited Edward VIII. The latter took it out in life and licence, the former in a controlled impatience. There is no doubt which of these is better for the nerves. . . .'[50]

Whether or not it was genuinely a factor in Eden's decision to remove Macmillan from the Foreign Office, jealousy was certainly one component of his personality on which many have commented. It had already shown itself during the war years in the numerous clashes with Macmillan over policy in the Mediterranean, notably over Greece in 1944. Harold Wilson was, however, more charitable about the motivations of Eden's jealous temperament; it was not the stigmata of a second-rate man, 'rather, concern for the job and for protecting the rights of the job. That was what had been at stake in his break with Chamberlain. . . .'[51]

Badly as he may have wanted the Foreign Office, and resentful as he was at having been removed from it, there is no indication that, in reverse, Macmillan harboured jealousy towards Eden. Indeed, as the second year of Eden's administration began in the spring of 1956, there seemed no prospect of his aspiring to the top job, with Eden three years younger than him and Eden's acknowledged heir, Rab Butler, some eight years younger. Moreover, it was only in the summer of 1954 that a popularity poll had given Eden a rating of 52 per cent to Macmillan's pathetic 2 per cent.

The fact remains that they simply did not like each other. Summing up in old age, Macmillan said that Eden:

> never contributed any ideas. He was a very good operator – charming, good company – would have made a perfect head of the Foreign Office – but basically not an interesting man. Unlike Winston, he never had a chance to read. As a negotiator he was like an excellent barrister, very nervous, making frightful scenes before going into Court, but once in Court arguing his case brilliantly. . . . Winston thought Anthony would wreck it – that's a reason why he held on for so long. . . .[52]

As Macmillan departed, unwillingly, from the Foreign Office, the rift between the two – however well concealed in public – was wide open.

At the Treasury

Diana Cooper, who back in 1944 had picked Macmillan as 'my horse' for the Prime Ministerial stakes, noted as her wartime hero moved into the Chancellor's quarters at No. 11: 'He looks so old and he shambles badly, but it is promotion and makes him nearer premiership.'[53] To Macmillan, the propinquity was purely geographic. To enhance his position, however, he had issued to Eden some terms that verged on the insubordinate before reluctantly accepting his new commission at the Treasury – and taking a month to do so. He had told Eden that he might want to make considerable changes, possibly bringing in outside advisers and reorganising the Bank of England: 'For there is no point in my leaving the Foreign Office to be an orthodox Chancellor of the Exchequer. I must be, if not a revolutionary, something of a reformer.' Since Macmillan thought that reforming the Treasury would be 'like trying to reform the Kremlin or the Vatican' – as many successive Chancellors would also discover – he stressed that he should have the dominant voice in the 'Home Front' under Eden. He could not agree that Rab Butler, now translated to be Leader of the House and Lord Privy Seal, should remain Deputy Prime Minister. Eventually a compromise, largely favourable to Macmillan, was arrived at, whereby Butler was denied the title but empowered to preside over the Cabinet in the absence of the Prime Minister, as heretofore. This was interpreted by Lord Kilmuir, who was to be one of the victims in Macmillan's 'Night of the Long Knives' in 1962 and thereafter bore little love for him, to mean that Macmillan's terms dictated nothing less than 'a step towards and not away from the Premiership'.[54]

Eden was soon regretting both the compromise and the presence in the quarters next door to him of a Chancellor with his own ideas who was far less malleable than Butler. Those who had read *The Middle Way* on the right-wing Tory backbenches were alarmed at the prospect of its author taking over the economic reins of the entire 'Home Front'. Brendan Bracken wrote to Lord Beaverbrook on 17 January 1956: 'It is undoubtedly a desperation appointment, but our financial affairs are in a pretty desperate condition. . . . you need no telling the difficulty of providing for an ambitious and potentially dangerous leading colleague. . . .' To which Beaverbrook replied: 'You will remember Macmillan served with me. He will do strange things and he will live to perpetrate a great deal of mischief. . . .'[55]

Britain was indeed having one of its regular economic crises. After 'a good morning at the Treasury', Macmillan confided to his diary on 30 December 1955: '. . . I am just beginning to get a glimpse of some of the problems. . . . The position is *much* worse than I had expected. Butler had let things drift, and the reserves are steadily falling. If and when they are all expended, we have total collapse, under Harold Macmillan! The best experts do not expect this to happen earlier than 6–12 months from now.'[56] It was a gloomy prognosis. He was also, privately, scathing about Rab: 'certainly a strange fellow. He seems to have little idea of the state of affairs or the financial and economic dangers which threaten us. . . .'[57]

To blame Butler, however, for what was the concerted Cabinet policy of Churchill and Eden was unfair. Provoked by accusations of being hostile to the working class, Churchill had appointed the bland and conciliatory figure of Walter Monckton as Minister of Labour, with the brief to keep the unions quiet by giving them more or less what they wanted. In 1951, Butler had inherited from the outgoing Labour government a bad balance-of-payments crisis, and had taken the orthodox steps of slashing imports and raising the bank rate. The following year – under pressure from Macmillan – he had flirted with convertibility, but had finally abandoned this cause, later admitting an error of judgement, in that if 'a floating rate had been accepted, Conservatives would have been saved some of the uncertainties and indignities of "stop–go" economics and Socialists the traumatic experience of a second formal devaluation'.[58] Butler's vacillations drew from Macmillan one of his earliest pungent criticisms of the old ally from Opposition days: 'This Protean Chancellor is impossible to pin down to any precise statement. He twists and turns, like the Old Man of the Sea. He . . . does not appear to have any views on anything himself. . . .'[59] Prophesying that the British standard of living could be doubled over the next twenty-five years, Butler's 1955 election Budget had allowed the economy to get thoroughly over-heated, and there were some economists who regarded its effects – reinforced by Monckton's 'softness' on the unions – as marking a turning point when the inflationary wage spiral began to get a hold on post-war Britain.

So the new Chancellor was installed against a backdrop of yet another economic crisis. To Harold Wilson, whom Gaitskell had appointed to be Macmillan's opposite number as Shadow Chancellor just a month after his arrival at No. 11, he camouflaged its scale with a self-assured display of jocularity, remarking in the Commons Smoking Room: 'After a few months learning geography, now I've got to learn arithmetic!'[60] At the end of 1955, Britain's dollar reserves stood at £757 million, which was only about 100 million dollars above what was regarded as the 'danger level'. February 1956 brought a further serious flight from the pound, making it impossible for Macmillan to pursue his dreams of convertibility. Yet there was still virtually full employment; costs and wages were rising at an inflationary rate, but productivity was not keeping pace. It was to become a depressingly familiar picture of the British scene. Meanwhile, this was the period when West Germany, under Professor Erhard's *Wirtschaftswunder*, was catching up; within the next two years her total exports would be exceeding Britain's. Warnings in such organs as the *Economist* were not heeded.

Macmillan came to the Treasury wanting to introduce a more dynamic policy than Butler's to cope with the crisis. He brought in some fresh air, and stimulated Treasury officials by his enthusiasm for planning. Six years of socialism had taken the edge off some of the more extreme planning elements in *The Middle Way* – which had been overtaken, anyway, by the disappearance of unemployment. Nevertheless, Macmillan's initial proposals were radical enough to shock Conservative orthodoxy. He was prepared to raise income tax and introduce a credit squeeze, in order to 'mop up purchasing power', and to slash public expenditure 'even in fields hitherto regarded as sacrosanct' – which meant defence. He was prepared to reintroduce controls, even on building. To increase productivity, he would resort, if necessary, to import controls; and he was determined to stimulate savings, to which end he was developing various ideas. Like many reforming Chancellors before and after him, however, he found that the mandarins at the Treasury – who had grown fond of Rab – could put up an imposing wall of resistance to new ideas.

Macmillan's first clash with Eden was not long postponed. In January 1956 he wrote a somewhat bossy critique of an important speech that the Prime Minister was about to make: '. . . I am sorry that it has been built up quite the way it has been. The public cannot expect more than a general approach. I also think you would not be wise to attempt an essay on economics. There are too many experts. . . .' He continued:

the tone of your speech could be, not that we are returning to restriction, not that we are trying to go back to a period of unemployment – all of us who lived through that would never wish to do so again; we are still preaching expansion, but it must be moderate and reasonable. The monthly growth of weight of the fine, well-grown bull is better than the temporary blowing up of the frog. . . .[61]

This was hardly the kind of advice a man as sensitive as Eden would relish.

The following month a major row was unleashed when Macmillan wanted to cut food subsidies on bread and milk in order to help stem the continuing flight from the pound. Butler, Heathcoat Amory (who had been Eden's first choice for No. 11) and Thorneycroft all warned Macmillan that Eden was absolutely determined against the cuts. 'In that case, I replied, he must get another Chancellor. . . .'[62] Eventually, a compromise was reached whereby part of the subsidies would be cut immediately, the remainder later in the year. Macmillan reckoned he had gained four-fifths of his demands. For Eden, according to his biographer, David Carlton, 'the most significant point was that he had been defeated by Macmillan.'[63] The row provoked another hostile exchange between the Tory mavericks, Bracken and Beaverbrook. Bracken wrote:

Your prophecy that our former Under-Secretary would make trouble for Eden has been swiftly proved. He sent in his resignation yesterday on a cunningly contrived issue which would have gravely embarrassed his boss and would have given your former Under-Secretary the credit for being the only virtuous and strong man in the government. A truce has been patched up, but how long it will last is anybody's guess. . . .

Beaverbrook growled back in reply: 'Be sure Macmillan will make trouble if he has the power. As long as he is kept in order he will be all right.'[64]

On the purely personal front, another small victory was won in the garden of No. 11 Downing Street by Dorothy. Glumly facing north and virtually sunless, the garden struck instant despair in the heart of so dedicated a gardener, and through delicate diplomacy and charm Dorothy eventually persuaded their neighbours at No. 10

The newly formed French Council, Algiers, 1943. Left to right, seated: General Catroux, General de Gaulle, Winston Churchill, General Giraud, Anthony Eden. Left to right, standing: Jean Monnet, André Philip, Harold Macmillan, General Georges, General Sir Alan Brooke, Admiral Sir Andrew Cunningham, Rene Massigli.

With General Alexander at the ruins of Cassino, 1944.

With General Alexander, Casablanca, 1943.

Casablanca Conference, 1943. Left to right, seated: *Sir Portal, Admiral Sir Dudley Pound, Winston Churchill, Field Marshal Sir John Dill, General Sir Alan Brooke.* Back row: *General Sir Harold Alexander* (third from left), *Lord Louis Mountbatten* (fifth from left), *Major General Hastings Ismay* (sixth from left), *Lord Leathers* (fourth from right), *Harold Macmillan* (third from right).

Civil war in Athens, December 1944. Churchill with Archbishop Damaskinos; Harold Macmillan behind; Osbert Lancaster on extreme right, behind Damaskinos' left shoulder.

The lantern-light conference to find a compromise. Harold Macmillan on General Alexander's left.

Back to peacetime politics: with Churchill during the Bromley by-election in 1945.

Low's view of Macmillan's proposal to change the name of the Conservative Party in 1946: 'Rechristening of Blimp'.

Labour in power: Foreign Secretary Ernest Bevin, Prime Minister Clement Attlee, and Home Secretary Herbert Morrison in 1945; and Chancellor of the Exchequer Sir Stafford Cripps and President of the Board of Trade Harold Wilson in 1949.

In opposition: the Tory Party Conference, October 1949.

Planning for the 1950 General Election. Left to right, back row: Harold Macmillan, Captain H. F. Crookshank, Sir David Maxwell Fyfe. Front row: Lord Salisbury, Lord Woolton (Chairman of Conservative Central Office), Anthony Eden and R. A. Butler.

Electioneering in Bromley, 1951.

Harold Macmillan, as Minister of Housing, at the opening ceremony of the 'People's Houses', Ealing, 1952.

The 300,000 houses: with Ernest Marples at the Ideal Home Exhibition, March 1953.

Counting houses: '. . . 299,998, 299,999'. Cartoon by Vicky.

Harold Macmillan, while Minister for Defence, in the Birch Grove Library, 1954.

Harold Macmillan as Foreign Secretary signing the Austrian State Treaty, Vienna, 1955, with Molotov and John Foster Dulles.

The Geneva Conference, July 1955. Left to right: *Molotov, Marshal Buganin, Khrushchev, Edgar Faure (shaking hands with Buganin), Harold Macmillan, Anthony Eden and John Foster Dulles.*

'I had often dreamed of sitting in this room.' At the Foreign Office, 1955.

Harold Macmillan, as Chancellor of the Exchequer, launching Premium Bonds in Trafalgar Square in 1956. He was piped to the platform by the Dagenham Girl Pipers.

Cartoon from a local paper during Harold Macmillan's visit to his mother's home town in Indiana at the height of the Suez Crisis in 1956 ...

... and in London, a Suez anti-war demonstration in Trafalgar Square.

Leaving No. 10 with 'Rab' Butler, 12 September 1956.

At the Tory Party Conference, 12 October 1956.

Arriving at No. 10.

to knock down the dividing wall, thus creating one large communal garden, which is how it exists today. To preserve the Edens' privacy, in summer the Macmillans would sit in garden chairs immediately outside their own windows, hugging discreetly to the wall.

Meanwhile, impelled by his experience as Minister of Defence, and determined to balance Britain's books, Macmillan was striving hard for draconian cuts of military expenditure. Writing to Butler about the 'deterrent' on 10 August 1955, he had declared: 'It has now become quite clear that there is really no protection against a nuclear attack, certainly in these islands. The only protection is the deterrent of the counter attack. What then is the purpose of spending these immense sums [on conventional defences]?'[65] Pursuing the same theme with Eden before the April 1956 Budget, he wrote on 23 March that he would like 'to make some precise reference to a new approach to the whole defence problem. . . . But if I cannot do that, I think I shall have to abandon all ideas of giving some reliefs in the Budget and content myself with a swingeing increase of taxation. . . .' He concluded by stressing again that 'it is defence expenditure which has broken our backs. We also know that we get no defence from the defence expenditure. . . .' Specifically, he wanted to cut the hallowed RAF Fighter Command, which he considered had been rendered obsolescent by rocketry. Eden flatly refused.

In the event, the Macmillan Budget contained neither the defence cuts desired by Macmillan, nor a 'swingeing increase in taxation'. Macmillan had had to climb down to Eden on both issues. But, speaking to the Foreign Press Association on 16 May, he warned that Britain was contributing a considerably higher percentage to her defence programme than the rest of Europe (West Germany, her booming competitor, was spending virtually nothing), and that if Britain cut hers from 9 per cent to the average 5 per cent it would provide an extra £700 million of spare resources. This could 'transform our foreign balance'. The following day he was writing to Eden:

. . . I feel I must tell you how anxious I am about the state of the economy. We are like a man in the early stages of consumption, flushed cheek and apparent health concealing the disease. . . . What we really need is relief to our system through the wholesale

> cancellation of defence orders . . . and by really tough cuts now. . . .[66]

Such statements are of interest given the charges made during the Thatcher era that it was Macmillan who was chiefly to blame for opening the Pandora's Box of inflation, by letting public expenditure rip.

The letter to Eden of 17 May went on to argue:

> Service Ministers, not being in the Cabinet, regard themselves, I am afraid, as in duty bound to support the claims of the Services. In the old days before the Ministry of Defence they had to share the political anxieties of the Cabinet. Now we have the worst of both worlds. They do not see the troubles that the Cabinet sees, and they are not really subject to the Minister of Defence. . . .

In a paper for Eden of 10 July, less than three weeks before Suez burst upon the scene, with the exacting demands it was to make of Britain's military potential, Macmillan returned to the theme of defence cuts. Suggesting that a serious reduction could be made in what Britain paid for NATO infrastructure, he concluded: 'If we do all this, we may escape our greatest danger – which is not war, but financial collapse.'[67]

The Macmillan Budget

'I stayed in bed most of the morning,' noted Macmillan when Budget Day on 17 April 1956 arrived: '. . . I could eat little. The nervous strain of these speeches seems to get worse as one gets older. Anyway, I have never attempted anything of the kind before – 2 hours or so.'[68] Nevertheless, he succeeded in disguising the gravity of his anxieties by couching his first, and only, Budget in positively cheerful terms. He began by remarking how surprised his 'great predecessor', Churchill, had been to find himself at the Treasury in 1924, 'but not half so surprised as I was, thirty-one years later.' Since Churchill's time, he had come to look on Budget Day as being 'rather like a school speech day – a bit of a bore, but there it is . . .'.[69] Macmillan soon had the House laughing with him; one commentator, Samuel Brittan, rated it as 'by far the most entertaining of the whole post-war series'.[70] The style was certainly something that had disappeared from Westminster by the 1970s. There was barracking from the Opposition benches: 'they sniggered at any literary turn of phrase or quotation and behaved rather like ill-bred schoolboys. . . .' 'However,' Macmillan recorded in his diaries, 'I went on and soon got them under control.'[71]

He had already, in February, struck at both public and private spending, and pushed the bank rate up to 5.5 per cent (the highest since 1931), and the Budget measures were not spectacular. Income tax was left alone; there was a twopence increase on cigarettes, a rise in taxation on profits, and promises of cutting government expenditure by a further £100 million. 'We must all be expansionists, but expansionists of real wealth,' was one of the key phrases Macmillan used: 'The problem of inflation cannot be dealt with by cutting down demand; the other side of the picture is the need for increasing production.'

But his most radical innovation was to introduce the Premium Bond, as a way of enhancing savings. 'Let me say at once,' he explained, 'that this is not a pool or a lottery, where you spend your money. The investor in the bond which I propose is saving his money. He will get it back when he wants it. But as long as he holds it saved, his reward, instead of interest, is the chance of winning a tax-free prize.' Macmillan's new adversary, Harold Wilson, delved into the quiver of party politics to fire off an arrow with all the skill in which he was later to prove unexcelled. 'In 1951,' declared Wilson, the victorious Tories had promised a Britain 'Strong and Free. Now Britain's strength, freedom and solvency apparently depend on the proceeds of a squalid raffle. They will be fighting the next election on "Honest Charlie always pays".'[72] To ward off disfavour from the Church quarters to which Wilson was addressing his remarks, Macmillan adroitly brought in from outside a leading nonconformist of impeccable virtue, Lord Mackintosh, to administer the new scheme. With a nice turn of humour, Mackintosh invented a maxim which delighted Macmillan: 'If we can't save sinners, let's make sinners save!' It was 'a great slogan,' Macmillan thought, 'and we never had much trouble.' Premium Bonds became part of the national way of life.

Although it was certainly less radical than he would have liked, Macmillan's Budget, and its presentation, were generally well received; 'the best press I ever had,' Macmillan noted in his diaries.[73]

Public interest in it was, however, somewhat distracted by the arrival of Bulganin and Khrushchev in London, coupled with the marriage of Grace Kelly and Prince Rainier of Monaco.

Shortly after the Budget, further distraction was provided by a bizarre episode on which Macmillan's diaries throw an interesting side-light. During the visit of the Soviet leaders, a frogman named Commander 'Buster' Crabb had apparently been examining the hulls of the highly modern warships which had accompanied Bulganin and Khrushchev, and were anchored in Portsmouth harbour. Crabb's headless body was later picked up in the sea, creating a long-lasting furore in the British press, coming as the event did so soon in the wake of the Burgess and Maclean revelations. Well over age for such an exploit, it appears that Crabb died of a heart attack, but the episode was adroitly used by the Russians as 'disinformation' – to demonstrate the sinister long arm of the KGB. There had supposedly been an undertaking not to indulge in espionage while the Soviet ships were in British water, and on 8 May Eden explained to a small group of Cabinet ministers what had happened. Macmillan recorded:

> PM was asked by Admiralty about such an undertaking a good few weeks *before* the visit. Next, he wrote a clear and precise minute, expressly forbidding anything of the kind. After that, you would have thought everything would have been all right. Not at all. The Secret Service (without proper liaison) and in touch with minor Admiralty officers, arranged this with Crabb (a retired officer, who has specialised in 'frogman' work). The Admiralty agreed – the PM's order had either been overridden – evaded, or merely not passed down the line. Then this gallant officer does the job – successfully, and without detection.

After this, Macmillan continued, Crabb:

> in an excess of zeal, undertakes another job – among the destroyers – and is unsuccessful. He is either killed by the Russians, or drowned by misadventure – we don't know for certain. Then the Russians complain. The Admiral at Portsmouth (knowing nothing about it) denies the charge. Then the Commander's relations ask questions. The Press begin. The Admiralty issues a

denial (the most idiotic thing possible, since otherwise we could have refused to know anything about it, as is always the rule with Secret Service work). Then the fat is in the fire. What makes it worse is that although all this happened on April 17th, nothing was said by officials to Ministers until the Press story broke. . . .[74]

The entry also gives some insight into Macmillan's instinctively low opinion of Secret Services activities, especially when it came to such 'boy-scout' blunders. He 'strongly advised' Eden to 'say nothing'.[75] Not without reason, Eden was thrown into a major rage by the Crabb episode. To a barrage of questions in the Commons, he replied simply that 'disciplinary measures' were being taken, stating in his memoirs, 'Beyond this I refused, and still refuse, to be drawn.'[76] When the Cabinet papers for 1957 were duly released under the thirty-year rule, all that could be found on Crabb was a note that the file was closed until 2057. The Macmillan diary entry remains one of the few chinks in this excessive wall of secrecy.

The Common Market

When Macmillan moved from the Foreign Office to the Treasury he also brought with him much of the responsibility for Britain's dealings with the six 'Messina Powers', and their moves towards a European Common Market. One of his first communications came from Lady (Juliet) Rhys Williams, whom he regarded as the 'Cassandra' of the pro-Europe Tories. In what he described as 'a letter of warning in prophetic terms', she wrote that 'the "protected by the Channel" mentality is so out of date that the risks of *not* going in with Europe are much greater than those of going in. . . . a 6-Power Customs union *with Britain out* . . . may go through unexpectedly soon if we don't take a hand to prevent it by coming in too while the door is still open. . . .'[77]

The reservations of the Eden government, and of Macmillan himself as Foreign Secretary, had led to their cold-shouldering the Messina Conference in June 1955. But as Chancellor, Macmillan, although still firmly opposed to the supra-nationalism of the Six, felt the time had come when Britain had to take a more constructive line. Accordingly, in February 1956, he asked the Treasury to prepare an alternative plan, but was promptly rebuffed by the civil service mandarins – on the simple grounds that it would be 'a huge task', for which they could spare neither time nor manpower.[78] Macmillan then persuaded Eden to short-circuit the recalcitrant Treasury by creating a working party that included the Foreign Office and Peter Thorneycroft's well-disposed Board of Trade.

By April they had produced a list of six options, of which one, option (e), was for a Partial Free Trade Area with Europe, 'by which tariffs would be removed on imports from the Six to the UK'. This still left Britain a long way behind the Six on planning, and it was not till the end of July that Macmillan and Thorneycroft were ready to circulate a memo backing option (e). Now redesignated 'Plan G', it proposed British 'association' with the Messina Plan, by means of a free-trade area, which got over the problems of the Commonwealth by ensuring its continued free entry of goods in the British market. This was the forerunner of what, under Macmillan's premiership, was to become EFTA (European Free Trade Area), or the 'Seven'. It also effectively closed the door to Britain joining the Messina Six. Macmillan explained in his memoirs that 'It was then universally believed that our obligations to the Commonwealth and our outside interests made it impossible for us to adhere to a tightly drawn plan for a Common Market, with all its supra-national apparatus.'

Macmillan was clearly not for kicking against the pricks at this moment. The day he and Thorneycroft submitted their memo was also the day Nasser nationalised the Suez Canal, and it was October before Plan G was paraded before the Party conference at Llandudno ('a charming resort, with . . . a fascinating type of jellyfish basking in the sea'), and November before it was put to Parliament. By this time, the country was in the throes of Suez, and, as Macmillan wrote, 'since the House of Commons finds it difficult to deal with more than one great issue at a time, there was a certain unreality about the discussions. . . .'

This covered over, however, the deep concern Macmillan now felt that Britain might find herself isolated if the Six went ahead. On 16 October he had sent a personal message to Spaak, 'pleading for a little time before final decisions are made'.[79] The Six replied by advancing a further step to embrace agriculture in their Treaty; but this was a step no British Cabinet could have taken at the time. It was the story of the Genii-in-the-Bottle: too late again. Gone was the time when, in 1955, the Eden government could have entered the Common Market, still being moulded, on favourable terms. On 1 January 1958, the EEC would come into being, with Britain excluded and always a lap behind, and no efforts by Macmillan then or subsequently would open the door.

Macmillan's period of office at No. 11 would last only until December 1956. How should one rate him as Chancellor? In place of the old, fusty tradition which he complained was like 'looking up trains in last year's Bradshaw', he had introduced a new streamlined system of statistics. By the end of a year in office, he had managed to make cuts – drawn almost equally from defence and civil expenditure – to within £7 million of his fairly ambitious target of £100 million. From a deficit of £78 million the balance of payments had risen to a surplus of £245 million. The critical gold and dollar reserves had risen substantially, though by not as large a figure as Macmillan would have wished.

In his endeavours, via the good offices of Iain Macleod, Monckton's successor as Minister of Labour, to get industry to accept a voluntary freeze, he had been less successful; the FBI co-operated, but in September the TUC rejected by a large majority any restraint on wage claims, which continued to rise. Harold Wilson, in the heat of the 1959 election campaign, claimed that the then Prime Minister's year at the Treasury had been, without exception, 'the most disastrous in our financial history . . .'[80], although in the mellowing of old age he was to write that 'there was never a dull moment. . . . In a strange way it was a happy and stimulating relationship between the Chancellor and his shadow. . . .'[81] There were other critics who thought that Macmillan showed himself to be more at home at the Treasury than at the Foreign Office; once again, however, the time was perhaps too short for him – with only one Budget to his credit – to be properly judged.

Eden's Star Wanes

As Macmillan involved himself in economic affairs over the first half of 1956, the situation in the Middle East was steadily growing more critical. In January, Jordan had refused to join the Baghdad Pact – a refusal which Eden saw as the diabolical handiwork of Nasser, via his powerful propaganda services to the Arab world. '. . . I played a big stake to try to get Jordan into the Baghdad

Pact, when I was Foreign Secretary,' wrote Macmillan in his diaries. 'But we have lost – at least we have lost the first round. However, the game is not over yet; and we have got to win. . . . For if we lose out in the Middle East, we lose the oil. If we lose the oil, we cannot live. . . .'[82] This was to be Macmillan's guiding principle throughout Suez, right until the last turn of the crisis. On 1 March (the same day that Makarios was exiled from Cyprus) there came still worse news from a Jordan that was showing increasing belligerence towards Israel and disenchantment with the West. Acting under the influence of Nasser (so Macmillan – and Eden – thought), the young Harrow-educated monarch, King Hussein, summarily sacked his British military adviser, Glubb Pasha, a legendary figure who had spent his life in Jordan and had created its excellent Arab Legion. This came as a body-blow to Eden. Fearing that the Russians might move into a vacuum here, too, if Britain in pique cut the financial subsidies on which Jordan largely depended, Macmillan, however, counselled Eden against taking any drastic action.

Suddenly the whole Middle East looked dangerously explosive. Stirred up by Nasser's 'Voice of the Arabs', rioters attacked the house of the British political agent in Kuwait, and Selwyn Lloyd was stoned while visiting Bahrain. By 16 March, Macmillan recorded 'alarming news' reaching London about Nasser's plans to weld the Arab world into 'a sort of League of Arab Republics', and for Egypt to attack Israel in June, as soon as the last British troops had left under the Treaty. He thought the putative Egyptian scheme had one flaw: 'If the Egyptians attack the Jews, they will probably (in spite of their superiority in weapons) get a bloody nose. They may even have a shattering defeat, which would tumble Nasser off his perch.'[83] But in the growing tension, Israel herself was far from being as sanguine as Macmillan about the prospects of an Egyptian attack on her.

Eden's 1954 agreement with Egypt – of which Macmillan, along with his son-in-law, Julian Amery, who was a leader of the right-wing 'Suez Group', had been critical – contained unhappily no provisions for lifting the Sharm-el-Sheikh blockade which sealed off the Gulf of Aqaba and the Red Sea to Israel. Mostly operating out of the Egyptian-controlled Gaza Strip, but later also out of Jordan, Fedayeen guerrillas had also been making increasing numbers of raids on Israeli settlements. The Israelis reacted with punitive retaliations. The threat of a concerted attack on her by a combination of her Arab neighbours (as had happened in 1948), now equipped with new Soviet weapons, became a nightmare to Israel's leaders.

As the threat of Soviet arms for Egypt mounted, so too did the haggling over the financing of the huge Aswan Dam project. When a beaming Bulganin and Khrushchev visited London in April, they promptly let it be known, according to Sir Ivone Kirkpatrick, that 'they would make as much trouble for us in the Middle East as they possibly could. They were as good as their word. . . .'[84] Macmillan related that Eden warned the Russian leaders 'explicitly that the Middle East oil was a vital British interest. If necessary, we should fight for our rights.' Macmillan added that, 'whether this was wise or not, it seemed to have made a deep impression upon our visitors.' June brought the evacuation of the last British contingent from the Suez Canal, in accordance with the 1954 agreement; Britain had already withdrawn from the neighbouring Sudan. Nevertheless Nasser's hostility remained unappeased, while from Washington, Macmillan – though no longer directly in touch as he had been when Foreign Secretary – received indications that 'Dulles was in one of his most indecisive moods'. So began the historic summer of 1956.

Eden had now been in power for little over a year and already he was experiencing a dramatic reversal in the tide of his political fortunes. When Macmillan had gone to see him at the end of December 1955, before moving into No. 11, he had thought that the Prime Minister looked ill but cheerful. Bouts of illness had increasingly dogged Eden over the next months, apparently exacerbated by occasional spasms of heavy drinking. His colleagues found him increasingly irascible. A visit to Eisenhower in Washington in January 1956 ended on a disastrously cool note; at the conclusion, a fairly banal communiqué was issued, incorporating a promise that would ricochet back on Eden: 'We shall never initiate violence.'[85]

In Britain the year started with a banner headline in the *Daily Mirror*: 'EDEN IS A FLOP: *Even the* TORIES *are saying it now*. . . .'[86] Always abnormally susceptible to criticism, Eden was particularly incensed by an article published by the nominally friendly *Daily Telegraph* on 3 January. 'There is a favourite gesture of the Prime Minister's,' wrote Donald McLachlan: 'to emphasise a point he will clench one fist to smack the open palm of the other hand – but the smack is seldom heard. Most Conservatives, and almost certainly some of the wiser trade union leaders, are waiting to feel the smack of firm government. . . .' The article continued: 'What are the actual criticisms that are heard wherever politics are discussed? They fall under three heads: changes of mind by the Government; half measures; and the postponement of decisions. . . .'[87] Faults that were beyond Eden's control, such as his lack of administrative experience, were now regularly paraded in the press. His relationship with Fleet Street had never been outstanding, and as it observed how Eden was frequently in a 'flap', it sensed – well before the crisis July brought – that his morale was cracking.

In the Commons, too, there were murmurs among the Tory backbenchers that his grasp was slipping. During the March debate on the sacking of Glubb Pasha, Eden made such a poor speech that the astute American correspondent, Drew Middleton, wrote to his Ambassador, Winthrop Aldrich, in prescient terms after talking to Tory MPs:

> My impression is that although they are profoundly gloomy about the state of the world and the state of their leadership, they are not now rebellious. That goes for the Suez group as well as the more moderate members. But I feel that another setback to British policy or to the home economy, coupled with any sign of indecision, will create an entirely new situation. I don't rule out the sort of rebellion that I watched in late April and early May 1940 [when Churchill replaced Chamberlain].[88]

Also criticising Eden's limp performance on that same occasion, a British political commentator, Ian Waller, concluded on an even more prophetic note: 'it is hard to avoid the feeling that the cards are mounting and that, if the year goes on as it has begun, it will be not Sir Anthony Eden but Mr Harold Macmillan who reigns in Downing Street in 1957.'[89]

On 5 July, after a Cabinet meeting when Macmillan had recorded charitably that Eden had been 'a good chairman – very fair and agreeable', he added that he was beginning to find that Eden's mind, though 'quick and versatile', was 'without depth. He does not "brood over things", as Churchill did.'[90] Two weeks later, he was writing that 'Eden gives no real leadership in the House . . .

although he is *popular* and respected in the country as a whole. . . .'[91] But even this popularity was waning, while Macmillan's stock had risen perceptibly since the April Budget. On the day Nasser launched his Suez bombshell, 26 July 1956, Harold Nicolson found himself at a party given by Bob Boothby, where Aneurin Bevan 'talked to me about the decay of the present government. He attributes it entirely to Eden, who, he says, is much disliked, weak and vacillating and, in fact, hopeless. . . .'[92]

For a leader and a government about to face a supreme test, the omens could hardly have been less auspicious.

Chapter Fifteen

Suez
July–November 1956

. . . if Nasser 'gets away with it', we are done for. . . . It may well be the end of British influence and strength for ever. So, in the last resort, we must use force and defy opinion, here and overseas.

(HM, Diaries, 18 August 1956)

Nothing so became Harold Macmillan in the Suez operation as his manner of leaving it.

(Harold Wilson, reviewing HM's Riding the Storm *in* The Times, *22 April 1971)*

Although Macmillan had played his part in warning of the dangers building up in the Middle East, during the early summer of 1956 his diaries are preoccupied not with Nasser but with continuing concern about the state of the gold and dollar reserves, cuts in spending and defence costs, industrial and labour problems, trouble in the steel industry and talk about a wage freeze, and the sale of Trinidad Oil to the US. No mention was made of the scheduled withdrawal, on 13 June, of the last British troops from the Suez Canal base. This evacuation was followed, on 28 June, by an event which, though far removed from the Middle East stage, was to have its direct bearing on the crisis period of Suez. Serious riots took place in the Polish city of Poznan, tanks had to be called in, leaving 48 dead and 270 wounded. President Eisenhower had meanwhile been taken into hospital, where he was subsequently operated on for an intestinal obstruction, and for much of June and July he was debilitated by illness.

On 5 July, Macmillan recorded briefly in his diary that after a three-hour rather rambling Cabinet, he had a long talk with Eden and Foreign Secretary Selwyn Lloyd about the Anglo-American Aswan Dam project: 'I gave the F.S. a line, which he promised to work up into a paper. I feel that we should neither abandon the project in a pet, nor be manoeuvred out of it. We and the Americans should have a *position*, and state it frankly and publicly.'[1] On 19 July, while Eisenhower was still recuperating, and without consulting Eden or even his own staff, John Foster Dulles summarily withdrew the US offer to finance the Aswan Dam. (Eisenhower later admitted that the way the cancellation was handled was perhaps 'undiplomatic'.)[2] Two days later, the British government also withdrew from the project; Macmillan glumly recorded in his diary: 'Government position very bad. Nothing has gone well. In the Middle East we are still teased by Nasser & Co; the colonial Empire is breaking up . . . Cyprus is a running sore . . . the people are puzzled. . . .'[3]

On 26 July, his diary entry was preoccupied with the strike that had broken out at the British Motor Corporation, after which he simply stated: 'Dined at Fishmongers' Hall – quite a pleasant party, but very hot. Read Jane Austen's *Northanger Abbey* – a great book. . . .'[4] That was the day Nasser launched his bombshell: the nationalisation of the Suez Canal. He used as justification the need for the income from Canal dues to finance the building of the Aswan Dam, following the Anglo-American cancellation of their offer. Macmillan, however, staunchly supported the line taken by the Eden government that the sudden US withdrawal from the project was not the prime cause of Nasser's nationalisation of Suez, but the consequence of his 'dangerous dreams of Arab imperialism'. Eden heard the news in the middle of a state dinner for King Feisal of Iraq and his Prime Minister, Nuri es-Said. 'Hit him, hit him hard and hit him now,' urged the veteran Nuri.

At this distance, it is easy to forget the tenor of the British reaction that followed Nasser's 'grab'. Britain was then the Canal's largest user, owning one-third of the 14,666 ships that passed through it in 1955; a 44 per cent holding in the Suez Canal Company also made her the largest single shareholder. The Canal, too, was of prime symbolic importance to an influential imperialist faction within the Tory Party. Across the board, immediate emotions were at least as violent, and the atmosphere as febrile, as in the dramatic days after Argentina invaded the Falklands in 1982.

Eden, who was already unpopular, and ill, at once came under the strongest pressure to 'do something'. The year of 1956 happened to be the twentieth anniversary of Hitler's reoccupation of the Rhineland, and – although the memories of men like Eden (and Macmillan) hardly needed jogging – the combative Ivone Kirkpatrick, standing out as a hardliner at the head of an otherwise traditionally cautious and pro-Arab Foreign Office, was swift to stress the tragic consequences of Franco-British inaction then. The parallels made were immediate. In his diary entry for the 27th, his first mention of the Canal's seizure, Macmillan described Nasser's nationalisation speech as 'very truculent – an Asiatic Mussolini . . .'.[5] Meanwhile the socialist *Daily Herald* declared forthrightly, 'No more Hitlers',[6] and Gaitskell himself used words before the Commons, on 2 August, that he later regretted: 'It is all very familiar. It is exactly the same that we encountered from Mussolini and Hitler. . . .'[7]

Eden Determines on Action

Thus encouraged and particularly mindful of the cruel gibe in the *Daily Telegraph* about the 'smack of firm government', Eden determined on the resort to force – not, as he made plain to Cabinet colleagues, simply to resecure the Suez Canal, but to 'topple' the Mid-Eastern Mussolini. ('I want Nasser destroyed, not removed, destroyed,' he had already declared in a rage at the time of the sacking of Glubb Pasha in March.)[8] In France Eden found unexpectedly vigorous allies. Premier Mollet was bogged down in the Algerian War, and he regarded Nasser mistakenly as the mainspring behind the Algerian rebels. Both he and his Foreign Minister, Pineau, were, in addition, ardent supporters of the infant state of Israel, whose very existence they believed was directly menaced by Nasser.

At the British Foreign Office, instead of the independent-minded Macmillan, Eden now had Selwyn Lloyd. Aged fifty-one, Selwyn Lloyd had spent most of his professional life as a lawyer and brought with him into politics the appearance, unremarkable but dependable, of the family solicitor, although he had risen to the rank of brigadier in the war. When Churchill had appointed him Minister of State at the Foreign Office five years before Suez, he had admitted with revealing modesty: 'I do not speak any foreign language. Except in war, I have never visited any foreign country. I do not like foreigners. . . .'[9] It was hardly the most promising qualification for the job. He felt himself unfitted to take over as Foreign Secretary after only eight months in the Cabinet, and certainly his Cairo visit in the spring – when he had tried to persuade Nasser of the innocence of the Baghdad Pact – had been a conspicuous failure. About all Eden had to say of his Foreign Secretary in his laconic memoirs was that, as a negotiator, Selwyn Lloyd was 'clear, firm and consistent'.[10] An honourable man out of his depth, he was also totally loyal, almost excessively so. He once complained that Eden had talked to him on the telephone the previous night from 10 p.m. to 2 a.m.; hearing which John Wyndham had muttered, 'Harold would have hung up on him!'[11] Thus during Suez Eden was virtually assured of being able to run British foreign policy without interference, disclosing only what he chose to disclose to even his closest colleagues. It was a great deal to handle for any one man – and certainly for a sick man.

Among colleagues at home, there was no one who supported Eden in his hard line more ardently than Harold Macmillan. On 27 July, the day after Nasser's nationalisation of the Canal, his diaries reveal that Eden 'appointed a "Suez" Committee of the Cabinet – himself, Salisbury, Home and myself . . .'. This was later to become the Egypt Committee, with a rather larger membership; but at first, significantly, the name of the Foreign Secretary was omitted. Macmillan expressed satisfaction with the 'firmness' Eden showed in a telegram to Eisenhower, which 'left no room for uncertainty or equivocation'.[12] From that moment on, as he stresses in his memoirs, he played a 'full part' in all the deliberations of the Egypt Committee that ensued, and shared 'to the fullest extent the responsibility of all the decisions, not merely from the normal responsibility of a Cabinet Minister, but because I was one of the circle of colleagues whom Eden consulted'.

The weekend of 28–29 July, Macmillan recorded that 'I was to have gone to Barnstaple today, to make a speech at a garden fête. Nasser at least saved me from that.' And on the Sunday, 'There was so much work to be done, that I did not go to church. I stayed in bed working till luncheon. . . . Finished *Northanger Abbey*; also read *Persuasion*. There was last night and through today, the most violent gale I ever remember.'[13]

The next day Macmillan's old wartime colleague, Robert Murphy, arrived in London, despatched by President Eisenhower as his personal representative. Macmillan invited him to dine that night at No. 11, bringing in as the only other British guest Field Marshal Alexander. Although retired, Alex remained closely in touch with the government's plans, and his presence – Macmillan calculated – would act as a further reminder of the wartime Anglo-American amity. Implicit, too, was the gentlest of hints that, in Greece in 1944, Macmillan and Alex – by taking prompt action – had been right, the Americans wrong.

According to Murphy, Macmillan declared that, if she did not confront Nasser now, '. . . "Britain would become another Netherlands." I was left in no doubt that the British Government believed that Suez was a test which could be met only by the use of force, and I was not surprised at this reaction, because it seemed not unjustified. . . .' Alexander, said Murphy, suggested that 'military moves might start in August and "would not take much" – perhaps a division or at the most two. And it would be all over in 10 days, with the Suez Canal returned to international control. . . .' To Murphy that night, his old chief and his British opposite number from wartime days clearly conveyed 'the impression of men who have made a great decision and are serene in the belief that they have decided wisely'.[14]

Murphy gained rather less from talks with Eden and Selwyn Lloyd, but he immediately filed, direct to Eisenhower, a full report on the Macmillan dinner. He also noted of Eden that he:

> was labouring under the impression that a common identity of interests existed among the allies. But that was not the American view, and I gave no encouragement to the idea. The Prime Minister had not adjusted his thoughts to the altered world status of Great Britain, and he never did. . . . Macmillan understood from the time I knew him in Algiers, and he never spoke the way Eden did . . . .[15]

The view of this important dinner party that Macmillan, however, confided to his diary was that 'it is clear that the Americans are going to "restrain" us all they can,' and that he and Alex 'did our best to frighten Murphy out of his life. We gave him the impression that our military expedition to Egypt was about to sail. . . .' But, recorded Macmillan, in fact it would take 'at least six weeks to prepare', and the Cabinet's chief problem was 'how to fill up the time before our striking force can be got ready . . .'. Concealing this from his American guest, he continued, nevertheless: 'we have succeeded in thoroughly alarming Murphy. He must have reported in the sense which we wanted, and Foster Dulles is now coming over post-haste. This is a very good development.'[16] When Macmillan realised what kind of gifts Dulles was bringing with him, his enthusiasm was considerably dampened.

Macmillan reported on 1 August on his first meeting with Dulles: 'We *must* keep the Americans really frightened. They must not be allowed any illusion. Then they will help us to get what we want, without the necessity for force. . . .' Latching on to this last sentence, Selwyn Lloyd claimed that misinterpretation of Macmillan's remarks led to a serious 'misunderstanding of our position, particularly by Eisenhower', on the grounds that 'the Cabinet had not yet decided to use force without delay'.[17] This seems to be a Jesuitical splitting of hairs, typical of Lloyd's lawyer's approach, as everything in Macmillan's diaries indicated the contrary. The entry for 1 August continued: 'But we must have (a) international control of the Canal; (b) humiliation or collapse of Nasser.' But how exactly was this last going to be achieved without recourse to force? Macmillan for one had no illusions. Meanwhile, revealing the first onset of the false optimism about the American position that was so dangerously to afflict him during Suez, he concluded his diary entry about the day's meetings: 'I have a feeling that Dulles and Co. are moving towards our point of view.'[18]

Who was deceiving whom? The immediate consequence of Macmillan's 'thoroughly alarming' Murphy was in fact to produce the first of President Eisenhower's eloquent letters to Eden, containing clear warnings of American opposition to the use of force – had the Eden Cabinet wished to regard it as such. 'Initial military successes might be easy,' wrote Eisenhower on 31 July for personal delivery by Dulles, 'but the eventual price might become far too heavy . . . .'[19] But Eden's interpretation, supported by Macmillan, was that 'the President did not rule out the use of force'.[20]

The second of August was the day when the Cabinet took the 'main decision' to use force 'if negotiations failed within a measurable time'.[21] Macmillan's diary entry for that day shows him, once again, the 'swordsman' and strategist expressing concern 'about the small force available to make the assault, and the extreme difficulty we shall be in for exploiting the position after a landing . . .'.[22] At the initial meeting of the Egypt Committee, it had been decided that the chief objective had to be nothing less than to bring about the downfall of the Nasser government, and the Chiefs of Staff were instructed accordingly. The first of three plans illustrated at once the potential problems of collaborating with a French ally; the chosen codename was Hamilcar, but when the British began painting their vehicles with an 'H' it was suddenly realised that the French spelt it without the first letter. Musketeer was substituted. The first Musketeer plan called for a landing at Port Said, but the British army commander, Lieutenant-General Sir Hugh Stockwell, was unhappy about this, describing it as a cork in a bottle with a very long neck. Macmillan too was unhappy when he first heard about it in the Egypt Committee on 1 August.

The third of August began with a furious confrontation between Macmillan and the directors of the Westminster Bank, who were now hesitant to pay out funds in their account to the Suez Canal

Company ('the legitimate one'). 'I told this story with particular glee to the Cabinet,' Macmillan recorded, 'because P.M. used to be a director of the Westminster Bank. But I was really shocked by their behaviour. . . .' He went on in his diary to express further anxiety about the military realities of the operation, notably the shortage of available shipping:

> . . . I am pressing the Admiralty to let us have all the ships (carriers, old cruisers, etc.) which they can find. It is tragic having to requisition liners at the height of the tourist season! . . . the fourth problem – the press – is very difficult. We have no censorship powers . . . and there is no way of stopping the most detailed accounts of shipping, troop movements and the rest. Personally I doubt that we shall get through all this without taking back the old war powers.[23]

The Macmillan Scheme

Clearly, Macmillan was substantially exceeding the normal prerogatives of a Chancellor of the Exchequer; moreover, it was he and Salisbury who were already charged with planning for the post-Musketeer organisation of Egypt and the Canal, once Nasser had been toppled. But Macmillan's diary entry of 3 August is of considerable importance for a further revelation. He states that at the close of the meeting of the Egypt Committee that day, 'a memorandum was read which I had sent to the P.M. about Israel . . .'. In this memorandum, Macmillan told Eden:

> . . . I was worried about the outline plan which we discussed last night. It seems to me full of hazards. Whatever the success of the air attack, two things are clear:
> (a) The number of forces that can be landed in the first wave even with an amended plan will be pretty limited.
> (b) The geographical situation makes the whole operation extremely difficult.
> This makes me feel that we ought not to reject any method of easing our position. The simplest course would be to use the

immense threat to Egypt that results from the position of Israel on her flank. . . .

Macmillan weighed the alternatives; if Britain were to warn Israel not to intervene, it might have 'very little effect'. He continued:

If I were in her position I should certainly intervene and get all the advantage I could. All history shows that Statesmen of any character will seize a chance like this and the Jews have character. They are bound to do something.
   Surely what matters is that what they should do is to help us and not hinder us. We don't want them to go off and attack Jordan.

As the Israelis were thus bound to do something, Macmillan argued that it was better that they were 'encouraged to attack Egypt'. Israel for her collaboration would have to receive, of course, 'some benefits', which Macmillan suggested should be at the expense of Egypt. He recalled the Alpha Plan of the previous year, under which Israel would have received 'a small benefit from Egypt', and could see no reason 'why they should not now get a much larger benefit out of Egypt'.[24] This was the first suggestion made of involving Israel. Eden was 'very shocked',[25] and Selwyn Lloyd was instructed to urge the Israelis to take no immediate action.
   After the reading of Macmillan's memorandum, the Committee talked about preparation of the 'Anglo-French ultimatum' to Egypt, where Macmillan expected 'Dulles's help' in the course of the imminent London Conference, which Dulles had advocated be held between the major maritime powers. Macmillan concluded his 3 August diary entry with some acid comments about Eden's handling of affairs:

For. Secy. has had a rough time and has got through well. He is very bitter about the P.M.'s interference, in small as well as in large issues. P.M. invited himself to the French Dinner at the Embassy (where he wasn't wanted and held up for two hours what was intended to be a business dinner) simply out of vanity and to get photographed. F.S. also feels that P.M. has talked too much in the H. of C. But I think he takes it (as we all do) in good part. Eden will never play Asquith to another man's Grey. He is too much of a prima donna himself. . . . I was absolutely worn out and took a sleeping draught which I rarely do.

The following day Macmillan was revealing his remarkable capacity to switch off in the midst of crisis:

> Woke at 11 a.m. Dozed on till lunch. This is the way to recover. Read a good life of Dickens – G. H. Pearson. What a character – restless, majestic, individualistic! Read *Our Mutual Friend*. . . . I am very tired and feel rather old. . . . It is almost impossible to believe that it is 42 years since 'our' war began.[26]

On the 6th, Macmillan started re-reading George Eliot (*Scenes from Clerical Life*), then went on to *Middlemarch*, which within four days he had finished, noting how it had been 'imitated' later by Arnold Bennett and C. P. Snow. By 24 August, after recording a particularly heated session of the Egypt Committee, he had finished *Adam Bede*. ('I found it rather heavy going. How inferior to Scott's *Heart of Midlothian*!') Two days later, worrying about the premature birth of twins to his daughter, Catherine Amery, which occurred a month early, he notes that he 'could not sleep very much, so read *Romola*. Not much George Eliot left!'[27]

By the mid-point in the Suez crisis he had already finished the whole of George Eliot, and moved on to Churchill's *History of the English Speaking Peoples* ('really most readable and dramatic. It gives the only intelligible account of the Wars of the Roses that I have ever read . . .'),[28] then Villari's *Life and Times of Savonarola*, followed by Villari's *Life and Times of Machiavelli*. On 16 September he was recording:

> Finished 'Machiavelli' yesterday. I have re-read Macaulay's Essay on Machiavelli – very flash and brilliant, but not very profound. But what a lot he knew! . . . P.M. rang up. He seemed a little depressed, so I did my best to comfort him. We *are* in a difficult position (particularly since we have no money). But we must have the courage to play the hand through. Sunday press very bad. . . . read a new novel by C. P. Snow (which M & Co. have just published) called *Homecoming* – well written, but rather depressing.[29]

Four days later, he was re-reading *Vanity Fair*. 'How good it is! I try to read an hour or two every day, however late, otherwise we would go mad. . . . A great deal of trouble in the party.'[30]

When asked why he omitted from his memoirs any mention of all this voracious reading during Suez, Macmillan remarked flippantly 'I didn't think it was of great interest . . . and it might have looked bad to let on that the Chancellor of the Exchequer had been reading books instead of being at his desk all this time. But if I hadn't, I'd have gone barmy!'[31]

Eden Raps Macmillan's Knuckles

On Sunday, 5 August, two days after the reading of his 'shocking' memorandum to the Egypt Committee, Macmillan dined with Churchill at Chartwell. Questioned about the current invasion plan, Macmillan 'said that unless we brought in Israel, I didn't think it could be done'. He rehearsed to the old warlord all the logistic problems of landing in Port Said, which would still leave Nasser in command in Cairo: 'Surely, if we landed, we must seek out the Egyptian forces; destroy them; and bring down Nasser's Government. Churchill seemed to agree with all this. We got out some maps and so on. C. got quite excited for a time, but he tired soon after dinner.' Late that evening, shortly after Macmillan's return to Birch Grove, Churchill's son-in-law Christopher Soames, then Under-Secretary of State for Air, telephoned 'to say that Churchill had decided to go to Chequers tomorrow, and put all the results of our talk and his own thoughts before Eden. Now the fat will be in the fire!'[32] The next day, Macmillan discussed his ideas further with Soames, who agreed with the good sense of marching on Cairo via Alexandria: 'Accordingly, I wrote a paper setting all this out, for circulation to the Egypt Committee.'[33]

In his biography of Eden, Robert Rhodes James speaks of a 'puzzling intervention by Churchill' on the 6th,[34] which is no longer puzzling when one matches it with Macmillan's account of the story. Instead of the 'strongly supportive attitude' Eden had hoped for from his old chief, says Rhodes James, Churchill read out a paper he had prepared, the principal feature of which was the need to involve the Israelis in a joint attack on Egypt. 'There was also some desultory historical reminiscence about Napoleon's invasion of Egypt.' Eden was described as being 'deeply disappointed and sad' at what he regarded as Churchill's mental deterioration. When pressed, Churchill admitted that his ideas had come from Macmillan.

Meanwhile, Macmillan, encouraged by his conversation with Churchill and Soames, had reworked his memorandum into a more detailed minute for submission to the Egypt Committee.[35] He began by repeating his concern at the 'practicality' of the first, Port Said plan, and urging the need to 'destroy Nasser's armies and overthrow his government'. He wanted the Committee now to consider the option of a landing at Alexandria, supported by a land attack with Armoured Division based in Libya; where, in the days before Ghadaffi, and under the then friendly regime of King Idris, Britain maintained substantial training areas and a considerable number of troops.

Relative air strengths and the need to knock out completely the Egyptian Air Force concerned Macmillan, but 'what worries me the most is that I feel that the directive on which the Chiefs of Staff have framed the Plan is perhaps the wrong one. It is to occupy the Canal.' Reminding the Egypt Committee of its earlier commitment, he continued: 'The object of the exercise, if we have to embark upon it, is surely to bring about the fall of Nasser and create a government in Egypt which will work satisfactorily with ourselves and the other powers. . . .'

Once 'humiliation' had been inflicted on Nasser, Macmillan thought that the Canal should be placed under international control, but a fair share of the profits 'set aside for the benefit of Egypt'. He concluded by repeating his earlier proposal for Israeli involvement: 'In view of the land armament at the disposal of Nasser, this is important. . . .'

On 7 August, Macmillan recorded that at the Egypt Committee:

As I expected the P.M. was in a very bad mood. He had refused to allow my paper to be circulated to the Committee or to the Chiefs of Staff. So I asked that it should be shown at least to Cabinet Ministers who were on the Committee. This was done. But by a very foolish and petty decision of this strangely sensitive man, copies were not sent to Service Ministers or to the Chiefs. (However, the Minister of Defence [Walter Monckton] had of course had copies made for them already!)

I discovered later that the source of the trouble was the Churchill visit. Eden no doubt thought that I was conspiring with C. against him. . . . P.M. was quite happy in the end about all this, and inclined to agree with my views. . . . I especially urged on him the need to appoint a Supreme Force Commander at once. The planning would be far better done by those who had to carry it out. . . .[36]

In this respect, at least, Macmillan's recommendation was followed, with the appointment shortly thereafter of General Sir Charles Keightley as Allied Commander-in-Chief – the man whose meeting with Macmillan at Klagenfurt in May 1945 was to provoke so much controversy.

On 9 August, after a meeting of the Egypt Committee, Macmillan was elated to find that a new military plan was being prepared; 'It seems that my paper has sunk the old plan, without trace – also, without a word being said about it, to me or to anyone else!'[37] Meanwhile, under pressure from Dulles, Eden had agreed to hold a conference of the eighteen major maritime powers; but Nasser refused to join it. Macmillan's diary entry for 9 August went on to give a glimpse of the stresses beginning to build up in the Cabinet as the British press grew more critical:

According to Walter [Monckton] P.M. was in a highly emotional state, and making life very difficult all round him. However, when we got to the meeting, he was in the best of good tempers and quite charming to us all. He is really a rather strange character – very feminine in many ways. . . . If Nasser accepts any plan which may emerge from the conference, well and good. If he turns it down flat, we may be able to justify our use of force. (Even so, we need a popular 'casus belli' – a sort of Jenkin's Ear) but if the answer is equivocal, how are we to negotiate with our invading Armada at sea? . . . No definite conclusions could be reached.

The following day there was a full meeting of the Egypt Committee, with Chiefs of Staff – 'and *maps!*' – at which the original plan of landing at Port Said and seizing the Canal was abandoned, in favour of a plan 'to seize Alexandria . . . and march on Cairo, to destroy Nasser!' This, Macmillan thought, had two immense advantages, 'in addition to it being the only way to obtain our purpose quickly. We need *not* stimulate the Israelites to do more than make faces. We need *not* invade Egypt from Libya. . . .' But, he concluded, 'the great thing is that last week's plan is dead and buried. The CIGS came up afterwards and thanked me. . . . "Chancellor" he said "no one will ever know what we owe to you".'[38] Thus the principle 'destroy Nasser' was translated into a military programme.

Eventually this plan was altered and re-altered, and finally it returned to a landing at Port Said, with full Israeli commitment. Macmillan, however, made no more specific mention in his diaries of any discussion of details of the military plan, and particularly of any further memoranda put forward by the Chancellor of the Exchequer. It is fairly plain that, following Churchill's unpopular intervention at Chequers on the 6th, and Eden's 'bad mood' of the next day, Macmillan had received a knuckle-rapping and more or less been told to mind his own business and leave strategic planning to others. On 16 August, Macmillan gave voice, with restraint, to his very real frustration: '. . . It is rather sad, in a way, for me to feel that I gave up the F.O. and am not *directly* responsible. . . .'[39]

In this characteristically low-key comment can be measured all the compounded resentment that had followed his removal from the Foreign Office by Eden. From his remarks in later years, it is evident that after early August, while totally loyal and continuing to provide the hard line buttressing Eden, Macmillan to some extent retired wounded from the diplomatic and military aspects of the crisis, accepting Eden's reproof and concentrating almost exclusively on Treasury matters. Herein may well lie one reason why, at the crucial stage of Suez in October, Macmillan did not occupy himself more closely with the details of the collusion plan or with its predictable impact on the Americans.

Delays

Macmillan's reckoning that it would take about six weeks to mount a strike force turned out to be optimistic. Joint Anglo-French planning began on 8 August, and the French were at once ready to earmark two elite divisions, including the 10th Para, battle-hardened in Algeria. The problems lay on the British side. Although the country spent 10 per cent of its budget on defence and had a military establishment of 750,000, its forces were designed to fight either all-out war in Europe or counter-guerrilla campaigns in Malaysia. The army was weak on fire-power and mobility. There was a shortage of troop-carrying planes and a worse shortage of airfields on Cyprus. At one point a private firm, Pickfords Removals, would have to be called in to help transport tank units. Worst of all was the shortage of deep-water harbours; nearby Cyprus might just suffice for parachute troops and RAF support strikes, but the main armada carrying most of the tanks and armoured vehicles would have to be mounted from distant Malta, several days' sailing away. If Macmillan's own intended defence cuts had already gone through, the strike force would have been still less capable of early action.

Egypt, with its newly purchased weapons from Czechoslovakia and the USSR, was – at least on paper – in some respects better equipped than Britain. Throughout, Eden's military advisers showed themselves unhappy with the projected operations. The débâcle of the 1944 airborne landing on Arnhem was less than twelve years behind them, and many had bitter personal recollections of what enemy tanks could do to unsupported units. The excessive caution on the part of the military was not revised when some ministers – and the French, case-hardened in Indo-China and Algeria – pointed out that the defences would be manned, not by the Wehrmacht, but by Egyptians.

The most powerful voice of all the Chiefs of Staff, that of the First Sea Lord, Mountbatten, was raised 'consistently and unequivocally' against the whole Musketeer operation – not just because of its technical shortcomings, but on political and humanitarian grounds as well. Hammering away at the 'political implications' of the British plan, Mountbatten caused Eden to flare up angrily and tell him that he 'would have no interference from the Chiefs of Staff on political matters'.[40] At the end of August, Mountbatten drafted a letter of resignation, but never sent it. (On 2 November, he would return to the fray again, urging Eden to accept the UN ceasefire call.)

Meanwhile Eden fretted and fumed with each fresh operational postponement. And with reason; as Chester Cooper, the CIA representative in London, commented, the British and French 'had already lost the game in late July. Whether or not Eden and Mollet could bring themselves to face it, the world had already accepted the nationalisation of the Suez Canal as a *fait accompli*. . . .'[41] When, after the first few days of nationalisation, Nasser proved that he had no intention of closing the canal and that his Egyptian pilots could – against all disparaging expectations in the West – bring ships through it just as competently as the Scots they replaced, so one of the few pretexts for force that might perhaps have proved acceptable to Washington (which meant Eisenhower) fell away. As time passed by and experts on both sides of the Atlantic cast more doubts on the illegality of the Egyptian action ('expropriation not burglary' was the general view in the US), so the pretexts looked ever more tenuous. In Britain, Eden lost the early support of the Labour Party, as well as of a growing section of moderate opinion. After Dulles had arrived in London at the beginning of August, a series of delaying – or 'spoiling' – actions were set in train from Washington – for which Dulles's style of contradictory utterances was admirably suited. There was an ironic reversal of roles between Eden, who had infuriated Dulles by talking peace over Indo-China in 1954, and Dulles the brinkman – whom Churchill once designated as 'the only case I know of a bull who carries his china shop with him' – now to be found preaching peace and patience. The London Conference, urged on Eden by Dulles, dragged on until 23 August; that same day in the States, Eisenhower was nominated again as Republican candidate for the presidential elections in November.

On 18 August Macmillan was continuing to speculate on the prospects of bringing Suez to a head, and with more deluded optimism about the American position, following a dinner, attended also by Douglas Dillon, the US Ambassador in Paris:

> Foster didn't think the Russians would press things to extremes. . . . All the same, the problem remains. . . . On what 'principle' can we base a 'casus belli'? How do we get from the Conference leg to the use of force? British opinion is uncertain – although some of the press are being firm. But it remains a tricky operation. Yet, if Nasser 'gets away with it', we are done for. The whole Arab world will despise us. . . . Nuri and our friends will fall. It may well be the end of British influence and strength for ever.
>
> So, in the last resort, we must use force and defy opinion, here

and overseas. I made this quite clear to Foster, who really agreed with our position. But he hopes (and he may be right) that Nasser will have to yield – in due course. This again lights up the frightful problem of how to keep a military expedition, brought together at huge cost, 'all dressed up and nowhere to go'.[42]

The next day he was noting that both he and Salisbury had the impression that Foster was getting rather 'sticky': 'I cannot help feeling that he really wants us to "go it alone", and has been trying to help us by creating the right atmosphere. . . .'[43] Although Menzies was 'much firmer in his attitudes', the Canadians were 'very wet', and Macmillan thought it very alarming that the 'weaker brethren' at the London Conference were now mooting the sending of a committee to Cairo to 'negotiate' with Nasser.

When the Egypt Committee met on 22 August:

It was decided to postpone D-Day by 4 days. This allows us to put off certain things (like photographing Egyptian ports from the air) until the Conference is finished. The question of certain French ships sailing was put off also for a day or two. They are to go to Cyprus. . . . The Conference should end tomorrow. The fact that Dulles has played such a prominent part certainly helps to commit the prestige of U.S. . . .[44]

This participation of Dulles gave Macmillan the impression that the Secretary of State was still 'determined to take a strong line'; 'if every peaceful means had first been used, and force then used, Dulles believed that the world would understand. . . .' Thus falsely encouraged, Macmillan (if Dulles's recollections are correct) evidently made an extraordinary, and – in many ways – incomprehensible, personal *démarche* to Dulles. In an office memorandum dated 21 August, Dulles reported:

As I was leaving Sir Anthony Eden's Reception last night, Harold Macmillan said he would like to speak to me privately. . . . Macmillan asked first of all whether I planned to stay on as Secretary of State. He said that he was thinking of perhaps going back to take over the Foreign Office in the reasonably near future and that his decision in this matter would be influenced by whether I would be his vis-à-vis in the United States. He spoke of the very happy relations we had together when we were both Foreign Ministers and that he would very much like to renew this.

Dulles replied that he had 'no definite plans', but that if Eisenhower was re-elected, he expected 'there would be no immediate change'. Macmillan then 'urged me most strongly to take on the negotiation with Nasser. He said he did not have confidence that anybody else could pull it off. . . .'[45]

Given the circumstances of Eden's shunting Macmillan from the Foreign Office the previous year, it was inconceivable that – under Eden – there would have been any possibility of his returning there. But the exchange seems at least to indicate, once again, where Macmillan's heart still lay.

At a meeting of the Egypt Committee on the 24th, Eden reported how he had told Dulles 'that we had no alternative, if we could not get our way by diplomatic pressure, but to resort to force. . . . Dulles had not seemed shocked. . . .'[46] Within the Cabinet, divisions were mounting:

Minister of Defence [Monckton] raised the general question. Could we use force? Would British public opinion support us? Would world opinion condemn us? Of course, if an 'incident' took place, that would be the way out. P.M. – strongly supported by me and Salisbury – and Home – took the view that we had no alternative. We must secure the defeat of Nasser, by one method or another. If not, we would rot away.

Macmillan came away with the impression that Butler was uncertain: 'he wanted more time, so as to show that every possible method had been tried, before the final decision to use force. I argued that if D Day were postponed too often or too late, it would never happen. We must be resolved. . . . Walter Monckton was calm, but obviously distressed.'[47]

Meanwhile, Macmillan was considering the economic position, especially from the point of view of the vital Middle East oil supplies. 'The truth is that we are caught in a terrible dilemma. If we take strong action against Egypt, and as a result the Canal is closed, the pipelines to the Levant are cut, the Persian Gulf revolts and oil production is stopped – then U.K. and Western Europe have "had it". . . .' On the other hand,

> if we suffer a diplomatic defeat; if Nasser 'gets away with it', Nuri falls, and the Middle East countries, in a ferment, 'nationalise oil' . . . we have equally 'had it'. What then are we to do? It seems clear that we should take the only chance we have – to take strong action, and hope that thereby our friends in Middle East will stand, our enemies fall, and the oil will be saved, but it is a tremendous decision.[48]

On 26 August Macmillan submitted his lengthy Treasury paper, 'The Economic Consequences of Colonel Nasser', which came – once again – to the 'clear conclusion' that 'without the oil, both the United Kingdom and Western Europe are lost. . . .'[49]

Following the London Conference, a second delaying action occurred with the Australian Premier, that staunch friend of Britain, Robert Menzies, being despatched to inform Nasser of the positions taken in London. Menzies forthrightly warned Nasser that Britain and France were not bluffing. As Menzies was pursuing his fruitless mission in Cairo, the Cabinet fretted at further delays. Macmillan recorded on 28 August that Salisbury 'referred to the "progressive decline" which might take place if we did not make a stand . . .'.[50] Afterwards the Egypt Committee was given an outline of a plan by General Keightley. This was presumably a new draft of Musketeer, originally scheduled to go into operation on 15 September. Macmillan was 'very much impressed' by the plan, but he recorded no details of it.[51]

On 29 August, Eden telephoned Macmillan late in the evening, informing him that Nasser had now accepted a meeting for Monday, 3 September. 'These delays are really intolerable,' Macmillan protested in his diary. 'Nasser's proposal is put forward in rather an impertinent way. This, combined with the arrest of British subjects on charges of "espionage", makes one feel that he is getting more and more truculent and may soon do something very foolish. . . .'[52] This was wishful thinking; Nasser was to continue playing for time.

After a long weekend at Birch Grove, where the two little Amery girls were staying ('They are very sweet and come to my bedroom in the morning "to pass the time of day" in the most friendly manner . . .'), Macmillan returned to work on Monday, 3 September, to discover:

> Things certainly look pretty grim. On the home front, the TUC leaders – out of timidity, not spite – have decided to turn down my approach. . . . meanwhile the Clyde strike looks like being long and bitter. . . . the press is getting very restive [about Suez]; the Sunday press was particularly bad – and very defeatist. . . . It's all very reminiscent of bad old pre-war days! Except that in some cases the roles are reversed![53]

The next day he was continuing in the same vein about the 'very violent' press:

> The P.M. is accused of deceiving the nation, and of preparing a military expedition which he has determined to use, at all costs. The President has sent a very hesitating and defeatist message, urging caution and appeasement. . . . Internally, the announcement of our loss of 120 million dollars in the reserves comes out this afternoon. It will be a shock to the market. I hope it will also be a shock to the trades unions.[54]

At a long meeting of the Egypt Committee on the evening of 4 September, Macmillan outlined the three possible courses of military action: to go to war without going to the UN; to go to the UN, but continue all the military preparations and face the accusation of preparing for an invasion; or to postpone the final arrangements for the invasion until after the UN failed, accepting a further delay of three weeks after that. It was generally agreed that the first course was impossible because of public opinion at home and overseas, and that the third course was also unacceptable because of 'the anti-war pressure that would build up' and 'the increasing Russian aid to Egypt of which we have evidence, which would make the operation dangerous if we leave it too long'. The second was thus 'clearly the only possible course'. As the Committee was breaking up, Mountbatten and his new civil First Lord, Hailsham, 'came in with the news of two modern Russian submarines, with Egyptian crews, sailing past Denmark. . . . the danger is that they may have really Russian crews and officers with a few Egyptians for show.'[55]

Opposition

On the following day, 5 September, huge headlines announced that Eisenhower at a press conference had unconditionally rejected the use of force. If Nasser turned down the proposals brought by Menzies, others would be pursued; because 'We are committed to a peaceful settlement of this dispute, nothing else.'.News of the failure of Menzies's mission was brought to the Egypt Committee on 7 September, when Macmillan in his diary makes the first mention of Dulles's latest proposal, to set up a body to organise safe transit of the Suez Canal by its users, a scheme that would end up as SCUA – the Suez Canal Users' Association. There was also further discussion in the Committee about the 'new' plan by General Keightley. Called 'Musketeer Revise', this third scheme reverted to a landing at Port Said, not Alexandria. It seems to have come largely as a result of pressure by Mountbatten, supported by Hailsham, who was persuaded in its favour by the unacceptable level of civilian casualties that would be caused by the naval bombardment of a major city like Alexandria. There is no indication from the Macmillan papers that he even participated in the discussion, and a week later the change of plan was accepted – only a few days before the fleet was scheduled to sail for Alexandria, and to the great confusion of all concerned.

Amid the crisis, Birch Grove continued to provide pleasant distraction for Macmillan. On Saturday, 8 September, he recorded 'a lovely day . . . a great host of children all the time – four Macmillans, and two or three Fabers . . .'. But he added: 'There are some very bad messages from Washington. It is vital to keep the pressure up on our American friends. As regards Cairo, it is now becoming clear that Nasser will not agree to anything.'[56] The bad messages presumably included Eisenhower's unambiguous statement to the US press on 5 September, which Macmillan claimed 'torpedoed' the work of the London Conference. A letter from Eisenhower to Eden of 8 September[57] was both eloquent (unlike his oral statements) and moderate, but it was equally unambiguous about his opposition to the use of force – as, indeed, had been all his communications to Eden since the end of July. A covering note from Eisenhower to Dulles, in which he wondered diffidently whether the letter was 'worth while sending', explained that 'the only usefulness it might have is in its attempt to destroy Anthony's apparent fixation that delay or long-drawn-out negotiations might

413

result in catastrophe for Great Britain and the West. . . .'[58]

It was unfortunate for the alliance that Dulles's utterances, alternately pacific and bellicose, continued to be as confusing as the President's were clear. Yet, during these first two weeks in September, the British Ambassador in Washington, Roger Makins, was also making it plain to London that the Americans would not provide either moral or material support for military action, and that without such support it could 'easily lead to disaster'.[59] What is extraordinary is that at this point neither Eden nor Macmillan, nor any other member of the Egypt Committee, is on record as having considered the consequences if the US were to decide actively to oppose British intentions.

Eisenhower's statements, Selwyn Lloyd stated, 'destroyed any chance Menzies might have had of success and made the mission futile'.[60] The Menzies mission, rejected by Nasser, finally collapsed on 10 September. The projected invasion date now had to be postponed from 15 to 26 September; in fact, to Eden's annoyance, the forces would not have been ready anyway, so the new delay could not entirely be blamed on the Americans. But Eden's renewed frustration was fanned by Ivone Kirkpatrick forcefully voicing the view that if Britain sat back while Nasser was allowed to consolidate his position, and gain control of the Middle East oil-producing countries, 'we can be wrecked within a year or two.'[61]

Meanwhile, from his bird-watching retreat of Duck Island in the middle of Lake Ontario, Dulles had hatched up a new canard, first mentioned by Macmillan on 7 September. Starting life under the acronym of CASU, until the Dutch Foreign Minister warned of the menacing proximity to *casus belli*, the Dulles egg was then amended to CASCU. The Portuguese then pointed out that it meant 'balls' in their language; and in French it sounded something like 'break-arse'. It was a bad joke that came to epitomise the whole story of Suez. So it ended up as SCUA – the Suez Canal Users' Association. Eden, supported by Macmillan, agreed to join, provided that the US would participate and that the dues collected would be paid to SCUA, not Nasser. The British remained convinced, however, that SCUA would work only if it had 'teeth'.

Macmillan showed increasing concern in his diaries about both the American position and the possible threat to the British economy. He had remarked on 6 September that the TUC Conference had

'gone very badly so far as "wages and prices" are concerned', and
the following Sunday, the 9th, after noting how his grandchildren
had greatly enjoyed the story of Daniel and the fiery furnace at the
church service, he was writing:

> the President has sent a reply to the P.M. It isn't bad. The more
> we can persuade them of our determination to risk everything in
> order to beat Nasser, the more help we shall get from them. . . .
> We shall be ruined either way; but we shall be more inevitably
> and finally ruined if we are humiliated.[62]

Back in London the next day, he was wishing the Presidential
election was over. His chief worry was oil. 'The Americans have
made proposals for switching us oil from the Gulf. But will it be
dollar oil? Who is going to pay for it?'[63] One of the many ironies of
Suez is that, if Butler as Chancellor – pressed by Macmillan – had
not accorded a degree of sterling convertibility two years earlier,
Britain would not have faced such menacing financial straits in the
autumn of 1956, as France, with an even rockier economy, did not.

Already by 8 August, the Permanent Secretary to the Treasury,
Sir Edward (later Lord) Bridges, had been warning Macmillan of
the costs of 'going it alone', without American support. Measures
to protect sterling, he cautioned, might be needed in the autumn
even if the country were not involved in hostilities. According to
Macmillan's memoirs, the Treasury at the end of August had
estimated the cost of the 'precautionary military measures' at no
more than £12 million for August and September, and had reckoned
on a total additional cost at a maximum of £100 million over and
above the defence estimates of £1600 million for the whole year.
Macmillan had passed these figures on to the Cabinet on 28 August,
in his paper entitled 'The Egypt Crisis and the British Economy',
and had also warned of the danger of the oil pipelines being cut,
together with the effect on dollar reserves. On 7 September, Bridges
gave Macmillan another detailed summary on Treasury thinking,
estimating that, 'at the worst', without US support, 'we should be
unable to maintain the value of the currency'. Bridges went no
further than that; he did not foresee total calamity. On the other
hand, given US support, 'our general feeling is that our action
would be regarded by world opinion as something likely to
strengthen sterling.' Bridges concluded by stressing 'the vital

necessity from the point of views of our currency and our economy of ensuring that we do not go it alone, and that we have the maximum United States support . . . '.[64]

Macmillan, who read Bridges's significant warning on 10 September, sidelined this last passage in the Chancellor's traditional red ink and wrote underneath: 'Yes. This is just the trouble. US are being very difficult.' That same day a hawkish letter from Kirkpatrick to Makins in Washington pointed out the misguidedness of Eisenhower, and declared: 'If Middle East oil is denied to us for a year or two our gold reserves will disappear. If our gold reserves disappear the sterling area disintegrates. . . .' In which case, he doubted 'whether we shall be able to pay for the bare minimum necessary for our defence. And a country that cannot provide for its defence is finished.'[65]

The effect of such a line on Macmillan would have been considerable. In the three weeks up to mid-September Macmillan admitted that the slender gold and dollar reserves had sunk by $170 million. But had he, 'hawk' that he was, made the Treasury warnings sufficiently clear to the Egypt Committee? And had Eden heard them? Certainly they did not diminish Macmillan's own enthusiasm for action, nor persuade him to take precautionary measures to defend sterling, such as drawing a tranche of funds from the IMF. On the other hand, he appears to have received no recommendation from his Treasury advisers to do so.

Meanwhile, he had supported going along with Dulles's proposals for SCUA, in order to gain US financial backing. Britain would then take the case to the UN, as a last measure before launching the military operation.

By mid-September opposition to the use of force against Egypt had reached a new peak, particularly during the short special session of Parliament. Macmillan described the proceedings in the Commons on 13 September:

> a good many Tories, mostly young and mostly sons of 'Munichites' – like Richard Wood* – began to rat too. . . . Under all this pressure, P.M. naturally began to waver. On the other hand, the militant wing (Waterhouse – Amery) of the party might well turn

* Son of Lord Halifax.

nasty if he were to change his position too noticeably. Meanwhile, Foreign Secretary had moved the vote of Confidence at 2.30 – in a fine speech – but Sir Lionel Heald (an ex-Attorney General) had declared himself unwilling to vote for the Government, and other Tories were following suit. There was a meeting at 6 p.m. Butler was for giving the pledge – 'no force, without recourse to U.N.'. I was for standing firm – 'What I have said, I have said.' If P.M. were to 'climb down' under Socialist pressure, it would be fatal to his reputation and position.

. . . the poor P.M. (already exhausted with all this 6 weeks' crisis and yesterday's debate) had only a few minutes to prepare his wind-up. . . .

Macmillan went on to record how Gaitskell had 'made great use' of the Dulles statement that day to the effect that American ships would *not* shoot their way through the Canal:

and P.M. was a little rattled. So – in reply to interruption – he said 'We will take it to the Security Council.' There was a roar of applause from the Socialist benches; silence on the Tories, except of course from the Waverers – Heald, Walter Eliot, Boothby, etc. (Boothby, characteristically, made a fighting speech yesterday and was in full retreat today.) I thought that all was lost, and so it nearly was. Fortunately, P.M. stuck [to] the tougher form of words, which I had drafted for him, and which formed the concluding passage of the speech. These words – although logically contradictory to what he had just said – seemed to hold the field, and had an air of confidence and determination. . . .

Macmillan reckoned that if Gaitskell had then risen quietly and said that in view of the assurance given by – or rather dragged out of – Eden, he would not press the motion, 'he would have dealt P.M. and the Government a mortal blow. But he wasn't quick enough, and the division saved us.' After the debate, Macmillan 'comforted' Eden over his 'pardonable slip', but he was anxious about the press reaction: it would be 'very bad if the headlines are "Eden gives in".'[66]

Over the next two days the ambiguity over whether or not the government had pledged itself to go to the UN before recourse to action was more or less smoothed over – with the help of a firm hand from Macmillan. On the 15th, he again stated in his diary that it was 'absolutely vital to humiliate Nasser' and that 'we must do it quickly.' 'But we must (if we possibly can) keep the Americans with us, or we shall have no chance of getting out of our financial ruin. . . .'[67] The next day he was trying to reassure Eden, who 'seemed a bit depressed'. 'We are in a difficult position (particularly since we have no money). But we must have the courage to play the hand through. . . .'[68]

On 18 September, the eve of the establishment of SCUA, Macmillan and Dorothy dined at the American Embassy, where he and Salisbury 'did our best to convince Dulles of the need to take a very firm line. . . . It is vital that the Americans should not think that we are weakening, in spite of the Socialist Opposition and the other defeatist elements here.'[69] Macmillan was about to leave for a ten-day trip to the States, officially to attend a meeting of the International Monetary Fund, and on 20 September, just before his departure, Eden called a meeting about defence expenditure. Macmillan's increasing anxiety is clear from his diary: 'We are trying to achieve far too much – beyond our capacity.' After the meeting, Eden talked to him privately, confiding that the Chief Whip was reporting 'a good deal of trouble in the Party' and that the Tory group 'opposed to force . . . even as "a last resort" . . . might be large enough to put us in a minority in a division. P.M. seemed, however, quite determined. It was 1938 over again, and he could not be a party to it.'[70] It was briefly considered whether in the circumstances Macmillan should cancel his trip to Washington, but Eden agreed with Macmillan's point that it would be bad for 'confidence'. So that night Macmillan set off for the States, due to return on 1 October.

Macmillan in the States

Macmillan's first call in America was a sentimental one, and perhaps surprisingly leisurely, under the circumstances – a demonstration of 'unflappability'. He flew direct to the Midwest, to receive an honorary degree at the University of Indiana, and then to visit for the first time the little town of Spencer where his mother had been born and raised. At Spencer he found old people who remembered both his mother and grandfather, a veteran of the Civil War, and was invited to the Methodist church which they had once attended, to read the lesson and make an address:

> I found it rather difficult to get through, without breaking down, and I really felt that my mother was there watching us and enjoying the satisfaction of so many of her hopes and ambitions for me. When I remember all that I owe to her, it's difficult to know how to express what she did for me. It was a most moving ceremony and the people were extraordinarily kind and sympathetic.[71]

His purpose in the Midwest was not, however, entirely one of personal nostalgia. Joined by Roger Makins in Indianapolis, Macmillan gave a strong speech about Suez. After making the parallels to Hitler and Mussolini, the Rhineland, Munich and appeasement, Macmillan warned his American audience that, if Nasser's action went unchallenged,

> . . . 'The determination to seize other property – whether it be British-owned, American-owned, Dutch-owned or what you will – will be too great; and before we know where we are it may well be that the control of vital oil supplies, on which Western Europe at any rate must live, will be in the hands of powers which have in effect become satellites of Russia. . . .' I then declared in the most solemn terms that Nasser must not get away with it. I could not believe that Britain and America would allow him to do so.

His words, reported coast to coast, were directed at the President and the Secretary of State. Macmillan noted how the *Indianapolis Star* had run 'some really bad isolationist leaders, about "Colonialism" and all the rest'.[72] If in Indiana he received any soundings on US reactions to Suez, these would doubtless have been written off as exemplifying Midwest isolationism rather than US public sympathies as a whole. Flying back to Washington with Makins, Macmillan judged from telegrams sent by Eden that 'the situation on Suez is calming down a bit,' but he recorded once again, 'The state of our Reserves and the pressure on sterling make me very anxious.'[73] A grim telegram from Leslie Rowan at the Treasury also carried the warning that, even if Nasser did fall, confidence in sterling might not return – unless and until there was some joint action by the US and Britain to deal with the Middle East generally.[74] But still no specific action was counselled on the monetary front. At dinner on the 23rd with George Humphrey, Eisenhower's Secretary of the Treasury, Macmillan found him 'a most charming man' but 'not very easy to persuade of the realities of our economic position . . .'.[75]

On the morning of the 25th, Macmillan received a private invitation to visit Eisenhower at the White House. Although they had met at the Geneva Conference the previous year, when Macmillan was Foreign Secretary, it was the first time he had had the opportunity of a real talk with his old wartime chief since before D-Day, nearly twelve years previously. He was gratified – and very surprised – to find that Eisenhower seemed in such good health; in photographs he had appeared very old and tired. Macmillan wrote that 'his manner could not have been more cordial':

> He talked quite a bit about 'the grand old man' [Churchill] – for whom he has obviously both respect and real affection. On Suez, he was sure that we must get Nasser down. The only thing was, how to do it. I made it quite clear that we could *not* play it long, without aid on a very large scale – that is, if playing it long involved buying dollar oil.[76]

In what, given the gravity of the circumstances, seems like a curiously unfocused and banal conversation, Eisenhower then ranged over nuclear defence, Germany, the United Nations, Singapore, and finally came back to domestic politics: 'He was "mad" with some of his critics. They always said what had been done wrong in the past, or made wonderful promises for future. But they never said what ought to be done now. (That's why they were not making Suez a campaign point. Democrats had nothing to suggest.)' According to Macmillan's diaries, there was no further talk on *the* critical issue of the time. Eastern Europe or Hungary was not mentioned at all. Macmillan concluded by enthusing how it was 'really an exhilarating experience to see "Ike" again, and have such a good talk with him. He is a most delightful character, and I felt had retained (or perhaps regained) all his old simplicity. I found him easier than when he was in Geneva. . . .'

To the surprise of the White House aides, Eisenhower kept Macmillan for thirty-five minutes or more, and then 'expressed a hope that he might have another "chat" before I left', an option that was, however, never taken up. Before Macmillan and Makins were 'smuggled away' via the same side door by which they had entered, the President proudly showed Macmillan 'one of the advantages of the garden in the White House. It was a narrow "fairway" – but, outside the railings, there was a street lamp which he could aim at – about 270 yards. He could drive his ball at the lamp – but would not reach it.' With the world about to erupt in the worst crisis since 1945, it seemed a superbly incongruous parting.

Makins, who, on Macmillan's instructions, had sat quietly taking notes of the conversation, was 'astounded' by its omissions: '. . . I was expecting Harold to make a statement, say something important on Suez – but in fact he said nothing. I was very much surprised. Nor did Ike say anything. I was amazed. . . .'[77] On the American side, in a telephone call to Dulles, Eisenhower merely remarked that he had had 'a nice chat' with his old buddy, Macmillan.[78]

Yet it is clear that Macmillan persuaded himself that he had had an important and sympathetic exchange of views about Suez and Nasser, as he explained to the Prime Minister. In a 'Top Secret' report to Eden the next day, based on Makins's notes, Macmillan stated that he had 'formed certain very clear impressions' of his talk with the President, and then went on to harden the criticisms which, according to his diary account, Eisenhower had made about the United Nations:

> he had reached the view that the United Nations had destroyed the power of leadership of the great powers, that under cover of all these international agreements for peace small nations like Egypt could do the most outrageous things, and that he felt that the great powers – US, UK, France and Germany – should get together to maintain order, peace and justice, as well as mere absence of armed conflict. This, of course, is the old Concert of Europe in a new form.[79]

In his diaries, Macmillan reported Eisenhower saying simply: 'Why could not US, UK, Germany and France form a group and try to settle all these things ahead of time before they reached crisis stage. . . .' Reviving the Concert of Europe seems to have been far from anything Eisenhower ever had in mind, and it was more likely to have been distilled from that deep sense of history of Macmillan.

He continued to Eden (also somewhat strengthening the words he had used in his diary):

> The next feeling I had was that Ike is really determined, somehow or other, to bring Nasser down. I explained to him our economic difficulties in playing the hand long, and he seemed to understand. I also made it clear that we *must* win, or the whole structure of our economy would collapse. He accepted this. . . .

To Roger Makins, staunch admirer and old friend of Macmillan, this despatch (which he did not see at the time) represented a 'failure in communication'; from the dialogue at which he had been present, he could see 'no basis at all for Harold's optimism' about Eisenhower's support: 'yes, the Americans were willing to see Nasser put down, *but* what they would not contemplate were military operations – especially ahead of the election.'[80]

The effect that Macmillan's version of this crucial meeting – coming from the strong man of the Cabinet – was to have upon the feverish Eden, then just returning from Paris where the French had applied the strongest pressures to act without more delay, can hardly be exaggerated; and it was to be further reinforced by what Macmillan had to say in person on his return to London.

After his meeting with Eisenhower, Macmillan spent the rest of the morning at his scheduled meeting of the IMF, and in the afternoon he and Makins went to see Dulles at the State Department. In contrast to his earlier meeting at the White House, 'we dealt chiefly with Suez.'[81] With Makins and State Department officials present, Dulles began with an outburst of indignation at Eden's having gone to the UN without forewarning him and contrary to what had been agreed. He thought that 'we should get nothing but trouble in New York; we were courting disaster.' From the way that the pious Dulles spoke, said Macmillan, 'you would have thought he was warning us against entering a bawdy-house.' Recovering his temper, Dulles took Macmillan into a small room, for a private talk.

In his report to Eden,[82] Macmillan recorded how Dulles then spoke

> about different methods of getting rid of Nasser. He thought that these new plans [i.e. SCUA] might prove successful. But of course

they would take six months. I said that I did not think we could stand for six months. . . . Dulles then observed that he quite realised that we might have to act by force. Indeed, in his broadcast on his return [from London] he had made that clear. He thought that our threat of force was vital, whether we used it or not, to keep Nasser worried. . . .

On the other hand, Dulles – so Macmillan reported to Eden – went on to warn that, although Suez was not playing much part in the election at present, 'if anything happened it might have a disastrous effect. He reminded me of how he and the President had helped us in May 1955 by agreeing to the Four-Power meeting at top level, which had undoubtedly been of great benefit to us in our electoral troubles. Could we not do something in return and try to hold things off until after November 6th?' Coming from Dulles, for all his contradictory utterances, this could hardly have been a more direct hint, and Macmillan in his memoirs admitted, 'Perhaps I should have attached greater weight to the date of the Presidential Election.'

When Macmillan stressed to Dulles the great financial strain which Britain was currently suffering, and pleaded for relaxation of the terms of the outstanding post-war loan, Dulles made it plain that nothing could be done until *after* the presidential election. This theme was replayed in a long session subsequently with Secretary of the Treasury Humphrey, who, Macmillan reported to Eden, 'has such a jaunty, amiable way of expressing himself that I found it difficult to estimate what was the real purpose of the talk'. Suez was never mentioned directly, from which Macmillan wrongly deduced that Humphrey 'had no very strong feelings about it. In this I was soon to be proved tragically wrong.'

For once, the highly sensitive antennae of Macmillan let him down; as the deadly month of October began, the British Cabinet Minister with whom both Dulles and Eisenhower could communicate most easily was not properly tuned in. Much as he loved and respected Eisenhower, Macmillan was often among the many to mock gently the presidential gaffes and relaxed style of government. In April he had written in his diary: 'Poor Ike! He holds these conferences . . . makes great pronouncements (often confused), and then leaves for a holiday. Unkind American commentators are calculating that his golfing holidays amount to 150 days or so out of the year! . . .'[83] Within two decades of Eisenhower leaving office, however, a revised view of the General as President emerged, from which it was clear that 'Ike', in his first term at any rate, was a more active President than the golfing images suggested, and that it was he, not John Foster Dulles or even the Secretary of State's brother, Allen Dulles, the powerful CIA chief, who called the shots at Suez. Over the Eisenhower years, the world – via the media – was probably misled by the garbled syntax of his press conferences into ignoring the articulateness of his orders as a Commander-in-Chief, and his letters. The key letters to Eden from Eisenhower during the Suez crisis were all drafted personally, and it perhaps typified the breakdown in the 'special relationship' when (on receiving Eisenhower's particularly important letter of 8 September) Eden was heard to snap acidly: 'The only thing that's true to Ike in that is his signature and that's illegible.'[84] But that letter was in fact as true to Ike as his policy over Suez was, while the small print was Dulles's. The tragedy was that, as in other presidential election years, there was no coherent US strategy for the Middle East.

History may remain harder on Dulles over Suez; certainly he infuriated all his British interlocutors, among them Macmillan, by his ambivalence and apparent duplicity – and not without reason. By appearing to blow hot and cold, he did a great disservice to the 'special relationship'; it gave Eden in his turn the excuse to be equally deceitful with Dulles, and through him the US. Yet if Dulles's tactics seemed slippery and devious, his purpose all along was pretty clear: to spin out talks so as to remove any basis for France and Britain using force – and this was on Eisenhower's explicit instruction. Eisenhower's motivation was simple; he had first been elected as the 'Peace' President during the Korean War in 1952, and he wanted to be re-elected in November 1956 on the same platform; but foremost was his constant nagging fear that action against Egypt, either backed by the US or with its tacit consent, would alienate the entire Arab world and incite it to call in the Soviets. Even with minimum hindsight, Eisenhower on almost every occasion in his correspondence with Eden had made his opposition to force unmistakable.

While in America, perhaps misled by US public comment and the views he picked up privately which called for British action against Nasser, Macmillan persuaded himself that they also represented Eisenhower's real position. Quite possibly, too, he had let himself be deceived by the somewhat arrogant general view of Americans that Richard Crossman had recorded back in Algiers in the Second World War, namely that, in principle, the American 'Romans' would do whatever the British 'Greeks' thought best. What was not clear to Macmillan when he flew back from Washington was just how far Eisenhower might be prepared to go to back up his disapproval. Certainly he *never* thought that his old friend would go to the point of applying sanctions against America's two closest allies – and he was not alone.

Breaking Point

On 1 October, Macmillan returned to London, tired but evidently reassured by what he had heard in the States. The following morning he reported to Eden, staying with him till nearly lunchtime. Eden was so encouraged by the discussion between Macmillan and the President that he promptly reopened their correspondence, to enclose an ugly letter from Bulganin, and returning to the theme that Nasser 'whether he likes it or not, is now effectively in Russian hands, just as Mussolini was in Hitler's . . .'.[85] But the next day, when SCUA was formally established, Dulles made an electrifying remark at a press conference: 'There is talk about teeth being pulled out of the plan, but I know of no teeth in it, so far as I am aware.'[86] In the words of Macmillan, this was 'a sentence calculated to destroy his own child'. Thereafter SCUA, Dulles's last delaying action, slid gently into oblivion, overtaken by other events.

Early in the crisis Eden had seized on a remark made to him by Dulles that 'a way must be found to make Nasser disgorge what he is attempting to swallow', and he held to this as a clear US endorsement of an Anglo-French resort to force. Murphy, however, dismissed this as a throw-away remark 'to be taken with a warehouse full of salt'.[87] Nevertheless, Dulles's statement of 2 October appears to have had a decisive impact on Eden, who now abandoned any hope of American support to make Nasser disgorge. If one may accept the account of Selwyn Lloyd's Junior Minister, Anthony Nutting, Eden flew into a rage, exclaiming, 'Now what have you got to say for your American friends. . . !' This was the 'breaking point', according to Nutting:

as the Dulles statement passed from hand to hand round the Cabinet table I could see that the last chance of retrieving an Anglo-American understanding had been lost and as the meeting broke up, I knew that henceforth Eden would be able to count on the overwhelming majority of his government for settling the issue by force irrespective of what the Americans might say. Dulles had provided him with an alibi which no member of his Cabinet was going to challenge.[88]

Eden himself seemed physically close to 'breaking point'. Three days later he was admitted to hospital with a temperature of 106°, and stayed there for three days. At various times during the Suez crisis his close colleagues went so far as to claim that Eden was 'intoxicated with drugs', or 'quite simply mad'. These allegations have always been sharply rebutted by his devotedly loyal widow, Clarissa, but there is no doubt that he was ill from a recurrence of his bile-duct problems, and little doubt that this impaired his judgement. It now seems that the doctors fed him alternately with amphetamines (which were not then recognised as possessing such potent side-effects), and with tranquillisers. Together, these medicaments could well account for the sudden alternations in Eden's moods during Suez, from feverish tantrums to bouts of almost unnatural calm.

Meanwhile (and the dates become increasingly significant), Britain and France on 23 September had at last brought a case against Egypt's 'unilateral action' before the UN Security Council. Dulles, with his lawyer's mind, had persuaded himself that the Anglo-French case was weak, and felt aggrieved that he had not been consulted in advance. The debate at the UN would drag on until 13 October, when the key resolution received a majority of 9–2, but the USSR interposed her veto. However you looked at it, the UN resolution, calling for 'free and open transit of the Canal' and respect for the sovereignty of Egypt, was a fairly anodyne affair. In the unadorned words of the *Annual Register*: 'The Security Council was thus relieved of the obligation to take any further steps in the matter and Egypt relieved of the obligation to pay any attention to the views of the majority.' Later in October, Fawzi, the Egyptian Foreign Minister, came forward with a new initiative, suggesting a meeting in Geneva. The historical parallels seem not dissimilar to Argentina's last-minute diplomatic moves in 1982. Nutting, among others, remains convinced that a compromise agreement was then within reach and Egypt was on the verge of climbing down. In what was virtually his last word, Selwyn Lloyd, however, designates this 'absolute nonsense'.[89] Whatever the truth, the UN resolution marked in effect the end of peaceful ploys by the British and French.

During all this time of talks, the military build-up had continued steadily, yet Nasser's behaviour had remained so exemplary as to provide no further pretext for armed intervention by Britain and France. British concern about a 'pretext' had been expressed in a personal letter to Macmillan, scribbled in the back of a car by Salisbury on 22 August. Salisbury, though every inch a hawk, said discouragingly that he had been through the Charter of the United Nations and had 'found very little in it that would seem to justify the use of forceful methods by a Member State until all the means enumerated in the machinery of the United Nations have first been tried . . .'. His exploration of all possibilities he found 'rather depressing'; 'It must, I feel, now be for the F.O. to produce one [i.e. some provocation] which is likely to exasperate Nasser to such an extent that he does something that gives us an excuse for marching in, either for the protection of the Canal and its employees or of British lives and property.'[90]

Neither the Foreign Office in its ingenuity nor Nasser had obliged; and a month later, Monckton, on being shown the latest plan, was heard to remark, lugubriously, 'Very interesting, but how do we actually start this war?'[91] Like Dulles, and Selwyn Lloyd, Monckton was a lawyer, and was now one of the foremost doubters about resort to force over Suez. Eden remained set on taking action to 'topple' Nasser, and it was still clear to others in the Cabinet – except, in varying degree, the 'waverers' or (in more modern parlance) 'wets' – that only force would make Nasser disgorge. But time was running out; the military were soon warning that, for operational as well as psychological reasons, Musketeer Revise could not be postponed, yet again, beyond the end of October. Then, on 3 October, the day after Dulles's devastating remark about 'no teeth', and two days before Eden's admission to hospital, Eden informed ministers: 'The Jews have come up with an offer.'

Since July, both in number and gravity Fedayeen terrorist attacks on Israel from Syria, Jordan and Egypt had been escalating, and Israel was now effectively blockaded in the Gulf of Aqaba as well as the Suez Canal. Her retaliations had grown more ferocious and there was serious talk about a major pre-emptive attack such as was to be launched by Israel against Egypt in 1967. If Israel were to attack Jordan, Britain was committed by treaty to the support of young King Hussein; and, indeed, up to the last days of October there still existed contingency plans in the War Office for British action against Israel.

Already in August the French and Israelis had begun exchanging discreet hints about concerting an attack on Egypt. In the first week in September, at French request, the Chief of Operations to General Dayan (then the Israeli Chief of Staff) flew to Paris to discuss a joint operation in detail. On the 24th, Mollet's defence advisers recommended action even if France had to act alone – on the assumption that Britain would then inevitably be compelled to join in. Two days later Eden and Selwyn Lloyd flew to Paris for overnight talks with Mollet and Pineau – 'to concert our tactics' in the words of Selwyn Lloyd.[92] From Paris, Eden reported to Butler, acting PM in his absence: 'My own feeling is that the French, particularly Pineau, are in the mood to blame everyone including us if military action is not taken before the end of October.'[93]

It is evident that the French did not then inform Eden about the growing collaboration with the Israelis, who were sceptical (and, indeed, always mistrustful) about the scope of the British involvement. Three days later an Israeli team headed by Dayan himself and Foreign Minister Golda Meir came secretly to Paris for two days, and got down to detailed planning. Chief among Israeli priorities was a commitment that the allies should provide some defence against Egyptian bombers, otherwise their cities could be devastated by Nasser's superior airforce. By the beginning of October, Franco-Israeli plans were far enough advanced for the French to bring the British in on the act, thus enabling Eden to inform his Cabinet of the 'Offer'.

In his memoirs, Macmillan stated simply that 'no event of great importance took place' during his absence in America; yet, given those crucial meetings in Paris, this could hardly have been less accurate. Although it was Macmillan who had first proposed the notion of bringing in Israel, which had so shocked Eden at the beginning of August, he appears to have received from Eden only the sketchiest information about these transactions, both while in Washington and on his return. Nor did he evidently enquire too deeply – wrapped up as he now was in his (to some extent self-spun) cocoon at the Treasury.

Macmillan's diary for 1956 ends on 4 October, and in the unprecedentedly brief final entry, he gave no details of the Cabinet discussions on Suez: 'Meanwhile, our anxieties are not growing less. The Suez situation is beginning to slip out of our hands. Nothing can now be done till the U.N. exercise is over. But by then the difficulty of "resort to force" will be greater.' He tried his best to dispel his own nagging doubts that, as in the Chamberlain days of the Second World War, Britain had 'missed the bus':

> if we have, it is really due to the long time it has taken to get military arrangements into shape. But we *must*, by one means or another, win this struggle. Nasser may well try to preach Holy War in the Middle East and (even to their own loss) the mob and the demagogues may create a ruinous position for us. *Without oil, and without the profits from oil*, neither U.K. nor Western Europe can survive.[94]

On 3 October, still shaken by Dulles's statement of the previous day, most of the Cabinet had little difficulty in accepting Eden's bombshell about Israel. From this decisive Cabinet meeting now logically followed the critical decision that Britain would act – without the Americans.

It was from 3 October that 'collusion' slipped into forward gear, and with it began an extraordinary silence in the British records. According to Anthony Head, who succeeded Monckton as Minister of Defence later in October and who was perhaps one of the few totally forthright witnesses on Suez, four Cabinet meetings dealing with 'collusion' were held without minutes; 'and it was very much on Eden's orders'.[95] There were, it seems, various meetings not involving the full Cabinet at which the Secretaries were asked to withdraw, or take no minutes, or following which minutes were destroyed. Anthony Nutting of the Foreign Office was quite clear that 'no records were kept, at least on the British side, of the discussions between Britain, France and Israel.'[96]

Macmillan's own reticence over Suez was, he always claimed, 'for Anthony's sake'; speaking of his published memoirs, he said that 'Anthony didn't give the whole story . . . therefore I didn't. It would have been bad manners of me to have produced the book in his lifetime, really contradicting or so adding to his story as to make his own volume seem rather . . . cheap. Therefore I gave all that I could without going into the details of the French and the Israelis.'[97]

Macmillan's diaries do not exist for the period from 4 October 1956 to 3 February 1957, when the entry explains that the events of the previous months had begun 'to move at such a speed and with such a pressure upon us all, that I was not able to keep up the diary. I mislaid the volume which began somewhere about the beginning of October – and was then caught up by the number of meetings which followed the Party Conference at Llandudno. . . .'[98] Many years later, he finally admitted that what he had written he had destroyed, and then discontinued the rest – at the specific request of Eden. The nearest he would come to an explanation was to say 'I thought it dangerous. . . . It was like the First War. When you went up to the front, as opposed to preparing behind lines, you stop keeping a diary. And in October we went into the operational stage. . . .'[99] Both veterans of the same war, it was clear that Macmillan and Eden had no difficulty in sharing the same understanding here.

But although Macmillan knew the Israeli–Franco–British 'collusion' plan in broad outline, and would afterwards never reveal the full extent of his knowledge, the details were also kept from him, as they were from other members of the Egypt Committee. Even the new Director of MI6, Dick White, was not fully informed, although his organisation was responsible for secret communications with Israel. When eventually briefed by Selwyn Lloyd, at a secret Cabinet meeting, on the final plans for Suez, White exclaimed, 'That's all a pretty tall order!'[100] On top of that, the French and Israelis made sure that the British partner knew no more than was necessary. All this secrecy would inevitably help shape the reactions of an open society like Eisenhower's America.

On 11 October Roger Makins was recalled from Washington to take up the top position at the Treasury in London, and until 8 November Britain had no ambassador in Washington. It seems an extraordinary error to have made at this key period, especially as Makins was a wartime colleague of both Eisenhower and Macmillan, and could have provided an inestimably valuable communication bridge between Eisenhower and Macmillan. On the other hand, Makins was in no doubt that, had he remained, he would have been forced to resign in the light of what transpired. His withdrawal marked the beginning of the active deception of the United States; the rapid shelving of a decade and a half of joint consultation, sharing of intelligence, the pooling of resources against a common enemy – in fact everything beneficial to both countries that was implicit in the 'special relationship'.

Having just given, as his last engagement in the States, a thoroughly optimistic speech suggesting that things were going to turn out all right, when he returned to London in mid-October Makins recalled his total mystification that 'absolutely nobody wanted to see me. . . . I couldn't understand why. Selwyn didn't want to see me – Anthony didn't want to see me – even Harold – who had after all called me back to be his "Joint Permanent Secretary of the Treasury"; I knew absolutely nothing, was told absolutely nothing, but I knew enough to realise that something very big was in the wind.'[101]

The Challe Mission

Sunday, 14 October, was President Eisenhower's sixty-sixth birthday, and he received a telegram from Eden declaring, 'Our friendship remains one of my greatest rewards . . .'; to which Eisenhower replied, rather more meaningfully: 'I know that nothing can ever seriously mar either our personal friendship or the respect that our governments and peoples have for each other.'[102]

It was also the day that – following a standing ovation for his tough talk at the Llandudno Party Conference – Eden had a surprise visit at Chequers from Albert Gazier, French Minister of Labour and a close confidant of Mollet, and General Maurice Challe, an airman of brilliance, distinction and integrity, who had won the DSO for smuggling out the Luftwaffe order-of-battle to Britain on the eve of D-Day. The plan they produced seems to have been Challe's own brainchild: the Israelis would attack across Sinai, and then Britain and France would call on 'both sides' to withdraw from the threatened Canal; if Nasser refused, as he surely would, the Anglo-French invasion force would interpose itself between the two belligerents, and the Suez Canal would be once again safely in their hands. Challe recalled that Eden was 'delighted' at the plan, and with Israel providing the 'pretext' he had been seeking.[103]

On the British side, apart from Eden, the Chequers meeting was attended only by Anthony Nutting and Guy Millard of the Foreign Office. According to Nutting, Eden requested that no notes be kept – thereby setting a principle of some consequence.[104] In the first instance, total secrecy was the Israelis' request; but they were the first to breach it. Later in the month, at the secret Sèvres meeting that formalised the collusion packet, the representatives of the three countries 'swore that none would in the lifetime of the others reveal what they had discussed'.[105] This almost boy-scout pledge was rigorously respected, if not by the others, certainly by the British principals – to the disappointment of historians and journalists when the Public Record Office files were finally opened in 1987.

Nutting was appalled by Eden's spontaneous enthusiasm for the Challe plan. Discussing it with Ivone Kirkpatrick the following day, he found that even he 'felt that it was a crazy idea. Never one to trust the French, he said that they would be certain to let us down. . . .'[106] At first, claims Nutting, Selwyn Lloyd appeared to support him, but was later swung round by Eden. When Nutting tried to see Selwyn Lloyd on the 22nd, he was told he had a 'bad cold'; in fact Selwyn Lloyd had been to the key conference at Sèvres. All that appeared in the Cabinet minutes of this historic meeting was: 'From secret conversations which had been held in Paris with representatives of the Israeli Government it now appeared that the Israelis would not alone launch a full-scale attack on Egypt. . . .'[107] Nevertheless, a written 'protocol' had been drawn up at Sèvres; a 'smoking gun' which Eden, enraged, sent Patrick Dean of the Foreign Office back to recover – without success.[108] On Selwyn Lloyd's return from Sèvres, Nutting warned that he would resign rather than be a party 'to this sordid conspiracy'. Monckton had already resigned as Minister of Defence the previous week; though he had loyally given 'health problems' as his official reason, and had agreed to another job within the Cabinet so as not to damage the government.

According to Eden's biographer, Rhodes James, Dean reported on Sèvres to a special meeting held at Downing Street at 11 p.m. on 24 October. Together with Eden, those present were Butler, Macmillan, Anthony Head, who had just succeeded Monckton, and Mountbatten. It was then agreed that the plan would be recommended to the full Cabinet on the following day. 'Although Macmillan wholeheartedly supported virtually any means of bringing Nasser down, Eden did not confide in him any more than he did in Butler, who was loyal, but doubtful and distant. . . .' Contrary to what he alleged later, Mountbatten 'willingly assented'.[109] Butler, too, went along unprotesting, even though his heart was never in the enterprise and he maintained to his official biographer that he had known nothing of the 'arrangements' made at Sèvres until afterwards.[110] 'The way Rab has turned and trimmed!' exclaimed William Clark, Eden's press adviser.[111] The trimming helped to lose Rab the premiership.

Nutting recorded in his book how on 24 October 'the Cabinet met in full to take the fateful decision about going in on the backs of the Israelis'; and he continued, in a passage expurgated under pressure from the Cabinet Secretariat: 'Such had been the secrecy of the discussions up to this point that for at least one half of its members, this was the first they had heard of what was afoot.' Hence, 'the matter was held over until the next day. . . .'[112]

Although Macmillan afterwards admitted that it was a 'bad plan', he had no qualms in supporting it at the time; it was the only plan of action available and he was the one who had consistently clamoured for action. Moreover, he had been the first to advocate bringing in the Israelis two months previously. He remarked much later: 'The plan of October 25th sounded alright, especially to a harassed Cabinet. . . . Collusion would not have been disreputable if Anthony hadn't said it wasn't true. . . .'[113]

On an unspecified date before the decisive Cabinet meeting of 24/25 October, William Clark recalled an important conversation at No. 10 between Eden, Selwyn Lloyd and Macmillan:

. . . H.M. casually remarked to Eden, 'I had a few words with Ike. Of course he's an ill man, but as brave as ever. . . . of course you saw the President too, didn't you, Selwyn?' This was very putting down of Selwyn for whom H.M. had total contempt, as being nothing more than 'Deputy Foreign Secretary to the Prime Minister'. Selwyn, blushing, replied 'No'; thus H.M. was very much one-up. He went on about the intransigence of Dulles – then H.M. came in, strong – 'I don't think there is going to be any trouble from Ike – he and I understand each other – he's not going to make any real trouble if we have to do something drastic.'

This reinforced the thought that was always in Eden's mind that Dulles was the enemy, and that he was not representative of American opinion.

Clark considered that the effect of this somewhat casual remark of Macmillan's upon Eden was 'very fundamental', as was the 'squashing' of Selwyn Lloyd – who was in fact 'more accurate in interpreting the American attitude' than Macmillan with the conviction he had brought back with him from America on 1 October that 'Ike will lie doggo until after the election.' Clark (who, it should be noted, was very disaffected and subsequently resigned in opposition to Eden's policy) also claimed that Macmillan made a fairly clear threat of resignation if Britain did not now go ahead with the military action.[114] Macmillan himself, however, consistently denied that he threatened to resign, either then or later when urging the necessity to halt the operation.

On 28 October, Macmillan summoned Roger Makins to tell him that 'now that the invasion fleet had already left, he could tell me what was happening. . . . He was like a man come out of a trance. . . . I think a lot of it was because of his curious fixation that he *had* to be loyal to Eden, because of the prickliness of the past.' Makins was staggered that the operation could not have been delayed those few days until after the American election, and asked Macmillan what he was going to say to the Americans. 'But he simply hadn't thought about the Americans. . . . I think I did give him a jolt by telling him what Suez would do to Anglo-American relations. . . .'[115] But why had Eisenhower not tried to get in touch with Macmillan, his closest contact in the Eden government?

The secrecy imposed by Eden proved all too successful in deceiving her ally, America. On 18 October Dulles had telephoned his brother Allen, head of the CIA, saying that he was worried about what might be going on in the Near East; he did not think 'we have any clear picture as to what the British and French are up to there. . . . they are deliberately keeping us in the dark.' He wondered if Allen had any real feel of it.[116] It was evident that Allen Dulles did not. Meanwhile intelligence provided by flights of the new U–2 spy plane seemed to indicate that Israel was mobilising against Jordan, not Egypt. In Paris, an important tip was leaked to the American Ambassador, Douglas Dillon, by a French politician, Jacques

Chaban-Delmas, during the last part of October. The information gave accurate details of impending Anglo–French–Israeli action, but (for reasons that remain unclear) the wrong date; i.e. that it would not take place until *after* the US elections in November. According to Dillon's subsequent testimony, the British when questioned, however, 'absolutely denied that there was any such thing in the wind. And for one reason or another I think our people were rather inclined here to believe the British over the French at that time.'[117]

Thus American intelligence was effectively thrown off the track; perhaps as much by the very confusion of the Franco-British planning itself as by the deliberate deception plans. In London, CIA representatives picked up vital hints; but evidence suggests that the CIA, not for the last time, was playing its own independent game. It was preoccupied with the anti-Soviet revolt building up in Hungary, while sympathies with the Franco-British design to 'destabilise' Nasser inhibited it from passing back to the White House everything it knew. After it was all over, a revealing telephone call between the two Dulles brothers (dated 15 May 1957) disclosed a CIA post-mortem on its performance at Suez: 'They agreed we knew about the military build-up. *A* [Allen Dulles] said the intelligence people in Britain told him they did not know about it. The Sec. said you can't expect the impossible – you can't read people's minds. . . .'[118] On Allen Dulles's recommendation, the post-mortem was discreetly dropped.

Until the last minute, in much the same way as the Anglo-American intelligence had fooled Hitler with their deception schemes preceding D-Day, Israeli and British 'disinformation', working separately, seems to have succeeded remarkably well in persuading Washington that Jordan, not Egypt, was the prime target of Israeli mobilisation. On 26 October, the CIA's veteran operative, James Angleton, renowned for his close contacts with the Israeli Mossad Secret Service, reported: '. . . I spent the last evening and most of the early hours with my Israeli friends in Washington, and I can assure you that it is all part of manoeuvres and is certainly not meant for any serious attack. There is nothing in it. . . .'[119]

Was this deception, or self-deception? The very success, however, of this disinformation would work against British interests when the crisis came, in terms of the rage it provoked in the Oval Office. And, at the heart of it all, was the fundamental failure of the Eden government to comprehend how Eisenhower would react, the responsibility for which rested heavily on Macmillan's shoulders and the messages he had brought back from Washington at the beginning of October.

Hungary Erupts; Action at Last

From the third week in October events assumed an even more rapid, and sinister, cadence. In Eastern Europe, on the 21st, Gomulka took power in Poland after a wave of anti-Soviet riots; a few days later Hungary erupted in a full-scale uprising against Communist domination. In America particularly, where there was weighty commitment to the Hungarian cause, thoughts and emotions were distracted from the Middle East. For two heady weeks hopes ran high that at least one East European country might shake off the Soviet yoke. John Foster Dulles and his brother Allen were heavily committed, but the Secretary of State spoke with the voice of Eisenhower when, on 27 October, he declared that 'the weakness of Soviet imperialism is being made manifest'.

That was the day Eisenhower, at the peak of his whistle-stop election campaign, heard the news of Israel's full-scale mobilisation. From Dallas he signalled Ben Gurion, urging him 'to do nothing to endanger the peace'.[120] Nevertheless, on the 29th, in accordance with the plan hatched at Sèvres, Israel invaded Sinai. Hastening back to Washington from an election meeting in Richmond, Virginia, an enraged Eisenhower summoned the US military and intelligence leaders and (according to Townsend Hoopes) 'ordered Dulles to let Ben Gurion have it with both barrels: "All right, Foster, you tell 'em that, God damn it, we're going to apply sanctions, we're going to the United Nations, we're going to do everything that there is so we can stop this thing. . . ."'[121]

The next day began the climactic week, with Britain and France issuing their ultimatum to Egypt and Israel. The British ambassadors in neither Cairo nor Tel Aviv had been warned in advance of what was afoot. As anticipated, Nasser rejected the ultimatum; Israel accepted it, but kept on moving. On the 31st Britain opened the five-day softening-up bombardment of Egyptian airfields and defence installations, while the ponderous Musketeer Revise armada sailed from Malta. In the House of Commons that day Selwyn Lloyd declared that there had been 'no prior agreement' between

Britain and Israel over the attack, and continued: 'It is, of course, true that the Israeli mobilisation gave some advance warning and we urged restraint upon the Israeli government. . . .' Anthony Nutting commented that 'it would be hard to find in the annals of parliament a more disingenuous pronouncement by a minister of the crown.' That day Nutting resigned, although, as he claimed, Macmillan had done his best to exhort him to remain silent, telling him 'you will lead the party one day.'[122]

In the subsequent vote of confidence, Eden won on straight party lines with 270 votes to 218. (In France, Mollet did rather better with 368 to 182, including 149 Communists.) British public opinion polls showed that 37 per cent of those questioned thought the British action was right, 44 per cent wrong, and 19 per cent did not know. When Eisenhower heard of the vote in the Commons, his comment was: 'I could not dream of committing this nation on such a vote.' According to Hugh Thomas, however, once the operation had actually begun, Eden became 'almost boyish, reminiscent of a young officer in the First World War, very calm, very polite, the captain of the first eleven in a cricket match', while his Chancellor was like the 'young Macmillan of the thirties again, hat thrown in the air'.[123]

As far as Macmillan was concerned, however, the reality was somewhat different. The government papers published in 1987 disclosed that, at the Cabinet meeting of 30 October, he had issued an explicit Treasury warning on the position of sterling: 'Our reserves of gold and dollars were still falling at a dangerously rapid rate; and in view of the extent to which we might have to rely on American economic assistance we could not afford to alienate the US Government more than was absolutely necessary. . . .'[124] Though still a hawk, Macmillan was showing that his hawkishness was already becoming modified by reality. The Cabinet was deeply concerned at having got so far out of step with America, yet it chose to ignore Macmillan's warning – delphic as the words 'absolutely necessary' may doubtless have seemed at the time.

Eisenhower Reacts

The lack of comprehension on the part of both the White House and State Department remains astonishing. Right up to the moment when the British bombing began, Eisenhower seems to have been deceived about the true Anglo-French intentions, and expressed faith in what the British position would be. On hearing of the Franco-British twelve-hour ultimatum on the 30th, Dulles told Eisenhower he thought it 'about as crude and brutal as anything he has ever seen'; Eisenhower agreed 'it was pretty rough'.[125] According to 'Scottie' Reston of the *New York Times*, probably the best-informed and accurate American political journalist of the time, 'When Eisenhower first heard of the ultimatum the White House crackled with barrack-room language the kind of which had not been heard since the days of General Grant.'[126] Yet later that same evening Eisenhower was apparently still hopeful enough to tell his speechwriter, Emmet Hughes, that he thought the problem 'will take care of itself if the Israelis stop fighting, and I'm sure they will, with this ultimatum from the British . . .'.[127] He could hardly have expressed a greater misconception of British intent.

Underlying the sternness of Eisenhower's reaction were three pragmatic factors: he did not want the US to be seen in the eyes of the Arab world as being in any way associated with the Israeli attack; he (and, more pronouncedly, the Dulles brothers) deplored the effect that the distraction of Suez might have on policy over Hungary, now in flames; and, as noted earlier, he wanted to be re-elected as the President of peace – and honour – who would not support war in the Middle East. But there was also a strongly personal element in Eisenhower's sense of affront. There was, to begin with, what looked like calculated rudeness on Eden's part in issuing the ultimatum without notification to Washington properly in advance. (Tory Party apologists for Eden later claimed that this was partly caused by the Foreign Office cipher lines being jammed.)[128] Once the rage provoked by the initial shock had passed, Eisenhower (who had always had a low boiling point) passed through stages of cold anger to a bitter sense of betrayal by Britain. 'I just cannot believe Britain would be dragged into this,' Eisenhower had remarked to Dulles before the British ultimatum, and – more explicitly – he wrote to his old friend, 'Swede' Hazlett, three days later:

> . . . I think that France and Britain have made a terrible mistake. . . . France was perfectly cold-blooded about the matter. She has a war on her hands in Algeria. . . . But I think the other two countries have hurt themselves immeasurably and this is

something of a sad blow because, quite naturally, Britain not only has been, but must be, our best friend in the world.[129]

Here was, in effect, the voice of the Anglo-Saxon warlord of the 1940s, still regarding the French as a liberated, client state, a 'lesser breed' of whom better behaviour could not be expected. Yet, while the French had actually told America *something* of what was afoot, the British had lied through their teeth and set out deliberately to deceive their closest ally. Roger Makins, with his knowledge of the wartime Eisenhower, and noting the information that Eisenhower had received via the CIA, reckoned that 'what he hated was having it concealed by his old friend'.[130] Matters might perhaps have taken a different course had the British only shown greater sensitivity. As it was, Eisenhower in his riposte specifically struck out at Britain, singling out the Achilles heel of Britain's reserves.

On 2 November an American resolution demanding a ceasefire was passed at the UN by an overwhelming majority of 64 to 5. For the first time in UN history, the USA combined with the Russians in voting against her two principal allies, Britain and France. The following day Dulles 'was rushed to hospital for an emergency operation on the abdominal cancer that would eventually kill him. Suddenly, on the verge of the elections, Eisenhower found himself alone in command of US foreign policy. On 4 November the Russians sent in four thousand Russian tanks to crush the Hungarian uprising with utmost brutality; hours later, hands still red with Hungarian blood, Bulganin cynically despatched to Eden and Mollet threats of an 'immediate resort to force to restore the situation in the Middle East', coupled with a crudely worded menace of rockets on London and Paris.

Only the previous day the warning had come through to London that the US was contemplating oil sanctions against her allies. According to Selwyn Lloyd, at the second meeting of the Egypt Committee held that day, 'Macmillan threw his arms in the air and said, "Oil sanctions! That finishes it." '[131] It was then decided to convene the whole Cabinet, at which it was agreed – after some dissent – that the landings, scheduled for the next day, would have to go ahead regardless. On the 5th, the first of 13,500 British and 8500 French troops landed at Port Said. There was some fierce opposition, but by the following day the invasion was well on its way down the Canal towards Suez. Spearheaded by a dashing young colonel called Ariel Sharon, however, the Israeli vanguard had characteristically exceeded its orders so that their forces had already reached their objectives near the Canal, and halted, four days before the Franco-British arrived – thus making a further nonsense of the Eden pretext of 'putting out the fire'.

On 6 November, Eisenhower's unyielding stand over Suez did not stop him winning an overwhelming re-election victory, carrying forty-one states (including New York with its influential Jewish vote). Pressures on London to call a halt reached their peak. When the full significance of Eisenhower's reaction was appraised in London that morning, Eden, Salisbury, Selwyn Lloyd, Head and several other hawks in the Cabinet were for persisting with the military operation, until Suez itself had been reached, notwithstanding. But it was Macmillan who decided the issue. He told the Cabinet that there had been a serious run on the pound, viciously orchestrated in Washington. Britain's gold reserves, he announced, had fallen by £100 million over the past week – or by *one-eighth* of their remaining total. His young Economic Secretary, Edward Boyle, had just resigned in distress at the military operation. Telephoning Washington and then New York, Macmillan was told that only a ceasefire by midnight would secure US support for an International Monetary Fund loan to prop up the pound. Secretary of the Treasury Humphrey, whom he had found so 'amiable' in Washington in September, was leading the pack against Britain. Macmillan is then alleged to have warned the Cabinet that, unless there were a ceasefire, he could no longer 'be responsible for Her Majesty's Government'[132] (though Macmillan himself always vigorously denied this – 'it was not my style').[133] At 5 p.m. on 6 November, in the teeth of strong French opposition, the allied high command gave the order to cease fire.

'Leader of the Bolters': Why?

Macmillan's intervention earned for him a harsh variety of slings and arrows both then and afterwards. His perpetual critic, Brendan Bracken, commented to Lord Beaverbrook:

> Until a week ago, Macmillan, whose bellicosity was beyond description, was wanting to tear Nasser's scalp off with his own finger-nails. He was like that character in O'Casey's play:

'Let me like a hero fall,
   My breast expanding to the ball.'
Today he might be described as the leader of the bolters. His
Treasury officials have put before him the economic consequences
of the Suez fiasco and his feet are frostbitten. . . .[134]

At almost every stage in the decisions taken by the Eden government over Suez, Macmillan had been a key figure, if not *the* key
figure. Within the Party, and indeed within the family, he had
throughout been influenced more by his forcefully right-wing son-
in-law, Julian Amery, a key figure in the 'Suez Group', than by his
more liberal son, Maurice. Within the Cabinet, he had instinctively
gravitated towards the hawkish constellation around Salisbury,
rather than to the moderate intellectualism of his old colleague in
opposition, Rab Butler. At about the time of Suez, a former Tory
MP recalled Macmillan remarking to him that all political leaders
'have to be either warriors or cardinals'.[135] In contrast to Butler,
whom he always relished seeing in the guise of a conspiring cardinal,
Macmillan regarded himself essentially as a warrior, and – as at
other times in his life – at Suez it was the swordsman that burst to
the surface, only to be replaced by the more prudent cardinal figure
when it suddenly appeared, on 6 November, that the accepted
course of action was confronting disaster.

What, then, was the motivation that caused him to swing from
being warrior to cardinal, from super-hawk to super-dove, at Suez
– or, in the cutting and oft-repeated comment of Harold Wilson,
'first in, first out'? Macmillan's own supporters and closest colleagues in the government at that time were equally baffled by
his sudden change of heart; many have remained so ever since.
Monckton's successor as Minister of Defence, Anthony Head, who
– as a dashing former cavalryman – combined something of the
vernacular of the stable with rare forthrightness over Suez, thought
that halting at Port Said was 'like going through all the preliminaries
without having an orgasm!' To him, Macmillan's switch was 'the
one thing he could not understand about Suez':

I could never believe it was just the US threat to withdraw money
from us. It wasn't naked ambition, though if you had a nasty
mind, you might have thought so. I didn't. And the 'fire was out'
excuse must have been likely to be untenable before the operation

actually began. . . . It's the big mystery. . . . But Harold was
very strong in his warning of what the US would do . . . he put
the fear of God into the Cabinet on finances, as Chancellor. The
Treasury must have got at him, from every direction . . . but I
simply could not believe that the US could wreck us, or would
want to wreck us, in two days. . . .[136]

In his own memoirs, discussing the various alleged motives
behind the Suez halt, Macmillan dismissed at once Bulganin's
threats of Soviet intervention, and his crude hints even of nuclear
attack on Britain. These were undoubtedly sheer bluster, designed
to distract gazes from the Soviet rape of Hungary. He admitted the
impact of the run on the pound, and he had some harsh things to
say of the US role in this: selling by the Federal Reserve Bank,
refusal to grant a temporary loan, and obstruction of Britain's right
to withdraw from the IMF. This last action by Humphrey he
stigmatised as a 'breach of the spirit, and even of the letter' of IMF
principles, as 'not so easy to forgive' and 'altogether unworthy'. Yet
Macmillan insisted that, although the losses in reserves had been
serious, they were 'by no means disastrous', and 'not the reason for
the ceasefire'. The true reason, he claimed, sprang simply from the
objectives behind the British ultimatum to Egypt and Israel, and
he let the matter rest by quoting Eden's own version for the ceasefire: 'We had intervened to divide and, above all, to contain the
conflict. The occasion for our intervention was over, the fire was
out. . . .'[137] Macmillan commented that 'there was no escape from
this conclusion.'

But, as Anthony Head pointed out, 'the fire was out' pretext was
untenable even before the Franco-British landings started, since the
Israelis – in jumping the gun – had already reached their target, and
thus effectively ceased fire. In one sense, however, the Macmillan
argument loyally supporting the Eden line does perhaps hold water;
by 6 November it was blindingly clear that the 'occasion for our
intervention' was indeed over, in that neither of its original objectives – the toppling of Nasser and regaining control of the Canal –
was going to be achieved. Macmillan was a sound enough strategist
to recognise that occupying the whole Canal would be pointless; as
indeed he had argued in his memorandum to the Egypt Committee
back at the beginning of August. More soldiers would be killed,
and eventual withdrawal would be more difficult. In the face of

such violent American opposition, sitting on the Canal was not a sensible option.

Despite Macmillan's own vigorous asseverations that it was *not* the run on the pound which precipitated the retreat from Suez, the weight of opinion among his eminent contemporaries ranging from Home to Wilson is, quite categorically, that it *was* decisive. The question that remains is, did he get it wrong? As early as 12 August, he was recording this minute to the Cabinet: 'It is clear that we are pretty well armed for Suez. But I feel more and more convinced that our economy is too weak for us to do without permanent powers. . . .'[138] What these 'permanent powers' might be seem not to have been specified, or any specific action suggested from the Treasury.

Again, as noted previously, at regular periods through August and September and into October, he had been voicing fears of Britain's vulnerability to any oil crisis or any run on her reserves. But no proposals emanated from the Treasury on prophylactic measures that might have been taken early on to prevent a flight from sterling, or to draw out a tranche of funds from the IMF in advance of any crisis. Macmillan could almost certainly have achieved this, the latter without objection from the Americans, while in Washington in September; the agile-minded French, with their shakier but less vulnerable economy, did just this in October and thus avoided any threat to the franc. But Macmillan seems to have been counselled *against* such a step by the Treasury. Even as late as 31 October when the bombing of Egyptian airfields had already begun, the Bank of England expressed the view that the time was still not ripe to make a drawing on the IMF, while the Treasury advice was that it should be delayed 'as long as possible to give tempers time to cool all round'.[139] By then it would be too late.

Misguidedly, as it now seems, Macmillan took the Bank's and the Treasury's advice, and did nothing. Equally, some critics feel that he was misguided in overreacting to the crisis when it finally occurred on 6 November, and casting the decision then to halt so precipitately. All along, it seems that Macmillan may have been getting bad, or at least inadequate, advice from those professional advisers. But, ultimately, it was he who was the Minister and he was responsible; it was a responsibility that, in his memoirs, he certainly never attempted to pass on down the line.

*

How much was Macmillan also swayed by public opposition at home? Again, at this distance it is easy to forget the bitterness of the divisions engendered by Suez. From 30 October onwards a deluge of letters – angry, incredulous or distressed – flowed in on Macmillan. They varied from a terse, 'Sir, A decent Englishman would resign,' to more lengthy, strongly worded protests, many from old friends. Violet Bonham-Carter wrote that 'knowing, admiring and *trusting* you as I have always done it seems to me inconceivable that you can be party to this madness – which has, by one stroke, destroyed all that we have patiently laboured to create during the last 10 years – Anglo-American unity, Commonwealth solidarity, the trust, goodwill and *respect* of other nations on every continent of the world. . . .' General McCreery, Macmillan's colleague from war days when he commanded the Eighth Army in Italy at the time of the Klagenfurt episode, felt 'shattered' by the government's 'most *fantastic* and colossal blunder'. Like most of the correspondents, he stressed the view that Suez had 'dealt a crushing blow to Anglo-American friendship and leadership'. To all, Macmillan replied along the lines that 'I am sure history will prove that we have taken the right course,' and, rather lamely, 'I am fortified in this view by the support for what we have done given by the man whose experience, character and knowledge I have more respect for than anyone else, Sir Winston Churchill.'[140]

As with the motivation for so many of Macmillan's actions, the truth was probably a combination of all these strands. But, in retrospect, perhaps no single factor weighed more heavily in Macmillan's decision that Suez had been a mistake which had to be reversed, than the American reaction. He had persuaded Eden that, at worst, America might show 'hostile neutrality' towards the British resort to force, but never that it would lead the opposition to it. He was appalled by his own miscalculation of Eisenhower's mood, stemming back to his Washington interview at the end of September, and there was a strongly personal element in his recognition of failure to judge his old friend correctly. Selwyn Lloyd was quite right in thinking that Macmillan 'was emotionally affected' when told that it was on instructions 'of his close wartime friend' that Britain's access to IMF moneys was obstructed in November.[141] In his own memoirs Macmillan did not spare the *mea culpa* of the American miscalculation – 'For this I carry a heavy responsibility' – and on television in 1971 he admitted that 'my judgement was wrong . . .'; his 'instinct [was] that the Americans didn't wish to be informed when we took the final action . . . because that would embarrass them . . . but would support us when action was taken . . .'.[142] Over the passage of the years, he was even more unsparing in private. He had been 'absolutely amazed', in November 1956, by America's 'not just lack of support but bitter violent lining-up with the Kremlin . . .'.[143] Burke Trend, Assistant Cabinet Secretary during Suez, thought that 'it never occurred to him that the old wartime relationship could be in danger.'[144]

With his parentage as well as this wartime connection, nobody in the Eden Cabinet was more wedded to the philosophy of the 'special relationship' than Macmillan and he determined that the danger to it had to be eliminated, whatever the immediate cost. Finally, it might be argued that his decision to be 'first out' on 6 November, recognising the error of his way, reflected possibly more civic courage than if he had attempted to soldier on.

Balance Sheet of Suez

With the passage of more than three decades, Suez still appears as *the* historic watershed of the post-1945 era, certainly for Britain. After the last troops left the Canal in the wake of the débâcle, Britain – and only to a lesser extent France – lost whatever pretensions they still might have had the previous July to be superpowers, capable of manipulating global destinies in the imperial manner of the past. Suez meant that henceforth Britain would find it hard, if not impossible, to pursue a foreign policy totally independent of the United States. Yet it was not only the Anglo-American 'special relationship' that was injured by Suez. All along, France – locked in war with the Algerian FLN – had seen the issue differently to Britain. The majority of the French solidly backed Mollet over Suez, and far less guilt was involved; where Suez divided Britain, it tended to unite Frenchmen. It was the first truly Franco-British joint military effort since the unhappy days of 1940, and the British decision to halt immediately raised echoes among elements in France that here was *Perfide Albion*, up to her old tricks again, repeating the desertion of Dunkirk. Jointly *les Anglo-Saxons* became the main object of obloquy, and neither were to be trusted again. As an American, John Newhouse, saw it, Suez 'did more damage to

France's relations with the Anglo-Saxons, especially the Americans, than any other episode in postwar history. . . . Washington was seen to have betrayed its chief allies, and Britain abjectly deserted France and Israel at the first sign of disapproval in Washington. . . .'[145]

The Franco-British *entente* was never to be quite the same again, with consequences that would rebound gravely during Macmillan's own premiership; it was historically relevant that, at the moment of the Suez ceasefire, Chancellor Adenauer of West Germany was in Guy Mollet's office, consoling him with an offer of 'Europe' in compensation for Suez. And, indeed, it was the Suez defeat which brought de Gaulle to power eighteen months later; from that would follow the first vetoes on Britain's entry into the EEC, withdrawal from the military structure of NATO, and refusal to support the US policy in Vietnam and, much later, the Lebanon. Meanwhile, in Britain as in France, the failure of the US defence umbrella at the critical moment forced both countries to concentrate on the independent deterrent as a measure of national survival.

As far as the unhappy Middle East itself was concerned, Suez also denoted the entry of the Soviet Union as a major influence; at the same time, the 4 November UN resolution of Canada's Lester Pearson was to introduce the notion of the United Nations' peace-keeping force – with the concomitance of repeated Arab–Israeli warfare that would accompany its failure. It was, moreover, from 1956 that the Arabs realised for the first time the full power of the oil weapon.

Constituting as it did such a crucial watershed in the post-war world, especially in terms of Britain's position, could Suez possibly have turned out differently? Historians will long debate the 'ifs'. *If* Britain and France could have acted with the swift brutality of the Russians in Hungary, without the embarrassment of Israel, and before world and domestic opinion hardened, they might have regained the Canal; but what then? Macmillan's successor, Alec Douglas-Home, felt things might have ended differently 'if Anthony had gone to see Ike in person, to get things absolutely clear'.[146] This was a view shared by Macmillan, who, in retrospect, felt that discussion should never have been allowed to remain at the Foreign Secretary level – Dulles to Selwyn Lloyd – and that if Eden had gone to see Eisenhower earlier, the issue would have been brought to a head in September.

Could Macmillan, would Macmillan, have done any better?

Former colleagues and critics alike are now generally agreed that, had he remained in charge of foreign affairs, the Suez crisis would never have been allowed to get out of hand. Coupled with the extraordinary misfortune of the overlapping illnesses of the Western leaders – first Eisenhower, then Eden, followed by Dulles – the replacement of Macmillan by Selwyn Lloyd may well have been the essential tragedy of Suez. Though publicly Macmillan disclaimed this, reckoning that he too would have been deceived by Dulles, the feelings he expressed in private were always quite different. If he had still been Foreign Secretary, he felt that the Anglo-American crisis would not have happened as it did: 'because I would have found out. I would have persuaded Ike, or Foster, to back us – or say to the Cabinet "we can't move".' He also thought that he would have been able to persuade the Cabinet to adopt 'a different plan': 'I think I could have reported quite early, "You must do it at once," or to say, "Let's wait till after the American election". . . .'[147]

There had been extenuating circumstances: he had been told, early on, more or less to mind his own business on the military plan; after the failure to find a pretext, there had been the frustrations and impossible pressures, affecting all members of the Cabinet alike, to get on with the ponderously prepared military action. So Macmillan had jumped at the October 'collusion' plan, without examining its details and implications too thoroughly. '. . . I can't honestly say I liked it, but I agreed to it – as I was all for going in.' But 'We got it tangled. . . . I now know that I should never have agreed.' It was a 'bad plan', he said, because of collusion with the Israelis:

> We went in on the wrong foot . . . it was a muddle – rather like Gallipoli. And I was in a difficult position; I took no part in the details (looking back on it, they weren't very clever) and therefore didn't wish to criticise. . . . I think if I'd perhaps had more experience, I would have taken a stronger position in insisting on knowing just exactly how they were going to bring it about; and what were the chances of its success and what were the dangers. I admit I didn't do that, in the final stages. . . .

To the end of his days, Macmillan regarded Suez with particular distress. It was 'a very bad episode in my life. I feel unhappy about the whole thing. That's why I look back to the start – to my leaving the Foreign Office. That was a great sorrow. . . .'[148]

Chapter Sixteen

Salvaging the Wreckage
November 1956–January 1957

Well, which is it, Wab or Hawold?
> *(Salisbury, interviewing ministers on Eden's successor)*

My belief is, when you get a chance, take it.
> *(HM, to author, 14 November 1979)*

With the collapse of his Suez policy, the full extent of Eden's illness became painfully apparent. He is described in the Commons as sitting 'sprawled on the front bench, head thrown back and mouth agape. His eye, inflamed with sleeplessness, stared into vacancies beyond the roof. . . .'[1] On the evening of 18 November, Sir Horace Evans, Eden's physician, called to see Macmillan at his study in No. 11 Downing Street. Macmillan was 'shocked' when Evans told him that he had just advised Eden that he had to take a holiday at once, 'if he was to avoid a serious physical breakdown', for the strain of the past months had brought on a return of some of the alarming symptoms of Eden's old illness. (According to Butler, Macmillan burst into a temper with Evans, expostulating that the Prime Minister could not possibly leave the country at that moment.)[2] Four days later Eden flew off to the Jamaican villa of the creator of James Bond, Ian Fleming. But before his departure, and immediately in the wake of the British ceasefire order, a last humiliation was inflicted on the sick man by Eisenhower rescinding an invitation (admittedly proposed by Eden himself) to confer in Washington, and – in effect – refusing to have any personal dealings with him.

In the meantime, someone had to undertake the painful task of unscrambling the mess left by the attack on Suez – the evacuation of the French and British troops, the clearing of the Canal (which the Egyptians had efficiently blocked), the salvaging of the pound, and the urgent provision of oil to Britain and France cut off by the Arab producers. On 19 November, the day after Sir Horace's visit to No. 11, Winthrop Aldrich, the American Ambassador, telephoned Eisenhower direct to report on a meeting he had just had with Macmillan, to discuss Britain's grave financial plight. Aldrich hinted excitedly at a likely change in the British leadership, reinforcing guesses he had already passed back, and reported that Macmillan 'is terribly anxious to see you as soon as possible'.[3] Macmillan wrote of these difficult days that Butler, in his capacity as Deputy Prime Minister, 'asked me to act as his main confidant, and we laboured together in complete agreement. . . . We made it a rule always to attend [the House of Commons] together and each to speak on the lines we had agreed.'

There now followed a series of triangular conversations between Washington on the one hand and Butler and Macmillan on the other, until Eden returned on 14 December. At a meeting in the White House the day after Aldrich's call, Secretary of the Treasury Humphrey offered the opinion that, as a successor to Eden, 'Butler would be the stronger of the two men mentioned'; to which Eisenhower replied with his preference for Macmillan, of whom he had 'always thought most highly', and who was 'a straight, fine man, and . . . the outstanding one of the British he served with during the war'.[4] But, with characteristic correctness, Eisenhower instructed Aldrich that he should communicate with the two men, equally and at the same time. Aldrich then followed up with cryptic messages that Butler/Macmillan were indeed required to cover up the acutely embarrassing nakedness of the British government, caused – said Macmillan with undiluted bitterness – 'by humiliations almost vindictively inflicted upon us at the instance of the United States Government'.

At the time the situation looked to Macmillan considerably worse than he revealed in his memoirs. On 21 November, he was telling the Cabinet that petrol rationing was unavoidable, and that the dissolution of the sterling area might follow. Eight days later, Treasury jeremiads about the danger of a forced devaluation of the pound precipitated the Cabinet into accepting unconditional withdrawal of the last British troops from Suez. With hindsight, Macmillan's fears may have been exaggerated; eventually he was able to obtain from Washington a lessening of pressures to withdraw, combined with immediate financial support to save the pound. Eisenhower instructed Aldrich to tell the British that 'as soon as things happen we anticipate we can furnish a lot of fig leaves' – the 'things' referring to the British evacuation.

Meanwhile, on 23 November, Churchill had made perhaps his last great contribution to the 'special relationship' in a moving letter to Eisenhower from his retirement at Chartwell. 'There is not much left for me to do in this world,' it began, 'and I have neither the wish nor the strength to involve myself in the present political stress and turmoil. But I do believe, with unfaltering conviction, that the theme of the Anglo-American alliance is more important today than at any time since the war. . . .' He went on to express fears that if the 'growing misunderstanding and frustration on both sides of the Atlantic' were allowed to continue, 'it is the Soviet Union that will ride the storm', and that the former Allies might well 'expect to see the Middle East and the North African coastline under Soviet control and Western Europe placed at the mercy of the Russians . . .'.

Macmillan believed that Churchill's appeal had a material effect on Eisenhower. On 4 December, Dulles – returned after his colostomy and apparently recovered – told Eisenhower that, on Humphrey's advice, the British immediately needed $500 million and that the US would have to cancel the principal and interest on the loan the following year. 'Even so,' said Dulles, 'Humphrey is not sure that will save the pound. Humphrey believes nothing but a change of government will. . . .'[5]

On the 12th, Dulles and Humphrey came to London. Macmillan made no attempt to disguise British bitterness about the American role at Suez, but clearly much progress had already been made towards dispelling what Eisenhower had still been complaining about on the eve of Eden's departure for Jamaica – 'a vagueness, not a frankness that he would have liked'[6] – in Anglo-American intercourse. Macmillan promptly reported, by letter, to Butler about his most private conversation with the US Secretary of the Treasury:

He said that it was like a business deal. They were putting a lot of money into the reorganisation of Britain and they would hope very much that the business would be successful. But, of course, when you were reconstructing a business that was in difficulties, the personal problems could not be ruled out.

I said: 'Don't you trust the board?' and he said: 'Well, since you ask me, I think it would be as well if we could deal as much as possible with the directors.' This rather cryptic observation he enlarged on to say that he would like to feel that he could always be on terms of private, and, where necessary, telephonic, communication with you and me.[7]

That is, not with Chairman Eden.

On 14 December, Eden returned, sun-tanned, from Jamaica. The financial aid required by Britain was granted, as well as new and satisfactory terms for repayment of the loan. The pound had been saved; and so was the Tory government. But for how long? And could Eden remain in No. 10?

Accusations have been made that Eisenhower, through his dealings with Butler and Macmillan at this time, behaved improperly by meddling in British domestic affairs to keep the Conservatives in power.[8] The situation has a passing resemblance to the relationship, initiated by Roosevelt in 1939, with Churchill while he was still only First Lord of the Admiralty. As Eisenhower had made quite plain even in his anger at the first British action against Egypt, 'those British, they're still my right arm,'[9] and Butler was – in Eden's absence – quite properly the leader of the British government.

Pulling the Carpet Out from Under Eden? And Butler?

Even more bitter accusations have long lingered against Macmillan – that he used Suez, and Eden's illness, to 'grasp the crown' for himself. There were even those Eden loyalists inside the Tory Party who went so far as to allege that Macmillan had actually pushed Eden into Suez in the hopes, all along, that it would bring about his fall.[10] But there is no evidence whatsoever for this. Anthony Sampson, an often critical biographer of Macmillan, pointed out that during Suez 'Macmillan seemed determined to be loyal to Eden – even to be leaning over backwards – the more so, perhaps, because he knew of Eden's jealousy of him.'[11] Philip de Zulueta, who as successive Private Secretary to Eden and Macmillan owed loyalty to both Prime Ministers, took this view; as did Robert Blake, who worked with Eden on his memoirs, and who 'never for a moment felt that Macmillan had pulled the carpet out from under Eden for reasons of ambition; Eden's principal complaint was that he should have calculated his finances better. . . .'[12] Even Eden's widow, Clarissa Avon, who remained unremittingly hostile to Macmillan, would not sustain the 'pulled-the-carpet-out' thesis, while Lord Carrington gave a characteristically unambiguous judgement: 'Rubbish! Anthony had clearly gone mad.'[13] In his diaries, Macmillan admitted that, after Eden's physical breakdown in November, he had recognised that Eden 'could never return and remain P.M. for long'.[14]

With Eden himself, once the poisoned air of Suez cleared away, Macmillan maintained overtly cordial relations until his death. Though those close to Eden were aware of the bitterness he continued to feel towards Macmillan, it was not in his nature to display his feelings.[15] They exchanged frequent letters, in which Macmillan would often send 'all my affection'. Together they honoured the pledge of silence; when Macmillan was preparing his account of Suez, he sent the draft of his chapter to Eden for comment and got the friendly reply: 'I thought it admirably done. . . .'[16]

More difficult to dispute are the assertions that Macmillan 'seized the crown' out of the gentler hands of his old colleague, Rab Butler. There is nothing to suggest that, before Suez, Macmillan had seriously regarded himself as a rival for the crown to the younger Butler. During the Churchill government, back in July 1953, Macmillan had observed the jockeying for position under the old Titan with detachment: 'The situation is really fascinating. Butler is, of course, playing a winning game. He has on his side his comparative youth, his oriental subtlety, his power of quiet but effective intrigue – and the absence of any real competition so well equipped.' And, a few days later: 'Monckton . . . told Lyttelton that he would always serve under Churchill, but would not serve "a slab of cold fish" (Rab). This is too hard on Butler – who is able and sincere but wildly and almost pathologically ambitious.'[17]

Macmillan once remarked, however, 'my belief is, when you get a chance, take it. It was always my philosophy. Chance played such a role in my life – Winston, the war, Algiers, housing . . . which made me Prime Minister.'[18] Bismarck expressed a similar view: 'a statesman has not to *make* history, but if ever in the events around him he hears the sweep of the mantle of God, then he must jump up and catch at its hem.'[19] There can be no doubting that after Sir Horace Evans's visit of 18 November, Macmillan must have heard the 'mantle of God' brush close by and, if he had not caught at it, he would have thought he was doing the country, as well as his own ambitions, a disservice. By that fateful third week in November, as Philip de Zulueta viewed it, the time had come when Macmillan 'saw that Eden could not go on, and Butler couldn't possibly take over'.[20] Butler himself admitted that Macmillan was quicker off the mark, 'quicker to notice the state of Eden's failing health than I was'.[21]

During a fiery debate on Suez on 12 November, Macmillan had

risen to give a spirited defence of the government's role and, resorting to a purely personal note on why he had eschewed 'appeasement', declared: 'It is because I have seen it all happen before.'[22] Some wondered whether this was an oblique shot at Butler and his mortal sin of the 1930s. Four days after Macmillan became Prime Minister, Harold Nicolson reflected 'that if Rab had not been so weak about Munich and Harold Macmillan had not been so strong, Winston would have given different advice to the Queen . . .'.[23]

As the absent Eden's deputy, Butler was in the unhappy position of having to answer, officially, to all the accumulated anger of the Party in the aftermath of Suez. During the brief, but critical, 'caretaker' interregnum, Macmillan admitted that he seldom entered the House, only spoke once – and then on purely economic matters. Thus Butler was left exposed as the government break-water; because of his record of 'wetness' earlier, the hawks held him, not Macmillan, responsible for the decision to halt; while – even more unfairly – the doves regarded him as the representative of the Cabinet that had erred in the first place. Butler later admitted that this was the most difficult period of his career.

The cool resilience with which Macmillan regained his political balance after the Suez débâcle, as well as his personal repute as the man who had been 'first in, first out', was truly remarkable by any yardstick. It stood him in good stead within the Party, in contrast to Butler. Equally remarkable was the ruthless skill with which he pressed his suit, while all the time co-operating with Butler in picking up the post-Suez pieces. On 22 November, he and Butler both addressed a 1922 Committee meeting. All Tory backbenchers were entitled to attend this off-the-record meeting, and most did. Hamilton Kerr, who was present, described it as being 'rather like going on board a steamer at the end of a very rough crossing. There was a slight smell of sickness in the Smoking Room and almost everyone looked green.'[24] Butler talked about the technicalities of Tory publicity, while Macmillan, emotional, uplifting and looking towards the future rather than the past, made 'a real leadership speech'. A government Whip recalled how:

Rab was not on his best form, whereas Harold was at his most ebullient and managed to win the day, not only on the merit of what he said (as it seemed to the Committee) but also physically in that his expansive gestures nearly caused poor Rab to fall backwards from the adjacent seat.[25]

The description spoke volumes. Anthony Howard, Rab's biographer, rated the joint appearance as 'a highly expensive mistake' on the part of his subject.[26]

At about the same time, Butler spoke disastrously – and with characteristic indiscretion – to twenty senior Tory MPs at a dinner of the Progress Trust, giving them (he said) 'some of the realities of the situation, particularly in relation to sterling, which no one had hitherto done'. For his pains, 'wherever I moved in the weeks that followed, I felt the party knives sticking into my innocent back.'[27] Macmillan gained points by being more reticent on the more sensitive aspects of Suez.

By 7 December, Macmillan's challenge was manifest to the hostile eye of Brendan Bracken, who wrote to Beaverbrook:

> Macmillan is telling journalists that he intends to retire from politics and go to the morgue. He declares that he will never serve under Butler. His real intentions are to push his boss out of No. 10 and he has a fair following in the Tory party. The so-called diehards think better of him than they do of Eden or Butler. . . .[28]

It was not just on his external performance that Butler lost; there was something self-defeating within the man himself – and this was to have an important bearing when the leadership stakes came up again seven years later. Friends and supporters maintained that – still afflicted by the death of his adored wife, and suffering from a virus infection – Rab had been only a shadow of his former self throughout Suez. Writing to his father Harold, Nigel Nicolson (then a Tory MP who later lost his seat because of his opposition to Suez) probably read Rab rightly when, in January 1957, after the succession was settled, he observed:

> I think the quality I most like about Rab is his melancholy. It wasn't the melancholy of personal disappointment, but the melancholy that right had not triumphed and that he was being obliged to contribute to a grotesque legend. The general feeling in the House is that he has mismanaged his attitude during the

past two months. He should have been one thing or the other, not a reluctant apologist. . . .[29]

While Macmillan, whatever the rightness of his position on Suez, always stated it clearly, decisively and persuasively, Butler – though unhappy about the use of force from the beginning – hedged. In Anthony Head's opinion, this was the deciding factor:

The whole time he was saying 'on the one hand, on the other'. It did him a lot of harm. If Rab had only been more forceful throughout the period, he could have been Prime Minister . . . but there was an ambivalence in him all the way – and it did him absolutely no good in the Cabinet. . . . Also, I have a sneaking feeling that he himself never really wanted the responsibility, deep down.[30]

Nicholas Henderson, who had worked under Rab in the Foreign Office, respected and held him in affection, noted how he made almost a positive virtue of his inability to make up his mind, or commit himself on an issue; he liked to think of himself as Tolstoy's Pierre Bezukhov, with his philosophy of 'delay and withdraw'.[31] These were not characteristics designed to impress a Cabinet under maximum stress, having to make decisions daily, even hourly. Over the big Suez issues, Butler would disagree but not forcefully protest, while there was also – according to Nigel Nicolson – a devious side to him: 'He played a double game, which lost him a lot of backing. He would speak up for the Government in the House, and then go into the Smoking Room and say to everyone how terrible it was. He thought that would get him support; in fact it did the reverse. . . .'[32]

There was another aspect of Rab that the average Tory did not like: he was often unable to hide his contempt for mediocrity. As Deryk Winterton of the *Daily Herald* wrote: 'They think he is too clever by half. An intellectual without the grace to pretend that he is not . . . a master of the dubious phrase and uncertain compliment. Sometimes indeed he seems to lose himself in a haze of words that can have no meaning even for him. . . .'[33] Yet for such an adroit politician, with so brilliant a mind, Butler seems to have been oddly blind to his own defects. He later rather plaintively said: 'I couldn't understand, when I had done a most wonderful job – picking up the pieces after Suez – that they then chose Harold.'[34]

Finally, both the Harolds of No. 10 agreed on the one outstanding defect of Butler: to Wilson, he 'did not have the killer instinct required to succeed';[35] and in Macmillan's words, 'He had the ambition but not the will . . . a sort of vague ambition – like saying it would be nice to be Archbishop of Canterbury. . . .'

But what chiefly mattered to the ruling Tories of post-Suez was that they wanted a man of action, not an academic; they also wanted somebody who knew the outside world – and one who, from his personal association with Eisenhower, could mend the gaping holes in the Atlantic alliance. When it came to the final choice, there was almost no disagreement.

'So It Was Settled . . .'

On the morning of 9 January 1957, Macmillan was working at the Treasury when he received a message summoning him to No. 10 at 3 p.m. He recalled:

> Eden was in the little drawing-room, the smallest of the three saloons which occupy the front of the famous house. All these face north and seldom see the sun; but in this room there is a window to the west, looking over the garden, and the afternoon and evening sun give it, even through the gloom of a London winter, a touch of warmth and glow. He told me with simple gravity, as a matter decided and not be discussed, that he had decided to resign his office. The Queen had already been informed. . . .

Eden told Macmillan that the doctors were inexorable; 'there was no way out.' Macmillan was 'deeply shocked':

> I could hardly believe that this was to be the end of the public life of a man so comparatively young, and with so much still to give.
> We sat for some little time together. We spoke a few words about the First War, in which we had both served and suffered, and of how we had entered Parliament together at the same time. . . . I can see him now on that sad winter afternoon, still looking so youthful, so gay, so debonair – the representative of

all that was best of the youth that had served in the 1914–18 War. . . .[36]

In that moment, all the discord, rivalry and jealousy of the past was forgotten. Macmillan 'walked sadly back' through the connecting passage to No. 11. The Cabinet met two hours later. Since Christmas, ministers had been showing signs of restlessness: 'There have been many meetings – no intrigue, but great concern at the apparent inability of the P.M. or anyone else to take hold of the situation. . . .' Nevertheless, no inkling of Eden's decision had leaked out and when the moment came the Cabinet was 'dazed':

> Eden spoke shortly, and with great dignity. The doctors' decision was irrevocable. He must resign. Salisbury spoke – with great emotion, almost in tears – of his lifelong friendship. Butler spoke next – very appropriately. I said a few words. Then it was all over. It was a dramatic end to an extraordinary and, in many ways, unique career. What seemed so dreadful was that he waited so long for the Premiership, and held it for so short a time.[37]

Macmillan then left No. 10, followed by Butler; after which Salisbury, as senior Cabinet Minister – in the words of Macmillan – 'invited the remaining Ministers to give their opinion about who should succeed to the vacant and, in the circumstances, not very alluring post'.

What ensued was, in comparison with subsequent procedure, a cosy and domestic way of selecting a new Prime Minister. Whereas in 1963 all Tory MPs would be canvassed by the Whips, the 1957 selection was essentially a straight Cabinet choice. Salisbury and Kilmuir, the Lord Chancellor, summoned ministers to see them, one by one, in Salisbury's room in the adjacent Privy Council offices. According to Macmillan, there was no attempt by either peer 'to use what one might call a prefect's influence. . . . They merely asked a question and received an answer.' Kilmuir recorded the historic simplicity of the scene:

> There were two light reliefs. Practically each one began by saying, 'This is like coming to the Headmaster's study.' To each Bobbety said, 'Well, which is it, Wab or Hawold?' As well as seeing the remainder of the ex-Cabinet, we interviewed the Chief Whip and

Oliver Poole, the Chairman of the Party. John Morrison, the Chairman of the 1922 Committee, rang me up from Islay the next morning. An overwhelming majority of Cabinet Ministers was in favour of Macmillan.[38]

According to Anthony Head's recollections, only one Minister, Buchan-Hepburn was for Rab.[39] (He was later made Lord Hailes by Macmillan, and despatched to be the first and last Governor-General of the short-lived Federation of the West Indies.)

The Chief Whip, Edward Heath, showing perhaps rather better political judgement than he would twenty years later and having received a number of MPs' letters opposing Butler, strongly advised the choice of Macmillan. Eden – as he later told Macmillan himself – had 'neither been asked for his advice nor had volunteered it'.[40]

The next morning Macmillan waited in lonely isolation under a portrait of Gladstone in No. 11, and 'read *Pride and Prejudice* – very soothing. At noon Sir Michael Adeane rang up and asked me to be at the Palace at 2 o'clock. So it was settled. . . .'

The Macmillans had come a long way from the humble croft on the Isle of Arran. Hardly less distant seemed the withdrawn and lonely child, the failure at Eton uncertain about his faith, the crippled veteran of the First World War, the diffident young man always on the fringe of things, the MP always at odds with his Party. He had struggled through those seventeen dispiriting years in the political wilderness, while struggling simultaneously with the wreckage of his marriage. A lesser man would not have survived. Then, on the eve of despair, had come the sudden opening of the Second World War and Algiers. But this late dawn had been followed by six more dark years of frustration, out of power. In 1951 came Cabinet office at last – though an apparent backwater, in the form of Housing. The steady climb though Cabinet ranks, stepping stones to leadership, had led him to the Foreign Office, which he himself regarded as the peak of political attainment. Never could he have predicted that, so soon, he would be moving upward into No. 10 – or under such unlooked-for circumstances. For a man on the threshold of his sixty-fourth year, at an age when many retire, burnt out, the auspices could scarcely have been less promising. As of January 1957, Tory pundits were giving him a life of three weeks; who could foresee then that the pedantic, unglamorous figure of the

1930s was about to become one of Britain's most extrovert, ebullient Prime Ministers, with nearly seven years of action-packed premiership ahead of him?

All, and more, of Nellie Macmillan's outrageous ambitions for her youngest son were about to be fulfilled.

Notes, Bibliography, Index

Notes

The following abbreviations are used in the source notes. For most works, the first mention within each chapter gives the name of the author and the title in full; thereafter, except in cases of ambiguity, the author's surname and/or shortened title is used. Where works appear in the Bibliography, details of publications are omitted.

AHC	author's conversations with Harold Macmillan (not taped), 1979–86
AHT	author's taped interviews with Harold Macmillan, 1979–86
CO	Cabinet Office
FO	Foreign Office
HMA	Harold Macmillan Archives
HMD	Harold Macmillan's diaries, unpublished, in Harold Macmillan Archives
HMWD	Harold Macmillan, *War Diaries: The Mediterranean 1943–1945*
P.M	Prime Minister
PRO	Public Record Office
T	Treasury
WO	War Office

Chapter 1 The Ripening Peach, 1894–1914

HM, *Winds of Change* (I), pp. 30–58, and:

1 Richardson report, 'Illness and Resignation', HMA.
2 HMD, 18 October 1963.
3 AHT, 15.9–10.
4 HM, *At the End of the Day* (VI), p. 515
5 AHC.
6 Ibid.
7 HM, VI, p. 515.
8 Thomas Hughes, *Memoir of Daniel Macmillan*, pp. 108–10.
9 HM, *The Past Masters*, pp. 11–12.

10   Hughes, op. cit.
11   HM, *Past Masters*, pp. 11–12.
12   AHC.
13   Philip Guedalla, *The Hundred Years* (London 1936).
14   *The Times*, 18 October 1975.
15   Ibid.
16   AHC.
17   *The Times*, op. cit.
18   Ibid.
19   Interview, Lord Richardson.
20   AHC.
21   Anthony Sampson, *Macmillan*, p. 6.
22   Interview, Lady Richardson.
23   Letter to Lady Waverley, 10 August 1962; Waverley papers.
24   Ibid.
25   *The Times*, op. cit.
26   AHC.
27   Letter from Caroline Hobhouse to author, 27 February 1987.
28   *The Times*, op. cit.
29   Interview, Julian Lambert.
30   AHT, 2.14–15.
31   Evelyn Waugh, *The Life of the Rt Rev. Ronald Knox*, p. 106.
32   Penelope Fitzgerald, *The Knox Brothers*, p. 67.
33   Waugh, op. cit., p. 106.
34   HMA.
35   Ibid.
36   Waugh, op. cit., p. 107.
37   Ronald Knox, *A Spiritual Aeneid*, p. 86.
38   AHC.
39   *The Times*, op. cit.
40   Quoted in James Morris, *Oxford*, p. 332.
41   Colin Coote, *Editorial: Memoirs*, p. 35.
42   *The Times*, op. cit.
43   Ibid.
44   Ibid.
45   Knox, op. cit., p. 117.
46   AHC.
47   Knox, op. cit., p. 195.
48   Ronald Knox letters, HMA.
49   Fitzgerald, op. cit., p. 121; interview, Penelope Fitzgerald.
50   Waugh, op. cit., p. 128.
51   *The Times*, op. cit.
52   Quoted in *Time*, 30 September 1966.
53   *The Times*, op. cit.

Chapter 2   Captain Macmillan, 1914–1918

HM, *Winds of Change* (I), pp. 57–105, and:

1   Interview, Reresby Sitwell.
2   Ronald Knox, *A Spiritual Aeneid*, p. 174.
3   Evelyn Waugh, *The Life of the Rt Rev. Ronald Knox*, pp. 139–41.
4   Ibid., p. 142; Mells archives.
5   Ibid.
6   Knox, op. cit., p. 254.
7   Waugh, op. cit., p. 142; Mells archives.
8   Ibid., p. 171.
9   AHC.
10 Ibid.
11 Penelope Fitzgerald, *The Knox Brothers*, p. 140.
12 AHT, HM 'Declaration'.
13 Letters to Helen Macmillan, 17 August 1915; HMA.
14 Ibid., 10 September 1915.
15 Ibid., 23 August 1915.
16 Ibid., 30 August 1915.
17 AHC.
18 Letters to Helen Macmillan, 26 September 1915.
19 Interview, Brigadier C. R. Britten.
20 Letters to Helen Macmillan, September 1915.
21 Interview, Britten.
22 Letters to Helen Macmillan, April 1916.
23 Ibid., 13 May 1916.
24 Ibid., 30 April 1916.
25 Ibid., 26 May 1916.
26 Ibid., 22 May 1916.
27 Ibid., 29 June 1916.
28 Ibid., 3 July 1916.
29 Ibid., 9 July 1916.
30 Ibid., 10 July 1916.
31 Ibid., 19 July 1916.
32 Ibid., 2 August 1916.
33 Ibid., 16 August 1916.
34 Ibid., 10 September 1916.
35 BBC1, 1 September 1966.
36 Letters to Helen Macmillan, 13 September 1916.
37 Ibid., 16 September 1916.
38 Ibid., 15 September 1916.
39 Ibid.
40 AHT, 1.13.
41 Ibid.
42 Letters to Helen Macmillan, 27 September 1916.

43 Ibid., 17 October 1918.
44 AHC.
45 Ibid.
46 *The Times*, 18 October 1975.

Chapter 3   Marriage and Publishing, 1918–1924

HM, *Winds of Change* (I), pp. 105–97, and:

1   HM, *The Past Masters*, p. 195.
2   Interview, Duke of Devonshire.
3   AHC.
4   Interview, Sir David Scott.
5   Interview, Lady Anne Tree.
6   AHC.
7   Interview, Keith Eccleston.
8   Letters to Dorothy Macmillan, Easter Sunday, 1919; HMA.
9   Ibid., 26 June 1919.
10 Ibid., 30 December 1919.
11 Letters to Helen Macmillan, 27 December 1919; HMA.
12 Ibid., undated.
13 Ibid., 6 January 1920.
14 AHT, 2.12–13; AHC.
15 Letters to Dorothy Macmillan, 20 April 1920.
16 Interview, Duke of Devonshire, quoting Lord Sefton.
17 Charles Morgan, *The House of Macmillan*, p. 87.
18 Ibid., p. 220.
19 Ibid., pp. 120, 126.
20 Ibid., pp. 119–28, 144–7.
21 AHT, 17.2.
22 Ibid.
23 AHC.
24 AHT, 18.5.
25 Ibid.
26 AHC.
27 Interview, C. P. Snow.
28 Letters to Dorothy Macmillan, 12 August 1920.
29 Ibid., 16 August 1920.
30 Ibid., 16 March 1921.
31 AHT, 2.20.
32 Interview, Maurice Macmillan.
33 Letters to Dorothy Macmillan, 25 August 1921.
34 BBC1, 1 September 1966.

Chapter 4   The Great Divide, 1924–1931

HM, *Winds of Change* (I), pp. 141–286, and:

1   Interview, Miss Amy Cooke, Stockton 1979.
2   *The Star*, 29 October 1959.
3   Interviews, Mrs Boyce, Miss Cooke, Mrs Ostle, Stockton, 1979.
4   Author's notes, Stockton, 1979.
5   AHT, 10.1.
6   BBC1, 1 September 1966.
7   AHT, 13.1.
8   HM, *The Past Masters*, p. 112.
9   Hansard, 2 May 1927.
10 Emrys Hughes, *Macmillan, Portrait of a Politician*, p. 33.
11 Harold Wilson, *A Prime Minister on Prime Ministers*, p. 141.
12 AHT, 19.6.
13 Interview, Lord Shinwell.
14 Interview, Lord Butler.
15 Interview, Lord Boothby.
16 Martin Gilbert, *Winston S. Churchill, 1922–39*, V, p. 214.
17 Interview, Dennis White.
18 Interview, Carol Faber.
19 Interview, Maurice Macmillan.
20 Interview, C. P. Snow.
21 Chartwell Trust, 18/85.
22 Ibid.
23 Gilbert, op. cit., p. 260.
24 Ibid., p. 296.
25 Ibid., p. 273.
26 AHT, 1.5.
27 HM, *Past Masters*, p. 64.
28 Hugh Dalton, *Call Back Yesterday*, p. 279.
29 Robert Boothby, *Recollections of a Rebel*, p. 203.
30 Ibid., p. 110.
31 Ibid., p. 160.
32 Ibid., p. 68.
33 Interview, Katharine Macmillan.
34 Interview, Lord Boothby.
35 *News Chronicle*, 11 January 1957.
36 Interview, Lord Boothby.
37 *Sunday Telegraph*, 29 January 1984.
38 Interview, Lord Boothby.
39 Interview, Maurice Macmillan.
40 *Daily Mail*, 10 May 1978.
41 AHC.
42 Interview, Robert Rhodes James.

43 Interview, Mary, Duchess of Devonshire.
44 Harold Nicolson, *Diaries and Letters*, I, p. 60.
45 AHC.
46 Interview, Duke of Devonshire.
47 Interview, Lord Butler.
48 AHC.
49 Hitchin papers; HMA.
50 Ibid.
51 Ibid.
52 Ibid.
53 R. A. Butler, *The Art of the Possible*, p. 26.
54 Boothby, op. cit., p. 81.
55 Letter of 20 March 1931; HMA.
56 Letter of 25 March 1931; HMA.
57 Nicolson, op. cit., p. 76.
58 HM, *Past Masters*, pp. 104–5.

Chapter 5   The Wilderness Years, 1931–1939

HM, *Winds of Change* (I), pp. 255–653, and:

1 Interviews, Pamela, Lady Egremont, Hugh Fraser, Carol Faber.
2 Letters to Helen Macmillan; HMA.
3 Stockton papers; HMA.
4 Interview, Maurice Macmillan.
5 Letters to Helen Macmillan.
6 Stockton papers, HMA.
7 Letter from Maynard Keynes, 6 June 1932; HMA.
8 Hansard, 21 November 1934.
9 Ibid., 20 November 1934.
10 Quoted in Anthony Sampson, *Macmillan*, pp. 42–3.
11 Martin Gilbert, *Plough My Own Furrow* (London 1965), p. 317.
12 AHT, 19.11.
13 HM, *The Middle Way*, p. 369.
14 Hansard, 23 March 1938.
15 HM, *The Middle Way*, p. 335.
16 Ibid., pp. 260–1.
17 Ibid., pp. 271–3.
18 Ibid., p. 286.
19 Ibid., pp. 373, 375.
20 Interview, Lady Anne Tree.
21 Philip Ziegler, *Diana Cooper*, p. 119.
22 AHT, 19.7.
23 Letter of 7 December 1936; HMA.
24 AHT, 19.3.7.

25 HMA.
26 Hansard, 17 June 1936.
27 AHT, 19.4.
28 Lovat Dickson, *The House of Words*, pp. 191, 210.
29 AHT, 19.4.
30 Hansard, 3 October 1938.
31 Martin Gilbert, *Winston Churchill: The Wilderness Years*, p. 234.
32 Hansard, 3 October 1938.
33 Alfred Duff Cooper, *Old Men Forget*, p. 249.
34 Hugh Dalton, *The Fateful Years*, p. 198.
35 Ibid., p. 200.
36 Ibid., p. 201.
37 Harold Nicolson, *Diaries and Letters*, I, p. 397.

Chapter 6   'Winston Is Back!', 1939–1942

HM, *The Blast of War* (II), pp. 1–217, and:

1   HM, *Winds of Change*, I, pp. 601–2.
2   AHC.
3   HM, I, p. 366.
4   Harold Wilson, *A Prime Minister on Prime Ministers*, p. 306.
5   Interview, Lord Longford.
6   AHT, 13.1.
7   Hansard, 18 October 1939.
8   Ibid., 17 January 1940.
9   Ibid., 1 February 1940.
10 Ibid., 8 February 1940.
11 Lovat Dickson, *The House of Words*, p. 219.
12 HMA.
13 HM, Finland diary, 12 February 1940; HMA.
14 Hansard, 19 March 1940.
15 Ibid.
16 HMA.
17 Ibid.
18 R. A. Butler, *The Art of the Possible*, p. 85.
19 Herbert Morrison, *An Autobiography*, p. 178.
20 Ibid., pp. 299–300.
21 Harold Nicolson, *Diaries and Letters*, II, p. 121.
22 Philip Ziegler, *Diana Cooper*, p. 94.
23 Interview, Michael Foot.
24 AHT, 9.20–1.
25 HMA.
26 AHT, 9.20–2.
27 AHC.

28 AHT, 9.20–2.
29 Ibid., 14.18.
30 Hansard, 24 June 1942.
31 CO 965 57 ERD/1350; PRO.
32 Ibid.
33 Nicolson, op. cit., p. 252.
34 AHT, 1.2–3.

Chapter 7   The Hinge of Fate, December 1942–June 1943

HM, *The Blast of War* (II), pp. 159–353, and:

1 Robert Glenton, *Sunday Express*, 19 October 1958.
2 Harold Evans, *Downing Street Diary* (London 1981), p. 31.
3 Interview, Robert Rhodes James.
4 HMWD, 26 January 1943.
5 Dwight D. Eisenhower, *The War Years*, p. 846.
6 FO 954/16; PRO.
7 Winston Churchill, *The Second World War*, IV, p. 579.
8 Oliver Harvey, *War Diaries*, p. 202.
9 Eisenhower, op. cit., p. 886.
10 Robert Murphy, *Diplomat Among Warriors*, pp. 163–4.
11 FO 954/16; PRO.
12 HMWD, 23 April 1943.
13 AHT, 7.2–3.
14 *Sunday Telegraph*, 9 February 1964.
15 AHC.
16 Philip Ziegler, *Diana Cooper*, p. 219.
17 Eisenhower to Bedell Smith, 9 November 1942; Eisenhower, op. cit., p. 677.
18 Quoted in John Ambler, *The French Army in Politics, 1945–62* (Ohio 1966), p. 78.
19 Churchill, op. cit., III, p. 653.
20 Churchill, op. cit., IV, p. 597.
21 Ibid., 573–6.
22 Letter to Dorothy Macmillan, 26 January 1943; HMA.
23 Murphy, op. cit., p. 166.
24 AHT, 7.20; 8.6–8.
25 Ibid.
26 BBC1, June 1957.
27 Murphy, op. cit., p. 167.
28 Ibid., p. 165.
29 Ibid., p. 145.
30 Ibid., p. 169.
31 Ibid., p. 170.

32 AHT, 7.3.
33 FO 371/36118, 26 January 1943; PRO.
34 FO 660/14; PRO.
35 Churchill, op. cit., IV, p. 609.
36 Ibid., p. 610; FO 660/88, 18 January 1943. The official record of the Churchill telegram differs slightly from the version printed by him in *The Second World War*, being, if anything, still tougher.
37 Ibid.
38 AHT, 7.2–3.
39 Charles de Gaulle, *Mémoires de la guerre: L'unité, 1942–44*, documents, p. 84.
40 Harvey, op. cit., p. 218.
41 John Wheeler-Bennett, *King George VI* (1958), p. 560.
42 Letter of 28 January 1943; HMA.
43 FO 660/88; PRO.
44 Pierson Dixon, letter to FO, 27 January 1943, FO 371/36118; PRO.
45 A. L. Funk, 'The "Anfa" Memorandum: An Incident at the Casablanca Conference', *Journal of Modern History*, xxvi, no. 3, September 1954, p. 250.
46 Ibid.
47 FO 371/36119; PRO.
48 HMWD, 23 February 1943.
49 Lord Egremont, *Wyndham and Children First*, p. 84.
50 Interview, John J. McCloy.
51 FO 954/16 ff. 318–21; PRO.
52 HMA.
53 Ibid.
54 HMWD.
55 HMA.
56 HMWD, 24 February 1943.
57 Ibid., 2 March 1943.
58 Ibid., 15 March, 6 April, 30 July 1943.
59 HMA.
60 HMWD, 25 February 1943.
61 Ibid., 29 July 1943.
62 Ibid., 1 April 1943.
63 HMA.
64 Quoted in Ambler, op. cit., p. 78.
65 Alistair Horne, *A Savage War of Peace*, p. 377; HM, *Pointing the Way* (V), p. 410.
66 HMWD, 26 April 1944.
67 Ibid., 23 April 1943.
68 Ibid., 26 April 1943.
69 Hopkins papers, Franklin D. Roosevelt Library.
70 HMWD, 3 May 1943.

71 BBC1, June 1967.
72 de Gaulle, op. cit., p. 102.
73 HMWD, 31 May 1943.
74 Ibid., 4 June 1943.
75 HMA.
76 Murphy, op. cit., pp. 180–1, 226–7.
77 Churchill, op. cit., V, p. 156.
78 Ibid., pp. 159–60.
79 Churchill to Macmillan, No. 20, 23 July 1943; HMA.
80 HMWD, 31 July 1943.
81 Quoted in David Carlton, *Anthony Eden*, p. 219.
82 Quoted in François Kersaudy, *Churchill and de Gaulle*, p. 297.
83 Ibid.
84 FO 371/36182; PRO.
85 L. A. Siedentop, 'Mr. Macmillan and the Edwardian Style', in *The Age of Affluence*, p. 21.

Chapter 8   Viceroy of the Mediterranean, July 1943–November
            1944

HM, *The Blast of War* (II), pp. 204–562, and:

1 Robert Murphy, *Diplomat Among Warriors*, p. 232.
2 Ibid., p. 234.
3 Richard Crossman in *Sunday Telegraph*, 9 February 1964.
4 Oliver Harvey, *War Diaries*, pp. 284–5.
5 Interview, Lord Gladwyn.
6 Murphy, op. cit., p. 237.
7 Ibid., pp. 242–3.
8 AHC.
9 See Richard Lamb, *War Monthly*, VII, 'Rome 1943', *et al.*
10 Memorandum, 30 September 1943; HMA.
11 Interview, General James Gavin.
12 Harvey, op. cit., p. 289.
13 HMWD, 5 September 1943.
14 Ibid., 3 November 1943.
15 AHT, 7.17.
16 HMWD, 12 January 1945.
17 Ibid.
18 Ibid., 1 January 1944.
19 Ibid., 21 April 1944.
20 AHT, 8.7.
21 HMA.
22 Murphy, op. cit., p. 257.
23 AHT, 9.2.

24 HMWD, 3 December 1943.
25 Ibid., 26 March 1944.
26 Murphy, op. cit., p. 214.
27 Ibid., pp. 263, 270.
28 AHC.
29 HMWD, 16 November 1943.
30 Alanbrooke diaries, 23 November 1943, quoted in David Fraser, *Alanbrooke*, p. 385.
31 Alanbrooke diaries, 8 December 1943, quoted in Arthur Bryant, *Triumph in the West*, p. 111.
32 Alanbrooke note, quoted in Fraser, op. cit., p. 390.
33 Alanbrooke diaries, 31 January 1945, quoted in Bryant, op. cit., p. 396.
34 HMWD, 15/16 November 1943.
35 Ibid., 21 December 1943.
36 Ibid., 23 December 1943.
37 Ibid.
38 Ibid.
39 Harvey, op. cit., p. 305.
40 Letters to Dorothy Macmillan, 3 October 1943; HMA.
41 Ibid., 17 August 1943.
42 Ibid., 11 and 14 October 1943.
43 Ibid., 23 November 1943.
44 AHC.
45 Ibid.
46 Nigel Nicolson, *Alex*, pp. 193–4.
47 Field Marshal Earl Alexander of Tunis, *The Alexander Memoirs, 1940–45*, p. 11.
48 HMWD, 16 July 1943.
49 Ibid., 9 July 1943.
50 Ibid., 18 July 1943.
51 Ibid., 16 January 1944.
52 Ibid., 11 February 1944.
53 Interview, Lord Richardson.
54 Letter from Robert Murphy, 1 September 1944; HMA.
55 Philip Ziegler, *Diana Cooper*, p. 218.
56 Lord Egremont, *Wyndham and Children First*, p. 109.
57 *Sunday Telegraph*, 9 February 1964.
58 Letter of 7 November 1943; HMA.
59 HMWD, 16 April 1944.
60 Ibid., 15 March 1944.
61 Letter of 15 January 1944; HMA.
62 HMWD, 19 April 1944.
63 Ibid., 28 April 1944.
64 Ibid., 3 May 1944.

65 Ibid., 21 July 1944.
66 Pierson Dixon unpublished papers, 2 January 1944.
67 Ibid.
68 HMWD, 16 March 1944.
69 HM telegrams 141, 'Saving', and 648 to FO, 2 and 7 May 1944; HMA.
70 HMWD, 1–23 May 1944.
71 FO memorandum, 9 May 1944; HMA.
72 HMA.
73 Fraser, op. cit., p. 429.
74 HMWD, 21 June 1944.
75 Robert Bruce Lockhart, *Diaries*, II, p. 324.
76 Ibid., p. 328.
77 HMWD, 19 July 1944.
78 Dixon, op. cit., 11 August 1944.
79 Churchill memorandum, 14 August 1944; HMA.
80 HMWD, 15 August 1944.
81 Ibid., 16 August 1944.
82 Dixon, op. cit., 16 August 1944.
83 HM memorandum, 16 August 1944; HMA.
84 HMWD, 21 August 1944.
85 Ibid., 22 August 1944.
86 Dixon, op. cit., 22 August 1944; Piers Dixon, *Double Diploma*, p. 112.
87 Martin Gilbert; Chartwell Trust, 20/138.
88 Lord Egremont, op. cit., p. 194.

Chapter 9   Greece and Victory, October 1944–May 1945

HM, *The Blast of War* (II), pp. 341–705, and:

1   HMWD, 15 October 1944.
2   Ibid., 17 October 1944.
3   Robert Bruce Lockhart, *Diaries*, II, p. 374.
4   Scobie diaries (unpublished), 14 October 1944; Imperial War Museum.
5   Reginald Leeper, *When Greek Meets Greek*, p. 90.
6   HMWD, 8 December 1944.
7   Ibid., 7 December 1944.
8   Ibid., 8 December 1944.
9   Ibid., 11 December 1944.
10 Leeper, op. cit., pp. 114–15.
11 HMWD, 9 September 1944.
12 Leeper, op. cit., pp. 70, 115.
13 Lockhart, op. cit., p. 460.

14 Field Marshal Earl Alexander of Tunis, *The Alexander Memoirs, 1940–1945*, pp. 42–3.
15 Quoted in Philip Henry Stanhope, *Notes of Conversations with the Duke of Wellington, 1831–1851* (London 1888), pp. 68–9.
16 AHT, 7.16–17; 8.9; 9.6–7.
17 HMWD, 11 November 1944.
18 Alexander, op. cit., pp. 142–3.
19 Scobie, op. cit., 13 December 1944.
20 HMWD, 13 December 1944.
21 Ibid.
22 Robert Glenton, *Sunday Express*, 19 October 1958.
23 HMWD, 8 December 1944.
24 John Wyndham, *Wyndham and Children First*, p. 126.
25 Ibid., p. 128.
26 Leeper, op. cit., pp. 110, 115.
27 HMWD, 16 December 1944.
28 Oliver Harvey, *War Diaries*, p. 399.
29 HMWD, 19 December 1944.
30 Winston Churchill, *The Second World War*, VI, p. 269.
31 Leeper, op. cit., p. 89.
32 Scobie, op. cit., 21 December 1944.
33 Ibid.
34 HMWD, 24 December 1944.
35 Ibid., 25 December 1944.
36 Quoted by Glenton, op. cit.
37 Alexander, op. cit., p. 143.
38 Churchill, op. cit., VI, p. 271.
39 Ibid., p. 276; letter of 26 December 1944.
40 Lockhart, op. cit., p. 381.
41 Churchill, op. cit., VI, p. 283.
42 Lord Egremont, op. cit., p. 131.
43 AHT, 7.21.
44 HMWD, 11 January 1945.
45 *Oxford Mail*, 7 September 1967.
46 Alanbrooke diaries, quoted in Arthur Bryant, *Triumph in the West*, p. 396.
47 HMWD, 20 and 25 January 1945.
48 Ibid., 3 and 4 February 1945.
49 Ibid., 14 February 1945.
50 Churchill, op. cit., VI, pp. 347–8.
51 HMA; Alfred Duff Cooper, *Old Men Forget*, pp. 174–6.
52 HMWD, 2 March 1945.
53 Ibid., 15 February 1945.
54 Ibid., 9 August 1944.
55 Ibid., 1–23 May 1944.

56   Ibid., 26 April 1945.
57   Ibid., 5/6 May 1945.
58   Ibid., 9 May 1945.
59   Ibid., 17 February 1945.
60   Interview, Lord Colyton.
61   HMWD, 23 April 1945.
62   Ibid., 29 April 1945.

Chapter 10   A Tragic Epilogue, May–June 1945

HM, *The Blast of War* (II), pp. 576–7, 659, 677, 685–98, and *Tides of Fortune* (III), pp. 10–22, and:

1   Nicholas Bethell, *The Last Secret* (London 1974).
2   Nikolai Tolstoy, *Victims of Yalta* (London 1974), *Stalin's Secret War* (London 1981), *The Minister and the Massacres* (London 1986).
3   The Tolstoy allegations were followed by Macmillan, only a few months before his death at ninety-two, being branded a 'war criminal' in a Tory student magazine (against which a writ was subsequently served by the Party Chairman, Norman Tebbit).
4   Interview, Julian Amery.
5   Winston Churchill, *The Second World War*, VI, pp. 351–2.
6   FO 371/40445; PRO.
7   FO 94/23; PRO.
8   Cabinet papers, 65/49; War Cabinet No. 13, 31 January 1945.
9   Martin Gilbert, *Road to Victory, 1941–1945*, p. 1160.
10   AFHQ/G–5 Section, Displaced Persons, microfilm reel 477; National Archives, Washington DC. The key first directive of 6 March, which appears not to have been seen by Tolstoy before writing *The Minister and the Massacres*, is erroneously referred to by him (notably p. 215) as dated May and not March; and from this flows a number of important false suppositions.
11   FO 1020/42; PRO.
12   Ibid.
13   HMWD, 12 May 1945.
14   Ibid., 13 May 1945.
15   AHC; AHT. (Author interviews with HM, 16 May 1979 to 25 May 1983.)
16   Interviews, Lord Aldington (by Serena Booker, 11 February 1981, and author, 27 January 1982). When initially questioned by Serena Booker, Lord Aldington said that he did 'not remember attending' the meeting. If he had been there, it would have been surprising that he had forgotten, given that he was a young man with political aspirations (let alone Keightley's chief executive) and that Macmillan was the most senior Tory minister in the vicinity. (Lord Aldington

later stated to the author that the first time he set eyes on Harold Macmillan was 'in a garret at Macmillan's', when he had already become a parliamentary candidate, having left the army.) There was indeed no surviving record, he declared subsequently, to show that he was present at the 13 May meeting with Macmillan, and he maintained categorically that he was *not*. In a letter to the author of 1 November 1987, he wrote that there was 'no reference in the files to what I was doing'. In his seventies, he recalled only the impression of a second-hand, ex-*post facto* account of the meeting given by Keightley, but he did 'remember being involved in the drafting of the signal to General McCreery' afterwards.

17 HMWD, 13 May 1945.
18 AHC; AHT.
19 HMWD, 13 May 1945.
20 John Colville, *Fringes of Power*, p. 599.
21 WO 170/4241; PRO.
22 AFHQ/G–5 Section, Displaced Persons, microfilm reel 477; National Archives, Washington DC. This telegram, which appears not to have been seen by Tolstoy, already shows that those in the know of Macmillan's dealings with V Corps belonged to a considerably wider circle than was alleged in *The Minister and the Massacres*.
23 WO 170/4184; PRO.
24 The study by the 'Cowgill Group' (see note 77) points out that the terms 'White Russians' and 'Russian émigrés' overlap but are not synonymous. General Vlasov's Russian National Army, which included a great many Soviet citizens, was commonly known as the 'White Russian' Army. References to 'White Russians' in V Corps communications at this time relate to the members of the 4000-strong Rogozhin Corps and not to the 'old émigrés' such as Generals Krasnov and Shkuro, who were members of the Cossack Corps. In military communications up to late May 1945, no reference in any way to 'Russian émigrés' has been found.

    The Cossacks (overwhelmingly Soviet citizens) were due for repatriation under the Yalta agreement, and were repatriated. The Rogozhin Corps, on the other hand, was not liable for repatriation under Yalta, as its members had left the Soviet Union before 1939 and were not 'Soviet citizens'. None, in the event, was handed back and this decision, in full accordance with AFHQ letter of 6 March 1945, was promulgated by V Corps on 21 May, well after the Klagenfurt meeting – a point which seemed to elude Tolstoy (see *Minister and Massacres*, p. 94).
25 AHC; AHT.
26 'On advice Macmillan' in the V Corps telegram of 14 May became a 'verbal directive' in a message sent on 23 May to Eighth Army (FO 1020/42); which it was not. Low, who had already left for England, was

not the signatory of this telegram; as he later pointed out, the imprecise language of 'verbal directive' would not have been used by him. This phrase in turn was translated by Tolstoy to read 'instructions', although, as political Resident Minister, Macmillan had no authority to give either 'directives' or 'instructions' to an army formation.

27   Macmillan had no recollection of having been informed of any such approach, as suggested by Tolstoy, by the Soviets to regain specific 'old émigrés'. And he considered it 'impossible' that anybody could have short-circuited Alexander to Keightley: 'Alex would have been furious. . . .' (AHC; AHT).

28   Interview, Lord Aldington.

29   It is also questionable whether in fact, as Tolstoy has suggested, the attitude of the allegedly more humane Alexander would have been markedly different. Alexander had been much more closely affiliated in 1919 with the essentially German *Landeswehr* in Latvia than with any White Russians, and there is no suggestion that he had any particular sympathy for them either then or in 1945. Had he known of the presence of the individual 'old émigrés' in Austria, he would almost certainly have asked what they were doing there – if not actually in German uniform or in some way having worked for the enemy cause.

30   Letter to author from Patrick Martin-Smith, 12 June 1980.

31   Letter No. 6 to Sir James Grigg, 18 May 1945; HMA.

32   FO 1020/42; PRO.

33   WO 106/4059; PRO.

34   Ibid.

35   WO 32/13749; PRO.

36   FO 371/48825; PRO. The reason for the untoward delay in the reply to Alexander lay in the order having had to be deliberated at top level in both London and Washington and by the Combined Chiefs of Staff.

37   Statement by Brigadier C. E. Tryon-Wilson to 'Cowgill Group' (see note 77).

38   WO 170/4241; PRO.

39   As Tolstoy himself stated (*Minister and Massacres*, p. 44), 'Neither General Krasnov nor any other old émigré was seeking to extricate himself from sharing whatever fate attended those of their comrades who were in the equivocal position of being Soviet citizens. At least no trace of an attempt to do so has survived among the voluminous Cossack and British sources.'

40   Interview, Lord Aldington.

41   WO 170/4241; PRO.

42   FO 1020/42; PRO.

43   Ibid. By the time of this request Brigadier Low had left for England, and demob.

44 FO 1020/2838; PRO.

45 WO 170/4241; PRO. To Nicholas Bethell (op. cit., p. 137), this order '. . . made clear that all officers without exception were to be sent back. It was this May 24 order which was the valid one.'

46 WO 170/484; PRO. The V Corps statement could be said to be correct in the sense of treating those handed over as formations, but no detailed screening within formations had been done – and this was not reflected explicitly in any signals from V Corps at the time.

47 HMWD, 16 May 1945.

48 Ibid.

49 Ibid., 19 May 1945.

50 Colville, op. cit., p. 600; diary entry of 19 May 1945.

51 HMWD, 21 May 1945.

52 Ibid., 22 May 1945.

53 Ibid., 19 May 1945.

54 Churchill, it can be assumed, would have been passed Macmillan's signal to the Foreign Office of 15 May, reporting the presence of 30,000 Cossacks in Carinthia and General Keightley's vulnerable position. (The 'Caserta' file, HMA, contains the uncorrupted version of HM's signal to the FO; only the corrupted version appears to have been seen by Tolstoy.) Churchill would therefore have been well briefed in advance of Macmillan's visit, and thus almost certain to have called for amplification on the subject. But in the lack of further documentation, one can only speculate.

Tolstoy's own disclosure is that on 20 May (the day after Macmillan arrived at Chequers), Churchill 'began to show an interest' in the Russian prisoner-of-war issue, writing to General Ismay for detailed information. 'Clearly something had disquieted the Prime Minister in connection with the captured Cossacks and the degree of guilt to be attributed to Russians accused of having served with the Germans' (*Victims of Yalta*, p. 343). What and through whom? Macmillan's three-day visit with Churchill may have been purely coincidental; nevertheless it is from this date that Churchill's 'sea-change' towards the Soviets and Tito is marked. Again, as Tolstoy concedes, somewhat against his own thesis, it is 'tempting to conjecture that it was during his visit to England that Macmillan received instructions which he relayed to Alexander on his return, thus bringing about the change in policy which ensued . . .' (*Minister and Massacres*, pp. 225–6).

55 Tolstoy, *Minister and Massacres*, p. 95 *et seq.*

56 HQBAF 699; Sir William Deakin papers.

57 Sir William Deakin papers.

58 HMA.

59 HMWD, 13 May 1945.

60 WO 170/4241; PRO.

61 WO 170/4184; PRO.

62 *Foreign Relations of the United States 1945, Diplomatic Papers*, V (Europe), (US Government Printing Office, Washington DC, 1967). Kirk, in his signal 2162 of 14 May to the State Department, creates the damning impression that Macmillan had recommended the repatriation of Yugoslavs as well as of the Cossacks. But, when read carefully, this appears to be a misinterpretation of General Robertson's telegram FX 75383 of 14 May, which does not mention Macmillan but which answered McCreery's signal 189, mentioning a recommendation by Macmillan relating to Cossacks only.

63 WO, 170/4183; PRO.

64 Memorandum from G–3 Division AFHQ, signed G. L. Eberle, Brigadier General, US Army, Assistant Chief of Staff, G–3, to Chief of Staff, 17 May 1945; Sir William Deakin papers.

65 Yet on 17 May, the day Tito accepted the hand-over of the 200,000 Yugoslavs, Alexander was also compiling his 'emergency' telegram to the Combined Chiefs of Staff and the British Chiefs of Staff, asking 'urgently' for direction regarding the final disposal of 50,000 Cossacks, 35,000 Chetniks (11,000 of them already evacuated to Italy) and 25,000 German Croat troops, for whom return to their country of origin 'might be fatal to their health' (WO 106/4059). It was as if General Robertson's hand-over order of 14 May, issuing from his own headquarters, had never existed.

66 WO 170/4185; PRO.

67 *Foreign Relations of the United States*, op. cit.

68 Ibid. The interpretation here, as in May (see note 62), is that Kirk, covering himself months after the events, was guilty of loose wording in inculpating Macmillan.

69 FO 371/48919, 48920; PRO.

70 WO 170/4241; PRO.

71 Ibid.

72 WO 170/4185; PRO.

73 Statement by Lord Aldington to 'Cowgill Group' (see note 77).

74 In a letter to the author of 1 November 1987, Lord Aldington, stressing the confused background against which V Corps was working, stated: 'The "deception" of the Yugoslavs has to be understood in military terms. In fact, all that the order which I signed, and which, of course, my General saw and probably initiated, did was to impose strict security on everyone as to the destination of the Yugoslavs who were to be repatriated.... We were under instructions from above to repatriate them, and had to carry out those instructions....'

75 An important insight is given in a letter (FO 371/44609) from Jack Nicholls, a Foreign Office representative sent up to V Corps, Klagenfurt, on about 17 May (in itself, further confirmation that Macmillan had played no further role since the 13th). Nicholls wrote on 21 May to Harold Mack, his superior attached to AFHQ, describing an

'agreement' that had been concluded two days previously '. . . while the BGS was sitting with two Yugoslav officers outside his caravan': the partisan 14 Division was ordered to withdraw behind the Yugoslav frontier, and to cease requisitioning civilian property; the Yugoslav GHQ was to be asked to withdraw all area HQs. On the British side, '5 Corps to return to Yugoslavia all Yugoslav nationals who had fought in uniform with the Germans, together with their camp followers (about 18,500 in all)'.

> The two Yugoslav officers stayed to dinner, and the atmosphere was friendly to a degree; they had brought a case of champagne, and in it we exchanged numerous toasts. . . . I doubt if two emissaries sent to climb down ever went away as happy as these two! Yesterday the withdrawal was in full swing. . . .

When it refers to repatriation of 'camp followers', however, the Nicholls letter seems to conflict significantly with the V Corps order of 19 May, which – by referring to the repatriates as 'these forces' – implicitly excluded civilians. Nicholls' letter was presumably sent upwards along the Foreign Office chain of communications, but there is nothing to suggest that any objection was raised.

Nicholls concluded with another interesting insight, concerning the Russian repatriates, put in the form of a question: '. . . if captured Cossacks fighting with the Germans are to be handed over to the Russians, what should be done with White Russians with French nationality?' This suggests that V Corps had by now discovered the presence of old émigrés; but there is no evidence to show that the information had ever been passed back to Macmillan, certainly not before he made his flying visit to see Churchill on 19 May, and the letter did not reach the Foreign Office until 10 June.

76   Interview, Julian Amery; letter from Lord Aldington to author, 1 November 1987.

77   Sparked by the Tolstoy allegations in *The Minister and the Massacres*, in 1986 a retired army brigadier, Anthony Cowgill, MBE, initiated his own study to examine the records. As of May 1945, he had been serving with Second Army GHQ in north-west Europe (and was therefore not involved) but, as a regular officer, he knew many of those who had been involved and was shocked at the serious allegations made over the years, which seemed to reflect particularly badly on the honour of the army. He felt that the army's role should be clarified, and if this were not done while some of the key participants were still alive, the truth would perhaps never be known. In the absence of any official enquiry, he decided to institute a study, at his own expense, with the aim of reviewing all available evidence from the official archives and other sources, and submitting surviving participants' testimony to detailed investigation. Cowgill invited to join him three people dis-

tinguished in their own different spheres: Brigadier C. E. Tryon-Wilson, the senior administrative officer (DA and QMG) at HQ V Corps in May 1945; Lord Brimelow, former Permanent Under-Secretary at the Foreign Office, who as Second Secretary had been concerned with the execution of the Yalta Repatriation Agreement and who had made a detailed study of the Foreign Office archives; and Christopher Booker, who as a journalist had written a number of critical reviews on the Tolstoy allegations over the years, and who wished to complete the work on the role of Macmillan which his late sister, Serena Booker, had been researching (for the official biography) when she died.

Full co-operation was received from all principal surviving army officers involved, in particular Lord Aldington (Brigadier Low) and General Sir Geoffrey Musson (who as Brigadier Musson had commanded 36 Inf Bde, the unit concerned with the hand-over of many of the Cossacks). Assistance was also received from the Thatcher Cabinet Offices, and for two years the 'Cowgill Group' sifted painstakingly all available sources, including a number of hitherto undiscovered documents, notably the key AFHQ instructions of 6 and 15 March 1945 (see note 10), which have kindly been made available to the author. A very detailed record was constructed, enabling for the first time the sequence and flow of events and decisions during the critical period of May 1945 to be seen in full perspective.

Though their brief was not in any way to 'clear' Macmillan (and, indeed, if the army were to be acquitted, the burden of responsibility could only have fallen the harder on the Minister Resident and his 'advice'), if anything the weight of military considerations – namely the need to clear the decks for possible operations against Yugoslavs – emerged even more strongly and was reflected in the resultant military decisions. Encapsulated, Macmillan's role at Klagenfurt had been to underline the delicacy of the developing political situation caused by Tito's territorial ambitions; to explain Alexander's order not to fire on the Yugoslavs, but also to agree the need for clearing the area at the earliest opportunity for possible operations against Tito; and to confirm that the Cossacks should be sent back in accordance with the Yalta agreement and government policy. In this last respect, the main thrust of Macmillan's advice to Keightley was that, in order to get quick action to move the Cossacks, it would be necessary to raise the level to Marshal Tolbukhin himself. Similarly with the Yugoslavs, the group found no evidence that Macmillan was involved in the repatriation of Yugoslav anti-partisans except in the broad sense of 'agreeing the need for clearing the area . . .'.

No evidence has been found that Macmillan had been shown a list of the émigrés wanted by the Russians. There was equally no evidence that Macmillan had been involved in any 'conspiracy'. The Eighth Army Chief of Staff (Harry Floyd) had been present throughout the talks with Keightley, as had the Head of Military Government (Con Benson) and other staff officers, including Macmillan's deputy, Philip Broad. The very full exchange of subsequent signals between AFHQ, 15 Army Group, Eighth Army and V Corps was also completely incompatible with the theory of a closed conspiracy. On the allegations by Tolstoy of a 'Klagenfurt conspiracy', the conclusion was that there was simply *no case to answer*.

In his old age, Macmillan may thus have incriminated himself unnecessarily by answering the wrong questions, based on false premises – as per his only public appearance on television on the subject (*Timewatch*, BBC2, 3 January 1984), when taken by surprise in some unscheduled questioning by Ludovic Kennedy. However reprehensible and brutal the consequences of the concessions made to the victorious Russians, at worst Macmillan was no more responsible than the signatories of Yalta. Macmillan was only the messenger.

On the V Corps directive of 21 May, the evidence showed that Macmillan had in no way been party to the decision to send back 'formed bodies' without positive screening, nor to the decision to use force in the repatriation, nor to the decision to indulge in deliberate deception against the Yugoslav 'anti-partisans'. These were all operational decisions.

Of all the surviving witnesses of the events of May 1945, the most important, Lord Aldington, wrote following the Cowgill Group investigations:

> I remain of the opinion that HM did not give any instructions about émigrés. I think the reference in his diaries to 'White Russians' was to the division formed by the Germans from Russian POWs who turned their coats, and to others like them. . . . I am certain I would not have issued the orders of 21st May defining Russian nationals, if HM had solved the problem. . . .

The last is a telling point in favour of Harold Macmillan.

78 Allegations of an official cover-up over the repatriations have also been made. Complaints by representatives of the Slovene Government in Exile in June 1945 seem to have been suppressed by the Foreign Office and the War Office, jointly or separately, during the Attlee years of 1945 to 1951. It was during that time that War Office files were discovered to have been 'tidied up' and an inquiry initiated under the Attlee Government effectively stifled (interview, Sir Arthur Drew; letter from Sir Robert Armstrong to author, 15 September 1980). Whatever the reasons for this, now buried in the sands of time, it can hardly have been either at the behest of Macmillan; then a fallen Tory minister, or to save his reputation.

Numerous documents alleged to have been destroyed were subsequently turned up by the meticulous researches of Brigadier Cowgill and his team, and many errors, half-truths, distortions of quoted material and suppositions not founded on fact were pinpointed. For instance, Tolstoy (*Minister and Massacres*, p. 94) writes that '. . . some forty pages of Macmillan's diary for this period are said to have disappeared'; in fact, these pages were in a bank vault, along with the other originals of the Macmillan diaries – exactly where they should have been.

Finally, in September 1958, an appeal for compensation on behalf of the few surviving repatriated Cossacks was made to the Prime Minister, then Macmillan. None was awarded and Tolstoy's suggestion is that Macmillan turned a deaf ear. In fact, this appeal was dealt with by the Foreign Office and evidently was never passed to the Prime Minister's office. (Letter from Sir Philip de Zulueta to author, 2 September 1983; FCO letter to author, 4 November 1983.)

79 AHC.
80 HMWD, 25 May 1945.
81 Ibid., 26 May 1945.

Chapter 11   A New Britain, 1945–1950

HM, *Tides of Fortune* (III), pp. 23–100, 278–318, and:

1 Letter of 5 April 1945; HMA.
2 *The Times*, 4 February 1984.
3 Hugh Dalton, *Memoirs*, II, p. 468.
4 Quoted in Anthony Sampson, *Macmillan*, pp. 74–5.
5 Emanuel Shinwell, *I've Lived Through It All*, p. 215.
6 Interview, Lord Shinwell.
7 Letter of 5 May 1945; HMA.
8 BBC1, 9 September 1969.
9 Quoted in Tom Pocock, *The Dawn Came Up Like Thunder* (London 1983), p. 166.
10 Ibid.
11 Harold Nicolson, *Diaries and Letters*, III, p. 3.
12 Sampson, op. cit., p. 75.
13 *The Times*, 8 March 1984.
14 Harold Wilson, *A Prime Minister on Prime Ministers*, p. 291.
15 AHC.
16 Hansard, 7 July 1960.
17 Michael Foot, *Aneurin Bevan*, p. 612.
18 Quoted in Pocock, op. cit., pp. 159–60.
19 BBC1, 9 September 1969.
20 Ibid.
21 AHT, 5.7.

22 Ian Gilmour, *The Body Politic*, p. 52.
23 From HM speech at Hatfield, 1 September 1946; quoted in Sampson, op. cit., p. 78.
24 Ibid.
25 *Sunday Telegraph*, 9 February 1964.
26 Interview, Michael Foot.
27 Emrys Hughes, *Macmillan*, p. 70.
28 Robert Bruce Lockhart, *Diaries*, II, p. 519.
29 Harold Nicolson, op. cit., III, p. 43.
30 Interview, C. P. Snow.
31 Interview, Michael Foot.
32 AHC; AHT, 5.5–6.
33 Ibid.
34 R. A. Butler, *The Art of the Possible*, p. 144.
35 BBC1, 9 September 1969.
36 HMD, 5 October 1950.
37 David Carlton, *Anthony Eden*, p. 268.
38 *Sunday Express*, 15 May 1947.
39 Author's private papers, 17 June 1958.
40 Letter of 5 February 1948; HMA.
41 Interview, Nigel Nicolson.
42 Sampson, op. cit., p. 82.
43 HMA.
44 Memorandum of 12 October 1949; HMA.

Chapter 12   The Cold World Outside, 1945–1950

HM, *Tides of Fortune* (III), pp. 100–278, and:

1   Hansard, 20 February 1946.
2   *Daily Telegraph*, 3 October 1946.
3   Hansard, 23 March 1949; Emrys Hughes, *Macmillan*, pp. 71–7.
4   Quoted in Anthony Sampson, *Macmillan*, p. 83.
5   Hansard, 16 May 1947.
6   Ibid., 1 August 1946.
7   The quotations in this section are from HM's letters to Dorothy Macmillan or from his unpublished diary of the Indian tour, January–February 1947; HMA.
8   Hansard, 17 November 1949.
9   Harold Wilson, *A Prime Minister on Prime Ministers*, p. 283.
10 Strasbourg letters, 24 August 1949; HMA.
11 John Beavan, *The Statist*, 18 October 1963, quoted in Sampson, op. cit., p. 85.
12 Quoted in Sampson, op. cit., p. 85.
13 Strasbourg letters, 10 August 1949; HMA.

14   Ibid., 24 August 1949.
15   Hugh Dalton, *Memoirs 1945–1960*, III, p. 323.
16   AHC.
17   Hansard, 20 February 1946.
18   Ibid., 23 March 1946.
19   HMD, 22 November 1950.
20   AHC.
21   Quoted in *The Economist*, 2 June 1979.
22   Ibid.
23   HMD, 13 November 1950.
24   Ibid., 16 November 1950.
25   Ibid., 23–30 November 1950.
26   Letter of 20 June 1950; HMA.
27   Hansard, 27 June 1950.
28   HM Strasbourg diary, 26 August 1950; HMA.
29   Quoted in Sampson, op. cit., p. 85.
30   Ibid., p. 86.
31   Dalton, op. cit., III, p. 327.

Chapter 13   Under Churchill: Houses and Defence, 1951–1955

HM, *Tides of Fortune* (III), pp. 312–578, and:

1   HMA.
2   HMD, 29 November 1950.
3   Interview, Julian Amery.
4   HMD, 12–17 March 1951.
5   Ibid., 10 April 1951.
6   Ibid., 16 April 1951.
7   Ibid., 21 June 1951.
8   Ibid., 27 November 1951.
9   Ibid., 30 November 1951.
10   Ibid., 6 December 1950.
11   Ibid., 11 December 1950.
12   Ibid., 13 December 1950.
13   Ibid., 6 December 1950.
14   Ibid., 14 December 1950.
15   Ibid., 17 January 1951.
16   Ibid., 25 January 1951.
17   Ibid., 7 April 1951.
18   AHT, 5.8.
19   Interview, Lord Soames.
20   HMD, 28 October 1951.
21   AHC.
22   HMD, 29 June 1951.

23 AHT, 9.23–4.
24 AHC.
25 Interviews, Lady Soames, Sir John Colville.
26 BBC1, 9 September 1969.
27 Anthony Seldon, *Churchill's Indian Summer*, p. 29.
28 *The Times*, 5 January 1983.
29 Hansard, 4 December 1951.
30 HMD, 10 July 1952.
31 AHC.
32 Anthony Sampson, *Macmillan*, p. 97.
33 AHC.
34 Philip Swinton, *Sixty Years of Power*, p. 179.
35 Interview, Margaret Thatcher.
36 Reginald Bevins, *The Greasy Pole* (London 1965), p. 29.
37 Hugh Dalton, *Memoirs 1954–60*, III, p. 358.
38 Kingsley Martin, *New Statesman Profiles*, p. 176.
39 Emrys Hughes, *Macmillan*, p. 83.
40 Emanuel Shinwell, *I've Lived Through It All*, p. 214.
41 Maurice Edelman reviewing HM's *Tides of Fortune* in *Punch*, 17 September 1979.
42 BBC1, 9 September 1969.
43 HMD, 20 November 1954.
44 Ibid., 30 July 1953.
45 Interviews, Lord Boothby, Lord and Lady Gage, Maurice Macmillan.
46 HMA.
47 HMD, 5 October 1953.
48 Ibid., 29 May 1954.
49 Ibid., 29 April 1954.
50 Lord Moran, *Winston Churchill: The Struggle for Survival*, p. 627.
51 AHC.
52 Interview, Lord Carrington.
53 Memorandum on 'The Economics of Western Defence', March 1955 (FM/97); HMA.
54 BBC1, 9 September 1969; HMD, 22 October 1954.
55 HMA.
56 BBC1, 9 September 1969.
57 HMD, 17 January 1952.
58 Letter to Eden, 15 June 1954; HMA.
59 HMD, 10 July 1954.
60 FO 953/1207; PRO; Richard Lamb, *The Failure of the Eden Government*, p. 63.
61 Robert Boothby, *Recollections of a Rebel*, p. 222.
62 Quoted in *The Economist*, 2 June 1979.
63 AHC.

64 HMA.
65 *Documents on British Policy Overseas*, series 2, I, 1950–52 (HMSO 1985).
66 Memorandum of 17 March 1952; HMA.
67 AHC.
68 HMD, 18 February 1952.
69 John Colville, diary entry of 31 May 1952. When this extract was to be included in Colville's contribution to *Action This Day – Working with Churchill* (1968), his publisher – Harold Macmillan – asked that it be cut out.
70 HMD, 7 December 1951.
71 Ibid., 4 June 1952.
72 Ibid., 17 January 1952.
73 Ibid., 2 July 1952.
74 Ibid.
75 Ibid., 13 December 1953.
76 R. A. Butler, *The Art of the Possible*, p. 173.
77 HMD, 31 July 1954.
78 Ibid., 27 February 1954.
79 Letter of 24 August 1954; HMA.
80 HMD, 9 January 1955.
81 Moran, op. cit., pp. 626–8.
82 HMD, 14 March 1955.
83 Ibid., 17 March 1955.
84 Ibid., 4 April 1955.
85 AHC.
86 Quoted in Seldon, op. cit., p. 93.

Chapter 14   Under Eden: From Foreign Office to Treasury, May 1955–July 1956

HM, *Tides of Fortune* (III), pp. 378–695, and:

 1 HMD, 26 and 27 May 1955.
 2 Anthony Eden, *Full Circle*, pp. 404–7.
 3 AHT, 10.16.
 4 Ibid., 10.17.
 5 HMD, 10 May 1955.
 6 BBC1, 9 September 1969.
 7 HMD, 14 May 1955.
 8 Ibid., 19 July 1955.
 9 Ibid., 22 July 1955.
10 Ibid., 8 November 1955.
11 Letters to Dorothy Macmillan, 5 November 1955; HMA.
12 HMD, 14 December 1955.

13   Cmd 952–5 (HMSO 1955).
14   HMA.
15   HM, *Riding the Storm*, IV, pp. 69–70.
16   Eden, speech at Norwich, 1 June 1956; HMA.
17   HMD, 3 April 1955.
18   HMA.
19   HMD, 2 September 1955.
20   Hansard, 7 November 1955.
21   *Daily Express*, Roy Blackman interview with Philby, 15 November 1967.
22   HMD, 8 October 1955.
23   BBC1, 9 September 1969.
24   HMD, 18 August 1953.
25   FO 371/115965; PRO.
26   Information produced by Egyptian and Israeli participants at a joint symposium on Suez by St Antony's College, Oxford, and the Woodrow Wilson Center, Washington, in Washington DC, September 1987.
27   FO 371/115879, minute by Geoffrey Archer, 20 September 1955; PRO.
28   HMD, 23 September 1955.
29   Ibid., 25 September 1955.
30   Ibid., 30 September 1955.
31   Ibid., 2 October 1955.
32   Ibid.
33   Ibid., 27 October 1955.
34   Quoted in Donald Neff, *Warriors at Suez*, p. 106.
35   HMD, 18 October 1955.
36   AHC.
37   Nicholas Henderson, *The Private Office*, p. 114.
38   Lord Kilmuir, *Political Adventure*, p. 243.
39   *The Times*, 16 December 1955.
40   HMD, 2 May 1953.
41   Ibid., 20 June 1955.
42   Ibid., 27 October 1955.
43   Ibid., 13 November 1955.
44   Roscoe Drummond and Gaston Coblentz, *Duel at the Brink*, p. 164.
45   Interview, Sir Philip de Zulueta.
46   Timothy Eden, *The Tribulations of a Baronet*, p. 23.
47   Patrick Cosgrave, *R. A. Butler*, p. 12.
48   AHT, 9.25–6; 3.8–10.
49   Interview, Sir Philip de Zulueta.
50   R. A. Butler, *The Art of the Possible*, p. 165.
51   Harold Wilson, *A Prime Minister on Prime Ministers*, p. 302.
52   AHC.

53   Philip Ziegler, *Diana Cooper*, p. 288.
54   Kilmuir, op. cit., p. 256.
55   Quoted in David Carlton, *Anthony Eden*, pp. 288–9.
56   HMD, 30 December 1955.
57   Ibid., 23 January 1956.
58   Cosgrave, op. cit., pp. 99–100.
59   HMD, 11–14 July 1952.
60   Wilson, op. cit., p. 308.
61   Letter of 12 January 1956; HMA.
62   HMD, 11 February 1956.
63   Carlton, op. cit., p. 396.
64   Ibid., pp. 396–7.
65   HMA.
66   Letter of 17 May 1956; HMA.
67   HMA.
68   HMD, 17 April 1956.
69   Hansard, 17 April 1956.
70   Samuel Brittan, *The Treasury under the Tories, 1951–1964* (London 1964),
      p. 182.
71   HMD, 18 April 1956.
72   Hansard, 18 April 1956.
73   HMD, 24 April 1956.
74   Ibid., 8 May 1956.
75   Ibid., 14 May 1956.
76   Anthony Eden, op. cit., p. 365.
77   HMA.
78   T 243/183; PRO.
79   FO 371/122035; PRO.
80   Quoted in Emrys Hughes, *Macmillan*, p. 178.
81   Wilson, op. cit., p. 308.
82   HMD, 12 January 1956.
83   Ibid., 16 March 1956.
84   Ivone Kirkpatrick, *The Inner Circle*, p. 262.
85   Quoted in Neff, op. cit., p. 155.
86   *Daily Mirror*, 5 January 1956.
87   *Daily Telegraph*, 3 January 1956.
88   Quoted in Carlton, op. cit., p. 399.
89   Quoted in Randolph Churchill, *The Rise and Fall of Sir Anthony Eden*,
      p. 227.
90   HMD, 5 July 1956.
91   Ibid., 21 July 1956.
92   Harold Nicolson, *Diaries and Letters*, III, p. 305.

Chapter 15 Suez, July–November 1956

HM, *Riding the Storm* (IV), pp. 99–174, and:

1   HMD, 5 July 1956.
2   Dwight D. Eisenhower, *The White House Years*, p. 33.
3   HMD, 21 July 1956.
4   Ibid., 26 July 1956.
5   Ibid., 27 July 1956.
6   Quoted in Donald Neff, *Warriors at Suez*, p. 277.
7   Hansard, 2 August 1956.
8   Quoted in Anthony Nutting, *No End of a Lesson*, p. 34. When Nutting's book was first published in 1967, some portions of the original text had been excised (apparently at the request of the Cabinet secretariat); the extracts used in this chapter include the excised portions where noted.
9   John Selwyn Lloyd, *Suez 1956*, p. 4.
10 Anthony Eden, *Full Circle*, p. 315.
11 Quoted in Philip Ziegler, *Diana Cooper*, p. 289.
12 HMD, 27 July 1956.
13 Ibid., 28 and 29 July 1956.
14 Robert Murphy, *Diplomat Among Warriors*, p. 379.
15 Ibid., p. 381.
16 HMD, 30 and 31 July 1956.
17 Selwyn Lloyd, op. cit., pp. 91–2.
18 HMD, 1 August 1956.
19 Eden, op. cit., p. 436.
20 Ibid.
21 Hugh Thomas, *The Suez Affair*, p. 55.
22 HMD, 2 August 1956.
23 Ibid., 3 August 1956.
24 Memorandum of 3 August 1956; HMA.
25 Interview, Robert Rhodes James. This reaction was not, however, incorporated in Rhodes James' official biography of Eden.
26 HMD, 4 August 1956.
27 Ibid., 24 and 26 August 1956.
28 Ibid., 25 August 1956.
29 Ibid., 16 September 1956.
30 Ibid., 20 September 1956.
31 AHT.
32 HMD, 5 August 1956.
33 Ibid., 6 August 1956.
34 Robert Rhodes James, *Anthony Eden*, p. 496.
35 Egypt Committee, Cabinet minute, 'Action against Egypt', 7 August 1956; HMA.
36 HMD, 7 August 1956.

37 Ibid., 9 August 1956.
38 Ibid., 10 August 1956.
39 Ibid., 16 August 1956.
40 Philip Ziegler, *Mountbatten*, pp. 537–46.
41 Chester Cooper, *The Lion's Last Roar: Suez 1956*, p. 151.
42 HMD, 18 August 1956.
43 Ibid., 19 August 1956.
44 Ibid., 22 August 1956.
45 State Department Memorandum, 21 August 1956, Dwight D. Eisenhower Library, Abilene.
46 HMD, 24 August 1956. By an apparent Freudian slip, Macmillan in his memoirs attributed these remarks to himself, not Eden.
47 Ibid.
48 Ibid., 25 August 1956.
49 Treasury paper, 26 August 1956; HMA.
50 HMD, 28 August 1956.
51 Ibid., 29 August 1956.
52 Ibid.
53 Ibid., 3 September 1956.
54 Ibid., 4 September 1956.
55 Ibid.
56 Ibid., 8 September 1956.
57 Dwight D. Eisenhower Library, Abilene.
58 Ibid.
59 Sir Guy Millard's report for 'UK Eyes Only' at the request of the Cabinet in 1957. *Contemporary Record*, I, no. 1, spring 1987, p. 5; PRO.
60 Selwyn Lloyd, op. cit., pp. 129–30.
61 Ibid., pp. 130–1.
62 HMD, 9 September 1956.
63 Ibid., 10 September 1956.
64 T 236/4188; PRO.
65 FO 800/740; PRO.
66 HMD, 13 September 1956.
67 Ibid., 15 September 1956.
68 Ibid., 16 September 1956.
69 Ibid., 18 September 1956.
70 Ibid., 20 September 1956.
71 Ibid., 23 September 1956.
72 Ibid., 22 September 1956.
73 Ibid., 24 September 1956.
74 T 236; quoted in *Contemporary Record*, op. cit., p. 4.
75 HMD, 23 September 1956.
76 Ibid., 25 September 1956.
77 Interview, Lord Sherfield (Roger Makins).
78 John Foster Dulles papers, Eisenhower Library, Abilene.

79 Report to Eden, 26 September 1956; HMA.
80 Interview, Lord Sherfield.
81 HMD, 25 September 1956.
82 Report to Eden, op. cit.; HMA.
83 HMD, 10 April 1956.
84 Quoted in Thomas, op. cit., p. 72.
85 Rhodes James, op. cit., p. 525.
86 Eden, op. cit., p. 499; Nutting, op. cit., p. 70.
87 Murphy, op. cit., p. 386.
88 Nutting, op. cit., expurgated text.
89 Selwyn Lloyd, op. cit., p. 79.
90 HMA.
91 Quoted in Neff, op. cit., pp. 307–8.
92 Selwyn Lloyd, op. cit., p. 150.
93 Ibid., p. 151.
94 HMD, 4 October 1956.
95 Interview, Lord Head.
96 Interview, Sir Anthony Nutting.
97 AHT, 11.10.
98 HMD, 3 February 1957.
99 AHT, 11.7,15.
100 Interview, Sir Dick White.
101 Interview, Lord Sherfield.
102 Dwight D. Eisenhower Library, Abilene.
103 Interview, General Challe.
104 Interview, Sir Anthony Nutting.
105 Thomas, op. cit., p. 114.
106 Nutting, op. cit., unexpurgated, p. 96.
107 CAB 128/30. CM (56) 72; PRO.
108 The 'protocol' was eventually published by Rhodes James, op. cit., p. 531.
109 Rhodes James, op. cit., p. 532.
110 Anthony Howard, *RAB, The Life of R. A. Butler*, p. 235.
111 William Clark, *Three Worlds*, p. 209.
112 Nutting, op. cit., unexpurgated, p. 104.
113 AHT, 11.10.
114 Interview, William Clark; see also Thomas, op. cit., pp. 95, 230.
115 Interview, Lord Sherfield.
116 John Foster Dulles telephone transcript, 18 October 1956; Eisenhower Library, Abilene.
117 Oral interview with C. Douglas Dillon, John Foster Dulles Library, Princeton.
118 Telephone conversations memoranda; John Foster Dulles Library, Princeton.
119 Quoted in John Ranelagh, *The Agency: The Rise and Decline of the C.I.A.*, p. 302.

120 Eisenhower, op. cit., p. 70.
121 Townsend Hoopes, *The Devil and John Foster Dulles*, p. 374.
122 Nutting, op. cit., p. 136.
123 Thomas, op. cit., pp. 127, 146.
124 T 236; PRO.
125 Telephone transcript, 30 October 1956; Eisenhower Library, Abilene.
126 Quoted in Randolph Churchill, *The Rise and Fall of Sir Anthony Eden*, p. 297.
127 Quoted in Hoopes, op. cit., p. 375.
128 Interview, Lord Aldington.
129 Quoted in Neff, op. cit., pp. 385, 396.
130 Interview, Lord Sherfield.
131 Selwyn Lloyd, op. cit.
132 Thomas, op. cit., pp. 145–6.
133 AHC.
134 Quoted in Patrick Cosgrave, *R. A. Butler*, p. 119.
135 Interview, Major the Hon. J. J. Astor.
136 Interview, Lord Head.
137 Eden, op. cit., p. 557.
138 Quoted in Richard Lamb, *The Failure of the Eden Government*, p. 281.
139 Ibid., pp. 280–3.
140 Letters on Suez; HMA.
141 Selwyn Lloyd, op. cit., p. 211.
142 BBC1, 23 April 1971.
143 AHC.
144 Interview, Burke Trend.
145 John Newhouse, *De Gaulle and the Anglo-Saxons* (New York 1970), pp. 7–8.
146 Interview, Sir Alec Douglas-Home.
147 AHT, 3.9; 8.4.
148 Ibid., 11.5, 10–11, 18–19.

Chapter 16 Salvaging the Wreckage, November 1956–January 1957

HM, *Riding the Storm*, IV, pp. 167–84, and:

1 Anthony Verrier, *Through the Looking Glass*, p. 158.
2 R. A. Butler, *The Art of the Possible*, p. 194.
3 Telephone transcript, 19 November 1956, Dwight D. Eisenhower Library, Abilene; Donald Neff, *Warriors at Suez*, p. 424.
4 Telephone transcript, 20 November 1956, Eisenhower Library; Neff, op. cit., pp. 425–6.

5   Dulles papers, John Foster Dulles Library, Princeton.
6   Eisenhower to Humphrey, 21 November 1956; Eisenhower Library.
7   Letter of 13 December 1956; HMA.
8   Neff, op. cit., p. 425.
9   Eisenhower to John Emmet Hughes, 31 November 1956; quoted in Neff, op. cit., p. 387.
10 Interview, Lord Rhyl (Nigel Birch).
11 Anthony Sampson, *Macmillan*, p. 115.
12 Interviews, Sir Philip de Zulueta, Lord Blake.
13 Interviews, Lady Avon, Lord Carrington.
14 HMD, 3 February 1956.
15 Interview, Sir John Eden.
16 Letter from Eden, 25 February 1969; HMA.
17 HMD, 3 and 6 July 1953.
18 AHC.
19 *Memoirs of Max of Baden*, p. 6.
20 Interview, Sir Philip de Zulueta.
21 Interview, Lord Butler.
22 Hansard, 12 November 1956.
23 Harold Nicolson, *Diaries and Letters*, III, p. 328.
24 Philip Goodhart, *The 1922*, p. 175.
25 Ibid.
26 Anthony Howard, *RAB, The Life of R. A. Butler*, p. 240.
27 Butler, op. cit., p. 194.
28 Quoted in David Carlton, *Anthony Eden*, p. 463.
29 Nicolson, op. cit., III, p. 329.
30 Interview, Lord Head.
31 Nicholas Henderson, *The Private Office*, pp. 650–73.
32 Interview, Nigel Nicolson.
33 *Daily Herald*, 15 September 1959.
34 Interview, Lord Butler.
35 Harold Wilson, *A Prime Minister on Prime Ministers*, p. 314.
36 HMD, 3 February 1957 (recording events from 9 January 1957).
37 Ibid.
38 Lord Kilmuir, *Memoirs*, p. 28.
39 Interview, Lord Head.
40 HMD, 3 February 1957.

Select Bibliography

Alexander, Harold (Field Marshal Earl Alexander of Tunis), *The Alexander Memoirs, 1940–45* (London 1962).

Beaufre, Général André, *The Suez Expedition, 1956* (London 1969).

Berding, Andrew, *Dulles on Diplomacy* (Princeton 1965).

Bethell, Nicholas (Baron Bethell), *The Last Secret: Forcible Repatriation to Russia, 1944–7* (London 1974).

Boothby, Robert (Baron Boothby), *Recollections of a Rebel* (London 1978).

Branyan, Robert L., and Larsen, Lawrence H., *The Eisenhower Administration, 1953–1961: A Documentary History* (New York 1971).

Brittan, Samuel, *The Treasury Under the Tories, 1951–1964* (London 1969).

Bryant, Sir Arthur W. M., *The Turn of the Tide, 1939–43* (London 1957).

——, *Triumph in the West, 1943–46* (London 1959).

Bullock, Alan (Baron Bullock), *The Life and Times of Ernest Bevin,* 3 vols (London 1960, 1967, 1983).

Butler, Richard Austen (Baron Butler), *The Art of the Possible: The Memoirs of Lord Butler* (London 1971).

Carlton, David, *Anthony Eden: A Biography* (London 1981).

Charmley, John, *Duff Cooper: The Authorised Biography* (London 1986).

——, 'Harold Macmillan and the Making of the French Committee of Liberation', *International History Review,* vol. iv, Nov. 1982.

Churchill, Randolph, *The Rise and Fall of Sir Anthony Eden* (London 1959).

Churchill, Sir Winston, *The Second World War* (6 vols): vol. I: *The Gathering Storm* (London 1948); vol. II: *Their Finest Hour* (London 1949); vol. III: *The Grand Alliance* (London 1950); vol. IV: *The Hinge of Fate* (London 1951); vol. V: *Closing the Ring* (London 1952); vol. VI: *Triumph and Tragedy* (London 1954).

Colville, Sir John, *The Fringes of Power: Downing Street Diaries, 1939–1955* (London 1985).

——, *Action This Day* (London 1968).

Cooper, Chester, *The Lion's Last Roar: Suez 1956* (New York 1978).

Cooper, Rt.Hon. Alfred Duff (Viscount Norwich), *Old Men Forget* (London 1953).

Coote, Sir Colin, *Editorial: Memoirs* (London 1965).

Cosgrave, Patrick, *R. A. Butler: An English Life* (London 1981).

Dalton, Edward Hugh John Neale (Baron Dalton), *Call Back Yesterday: Memoirs, 1887–1931* (London 1953).

——, *The Fateful Years: Memoirs, 1931–1945* (London 1957).

——, *High Tide and After: Memoirs, 1945–1960* (London 1962).

Dayan, Moshe, *Story of My Life* (London 1976).

Dickson, Lovat, *The House of Words* (London 1963).

Dixon, Piers, *Double Diploma: The Life of Sir Pierson Dixon, Don and Diplomat* (London 1968).

Drummond, Roscoe, and Coblentz, Gaston, *Duel at the Brink* (New York 1960, London 1961).

Eden, Robert Anthony, Earl of Avon, *Full Circle: The Memoirs of Sir Anthony Eden* (London 1960).

Eden, Sir Timothy Calvert, Bt, *The Tribulations of a Baronet* (London 1933).

Edwards, Ruth D., *Harold Macmillan: A Life in Pictures* (London 1983). (Introduction by Alistair Horne.)

Egremont, Baron. See Wyndham, John.

Eisenhower, Dwight D., *The White House Years: Waging Peace, 1956–61.*

——, *The War Years* (papers, ed. A. D. Chandler) (Baltimore 1970).

Farrah-Hockley, General Sir Anthony, *The Somme* (London 1986).

Finer, Herman, *Dulles Over Suez* (Chicago 1964).

Fisher, Sir Nigel, *Harold Macmillan: A Biography* (London 1982).

——, *Iain Macleod* (London 1973).

Fitzgerald, Penelope, *The Knox Brothers* (London 1977).

Foot, Michael Mackintosh, *Aneurin Bevan, 1945–60* (vol. I, London 1962; vol. II, London 1973).

Fraser, General Sir David, *Alanbrooke* (London 1982).

Fullick, Roy, and Powell, Geoffrey, *Suez: The Double War* (London 1979).

Gaulle, General Charles de, *Mémoires de la guerre: L'unité, 1942–44* (3 vols, pub. London 1954–9).

Gilbert, Martin, volumes of the official biography of Winston Churchill: vol. V: *Winston S. Churchill, 1922–1939* (London 1976); vol. VI: *The Wilderness Years, 1929–1935* (London 1981); vol. VII: *The Coming of War, 1939–1941* (London 1983); vol. VIII: *Finest Hour, 1939–1941* (London 1983); vol. IX: *Road to Victory, 1941–1945* (London 1986).

——, *Winston Churchill: The Wilderness Years* (London 1981)

Gilmour, Ian, *The Body Politic* (London 1969).

Goodhart, Philip, *The 1922: The Story of the 1922 Committee* (London 1973).

Grigg, John E. P., *1943: The Victory That Never Was* (London 1980).

Harrod, Roy (Sir Henry R. F.), *The Life of J. M. Keynes* (London 1951).

Harvey, Oliver (Baron Harvey of Tasburgh), *War Diaries (1941–45)* (London 1978).

Henderson, Sir Nicholas, *The Private Office* (London 1984).

Hitchens, Christopher, *Cyprus* (London 1984).

Hoopes, Townsend, *The Devil and John Foster Dulles* (London 1974).

Horne, Alistair, *Death of a Generation* (London 1970).

——, *A Savage War of Peace: Algeria 1954–1962* (London 1977).

Howard, Anthony, *RAB: The Life of R. A. Butler* (London 1987).

Hughes, Emmet John, *The Ordeal of Power* (New York 1963).

Hughes, Emrys, *Macmillan: Portrait of a Politician* (London 1962).

Hughes, Thomas, *Memoir of Daniel Macmillan* (London 1882).

Kersaudy, François, *Churchill and de Gaulle* (London 1981).

Kilmuir, Lord, *Political Adventure: Memoirs* (London 1962).

Kirkpatrick, Sir Ivone, *The Inner Circle: Memoirs* (London 1959).

Knox, Ronald, *A Spiritual Aeneid* (London 1958).

Lamb, Richard, *The Failure of the Eden Government* (London 1987).

Leeper, Sir Reginald, *When Greek Meets Greek* (London 1950).

Lloyd, Selwyn. See Selwyn-Lloyd.

Lockhart, Sir Robert Bruce, *Diaries*, ed. Kenneth Young: vol. I: 1915–38 (London 1973); vol. II, 1939–65 (London 1979).

Macmillan, Harold (Earl of Stockton, OM), autobiography: vol. I: *Winds of Change 1914–39* (London 1966); vol. II: *The Blast of War 1939–45* (London 1967); vol. III: *Tides of Fortune 1945–55* (London 1969); vol. IV: *Riding the Storm 1956–59* (London 1971); vol. V: *Pointing the Way* (London 1972); vol. VI: *At the End of the Day* (London 1973).

——, *The Middle Way* (London 1938, New York 1966).

——, *The Past Masters: Politics and Politicians* (London 1975).

——, *War Diaries: The Mediterranean 1943–1945* (London 1984).

Martin, Kingsley, *New Statesman Profiles* (London 1957).

Moran, Lord, *Winston Churchill: The Struggle for Survival* (London 1966).

Morgan, Charles, *The House of Macmillan, 1843–1943* (London 1944).

Morin, Relman, *Dwight D. Eisenhower and the American Crusade* (New York 1972).

Morris, James, *Oxford* (London 1965).

Morrison, Herbert, *An Autobiography* (London 1960).

Murphy, Robert, *Diplomat Among Warriors* (London 1964).

Neff, Donald, *Warriors at Suez* (New York 1981).

Nicolson, Hon. Sir Harold, *Diaries and Letters* (3 vols): vol. I: *1930–1939* (London 1966); vol. II: *1939–1945* (London 1967); vol. III: *1945–1962* (London 1968).

Nicolson, Nigel, *Alex: The Life of Field Marshal Earl Alexander of Tunis* (London 1973).

Nutting, Sir Anthony, *No End of a Lesson: The Story of Suez* (London 1967).

Parmet, Herbert S., *Eisenhower and the American Crusades* (New York 1973).

Ranelagh, John, *The Agency: The Rise and Decline of the C.I.A.: From Wild Bill Donovan to William Casey* (New York 1986).

Rhodes James, Robert, *Anthony Eden* (London 1986).

Sampson, Anthony, *Macmillan: A Study in Ambiguity* (London and New York 1967).

Seldon, Anthony, *Churchill's Indian Summer: The Conservative Government 1951–55* (London 1981).

Selwyn-Lloyd, John Selwyn Brooke Selwyn-Lloyd (Baron), *Suez 1956: A Personal Account* (London 1978).

Shinwell, Emanuel (Baron), *I've Lived Through It All* (London 1973).

Shuckburgh, Evelyn, *Descent to Suez: Diaries 1951–56* (London 1986).

Siedentop, Larry A., 'Mr. Macmillan and the Edwardian Style', in *The Age of Affluence*, ed. Vernon Bogdanor and Robert Skidelsky (London 1970).

Soames, Mary, *Clementine Churchill* (London 1979).

Swinton, Philip (Earl of Swinton), *Sixty Years of Power: Some Memories of the Men Who Wielded It* (London 1966).

Thomas, Hugh (Baron Thomas of Swynnerton), *The Suez Affair* (London 1967).

——, *The Beginnings of the Cold War* (London 1986).

Tolstoy, Nikolai, *Victims of Yalta* (London 1977).

——, *Stalin's Secret War* (London 1981).

——, *The Minister and the Massacres* (London 1986).

Verrier, Anthony, *Through the Looking Glass: British Foreign Policy in an Age of Illusions* (London 1982).

Waugh, Evelyn, *The Life of the Rt Rev. Ronald Knox* (London 1959).

Wheeler-Bennett, Sir John, *Munich: Prologue to Tragedy* (London 1963).

Wilson, Harold (Baron Wilson of Rievaulx), *A Prime Minister on Prime Ministers* (London 1977).

Wyndham, John (Baron Egremont and Leconfield), *Wyndham and Children First* (London 1968).

Ziegler, Philip, *Diana Cooper* (London 1981).

——, *Mountbatten: The Official Biography* (London 1985).

Index

Index

143; Macmillan spokesman
for Colonial Office in, 147,
151; Macmillan's speeches in
opposition, 293–4; Burgess
and Maclean affair, 365–6;
Eden's popularity wanes, 390;
Suez crisis, 416–17, 436–7
housing, 103, 331, 332–3,
335–40
Howard, Anthony, 456
Hughes, Emmet, 438
Hughes, Emrys, 294, 340
Hughes, Thomas, 7
Hull, Cordell, 172
Humphrey, George, 420, 423,
440, 442, 451, 452
Hungary, 361, 420, 435, 436,
438, 439, 442
Husky, Operation, 192–3
Hussein, King of Jordan, 388,
428
Huxley, Aldous, 309
hydrogen bomb, 345, 346

ICI, 74
Idris, King of Libya, 404
Inchon, 328
India, 52, 59, 109–10, 146, 289,
305, 309–12
India Independence Bill (1947),
312
Indiana, 55, 158
Indiana, University of, 418
Indianapolis, 419
Indianapolis Star, 419
Indo-China, 207, 304, 329, 346,
347, 349, 358, 372, 407, 408
Industrial Capacity Committee,
141

Industrial Charter, 299–300
industry, Derating Act, 82–4
Industry and the State, 78–9, 82
inflation, 333–4, 382, 383
International Monetary Fund
(IMF), 290, 416, 418, 422,
440, 442, 443, 444
Intourist, 101
Iran, 309–10, 327–8, 358, 369
Iraq, 369
Ireland, 41, 53, 68
Irgun, 308
Irvine, 6
Isis, 23
Ismay, General, 156
Israel: creation of, 305; Project
Alpha, 367–8; and the
Egyptian–Soviet arms deal,
370; Middle Eastern
instability, 388–9; Suez crisis,
396, 400–1, 403, 404, 406,
427–40, 442, 446
Istanbul, 364
Istria, 219, 245
Italian Communist Party, 204,
244
Italy: invasion of Abyssinia,
111, 113; invades Albania,
120; peace negotiations,
193–6, 199; Allied landings,
196–9; Allied administration,
200–6, 243–4; Allies advance
in, 242; White Russians in,
252; Cossack troops in, 262–3
Izmir, 364

Jamaica, 450
James, Henry, 58, 63–4
Jameson, Storm, 129

Yeats, W. B., 59, 62–3
'YMCA', 79
Yorkshire Post, 78
Young, Allan, 95, 100, 101, 103, 106
Ypres, 39, 41, 338
Yugoslav Army, 274
Yugoslavia, 206; threat to Trieste and northern Italy, 244–7, 256–60, 267–8;

anti-Communists repatriated to, 249, 269–77; White Russians in, 252; settlement of boundaries, 278

Zanussi, General, 194, 195–6
Zionism, 309
Zulueta, Philip de, 374, 375, 453, 454
Zurich, 304, 313

Picture Acknowledgements

Plate section I: Associated Newspapers Limited page 4 above. BBC Hulton Picture Library pages 8, 9, 12 above, 13 above left and below. Imperial War Museum, London, pages 15 below, 16. Keystone Collection page 14 below. Macmillan Archives pages 1, 2, 3, 4 below, 5, 6, 7, 10, 11, 12 below, 13 above right, 14 above, 15 above.
Plate section II: BBC Hulton Picture Library pages 6 above, 8, 13, 15 above. Crown Copyright Reserved pages 12, 16. *Evening Standard/* Solo page 9. Imperial War Museum, London, pages 1, 2, 3. Keystone Collection pages 5, 6 below, 10, 11, 14 below, 15 below. Macmillan Archives pages 4 above, 7, 14 above. Solo page 4 below.